Park Maker: A Life of
Frederick Law Olmsted

Park Maker: A Life of

Frederick Law Olmsted

by ELIZABETH STEVENSON

MACMILLAN PUBLISHING CO., INC.
NEW YORK
COLLIER MACMILLAN PUBLISHERS
LONDON

Macmillan Publishing Co., Inc.
866 Third Avenue, New York, N.Y. 10022
Collier Macmillan Canada, Ltd.

Library of Congress Cataloging in Publication Data

Stevenson, Elizabeth, 1919–
    Park maker—a life of Frederick Law Olmsted.

    Bibliography: p.
    Includes index.
    1. Olmsted, Frederick Law, 1822–1903. 2. Land-
scape architects—United States—Biography. I. Title.
SB470.05S73   712'.092'4 [B]   76–52942
ISBN 0–02–614440–9

FIRST PRINTING 1977
Printed in the United States of America

To Dorothy and Hugh Joyner

Contents

Illustrations

Acknowledgments

My thanks are due:

to the Emory University Faculty Research Fund for awards during 1967–68, 1969–70, 1970–71, and 1972–73; to the National Endowment for the Humanities for an NEH Summer Stipend in 1974; and to the American Council of Learned Societies for an award in the year 1975;

to the Manuscript Division, the Library of Congress, for unstinted use of the Frederick Law Olmsted Papers and supplementary papers, to successive Directors, Roy P. Basler and John Broderick, and especially to Carolyn H. Sung, Head, Reference Section, and Librarian Mary M. Wolfskill; Olmsted family members and editors for their devotion and skill in collecting and arranging these papers and for dedicating them to the public.

to the Olmsted Associates, Brookline, Massachusetts, for permission to visit the Olmsted house, library, and grounds at 99 Warren St., in particular, Artemas P. Richardson, Landscape Architect, and Mary J. Tynan, Administrative Assistant;

to the Frances Loeb Library, Graduate School of Design, Harvard University, for permission to read the unpublished diary of Charles Eliot and access to other Olmsted materials, and especially thanks to Caroline Shillaber, Librarian; to Charles Eliot II, Landscape Architect, for permission to quote from this diary;

to the Manuscripts and Archives Division, The New York Public Library, Astor, Lenox and Tilden Foundations, Robert W. Hill, Keeper of Manuscripts, for the use of materials from the Calvert Vaux Papers;

to the Bancroft Library, the University of California, Berkeley, J. R. K.

Kantor, University Archivist, for access to Olmsted reports not available elsewhere and for materials on the gold-mining days at Bear Valley and Mariposa;

to the John M. Olin Library, Cornell University, George Healey, Curator of Rare Books, and Barbara Shepherd, Research Assistant, for access to the Andrew D. White Papers and a collection of Olmsted plans;

to the Gallaudet College, Washington, D.C., Carolyn Jones, Librarian, for a view of the original report and plan for the college by Olmsted and Vaux, and for a sight of Vaux buildings on the campus;

to the Henry E. Huntington Library, San Marino, California, Barbara P. Coucot, Department of Manuscripts, for the microfilm of ten unpublished letters of Frederick Law Olmsted;

to the Stanford University Archives, Susan R. Rosenberg, Assistant Archivist, for access to the file of Olmsted-Stanford letters and other materials; to the Stanford University Museum, Betsy G. Fryberger, Curator of Prints and Drawings and Anita V. Mosley, Curator of Photography, for a view of the original Olmsted firm drawings and plans of the Stanford campus;

to the Yale University Library, Sterling Memorial Library, Rutherford D. Rogers, University Librarian and Judith A. Schiff, Chief Reference Librarian, for the use of Olmsted letters and other materials in the Samuel Bowles Papers, the Whitney Family Papers, and the Stokes Autograph Collection;

to the Berkeley Plantation, Virginia, for access to photographs and paintings of the house and grounds during the Civil War and for access to the James River plantation dock, the site of Harrison's Landing;

to the Woodruff Library, Emory University, for prolonged use of Frederick Law Olmsted materials and the use of a study;

to the Friends of Central Park, especially Estelle Woolf, and the Friends of Prospect Park for special occasions in the parks, and for materials about Olmsted, Vaux, and all the green spaces of the New York metropolitan area;

to Henry Hope Reed, then Curator of Central Park, for the benefit of his advice and knowledge of the New York parks and of the careers and personalities of Frederick Law Olmsted and Calvert Vaux, and for suggestions of lines of research;

to John G. Zehmer, Senior Planner, Historic Preservation, City of Richmond, Virginia, Department of Planning and Community Development, for searching the records and confirming a hunch I had that Richmond's Sherwood Park was an Olmsted design, a fact lost to knowledge for some decades;

to my friends, Gladys and Howard Teeple, for giving up a day devoted to helping me see Olmsted's Chicago sites;

to Robert P. Nicholls, Dean of the School of Environmental Design, The University of Georgia, for a letter concerning Olmsted's influence on present-day environmental design;

to George B. Vaughan, Landscape Architect, Boothbay, Maine, for a letter of professional and personal memories about his service with the Olmsted firm;

to Edward L. Daugherty, Landscape Architect, Atlanta, Georgia, for a conversation about his apprenticeship semester in the Olmsted firm during his enrollment in the Harvard School of Landscape Architecture;

to the Connecticut Historical Society, Hartford, Connecticut, Melancthon W. Jacobus, Curator of Prints, for access to several Olmsted items;

to Louis W. Buckowitz, Director, the St. Louis Department of Parks, for information about the city's parks;

to Victoria Ranney, for information and encouragement in the Chicago search;

to the Olmsted Sesquicentennial Committee, Frederick Gutheim, Chairman, and Jane Loeffler, Executive Secretary, for helping to reintroduce Olmsted to the American consciousness;

to an enthusiastic Boston taxi driver, whose name I do not know, who went above and beyond commercial duties in helping me see the Boston Back Bay parks, the Arnold Arboretum, and Franklin Park.

My gratitude also:

to Emory University colleagues who helped with encouragement and incitements to further study: to Dean John C. Stephens, Jr., and Vice President Charles T. Lester; to Professor Bell I. Wiley, for his expert perspective on Olmsted's southern travels and Civil War service; to Professor Harvey Young for keeping me abreast of bibliographical items and for his guidance in intellectual and social backgrounds; to Professor Dana White, for sharing his own irreverent admiration for Olmsted and for the stimulus of his researches in Olmsted's urban work; to Dr. Elizabeth Lyon, for her knowledge of Olmsted's works and influence in the South; to Professor Timothy Crimmins of Georgia State University, for sharing his specialized knowledge of J. B. Harrison and his relations with Olmsted and Charles Eliot Norton;

to the company of Olmsted scholars who are presently engaged in important labor in the field, or have recently been delivered of works, for their generosity and encouragement: Laura Wood Roper, Albert Fein, Charles McLaughlin;

to Lewis Mumford, for what he has done in the past to make Olmsted a living figure in the American present, and for a word of encouragement;

to my mother, Bernice Upshaw Stevenson, and to my sisters, Joan Stevenson Wing and Martha Stevenson Fabian, for standing by and wishing me well; without them, not much.

My thanks are due also for permission to use the following illustrations:

to Jacques Hnizdovsky for his graciously giving the use of his etching of Frederick Law Olmsted;

to Dr. Stephen P. Gill, representing the Olmsted family, for a photograph of Mary Perkins Olmsted in the custody of the Olmsted Associates; to the Olmsted Associates also, for the reproduction of that photograph;

to the Olmsted Associates, Brookline, Massachusetts, for photographs of the Olmsted house at 99 Warren St., and of John Charles Olmsted, Frederick Law Olmsted, Jr., Henry Sargent Codman, and Charles Eliot;

to the Manuscripts and Archives Division, The New York Public Library, Astor, Lenox and Tilden Foundations, for a photograph of Calvert Vaux in the Calvert Vaux Papers;

to the Bancroft Library, the University of California, Berkeley, for a photograph of the OSO House, Bear Valley, California, in the 1860s;

to the John M. Olin Library, Cornell University, Collection of Regional History and University Archives, for the reproduction of a number of Olmsted firm plans: the Harvard (Arnold) Arboretum, Jamaica Park, Logan Place, Seneca Park;

to the Berkeley Plantation, Virginia, for a print of Harrison's Landing during the Civil War;

to William A. V. Cecil, The Biltmore Company, for a reproduction of the John Singer Sargent portrait of Frederick Law Olmsted in Biltmore House;

to the Museum of the City of New York for a reproduction of the Bridges Map or Randel Survey, the 1811 plan of New York City, and for a print of the J. M. Culverhouse Skating Scene, Central Park, 1865;

to the Onondaga Historical Society, Syracuse, New York, Richard N. Wright, President, for a reproduction of the Charles Loring Elliott portrait of George Geddes, 1836;

to the New York Parks, Recreation & Cultural Affairs Administration for a photograph of the Prospect Park Centennial Plaque, Neil Estern, sculptor;

to the Yale University Library, Stokes Autograph Collection, for an engraving originally published in *The Century* of Frederick Law Olmsted in his later years;

to the Library of Congress, as reproduced from the collections of the Manuscript Division, Frederick Law Olmsted Papers: a page from a letter from Frederick Law Olmsted dated from Hongkong, September 3, 1843; a sketch, probably by Olmsted himself, of the Southside farmhouse; a portion of a letter from Frederick Law Olmsted to Mariana G. Van Renssalaer dated December 21, 1887.

Note: parts of Chapter XV, "Secretary of the Sanitary Commission," appeared in different form in an essay, "Olmsted on F Street," in the 1973–74 edition of the *Records* of the Columbia Historical Society of Washington, D.C.

Preface:
A Search for Olmsted

I T IS CURIOUS to see how scenes, events, persons in the remote past persist to help make the structure and theme of work done years later. In this case it was another book to write. It had seemed to me that after five books this one was going to be a departure. Instead, after having spent eight years in writing it, I found that I had dipped back into my childhood, pulled out what was left to me of the longest lasting experience from that time and poured it into a book about one of the lost heroes of American history, Frederick Law Olmsted, the man who made the art of land design into a profession and who did many other things during a battling life lived out against the background of the American nineteenth century.

My first book, when I was very young and inexperienced and thought that a writer simply plunged in and did what he wanted to do, had been about man and art, a study of Henry James. It was eighteen years later that I began to think about another kind of book, concerning another private interest, a book about man and nature. It was not for nothing that the memories from my earliest years were of the five of us in my family camping at the end of unpaved roads in remote, unpeopled wilderness in the Rocky Mountain West. I had carried that happiness with me through all the later years of city living. Therefore, when the years of work on another book, a study of the American 1920s, had ended, I thought about writing a book about man and his artifacts and the ultimate wilderness which surrounds them, about a relationship which I had come to think of as fundamental and nourishing to the well-being of the human race.

The process by which I changed my mind was, I thought, quite cut and

xvii

dried. I tried out the idea of a study to be called *Americans in the Wilderness.*
Then I found that Roderick Nash, in the year of my decision, 1967, had
done something of the kind in writing his *Wilderness and the American
Mind.* I dropped my plan and looked about again. My editor of that period,
Peter Ritner, suggested that I take one of my three or four principal heroes of
the movement toward conservation and preservation and write a biography
of him. I considered George Perkins Marsh, Gifford Pinchot, and Frederick
Law Olmsted, and although the last one named seemed the remotest from
my original theme, yet I chose him. His life seemed the richest and fullest
in events, there seemed to be sufficient material to ensnare me for some time,
and he had, after all, helped preserve the Yosemite, the Adirondacks, and
the Niagara Falls area. And I saw in Olmsted's interest in the environment,
in the raw materials of land itself, and in the transformation of these materials, a richer theme than I had supposed, the life of a man who had lived in a
tension between the claims of nature and art. Also in him I found a man
who had lived variously over a great stretch of time. The narrative would
have to concern itself with every aspect of that existence. I found that I was
not going to write my book about the wilderness. I was going to write a life,
however, which encompassed many aspects of the American procession across
the nineteenth century, and which included the story of what man did for
good or ill to his land during that time.

I began writing to libraries and other institutions in a methodical way
to try to locate Olmsted materials. At this beginning of my search occurred a
fortunate happening which I took to be a lucky omen. On November 29,
1967, I inquired of the Library of Congress what were the prohibitive
restrictions placed upon the collection of Frederick Law Olmsted Papers
which I knew were in the custody of the institution. On December 4, unexpectedly, came a telephone call from the library telling me that the
Olmsted family had recently "dedicated to the public" the great collection of
papers which had been held restrictively for almost fifty years, first by the
family, and then, since 1947 and 1948, by the library. The papers, a most
remarkable collection of letters written not only by Frederick Olmsted but
by family members and friends, and including other kinds of documents,
had been put together through the foresight of Frederick Law Olmsted, Jr.

While I continued my search for other Olmsted papers, I knew that the
collection in the Library of Congress would occupy me considerably. I did
not know that I would make twenty visits to the Library of Congress in the
next eight years, that I would come to be very much at ease in the Manuscript
Room on the third floor of the Library Annex Building, and that I would
come to find Washington, D.C., in the midst of its subway construction,
almost a second home. But I knew, as the year 1968 began, that I was
committing myself to a long and difficult search for Frederick Law Olmsted
in his own words and in his designs scattered across the face of America.

In March, 1968, I took my first look at the Frederick Law Olmsted Papers in the Manuscript Room of the Library of Congress Annex and, during a lunch break, walked from the Library to the United States Capitol, to spend some time standing on the west-front terrace which was one of Olmsted's creations, looking at the vista that he had helped create for the building.

In May, I was in New York City seeing it differently from the way I had seen it so many times before, gazing at the remarkable, city-enclosed green spaces of Central and Prospect Parks more thoughtfully than I had in other years, before knowing anything about the creator of these first city parks of the United States. In the New York Public Library, I began exploring the Calvert Vaux papers, knowing that I would have to try to unravel the long, intimate, and complicated relationship of Olmsted and Vaux, the partners and friends in many projects, who remained attached to each other even in their years of mutual exasperation and alienation.

In June, I went to Asheville for my first visit to the Biltmore Estate, one of Olmsted's last creations. I would go three more times in the next few years.

In July and again in November I was at my now accustomed seat in the Manuscript Room of the Library of Congress, opening folder after folder containing the early letters of a very young Olmsted, learning to like the rhythm of work in that accommodating and gracious room, with the good quiet help at hand, the papers spread out at my convenience on the table, at my back the third floor windows from which I could look occasionally away from crabbed handwriting to the westward sky, traced by gulls at sunset, as I worked in winter months almost to dusk. In these three- or four-day visits, I worked miner's hours, or at least banker's hours, from 8:30 AM when the bell rang to open the library to 4:30 PM, time to catch the bus taking me back through downtown Washington with all its vital, lively life filling its broad sidewalks. Lunch was in a delicatessen or a small restaurant on the Pennsylvania Strip around the corner from the Library where the air was always lively with Capitol Hill gossip.

In 1969, I visited New York City twice. I explored Central Park in sections, seeing parts that were not familiar to me. I went to look at the paintings of the Hudson River School, finding Cole and Church and the others precursors and contemporaries of Olmsted and Vaux in spirit. I ventured downtown on a drowsy Sunday, across the harbor on a ferry to Staten Island, where, finally the last passenger left on a bumpy bus, I talked to a friendly driver who parked at the waterfront in a vague area called Southside. There I tried to imagine some of Olmsted's countryside when he was an ambitious young farmer on this shore of Staten Island. At the Arsenal in Central Park, I saw Olmsted and Vaux's original design, "Greensward," nine feet long, which had won the Central Park competition, and I heard Professor Albert Fein talk about Olmsted. I also met there Henry Hope Reed, then Curator of Central Park, full of sharp and pertinent leads for the various directions Olmsted research might take. This was the beginning of encounters with one Olmsted scholar after another, people who have seemed to me unusually generous and open-hearted. I visited the rounded hill of Mount St. Vincent in Central Park another day, the place where once stood old convent buildings which were converted into a residence for Olmsted and his young family when he was overseeing the completion of the basic design of the park; this was after a visit nearby to the Museum of the City of New York on the other side of Fifth Avenue where I found some early New York City prints.

Late in the year I was again in Washington, by this time an old hand in the Manuscript Room, where I was becoming an inhabitant of Frederick Law Olmsted's world as I traversed with him in adventures across the years. I learned to recognize traits of his personality in the same way I learned to read his difficult handwriting almost by osmosis. Quirky and decided, I found him, and I began to enjoy the sensation, perhaps a happy self-deception, that I knew him well enough to predict what he would do, what he would feel, in crises as they loomed.

My most important exploration of 1969 was a long summer drive by automobile into parts of upstate New York and New England, assimilating geography and scenery which had once operated upon the mind of Frederick Law Olmsted, and which he had in some way touched or altered in the alembic of his imagination.

This does not mean I failed to make mistakes. In Owego, New York, and the country roundabout, lush, green, gentle folds and hills surrounding the upper reaches of the Susquehanna River, I was off on my wildest goose chase. I thought mistakenly for a few days that I had found here the site of Olmsted's apprenticeship at "Fairmount," George Geddes's farm. This mistake, possible only in the earlier, tentative stages of searching, was due to Frederick Olmsted's easy habit of misspelling words; he had written "Owego" instead of "Oswego" and I should have been some distance away in a community now suburban to Syracuse, as I discovered in time. However, being in Owego was not a total loss. The town was interesting with its old stage-coaching inn, its cottage where the genteel Nathaniel P. Willis had lived, its horse farms and broad fields of hay, its historical society, the lawns of which swept down to the margin of the river; all gave me the proper setting for Olmsted's idealized Northern farmer, his "Yeoman," whom he impersonated in his writings from the South of the 1850s, and whom he contrasted with the improvident, slave-owning farmers of this other region. Owego gave me a perspective, as had also my own Southern background of great-grandfathers who had stood in the path not only of Olmsted's journeys but of Sherman's march.

During this same wandering journey across New York, I stopped a half day at Albany to look at the solid embodiment of nineteenth century pride and power, the state capitol. Here Olmsted, H. H. Richardson, and Leopold

Eidlitz had supervised, and the two architects had re-designed the building. This set me musing on the happy teaming of Olmsted and Richardson in other projects, and their friendship. I drove on across the Berkshires, turned south to follow the Connecticut River, after a few days at Hartford, all the way south to the coast, remembering how young Frederick and his friend Charles Loring Brace had sailed the river and camped along the shores, the boy who would be the landscape architect storing up this scenery in his imagination; Connecticut River meadows with free-standing trees in splendid isolation bordering moving water prefigured for him an ideal kind of park landscape. In Hartford, Olmsted had been a child and youth. I visited the historical society and garnered what scant memoirs they had there of this son of the city, a place his ancestors had helped found in the seventeenth century. Reading a few Olmsted letters in the Yale Library, I tried to vanquish in my imagination the new buildings on the Yale grounds so as to see the little college where Frederick had been an irregular student, an aspiring but uncertain young man; below New Haven I drove south onto the rocky peninsula of Sachem's Head where Olmsted first tried farming on in-hospitable soil, and also first designed the layout of a homestead—his own farm.

This year, 1969, was also the year that slowly, day by day, week by week, I began mastering all of Olmsted's published books and articles, finding in the well-endowed nineteenth century collection of the Woodruff Library at Emory University all the original editions and many other writings of the period which began building up in my mind a rich context for the adventure of the life I was following.

By the beginning of 1970 I had settled into a routine of leaving my job several times a year to visit the Olmsted Papers in the Library of Congress for several intensive days of work. I tried, on those visits, to hold myself to a strict chronological reading of the manuscript letters, folder after folder, box after box, writing my notes on letter-size pads of ruled paper. As I brought home sets of notes to add to the stack already accumulated, I began in my mind to fill in details and color of a life from these letters to and from Frederick Olmsted, and from all the other papers of a lifetime, titles to farms, contracts for books, correspondence with clients. It might have been difficult for an observer in that quiet room to have seen the electric excitement generated in the mind of one well-behaved reader who, with difficulty, sometimes restrained cries of elation at certain discoveries. In 1970, I was in the Manuscript Room three times, in April, August, and December.

The next year, in June 1971, I was in New York City again, this time walking Central Park and Prospect Park with that small-town group in the heart of a great city, the Friends of Central Park, even helping them take up the one-dollar contribution from those who wanted to join us. As I tramped the grass and walked in the shade of the one-hundred-year-old trees, I walked deeper also into the interior tangle of human relations in which

Olmsted had lived: Frederick and his father, Frederick and his stepmother, Frederick and his brother, Frederick and his wife, Frederick and his friends.

A long summer drive in 1971 took me through Buffalo and the Niagara Falls area, on to stops in Rochester, Ithaca, and in Montreal. South Park in Buffalo was sadly deteriorated but was situated where the poor of today get a breath of air and open space to walk in. Niagara was commercialized but not entirely ruined. Seneca Park followed the Genesee River sinuously through a part of Rochester and was faithful to Olmsted's idea of *rus in urbis*. In a soft rain, the green mountain top which is Mount Royal seemed more necessary than ever to the large city below its modest height. I had stopped on the way to Montreal at Ithaca to spend three days in the Olin Library at Cornell University, learning a bit more than I had known before about Olmsted's part in the original plan, reading a number of his manuscript letters in the Andrew White Papers, and having spread before me in generous profusion the library's collection of Olmsted plans.

September saw me in Washington again, snatching time away from the occasion which had brought me there to spend some hours in the library; the occasion was a lunch-meeting of the group planning Olmsted's sesqui-centennial year as a national celebration. There I met Charles McLaughlin, open and generous of help, Albert Fein again, full of trenchant ideas and good talk about Olmsted and cities, Laura Wood Roper, nearing the end of her long journey through Olmsted's life, William Alex, who was to be the designer of two Olmsted exhibitions, and Julius Fabos, who had already brought out a book of splendid pictures of Olmsted as the "founder of land-scape architecture in America." Next day, McLaughlin, Fein, and I had Olmsted and hamburgers for lunch.

An appendix to this trip was a flying visit to the New York Public Library to look over that institution's collection of the papers of the United States Sanitary Commission.

In the spring of 1972, I began to know Laura Wood Roper as a friend as well as a meticulous scholar. She was bringing to a conclusion her life of Olmsted, about which I had soon heard after I began my search. She had known members of the Olmsted family, she had persuaded Frederick, Jr., to turn over the papers to the Library of Congress, she had begun her journey through the life long before the rest of us. Yet she was generous and stimulating in ideas to all of us. Among all the Olmsted searchers I was to find a remarkable comradeship. We were finding our hero large enough and various enough to reward many explorations and several points of view.

In June, I visited the Biltmore estate again, going out into the grounds, ignoring Richard Morris Hunt's castle, fantastic yet in the North Carolina mountains, but deserving respect by its solidity and honesty of construction. I began to appreciate in this deepening of my interest in the place how Olmsted, with a free hand given him by George Vanderbilt's millions, had used with grace and authority here all the elements of land design which had interested him and had made also a pleasing unity of this obsession of a rich young man. I guessed that this was also, thanks to the Cecils, grandsons of George Vanderbilt, the best preserved of Olmsted's designs.

A long drive into the vibrant heat of the Midwest in July took me to St. Louis and Chicago. I added the old inner quadrangles of Washington University to the remnants of Olmsted's other college and university work which I had seen, at Smith, Amherst, Cornell, and Trinity of Hartford. The magnificent public parks of St. Louis, particularly Forest Park, not a design of Olmsted, reminded me how pervasive his influence had been in the nineteenth century; all had the informality, irregularity of the romantic, humanistic influence Olmsted had inculcated. In Chicago, there was satisfaction in seeing people enjoying Washington Park and Jackson Park in the everyday fashion the designer had wished. Here were families "bivouacking" in little groups on the grass. Here was the green channel of the Midway which Olmsted had meant to be a waterway. Here, most generous in open space and a vista of the city to the north, was the lakeside park which had served in 1893 as the site of the great Columbian Exposition and which, as Olmsted had planned, reverted to parkland afterwards. Here was the neglected but still delicious "Wooded Isle," which Olmsted cherished during the peopled frenzy of the fair as a place of solitude and withdrawal. At the end of a long day of looking I found myself in the quiet, shaded, curving streets of Riverside, still livable, one of its streets Olmsted Drive. Riverside is probably the best example as well as the oldest of the designer's suburbs.

In October, 1972, I returned once again to Washington, for the occasion of the Olmsted exhibition in the National Gallery. I made the visit the excuse for two more days of seclusion in the Manuscript Room of the Library of Congress.

By 1973 I had some sense of mastering the sequences of the life and of beginning to understand my own attitude toward Frederick Law Olmsted. This was also the year of my most adventurous journeys, expeditions whose daring and excitement were only interior and would not have been obvious or visible to others.

In April, a cold day, I walked the grounds of the Gallaudet School, one of Olmsted and Vaux's earliest designs as an independent firm. The grounds were greatly different and many new buildings had been added, but two old structures designed by Calvert Vaux remained and were designated historic treasures. In the library I sat down to read Olmsted's original report and look at the original plan.

During this year, researches by Emory University scholars, particularly Dana White, Elizabeth Lyon, and their graduate students, had revived a long lost knowledge of the amount of Southern work Frederick Olmsted, and subsequently the Olmsted firm, had done. Familiar parts of the Atlanta landscape took on the excitement of discovery: Piedmont Park had a new meaning because we knew now that Olmsted came south to advise the local commission planning the Cotton States Exposition to be held on these grounds; Druid Hills, through which we drove every day, rewarded thought and emotion, for its basic design and aspect were the result of Olmsted's visits in 1894. Dana White was gathering articles by several hands about this Southern work by Frederick Olmsted. Albert Fein came to Atlanta in May and Charles McLaughlin in October to visit, talk, and see firsthand these aspects newly discovered of Olmsted's later career.

Sargent's living likeness of the bearded Olmsted among the blooms of mountain laurel outdoors at Biltmore held my attention in another visit to the estate where the old man himself first became aware of his failing abilities. There was poignancy and vividness in that portrait: Olmsted striding forward forever among trees into whatever his life was yet to bring him. Not far from the Biltmore house, high up near the Blue Ridge Parkway in the Museum of the Cradle of American Forestry, I found that the National Forest Service had commemorated the work of Olmsted and Gifford Pinchot in beginning the work of that branch of the government. I remembered that at one time the Biltmore Estate had stretched all the way from the French Broad River to Mount Pisgah, and it was in this area that Olmsted directed Pinchot to begin the practice of scientific forestry in the United States.

My midyear drive took me south of Richmond into the area of the Peninsular Campaign of 1862, where Olmsted spent hectic weeks as chief of the hospital ships of the United States Sanitary Commission. I drove to within a quarter of a mile, and the barrier of a muddy dirt road, of the site of White House Landing on the Pamunkey River, and came away with the satisfaction of knowing that this part of the Peninsula was as primitive, perhaps more so, than in 1862. At the Berkeley Plantation on the James, the site of Harrison's Landing, where Olmsted observed the Union troops camped after their retreat from Richmond, I walked down to the water's edge and tried to recreate the scene as it had been to Olmsted's eyes. In Washington, D.C., a picnic in the National Zoo was a reminder of another Olmsted effort.

An August trip to Boston gave me my full share of indoor and outdoor work: a morning at the Olmsted house and grounds, a day of reading Charles Eliot's diary in the library of the Graduate School of Design. Another day's tour of the Back Bay parks, the Arnold Arboretum, and Franklin Park gave me vivid hints of the attention and love Olmsted had poured into these Boston ventures in his later years.

In October, a week in California was rich again in books and views. Two afternoons I spent in the Bancroft Library at the University of California at Berkeley, and one morning in the Museum and Library at Stanford University, gave me help in filling in with rich detail Olmsted's California years. I saw Olmsted's Mountain View Cemetery in Oakland as well as the Berkeley campus, both of which Olmsted had seen first as bare brown hillsides. A drive into the foothills and then on into the Sierra reminded me of Olmsted's saying of these mountains: "They are to be remembered." Fortunate weather, fortunate seeing: I drove about as I pleased in a rented car in Mariposa, Bear Valley, and what I thought of with partiality as Frederick Olmsted's Yosemite Valley, keeping in mind all the way the associations I had with Olmsted's experiences in these places.

My visits to the Library of Congress in 1974 numbered six: in January, April, June, July, September, and December. I could by now regard Olmsted as an old friend, crotchety, quick to anger, warm in his enthusiasms, tireless in his ambition to do what he wished to do, sudden in his exhaustions, sensitive to beauty, hopeful of his fellow men even in the face of the robust corruption of his century. My writing accelerated during this time. I had earlier blocked out episodes and sequences. Now I modified these divisions of my subject and found new transitions reflecting real events in the mind of my hero.

In 1975 I visited the Library of Congress three times: in March, in May, and last in October. When I came out slightly dazed into the cool sunshine of a late day in fall, I realized with a shock that if I had not done everything, I had, at last, done all I could reasonably do. My search had led me not only a long course through these and other documents but out into physical spaces. This had been a double kind of looking. My book would be my way of showing the result, a long and enthralled consideration of a man who thought two matters of great importance: the proper use of land and the proper use of man.

ELIZABETH STEVENSON

Atlanta
July, 1976

Park Maker: A Life of
Frederick Law Olmsted

CHAPTER I

A Boy in the
Connecticut Woods

Such a bothering little chap as I must have been.
—F. L. O., "Passages in the Life of an Unpractical Man"[1]

A BOY CALLED FREDERICK, Fred-Law, or Fred, liked to wander in the woods. The trees under which he walked in his vagrant fashion one day in 1829 or 1830 were in a rural part of southern Connecticut near the town of North Guilford. And although this was a long settled part of President Andrew Jackson's America, these rural spaces were often lonely, for many farmers had departed westward. Not many mills had been set up to dam the streams. It was not difficult for a boy of seven or eight to get away from a house where he had been placed to learn reading and writing from the local parson and to lose himself in looking for fishes in the brooks and birds in the trees, and to wonder about the tramps he met on the roads or about the deserted farmhouses he found swallowed up by the forest.

The name given to the child, Frederick Law Olmsted, was a large and impressive one for so small a body. He did not belong to the village. In fact, the inhabitants looked at him somewhat askance. He belonged to a family in Hartford. His father, John Olmsted, a prosperous dry goods merchant, had sent the child away from a comfortable house and a busy city to this country place to be taught by the schoolmaster-minister, who took a few boys into his house in an informal sort of way. This was to be the pattern of Frederick's childhood, a going away from home each year to one or another "school" in primitive circumstances in the less-peopled parts of Connecticut. He did not care much for the lessons given him. He spent all the time he could wandering the woods.

One day in summer, he strayed away in his usual fashion and found out in time that he was lost. He was not afraid, or so he later remembered the

I

adventure. It had begun when he kicked off his shoes at the door of the minister's house where he boarded and followed one scent of interest after another like a little dog. A town boy, he was curious about country sights and sounds and smells. He crept to the back of the crude circle of log cabins —"Sunday houses"—put up for the families who came into the village for services from remote homesteads. He saw through a window the "drunken poor family" who had traded skins for rum and had now drunk themselves privately into a stupor. They could not resist the drink, but they kept themselves out of sight of the villagers. He gave up the sight of this un-understandable shame, concealed from curious and censorious sight, and ran after some bigger boys who had trapped a weasel and now lifted its limp body to his awed and shocked view. He flung himself away from them and stopped only at the little brook dammed the day before by a crowd of boys and girls, himself among them. He paddled his hand in the shallow water and felt for crayfishes under rock ledges. Leaving off playing with the moving stream, he followed the dusty road. He passed the last house and said hello to a farmer leading a tired horse pulling hard to drag stones from a field on a sledge. On the road before him under the tall elms, he saw approaching the bedraggled bravery of the militia practicing for the spring muster. Their uniforms of 1812 were patched, their plumes of a gaiety and jauntiness reduced by age and dust and the packing away year after year between musters. The boy turned off the road when they had straggled by, potbellies on thin shanks making an effort not to betray age. He struck out through the woods. In looking so closely at one thing after another he had tired himself out. He curled up in a hollow under a tree and went to sleep. He woke in the half dark of evening, not so frightened as a boy not used to wandering might have been. He knew that any lighted house would take him in. He knocked at a door, was fed on milk and pudding and put to bed with the boys of the family under a faded quilt. The farm parents must have looked with some wonder at the child who was let wander so freely.

There was a strangeness about his upbringing although he was a member of a large and secure family. There were, at home, John, his father; Mary Ann, his stepmother; John, Charlotte, Mary, Bertha, and the others, a growing succession of brothers and sisters. Yet even as a very small boy he—the eldest son—was sent away, almost as if he were an orphan child, and boarded with one country parson after another, the father taking a chance each time on the kind of schooling that Fred might receive. Only by luck, and for short periods, was the schooling good. Only occasionally did the child receive the benefit of the excellent schools of Hartford, where John Olmsted, the father, was a prosperous merchant. In such places as North Guilford, Ellington, Newington, Saybrooke, and East Hartford, the child was sent to live away from his family from the time he was seven years old, attending a hit-or-miss succession of schools. In each place he boarded with a local minister, picked out with a sort of superstitious but unguided reverence by his father, who had the idea that such a man might be good for his son. The minister-guardian tutored the boy himself or sent him to the public school of the town.

His father's journal recorded for 1829–30 the event of Frederick's first going away from home: "To Rev. Z. Whittemore, No. Guilford."[2] It was from this first stay away from home that Frederick thought he remembered seeing, one Sunday, the poor drunk family, the trapped weasel, and the militia practice, watching the minister bury a child, going to the grist mill with rye, and, on a sleighing party, being tumbled in the snow by a bigger boy. The minister was not only kind to him but exemplary in his own life, and no family in the village failed to be self-supporting and self-respecting (the drunken family had come from some unimaginable wild area beyond the decent bounds of the village). It seemed a little Eden, even to a brooding memory, as he thought of the place later, and the experience of such primitive if limited goodness shaped some of his ideas the rest of his life. The place belonged even in 1830 to a past further removed. The elders of the place remembered and lived by the emotions of the war of the Revolution. Veterans of 1812 mustered on the green and were given a benediction by the parson. The divisions which were to disturb his own growing up had not arrived, neither the fierce opinions about abolition, nor the intolerance concerning drink. The minister's daughter drank flip at a party and was "merry"; people played "romping games" around a fire and rode home through snowstorms, going gaily and recklessly along white roads. The parson was on good terms even with the town drunk, and the drunk with him. The gentle man preached temperance, but not abstinence, and did not know of evils beyond his horizon.

The memories indicated belong to some fragments of an autobiography written by a man past middle age. In the memory-laden pages, stray bits and pieces were gathered into a shifting kaleidoscope, with much vividness and little continuity: "I do not know whether it was before or after this [the stay in the village where he looked into one of the Sunday houses] that I spent several months with my uncle at Geneseo, where I remember being taken to see Indians making baskets, to visit at a house in the dooryard of which there was a fawn and at which a beautiful woman gave me sweetmeats, and that I was driven rapidly and silently over the turf of the bottom lands among great trees."

Frederick Olmsted had only a part of two years in his happy little paradise. Afterwards he was sent for obscure reasons from one parson and school to another, and the experience was not often as happy as the first time. He was a particularly small boy among sixty others at one boarding school. There he earned scars both mental and physical from unnecessary and callous cruelty: "I was taken away suddenly when one of the big boys wrote to his father, who sent the letter to mine, that a teacher had lifted me up by my ears and had so pinched one of them that it bled." He recalled that he had been so worked upon by fanatical religious fervor at this cruel place that his first letter from there to his father was an attempt to "convert" him.

He stayed some months at home that year and successive years, home being all the branches of a numerous family within the circumference of the countryside surrounding Hartford, a city which then was a place which could be easily walked out of into the woods, or skated away from on the winter surface of the river. All the times at home between exile to schools melted into a continuous memory for the older man. He recalled a gallery of grandparents, granduncles, uncles, aunts, all seeming to have been solitary, independent, and individual persons who had lived mightily in a far-off past and who were friends now, without loss of dignity, with a small boy who came and went freely in their gardens, libraries, laboratories, barns, and attics. He had no less than five great-uncles who had been "seafaring men before the Revolution." Each one had a story to tell, about himself or another relative. One sailor of the old war had died a prisoner of the British in a hulk. One made a famous capture of a vessel on the high seas. His own grandfather, old and "infirm from wounds and rheumatism," got up from his chair to show Fred a bird's nest in an elm he had planted. Fred ran home to tell his father that he wanted to plant trees too. Somehow he had learned to read quickly and easily, and taking delight in that ability, he found old English books in his grandmother's attic, Goldsmith's *Vicar of Wakefield* and Sterne's *Sentimental Journey*.

At eight or nine Frederick was sent to board with the Reverend Joab Brace at Newington. Four boys were boarded, and "school" was in a ramshackle, country-store building next to the parson's house. In the cellar, cabbages; on the second floor, harnesses and saddles; on the third, the boys and their desks. Fred cut and split logs and kept the fire going, "all in playtime," as he said. The parson was not deliberately cruel but petty and lazy. He left the boys to shift for themselves in the classroom, but he crept upstairs occasionally with his shoes off to listen at the crack of the door. He would pull it open suddenly to surprise them, and when he found them, as he often did, being entertained by one of Fred's stories, he burst in, flailing them with a ruler, a piece of firewood, or a broom, "shouting 'Oh! the depravity of human nature!' "

The little boy who got willingly lost outdoors, and who told stories indoors to fellow captive schoolmates, was small for his age, but quick, deft, and supple in his movements. His thin, expressive face was topped by a shock of bright brown hair with an unruly wave. His dark, intense eyes showed as blue gray only in a fair light. He moved with a springy, nervous energy but did not look hardy. He took in everything he encountered, absorbing sensations and catching at ideas eagerly.

Although the child was often separated from his father in childhood, it was the father who was to him the most important figure of that time. For Fred, although posted from one little Connecticut village school to another, was not a neglected child, but the eldest son of a seventh generation Hartford family. It was true that he and John Hull were orphaned at a young age by the death of their mother, and their stepmother was perhaps diffident about the care of little boys. But Frederick was neither unloved nor unnoticed. The difficulty was in the father's abnormal distrust of his own ability to guide not only his children, but anyone else, in the direction of morality.

The elder Olmsted was a late descendant of New England religious orthodoxy. His ideas of right living were simple and clear-cut. Because of his rather winning modesty, feeling himself unable to show others how to live, it might have seemed to an outsider that the father neglected Frederick or shirked his duty to him. But John had an anxious care for every movement of his son and recorded this care in a journal. But a result of his fastidious self-distrust was sometimes unfortunate (and Frederick never recovered in later life from a wondering unhappiness about this aspect of his childhood). The child, through the father's well-meaning care, sometimes fell into the hands of men either physically or mentally cruel. When Frederick was a grown man, he analyzed his father with a mixture of cool distance and a kind of pitying love: "He lived in perplexity between his self-distrust and disposition to acquit himself fully in his proper part, and the supposed demands of Society, Religion and Commerce." Frederick went on to describe how his father shrank from asserting himself in company; his steady worth was given less credit than he deserved. Yet this man was a quiet, good friend, and "a decided companionship was always necessary to his comfort." He had one deep, almost inexpressible passion, a love of natural beauty. The child learned from the father the one thing that was to be of most importance in his life. About this he wrote, "On a Sunday evening we were crossing the meadows alone. [This would have been the river meadows of the Connecticut River, of which scene Olmsted was to say later that it had the greatest influence in determining the kind of landscape he would love.] I was tired and he had taken me in his arms. I soon noticed that he was inattentive to my prattle and looking in his face saw in it something unusual. Following the direction of his eyes, I said: 'Oh! there's a star.' Then he said something of Infinite Love with a tone and manner which really moved me, chick that I was, so much that it has ever since remained in my heart."

In searching for beautiful places to look at, the family took vacations together: "We were our own servants, my father seldom fully trusting strangers in these journeys with the feeding, cleaning or harnessing of his horses. We rested long in pleasant places; and when at noon we took the nags out and fed them by the roadside, my father, brother and I would often wander far looking for a bathing place and an addition of fresh wild berries for the picnic dinner which my mother would have set out in some well-selected shady place." They traveled by coach, canal boat, and steamer, as well as in their own coach or wagon, but it was always the homely, unheralded scenes that they freshly admired. Before Frederick was twelve, he was a traveler who had seen much of New England, New York state, and eastern Canada.

On the family travels, the members read to each other, gravely and enjoyably, the travel books of their time and earlier times—"the travel books of President Dwight, Professor Silliman and Miss Martineau, in all of which the observations on scenery with which I was familiar had helped to make me think that the love of nature, not simply as a naturalist but as a poet loves it, was respectable."[3]

Benjamin Silliman, who was a public lecturer widely venerated and respected, as well as the first and founding professor of science at Yale, wrote, "Natural scenery is intimately connected with taste, moral feeling, utility and instruction."[4] And President Dwight wrote, "Surely travel is an enriching, an ennobling, an exalting, as well as a delightful employment, when properly used."[5] The innocent family group, behind their slow-moving horses, believed such sayings implicitly.

One should step back and place this family, this child, in the time and the scene through which they traveled. Connecticut in 1834, when Frederick was twelve and keenly enjoying such a trip, was a relatively old and traditionminded part of a youthful and bumptious land that was beginning to crow over its destiny. The state was one of rural fields and woods, in part deserted by people who had moved on to new areas farther west. It was a state of small cities. Hartford was already old and dignified, and a member of the Olmsted clan could feel that he belonged there, his family having lived there for generations. Connecticut, Hartford particularly, was strongly etched into the character of its citizens. Connecticut in Frederick Law Olmsted might be recognized one day in traits of reticence, in concern about belief and morals, or at least the quality of life, in a respect for work, in a cleverness with tools and things. Although he was to leave that city in his youth and never again live there regularly, Hartford rightly claimed him. His first American Olmsted ancestor was one of the group of one hundred colonists from Newtown (now Cambridge, Massachusetts) who, with their pastors, Thomas Hooker and Samuel Stone, left the already too settled colony of Plymouth (circa 1635–36) and made a settlement on the Connecticut River, a new place on the map which became Hartford.

Frederick's father, John Olmsted, was born in 1791, during the presidency of George Washington. In 1807, at sixteen, he was apprenticed to a dry goods firm. In the year of the battle of Waterloo, young John Olmsted went into the selling of merchandise on his own and was thereafter self-supporting and, in time, prosperous. In 1821, when he was thirty, during the fourth year of James Monroe's presidency, he married Charlotte Law Hull, who was born in 1800. Her family was that of Commodore Hull. On April 26, 1822, the first child of this union, Frederick Law, was born in the "Dodd" House, College Street, Hartford. On September 2, 1825, a second child, John Hull, was born. On February 28, 1826, when Frederick was not quite four and John

Hull in his first year, Charlotte died. She was twenty-five years and five months old. This ended the growth of the merchant's first family. In a sense Frederick and John Hull were always a distinct unit under John Olmsted's roof. John Olmsted married a second time on April 25, 1827, to Miss Mary Ann Bull. John and Mary Ann were to have seven children: Charlotte, Mary, Bertha, Owen, Ada, Theodosia, and Albert Harry. The tie between Fred and John Hull on the one hand and the second and growing family on the other was warm and friendly, but cousinly rather than brotherly. Fred's letters as a boy and young man were to tease, instruct, advise, and worry over the younger generation of children as if they were somehow partly his responsibility, as well as his father's and mother's. He did not remember his own mother. He remembered only that once he had had a memory of her, a recollection of her sitting under a tree sewing. Mary Ann was indeed mother to him: a conscientious, upright person, a decided and forceful person, in her relations both to her children and to her husband. Frederick traced his love of nature both to his father and to his stepmother. "My step-mother's character was simpler than my father's, but she also had a strong love of nature and her taste was more cultivated and had more of her own respect." As he grew older, Frederick was to define his character not only in yielding to certain influences of Mary Ann but also in resisting certain claims she made on him.

The child's memories of finding his way in the woods and fields of Connecticut or listening to tales of elderly veterans of the revolutionary war might seem a frail pivot on which to rest a description of the changing character of a land stretching out from his little world in Hartford to various points of the compass of America; but the attempt to relate the life to the land is not unfair if one considers what the child later became. James Monroe, president the year Frederick Olmsted was born, promulgated his famous doctrine in the first year of the child's life, and placed the United States aggressively in foreign affairs, proclaiming that this new country was worthy of great affairs. Also, in 1823 a novelist, James Fenimore Cooper, peopled the land with a past, a past of imagination in *The Pioneers*. He made over the grubbing life of ancestors into a dignified and satisfying vision, to be contemplated with some complacency. Cooper redirected the inner sense of what people were as surely as Monroe redirected the same people's outward energies. As a sign that this was to be a complex country, not just a large one, while the bulk of his countrymen still sweated away as "pioneers," Edgar Allan Poe in 1827 (Frederick Olmsted was five) wrote and saw published his first book of poems, *Tamerlane and Other Poems*. It was to be a land of creations, then, as well as aspirations, a country of exquisitely made things, sailing vessels and artificial verse, Connecticut clocks, and Mardi Gras costumes in New Orleans. American character expressed itself in Andrew Jackson as president (the growing Fred Olmsted was seven when this president was inaugurated and fifteen when he left the White House). American talk defined itself in Noah Webster's dictionary in 1828. Within the larger national destiny, American regions characterized themselves in various writings: Whittier's *Legends of New England* in 1831, Longstreet's *Georgia Scenes* in 1836. The Civil War was foreshadowed in the election of former president John Quincy Adams to the House of Representatives in 1831, by Nat Turner's rebellion in the same year, by the state of South Carolina's nullification attempt the next year, the Texas rebellion against Mexico in 1836, and the murder of E. P. Lovejoy in 1837. From the fight which Massachusetts Congressman Adams carried on to kill the parliamentary gag rule which barred petitions to end slavery, to the murder in his shop of an editor who wrote against slavery, the way was toward division. The war of 1861 was foreshadowed in the 1830s, and whether it was inevitable or not, its causes disturbed the lives surrounding a growing boy. To be what he was to be, the man Olmsted, imprisoned in the kernel of the boy, required a country rich and complex in causes, even conflicts, complicated enough to differentiate itself in ways of life and thought. This enrichment and differentiation was accomplishing itself as he looked about and became aware both of himself and of other people.

Customarily the sons of prosperous fathers in the 1830s and 1840s finished their preparation for college in their early or middle teens and set themselves with perfect resolution toward being doctor or minister or perhaps dry goods merchant. Frederick Olmsted did not feel called to any of these activities in the apparently easy way his brother John was to medicine. Fred did not know what he was to be, and his indulgent father, in distrust of setting a way for his son, simply let him be. Frederick's situation in his young adolescence was only a more sophisticated version of the little boy lost in the woods. He was a thirteen- and fourteen-year-old who had everything to learn, who was open to learn anything he chanced upon, in danger of he did not know what; but miraculously, the tree did not fall, the snake did not strike, the freeze did not overtake him as he curled up to sleep at the foot of a convenient tree. More literally, Frederick became a good woodsman. He fished and hunted and walked in the neighboring woods with reasonable security or went on hunting or ice-skating expeditions with cheerful independence, an amateur of the outdoors.

He was a reading boy also. In the public library of Hartford he "found . . . certain books, which it is a strange thing that I should have looked into, stranger that I should have assimilated as much as, when re-reading them perhaps twenty years later, I found that I had. They were Price on the *Picturesque* and Gilpin on *Forest Scenery*."[6] He lost himself in reading as entirely as he had as a child in a forest—a place in which to wander.

At fourteen, Frederick Olmsted was precocious and naive, stuffed full of attitudes from books of romantic feeling and impracticable skills. His father, nevertheless, was proud of his son and thought that the bright and independent boy should be ready soon for entering Yale College. (Fourteen was young even for the Yale of that time. When the second Timothy Dwight entered the college a few years later, he was, at sixteen, the youngest boy in his freshman class.) But John Olmsted brushed aside imaginary obstacles. He sent Frederick away from home again, this time to board with the Reverend G. C. N. Eastman at Saybrooke for some months, to be tutored to go to Yale.

It was in Saybrooke, careless about a danger that surely he knew, that Fred walked into and involved himself in a tragedy which changed the course of his life.

CHAPTER II
Idler

I was strangely uneducated—miseducated. Because of an accident
putting my eyes in peril, I was at the most important age left to
"run wild.". . . While my mates were fitting for college I was
allowed to indulge my strong natural propensity for roaming afield
and day-dreaming under a tree.
            —F. L. O., to Elizabeth B. Whitney, December 16, 1890[1]

WHEN FREDERICK OLMSTED entangled himself in a thicket of poison
        sumac, he embroiled himself in consequences. With his country
rearing, he should have known better. The handsome plant, oozing juice
along its strong stems, was notorious and to be avoided, however beautiful its
leaflets and its handsome head of white blossoms. The effect of its touch was
worse than that of poison ivy. Somehow, Frederick, looking for something,
thinking of something, stumbled into the fire-producing grasp, which within
a few hours caused all the skin surfaces which the plant had touched to be
blistered and swollen. His face was worst, puffed beyond recognition, his eyes
closed. He was almost blind. He looked frightful, he was in pain, and nothing
could be done except an alleviation of the suffering while the poison worked
its way through a succession of afflicting effects. When the passing of weeks
and months made him better, sometime in 1837, his father took him to New
York to see a Doctor Wallace.[2] The doctor advised sea-bathing. This was tried
at Saybrooke, where once again Frederick stayed with Reverend Eastman.
Disconsolate beach-wandering did not make up for plans abandoned. Frederick returned home and remained at Hartford for some months. The principal advice given the father of a son so spectacularly afflicted by this common
woods-poisoning was for him to give up reading and to put off attending
college. So a pause was given to his life.

A difficulty with his eyes lingered. He seemed later to have doubted that
the long-lasting eye trouble was due altogether to the sumac poisoning. His
wording is interesting: "When fourteen I was laid up by an extremely viru-
lent sumach poisoning, making me for some time partially blind, after which,

10

and possibly as a result, I was troubled for several years with a disorder of the eyes, and the oculists advised that I should be kept from study."[3] Yale College was out of the question in the immediate future. Frederick at least pretended not to care. His illness gave him great quantities of freedom. He had a sensation of the world's largeness, for he had no place in it. He tried to learn some things on his own. "I tried to learn Euclid by rote, without trying to understand what it meant,"[4] he wrote. A furious energy burned his mind. It battered him, for he found no object for it, and was excluded from the school life of his contemporaries.

He made a new start in November, 1837, when he went away from home again for another try at private tutoring. He was fifteen and a half. Not so very different from what he had been, but no longer a child. He wrote of this time, "I was nominally the pupil of a topographical engineer but really for the most part given over to a decently restrained vagabond life, generally pursued under the guise of an angler, a fowler or a dabbler on the shallowest shores of the deep sea of the natural sciences."[5] His teacher was Frederick A. Barton, a minister who had been a civil engineer. Almost by chance, the pupil learned at least the rudiments of skills which would serve him in a profession which did not as yet exist in his country and which he had no idea that he would one day practice. He learned surveying. He played at laying out towns on paper.[6] It seemed not quite serious, and his energies— encouraged because his eyes were bad—went into hunting, fishing, skating, walking, and looking. However, he exercised the eye that was to judge the line and texture of scenery.

Frederick lived with Professor Barton, as he was called, first at Andover, which was north from Boston, near to the growing mill towns of Lowell and Lawrence, not too far from Cambridge for the student of topography to think of trying to attend some of Asa Gray's classes in botany. Because there were good coaching roads for this civilized section of the United States, Frederick visited his family often and always joined them in their long sightseeing tours of New England and Canada. It was a pleasant life, but a boy of sixteen did not hanker for comfort. He felt deprived and wished that he were going to college.

Almost a year after beginning his desultory studies with Professor Barton, in August, 1838, Frederick, sixteen, and John Hull, thirteen, accompanied their father and mother on a customary August holiday, this time to the White Mountains by way of Springfield, Northampton, Hanover, Franconia Notch, Conway Center, and back by way of Portsmouth, Nahant, and Boston. After the holiday, Fred continued his studies with Mr. Barton. There was trouble at home in Hartford in September. On the thirteenth, his father wrote to Frederick that "dear little brother Owen" had died. "My son take this affliction to heart and improve upon it"[7]—this seemed a summary way to deal with little Owen and somewhat hard on the older brother. It was a chilling admonishment at sixteen. Owen was the fourth child born to the second marriage, coming after Charlotte, Mary, and Bertha. He died as easily as many children did in the 1830s, and the only family resource was religious resignation. If Frederick had as yet awakened to adolescent disagreement with family attitudes, there was no sign. But his dreaming, leisurely life acclimated him to a new way of thinking. One can only name his attitude as romantic, a divergence from parents' and grandparents' ways.

Frederick was restless and bored with Professor Barton. He let his father know his dissatisfaction. John Olmsted wrote in reply, "If you will not go back in your surveying, by giving it up this term, and pursuing other studies, and if Mr. Colman *strongly advises* to that course, I have *no objection*. It will be an excellent chance for you to study Rhetoric, and you may not have another. . . . I am sorry however to have your mind unsettled on the subject of your studies. . . ." The father probably wished for Frederick to join him in his business in Hartford but was held back from urging this course by a delicacy of perception which saw something unsuitable in his son for such a life. He concluded his letter with generous advice: "Be desirous of pursuing such studies as will most tend to your intellectual and moral improvement and to fit your usefulness and enjoyment when you take your place in the great theatre of life. . . ."⁸ Fred did not know what he wanted to do. Mr. Colman, whoever he was, did not tip the scales in persuasion against his easygoing life. In December, when Professor Barton moved from Massachusetts to Connecticut, he took Fred with him to Collinsville. This was a village just west of Hartford, near the activities of his delightfully growing sisters, who teased Fred but deferred to him, and near John Hull, the younger brother who was becoming a companion.

A year after, a year in which to outward view Fred vegetated, the father broke into his son's settled irregularity to take him on a trip to Washington, D.C. They set out from Hartford on December 9, 1839, and returned only on Christmas Eve. The older man and the fresh young boy shared an eagerness to see all that they could of the capital city of President Martin Van Buren. John Olmsted was not beguiled by Van Buren as the standard bearer of old Andy Jackson's Democratic party. Even this president's manners, smoother than Jackson's, condemned him. He not only led the wrong people, he was, as opposition sentiment said, a hypocrite too. A silk purse, the grudging new Whigs said of him. Thus political partisanship was passed on to Frederick early. Only a couple of years later at eighteen, the boy was to be an enthusiast for the Whig party and its candidate, "Old Tip," General Harrison, who was to defeat Jackson's party.

Frederick finished his time with the minister-engineer in April, 1840. He was eighteen, and he came home to spend the summer in Hartford, and to be the hero of Charlotte, Mary, and Bertha. On May 9, John Hull, only fifteen years of age, through some stroke of luck, set out on a trip to Europe in the company of some friends of his parents. Frederick remained at home. He wrote John Hull on May 14, "I hope you will as soon as possible write me a long and particular account of your adventures and afterwards keep a kind of journal of your proceedings; that is write us an account of each day or part of a letter every evening, and when you fill the sheet send it. I will do the same if you wish."[9] Meanwhile he cultivated the family garden. "I hear Fred'k coming (whistling)," wrote the father to John Hull abroad, giving him a picture of home. "He has been down to spend the evening at Aunt Law's. He works in the garden (with great moderation) in the morning and this P.M. has been breaking the laws of our town, shooting poor blackbirds."[10] In midsummer, from Sachem's Head below Guilford, an area that Frederick was learning to enjoy for its hunting, he wrote John Hull, still in Europe, news of the presidential election—warming up to partisanship: "Hurrah for Tip. . . . He *goes it,* strong. I hope you will be back to *help* him. We've got a Tippecanoe Club in Hartford."[11]

It is probable that the older brother felt a pang of brotherly envy at what John Hull was doing, and he translated his emotion into a sudden decision to do something himself. He decided to try what his father would like him to attempt, a career in a store. The next time Frederick wrote to his brother, on August 29, it was a Fred-Law transformed. "I write you from Pine's Coffee Rooms where I dine,"[12] he announced from New York City. A week and a half before, his father had brought him to the city, introduced him to old and trusted colleagues in the dry goods business, Benkard and Hutton, French importers at 53 Beaver Street, Manhattan. He established Fred in a minor position with the firm and found his son a boardinghouse in Brooklyn, Mrs. Howard's, at 120 Henry Street.

In his new job, Fred traveled daily the quiet, villagelike streets of Brooklyn, the busy streets of Manhattan, and crossed, morning and evening on the ferry boats, a harbor being looked at and written about by another Brooklyn man of these years, Walt Whitman. At Benkard's, French was spoken, as Fred wrote to John Hull, "almost as much as English," and he was determined to learn French and thought he would do so quickly. Frederick as clerk had to copy French letters, "a troublesome job for one that don't understand it. Tonight I expect to sit up till towards 10 o'clock copying letters. . . . I shall have nothing to eat till I get home in Brooklin, unless I call at Delmonico's and get some coffee (in French style)."[13]

It was not long until Mr. Benkard or Mr. Hutton saw that young Frederick could handle responsibility. He was put to totting up figures as cashier. The young clerk had some pride in the trust put in him. But the duties were tedious. Eighteen-year-old sensibilities were offended. An outburst five years later against business in general showed his feelings: "Business—which I suppose amounts to writing at a desk all day and half the night, practising a pained politeness, or eulogising a piece of silk, or barrel of lamp oil—I would sooner recommend [that is, recommend for John Hull, who was considering then various professions] to study the proffesion of butcher and learn to stick a hog with accuracy and dispatch, or something as manly and refined."[14]

He could not like it but stuck with it for a year and seven months. He pretended to an independence he did not have. He was interested in the busy city and during that year saw the end of the heated presidential campaign. Speeches upon street corners, processions, crowds, slogans enlivened the scene. Daniel Webster spoke for General Harrison in front of the Exchange Building only one month after Frederick arrived.[15]

The life of the streets fed him, for the daily job starved his senses. The variety of people to be encountered on Broadway educated him. He had known the woods and fields of Connecticut. New York added a dimension of insistent human life he had not known before. A contemporary New Yorker, George Templeton Strong, another young man with eager eyes and ears, wrote of Broadway, "The street is always crowded, and whores and blackguards make up about two-thirds of the throng."[16] The human movement in the street and the solid, heavy buildings framed his life. By spring he began to chafe at confinement. The need for some wild and natural thing pulled at him. He wrote home in March, 1841, "Dear Mother, I have succeeded in seducing a pair of doves into a coop in our tower, and they have commenced laying. Could you spare me one of the canary's this summer. I think I could take good care of it." He broke into parody in his best Sir Walter Scott manner, "Oh, how I long to be where I was a year ago. Midst two lofty mountains, pursuing the uneven course of the purling brook, gliding among the fair granite rocks." He was not exactly homesick, but he was not at home in the city. Mary Ann sent food boxes to Brooklyn. "If you had heard all the compliments, thanks, etc. bestowed upon you and yours, for those last nut cakes, you would—(guess)—do pretty much as you pleased without any hints perhaps." He signed the letter, "Your affectionate son, Frederick L. Olmsted."[17]

Unmoved by his younger brother's advice that he locate another job before he quit this one, Frederick in March, 1842, left Benkard's employ. He could not think or behave like a dry goods merchant. He had no prospects except to go home or visit New Haven and try a few Yale classes. He knew that his brother John was going to enroll there in the fall. He visited some friends and was allowed to attend some classes without being enrolled.

After dining in Hartford with a group of local worthies—among them, John Olmsted—Charles Dickens in February, 1842, visited Yale College shortly before Frederick began to attend classes there. He was to report his impressions of this "establishment of considerable eminence and reputation." He liked the woodsiness and spaciousness of town and campus: "The various departments of this Institution are erected in a kind of park or common in the middle of the town, where they are dimly visible among the shadowing trees. The effect is very like that of an old cathedral yard in England; and when their branches are in full leaf, must be extremely picturesque. Even in the winter time, these groups of well-grown trees, clustering among the busy streets and houses of a thriving city, have a very quaint appearance; seeming to bring about a kind of compromise between town and country...."[18] Elm trees were not enough for Frederick, and he was soon impatient of what seemed to him dry-as-dust instruction. He was not docile to rote learning. He was both more intellectually advanced and somewhat more behindhand in his growing up than the regular students. Another student of the time, who would one day be president of the college, wrote that in that time teaching at Yale "limited itself to the means ... instead of reaching out towards the end. ... The memorizing of rules and the solving of problems had the largest place for themselves—even, as it were, to the exclusion of everything else."[19]

Frederick was becoming opinionated. His lack of experience coupled to a wide range of reading encouraged youthful disgusts. He was immoderate in his expression of dislike three years later: "I do think colleges are a most gregious nuisance, and I'd almost make one of a mob to rase 'em all down about the besotted faculty's ears, if I could not make reason reach 'em any other way."[20] But he was to owe something to Yale. After his brother began attending, Frederick was to visit there often, go to classes without enrolling officially, and to fall under the sway of Yale friendships at least. He was to owe a good deal even to one particular professor who was kind to the irregular student.

The college was a small, democratic, relatively plain-living community. The business crash of 1837 had caused the living standards of many students' fathers to become frugal out of need, if not habit. Costs were low. Tuition was $11.00 for each term, $33.00 for the year; meal charges at boardinghouses and clubs were from $1.50 to $2.50 a week.[21] The young men of Yale invented all their own extracurricular activity. The college fostered mental effort only and inculcated strenuous self-examination. Yale's worship services furnished a forum for outstanding preachers, men who had made a mark upon their generation. Religion stimulated thought as well as feeling. Such a man as Horace Bushnell, the Hartford minister, awakened youthful social consciences. While Yale was narrow, it was not a superficial place. And the surrounding enlivening society of the young ladies of New Haven was a civilizing influence upon the young gentlemen of the college.

This effect of Yale community life was to benefit Frederick, but his first spring term was not satisfactory. He was restless and broke away gladly. He spent the summer in outdoor activities; in August he engaged his energies and interests in handling a small boat on the Connecticut River and on Long Island Sound with John Hull. The two boys camped out on Faulkner's Island. John fell sick and went home. Fred stayed on alone. In the fall, his brother was a regular student and was bound to the routine of classes and chapel, but Frederick set out in October on a walking tour. He visited an uncle at Cheshire who had a farm. From a cousin there he borrowed a sextant and carried it home to Hartford. He was to be seen thereafter on the city's pier navigating the horizon of the Connecticut River. He already had an idea of going away to sea. In the meantime he idled but was willing to laugh at himself. He wrote to John that "Mary and Bertha are taking Drawing Lessons with lectures by that eminent artiste and savan 'Sig. F. La Olmstadi.' "22 "The venerable Audubon dined with Mr. & Mrs. Ayers short time since," he wrote John Hull in December, and "next spring starts for Council Bluffs— Yellowstone & Rocky Mts. in search of materials for his magnificent 'Zoology of America.' Might I be there to see."23

By spring he had found a destination. On April 8 he wrote in a letter to John Hull: "I have ship'd or engaged to—anyway—& must be in New York on the 18th inst.—to sail as soon after as may be."24 He sounded cocky, crowing a little to the sedentary brother who was going to daily classes at Yale College. Frederick and a friend had scrambled about the docks of New York, asking at one ship after another about passage for apprentice seamen on ships bound east to China. They were told that "one more could go on the *Ronaldson* sailing soon for Canton." Captain Fox behaved as if he were doing them a favor. " 'We always dislike,' he said, 'to take a green hand, but somebody must now and then, and we may as well as any else I suppose.' " Fox must badly have wanted one boy more, for he accepted Fred Olmsted without much more talk. He told him he had three boys already, but that they had all been to sea before. He, young Olmsted, would make a fourth. Frederick, eager to get on board, asked where he should stow his things and was told—if he could have known, ominously—in the steerage, but that the boys, as learners, apprentices, young officers of the future, were to have a "house on deck" when it could be built. Captain Fox implied a consideration which quite dazzled Frederick: "I was much pleased with him." The friend who had hunted a berth with him had to give way to Fred's impetuosity. The deal was made. Frederick went home to Hartford to get ready to be away from home for a year.

CHAPTER III

Sailor

I think I shall be calculated to appreciate rural comforts, if no other when I return.
—F. L. O., to his brother, from Whampoa beach, September 8, 1843[1]

O N THANKSGIVING DAY, 1843, a very thin young sailor on the deck of the American sailing ship *Ronaldson* started to write a letter home. He pictured his family sitting down to turkey and cranberry sauce. So real did the image become he turned blind eyes from the paper to the shore of muddy swamp off which the ship was anchored. He failed almost to see the hard-gazing mate coming toward him and hid pen and paper only just in time to avoid being caught. If the mate had found him well enough to write a letter home, he would have thought him well enough to work and would have set him to manning the pump or filling the water buckets. Taking good care to find a place on the deck hidden from the mate's eyes, Frederick Olmsted continued his letter a week later from the same anchorage off the south China coast.[2]

Frederick had told his "Dear Parents" in an earlier letter (November 20) that he had been ill for three weeks with typhus fever: "For two weeks I eat nothing, but now I have appetite enough to eat a bowl of weak Soup. I am getting better having little or no fever." He tried to make little of his illness, but his homesickness burst through in this and earlier letters long delayed in arriving at Hartford: "Oh! Aunt Maria, Oh Johnny, Fanny, Mary & Bertha, how I grieve that I cannot answer your invaluable letters." And "Oh! Aunt Maria, to be sick in a ship's forecastle is the extent of human misery."[3]

His news after Thanksgiving was slightly more cheerful. The evil mate had gone to Canton, and he was allowed the rare chance of getting off the ship. This was through the intervention of a passenger who had come out on

17

their ship, a Dr. Green, who had tended to the forlorn young sailor during the passage. Through the doctor's kindness, he saw the harbor from this gentleman's sampan, himself resting in state on a mat with a bamboo pillow. He visited the doctor's house and even managed a short walk through the streets of the port of Whampoa. "You must recollect I'm a sailor," he wrote, "swinging [along] in tarry trousers, check shirt, with the lanyard of a jack-knife in place of a cravat, monkey jacket, etc."[4]

Frederick wrote John Hull a franker letter and warned him not to pass it along to their parents but to let their friend Charley read it (Charles Brace, a classmate of John's at college). He had been seasick the first weeks out. He had had a fall on deck. He had had rheumatism. At anchor off China, five months out of New York, the seamen, and among them the apprentice officers, were not allowed off the ship for long weeks but could only gaze at the sticky, oozy mud shore and wish for freedom.

Although, after typhus, his hand trembled from weakness and his words slid downhill on the page, he continued to write. It was his escape from a misery that had descended on him almost as soon as the ship left New York. It was not a happy ship, and it had been for Frederick an unhappy voyage, not what he had expected from Captain Warren Fox, who had spoken so smoothly to him on the dock in New York. The boys, as the captain referred to his apprentice officers with apparent benevolence, were to have a "house" upon the deck, separate from the crew; they were to be learners in an honorable trade; they were to be under his special care. To Frederick's family as to him, the voyage promised a safe journey into adventure. John, Senior, thought this a splendid opportunity for Fred to observe strange peoples and their ways. He advised his son to take every opportunity to go ashore and to take careful note of the natives.

In April, 1843, Frederick had boarded the *Ronaldson* at the Pike Street dock just a few days before his twenty-first birthday. Intoxicated with excitement, full of his recent reading of Richard Henry Dana's *Two Years Before the Mast*, he expected a strenuous but enjoyable and costless lark. It would be full of discovery, of other peoples and places. Although the family circle of the Olmsteds had been earthbound and city bred for at least two generations, before that time they had had much experience of the sea. Frederick himself handled small boats with ease. He had sailed up and down the Connecticut River and on Long Island Sound. Such a journey was often the initiation into life of many a well-bred young son of good New England family. Dana sailed around the Horn to California in 1834 and then returned to Harvard and the study of law. Herman Melville shipped out in the whaler *Acushnet* in 1841.

Frederick learned the first day out how hard it was going to be to handle the stiff, awkwardly placed pump, low on the deck, requiring an unnatural bending position and straining arms and back unused to the motion. He learned also how splendid another sail looked running across their stern. He began keenly to study his shipmates, the other "boys," the mad steward, the cruel mate, and the selfish and hypocritical captain in the little world of their ship cut off completely from the world.

Meantime and very soon, he was severely seasick. Even the harsh mate ordered him below. He gagged at the smell of the boxlike room in which he belonged, with the other apprentices. His chest was crammed under two others and was usually unreachable. Four boys were as crowded as the chests. The first time ordered below he did not wait to change into dry clothes but crawled again on deck and found refuge in a friendly sailor's bunk—"Tim's bunk (fortunately very wide one) where I remained nearly two weeks, hardly eating, drinking or thinking."[5]

By early May he was on duty again. He lifted up his head and looked about. A sailor had said to him roughly his first morning at the pump, " 'You an'n't tired yet, are ye? You may think yourself d——d well off if you get through before 8 o'clock. So look about ye—you bloody young ——.' Acting on his suggestion I looked about me."[6] Having survived seasickness, especially grateful for daily visits from the passenger, Dr. Green, he learned to eat with shudders the gruel made from sour meal "which it was hoped the pigs would take off their hands." As he said, "One of the pigs died that night." But he began to learn the language of the ship and the names of all the sails and included minute descriptions of the ship and all its parts in his journal-like letters. The *Ronaldson* was "about 330+ tons, pretty good form, but nothing clipper. Rakish rigging, long black yards . . ."[7]

On August 6, he noted: "Saw first tropical bird."[8]

So it was not all bad. He endured the passage of the Horn well. He enjoyed a splendid sail before monsoon winds through the Straits into the China Sea. He was aware of the danger of Malay pirates and relished the sensation. Arrived at anchor off Hong Kong, he was given a job as captain's clerk and "made an enlarged (800%) chart of the entrance to the Canton River, including Macao and Hong Kong."[9] The ship was 132 days out of New York when they arrived there. All the men were eager to go ashore, but the captain held them on board day after day.

To his father Frederick wrote, "My opportunities of observation and investigation are very similar to those enjoyed by Mr. Pickwick while a resident in his Majesty's Fleet Prison. . . ."[10] He stared hungrily at the shore and had written to John Hull: "I shall surely do something 'disprit' before long—such as paddling ashore in my anchor some night to *wallow* in the . . . paddy swamp along shore here."[11] However, one day the captain, himself impatient to go ashore and needing a hand to man an oar to fill up the boat's crew, discovered that Olmsted could row; so Frederick found himself bending rapturously to his work, aware of the strange sailboats in the estuary and the people on them eating, fishing, going about the daily chores of life. After this visit there followed his bout of illness from typhus, long weeks of quarantine on board ship, and the bonus he had from this suffering in the visit to the doctor on shore. During this time he saw no "natives" except those who sailed out to their ship in their curious sampans, anchored under the swaying bulk of the ship, and sold food and other goods to the men when the captain was not looking.

The relationship between the men and their captain was a kind of war. One time they bought two green turtles among themselves and were going to enjoy the luxury of the meat. The captain coolly commandeered the best part of the anticipated meal. On the way east, in tropical waters, they had been given the gift of fruits and fowls by the people of Anjer, a port in Java. The captain this time too had stepped in and taken the best for his private table, "and we were welcome to the cocoa nut shells, rinds, I should say, after the Capt. had drank their contents...."[12] Seaman Olmsted's sense of fair play was outraged. And not by the captain's gluttony alone. He had opportunity in the cramped quarters of forecastle and deck to witness the injustices practiced by a man using power unwisely and callously. Ignorant, helpless men were the victims almost by accident of one other man holding absolute power over them in their little world. Frederick was hotly indignant over the fact, but could not express the emotion, being himself shiveringly near being whipped, as most of the men and boys were from time to time.

The midshipmen's "house" was built at last, but those for whom it was built did not enjoy it long. The captain had them routed out when he found another use for it. The boys were moved into the forecastle, which was already overcrowded with seamen. The ship was not a cleanly, well-ordered ship. The hold was dirty, ill smelling, and cluttered. No special training was given these officers-to-be of the American merchant marine. Treatment was rough. Punishment was physical. Young Olmsted's main duty was a stupid kind of exercise, the handling of the pump, a motion at which he fell asleep while filling his bucket and woke in a sort of rhythmical start, like the pump's, upon each filling up of it. "However, I succeeded pretty well after all—for I have not been ropes' ended yet—as two of the boys were for being caught asleep."[13] Worse than ropes' ending was the sight of land when one was deprived of standing on it. Olmsted discovered at sea that he had a physical need to feel the earth under his feet.

The illnesses which plagued his voyage of discovery were perhaps more serious than he admitted to his family. Dr. Green, who attended Fred kindly during the journey, wrote a postscript in one of Fred's letters to his parents: "I am happy to say that he is convalescent from a slight attack of paralysis."[14] As a fourteen-year-old he had suffered from eye trouble that had had in his own understanding only a partial cause in the sumac poisoning which had begun it; now, on a voyage that made him suffer, the young man endured a paralysis which afflicted him and then went away. No more mention was made of it in his letters. This is a possible indication that Frederick was prone early, as he would be later, to suffer in his body when his mind or his feelings were disturbed. Whatever the accumulation of ills the boy endured—seasickness, a fall, rheumatism, typhus fever, paralysis, or general homesickness—the good doctor returned several times to the ship to nurse him and cheer him, although the captain allowed no repetition of the sampan sail across the harbor, the walk through the streets of the Chinese city, or the visit to the doctor's house.

As Frederick endured, he roused himself to an interest in things outside himself and set himself to writing down what he had seen in glimpses of what he called the "real China." He carried home with him a thick sheaf of papers containing his impressions, hoping to get an article published. The essay was never to be printed but was carefully saved. It exists, an early piece of writing by a young man who as yet had only vague ambitions as to being a writer, or engineer, or merchant like his father.[15] But he had indeed already given that last career up at Benkard's. Nor was sailoring to be in his future, he knew with finality. But he was going home; he learned this toward the end of December, 1843, and he gave up the idea he had seriously entertained of jumping ship in Canton. His whole mind was taken up with expectation. He wrote a general letter home on the twenty-seventh to "inform you [the family] of my returning health and strength and the prospect of our soon being on our way home—home! . . . Oh my, I can't sit still, to think of it." An interruption called him off to work. "Have a kissing match all round and tell each other Fred sent it."[16]

He hoped that the voyage home would be better than the trip out. At any rate it was a turning back, and he could at least endure the going with more equanimity and notice with more tranquil attention the vagaries of the odd crew scraped together to man the *Ronaldson*. Unlike Richard Henry Dana, whose *Two Years Before the Mast* had in part inspired his own voyage, he failed to respond to the purely physical rhythms of the ship's routines. Dana had loved the work of his ship, and he had acquiesced in the discipline of the sea, however misapplied it was. His was a relatively uncomplicated, unthinking, richly endowed physical nature. His two years' voyage was a straightforward effort of mind and body to encompass new ways and find enjoyment in finding out how much he could endure. Olmsted was somewhat less lucky in his circumstances than Dana (although Dana did not have an easy time), and his temperament was more one of nerves and sensitivities than Dana's. He suffered boredom as well as hardship from the monotony and poverty of conditions on the *Ronaldson*.

What interested him, and perhaps more richly on the journey home when he had lived past his worst experiences and had hope, were the human relations on board ship and his own reactions to conditions, ugly things, beautiful things. They were reflections he could not very well share with anyone aboard, but he showed something of these interests in letters written to the family at home. This was his only outlet for deep feelings or keen emotions. He knew that the letters could go no faster than he did, but he wrote them nonetheless.

"The Steward is sick, and pretends to be crazy, the Captain of course sent him to the forecastle (where he has no more right to be than the livestock) where he keeps all hands awake all night."[17] Captain Fox was an intelligent man. He spoke well at the religious service, which in his office he was bound to conduct. Was this hypocrisy? The man was selfish, violent, callous in his daily relations with the men. Toward the end of the voyage, Captain Fox fell ill. Frederick ventured to pity him. "Well, how do you like the Sea?" he asked himself ironically, in a letter of December 10, 1843. "The Sea—On the whole I believe that if I had been in some ships, with some officers, and some crews, & those not very uncommon, and enjoyed the health I might have expected, I should have been *agreeably* disappointed. . . ."[18]

CHAPTER IV

Company and Solitude

I've considerable faith that I shall make a good Farmer.
—F. L. O., to Charles Brace, July 30, 1846[1]

T HE VOYAGE TO CHINA had ended when the *Ronaldson* nosed against the Pike Street wharf. It was April, 1844, a year from the time the hopeful young man had set out. Now the damaged sailor was home. He rested for the summer, restored to the love and care of his numerous family, the girls growing up, John Hull almost a young man, father, mother, and the good Aunt Maria attentive. He had dreamed of his aunt's pudding on shipboard. Now he enjoyed good food, a clean bed, and the right to walk out on any road leading out of Hartford. No one pushed him, but his own energy surged back. By fall he was ready to try something new. The sea seemed to make the land a good alternative. He had a kind uncle in Cheshire down below Hartford, nearer to New Haven. In October he picked up a few things and moved down the road to Cheshire to help his uncle with farming odd jobs. He was near Yale and his brother and might try some classes again when cold weather killed the life of the fields.

The growing up he had accomplished on board the *Ronaldson* brought him home from Whampoa Beach a formidable young man, doing whatever he set out to do with an intense drive and relish, however little he knew, beyond immediate ambitions, where he was going. The way he had now of going about his purposes, with a forgetful, wholehearted effort, attracted the respectful attention of immediate family, uncles, and friends. He groped in his understanding, but he pushed ahead doing one thing after another.

He came back to a nation which was running a higher temperature than in 1843. Everyone seemed obliged to get into arguments. Even physically, the country was changing rapidly. Boundaries had stretched and communi-

23

cations had improved. In the previous winter, the worst time for completing his trip, Fremont had crossed the Sierras and descended into Spanish California, from this moment a hero. A telegraph line was strung to connect Washington and Baltimore for the first time in 1844. So quickly did such lines multiply that by 1850 all areas in the East were tied together. Behind the moving line of new settlement, people could not agree. The Baptists and the Methodists split, North and South, in 1844 and 1845. Congress unstoppered debate on slavery by repealing the gag rule on December 3, 1844, thus allowing petitions for the end of slavery to be presented. The acquisition of Texas was variously hailed as a blessing and a curse. Inevitably Yale students joined in these debates, although on-campus division was funneled into the debating societies. It was a time when students had sport and refreshment in public speaking. Slavery was an irresistible topic. "We college boys discussed the question," wrote the second Timothy Dwight. "We contended about it. We exercised and cultivated our oratorical powers. We divided into parties, according to our residences whether in the north or south, and our prejudices whether on the conservative or progressive side."[2]

If at this time the debate on slavery touched Fred Olmsted, it was in his mind and not in his emotions. He expressed a lively interest in what might happen in Texas, but he spoke as an observer unwrung by feeling. It was a kind of game, a rivalry like the freshman-sophomore football game which took place on the Green, the only sporting event at which the whole college looked on. His was a private mind, but he was not as lonely as he had been before John Hull enrolled. He found friends among the classmates of his easily sociable younger brother. He had perhaps an advantage among these younger boys in having had the adventure of sailing to China.

"We are a most uncommon set of common friends,"[3] wrote Charles Loring Brace. These young men gaze out of a studio picture with candid young eyes. They are five friends, three standing, two seated, and in front of them the photographer's standard table. Frederick is the young man seated on the right who has turned momentarily to look at the others, while the four others look forward at the large black box on the tripod. The photographer has grouped them companionably about the table on which is placed an open book. Fred holds another book. Seated next to Fred on our left, Charley Brace looks straight at the camera with steady seriousness. Behind, standing, but leaning forward in comradely fashion are Charles Trask, Fred Kingsbury, with a hand on Charley Brace's shoulder, and on the right, resting his arm informally on Fred Kingsbury's shoulder, John Hull Olmsted smiles an easy smile. He has a natural grace and ease. The others have struggled into their best clothes, but lack John's ease. Various degrees of disarray in expanses of white shirtfronts and awkward neck-pieces glare at the camera. Frederick's half-averted look is of an exposed and somewhat defiant sensibility. The lift of his head is determined, the mouth and eyes, vulnerable. He has the open good looks of youth, clear eyes, mobile mouth, turned-up nose, an un-wrinkled forehead from which brown hair is brushed back in unthinned luxuriance. Yet of the five, he looks the one somewhat at odds with some-thing or everything. On the other hand, his brother John looks supremely happy and carelessly easy. He is strikingly handsome in a way his brother has missed. His dark hair is thick and short for the time, his eyes dark with a quick, direct look, his nose straight, his face well assembled in pleasing lines, his smile charming.

Charles Brace observed John Hull Olmsted when they first became freshmen at Yale. "I think John's father must be very rich, for John has a great deal of money." So he wrote home. "He treats fellows considerably to pies and that kind of thing, and is very generous with it. I have refused, except once or twice, to be treated, because I could not afford it in return (not that I ever said so), but he buys great quantities of confectionery. . . ."[4]

The younger brother became for Fred—after his return from China—the most important individual in his life. It was as if they were a family to each other, within the larger family group which was growing so that it seemed like a company of cousins. They loved each other and had also a kind of emulative jealousy, one of the other. Being somewhat unsure of himself, while the younger boy seemed sure and easy, Fred reacted in everything he did to what John did.

John Hull's roommate for four years, Charles Brace, became Fred's firm friend too. The other inseparables remain a little hazy. Charles Trask is a name only. Fred Kingsbury, in the light of letters written to him and by him, reveals himself as a stimulating, abrasive personality. In his friendship with Charley Brace, Fred reacted to an attractive opposite. Theirs was to be a firm, long-lasting friendship.

Charles Brace looks out of the group picture as if he had just been assaulted hard by life and was promising life that he would not back down. The blue eyes, clear and steady, are a little frightening. In his first year he had become a convinced and formidable Christian and joined the church (Congregational). The act was not empty form for him, but the bedrock base of his being. "Last Sunday I joined the church, and I humbly hope that with God's aid, I shall keep up to my professions."[5]

Charles was quite capable of saying something priggish and yet not being a prig at all: "I have to be much more careful of myself than I would be at home, or than persons generally would, for John notices very particularly, and is influenced in his own conduct by what he sees in mine." He was a young man in love with a goodness which he called God. He was to define his goodness in later years with much originality as well as earnestness.

He came to Yale from the careful nurture of an unusual father. His mother had cared for a sick younger brother while Charles was growing up. He him-self came under the tutelage of the father who, a Williams graduate, became a minister, a teacher, and a newspaper editor. The father exercised his talents most plastically on Charles, his eldest son, and in spite of his duties as principal of the Hartford Female Seminary, he read aloud to him at least two hours a day; he imparted to him a love of languages and history and shared with him rambles and trout fishing. Charley came second in a family of four, after his sister Mary, who became a mother to the others after their mother's death when Charley was fourteen; the younger ones were Emma and James. The Braces had been a Hartford family for seven generations, as long as the Olmsteds, although Charles was born in Litchfield. Even though Charles Brace was a year younger than John, four years younger than Fred, it was not surprising that a quick intimacy sprang up between the Olmsteds and the Braces. Their growing up in Hartford had been similar. When they went from New Haven to Hartford, they often went together. Soon there was much visiting back and forth between the two families. Frederick Olmsted introduced his own preferences in outdoor life to the new friend and found that Charley agreed well with him. He discovered that friendship was possible in solitude. The two walked together, skated together, and sailed together. One can imagine them talking fiercely. It was to be their habit of friendship later. Frederick was learning to enjoy a good swinging argument. John Hull was perhaps too agreeable and too pliant to be a good arguer. At home, John, Senior, and Mary Ann were not amused by audacious talk, especially in matters of faith and morals. But Charles Brace had as strong opinions as Fred and a passion for arriving at positions. The two young men stood up to each other with thorough enjoyment. They found themselves allies in a world they were beginning to explore.

Beyond Yale were all sorts of possibilities. Meanwhile, "I remember once being with him," Frederick wrote of his early friendship with Charles Loring Brace, "for a week or two on a walk which took us through Litchfield, Stockbridge, and Lenox. I remember also vividly a fine run of fourteen miles on skates, ending in a cold bath."[6] Frederick had discovered the joy of sailing from New Haven to Hartford and had Charley's company for one trip. In this version of going home from school, the longest way home was by far the most fun. Frederick kept a sailboat docked on the Sound. He took her out into the channel, zigzagged east to the mouth of the Connecticut River at Old Saybrooke, and then, stopping along the way at night, sailed up the broad river. The two friends camped below Haddam in a pasture. Their sail made a tent "and [we] turned in on a blanket under it. It was a most beautiful place, a green grassy dell [or] glen sloping gently up, lofty and picturesque trees opening a way for it back to a most lonely vista. A most charming prospect of our Rhine in front and on either side. Lots of wild pigeons, meteors, owls, sturgeons, mosquitoes, whipporwills, methodists, and hydrophious quadrupeds to lull us to grassy sleep."[7]

Emma Brace, two years younger than Charley, helped civilize Fred Olmsted. She was pretty, spirited, and intelligent. Every week she wrote a letter to Charley at Yale and sent it along to him in his weekly trunk containing his fresh linen and a supply of pies. She had no intention of being a passive kind of person. She had ambitions to teach and in a couple of years would be setting off to Kentucky to do so. Until then Fred came into her orbit and found it delightful to be able to talk to and laugh with a young woman. A year after he returned from China, he wrote to John about Emma: "You'll say I'm in love with her. Yes certainly, I really *love* her, love her dearly, but I've no intention of marrying her, and she knows it, and moreover I know that she's no intention of marrying me, whatever I wish."[8]

Fred's experience was enlarged by finding that he could be friends with a girl. But he found that he was susceptible also to the shakier, more violent forms of affection. It was this or that one, depending principally upon propinquity, who engaged his transient feelings. His stepmother spoke of the easy way Fred had of finding nearly any young lady irresistible. During his first summer home after the China voyage, she wrote, "Freddy seems head and ears in love with Frances Condit."[9] The same condition held sway later when Fred discovered a "Miss Abby," probably in New Haven. She had made it a little difficult to keep his mind on farming in Cheshire. "I feel as if I had returned to common air," he wrote to her, "after breathing in an atmosphere of exhilarating gas for a couple of weeks.... (Pray, Miss Abby, do they breathe anything else at your house?)"[10]

Forty-five years later he recalled what another young lady of New Haven had been to him at this youthful, aspiring age. To Mrs. Elizabeth B. Whitney, who had once been an adored and respected "Miss Baldwin" to him, he wrote, "You lifted me a good deal out of my constitutional shyness and helped more than you can think to rouse a sort of scatter-brained pride and to make me realize that my secluded life, country breeding, and miseducation were not such a bar to an 'intellectual life' as I was in the habit of supposing." Learning, leavened with affection in the banter of conversation, had a wonderful effect: "In some way in which you had to do, I was led up at that time to Emerson, Lowell, and Ruskin, and other real prophets who have been familiar friends ever since."[11]

Reading, writing letters to young ladies, Fred also wandered out as was his old habit. He explored the woods, fields, and streams around Cheshire when farm work was light. And he breathed in what he needed, great gusts of freedom. On a February expedition with someone named Alonso, his uncle's hired man probably, he found himself in a *shantee*, a mile from anyone, reading a book. Alonso was not happy with the poor little place in which the two had taken refuge from the weather, but Fred was: "I liked it very much—sat up with a hot fire and reading Zimmerman on Solitude, which will rank next to the Bible and Prayer book in my Library—I think it is one of the best books ever written." He had breakfast at sunrise, washed the dishes, "after which I take my gun and dog and go exploring—and I found some of the most picturesque and sublime scenes I ever saw."[12]

From the books he had been reading, he had found words to apply to pri-

vate experiences. He had lived nakedly, almost without words, as an infant
and a child. The experiences were now richer in his having acquired words
to describe things to himself. He found in the words of others, which he ex-
propriated, the assurance of the worth of his own bare, sensuous responses.
The book for this time was a curious, cramped reprint in small print of a
German book by Johann Zimmerman, *Solitude; or the Pernicious Effect of a
Total Seclusion from Society Upon the Mind and Heart.* In spite of the title,
the book was written by an eccentric who had relished the deliciousness of
solitude. As if speaking to himself, the author admonished: "Social happiness,
true and essential social happiness, resides only in the bosom of love and in
the arms of friendship." Fred was at this time most anxious to prove the joys
of love and friendship. But he shyly believed himself also to be of the select
few who wandered in solitude and whom Zimmerman ranked as made of
finer stuff than those who found the bosom of love and the arms of friendship too easily. Something in the young man responded to Zimmerman's
axiom: "Alternate society and solitude are necessary to the full enjoyment
of both the pleasure of the world and the delights of retirement."[13] And did
not the community of Yale College, in Fred's biased experience, answer to
the Zimmermanian description: "Those self-created wits, who proudly place
themselves in the professor's chair, look with an envious and malignant eye
on all the works of genius, taste, and sense." And the following words spoke
to an obscure ambition in the young man: "The world is the only theatre
upon which great and noble actions can be performed." Also appropriate for
the park-maker of the future, who did not know that he would be one, were
these words: "Daily observation proves most clearly, that many of the charms,
and some of the benefits, of rural retreat, may be enjoyed without retiring to
any very considerable distance from the metropolis, the seat of social joys and
interested activity." Such sentences, read and reread, sank deep into Olmsted's
consciousness, and constituted a lasting influence upon his thought. In this
curious correspondence of temperament, a crotchety, embittered German
philosophe was to have a lasting effect upon the shape of a life and the shape
of some considerable acreage of American land.

Happiness broke in, and playfulness. "I do believe I am as happy as any
body in it (it is a good world)," Frederick wrote to Charles Brace in February,
1845, during the separation of a midwinter break. "I don't know hardly anything I want unless it is, of course, the welfare of my friends, besides a wife
—Yes! that's what I want[!] somebody that'l love me as much as I want to
love her. Oh dear! I wish she was here now that I might tell everything to
her. I don't care about being married to her! no! hang ceremony, now—I am
in no hurry for that—I go for the largest liberty—how I do hate these stiff
laws of etiquette and society.... Hurrah! then I'm free!... [But] I am des-
perately in love—now, and no mistake, only I can't for the life of me tell
who it's with—the whole of 'em, I believe...."

The young man who was grateful for invitations in New Haven rhapso-dized humorously: "Any young woman, with tolerable attractions including a sweet expression and eyes that can tell—that has no hereditary ailments, if she feels at all as I do, and can make bread, milk cows in case of necessity —is a member of no Temperance society—can read, write, sing, ride, and drive, and loves cats and dogs and has read and can appreciate and feel the beauties of Zimmerman on Solitude—is earnestly requested to apply forth-with to the subscriber (if by mail never mind the postage) at his castle— 'Villaligni'-'Montursi'—Walcot Post office—Connecticut."[14] All this to Charles Brace.

In May, 1845, Fred found a second farmer, Joseph Welton of Waterbury, who promised to take him on as an apprentice on a more serious basis than his uncle had. This place was located through the exertions of Charley Brace and Fred Kingsbury. Yet before the arduous, short Connecticut summer began to engage him in earnest in plowing and hoeing, Fred was at New Haven again with his friends.

The little circle to which Fred and his brother belonged encountered al-most their only exciting educational adventure at this time in being given the freedom of his laboratory by the great and magnanimous Professor Benjamin Silliman, who was "the science professor." There they did their own awkward little experiments in the shadow of his elegant public ones. Students *watched* experiments normally, and did not perform them at Yale in 1845. Yale in this year was one of the few places in America where science to any extent was encouraged. Tall, handsome, gracious in manner, the sixty-six-year-old Silli-man, in the last decade of his fifty years of teaching, commanded love as well as respect. He was the only instructor at Yale to touch Frederick Olmsted deeply. He related science to general culture. He implied that God worked in nature, yet what the young men did mostly was wash test tubes, sweep out the lab, arrange books and papers, and sit, consciously privileged persons, at the public demonstrations of his experiments. These, Silliman performed with grace and economy. It was the example of his person they remembered and his attitude. He was a commanding presence who had routed the old theology-bound guardians of a narrow curriculum and had enlarged education to in-clude knowledge beyond the classical languages and mathematics. Even a small experience of such a man as Silliman was important to the person Fred Olm-sted became. Olmsted was to have a large, experimenting mind, working out-ward from facts, anchored in them, but unafraid of large results and effects reaching in unimagined ways beyond what other men might see. Fred Kings-bury, of the circle of friends, was to say, "We read and studied, and talked and experimented beyond anything required by the regular courses. College students always get a large and valuable part of their education from each other, and perhaps this set to which he belonged did this more than most. We discussed things endlessly." Kingsbury wrote about Brace, but his words applied to all of them. Perhaps due to Silliman, Fred Olmsted's innate esthetic bent encompassed and easily made use of the tools, the methods, and the attitudes of science also.

The friends began talking of the future. Brace thought he might go into the ministry. John Hull's ambition was to be a medical man. Frederick took seriously the prospect of farming as a career. His idea of farming was that it should be a profession in harmony with his new scientific interests. He didn't scorn labor. "I like ploughing better than any work I do here," he wrote his sister Mary, not abashed by homely operations and enjoying some playful inventions of his own. "I've got a trap set for woodchucks and I'm anxiously waiting for their steaks, which are said to be very good." But to take on farming as an intellectual operation was his ambition: "I grow more contented— or more fond of my business every day—really for a man that has any inclination for agriculture the occupation is very interesting—and if you look closely you will be surprised to see how much honorable attention and investigation is being connected with it. The 'Cultivator' has now *five regular* monthly European correspondents. Scientific men of the highest distinction are devoting their *undivided* attention to its advances, and I think here, the coming year will show a remarkable progress."[15] By *here* he meant *America;* he shared in the contagious American pride of the 1840s.

At Waterbury on Mr. Welton's farm, or at home in Hartford, he tried at least sporadically to follow the college courses of John and Charles and the others. In the fall of 1845 he wrote his brother from Hartford that he had "finished the architecture" and thought it had "been entertaining and probably very useful to me."[16] He had not learned much of mineralogy although he had looked at Fred Kingsbury's and Charley's specimens. Chemistry had been the same. Scientific studies in solitude were difficult. However, after a summer spent outdoors, Frederick seems, in September, to have rejoined the friends in New Haven and perhaps gained a more regular irregularity in sitting in on their courses.

At this time, John, Senior, had cause to worry about the health of both sons. John Hull was ill intermittently, and thought of leaving Yale to do something undemanding to make a living. Suddenly, Fred fell ill too. The father wrote to his "Dear Boys": "You may well suppose that we were not a little surprised to get your letter this evening informing of Fred's alarming attack. I hope he is well over it by this. If not, I shall expect his immediate return home, this is the third he has had within a few months, all proceeding from same cause, no doubt. I beg and pray he will now consider himself a vulnerable man and in danger of his life."[17] He gave Fred advice on keeping to a regularity and moderation in his habits. What the attack was, it is impossible to discern at this distance. By hindsight, judging by the interruptions he had in his lifetime from illnesses, one might hazard a guess that he was already in the habit of putting every ounce of mental and physical energy into whatever he was doing, and so occasionally exhausting both nerves and body.

In February, 1846, another child of the family, Ada, died. Orthodox faith, as handed down in the family, provided a frame of reference for such a death, or at least words to say. These words induced resignation if not comfort. But occasionally religious feeling in the family became a nag and a worry, almost an obsession, passed along from one member to another like a disease. During the year 1846, perhaps stimulated by the sad death of the child, such an epidemic of religious fervor seized the circle of the Olmsteds.

Fred was twenty-four and susceptible to the attention which centered anxiously now upon his spiritual state, his brother's, and his father's. It was Mary Ann Olmsted who promoted fervency. On April 2 his stepmother wrote to John Hull full of worry about his and Frederick's questionable faith. The next day, Frederick, at home in Hartford in the house with his anxious stepmother, in turn wrote to John Hull: "We are all constant in prayer for you." That day, John Hull gave them the news that he had achieved salvation for himself. His mother answered, "And can it be so? Is *your* name written in the Lamb's book of life? . . . Now, if your father could be persuaded to follow your example . . . should we not be a *happy, happy* family? For Frederick if not already entered in, is, I trust, nigh, very nigh to the kingdom." Fred was near, at least, to succumbing to Mary Ann's concern. He wrote with mimetic fervor on the seventh to John Hull: "My faith is much increased . . . I do believe that I love God and our dear Saviour much more, and I hope I shall live more to his glory. How wrong, how foolish I have been!"[18]

This same month Fred moved to Mr. George Geddes's farm, Fairmount, near Syracuse in New York state, to learn more about scientific farming. New interests adulterated pure religious fervor. He wrote in a letter to Charles Brace that he was glad that Charley's uncle had been converted before he died, but he said, inconsequently, in the next breath that there were no girls in Fairmount.[19] He was lonely in this new place, but that fact was soon mended.

One day in mid-June the apprentice farmer was engaged in the interesting and difficult operation of sheepshearing. He lay sprawled, as he described his position in a letter to his brother, "on the barn floor laying across a sheep's belly."[20] He looked up to find that Mr. Geddes had ushered a well-dressed party of young people into the splendid barn and the sheepshearer, looking up, found that they had gathered in a circle around his prone body and were looking down at him, dirty, disheveled, and in no condition to make conversation.

Mrs. Geddes's niece, Sarah, a very pretty young woman, was being introduced to him. Mr. Geddes was kind and said: " 'Come Mr. Olmsted—supposing you knock off—come in and cool off and see what's in the papers.' " So Fred scrambled up, disappeared out of the barn a rumpled hired man and reappeared soon in the parlor "washed and 'slicked up' " and found no difficulty in joining the company and the conversation of Mrs. Geddes's brothers, one of whom was a young doctor, and her niece, the attractive Sarah, who turned out to be a capital girl, who could talk well, but who also liked to listen to a young man who could talk well. The medical man, the apprentice farmer, and the pretty girl all forthwith retired from the parlor to go swinging. The swing broke. They all fell in a heap. Frederick showed off his sailor's skills by shinnying up a supporting pole and repaired the rope, and presumably the three young people continued to swing. It was no wonder that before the afternoon was over Fred was more than half in love with Miss Sarah: "Somehow these hearty open souled girls that are not afraid folks'll think something—always do meet me right down—and all others too, I suppose you'll say."

In the parlor, the young people had talked religion. It was the avocation of the time. Apparently Frederick expounded some eager new ideas under Miss Sarah's clear gaze and enjoyed her forthright responses. All through the year at Mr. Geddes's, he moved step by step toward a position of his own. Finding his own way, he moved farther and farther away from the views pushed toward him by his stepmother. Resisting Mary Ann's stiff, loving pressure, Frederick found his own beliefs, and he never acceded to her desire that he join the church, as John Hull had done. His father never did either, although in his case it was through a humble sense of his own unworthiness.

Farming, even the rough physical side, interested Fred and crowded introspection out of his mind. "I can cultivate and hoe corn—as well as plough—and wash and shear sheep. . . . etc. as well as most farmers though not very quick. . . . Tomorrow I have a field to harrow and next day sow corn broadcast." The next sentence of the young farmer's letter to his father on June 16, 1846, concerned a possibility of owning a farm of his own: "I hope you will visit and see the Akerly place but I do not fancy living on Staten Island."[21] (This was in fact the farm he would one day own, but not before a try in Connecticut.)

Three days later Fred, showing off his new religious sophistication to John Hull, wrote that as for himself, if he could put aside hereditary prejudices, he might become an Episcopalian. By the end of the month he wrote his brother that it did him, Fred, more good to stay home from church and read and criticize a sermon than to attend the service.

Like a good New Englander, which he was, indeed, to his bones' marrow, he exercised himself critically on his friends as well as himself. He scolded Fred Kingsbury for liking coffee and tea and urged him to give them up, saying that, as for himself, he enjoyed water. He admitted to having drunk his quart of coffee and tea on board the *Ronaldson,* and brandy and wine too, and said that he would prefer brandy-drinking or wine-drinking to coffee.[22] But he contradicted himself in a letter of this same summer to his father, expanding on how well one lived at Mr. Geddes's. "We have tea three times a day—and very good coffee for breakfast." Mr. Geddes, his farm, his hilltop, his niece, his habits captivated his imagination: "We have fresh meat well cooked and served, half the time at least—and *silver forks every day....* We have excellent water and an ice house so handy that they never think it is not worth the trouble to use it. Mr. Geddes drinks Congress water and a little brandy for the stomach ache."[23]

Fred was free to invite friends to stay at Fairmount. He was treated as a friend of the family. And for companionship, he acquired a dog, a terrier, "the finest pup you ever saw. I call him 'Pepper.'"[24] He read about farming as well as practiced it, in a magazine called the *Horticulturist,* with a column which much impressed him by a writer named Andrew Jackson Downing. The general expansion of his world was largely due to his employer and patron, George Geddes, who was a great man in his local community, an investor in canals, a speaker on public occasions, a prize-winning farmer. He was a gentleman of large interests and he shared these concerns with Fred Olmsted. He asked Fred to accompany him on a fishing expedition to Lake Oneida. He introduced Fred to the world of county and state agricultural fairs. He talked, probably, about his economic interests in the region; he had been a strong backer of the Erie Canal. (His father had been the canal's engineer.) He stimulated a latent interest in politics in his young helper; Geddes was strong against the "slave power."

It was inevitable that the bright young man grow mentally during his time at Mr. Geddes's farm. He threw off, almost without knowing it, the anxious religious gloom which had shrouded the whole family early in the year after the death of Ada. He reached out to learn all kinds of new things. He began to find a number of firm points of reference, which living wove together into an individual and strongly held personal morality and faith. To his father, who was very quiet during the family religious crisis, Frederick wrote from Fairmount, "I am at war with all sectarianism—and party trammels. The tyranny of priests and churches is as great a curse to the country and the world as negro slavery. I very much doubt if I shall join or array myself under any communion that is not open to any follower of Jesus Christ." Then irrelevantly but only superficially so, he followed with, "I have been reading Sartor Resartus."[25]

He was thinking, he told his father, of writing a piece on an agricultural topic. He found his taste for study had increased. Outdoor work had not decreased but only sharpened his critical faculties, or so it seemed. "This has been a good place for me." So he wrote Charley Brace as he saw the end of the summer. "I have looked on and talked more than I've worked; but I've considerable faith that I shall make a good Farmer. In fact I don't doubt it at all, if I can only get a good wife and a place to suit me and am not badly shaved in purchasing it."[26]

He was turning his gaze outward from solitude toward all the engrossing affairs of the world, one of which at this time was the politics of freedom versus slavery. "Texas with Slavery, will I hope give us California as well as Oregon *without.*" (He was to feel more keenly about Texas with slavery, and would not, several years later, give it up so easily.) "If we can but secure that before the lines are irretrievably drawn [this was still 1846] then at least I hope it will be North and freedom vs. South and Slavery, and then Hurrah for gradual Emancipation and a brisk trade with Africa."[27] He was thinking, apparently, as many people in the North were, of a return of freed slaves to Africa.

Frederick finished up his apprenticeship in a blaze of glory. He went to the Auburn, New York, fair, was a committeeman for the arrangements under George Geddes's friendly sponsorship, and was made much of by the portly, successful men of affairs taking part in the judging and awarding of prizes. He was beyond the reach of his stepmother's now pitiful query (for she was in deadly earnest): "Can you tell me," she wrote her other son, "why Frederick has never made a profession of religion? I supposed it was his intention, when he left here in the spring, to do it as soon as he was settled for the summer."[28] And she wrote again a little stiffly, from disappointment, "With respect to Fred I regret with you that he did not connect himself with the church last summer as he intended. I fear now that he never will."[29] But Frederick was walking into his own life. In the experience of living he would create his own faith. That it would be infused with a religious feeling would be true, that it would be individual would be seen.

As he left the Geddes farm, he was most eager to have a place of his own. To his father he had written in July, "In regard to the winter—If you should find a sea shore farm—that would make some difference. Wherever I am I shall study more than I work, a good deal. . . . The greatest objection to the Sachem's Head Farm is its smallness and perhaps its bleakness."[30] But it was to Sachem's Head that he went.

CHAPTER V
Scientific Farmer

He won't be content with less than infinity—while he himself is only finite and a farmer.

—John Hull Olmsted on his brother Frederick,
to Fred Kingsbury, December 11, 1849[1]

SACHEM'S HEAD was a spiny serpent of a peninsula pushing its rocky ledges by twists and turns into the blue Sound below the old town of Guilford, which lay thirteen miles east of New Haven, accessible to Yale men as a good fishing and hunting area. It had bad roadways and scattered acres of oats and hay struggling to separate themselves from rocks and swamp. In fall brilliant tufts of maples separated fields and fringed miniature bays. It was an area as difficult to farm as when seventeenth century settlers first tried to plow its resistant acres, as isolated in 1847, when Frederick Olmsted determined to live there and farm a small acreage. His father very willingly purchased the farm, and Frederick pledged by note to repay his father.

In January, this transaction completed, he made trip after trip down to Guilford where he stayed while scouting the place. Not noticing his father's and mother's mild upset at his leaving home, he wrote Charley Brace on January 12, "I have got so much that I must do this week before I leave home (*forever*)—I can't keep purchasing a letter from you to cheer me in my voluntary exile to the rock bound head of Sachem." But he confessed also, with a little complacency, that he had enjoyed himself "a great deal at the little dancing parties this winter."[2] Dancing parties, at least for a time, were to be left behind, as well as his family. "We miss Fred a good deal," the father wrote to John Hull. "The idea that he has gone to a new home and perhaps to be with us no more permanently, is rather gloomy. This dispersion of children is to a parent fond and devoted to the domestic circle one of the most melancholy circumstances in life."[3]

Fred, burned brown with sun, full of a purpose that had nothing to do with the kind of gentlemanly activities John Hull was engaged in at Yale, shocked his younger brother by his energy. John had come from Yale for a visit and saw Fred arrive from Sachem's Head talking of nothing but farming—"tool-and-horse-and-cattle, etc. buying."[4] As soon as he had gathered his needed supplies together in Hartford, Fred left immediately driving a horse cart, with a "yoke of oxen behind and a led-horse beside."[5] John described his brother as nattily attired for the occasion, "When he drove those oxen to Guilford he had on a nice cap and dress-coat, etc. which made it all the more ludicrous, though perhaps not less 'dignified.' "[6] John Hull wrote about his brother to Fred Kingsbury, worrying overmuch about Fred's dignity in this letter and another one in May: "The life down there is just such as to rid him of all dignity. He is 'well met' with everyone—everyone calls him 'Fred'—and everybody likes him. Which last perhaps compensates for the loss of 'dignity.' " John, filled with himself, ended, "I'm sorry he didn't have the College Education as well as I, or rather than me. He has fine capabilities naturally I think, but they want training now most shockingly. Still, Fred will make a good farmer—a good citizen and a good husband, one of these days."[7] The complacency of twenty-two and a Yale degree about to be earned spoke thus.

As fascinated as John Hull, his friend Fred Kingsbury, to whom he had written about Fred, wrote back on the same subject. He saw a little further into Fred, perhaps. "It's pretty much all true what you say about Fred. But living and growing and experience will have to answer for him instead of College discipline. He is an enthusiast by nature—though, and all the Greek and Latin in the world wouldn't have driven that out of him. Well the world needs such men. And one thing is curious—disappointments never seem to trouble them. They must in the nature of things meet with them often and yet they go right on in the same old way just as if it had not happened. I think Fred will be one of that sort. Many of his favorite schemes will go to naught—but he'll throw it aside and try another and spoil that and forget them both while you or I might have been blubbering over the ruins of the first."[8]

John was to graduate in August. His health was poor again. Fred offered him the hospitality of the farm for the summer. John was not sure he wanted all that much outdoor life. Fred himself saw the drawbacks of the place in his preliminary visits. The house looked "nasty," his fields had rocks in them, and what was not rock was swamp. In late winter, during thaws, the land was "juicy."[9] He would have to look to draining his fields. It was a subject on which Frederick Olmsted would expend much thought and effort in the next few years, and one of the esoteric subjects on which he made himself an expert. Besides, the wastes from the barnyard flowed malodorously past the front door of the house on the way to the sea. He hoped his friends would come to stay with him from time to time, but also that they would all—except John—wait until summer was over. He had too much to do during that time to entertain guests. But "there's a splendid view from the top of the hill."[10] So he wrote to Fred Kingsbury, the other Fred, with the sharp tongue and the keen mind, with whom Fred Olmsted enjoyed mental fencing.

With or without the approval of his friends, Fred Olmsted began his new life. He came into his ownership of the farm at the most forbidding season of the year on Sachem's Head. Winter was hard here, doubly hard from the assault of the sea on one side and of inland snows on the other. Neighbors were scattered and turned in upon themselves. Frederick made the acquaintance early of a nearby minister named Hall. He found him a narrow, prating man, with hardened opinions: "It seems as if a minister almost always spoke for effects like a politician. I *scarce* know a clergyman that I think an honest man. There's just the *damdest* kind of Christianity here raging."[11] Fred found companionship, though of a limited kind, in a young couple whom he hired to help him, the man with the clearing of the fields, the woman with the housework. She was "a nice young wife," and Fred was interested in her and the progress of her pregnancy. He sat at breakfast and supper with the couple and talked farm work with them almost as if they were his family.

Fred, with the new hired man, was soon hard at work casting manure, using seaweed for dressing his rocky fields. He rose early and went to bed early, tired out at the end of each day by the hard physical labor made necessary by the rough state of the land and the house. Sitting by lamplight at the kitchen table after a milk and pudding supper, he pulled paper to him and worked at his plan for the farm, sketching the form toward which their daily labor was working. As a boy he had designed imaginary towns. This was his first effort at the design of a real place. He wrote of his plan to his brother, "I intend to plant (trans-) but few ornamental trees and with them to take great pains—until I know where to put my house exactly I cannot arrange the lawn very well. The *Lawn* is to be the grand feature of my gardening."[12] His drawing of the location of the house, the disposition of the trees, the placing of the outbuildings exists on a part of a letter, probably Frederick Olmsted's first landscape design, not that he called it that, or thought in such terms. He was doing something as natural as breathing.

Rather than go home to Hartford, John Hull came to stay with Fred in the summer break of his senior year at Yale. To the other Fred, John Hull wrote, "Fred is altogether too busy to write. The pigs are growing nicely. The calves in the clover—cows yielding a good quantity of butter, for which there is no market." He added, "Farming does not suit my health at all." John's eyes were bad, and he was given to coughs and fevers. He had also a languid disdain for Fred's too enthusiastic energy. *Enthusiasm* was a word with a bad meaning in the Olmsted family. It was understood by them in the eighteenth century sense, as a rash, imprudent, unthinking, irrational quality to be discouraged and disapproved. Frederick had been reading new writers who defined the word differently and for whom the quality of enthusiasm was a sacred gift.

John Hull was pulled into Fred's wake more and more. In the lazy summertime between presentation day and commencement, the senior class of Yale College had long weeks of leisure, while the other classes drubbed away at regular tasks. John spent this time down at the farm, not too much caring for the spartan tone of existence: "We live on bread and milk and those who choose on cold salt pork and cold boiled potatoes or 'nothing else.' It is horrid in that respect. Davis is a very decent man—but never saw any luxury (except stale coffee) in his life and don't know why anybody wants any." Davis managed the practical farming while Fred pitched in and did whatever was needful from morning to night, as well as laid out on paper a lawn and drives and ponds. John Hull was privileged by bad health to dawdle. "I generally study part of the forenoon—then work in the garden or go sailing, fishing, etc. Same in the afternoon."[13]

Frederick was not averse to getting offshore whenever the opportunity offered. He enjoyed rough, dangerous sailing. He exulted to Charley Brace, "I harpooned *seven* sharks (all of which we got aboard) the other day. It was almost equal to whaling, for some of them were very wild and fierce. The very most exciting sport that I ever had a hand in. Leave woodcock and trout, my boy, and come down here."[14]

After clearing fields of rocks or spearing sharks, it was no hardship to go to bed by nine o'clock. But plain living did not tire out the brain. The Olmsteds in Hartford and the brothers at Sachem's Head shared an interest in the preaching and writing of Horace Bushnell, the minister of Hartford's North Church since 1833. Here Frederick could take part, and had perhaps led his father and mother into this interest, for Bushnell was already stirring up some disapproval among orthodox Congregationalists. Frederick to begin with was probably influenced by Charles Loring Brace's youthful enthusiasm for the minister; Charles had grown up under his teaching and preaching. "Those were the eager and powerful days of the great preacher," Brace wrote later about Bushnell. "We were withdrawn from the overpowering control of external formulae and formal statements, and began to search for the realities as for hidden treasures." The man fascinated his young followers. "Proud, at times almost disdainful; full of powerful feelings; simple; witty; tender as a woman to real misfortune, but biting in his sarcasm against pomposity and falseness; self-willed, thoroughly independent, a true leader of men"[15]—this was Brace's description. Frederick was not willing to join a congregation, but he drank in Bushnell's teaching by reading his close-knit, eloquent, and intellectual sermons as he sat at the scrubbed kitchen table.

The parts of Bushnell's message which made uneasy the adherents of an older Calvinism were those parts which Frederick took to himself and made part of his wider creed of unchurched faith. It was at this time (1847) when Frederick began his independent life that Bushnell's *Christian Nurture,* originated as a periodical in 1844, was widely disseminated by the Massachusetts Sunday School Society. Bushnell said quite simply that "the child is to grow up a Christian and never know himself as being otherwise."[16]

Why should this proposition have thrown consternation into the camp of New England orthodoxy? And why should it have attracted the allegiance of a New Englander moving away from the religion of his childhood, wary of all attempts to coerce him into any kind of religious fold?

The first question is easy to answer. By saying that a child, rightly reared, could grow up in the love of Christian goodness and be a Christian from the time his consciousness awoke, not knowing otherwise, Bushnell rebelled against the straiter New England conscience, that self-tortured growth, influenced by Jonathan Edwards into an exaggerated sense of sin, holding children depraved until converted, saying that the conversion could not come to that growing member of society until he was mature, consigning him meanwhile to perdition—at least as his predestined fate, until and unless with violence and as an act solely of God he was transformed in conversion into a Christian. Bushnell said he went back to an earlier New England tradition of faith, in which society gently nurtured the child in his faith from birth onward. His words, which describe what he considers the corruption of that earlier kind of nurture, crackle with emotion.

God leaps from the stars, or some place above, to do a work apart from all system, or connection with his other works. Religion is thus a kind of transcendental matter, which belongs on the outside of life, and has no part in the laws by which life is organized,—a miraculous epidemic, a fireball shot from the moon, something holy, because it is from God, but so extraordinary, so out of place, that it cannot suffer any vital connection with the ties, and causes, and forms, and habits, which constitute the frame of our history. Hence the desultory, hard, violent, and often extravagant or erratic character it manifests. Hence, in part, the dreary years of decay and darkness that interspace our months of excitement and victory.[17]

There had been dreary months in the Olmsted household recently when they had all been under the spell of the sense of sin out of which they were to be rescued by conversion. It did not come to Frederick; he resisted the experience, or was honest in admitting to himself that such a thing had not happened to him. Yet he yearned for meaning and significance in his life. Here was a presentation of religion he could understand. Through Bushnell's teachings he learned to add a sanction of Christianity, or at least religion, to another deeply felt belief: that men could be taught or nurtured by society to do well. He was to show in his writings later that he thought that the child, the worker, the slave, could all be taught, and thus become worthy members of society. This was the basis of his belief in democracy. It was a faith that would inform the work of his life; he was to build parks for people who could find in landscapes a force to educate and to transform. He would act as an agent of society nurturing people by influences of beauty, order, and release from the pressures of ugliness and disorder. But all this (while contained in the germ of a few words caught from a Hartford minister's weekly sermons, or published discourses) lay far in the future. As he read

and applauded Bushnell, it seemed to Fred Olmsted that the preacher buttressed his other teachers—Emerson, Lowell, Whittier, and Bryant. Bushnell,
as well as these purely literary men, gave a religious sanction to a contemporary hopeful feeling that the processes of human life were important. He,
and they, were a part of a background that made other more radical departures possible. But although Frederick Olmsted was to meet Bushnell and
find him a conversable human being, the minister was somewhat remote from
his daily life. On the other hand, his friend Charles Brace was a part of the
everydayness of living, and Brace's developing social and religious thought,
somewhat like Bushnell's, but more radical in its application of faith to life,
was an immediate part of his own development.

Charles Brace helped Fred Olmsted along the way that his instincts and
his mind were leading him. Thoughts, exhortations, encouragings were tossed
back and forth between the two young men, each anxious in youthful idealism
to live well. "Throw your light on the path in Politics and Social Improvement," wrote Fred to Charley, "and encourage me to put my foot *down* and
forwards. There's a great *work* wants doing in this our generation, Charley,
let us off jacket and go about it."[18] This eagerness to improve oneself and to
improve society was endemic in New England at this time. It lasted into the
early years of the Civil War when young Henry Adams wrote to his brother
Charles, "We want a national set of young men like ourselves or better, to
start new influences not only in politics, but in literature, in law, in society,
and throughout the whole social organism of the country—a national school
of our own generation."[19]

However difficult and rough the life was at Sachem's Head, Frederick
Olmsted looked past impossibilities at this time, full of ideas and hopes and
energies. The mistaken directions he had taken, and the harsh experiences
he had gone through, had not hurt him but tempered and fired adolescent
dreaming into a willingness to act. The young man was full of confidence,
even willing to give Charles Brace advice. His friend, in 1847, having tried
teaching, and not particularly liking it, was planning to go back to Yale for
a year of divinity study. Fred wrote to him, "I tell you what Charles I believe
would do you more good than something else—a vast deal—to spend a year
or a season in some well conducted though rough business or mercantile
establishment. The fact that it would be repugnant to your tastes is evidence
of the benefit it would be, the discipline would be to you."[20] He was thinking
of himself, reconciling to himself what he had formerly thought wasted, the
year in New York at the Benkard establishment, the year at sea, the summer
months working for other men on their farms. He felt stronger now, and
retelling the story of his past years to himself, he put those years behind in
a surge of energy. A passage from Emerson's *Self Reliance* might have hit
him fresh, it agreed so with his experience. "If our young men miscarry in
their first enterprises they lose all heart.... [But] a sturdy lad from New
Hampshire or Vermont [or Connecticut, Frederick might have added], who

in turn tries all the professions, who *teams it, farms it, peddles,* keeps a school, preaches, edits a newspaper, goes to Congress, buys a township, and so forth, in successive years, and always like a cat falls on his feet, is worth a hundred of these city dolls."[21]

Frederick and his brother not only read Horace Bushnell's sermons, they captured the man himself. In the fall of 1847, they invited him to Sachem's Head for a visit. The minister came down from Hartford and met the young men whom he had previously known in their family circle in the city. They had also invited down from his Fairmount farm George Geddes, another person whom Frederick admired. The four played nine-pins together, and Bushnell was so excellent a player that the others teased him; you missed your calling, said Fred to him, you should have been a professional gambler, for you would always have won. So Fred said to Charles Brace, who admired the minister as much, or more than the Olmsteds did. To Charles he related also their perfectly serious conversation. "He was not prepared to say that the local churches should be abandoned [as perhaps Fred said, in the grip of a new idea]—but he had made up his mind that a member of the *church* at large (i.e. any who *himself* called himself a follower of Christ) should not be excluded from the sacraments because he was not a member of a particular association of believers—(local church). . . . He was very glad indeed that I had joined his church in communion although I had not proffess'd to join it in faith."[22] Frederick is difficult to understand here. But from this statement, and others he made later, one must take his Christianity to be what would later be called a pragmatic act, or perhaps even an existential leap; he behaved as if in communion, even if he did not hold what another would identify as belief. In feeling that communion was sufficient, faith came to seem superfluous and even impertinent.

While arranging his inner life to his satisfaction, Frederick did not hang back from a new arrangement of his outer life for a more practical, everyday existence. Sachem's Head—well tried during the year 1847—had proven itself after all too small, harsh, and isolated. Some time toward the end of the year he decided to give up the place and find another. The Akerly farm, called Tosomock, at Southside, Staten Island, was one his father had mentioned to him while he was still at Fairmount. The senior Olmsted had vacationed on Staten Island on the south shore at a comfortable family hotel, and out of curiosity examined a farm for sale, told about it by people at the hotel. Frederick had refused the bait at that time; now he thought he might take a look at the place. But he asked George Geddes to give him advice. If his older friend and patron should find the farm a good buy, then Frederick would give Staten Island a second thought.

Frederick liked what he saw. Geddes gave his approval. John Olmsted, hopeful as always for his son's projects, agreed to lend the money for the purchase. Fred resolved to leave Connecticut and try farming in New York. The older Olmsted paid twelve thousand dollars for one hundred thirty acres, and Fred signed a note to repay his father. The sanguine father began immediately advancing further sums to outfit the place, furnish an already existing house, and pay for the move which was to be accomplished by sea from one waterfront farm to another.

In addition to being more farmable than Sachem's Head, the Akerly place (as Frederick first heard it named) had a sea view. It was also comparatively extensive and varied in its acreage. Frederick was to remember his first landside impression of the place. Far down the island from Manhattan, heading on the Main Road toward the southwest shore, a farm track turned off through a generous woods of oak, maple, sweet gum, sour gum, and sassafras. He came this way first in wintertime, when there were only a few stiff brown leaves on the branches of the hardwoods. The holly shone green in the sunlight. Beyond the woods was open farmland. Here the newcomer paused. He was on a plateau with a clear view down a slope to the shore. In this high open area, he examined the soil eagerly and found it to be red clay, good for growing grain, he had been told. His eyes turned down the hill toward the farmhouse which had a sparse tree or two near it. This structure was an old stone house, standing near the edge of the land, but on a last six-foot height of land which broke off to make the beach. The house had extensive porches surrounding the old core and was built up in wood on one side also. Beyond the house were all the white sails and black or painted hulls of New York harbor. One could see all the ships coming and going from the docks of Manhattan. The farm was an Atlantic Ocean farm, on the southwest quadrant of the island, westward from the hook of Sequine Point, within the rounding of Prince's Bay (Princess Bay) near the village of Tottenville. The large body of water southward was Raritan Bay, which widened eastward into New York's Lower Bay outside the Narrows and beyond that into the horizon of the whole Atlantic. In sight a few miles southward across the glittering water were Sandy Hook and the little hills of New Jersey.

The house in which Frederick was to live was an old Dutch farmhouse, built of rough stone, covered with plaster. The Akerly family, which had been a large one, had added a story and a half in wood, with nine bedrooms. "Outside the junction of the stone and wood was disguised by the roof of an all round piazza." Thus the future Mrs. Olmsted (twice Mrs. Olmsted), who was to keep house here, described it. "Inside the effect was rather odd for the stone wall a foot and a half thick came up nearly three feet and on top of it were built closets convenient, but queer." East to west was a large entrance hall, twelve by sixteen feet, going through the entire structure. On each side was a square room, sixteen by sixteen, high ceilinged and spacious, and opening upon the land "windows with deep seats looking east and in one room a window looking south either side of the fireplace."[23] So the future housewife was to remember the place, strange, but substantial, and comfortable.

John Hull had looked over the Akerly place with Fred and endorsed it. But he had to go off to Northampton and then to doctors on Fourteenth Street in New York City for a vague kind of cure. Fred tried to cheer him up by asking him to look about for a wife for him, since as a Staten Island farmer, he would need one! Meanwhile, he exercised himself in fierce exertions in order to bring equipment and supplies from Sachem's Head to Southside. He hired the sloop *Juliet,* loaded animals, plants, and furniture on board, and sailed with the captain into a storm of ice and snow. It was a storm which at one time blew them almost out into the Atlantic and at another time had them taking refuge in New York harbor off Hellgate. They ended up grounded, in sight of the farm, forced too close in near the hook of Great Kills. At last they safely put off the supplies during a lull, and Fred had to have the things hauled laboriously along the shore from some distance. Safely in the house, he found no comfort or relief at first: "The kitchen attick is full of bedbugs! don't tell John of it. There are none in the new house (tell him that)."[24] This to his father.

In the coming year Frederick would have company on the weekends. John was to be studying medicine in the city with Dr. Willard Parker; Charley Brace was studying divinity on his own and teaching in a private school, the Rutgers Institute, to make expenses. John and Charles lived in the same boardinghouse, full of "a curious mixture of Theologs who are 'Brothers' and eat fast, and music teachers who are indignant at the prevailing want of taste in music."[25] The two young men got away from such barbarities by going down to see the progress Fred was making on his new farm.

Joking about having to call his place "Connecticut" or "Hartford," the Staten Island farmer soon began to feel a native and fell easily into the habit of calling his homestead "Southside" from the general geographical designation of the area. The nearby inhabitants, at least the farmers of medium or large holdings, were an open, cheerful, and helpful lot, and Fred responded eagerly. He had been lonely at Sachem's Head. The substantial farmers of Staten Island, of Huguenot or Dutch descent, from the first did not give him a chance to be lonely here. "I met about a dozen of the neighbors with three or four from the city and Clifton,"[26] he informed Charles Brace shortly after unloading his supplies. At a friendly neighbor's house there was a sit-down supper and sober conversation among practical men who were all interested in the welfare of Staten Island as well as their own farms, and who were ready to help a likely newcomer. The men sat down to a smoke after supper, and as he left, bundled up against the weather, he was given a farewell brandy at the door. A week later, Frederick told John Hull that he had *"tea'd* and *evening'd"*[27] at Dr. Cyrus Perkins's. He could not know the momentous importance of this announcement both for himself and for John.

The doctor's was a household of more than average refinement. The doctor had been a professor of surgery at Dartmouth and "perhaps at Harvard," as Frederick reported somewhat vaguely to his brother on March 16. His house had a library and pictures and a piano. Not the least of the attractions of the doctor's house was his granddaughter Mary who as a child had lost both father and mother. Within two weeks of having moved into the neighborhood, Frederick was included in a birthday party for the young lady. He had a high-spirited time. There was piano music and singing, a little dancing, games— "goose and fox" and "who can do little" and "much romping nonsense—and a good deal of sensible conversation. . . . We . . . had a 'little quiet spree' quite in the Charley Brace style, in the supper room about 12 o'clock—and got merry with bumpers to Miss Perkins."[28] The doctor gave him four grape vines when he left. Young Olmsted and the old doctor agreed to share the cost of shipping their vegetables to the city market the next year.

Fred brought his sister Mary, visiting him at Southside, to see the other Mary. Mary Perkins later recalled that Fred had first come to see them on a spur-of-the-moment occasion. Irrepressibly, he arrived at their door to tell them at Holly Hill, as the Perkinses called their farm, that Louis Philippe had fled from Paris. The quickly-arrived-at friendship was to be a steady, warm, and genial one. The tie became a general family one, with Olmsteds and Perkinses visiting back and forth between New York and Connecticut.

Fred's sister Mary became a frequenter of the farm too, for she was enrolled in the Abbott School in the city, spending her first year away from home. Mary Olmsted, younger than Fred and John, was a girl of independent spirit, who expressed herself with delicious straightforwardness. She helped Fred civilize his house. A more or less permanent guest throughout the summer, John was at home there too. Between terms as a medical student he enjoyed the sea bathing and the horseback riding along the beach. In September a prime addition, who became the mainstay of the house, was Aunt Maria, the delightful Aunt, "who will kill you with kindness and herb drink,"[29] as John Hull said of her. Miraculously, then, the house became clean, ordered, beautiful.

The transformation of Frederick Olmsted into a householder with a large "family" and workmen and various interests in the community as well as on the farm can be seen through the eyes of Mary Perkins, who had become a friend to all of them. She saw the arrival of his brother, the visits of his sister, the auspicious advent of Aunt Maria, and the installation of "two jolly green imported Irish maids" and the hiring of "three or four farm laborers." The young man himself made an impression on Miss Perkins: "Frederick was at this time 26 years of age full of life and fun. He threw himself into farming with enthusiasm, introduced system and order to his men, expecting for one thing that at knocking off time every tool used should be returned to its appointed place and that every 'chore' should be done at the hour fixed, the foreman to report progress before going in to supper."[30] This is memory, and system did not come all at once although Frederick, in any kind of effort, invested a tremendous amount of push at the beginning in ordering and organizing. But there was a great change in a short time. Within months, the place was hardly remembered as the dirty, unkempt, and neglected farm dwelling it had been.

What Frederick Olmsted said on first assessing his new home—"There is no tool room, no shop, no harness room"[31]—was no longer true. Busy every day, stopping only for his hospitable Sundays, he laid out fields for wheat, he priced potatoes, he planned a dock, he remolded even the shape of the land. He would move a barn from his front door and put it out of sight; he would seed with grass the edges of the pond that was now only a mudhole; he would bring a curving drive to the door; he would fence the grazing land; he would, above all, plant trees. Olmsted was as soon involved in doing these things as thinking of them.

But all this activity did not fully engage his mind. He was heartily glad when John and Charley fled the heat and mosquitoes of the city to come down to spend the weekends. The farmer foreswore work on Saturday evenings and all day on Sundays for long sessions of walking, riding, or sitting by the fire with his guests. They talked of everything they were interested in. Fred reported every stage of his work at Southside to the two young students, and they, in turn, told tales of their city experiences to the farmer. John Hull was apprenticed to a physician and accompanied him on his rounds among his patients, in their homes and in hospitals. Practical experience among the sick and the dying, the rich and the poor, broadened his knowledge of life and gave him stories to tell. Charles taught little boys Latin four and one-half hours a day for six dollars a week in order to study theology and to volunteer his services to various kinds of city mission work. More direly even than John, Charles began to see, touch, feel the life of the city poor, in hospitals, prisons, and in the streets. These experiences of his younger brother and his best friend entered Frederick Olmsted's life and touched him in his sympathies and in his understanding.

The three young men were never narrowly practical or personal in their talk. They swung off easily into larger concerns, which were often either politics or religion, with the slavery controversy as the catalyst which turned every discussion into an affair of passion. The intensity of feeling centering around the great national conflict gave a religious tone to politics, and religion itself reached out to apply itself to this cause and others of everyday life. The two Olmsted brothers and their friends were wholeheartedly of the generation of young men who had Emerson and Lowell as personal seers to give a tone to their behavior, and who applied standards of high principle to every political instance. The last few years of conflict in Texas had heightened both aspirations and tensions. Frederick, however, approached certainty by zigzags. He was never to be as sure of himself as Brace, for instance. In a letter to the other Fred (Fred Kingsbury) in the year of his move to Staten Island, Frederick Olmsted labeled himself in this year, which was the middle year of the war with Mexico, a "peace man"; also he said he was growing into "an abolitionist"; he was however "a Whig," although this was now a weak rope to hang on to; yet he was most deeply, and contradictorily, a "patriot." (Rather than be a patriot, Henry Thoreau went to jail—if but for one night.) What Frederick wrote half deprecatingly about being a patriot should be believed. The conviction informed his prejudices as well as his insights at this time and later. "I am tremendously patriotic (I am, if you'll believe me, it's the strongest principle in my nature, if it is a natural instinct. It's stronger than love, hatred, selfishness, or even I do confess Religion or the love of life itself—now laugh) and wanting to do something for my country I fall hold of the Whig rope because I can clutch that easier than any other. I am going to be a Peace man too—I am afraid—afraid I say—because it will not be pleasant for me—as I have naturally a wonderful taste for the pomp and circumstances of glorious war."[32]

Arguments about belief roused even fiercer swingings and slashings than those about the war. Frederick and Charles argued each other into a state of exhaustion, but did not release the grappling love they had for each other.

The groan I gave on noticing how much importance you do in your heart attach to matters of belief—[so Fred to Charles] questionable matters which cannot be decided in this world and which I think it is right down wicked—absurd—filthy to look upon and act upon as absolutely decided. . . . Now I thank God, Charley, you are not *settled* yet, not absolutely pinned down to any or but comparatively few Theological dogmas (I hope *political* too). For if you reach this state it will be perfectly impossible for you practically to have charity for those that differ from you—and I believe that one spark of charity is of more value than all the settlings of all the study, the light, or Grace of Belief—of Drs. Taylor, Edwards, Luther, Calvin (whose opinions have been a terrible curse).[33]

John and Fred had got through their year of religious crisis and were comfortably beyond it. Fred had been left with his mind set against belonging to any Christian sect, but with an allegiance to Christian behavior. And as one who had grown up under Congregational ministers' weekly preaching, he had a nice appreciation of a good sermon, an awareness of what was a decent service. He was to be very critical of the forms religion took, and to abhor emotionalism in the religion as well as strict dogma. His religion was to be henceforth personal, taking the shape of his mind and his life. John Hull had adhered to the family's Congregationalism, but was gentle and tolerant.

Charles Brace was a different case altogether. From his awakening at Yale, when he declared his faith and joined the Congregational church, his religion was to be the center of his life and to have an individual growth and an original application in the life of society. What he saw in Christianity was a vision of goodness. In this year after he had left Yale and tried teaching at Ellington and moved to New York, he was searching for some action in which to trap the beautiful prey of goodness. John and Fred admired him and yet teased him and tried to pull him down to common earth. He took their laughter at his uncommon seriousness in good part, and in turn his intensity about certain things colored their lives as well as his. During his divinity year at Yale, he had heard a quantity of oratory bearing upon the slavery question. Cassius Clay, the Kentucky abolitionist, Henry Ward Beecher, and others had spoken to the students. "But, Fred," Charley wrote to Fred Kingsbury, "why won't you follow your reason in the Negro Suffrage question?...I do most devoutly hope for a knocking to pieces of the old parties, and as Bushnell says, 'I'll swing my hat over the ruins.' But if once a grand free-state party can be formed, I shall feel like being a politician. I could fight then."[34]

It was a cooler situation but yet an energetic intellectual atmosphere that prevailed on the farm. Fred was radiantly energetic about work on the farm, the pond to be filled with lily pads, the barns to be moved behind a hill, a new drive to be put in. But on the piazza on Saturday evening, peace reigned, except for the delightfully fierce talk. The sea broke on the sand within sight and hearing. To those who looked up from apples and a drink, sails or steamship smoke were always visible from ships in the outer harbor, pausing before going into the city or on the voyage out. At night, Fred would point out to his guests the six familiar lights offshore which he had come to love and to think of as his lights, finding these sentinels neighborly to him.

To Fred Kingsbury Charles Brace wrote about an early visit to the farm:

Just wear your feet out, Fred, in tramping over the hot pavements of New York for a day, and become thoroughly stunned by the unceasing din; then let a kind hobgoblin transplant you to a cool piazza into a comfortable armchair and slippers, with a quiet country scene before you of meadows and cattle and grain-fields, and beyond, the blue waves and the white sails, and, "some more peaches in that basket, yet, Charley," and you will get a faint idea of my feelings on the evening of Thursday, Aug. 28, 1848.[35]

Whether in good weather or bad, the talk went on. No churchgoing stopped it on Sunday. Brace, to Fred Kingsbury, described life at the farm during his weekend visits:

A wild, stormy day, and we spent it at home. A sea-beach in a storm is no unfit place for worship, is it? But the amount of talking done upon that visit! One steady stream from six o'clock Saturday night till twelve, beginning next day, and going on till about twelve the next night, interrupted only by meals and some insane walks on the beach! And this not like ours together, easy, discursive, varied, but a torrent of fierce argument, mixed with divers oaths on Fred's part, and abuse on both! However, I must say Fred is getting to argue with the utmost keenness,—a regular Dr. Taylor in its analytic power!...I shouldn't be surprised if he turned out something rather remarkable among men yet.[36]

Another day, the weather calmer, Charles wrote, this time to his younger sister Emma, "Sunday again at the Island, about nine o'clock in the evening, and such a beautiful day! Since I have learned to look more on beauty as an expression of God to us, I have explained many of the peculiar feelings I have always had about it." If he did not learn this connection between beauty and God from Frederick Olmsted, his learning of it went along with Frederick's own learning the same lesson. Charles: "I took a long walk alone on the beach this afternoon,—the old golden light on everything, with the blue, dreamy highlands, and the gray sky in the east, against which everything stood out so beautifully, the sea sparkling and deep blue, with the same unceasing whisper on the beach—hush, hush."[37]

Between them, John and Fred softened Charles Brace's uncompromising rectitude. They made him more human, more aware of beauty, more companionable, more flexible. In his turn Charles taught the brothers facts about life in the great city north of them. In October, 1849, Charles began helping a chaplain who visited the paupers and prisoners and sick people of Blackwell's Island in the East River. He wrote his sister, teaching in Kentucky, "You can have no idea, Emma, what an immense vat of misery and crime and filth much of this great city is! I realize it more and more. Think of *ten thousand children* growing up almost sure to be prostitutes and rogues!"[38] He wanted to help these children. He groped toward the idea that his ministry might be in the streets, not in a pulpit. The professed religion of comfortable men repelled him. He was uneasy about a faith "so seldom making a merchant exactly honest, so seldom inspiring men with genial kindness and charity towards one another; no, never hardly entering the least in a politician's duties."[39]

Charles Brace's firsthand reports of the life of the poor touched Frederick to the quick. For John Hull the effect was perhaps superficial. When John was easy about his own health (which was not often), he turned the gayest, most charming part of himself outward and pleased people easily and without the effort of thought. He pleased Mary Perkins, the neighbor's granddaughter, who often visited the farm at Southside. She was eight years younger than Frederick, five years younger than John; in 1849, nineteen years old. She was accepted into the circle on the piazza, as an excerpt from a letter of Fred's to his father on November 4, 1849, shows: "We had an excellent Sunday with Charly & John. Charly has undertaken to do considerable among the all sorts at Blackwell's Island and has very interesting and promising times. Mary Perkins spent the day with us yesterday."[40] John progressed rapidly from finding Mary good company to finding her indispensable company.

He wrote Fred Kingsbury what he had missed by not coming down to see them so far; he detailed attractions of the life on the farm "and the acquaintance of a beautiful and very intelligent young lady about whom I decline particularising as that loss may perhaps be repaired on some future occasion."[41] While Fred continued to be attracted by this one and that one, John narrowed his attentions. He saw Mary with casual and almost daily ease when visiting at Southside. But soon he was calling on her in New York when she was in town. There is in his letters a glimpse of growing intimacy in the enjoyment the two young people shared in a comic experience they had one night in a cab the driver of which did not know the city and drove them up and down Manhattan looking for an address he could not find. By the spring of 1849 John, describing to Fred K. the beauties of the farm outdoors—sunsets on the water, green wheat springing up—added also that, "Indoors too there were attractions, in the shape of Miss Mary Perkins, her honored parents [grandparents?], and new sponge cake."[42] By winter, people were congratulating John Hull Olmsted and Mary Cleveland Perkins on their engagement.[43]

Fred was not content "with less than infinity"[44] in young ladies and enjoyed being in love with a safe number of them. In midwinter, when the weather was grim and he was alone on Staten Island, he threw up the struggle against weather and solitude and went home to Hartford for Christmas and New Year's. If he went to church to hear Horace Bushnell preach, he also went on sleighing parties. To Charles on January 7, Fred wrote, "Since you were here I have only fallen in love with—let me see—Miss Stevens—Sarah Day— Emily Perkins—and Sarah Robinson. . . . I might also imagine I had a latent passion for the Widow Cook. She is *very* pretty."[45]

Thawing spring brought activities and life back to Southside. Friends were taught to admire the emerald green wheat growing in the field between the house and the sea. One day an expedition sailed across the bay to Sandy Hook. Wrapped warmly, for it was cold on the water, Fred, John, Charley, and a small boy who captained the boat made up the party. They had to spend the night, for the winds got up, and they could not sail safely back. Crammed in the small cockpit of the boat in a snug inlet behind the white sandbar, they lay in cramped positions through an uncomfortable night. But a farmer brought strawberries to them on the beach, and they picnicked with enjoyment on a stretch of land as virgin as it had been before men first sailed into the region, or so it seemed.

Frederick did not narrow his horizons to planting and sailing. He was keen about good prices for his cabbages. He attended a "fruit convention." He helped organize a farmers' society in Richmond County and was recording secretary. He voted "the straight Whig ticket and for the new school."[46] He became a school trustee. He wrote a letter to the *Staten Isler* about the need for "a plank road" for the Island.[47] Thus he fulfilled his role as a "scientific farmer." But the part he played at Southside did not contain him. His ideas, emotions, and desires outran the aims with which he might have been content if he had been only a farmer. A native restlessness stirred in him and perhaps disquieted his family. Influences played upon him, enlarging him and making him not quite fit to play only the role that he had first imagined for himself at a place such as Sachem's Head or Southside. He might have been a reasonably prosperous, enterprising landowner on the south shore of Staten Island, getting his crops to market, associating himself to advantage with other landowning men, speaking to school boards and agricultural societies, writing an occasional piece on fruit culture for horticultural journals. He talked knowledgeably of land values and population growth and worried about the reputation of the area suffering from the supposed prevalence of malaria. By the end of 1849, he seemed thoroughly settled in his place, a member of the community, a householder with the cares of workmen, land, animals, a house and barns, and a pleasant life of daily work, with intervals of visits from friends who brought the breath of the outside world with them. But he asked himself questions which disturbed the surface of what might have been a settled life. The politics of suffering troubled him. In a city such as New York, in a land with the principles of democracy, why should such things be? His sense of what was beautiful or fitting also disturbed him; he was not quite average in his reactions to pleasing sensations. He craved friends to whom he could "talk esthetically," and found few near Tottenville. He went to exhibitions in the city. "The Art Union collection" in March, 1849, was, as he wrote his father, "not very large yet, but the finest yet exhibited."[48] He admired a landscape by Church. He found a shop which owned several Turner engravings and returned several times to look at them.

The year 1850 was to shake up the friends and to widen Frederick's experience of life. First Emma Brace died. After teaching in poor schools in Kentucky, enlivening her surroundings with gaiety and her own kind of bravery, Emma was beaten in both her lightness of heart and her health, her work terminated by consumption. She came north to die and found refuge at Cambridge in the home of the Asa Grays, cousins of the Braces. Charles was at first overturned emotionally. "How strange it seems to me that I shall make new friends and shall speak to them of her, and she will seem to them like some one who never existed, or a character in novels or in history. The most warm, living character which will ever be in my memory!...I do not see how those can bear such losses who have no religious hopes."[49] It was hard for him to apply the consolation of religion. But he wrestled to achieve an equilibrium. John commented to Fred, "Before getting this state he went through a week of very unpleasant doubt and loneliness."[50]

John and Mary Perkins's decision to be married was made known to their friends in the month—February, 1850—of Emma Brace's death, so that for John, sadness was tempered by joy. When Fred, on February 29, stopped on a stormy night at Judge Emerson's house, he received from the judge and his wife warm congratulations on John's engagement, of which they had just heard. (The circle of Frederick's friends had widened and the lines of connection crisscrossed from New England to Staten Island and then to Hartford to Cambridge to Boston. Judge Emerson was the poet's brother. He had for a time employed his brother's improvident friend, Henry Thoreau, as a tutor in his home.)

For John Hull's and Mary's sake the Olmsteds and the Perkinses drew closer together. During the winter of the engagement, there were parties for the young couple in Hartford, including sleighing outings on the snowy roads leading out from the city into the Connecticut countryside. Spring coming on, Charles Brace and John Hull planned a trip to England and Germany. They talked carelessly; perhaps Mary might go too, but they did not really mean it. It was decided that it was to be a walking tour, and therefore it became an impossibility for Mary to accompany them. The two young men alleged practical benefits to accrue from the trip: not only was John Hull to regain strength and vigor, Charles would find out about English and German prisons and foundling homes, matters in which he was interesting himself, feeling his way toward a ministry among the unfortunate. But what about Frederick? Would he not go too? Frederick almost burst at the thought that he might be left behind.

The farm needed looking after. And he did not have, as he was embarrassed to discover, enough money to buy even cheap passage across the Atlantic and travel economically, as John and Charles were determined to do. He got quite wild with longing and wrote a strange letter to his father, reverting as grown men do to a childish state of frustration, jealousy of a brother who had already gone once before abroad, when he the older brother had stayed home. Hard times made the trip inappropriate. He had not sold his crops advantageously in the New York market. Yet, in his bones, he knew that the trip would benefit him. He was certain that he was a better manager than either Charles or John Hull would be. He had, in the end, to ask his father to make it possible to let him go. Frederick was twenty-eight years old, still asking his father for privileges, and more to the point, asking him for pocket money. In this letter, so different from the everyday confidence and independence he had gained, it was as if he begged his father for a chance—as if again he were a dependent: "The use I should be to John is worth some dollars. My experience and aptitude to *roughing it,* his diffidence, and Charley's awkwardness in obtaining information and services of men, would make my confidence and sympathy and experience with common and rough men of great assistance,—to his comfort, his health, and his purse." He thought he would need only one hundred forty to one hundred sixty dollars for the trip. "I did not mean to argue the matter much, but I hope [you] won't consider my opinions as if they were those of a mere child—nor my desires as senseless, romantic impulses only." He mentioned selling the farm and using part of the money to go, for "The idea of settling down for life without having seen England seemed to me cowardly and unreasonable."[51] Such a deed was unnecessary. His father quietly agreed that Frederick should go. In replying, Frederick put on an air of judiciousness that fooled no one. The remainder of the spring and summer was filled with a whirlwind of activity preparatory to the departure for England. Fred found a foreman for the summer work of the farm. He planted and gathered and sold vigorously so that the farm should be shipshape while its master was away. When he boarded the ship *Henry Clay*, with John and Charley, he turned his back decisively on the cares he had heaped on himself as a conscientious farmer and sailed out of his daily life into new worlds of sensation and experience.

CHAPTER VI
A Walk in England

Like children in a garden . . .
—F. L. O., *Walks and Talks of an American Farmer in England*[1]

O N THE THIRTIETH OF APRIL, 1850, in the highest spirits imaginable, Fred and John Olmsted and Charles Brace went on board the sailing ship *Henry Clay* and began a sea voyage which in their time was still a considerable adventure. The captain reluctantly agreed to deliver to them the keys of the second class cabin which had been promised to them by an agent on shore. The steward tried to push other passengers in with them while the captain argued. They compromised and accepted one other cabin mate, a prepossessing young Irish surgeon. Looking into the cabin, they found it half choked with cotton, spare sails, and lumber. By persistent talk, they had the ship's stores removed. Even before the ship sailed, while becalmed in the harbor, Frederick, who was still half the sailor he had been in earnest for a year, scrambled above and below decks, inspecting critically the way the ship was handled. (He was to say in his preface to the book written to describe the journey that he had traveled on one farmer's leg and one sailor's leg.) Drunk seamen delayed the departure. The captain knocked down a cook he thought impertinent. Frederick roamed the passageways as the ship got under way and sailed out through the Narrows. He met everyone, talked to everyone, and was soon engaged in taking notes, for he was determined to make a book out of his travels.

For quiet hours, John and Charley set up an improvised chessboard, with handmade cork men stuck with pins into the board. The surgeon, who fortunately played chess, joined them at the homemade game as the lights shifted and the boards creaked. John's eyes were bad, so Fred and Charley read aloud when the light would allow it. But most of their amusement came from mixing with the people on board. They took a whirl in the saloon, dancing with young and old ladies. Long hours and long days followed with much sameness. Expectations rose toward the end of the voyage. Frederick put on oilskins to wait on deck for the first sight of land. At three o'clock, "There was LAND—dark and distinct against the eastern glow—no more 'imagination.' It was only a dark ledge of rocks, with a white light-house, and a streak of white foam between it and the dark blue of the sea; but it seemed thrillingly beautiful."[2]

Everything to be seen and heard and smelled was new and wonderful as Liverpool unfolded before them. Its solidity struck them at once, very un-American. "It was a real pleasure to stamp upon the neat, firm, solid masonwork of the dock," a contrast to the "shabby log wharves we had stumbled over as we left New York." To Frederick, Britain was not only the past, it was the most modern of nations in the year 1850. "The landing-place was spacious, not encumbered with shanties or piles of freight, and though there was a little rain falling, there was a smooth, clean stone pavement, free from mud, to walk upon. There was a slight smell of bituminous smoke in the air, not disagreeable, but, to me, highly pleasant. I snuffed it as if passing a field of new mown hay."[3] Stocks and stones, and people, he missed nothing. His eye was caught by a huddle of women, prostitutes waiting quietly at the dock. "I was surprised at the quietness and decency of these 'sailors' wives,' as they called themselves."[4]

Being allowed to leave the ship, the young men walked about the town a little until they were tired. They found a "Temperance Hotel" in which men were, in a jolly, noisy way, drinking beer, and slept in good beds in rooms for which they paid 25¢ the night. They were now confident that they might travel cheaply. They were going to allow themselves 75¢ to $1 a day, and perhaps could spend less. They repacked and balanced their knapsacks, they tested their socks and boots, and for two or three days walked about Liverpool to get used to being on land. In the new suburb, Birkenhead, they walked for hours. The city planner of the future, not knowing he was to be one, viewed with great interest a city which had been designed. This planned growth was what the wealth of the new steam packets and the slave trade had brought to Liverpool.

Birkenhead was not only a new city, where there had been only half a dozen houses before, but a planned city. Frederick recorded the name of the architect-planner, Gillespie Graham, and noted, "There are several public squares, and the streets and places are broad, and well paved and lighted. A considerable part of the town has been built with reference to general effect."[5] Everything was a discovery. The young men went into a bakery and fell to talking with the baker about the kind of flour he used. He, in turn, joined their walk and showed them through the public market with its glass roof supported on slender iron pillars. As they said goodbye to this guide, he "begged us not to leave Birkenhead without seeing the New Park, and at his suggestion we left our knap-sacks with him, and proceeded to it."[6] The people in the park and the park itself filled Frederick with admiration. It was a beautiful, civilized place, and the city poor as well as rich were perfectly at home in it. He admired two achievements in the park: the beauty of an adaptation of lawn and trees and slopes from nature and the accommodation of this creation to the needs of human beings. He scribbled in his diary, "Five minutes of admiration, and a few more spent studying the manner in which art had been employed to obtain from nature so much beauty, and I was ready to admit that in democratic America there was nothing to be thought of as comparable with this People's Garden."

After surveying the New Park, they departed by train and were let off at an appropriately rural station to begin their walking. "There we were right in the midst of it! The country—and such country!—green, dripping, glistening, gorgeous! We stood dumb-stricken by its loveliness, as, from the bleak April and bare boughs we had left at home, broke upon us that English May—sunny, leafy, blooming May—in an English lane; with hedges, English hedges, hawthorn hedges, all in blossom; homely old farmhouses, quaint stables, and haystacks; the old church spire over the distant trees; the mild sun beaming through the watery atmosphere, and all so quiet—the only sounds the hum of bees, and the crisp grass-tearing of a silken-skinned, real (unimported) Hereford cow, over the hedge." They walked and stopped and pointed and talked and looked, seeming to themselves "like children in a garden."[7] They were delighted that the English inn in which they stopped the first night was very English and traditional. Frederick sat up to write his diary, enjoying the sensation of so sitting up in such a place: "The landlady has sent me up a glass of her home-brewed beer, with a nightcap, which I noticed she hung by the fire when I left the kitchen. The chambermaid has drawn down the bedclothes, and says, 'The bed has been well aired, sir.'" Next morning kneeling at a "little, low, latticed window" he gazed at village roofs and a misty gray unemphatic landscape with great emotion. It was the landscape of literature, "all its parts as familiar to me as my native valley."[8]

But one must not think of Fred or John or Charley Brace with their keen Connecticut practicality as walking through the English landscape in a state of dreaming. The very morning after the first night on the walking tour, Fred met a farmer in a lane near the inn and very characteristically "asked him to let me see his cows." The farmer was obliging and took him along to his barns, where he allowed Fred to inspect everything—the animals, the buildings, and all the arrangements. Sharpness began to come through. "The arrangements for saving manure were poor." Frederick approved the use of bones for fertilizer. But the farmer's carts were clumsy and heavy for the horses. The plow was "a very beautiful instrument"[9] suited for the deep, rich loam of the area. It would not have done at all on the rocky Connecticut fields. So the first day and night of the walks and talks of the young American farmer set the tone of the several weeks' expedition.

Each morning, the walkers repacked their knapsacks with care, strapped raincoats on top of the knapsacks, and set out for whatever new things might happen on their way. They measured roadways and paths, climbed stiles, waded brooks, threaded fern-floored forests in their stout Connecticut-made boots. And everywhere they went, they talked with people, or listened to what people had to say. People, animals, habits of living, modes of work and play, and pure unadulterated scenery caught their attention in turn. Starting at the end of May, they walked about two hundred miles in the next four weeks. They had fast days, slow days, intermediate days on trains to get from one good walking area to another. Peddlers on the road, farmers in fields, evangelical laymen who invited them to spend the night (and they did), gentlemen, sextons in cathedrals, landladies, ditch-diggers, herds-men—all were part of the movement of their pilgrimage. They looked at churches and manure piles, they studied drainage systems and farm tools, they asked about breeding-stock and orchard trees, about prisons and children's homes (this principally for Charley Brace). Frederick stopped to sketch scenes. He decorated his notes with drawings in the margin. He was to use the sketches in his book describing the trip. Unable to be mere passive observers of the scene, the three young men entered into more than travelers' relations with people along the way. They gave back to those who opened to them on religion or politics something of their own opinions. Their clever hands did not balk at doing some practical repair work on a clock in an inn where there was a Connecticut clock which, as the landlord said, "had got a-going too fast." "We have set it back to the landlord's notion, lengthened the pendulum, and oiled the 'pallet,' all to save the reputation of Mr. Welton [the brass plate on the clock said 'H. Welton, Terryville, Connecticut (warranted, if well used)] and the universal Yankee nation."[10]

The general direction of their walk was southward from below the crossing of the Mersey, setting a course mostly just to the east of the border of Wales, although John and Charles left Fred temporarily to make an expedition into the mountains of Wales, going off course at Wrexham. Fred kept going straight southward to Shrewsbury where the two others rejoined him. They continued through the cheese country of Chester, the orchards, grains, and pastures of Shropshire, Hereford, and Gloucester. They crossed the Severn and went into the Cotswolds from Bristol. They traveled by rail to Bath, then walked southeastward across Wiltshire through the Salisbury Plain into Hampshire to Winchester. From Portsmouth, where ships of all kinds attracted Fred's professional seaman's eye, they crossed to the Isle of Wight and walked all round the island. They came back to Portsmouth, journeyed almost to London by rail, enjoying the humor and byplay of some pale, sharp factory-working "London lads." They detrained at a country stop south of the city, with the express purpose of walking into London to which they thus came for the first time by a purposefully round-about path. Little by little, the houses, the people, and the street activities increased until they came at last to a parapet on the south bank of the Thames and they looked across the river at the dome of St. Paul's. At this moment of high drama for the young pilgrims, Frederick Olmsted was to end his written account of his "walks and talks" in England. In actuality, they went on beyond this point, to an experience of other parts of England, of Ireland, Scotland, Belgium, France, and Germany.

What Frederick Olmsted brought to this homely expedition was all the force of his nature as it had developed. He was twenty-eight, an unusually youthful twenty-eight, having the fire and spontaneity of eighteen, tempered only slightly by experience. His was a temperament still absorbing stimuli from the outside world; he had not yet decided which way to turn himself. For this reason, being so impressionable, yet with decided and mature reactions, he was at the very time of life for various inchoate ideas to begin to fall together into a pattern and to give his character force. The journey abroad (not only to England, but to other parts of the British Isles and to the Continent) was an important event. It was in a sense the end of youth, the beginning of maturity. Fortunately, he put a book together out of his travel experiences, and in the book is fixed the crystallization of his mature personality. He was immediately and sensuously interested in everything he saw; he was also instantaneously critical and discriminating. His interests were spontaneously double—esthetic and intellectually critical. He saw towers, battlements, castles, moats, and, in his American plainness, was charmed and, almost at the same moment, irritated. He found the gateway structures of the Marquis of Westminster's Park "bombastic."[11] In the house at Eaton Park, "We found little to admire. There was no great simple beauty in it."[12] Chester Cathedral was admirable for its grandeur, but its effigies and monuments were ugly. Sails off Portsmouth were beautiful, but he dared to say not as practical as Yankee sails off the New England coast. There was even, to his unfettered eye, something wrong with the proportions of the much-praised cathedral at Salisbury, which he and John and Charley spent the afternoon looking at, sometimes from a prone position on the green. Fred eyed the famous pile from every angle, testing the cathedral to see how it fitted to the landscape around it. Testing Winchester Cathedral severely, he found his satisfaction in it due "to the connection and harmony of the mass with the ground upon which it was placed."[13]

A strange mixture, the young man who noted vermin in the picturesque straw thatching of cottages, who took down the price of butter on sale in the marketplace, who registered the wages of farm laborers and did not wonder that they lacked patriotism—starved out of it he judged—who also reacted to the line and color of every landscape to which the turn of the road opened. Hardheaded, clever handed, able to repair a clock, find a cheap lodging, plan an itinerary, bargain with an innkeeper, converse with farmers about cows and pastures, the practical side of Olmsted in no way inhibited the generous attention he paid to beauty in nature. He puzzled over the English landscape, what were its elements, why it was slightly, mysteriously different from the American landscape. Looking down a slope at a particular scene, he noted the hedges, the free-standing trees, not so much broad water as at home (he was thinking, inevitably, of the Connecticut River Valley), but plentiful watering in small brooks, the foreground of the scene containing always interesting old buildings, ivy-draped, and a tidy agriculture visible in its system of rows and ditches. Perhaps the general, dreamlike quality, he thought, musingly, was the way in which the leaves of English trees grew: "It is as if the face of each leaf was more nearly parallel with all others near it, and as if all were more equally lighted than in our foliage. It is perhaps only owing to a greater density, and better filling up, and more even growth of the outer twigs of the trees, than is common in our dryer climate."[14] In this close and searching way, the young man reasoned about the esthetic effect of a landscape view.

In keen responses he reacted to sensuous stimuli: "See! the sparrow lighting on the iron roof burns her feet."[15] A figure only glimpsed in a doorway is "a dirty peevish-looking woman."[16] He is disturbed by the listlessness of over-tired workmen. On the downs, they march past him like automatons after a day's work, too tired to pay attention to a stranger. It was hard times in England. He noted the human consequences, "Instead of stout, full-faced John Bulls, we had noticed few who were not thin, meager, and pale."[17] The dreariness of a poor street recalled a different kind of poverty at home. The poor city street in his own country would have been dirtier; it would have been livelier too: "Hand organs would be playing, hogs squealing, perhaps a stampede of firemen; boys would be crying newspapers, and the walls would be posted with placards, appealing, with whatever motive, to patriotism and duty, showing that statesmen and demagogues could calculate on the people's reading and thinking a little there."[18] Here he encountered a political atmosphere darker than anything he had yet known at home. Poor people were indifferent or hostile to the crown. A "coarse joke"[19] about the queen was not unusual. So the trip was not all sights or sensations. He came to England not long after the great Chartist demonstrations, when the aspirations of the poor had been frustrated. England in 1850 awoke Olmsted's conscience and started him thinking of social arrangements. He had not personally known conditions as dark as he found here, but he was aware of the invidious circumstance of slavery in the American scene. Writing about England and criticizing English customs forced him to make an avowal of belief about the knottiest American problem.

He was not an outright abolitionist, although his friend Charles Brace had moved in that direction, and had tried to convince him that this was the only possible decent position. He believed in some kind of amelioration of slavery, a restoration of slaves to freedom, he did not know quite how. He could not please absolutists on either side: "The law of God in our hearts binds us in fidelity to the principles of the Constitution. They are not to be found in 'Abolitionism,' nor are they to be found—remember it, brothers, and forgive these few words—in hopeless, dawnless, unredeeming slavery."[20]

His position was as follows:

In America we hold that a slave, a savage, a child, a maniac and a condemned criminal, are each all born—equally with us, with our President, or with the Queen of England, free and self-governing; that they have the same natural rights with us; but that attached to those natural rights were certain duties, and when we find them, from whatever cause—no matter whether the original cause be with them, or our fathers, or us—unable to perform those duties, we dispossess them of their rights: we restrain, we confine, we master, we govern them. But in taking upon ourselves to govern them, we take other duties, and our first duty is that which is the first duty of every man for himself—improvement, restoration, regeneration. By every consideration of justice, by every noble instinct, we are bound to make it our highest and chiefest object to restore them, not the liberty first, but the capacity for the liberty. . . . We must not wait till a child can walk alone before we put it on its legs; we must not wait till it can swim before we let it go in the water.

He went on to say that we never govern, except in trust, and in the hope of restoring to the governed their self-direction. He had a New Englander's faith in education. He believed the link between deprivation and restoration to be education: "Education, then, with certain systematic exercise or discipline of the governed, having reference to and connected with a gradual elevation to equal freedom with the governing, we hold to be a very necessary part of all rightful government. Where it is not, we say this is no true and rightful government."[21]

The poverty of the working class in England, the fact of slavery at home, these were blots upon the conduct of life. But Olmsted was not pessimistic of the future, at least the American future. He believed in his country's ability to be great. His mood was of his generation—Emersonian—and chimed with Emerson's own words: "Why should these words, Athenian, Roman, Asia and England, so tingle in the ear? Where the heart is, there the muses, there the gods sojourn, and not in any geography of fame. Massachusetts, Connecticut River and Boston Bay you think paltry places, and the ear loves names of foreign and classic topography. But here we are; and, if we will tarry a little, we may come to learn that here is best."[22]

Walks and Talks of an American Farmer in England suggests more of unity in the English experience than Olmsted had in living it; it was written to exclude what came after: further exploration of London, experience beyond England in other countries. The three young men spent eight weeks outside England, two in Germany, two in Belgium and France, three in Scotland, and one in Ireland. Frederick Olmsted filled his mind with impressions wherever he went, yet nothing impressed him more than the London parks. It was an interesting fact that two other Americans looked at the London parks, had strong reactions, came home, and publicized these ideas in essays and books in this same decade. In 1845, a few years before Olmsted saw the green spaces of London, William Cullen Bryant, as editor of the New York *Evening Post,* wrote, "Nothing can be more striking to one who is accustomed to the little inclosures called public parks in our American cities, than the spacious, open grounds of London. . . . These parks have been called the lungs of London, and so important are they regarded to the public health and the happiness of the people, that I believe a proposal to dispense with some part of their extent, and to cover it with streets and houses, would be regarded in much the same manner as a proposal to hang every tenth man in London."[23] The same summer (1850) when the three young men from Connecticut walked the roadways and paths of the countryside in perfect obscurity, another American was received in England with much acclaim. This was Andrew Jackson Downing. He was the editor of *The Horticulturist* and the author of *A Treatise on the Theory and Practice of Landscape Gardening, Adapted to North America, with a View to the Improvement of Country Residences* (1841), *The Fruits and Fruit Trees of America* (1845), and the about-to-be-published capstone of his writings, *The Architecture of Country Houses.* The young, handsome, and diffident young agricultural designer came as a conqueror of English society. He was admired by the country's architects and landscape designers. He was greatly feted and celebrated in his months in England in 1850. At this time, he had not met Frederick Olmsted, but had answered his letters. He had kindly given him a letter of introduction for his more obscure English tour. There is no evidence they met in England. The connection they were to have lay in the future, when interests they shared would draw the "scientific farmer" out of his exclusive interest in tilling and harvesting. Downing wrote about English parks and gardens for *The Horticulturist.* An essay on Kew Gardens in the issue of August, 1850, conveyed the largeness of these creations to his American readers when he spoke of "the enormous parks of London . . . absolute woods and prairies, in the midst of a vast and populous city." Downing had written in July, 1849, about America's cemeteries, such as Greenwood in Brooklyn, serving in place of needed parks "such as we must surely one day have in America."[24] The year after his summer in London (and Frederick Olmsted's) Downing in his magazine campaigned for Mayor Kingsland's proposed park for New York. "Deluded New York has, until lately, contented itself with the little door-yards of space—mere grassplats of verdure, which form the squares of the city, in the mistaken idea that they are parks"[25] (August, 1851). Bryant, Downing, Olmsted walked toward a common future, the building of Central Park in New York. Each would play a part in turning vague dreams into reality.

Nothing of this could be known to Frederick Olmsted at the end of his wandering summer abroad. When he returned to Staten Island, he seemed consigned to a future of farming. Yet he determined also in his spare time to write, to make a book of his "walks and talks" in England. He had taken careful notes with that purpose in mind as he traveled. Now, with hasty energy he set to work. A fire laid in the fireplace, paper and pen set before him, Frederick decided to write rapidly fifty or a hundred pages and try for a publisher before going further. He did not desert the original raw form of his diary but enlarged his daily jottings to give the book the variety of observations and reflections about people and places. He included all the diverse things which had amused him: landscape appearance, soil use, school and prison practice, poverty, the talk of a stream of people passing by on the roads. It was a loose-limbed organization, but it had easy manners. One sauntered through England at footpace with the writer. Olmsted as a writer was never to be obsessed with the desire to be perfect. But he was, indeed, from this time, a self-conscious and conscientious writer. He was a good workman in words, cheerfully professional in attitude, building with the bricks of experience, slapping off mortar when he had laid it on too thick, shaping the boundaries of episodes to fit an idea.

Frederick's own trip had ended, but he continued to have vicarious experience of further travel in Charles Brace's wanderings; these were to be an adventure before he came home again. Charles stopped first in Germany, spending some months in Berlin, lonely but interested in the "home life" of the German people. Frederick advised his friend, "Tell us what you do, and what people do to you, and in what way your impulses are moved, as much as you can. It's worth more than your thoughts to us who know you. . . . Do walk out and talk with the farm servants and the waiters and the soldiers and the beggars. What their wants, and what do they think?"[26] Charley wrote back: "I am just exactly the same abstract, straight-to-the-mark, simple-minded, coffee-loving individual which I ever was."[27] Straight-to-the-mark Charles Brace got more than he bargained for in the area beyond Vienna, which was still seething with the aftereffects of the Hungarian revolution. He looked suspicious. Police searched his luggage, found what they considered inflammatory pictures and writing, locked him up with other political prisoners in the castle in Gross Wardein. He found himself held incommunicado in the midst of an interesting collection of supposed enemies of the Austrian rule, interrogated, and threatened over and over again with execution. He was able, at last, to smuggle out letters in the shoes of a prisoner who was released. His father had been exerting pressure to find his son. The American consul in Vienna made inquiries. Interested, somewhat shaken up, but also furious at this firsthand experience of tyranny, Charles Brace walked out of prison.

Before Fred at Southside knew the seriousness of Brace's situation, he wrote half jokingly, thinking of his friend's adventure as a comic opera affair: "I anticipate your most interesting letters now, describing Austrian prison discipline, the size of your cell, weight of your chain, etc., your conversation with your keeper; how you were fed; the visits of the chaplain, ..."[28] But he learned soon that Brace had been in real danger. When he came home, Brace was a fiery propagandist of the Hungarian cause. Through him, his friends learned that political life elsewhere was not like a New England town meeting.

Before he returned to the company of family and friends, Charles deviated toward England again to get himself engaged to Letitia Neill. Her father, Robert Neill, had entertained the Olmsteds and Charles Brace in Belfast. After his experiences in an Austrian prison, the released prisoner had an irresistible desire to see Letitia again. He succeeded in doing so in England, where the Neills were staying. He went home with his domestic future solid and sure, and he went home a more impressive person than he had been before his sharp adversities. "I suppose many of my friends were almost surprised at such a quiet man as myself making such a noise about the affair. If it had been a mere matter of personal pique and inconvenience, I should have dropped it, as I have the cheating of Italian waiters or anything else of the kind. . . . But it seemed a question of universal justice."[29] Charles Brace wrote a book about his experience of Austrian justice. He lectured in America for the Hungarian cause. He even, when the revolutionary Kossuth visited the United States, shared in that visitor's glory. But this was an eddy only in the quiet man's pursuit of his chosen profession, the highly original one of being a minister to the children of the streets.

He, as well as his companions of the walk in England, came home from the trip matured, more their own men. Like Charles Brace, Frederick Olmsted was a more interesting and capable person than he had been before his summer of travel abroad. He did not know yet that there was another future before him than farming and the activities of his own particular farming life—planting fruit trees, designing his neighbors' farm grounds, writing articles for agricultural papers, taking time to travel occasionally and to write a consequent book, as he did in the fall of 1850 and the succeeding winter. But he followed up each opportunity for enlargement. Everything he saw or experienced added something to him. He grew out of an accustomed life and into a new one, shedding his skin of habit bit by bit.

CHAPTER VII

A Visit to Newburgh

I liked Downing and Newburgh.
—F. L. O., to Fred Kingsbury, August 5, 1851[1]

T
HE YEAR AFTER his walking tour in England was a complex one for
Frederick Olmsted. Several things happened to cause shifts in his
impulses and aims.

For one thing, in January, 1851, the senior John Olmsted retired from
business. This meant that his father visited Frederick more often at Southside. He came sometimes alone and sometimes with various members of his
family. It was as if the center of family life and interest shifted toward the
older son. In some sense, the retired merchant was freer, having shed an
absorbing business life, but he was also more dependent, in that his emotions
centered more narrowly upon his children, and particularly upon the two
eldest, Frederick and John Hull. He continued also, generously and practically, to bolster the two young men with his money. Fred had not succeeded
in making a profit as a farmer. Nearly every year he had acquired debts
which the father shouldered. John Hull was a nagging care to both the
father and the older brother.

Normally cheerful, in spite of bad health, John Hull was full of hope in
the spring of 1851. He had got himself engaged more than a year before to
Mary Perkins. After completing his medical training in New York City, he
accepted a position as assistant physician at the Seamen's Retreat at Stapleton,
Staten Island. His position was an easy one, without much responsibility,
and he had time to study before a window which opened on a view of the
Narrows.

John's fortunes interested Fred keenly. He wrote to Charley Brace, the
friend of both of them who had shared their walking tour and had remained

abroad, "John has had another dismal turn, and Mary has been unwell. Otherwise they prosper greatly. I like John's berth very much, a most excellent opportunity for education it seems to be, and quite agreeable position. Morally they are thriving too; the discipline of hospital practice is good for John's character and Mary is thinking. She has been reading Ruskin's Stones of Venice."[2] No doubt the book was lent by Fred, who was a great reader of Ruskin at this time.

Mary stayed nearby or at the farm. John Hull came down from Stapleton every weekend. Bertha and Mary Olmsted were also frequently with Fred. It might have been a happy summer. But Fred himself was ailing. He had intermittent chills. It was thought that the farm was malarial. He went home to Hartford to be nursed. Mary Perkins traveled with him to stay for a while with the senior Olmsteds. And John Hull's cheerfulness wore thin when he spit up blood in an attack of coughing.

Diagnosis of "consumption" was vague, but Frederick wrote to Fred Kingsbury that it was thought that John had the disease in an "incipient" form. "Dr. Parker judges that his lung is not so far diseased but he may cure it and at all events there is a reasonable hope that he may live to a good age. . . . He raised blood decidedly from his lungs week before last for the first time and again a few days after. He is in pretty good spirits. Mary I think is in misery. She has been far from well all summer."[3] Fred wrote this letter on August 5. There was talk of John's going south for the winter, but it was decided, after all, for him to go to the Berkshires at Pittsfield and get what benefit he could from fresh air and horseback riding. He went off obediently.

All the affairs of his family were a concern, particularly those of John, but Fred lived and breathed other interests in spite of his worries. As a citizen of Southside, he was deep in Staten Island affairs. There was to be a road from near his farm to the North Side, and there was the possibility of a railroad across the Island, connecting "with the Amboy road between New York and Philadelphia." Also Cornelius Vanderbilt no longer held a monopoly on harbor traffic, and Fred was interested: "The ferry opposition to Vanderbilt is doing well." He was concerned about the future of Staten Island and noted that on bright days as many as five to ten thousand came there.

Amid such news of local and civic interest, Fred wrote to the other Fred (Kingsbury) almost incidentally, in a letter on August 5: "My engagement with Emily Perkins is not out yet, but I don't think I shall be married before thanksgiving. I have too many cabbages to be sold—about 60,000 planted."

The incongruity of the cabbages getting in the way of his marriage apparently did not strike Fred as absurd when he wrote the letter, but the remark indicated that the engagement, however seriously he believed in it at the moment, was more a product of his youthful desire to be married than to marry a particular young lady, Miss Emily Baldwin Perkins. No kin to John Hull's fiancee, Mary Cleveland Perkins, she was one of the young women to whom he had devoted himself successively with sincere and ardent if interchangeable devotion. She was of good family; the granddaughter of Lyman Beecher, the niece of Harriet Beecher Stowe. The sixty thousand cabbages were significant. Miss Emily did not take to being engaged to Fred Olmsted. In September she broke off the engagement. Fred and Emily had had a long and interesting correspondence, according to his brother's testimony. The letters are not preserved.

There is only John's oblique explanation, after the fact, in a letter to Fred Kingsbury. All had seemed well. "Then came a letter from Mrs. Perkins [the mother] announcing a revulsion of feeling in E. and desiring a break off. Fred answered this and went to Waterbury. . . . It was found that this change had not been temporary as Fred supposed, but that E. really desired to be released. Which of course she was. Fred was very much stunned, but on the whole has borne it like a philosopher." John feared "it will spoil both their lives,"[4] but the results were not so bad as John thought they would be. Fred held back from marriage longer than he might have. Emily Perkins, who had met Edward Everett Hale after her engagement to Frederick Olmsted, married Mr. Hale on October 15, 1852.

Fred's worries over his brother's health and his sympathy for both John and Mary Perkins distracted him from his own trouble. John agonized, as much as one with his cheerful disposition could, over his prospects. He doubted momentarily that he should marry. At the Seamen's Retreat, he had seen men die; he had even held one in his arms when he died. He admitted the fact of his hemorrhages and the danger they were. "Marriage is a hard hard question, Fred [to Kingsbury]—under the circumstances."[5] After his weeks of rest in Pittsfield, he felt better, and the wedding was set. "I am to be examined by Wednesday, married on Thursday (probably) and am to sail for Italy Thursday week."[6] John, Senior, came down from Hartford. The ceremony took place on October 16, 1851, and John Hull and Mary departed for Europe. Fred was left to worry about his cabbages, still in the ground and unharvested, when a sleety snow hit Southside in November.

The world beyond cabbage rows widened, however. Charles Brace had come home from his imprisonment. He involved Fred in the reception of the Hungarian revolutionary hero, Kossuth, when he came to New York in early December. Fred was appointed to the committee of reception. He marched in the parade. "I carried the large Hungarian color immediately behind the carriage in which he rode. While there he turned and took my hand and I had some conversation with him about the harbor and fortifications. Mentioned Charley, he didn't seem to know anything about it. Afterwards I had the honor of kissing Madame Kossuth's hand."[7] Charles's Hungarian adventure had some effect on Frederick Olmsted's thought. He had an inherited New England and Hartford idea of a simple, natural kind of town hall freedom as what all men strove for. His idea of freedom was enlarged to include the social-democratic mid-European yearnings of 1848. The enlargement showed in his comprehension of the Germans he was to meet in Texas.

It was to show also in his better understanding of the poor of the city, who were mostly immigrants from conditions in Europe not covered by the transactions of town hall meetings.

Excitements like the Kossuth reception interrupted only briefly his work on the book about his experience in England. He was able to tell his father on December 4 that he had arranged with the Putnam publishing company to bring out his book, which was to be called *Walks and Talks of an American Farmer in England*. The publisher George Palmer Putnam was a cousin of the Olmsteds. Frederick felt the need of placing the evidence of success before his father. But in other ways his confidence increased as he widened his world.

He had sent an excerpt from the book to Andrew Jackson Downing, the editor of the magazine he admired, *The Horticulturist*. Sometime in the summer before publication of his *Walks and Talks* he determined to make a visit to Newburgh-on-Hudson, a kind of pilgrimage to meet the writer he admired.

When Frederick Olmsted walked up from the town to Highland Acres, he saw embodied the ideas Downing preached as an advocate of "landscape gardening." It was a modest example of the art, but a fit and winning one. Downing's place was an estate only five acres in extent, but cunningly designed to take advantage of its setting, a hill above a great river. "The town lay at the bottom of the hill, between the garden and the water, and there was a road just at the foot of the garden. But so skillfully were the trees arranged, that all suspicion of town or road was removed . . . . The enchanted visitor [in this case the writer, George William Curtis] saw only the garden ending in the thicket, which was so dexterously trimmed as to reveal the loveliest glimpses of the river, each a picture in its frame of foliage, but which was not cut low enough to betray the presence of the town."[8]

Within his tall house with its suggestion of "gothic" towers, Downing was a quiet, modest host. He impressed visitors with his reserve and his authority. George William Curtis found him "a tall, slight Spanish gentleman, with thick black hair worn very long, and dark eyes fixed upon me with a searching glance." His manner was perhaps "Spanish,"[9] but he was a product of Newburgh, as native to that city as Fred Olmsted was to Hartford. His father was a nurseryman, who died when Andrew was seven. His mother conceived the idea of Andrew's being a merchant and, like Olmsted, he was apprenticed to a dry goods merchant. He liked this as little as Olmsted, joined his brother in the raising of plants, painted and botanized outdoors along the river he loved, and taught himself a profession which hardly had a name yet. In 1841, his reputation was made by his *Treatise on the Theory and Practice of Landscape Gardening*. He was praised abroad as well as in America.

He was a famous man, but his reserve hid a certain shyness. He had traveled into renown with complete unselfconsciousness and with a simple rectitude of belief and aim. He was also hopelessly incompetent in managing his business affairs. His friends had to band together to save him from bankruptcy.

Andrew Downing came out of the same generation which produced Thomas Cole, William Cullen Bryant, and James Fenimore Cooper. His writings called the attention of his fellow countrymen to the beauties of a native landscape at which they had rarely looked although they had lived on it and off it. He designed houses and laid out grounds for men of modest success. He thought the good man, when he was able to do so, should live in the country. He would become a better man for doing so. Downing had a thorough knowledge of the works and attitudes of the landscape designers of England of the last two centuries, but he adapted the practice of these men to a wilder and larger land. He believed that a country residence should fit into an unobtrusive, man-made garden, which in turn should blend with the broader view of wild nature. He attempted to train bourgeois bankers and merchants to look across their hedges to the hills and rivers beyond, a grander view, he thought, than that possible from the windows of an English country house.

When Frederick Olmsted made his visit to Highland Acres, he carried some quantity of reverence for the man from reading his words. He saw exemplified in Downing's estate all that he had admired in his writings. In the man himself he found a mentor to ideas only half formed in his own mind. Downing had concerned himself not only with horticulture and architecture for private persons but with matters affecting public welfare: the need for a state agricultural school, the desirability of having a federal agricultural bureau, and the necessity for New York City to have a large public garden or park. He was also at present engaged in an important work in the national capital, in improving the grounds of the Smithsonian Institution. No doubt a partaker in this conversation was Downing's young English architectural partner, Calvert Vaux. Very probably, as was his habit, Downing tossed the ball of an idea in the air and let the others in the room play with it in words, while he sat and listened. In any case, Olmsted found himself in an element of talk in which he thrived. Here were new friends, here were new ideas. He kindled in the stimulation of the moment.

Vaux remembered this as his first meeting with Olmsted. "I first met Mr. Olmsted at the house of Mr. Downing at Newburgh,"[10] he wrote in a memorandum in November, 1894. It was a meeting of importance for the future of both men, but at the time it must have seemed nothing more than the chance meeting of a congenial acquaintance.

Downing had gone to England in 1850 to find an architectural assistant. Much of his work was the design of houses. Calvert Vaux was recommended to him as a promising and able young man. Vaux had progressed through the rigors of a conventional, thorough training. He had entered the firm of Lewis N. Cottingham as an articled pupil, and in 1850, he was a member of the firm. Vaux at twenty-four welcomed a new field for his endeavors and accepted Downing's offer. He found a friend in Downing as well as a generous employer. He was soon made a partner in all Downing's endeavors. One or the other of them was journeying regularly to Washington, D.C., to tend to the redesigning of a portion of the Mall at the time Olmsted visited Newburgh.

Apparently Vaux and Olmsted hit it off well at this first meeting. One can imagine that they, with Downing in the background, found plenty to talk about. Olmsted never hung back from telling his opinion. And Vaux was always ready for a joke or an argument or a passionate statement of belief. To reconstruct—perhaps Olmsted, with a slight touch of envy at Vaux's professional education, let the other man have the benefit of his own experience in the design of farmers' grounds. He might also have talked about his luck in raising pear trees in an area raked by sea winds. One can imagine Downing, who knew much more than Olmsted about growing fruit trees, listening to the younger man with a grave courtesy.

It is probable that they talked of parks. In his column in the October, 1848, issue of *The Horticulturist,* Downing had written about city parks as "public enjoyments—open to all classes of people, provided at public cost, maintained at public expense, and enjoyed daily and hourly, by all classes of persons."[11]

A park for the city was much in the air. Andrew Jackson Downing in *The Horticulturist* and William Cullen Bryant in the New York *Evening Post* were the principal exponents of the idea. Official action had at last been taken. In April of the year of Olmsted's visit to Newburgh, Mayor Kingsland of New York had recommended an actual park for the city. In August, Downing wrote a column entitled "The New-York Park," which included these words: "The fourth city in the world (with a growth that will soon make it the second) . . . has not hitherto been able to afford sufficient land to give its citizens . . . any breathing ground for healthful exercise, any pleasant roads for riding or driving, or any enjoyment of that lovely and refreshing natural beauty from which they have, in the leaving the country, reluctantly expatriated themselves for so many years—perhaps for ever."[12] And during the summer of 1851, either just before or shortly after Olmsted's visit, Downing printed the Staten Island farmer's description of Birkenhead, the English public park, from the book soon to be published, *Walks and Talks of an American Farmer in England.*

Olmsted sent another essay to Downing, on pear tree culture, to appear in January, 1852, in *The Horticulturist.* This association, which was to mean so much to Olmsted in memory, was cut short by Downing's death. On the twenty-eighth of July, 1852, Downing, his wife, and his mother-in-law boarded the *Henry Clay,* a Hudson River steamer southbound from Albany to New York, stopping at Newburgh. Like the other captains of the powerful if unreliable new steamships, the captain of the *Henry Clay* could not resist a race. He fell in with the *Armenia,* and the two vessels began racing downstream, trying to beat one another to the landing at Kingston. The *Henry Clay* crowded the *Armenia* and grounded her. Below Kingston, the race was resumed. Heavy fires were built in the *Clay*'s boilers, and the ship caught fire near Yonkers. The passengers were pushed to the rear of the burning midsection, and the ship ran aground head on. Flames swept toward the rear. More than ninety passengers were burned or drowned in leaping overboard to swim ashore. Downing's wife and her mother were saved, after jumping overboard, by clinging to chairs which had been thrown in the water. The last sight of Andrew Downing was of his standing on an upper deck throwing chairs overboard to passengers already in the water. One rescued man said that he saw him in the water with others clinging to him. His wife survived and waited for hours for him to be found. His body was discovered among the many others in the river. He was brought home to be buried in the garden at Highland Acres. He was thirty-seven years old when he died. It was the sudden end of a brilliant life, to be carried on in some sense through the future work of Calvert Vaux and Frederick Olmsted.[13]

Meanwhile, Frederick Olmsted, with not much support from anyone for what he was doing, pursued his own course. He had the satisfaction of seeing his book on England published on February 18, 1852. The book was widely read and well received. The first attempt he had made to write when he was a sailor on the *Ronaldson* had not been pointless. His *Walks and Talks* had ease and grace and imitated in its gait the sauntering tempo of the three young men who had strolled through western England. The fact of having had the book published made an important difference in Olmsted's life. He could not only mold earth with his hands. He would henceforth use words as tools, readily and cleverly.

A sign that Frederick Olmsted was no longer an entirely private person was the anonymous review in the back pages of *Harper's Magazine* in December, 1852. It said that the successive chapters of the book were "desultory, but frank and genial papers. . . . Mr. Olmstead [sic] is a shrewd, observing, free-spoken Yankee—with none of the stiffness of the professed author—and rejoicing in the fragrance and beauty of the orchards and grain-fields of old England. Some of the best things in his book are the descriptions of his off-hand conversations with people he met by the road-side, at cottage-doors, or in stage-coaches; and the next best, are his remarks on English agriculture. His book is eminently popular, in the true sense of the term, and cannot fail to be a favorite with the great mass of readers."

CHAPTER VIII

Journeying South

Let the reader understand that he is invited to travel in company with an honest growler. But growling is sometimes a duty.
—F. L. O., Preface, *Seaboard Slave States*[1]

DURING 1852, Frederick Olmsted's brother and sister-in-law were abroad. They settled in Rome, and John Hull Olmsted wrote impressions of Italy for the Philadelphia *Bulletin,* an assignment which Charles Loring Brace had secured for him.

John was by no means cured of his lung disease, and Mary was pregnant. One of John's newspaper essays paints a portrait of the two young people in a foreign land—"two strangers, with light hair and odd thin faces"[2]—as John saw themselves reflected in the curious eyes of a Roman girl who was their neighbor.

In September, in Geneva, Mary's baby was born. As soon as the news reached Staten Island, John's brother wrote proudly and fantastically about his nephew. To Fred Kingsbury: "Fine fellow, very handsome, looks like me and if they could have had their own way they would have called him after us. [The child was named John Charles.] Has a scowl . . . 'as if he already found life a bore.' Mary was all right and was eating steaks and chickens enough for two ordinary sized mortals—the baby got mad at her in five minutes after he was born, snatched her up—laid her over his knee and spanked her so she had to give it up on natural depravity but thinks there may have been something in the air of Geneva."[3]

Frederick was lonely for his brother's company, and the sister-in-law's too. However, his father was three times at the farm in 1852—in March, in midsummer, and in late November and early December. The last time was to say goodbye to his farmer son going South to write his impressions of a slave society.

It is not surprising that various reasons persuaded Fred to desert as beautiful a farm as Southside. He had written successfully about travel in England, and since publishing *Walks and Talks,* he had thought of himself in the character of a writer. It would be tempting to try his reputation again in articles about a region perhaps more foreign than England. The subject of the South held more than casual interest for him.

He and his friends on the comfortable piazza at Southside had had hot discussions about the slave question. Fred was disturbed by the political behavior of the South, but he held off from the abolitionist extremity of opinion. He did so even when Charles Brace had brought down William Lloyd Garrison to the farm to add his fire to their talk.

Apparently it was Brace who pushed his friend Frederick Olmsted the last step toward going on the journey. He already knew Henry J. Raymond, the vigorous, politically liberal editor of the New York *Daily-Times,* and he introduced Frederick Olmsted to him. Raymond and Olmsted came to an agreement; the ambitious editor engaged the young man to do a series of letters which he would display prominently on the first inside page of the newspaper on the "production, industry and resources of the Slave States." Editor and correspondent agreed that the series was to be sensible, unemotional reporting, quite different in tone from recent writing about the South, which had been often either moonshine about cavaliers or impassioned abolitionist rhetoric. (Mrs. Stowe's book was published earlier the same year.) In any case, more news from the South was welcome. Mrs. Stowe and the general political struggle had ensured an audience for almost any writing from the South. Raymond, with a large view of what his new newspaper should accomplish, and Olmsted, ambitious for his reputation as a writer, were both determined to do the kind of objective job of reporting which had not so far been done in the North on the ever-teasing, ever-worrying subject of one's fellow Americans to the southward.

In April, Frederick had hired by contract a couple, William Carter and his wife, to live and work on the farm. He did not have to remain physically bound to the land all the year round, for he had thoroughly tested Carter's abilities to act as manager in his absence.

Before agreeing to write for the *Daily-Times,* Frederick ascertaned that, traveling at his own direction, he should be able to write as he pleased. He chose the name "Yeoman" to use in signing the articles. The label pleased him. He would go in the character, in part his own, of a small, independent farmer, with his eyes focused sharply on everything he saw. The other part of his character, which he would not emphasize in the "I" of his articles, was an already self-conscious, professional writer. He was annoyed by the Boston *Courier's* reviewer speaking of his "unaffected simplicity." Why, Fred wrote to his father, "The most *simple* parts are those I worked hardest at to make simple."[4]

An October letter to Fred Kingsbury explained to that friend the state of mind he would try to maintain; he would go "mainly with the idea that I could make a valuable book of observations on Southern agriculture and general economy as affected by slavery—the condition of the slaves—prospects—tendencies—and reliable understanding of the sentiments and hopes and fears of sensible planters and gentlemen that I should meet. Matter of fact matter to come after the deluge of spoony fancy pictures now at its height shall be spent."[5] He would not do exactly what he set out to do, but he would do a formidable part of it. Part of the interest in following him is in seeing spontaneous departures and additions, growths, discriminations, judgments which closer knowledge fostered.

Before he departed, he rated himself in the scale of emotion, in the same letter to Fred K., "I am not a red hot abolitionist, like Charley, but am a moderate Free Soiler—going to vote for Scott and would take in a fugitive slave and shoot a man that was likely to get him. On the whole I guess I represent pretty fairly the average sentiment of good thinking men on our side." It was already a matter of sides.

Ready in mind and in arrangements (carrying a certain amount of money to get him started, having arranged with Raymond about his sending copy to him by mail, and where he might, along the way, cash a draft on the *Daily-Times*), on December 11, 1852, Frederick Olmsted set out on the journey which was to be as interesting and as arduous as anything he ever did in his life, and was to result in the writing by which he would be known in American history and literature, if he had done no other kind of work. His "Yeoman" letters would begin to appear in the *Daily-Times* on February 16, 1853. He would return home from this first Southern expedition on April 6, 1853. The letters would continue to appear in the newspaper until February 13, 1854. And this first trip was to be followed by a second trip, of a more ambitious scope, and more letters. But in December, 1852, the sensation was all of beginnings.

He had practiced the art of recording impressions on his English journey and was eager to expose himself to new situations in which he would be a transparent recorder. He carried along with him some preconceptions, he could not help that fact. But he tried consciously to have as few as possible. And he made conclusions along the way; he could not help that either. Yet he was ready to let life itself make its impressions on him. He was to write his journal each night, no matter how uncomfortable he was, and much of the quality of his writing about the South would be due to this willingness to leave himself open to the accidents of life. He was thirty years old, wiry from outdoor work, slim, small, and youthful in appearance, unobtrusive but keen to explore a land which he sensed at once was as foreign as a place could be where he could still understand, more or less, the language of the natives.

His first bath of strangeness was in the national capital of the United States. Washington, D.C., seemed essentially a Southern town. A towel with a hole in the middle, no water for bathing, dirt in the corners of the room, tobacco juice in the unlit grate, a hotel servant who was also oddly a slave: such was the collective set of impressions made on him by his hotel. He was cold in his room and asked three successive Irish boys to bring him firewood. Each made off and did not come back. He sat and shivered. At last, an ancient black man came in bearing kindling and coal in a hod on his head. Here was his first Southern Negro, his first slave. " 'Tink I can make a hundred fires at once? . . . Nebber let de old nigger have no ress—hundred genmen tink I kin mak dair fires all de same minute; all get mad at an old nigger; I ain't a goin to stan it—nebber get no ress—up at night—haint got nautin to eat nor drink dis blessed mornin—hundred genmen—.' "[6]

Olmsted was annoyed yet fascinated. He let play upon him all the emotions that the old creature aroused—irritation, amusement, pity—and when he had a chance, transcribed the feelings into words. It was not that he held off making judgments. The hotel was a poor sort of place, and it should have been otherwise. He sensed that he was touching only the edge of a great mass of things that would be somehow immovable, unchangeable, and indifferent to his wishes: "But my perverse nature will not be content; will be wishing things were otherwise. They say this uneasiness—this passion for change—is a peculiarity of our diseased Northern nature. The Southern man finds Providence in all that is: Satan in all that might be."[7]

Having had his first taste of the South in Washington, Olmsted traveled farther south, a self-conscious Yankee interested but already somewhat affronted by the nature of this region which had been shaping the laws of his country for decades. Or so it seemed to the Connecticut citizen, who had heard only the Northern side of the quarrel which had irritated the relations of the two parts of the nation. A Southern gentleman of Frederick's generation would have argued that it was the North that was trying to impose its ways on the South. Already, Fred Olmsted noted almost with relief that the humble Yankee virtues were not so bad. The great South could well do with an intermixture of these traits of promptness, cleanliness, carefulness. Yet this happy discovery of faults was only a flavoring in an essential fairness, or at least openness. And there were to be discoveries of some unsuspected Southern virtues which made him uneasy, so wanting were they back home.

Of course he traveled with slavery on his mind; he could not help that. But his advantage was that he actually looked at it; these Southerners were so used to it they did not look at it any more, but simply took it for granted. In the end he was unable to be neutral in his reactions, although he remained all the way through his travels remarkably rational in his attitudes. Southerners often shared with him their thoughts on the institution of slavery because, chameleonlike, he seemed to belong to the scene, and did not ever seem very strange or foreign to most of the people he met along the road. Any hint of probing dried up answers. He believed that Southerners simply could not be coaxed to talk on the subject. (But his own pages belie that fact.) The events and mood of the past twenty years had put the South on the defensive. Public self-criticism was rare, considered a species of treason to one's region, since there was criticism offered in plentiful profusion from outside the area. Yet privately, as a reader of Mary Boykin Chesnut's diary might discover today, there was much frank discussion of the subject, and an expression of disapproval or even abhorrence of slavery was not taboo in the seclusion of family circles or those of close friendship. It was only to out-siders, to whom an admission of cracks in the smooth surface of Southern unanimity seemed a kind of self-betrayal, that one kept one's mouth shut. Thus, all the more remarkable was it that as he traveled Frederick Olmsted received from all kinds of people frank expressions of views on the subject. There must have been, in him and his appearance and manner, something singularly disarming.

Perhaps it was that he was so genuinely interested in everything, but also unobtrusive in showing the fact. Impressions flooded in on him as he traveled by the regular route from Washington to Richmond, first by steamboat on the Potomac to Acquia Creek, then by railroad to the capital of Virginia. Fields, houses, people interested him. The fine houses were less fine generally than he had been led to believe, but there was an occasional one with a portico of columns like Mount Vernon. The scattered plantations seemed to occupy only one quarter of the land; the rest was pine forest. The poorer, commoner houses were "either of logs or loosely-boarded frames, a brick chimney run-ning up outside, at one end; everything very slovenly and dirty about them. Swine, fox-hounds, and black and white children, are commonly lying very promiscuously together, on the ground about the doors."[8] Blacks and whites lived intimately together. "I am struck with the close co-habitation of the black and white—negro women are carrying black and white babies together in their arms; black and white children are playing together (not going to school together); black and white faces are constantly thrust together out of the doors, to see the train go by." A family party entered the train looking for a place to sit together. The lady leading the group looked about expec-tantly, as Frederick soon found that Southern ladies often did. He got up and offered her his seat, thus making room for the group. "She accepted it, with-out thanking me, and immediately installed in it a stout negro woman; took the adjoining seat herself, and seated the rest of her party before her. It consisted of a white girl, probably her daughter, and a bright and very pretty mulatto girl. They all talked and laughed together, and the girls munched confectionery out of the same paper, with a familiarity and closeness of in-timacy that would have been noticed with astonishment, if not with manifest displeasure, in almost any chance company at the North." It seemed that personal relations in a slave state were more difficult to understand and more interesting than he had bargained to find.

He thought that the better treated, generally lighter Negroes, who had obviously made a place or made a way for themselves under slavery, had an expression of "counsel-keeping," as if they had won place and position at cost. But the majority of field hands seen at work were pitiable—"dull, idiotic, and brute-like."

The land seemed very poor on the way to Richmond, the poorest land he had ever seen in the distance traveled. The fact made a great continuing impression on him, and he set himself to finding out why. Here were great stretches of farming land used, misused, worn out, and in the midst of continued settlement, abandoned. Broom-sedge and field pines had grown up to cover the nakedness of abuse. To the farmer it seemed a sacrilege. To the student of human manners, a puzzle. Why had an intelligent people allowed this to happen? At once the condition of the land in the South seemed the clue to his continuing study: was this what slavery did to a land and to a people?

In Richmond, he walked about the streets. On a Sunday he saw well-dressed Negroes strolling and an old Negro man pushed off the sidewalk by three rowdy whites. He heard the old man complain: " 'Cain't you find anything else to do than to be knockin' quiet people round! You jus' come back here, will you? Here, you! *don't care if you is white.* You jus' come back here and I'll teach you how to behave—knockin' people round!—don't care if I does hab to go to der watch-house. . . . You come back here and I'll make you laugh; you is jus' three white nigger cowards, dat's what *you* be.' "9

On the outskirts of town, he saw a Negro funeral procession and followed it. There were no whites along but him. The singing over the grave reminded him of something he had almost forgotten, the responses sailors made in "heaving at the windlass." The song, like a sea chantey, divided into the leader's part and the followers' responses, was "wild and barbarous, but not without a plaintive melody."

Olmsted did not see any slaves being sold in Richmond or elsewhere in all the months he spent in the South. But in quick order in Richmond he saw three sights he did not forget. First he was stopped in his tracks by the sight of a line of three Negroes roped together, scantily clad in cold weather—icicles forming on the awnings of nearby stores. The three were a middle-aged man, a girl of twenty, and a young boy. They were led by a well-dressed Negro holding the rope, the confidential servant, as he assumed, entrusted with the transferral of these slaves from boat to removal point southward. He heard the boy complain and the girl turn and say angrily: "O pshaw! Shut up!" Farther along, he saw a group of men and boys lounging on a corner, their personal belongings wrapped in a white blanket which each grasped to him. They were slaves waiting to be hired out for city work. Olmsted found all through the South, but particularly in the cities, a considerable business of hiring out Negroes for labor by the day, month, or even year. He looked into some slave dealers' rooms where Negroes sat on benches along the walls, comfortably dressed and cheerful in manner, not a bit downcast, "each grinning obsequiously, but with a manifest interest or anxiety, when I fixed my eye on them for a moment." He had never before found himself being gazed at as a possible buyer of human flesh, and the sensation disconcerted him. He looked up written accounts of the sale of slaves, and found they were horrible only in the perfect ordinariness of the transaction, the manner in which everyone accepted the operation as an everyday kind of business. There was not much cruelty in it except of the totally unconscious kind. He was to include such accounts later in the book he wrote.

Near Richmond, Frederick visited a James River plantation where the owner acted as his own overseer, where the land was farmed admirably, and where the relationship between master and servants was intimate and cordial. The planter was not shy of talking to his Yankee visitor, who observed with amazement how pestered the man was by interruptions from his servants, noting that he was called away from his dinner three times. " 'You see,' said he, smiling, as he came in the last time, 'a farmer's life, in this country, is no sinecure. . . . I only wish your philanthropists would contrive some satisfactory plan to relieve us of it [slavery]; the trouble and the responsibility of properly taking care of our negroes, you may judge, from what you see yourself here, is anything but enviable.' "[10] He thought those Negroes in the South who were free were worse off than those in bondage, and he thought that Negroes in the South—whether in bondage or not—were better off than most laboring men in the North. Olmsted thought this a specious argument, but it was hard to answer, and it caught most Northerners off balance, for there was some grain of truth in it. Charles Brace had made him aware of the woe of New York's streets—in fact, as Olmsted traveled South and wrote about slavery, his friend was doing a series of articles for the *Times* called "Walks Among the New-York Poor." (For several weeks, in fact, Fred's Southern articles and Charley's New York City articles alternated with each other in the same good position on page two of the newspaper.) Frederick had also seen poor living on farms in New England and New York, and he had himself experienced, and felt keenly, a kind of servitude as a sailor on a sailing ship. Yet he still thought the argument false, even if many slaves were better fed and better clothed than dirty, hungry, illiterate, and unemployed Irish immigrants in the city he had left behind. He was, however, going to have to work out his rebuttal to the argument.

His host illustrated all the confusing virtues of slavery: candor over its shortcomings, attachment to his own people, and an admitted sense of being caught in a system that he had not made himself and did not know how to get out of. This kindly and intelligent man was perhaps not representative, but he was not very much out of the ordinary either. He consulted the black servant behind his chair as if he were a family friend, relying upon him for knowledge of certain affairs that he did not bother to keep up with, and he laughed with him, liked him, and communed with him as a fellow human being on easy terms. (And yet he owned the man; that stuck in the craw of his guest.) Outdoors, the servants when they approached him were apparently fond of him. Still the whole thing raised the hackles of Fred's sensibilities. At best, he could not be easy about it—*it* being the whole complex of slavery.

But Fred Olmsted could not be a grave student all the time. He craved adventure. He found one soon after leaving Richmond in backwoods country when he was searching for a particular plantation which seemed to retreat from him beyond woods and fields while he rode deeper and deeper into the Southern wildness and differentness.

Thomas W.'s place, he was told at the Petersburg station, was on yonder through the woods, up a hill or two, an easy ride of several miles. He rented a lively mare from a convenient landowner who happened to be in the general store next to the station. After receiving long and involved instructions, he set off alone, exhilarated by a bright winter morning. He felt well and was, at this moment in his life, in fine fettle, a youthful, life-loving, life-exploring, observing "I," who missed nothing, ducked nothing, and set it all down in his notes later. He enjoyed the companionship of the filly Jane "bounding over the fallen trees as easily as a lifeboat over a billow, and all the time gracefully playing tricks with her feet, and her ears, and her tail, and evidently enjoying herself just like any child in a half-holiday ramble through the woods."[11] As Jane's rider soon got lost, he found himself talking to the mare, explaining to her the predicament into which the two of them had fallen, and which he half enjoyed. The sights were varied and interesting, teaching him what a country looked like which had been farmed over, grown over, abused, half abandoned, and was still beautiful.

"First, we picked our way from the store down to the brook, through a deeply corrugated clay-road; then there was the swamp [and] among pine trees, we discovered a clear way through them."

Then there were " 'old fields'—a coarse, yellow, sandy soil, bearing scarce anything but pine trees and broom-sedge." The inhabitants of the fields were lean, razor-backed hogs.

"We then arrived at a grove of tall oak trees." There was a grist mill under it and an idle slave, who gave vague instructions as to their way. Mr. W.'s plantation seemed farther away than ever.

Fred began to feel that he had indeed come away from Connecticut. The land was gigantic and unkempt. What had been tobacco plantings had robbed the soil of fertility, and those who had worn out the land with tobacco farming had moved on, confident that new and unused land westward was limitless. This was not a particularly Southern idea, but an American one North and South. But the one-crop concentration of Southerners (whether tobacco, rice, indigo, or cotton) had speeded up the misuse of the land, the moving on, and the beginning again of the process.

Slavery, as Frederick Olmsted began to see firsthand, had intensified bad land use. Slaves worked best in gangs put to simple tasks with primitive tools under close supervision with no allowance for initiative or judgment. This abused not only the human being but the land he worked. It was a crude but effective system for getting the most out of new land in the shortest length of time. After initial profits, landowners might become land-poor and labor-poor unless somehow they piled up supplies of new labor and new land. As he traveled southward and westward from this beginning in Virginia, Frederick was to move from poor land where slave usage had softened into some humanity to new land where slave treatment was severe and businesslike. In the whole shifting system, little money was held back for diversification of crops, or to the conserving of one's fields. (There were honorable and notable exceptions: Ruffin, of Virginia, was a great advocate of good agricultural practice, and introduced or publicized the use of marl to restore old fields.)

It was to seem also to Frederick, an intensely city-bred man in spite of his rural childhood, that life, as it had been lived in the South, had prevented the development of many of the institutions which in Hartford and New Haven and Guilford and Ellington he had taken for granted: fair to excellent schools for all the children of the community, intelligent preachers, lecture societies, agricultural and other self-help groups, ease of transportation, close-knit town life and village cooperation. In this strange area everything was ordered differently. Life was organized in clusters of families, living at great distances one from the other. Education, taste, manners, the arts of conversation, politeness, the refinements of personal relations might flourish in certain idiosyncratic circles, but were unknown to the great majority of plain folks and poor folks who lived nearby but completely outside a high culture. These *people* of the South (white people—blacks were a different matter altogether, and an even more difficult problem to fathom) had a folk culture of considerable vitality and charm, but lived also in very plain poverty, both of material goods and of knowledge. Even many of the planters, most of the small to middling ones, lived as comfortlessly and as deprived of the delights of culture as the poorer folks roundabout.

It was a puzzle to the newcomer, and young Olmsted only began to probe the difficulties of his problem as he lost himself and found himself again on a winter's day ride out from Petersburg, Virginia. His early judgments were as yet only perceptions. But he was an apt student. What he saw early was what he built later into the content of three books.

He did not find Mr. W.'s plantation the same day he set out. Stumbling into an unexpected courthouse town, he dined at an inn in solitude, except for the landlady, who was pretty and amiable, and willing to talk to him as he ate. She explained that it was not court day and so the place was empty. He rode on into the afternoon and evening, admitted himself lost, and sought a night's shelter in a house that had once been grand but was now run-down and neglected.

In a room bare of comfort young Frederick was entertained by the conversation of a little girl and joined her in playing with her kitten. Talk before the plain meal was of labor. You could not, said the owner of the plantation, get satisfaction out of white labor. They would not do certain things, such as bring water or wood to the house, for that was "nigger" work. White labor was unreliable; it could not be driven. Black labor was the only reliable kind.

After talk, it was time to go to bed, and Mr. Newman (as Frederick called him—beholding a new type in the man) accompanied him to a room partly filled with goods but holding also a feather bed. "Mr. Newman asked if I wanted a candle to undress by, I said yes, if he pleased, and waited a moment for him to set it down: as he did not do so I walked towards him lifting my hand to take it. 'No—I'll hold it,' said he, and I then perceived that he had no candle-stick, but held the lean little dip in his hand: I remembered also that no candle had been brought into the 'sitting-room,' and that while we were at supper only one candle had stood upon the table, which had been immediately extinguished when we rose, the room being lighted only from the fire.

"I very quickly undressed and hung my clothes upon a bed-post: Mr. Newman looked on in silence until I had got into bed, when, with an abrupt 'good-night, sir,' he went out and shut the door." He found in the morning that pay would be expected. " 'I reckon a dollar and a quarter will be right, sir.' " He was not to receive here or anywhere else the "planters' hospitality" he had been led to expect. He sourly commented on this fact throughout his narratives of Southern travel. It was a count against this society, or at least against what he had, perhaps unreasonably, expected.

When his host withdrew, taking his light with him, Frederick might have wondered before he went to sleep how he came to be here. Muscles and bones aching from an unaccustomed day in the saddle, his mind slowing down the race of images of all the things he had seen, he might have recalled as the beginning of this journey the apparition, upon his Southside piazza, of the visage of William Lloyd Garrison, a cold, bleak face, the eyes behind rimless glasses burning with the fire of conviction. He talked tirelessly the kind of things he said in his writings. On the Constitution (because it enshrined the fact of slavery in the structure of government): "A sacred compact, forsooth! We pronounce it the most bloody and heaven-daring arrangement ever made by men for the continuance and protection of a system of the most atrocious villainy ever exhibited on earth."[12] How could one be so sure? How could one be so simple? So Frederick had reacted on his comfortable porch surrounded by his reasonable vegetables and flowers. Garrison had not convinced him, but had seemed rather a phenomenon who made statements and left opinions trailing behind him. Now, traveling in the South, he found men much like himself caught in a system they had not made, sometimes criticizing it, more often stiffly defending it, principally against the righteous accusations of men like Garrison, who assumed that the Southerners as men were deliberately wicked. Wickedness there might be, and Frederick had already seen that the fact of legal slavery allowed individual evil a chance to bloom strangely, as well as for goodness and benevolence to exert themselves. But how had the thing come about, how did it work, what did it do, and could it be cured? Already, in this early part of his journey, he knew that the answers were not going to be easy.

He went on the next day, postponing reasoned conclusions while bathing all his senses in impressions. His passage across North Carolina through swamp and piney woods and farmland tested his endurance. He crossed the river from Norfolk to Portsmouth, and the ferry stopped in midstream, drifting with the current. The fireman was asleep. He found stagecoach transportation on the other side to take him on. At Welden, hungry and tired, he tried to eat a hasty meal. Cold sweet potatoes were the fare. He looked up from this dinner to see his coach leaving, taking his bags farther into the wilderness. "I am pretty good on the legs for a short man, and it didn't take me long, by the *pas gymnastique,* to overtake the coach."[13] It was a dubious comfort to have caught up. The driver greeted him: " 'Ortn't to be so long swallerin' yer dinner—mind, next time!' " And the comfort of the coach was a minor form of torture: "The road was as bad as anything, under the name of a road, can be conceived to be. Wherever the adjoining swamps, fallen trees, stumps, and plantation fences would admit of it, the coach was driven, with great dexterity, out of the road. When the wheels sunk in the mud, below the hubs, we were sometimes requested to get out and walk." It lurched along on firmer ground in danger of tipping over. When this happened, "the driver, climbing on to the upper side, opened the door, and asked, with an irresistibly jolly drawl—'Got mixed up some in here, didn't ye? Ladies, hurt any? Well, come, get out here; don't want to stay here all night I reckon, do ye?—Ain't nothing broke, as I see. We'll right her right up. Nary durn'd rail within a thousan' mile, I don't s'pose.' "

The coach made only fourteen miles in four hours, and came to a stop at the banks of the Roanoke River. Here the jolly driver deposited his passengers and dexterously turned about, preparing to leave them in a howling wilderness on a deserted river bank. His victims asked: "Where are we—not in Gaston?"

"Durned nigh it. That ere's Gaston, over thar: and you just holler, and they'll come over arter you in the boat." He retreated. All was dark. No sound. It turned out that Gaston was "a mile above us, and on the other side of the river.... And away he drove, leaving us, all strangers, in a strange country, just at the edge of night, far from any house, to 'holler.' ... The only way to stop him was to shoot him." And they would have been glad to do it.

So went Fred Olmsted's initiation into Southern travel. Strange delicacies floated upon the surface of much discomfort and rawness. He observed curiously that, "Among our inside passengers, in the stagecoach, was a free colored woman; she was treated in no way differently from the white ladies. My room-mate [as he termed a garrulous fellow-traveler with whom he had to share bed and board along the way] said this was entirely customary at the South, and no Southerner would ever think of objecting to it."

Hardened somewhat to the hardships he met along the way, he began to enjoy some sights and some experiences. Pine knots burned in the woods around the camps of turpentine-workers. These slaves hired out by plantation owners sang mournful songs around the fires, but thrived in semifreedom.

He broke ice in a pan in a lean-to in one hostel. In another the food was good, a fire glowed, warm water was placed before him for his tired feet to soak in. Such contradictions were scattered with dreamlike inconsistency along his path.

All the while, his senses and his critical instinct were awake. He noted the glossy, evergreen foliage of the Great Dismal Swamp and was grateful for the sight. In the North Carolina capitol grounds he regretted that the city fathers had not laid out the area better. The place was a hog pasture, and not the proper setting for a building he liked. One planter offended him by having cut down original giant oaks and planted poor, sleazy ailanthus trees along a drive.

Beyond the poverty of North Carolina, whether in South Carolina or Georgia he does not make clear, on a coastal rice plantation he found respite in an invited stay with the master of a "good" plantation.[14] Here he was a guest and treated in kingly fashion. He found that life here was an esthetic experience. Grace and economy of force always strongly attracted him. Here slavery with a beautiful face on it almost lulled him into happiness. The land itself was as beautiful as any he had ever seen and glowed with blooming camellias. It was winter at home, he reminded himself, and people went wrapped in bulky clothes against the cold. Here, on a Sunday morning, one laid one's coat aside and rode to church comfortably in an open carriage.

Indoors a bright fire burned in his bedroom when he awoke, and his window gave upon jasmine smell and mockingbird song. A pleasant family gathered around a table made delightful by conversation and varied and interesting food, including for dinner even possum roast, new to his inquiring taste. For a number of days in the morning or in the afternoon either the master or his overseer rode out with him willingly to show Olmsted everything he wished to see: how the rice was planted, how the hands were worked, what kind of clothes were issued to them and how often, what were the working hours and what kind of discipline was used to keep field hands at their tasks, what were their rest times and their sleeping hours, what kind of food they ate. He looked in slave cabins—feeling slightly embarrassed to do so—and sketched the "nursery" building where children tumbled about from porch to hard-packed ground under the tolerant and not too watchful eyes of an older woman. He saw healthy, cheerful workers greet the master with solicitude—he had been ill. He learned the routine of the hours, what time work started and ended, what time was left over for tending personal gardens from which fowl and vegetables might be gathered and used or sold in the markets of nearby towns. He saw the trinkets bought with this personal money: handkerchiefs and caps and good dresses. He heard about the whiskey and tobacco bought too. He saw that slaves were too valuable here to be treated badly. But——

He felt that some deep spring of ethical purpose was lacking in the lives of these other folk. They lived and died as well as worked for the purposes of other men; they had none of their own. It seemed a completely accepted system. The questions which were allowable were only how to improve the system, including how to make it reasonable and fair. No questions cut at the roots of the system itself. If he had been traveling thirty years earlier, before Eli Whitney's invention, before Garrison and Stowe and others had poured criticism on the South, he might have been able to discuss more often with thoughtful Southerners the basic wrong of slavery. As it was, comments came to him most often from unsophisticated folk. The Southern ruling class had grown defensive. To outsiders, and to themselves, they exaggerated the benevolence of the system.

However, as he traveled, Olmsted accumulated copious notes substantiating the beginning of a theory; that the labor system itself created the troubles of the South which he saw visibly exhibited in poor fields, poor people, and a static condition of society. Yet Olmsted was a various person. He could not always be arguing himself into considered judgments. He often, simply as an appreciator, let life roll over him in all the sad, funny, grotesque, or picturesque plenitude which came along the ways he followed. His liveliest interest was in the variety of the people he met.

He was struck by the difference in dress and even in physical appearance of the "crackers" and the cultivated planters. Yet in the poorer white folk he found a self-considering pride as pronounced as in the large landowners. It was a sense of distinctiveness founded upon the mudsill of slavery even when, in the case of the small farmers, they owned no slaves. They had an emotional benefit from slavery. They took a vicarious pride in the fact of slavery's existence even if the system hurt them.

It was going to be hard to puzzle out the mental and emotional quirks of these people. Olmsted assured himself from experience that the poorest whites were often proud people. Their clothes were ill cut and homespun, but wearers of butternut-dyed suits and shapeless brogans were not hangdog in manner. They had as good an opinion of themselves as any landowner in fine linen. On one road he was a keen noter of details: "The men with the carts [on the way to market, having spent three days coming from their backwoods homes] were generally slight, with high cheekbones and sunken eyes, and were of less than the usual stature of the Anglo-Saxon race. They were dressed in long-skirted homespun coats, wore slouched hats, and heavy boots outside their trowsers. As they met me, they usually bowed, and often offered a remark upon the weather, or the roads, in a bold, but not uncourteous manner—showing themselves to be, at least, in one respect better off than the majority of European peasants, whose educated servility of character rarely fails to manifest itself, when they meet a well-dressed stranger."[15] He could barely understand their talk, but their manner was unmistakable. They addressed themselves to the young New Englander with as much curiosity and self-possession as he in looking at them. He was to notice later the same quality in riverboat travelers. Some had money, some had none, but all carried themselves with self-assurance, a strange mixture of earthy coarseness and gentility.

One instance remained in memory of a personality pressed by life into idiosyncracy, an old woman of the road, driving an ox cart, wearing a man's hat, smoking a pipe, carrying her own goods to market, greeting his road companion, the plantation owner, with as much straightforward friendliness and familiarity as he used to her—the two on a perfect equality of understanding although their clothes, manners, and language were as different as possible. He saw the strange contradiction of the South: a society built upon inequality, yet above that base, the personal equality of individuals surpassing anything he had ever known in his own Connecticut.

Georgia surprised him. He cast back to its "free" status under Oglethorpe to understand it. There was "more life, enterprise, skill, and industry in Georgia than in any other of the old Slave Commonwealths"[16]—perhaps from its origin in a colony that forbade slavery, as he thought, and he was beguiled both by the planters and the unsubservient free crackers. He was amused by the show of a country evangelical church service, and was to preserve in his notes the sights, sounds, and displayed emotions to be seen by a sharp observer. Yet this spectacle of life and vitality seemed a caution and a warning of the kind of thing religion could be without rationality curbing it.

As he traveled, a contradiction in his reactions occurred. Rationality was affronted, even shocked, by many things seen. Sights seen fed the mind with instances of why the South was backward when compared to his own New England or New York. On the other hand, it was irresistibly interesting, and he was drawn to a relishment of the everyday encounters of life. People seemed to get more out of talk, casual meetings, and any and every occasion for sociability. His notes were to be a dialogue between sensuous enjoyment and cool analysis. Fascinated by the rich display of human life, Olmsted was compelled to attempt to grasp in words the very way a scene hit his senses. Here was his country church service:

During the exercises, people of both classes were frequently going out and coming in; the women had brought their babies with them, and these made much disturbance. A negro girl would sometimes come forward to take a child out; perhaps the child would prefer not to be taken out, and would make loud and angry objections; it would then be fed. Several were allowed to crawl about the floor, carrying handfuls of corn-bread and roasted potatoes about with them; one had a fancy to enter the pulpit; which it succeeded in climbing into three times, and was as often taken away, in spite of loud and tearful expostulations, by its father. Dogs were not excluded.

The observer was caught up in the very rhythm of the words and phrases of the preacher—this young man who rejected even the most reasonable of church-contained religion at home. " 'A-ah! why don't you come to Christ? ah! what's the reason? ah! Is it because he was of *lowly birth?* ah! Is that it! *Is it* because he was born in a manger? ah!' "[17]

Language itself fascinated him. He prided himself on adapting or blending so well that wayside people took him for a Southerner. He heard many varieties of Southern speech along the roads. The cultivated planter, the cracker, the Creole, the frontiersman, the mountaineer of his later travels, and all the way, the Negroes. A Negro of the swamp had run away even when shot at. The explanation was succinct and vivid from the white woodsman: " '*But some on em would rather be shot than be took, sir.*' "[18] A hospitable and self-possessed slave on a riverboat offered sustenance to the white passengers: " 'Does any of de genmen want some o' dese potatum?' "[19] One of the passengers had as curious a way of expressing himself as the Negroes. He complained about the conduct of a boat in which he had recently journeyed: " 'She's a right pretty boat, and her capting's a high-tone gentleman, that's what he is. But the pilot—well, damn him! He run her right out of the river, up into the woods—didn't run her in the river, at all. When I go aboard a steam-boat, I like to keep in the river somewar; but that pilot, he took her right up into the woods. . . . I was in my berth, and he run her straight out of the river, slap up into the forest.' "[20]

Olmsted savored the experience and the expressions of life. Alone among many people, unobtrusive, accepted, he was talked to everywhere he went, and he was known for his purposes only on the large plantations where he had letters of introduction. The large owners were usually courteous to him, and often uncomprehending. He saw well how all the psychological adjustments of life were affected by slavery. He explored this rich field for the operation of human nature with an economic explanation at the back of his mind, giving his searchings scope and shape. But his reactions took on an emotional color he had not anticipated.

By the time he reached New Orleans, he was tired, and being tired, discouraged. He thought that he had learned and seen little. He was uneasy that editor Raymond might not like his letters to the *Daily-Times.* He had seen the first one and feared an effect of superficiality in the early ones when his only news from the South was of the difficulties of travel. "You can't imagine," he wrote Charles Brace, "how hard it is to get hold of a conversable man and when you find [one] he will talk about anything else but slavery."[21] He worried too that he had not yet, as he thought, got inside the life of the slaves. He could not brazenly talk to them in the fields in their day-long work shifts, nor could he go to their cabins at night. The masters of the plantations, particularly those with large work forces, were not anxious for even their neighbors to know too much about how their slaves lived. They were sensitive to criticism one from the other, and much more so from an outsider.

Olmsted achieved his reporter's task by learning much from small indications, by being sensitive to nuances that many would have missed. Even reluctances were enlightening. He performed much better than he thought in his fit of discouragement, but he saw realistically the difficulties of anyone's penetrating the bland surface of a united South. He had to make much of glimpses, and this he did. Much of his writing about the South, assembled later from his daily notes, was indeed a surface picture of genius, a surface presented so clearly and multiplied with so many instances, a reader could come to conclusions without the writer vulgarly prompting him. As author, Fred Olmsted was, in his best passages of description, an eye without prejudice. Even in his judgments, he reflected not extreme positions as taken and held by the abolitionists, but the simple habits of his background, the morality of his bringing up, the virtues of hard work, efficiency, and some maturing notions which were beginning to take hold of the direction of his life, the proper use of man, beast, and soil, and the proper self-governing of every man. Although he was young and relatively unworldly, although he was seeing the South for the first time, his breadth of vision was not to be surpassed by any other traveler in the region in the two decades before the Civil War.

But he did not travel unscathed. His experience in "journeying south" was in some sense an ordeal of the mind as well as of the body. By the time he was in New Orleans, he was a somewhat different person from the young man who had set out carefree on the dancing, light-footed filly in Virginia to see for himself what life was like in this land so different from his own.

He tried one more adventure before he turned back home. He resolved to try to get up at least to the edge of the Texas open country. He engaged to travel upriver from New Orleans on the *St. Charles,* an overcrowded steamboat, which was setting out for a voyage to the Red River. The ship repeatedly delayed its departure. He made regular and useless trips to the dock. But there he amused himself with the human scene.

The book peddlers on the dock amused him by selling surreptitiously the forbidden *Uncle Tom's Cabin*—doing a brisk business with the slave owners boarding the ship. "They did not cry it out as they did the other books they had, but held it forth among others, so its title could be seen."[22]

When the boat finally backed away from the dock, he leaned upon the railing and watched the Negro stevedores on the lower deck. They sang a chant:

> Ye see dem boat wat dah ahead.
>   Chorus.—Oahoiohieu.
>
> De San Charles is arter 'em, dey must go behine.
>   Chorus.—Oahoiohieu.
>
> Dey's burnin' not'n but fat and rosum.
>   Cho.—Oahoiohieu.

> Oh, we is gwine up de Red River, oh!
> Cho.—Oahoiohieu.
>
> Oh, we mus part from you dah asho'.
> Cho.—Oahoiohieu.
>
> Give my lub to Dinah, oh![23]

And so on and so on. It went, endlessly, with a rhythm and with words and sounds he tried in vain to take down. One can see the rapt young man, stub of a pencil in his hand, scribbling rapidly in his notebook, struggling to transcribe an experience into words on paper.

The usual kind of overcrowding caused trouble on the passage upriver. He had engaged a berth but found it occupied by a gentleman who "was a good deal bigger fellow than I, and also carried a bigger knife." He was pushed, after supper, into the excess of passengers who occupied cots in the converted dining room. After the food and tables and chairs had been cleared away, cots of the meanest size were jammed together. He tried this dubious arrangement but was driven out by the bad smell of the crowded room. He wandered first in his restlessness into a part of the cabin used as a gambling bar. Under a placard forbidding "smoking, gambling, and swearing in the cabin," was "a close company of drinkers, smokers, card-players, and constant swearers." He tried the boiler deck next and talked to the poor Irish- and English-born firemen, learning about their hard life. "The regular thing was to make two trips, and then lay up for a spree." He explored the territory behind the furnace and found miscellaneous freight and hot steampipes all mixed together with exhausted Negroes and whites asleep amidst this tangle. There were two hundred deck passengers who had no more sleeping space than he had. Finding a corner he lay down to sleep but was awakened at midnight by the excitement generated by their boat's being in a race with another steamboat, the *Kimball*. At four o'clock the cot sleepers in the dining saloon (where he had settled at last) were roused and routed out so that the room could be made ready for the first session of breakfast. After this first difficult night, he found a place to sleep in the "social hall" rather than in the dining saloon. It was not an easy voyage. But still, in daytime, he enjoyed himself.

He watched ducks flying ahead of them. He assessed the skill of a passenger who sat in the prow taking shots first to one side then to the other at the flying birds. One or another of the passengers would start talking in the long boring hours of confinement. He made a mental note that everyone in the South, whether he talked to the purpose or not, enjoyed talking. Often enough, with him, this one or that one talked about slavery. The third day out a "well-dressed middle-aged man" asked him if he were reading *Uncle Tom's Cabin*. He understood that several of the gentlemen on board had the book. He supposed he might have picked it up if he had wished. He then plied Olmsted with questions about the book. From the book, he moved on to the general topic of the Northern belief in the cruelty of slavery. "He just wished I could see his Negroes.

" 'Why, sir,' said he, 'my niggers' children all go regularly to a Sunday-school, just the same as my own, and learn verses, and catechism, and hymns. Every one of my grown-up niggers are pious, every one of them, and members of the church. I've got an old man that can pray—well, sir, I only wish I had as good a gift at praying! I wish you could just hear him pray. There are cases in which niggers are badly used; but they are not common. There are brutes everywhere. You have men, at the North, who whip their wives—' " Frederick would have agreed with him that, from his observation, Negroes were not generally ill used. But the man's comparisons gave him his chance for a rebuttal. Did not the law, at least, protect women from cruel husbands? What law protected a black man from a cruel master? This, for Olmsted, was the rub; no law at all under heaven protected the slave, who was a chattel, a thing, not a man, in Southern law. Of course no man was respected by his neighbors if he treated his people badly. Yet the planter with whom Frederick was talking himself gave the instance of a case of cruelty which no law punished.

A planter in his neighborhood had had a favorite among the girls he owned. He became, rightly or wrongly, jealous of a black man for receiving her attentions. "Under an impulse of jealousy, he mutilated him." The court had not enough evidence to convict him, said his deck companion, ruefully, seeing evil here. " 'But . . . everybody believes he was guilty, and ought to have been punished. Nobody thinks there was any reason for his being jealous of the boy.' "

A more cold-blooded reasoner than the Southerner was a transplanted New Englander, who had entered enthusiastically and profitably into the life of the planter; he joined Olmsted in conversation one day. His justification for slavery was plausible and reasonable. Olmsted liked him less than the Southerner. He argued that the basis for all the prosperity not only in the South but in the North too was cotton and slavery and that, therefore, the combination of cotton and slavery was the basis of all the moral and intellectual growth of the North. They—those Northerners—then, had no right to sneer at the necessarily lower level of life in the South; it fed them. "Men gave more time to study and thought, because they gave less to providing themselves with shirts."

This talk, chilling in its reasonable acceptance of evil as the basis of all kinds of higher life, occurred after Frederick had left the crowded *St. Charles* without regret. He transferred to an orderly, well-run boat, the *Dalmau,* to return from Grand Ecore to New Orleans. He had not achieved his purpose of reaching the beginning of the West. He had gone only part way up the ladder of rivers to a point near which men struck out for Texas. He had a desire to return to that place.

Going downstream he felt already that he was turning toward home. But he spent some time in little Creole towns and had a stay at a sugar plantation. Luck had little to do with the owner's success. Here, on new land, with prime hands, and with intelligent direction, the slave economy—contradicting his leading theory—was brilliantly successful. This troubled him.

Wet land had been drained and made productive. Hands had neat clothes, good food, sound houses, and Christmas gifts. A family feeling united master and servants. The master's house reflected esthetically the good sense of his arrangements. It had attractive grounds. A rear yard held "houses for the family servants, a kitchen, stable, carriage-house, smoke-house, etc. Behind this rear-yard there was a vegetable garden, of an acre or more, in the charge of a negro gardener; a line of fig-trees were planted along the fence, but all the ground inclosed was intended to be cropped with vegetables for the family, and for the supply of 'the people.' I was pleased to notice, however, that the negro-gardener had, of his own accord, planted some violets and other flowering plants."[24]

When Olmsted came to New Orleans again in the springtime blooming of violets, he had much material set down in notebooks to carry home. He had seen varieties of management of both land and men. Within the chaos of material gathered hastily along the road—sights, sounds, impressions—there were a number of involuntary judgments. Now these must be sorted out and the material arranged into patterns to explain the South of 1852–53 to himself as well as to others. He had listened to and even provoked impassioned or casual talk about slavery. He had noticed every interrelationship between men and men and between men and the land. The book he was to write as a result of this journey (and the two others that would be written after a second journey) would be the result of honest observation and his own independent judgments based on his experience of men and land as well as extensive reading.

What he had seen was a magnificent region varied in fields and forests, hills, swamps, and seacoast. (He was to see the great shaggy mountains of the South on his second trip.) Splendid temporary fields of hundreds of acres had been carved out of wilderness; in the newer areas, where such work was possible, fields uniform in cultivation yielded rich crops of regulated quality. Yet this kind of agriculture drained the land of fertility. Behind the movement westward of the profitable part of this society were areas where once great and splendid fields had passed back into disuse, and the land left lonely and desolate. Southerners, rich, poor, or middling, either stayed on in the older regions in fierce loyalty to an impoverished land, or picked up all their belongings and moved westward. These people were endlessly interesting, a rich and developed humanity presenting itself to his view, a wide range of *folk* which delighted in being itself, a mix of good and bad and amusing, expressing itself—white and black—in endless drawling talk and in idiosyncratic acts which defined character.

CHAPTER IX

New York Streets
and Texas Trails

Scene, the South; bound West.
—F. L. O., *A Journey Through Texas*[1]

TWO EXUBERANT YOUNG MEN turned up in the backcountry of Louisiana in December, 1853. Fred and John Olmsted were leaving behind any number of cares. Fred left his farm to an overseer; John, who had returned from Europe in midsummer, left behind his wife and child. The younger brother tried to leave his bad health behind too, or to forget it in this desperate cure. It was to be a journey of many months upon horseback into country partly settled and even, they hoped, beyond into Indian country. In Natchitoches, on December 15, where public conveyances were still available, a traveling companion, who had volunteered to go along with them part of the way, went on ahead by coach to San Augustine with some of their gear. However, the young men from Staten Island scorned to travel on from this point except by horseback. They began assembling the supplies and necessary equipment of western horseback travelers and completed their purchases a little farther along the way across the border in Texas. They had great joy in outfitting themselves in frontier style, preparing to live in a free and independent fashion on what they could carry with them. From a passing Missouri muletrain they picked "Mr. Brown,"[2] who was to be steady and faithful, "a stout, dun-colored, short-legged, cheerful son of a donkey, but himself very much of a gentleman.... A saddle, saddle-bags, and the doctor, were temporarily put upon his back until the pack was overtaken." They soon grew fond of the willing beast who turned aside only when passing farmers' corn cribs. As if bred to it, he bore their strangely styled packsaddle with its side hampers attached and refuted all the scoffers at the crossroads where first saddled.

In Natchitoches, they found their number one horse for Fred—"a sturdy but gay little roan 'creole pony' . . . an animal of excellent temper and endurance, full of boyish life and eagerness, warm in his friendships with man and beast, intelligent, playful, and courageous." Nack was so splendid a companion that "tears stood in our eyes, as well as his, when we were forced to part." This was to anticipate. When they first saddled Nack, all was eagerness for the long journey. They tried to provide themselves against all difficulties, but made their preparations in the spirit of boys playing a game. They acquired Sharps rifles and Colt pistols and practiced marksmanship at the town edge, delighting all the little boys of the neighborhood. They were modestly proud that "after a little practice we could very surely chop off a snake's head from the saddle at any reasonable distance, and across a fixed rest could hit an object of the size of a man at ordinary rifle range."[3] They were to acquire another horse, Fanny, for John Hull, at San Augustine, an animal of dashing but uncertain temper, and at Centreville, they added a dog, Judy, to their company, "a sturdy bull-terrier"[4] to protect their camp from hogs. The terrier was not only a terror to hogs, but to all strangers to the camp. Judy was reluctant the first day but transferred her allegiance to them and accompanied the two brothers on their travels of two thousand miles, and Fred alone, when he parted from John Hull, and went on by himself through the "back country." Judy was to go home to Staten Island with Fred.

On December 26: "We sallied forth from the inn-gate . . . at San Augustine amid the cheers of the servants and of two small black boys who had watched with open eyes all our proceedings."[5] John Hull on the lively Fanny took the lead. Then came their friend B. (whom they had met traveling) leading the mule, while Fred-Law on Nack took up the rear. Frederick, this time with a good companion, was on the road again, directing their little party toward Texas at last, the region of controversy and myth, about which they had heard all their lives.

Frederick had returned to Staten Island only the previous spring tired out from his solitary journeying from Washington to New Orleans. But he had rested. His newspaper articles had done well; they excited attention North and South and raised a pleasant fuss. Only his family and friends knew that he was "Yeoman." He imagined that these folk thought at last that Fred might be amounting to something after all, making up for having lagged behind the younger, more brilliant-seeming John Hull, who had gone to Europe first, graduated from Yale, gained a medical degree, married a pretty girl, had a son, and was an easy charmer, making people expect more from him than he ever accomplished.

Frederick had planned to write a book about his "journey through the seaboard slave states" and had begun almost at once looking through his notes and the newspaper articles and going to Manhattan to libraries to supplement his observations with statistics and other information. Interferences of living and traveling held back completion of the book, however. He was not to see it published for almost three years (January, 1856).

Returning from his first southern expedition, Frederick had found himself looking at the hills of Staten Island with a stranger's eyes. He had looked about himself searchingly in the South in the piney woods and open fields and in the considerable cities of Richmond, Savannah, Columbus, Montgomery, and New Orleans. The habit took hold. Why are we as we are, and they, down there, as they are? Since he had asked so seriously: what is the Southern character? he now might ask: what is the Northern character? This kind of restless self-examination—for he included himself in the scrutiny—was a part of his preparation for writing the book which was to be larger than the sum of his newspaper articles. It was not a comfortable process. All the buttressing of his observations by statistics and other men's opinions did not spare him making his own conclusions.

Visiting Manhattan from peaceful Staten Island was a disturbance and an exhilaration. The Island itself was backward enough, its people isolated enough, to be found kin to the rural folk scattered across the great regions of the South. There was likeness—leaving aside slavery. And it was true, some of the "help" on farms nearby were hardly as well off as some of the slaves he had seen. His ideal yeoman was not always visible to him when he came back north. And yet he thought: we hustle, we change things, up here. He had entered again into the seasonal activities of Southside, growing grains, fruits, and vegetables, getting products to market, meeting with his fellow farmers to agitate for a new road from the ferry on the north shore to the farms on their side of the island. But he also got away more often than in his earlier years from the confining round of the farmer's life. He let New York buffet him with its life.

The city was changing rapidly, a fact he could discern even in his casual experience of its streets, shops, and museums. It was a city different in kind from the cities in the South. Already the characteristic note of New York was competition. People had to step lively to avoid collision in the streets and in all the accidents of living. A new mode of transportation struck the note of the city. There were too many people to be accommodated only by private carriages on the very long avenues now running north and south. Private vehicles remained for the wealthy. The democracy of New York rode up and down Broadway now in horsecars, heavy omnibuses pulled by multiple yokes of horses. In crowded blocks the once open street was filled by "a continuous chain of omnibuses . . . you often have to wait ten minutes before you are able to cross the street."[6]

Broadway not so long ago, as recently as when twenty-year-old Frederick Olmsted was a clerk for Benkard and Hutton, had been a "thoroughfare of small frame dwellings and three-story brick buildings, [and] it now offered a succession of imposing marble, stone, or cast-iron-faced structures rising five or six stories in height." "Horse railways," as they were called, rivaled the omnibuses on avenues parallel to Broadway. These "monster cars" on tracks held up to thirty people.

New York pushed and shoved to meet new conditions. Olmsted could not but contrast this turmoil with the slower pace in the South; and yet the South moved in its own way westward, with all its paraphernalia of family, furniture, servants, loaded on unchanging wagons and coaches; and people repeated honored and unaltered ways of doing things as they moved from rice to tobacco to the newer cotton plantings as far west now as Texas. Although his eyes beheld New York horse cars, Olmsted recalled Southern sights. He ached to get it all straight and in order. He continued to turn out the slighter newspaper articles while studying Southern political and economic history.

The city in itself was so interesting that it was a distraction. In the early weeks of 1853, while Olmsted was in the South, a new magazine made its first appearance. This was *Putnam's Monthly Magazine*. Frederick was to have a connection with this publication within two years. In July the city government arrived at a decision which would, within five years, have a radical effect upon Olmsted's life. After much public talk and effort by such men as the *Post's* editor, William Cullen Bryant, and by the landscape gardener, Andrew Jackson Downing, the state legislature (which was required to act in city matters) specified a site for a "central park" for the city.

The city was so various now, and with so many problems, that a citizen such as George Templeton Strong, fond of the life and movement of his place, yet characterized New York, which he would not for the world have deserted, as "the roaring chaos of corruption it is now."[7] The date of his diary entry was December 23, 1853. In this "chaos"—very real and terrible in the poorer streets—Fred Olmsted's friend Charles Loring Brace was committed to saving as many boys and girls of the streets as he could.

The world of the poor children was one that haunted Brace, not from hearsay, but from having thoroughly explored its innermost recesses. And he discovered then that "after awhile the world, which is seen, the busy, well-to-do, comfortable, luxurious world, appears only the surface. Beneath, far and wide, deeper and darker as one penetrates it, flowing under everything, is the current of poverty and wretchedness and rioting crime. One wonders how the society can long exist which is built on such slippery foundations."[8]

Just above the level of the most wretched were those children who earned a living of a kind in the streets. There was, for example, a whole way of life lived by the prematurely wise newsboys, who hawked the many thriving and not-so-thriving daily papers of the city. Brace found out their "lodgings." One night's exploration took him to a sleeping place "down a dark stairway under the sidewalk, in a great charcoal box, where usually six or eight sleep, with the huge steam-press clanging all night in their ears. Another was a little corner in the alley of a printing office, where refuse and old paper is thrown; another, the floor of the press room. Sometimes you will see them curled up around the grating on the side-walk, where the steam comes through. In summer they sleep in the Park [City Hall park] and on the Court House steps." Yet these strays and waifs were experienced business-men. They picked up their pennies shrewdly; they spent them on cigars and theatre tickets and gambling. There were little "coffee-and-cake" cellars where these ten- to thirteen-year-old boys gathered.

While Frederick Olmsted was still in the lower South, the gentlemen who organized the Children's Aid Society asked Charles Brace to be its active head. He accepted at once, determined to use his brains, his powers of per-suasion, even the fame he had won in the Hungarian cause, and his own magnetism and good looks to dragoon others into helping him. This was going to be his life's work, to invent new ways to get boys and girls out of the dirt of the streets and into clean and decent ways of living. This was what he had aimed for without knowing it, and he had been wise all along to avoid the commitment to a pulpit.

It was about the time of Frederick Olmsted's return to Staten Island from his first adventure in the South—an experience which deflected him from his future in farming—that Brace, unsettling himself in a fruitful and satisfying way too, began to devise means to make the Children's Aid Society work. He began everything on a small scale: first a school for little girls, dirty, wild, foul-mouthed, almost uncontrollable children; then, a lodginghouse for newsboys. He persisted with various experiments in industrial and voca-tional education for both boys and girls, compelling delicate ladies of his acquaintance to become teachers of classes set up in poor neighborhoods, but his first great success was in the imaginative way he devised a kind of home for the boys who sold papers and customarily lived on the streets as well as worked on them.

The principle by which Brace did his work was that of making the poor boys of the "newsboys' lodging-houses" more knowledgeable, more self-respect-ing, and more able to do for themselves in a difficult world. Brace indeed disapproved of charity. He wanted ruggedly independent men to grow from his urchins, who, so far as they could, had already fended for themselves against weather, bigger boys, police, and, in fact, all the world that threatened them from above. Brace's idea was that the boys who were to live in one of his lodginghouses were to pay a few pennies for the privilege. They were to help govern and maintain the place. They were to learn together as well as live together.

The first of these lodginghouses was "an old begrimed loft in the top of a building at the corner of Fulton and Nassau streets."[9] He spent one thousand dollars and divided the loft into "schoolroom, bedroom, office, and bathroom." He put bunks in the bedroom to take care of seventy-five boys. He was lucky in finding C. C. Tracy, a self-educated mechanic, to be the first resident supervisor and landlord. Brace had a kind of talent for finding the right people to help him with his work. He was to hire later a couple to be resident supervisors, and they too were excellent helpers.

To get together his first group of lodgers, Brace used newspaper ads. These boys—at least some of them—read the papers as well as sold them. Tracy helped find some others. The scrappy, compassionate mechanic gathered together his first rebellious, questioning group of boys and told them right off that they were not objects of charity, "but each one a lodger in his own hotel, paying his six cents for a bed, and the only rules were that they should keep order among themselves and use the bath." A few who had come "merely to make a row, left in disgust." The others stayed, wary as little animals, but willing to try this strange place.

"When they turn in, the Superintendent could hear their exclamations of satisfaction. 'Better than bumming—hey, Jim.' 'Rather warmer than the soft side of a plank, ain't it?' 'Did ye nivir see a bed afore?' and the like. The next day several said they 'couldn't sleep, the beds were so soft!' During the night there was 'larking' going on in the stairways by the outsiders: the gas-burner twisted off, which might have been followed by serious consequences if Mr. Tracy expecting this, had not provided a cut-off in the inside." The boys were suspicious at first. What was all this for? "Some whispered, 'It's a House-o'-Refuge trap!' Another, 'I know—it's worse 'an that— it's a Sunday-school-trap!' "

Gambling on policy tickets was their great amusement. Tracy introduced checkers and backgammon and constructed an ingenious wooden bank table with a drawer for each boy to put his savings in. They grumbled but voted to keep the bank locked for two months. They were amazed when it was opened and they counted out each one his own account, fierce and fascinated little capitalists. The superintendent soon instituted a system of paying interest on savings to each one.

All this Brace tumbled out to Fred and John. He told them how he had introduced lectures at night and persuaded teachers to teach. He gave the boys of the lodginghouses simple religious instruction in his own straightforward, unselfconscious way. His plan, he told his friends, was to gather the boys in the lodginghouses for only limited periods, then to scatter them throughout the country in good foster homes. He would rescue them from the streets; have them taught, to the extent that he could find teachers in the ordinary subjects of schooling; then pass them on to more normal home life and chores and jobs. He accomplished this in the end with thousands, tens of thousands, finding places for generations of boys (and girls) "with farmers, others in factories, others in shops, on railroads, and in telegraph offices. They generally succeeded. Their shrewdness and quickness, with the self-reliance they had acquired in their rough life, made them very efficient in whatever they undertook."[10] He was making his small boys able to grow up to compete in the world which Brace knew that he would not be able to change fundamentally. He did not wish for a transformation of that world, only an improvement of its lower depths.

Brace's view of the deprived poor became a part of Frederick Olmsted's mental furniture. The needs of children and of women and men living in crowded, unsanitary, and ugly surroundings became one motive for work he was to do later.

In 1853, Olmsted did not know what he wanted to do. Farming did not seem to be enough to occupy his restless mind. Writing, perhaps, was necessary too. He knew that he had not finished with the South yet, and that he had more writing to do about that section of the country. If he could have seen into his future, he might have found prophecy in George William Curtis's preface to A. J. Downing's collected horticultural writings, published in 1853 by the Putnam publishing house: "To touch the continent lying chaotic, in mountain, and lake, and forest, with a finger that should develop all its resources of beauty, for the admiration and benefit of its children, seemed to him a task worthy of the highest genius."[11]

The future was unclear, but the present held interesting problems, which Olmsted's recent trip south had quickened for him. Slavery was more than ever a topic of conversation among Fred's, John Hull's, and Charley Brace's circle.

Charles Brace brought the abolitionist minister Theodore Parker to see Fred and John. The young men resumed their enjoyable, nonstop talks about such things as whether one must support slavery in order to support the Constitution or, whether, instead, one should disobey the law of one's country in order to obey a higher law of morality. Frederick spoke with some authority now. He had seen slavery. He had come home sobered but puzzled by the experience. He was not sure of solutions; he groped toward the idea of a gradual containment of slavery and diminution of the system. He was impatient of those who had no firsthand knowledge of the South and who wished to abolish the system without planning an orderly future for the region and its people. He felt a shuddering horror at the sureness of those extreme abolitionists who wished to put down the "slaveocracy" in blood. It was perhaps as great as that he had felt toward even benevolent slavery. More knowledge was needed. He would go back.

"Texas" was a great part of the argument in the North. Frederick had got to the edge of Texas on his first trip, but had not stepped into that land which had been the scene of so much violence and was yet the subject in the North of so much talk. He wanted to see the physical spaces of that new state, which was almost an abstract idea to those who had never been there. In the North, Texas was at once the romance of going west, and the very symbol of Southern wickedness in doing that very thing, going west with family and slaves and settling the Southern way of life on vast open spaces. If Texas, why not Kansas and Arizona, California and Oregon? All through the decade of Olmsted's Southern travels, disagreements north and south burned fiercest not so much about the fact of slavery, but the extension of slavery geographically. This was particularly true after the election in 1853 of President Pierce, a New Hampshire man, who was thought to be compliant to the South.

Sober men were still convinced that abolishment of slavery was unconstitutional and impractical, but forbidding its expansion was a different matter; that might be done. Here one should draw a line, even fight if necessary. Southerners, under the pressure of moral disapproval, insisted upon the right to take their servants anywhere. Federal law, they believed, should protect their right of ownership outside the South. And they insisted, with even worse effect upon the nerves of men in the North, upon the right to reclaim runaway slaves under federal law, with the protection of federal troops. Frederick found an irresistible interest in the scenes where such ideas were not abstractions but were actually embodied.

He resolved to go back for the sake of deeper and sounder conclusions. He had not been paid very much for his first series of newspaper articles, nor gained much fame, but he had received a supplement to his income and enough money paid in advance and along the way to accomplish the trip. This summer, after a vacation trip to upstate New York, Mrs. Geddes having welcomed him with open arms at Fairmount, he came back to the city and conferred with Henry J. Raymond of the New York *Daily-Times*. He stayed with Charles Brace for a few days, and the editor of the paper paid him the compliment of coming to Brace's house to talk with him. Olmsted's letters, the editor told him, "were being read with much interest at the South. The papers had done talking of them because they were afraid to touch them."[12] Raymond agreed to accept additional letters from a second journey. He talked also of commissioning Frederick to do other correspondence for the *Daily-Times* in the future, perhaps letters from London. A different kind of future seemed opening up. From this time on, Fred saw the possibility of selling his farm and living altogether by means other than farming.

In the meantime John Hull and Mary and their baby had come home from Europe. Apparently, Southside was their home after their return in mid-summer. John was hopeful of accompanying his brother to Texas. Would not the dry western air, the open, invigorating life, do him good, and would he not come back to Southside improved in his health? It seemed a chance worth taking.

On November 10, the brothers started south. Their real journey began upon catching the B & O train in Baltimore.[13] Inside the coach they were already "south" it seemed. A Virginia "gentleman" (Frederick's sarcastic designation) successfully aimed a generous squirt of tobacco juice across the aisle and upwards over their heads through a hinged ventilator above the window. A nurse and her charge sat opposite, a "white baby drawing nourishment from a black mama." The train carried them to Harper's Ferry, through the mountains, and on to Wheeling. They boarded the *David L. White* on the Ohio and traveled for a time in the comparative luxury of a well appointed steamboat. Here they were in the "North" again. Along the Ohio, Frederick found: "The towns, almost without exception . . . [were] repulsively ugly and out of keeping with the tone of mind inspired by the river." This seemed to be a people on the move toward better conditions, but in going there they had thrown overboard all the amenities. They did not seem to have any fun either. They did not sit back and talk as did the beautifully idle jawers and storytellers of the South, who were content to *be*, without anything to *do*. Contrasts and comparisons, North and South, touched him on the quick. He was going back determined to seek out the meaning of the Southern character. But he also asked: what is a Yankee? What were the qualities of the North to which he could be loyal? It was already a matter of loyalties and a declaring of sides.

An encounter with a prepossessing young Southern gentleman who had been a classmate of John's at Yale brought together all the elements of a personal crisis of confidence and belief. Frederick poured out his thoughts and feelings in a long private letter to two friends (Charles Brace and Charles Elliott).[14] He described how he and John had spent two days in Nashville in the company of young Samuel Perkins Allison, who had shown them about, taken them to dinner, and talked with them as they liked to talk to friends on the piazza back home. Giving hard blows with words, enjoying the zest of controversy, Frederick, who took it all to heart, savored this frankness of exchange. On the boat trip below Nashville, penetrating the South, he poured out ideas pell-mell in spite of the activities of the riverboat gamblers who made the night noisy with cards slapped on the table, money jingled, oaths uttered, cries and curses exclaimed, and loud laughter. And there was a congenial torrent of feeling in the heart of the young man trying to write a letter—a message to himself as much as to friends back home—trying to explain his personal reactions to a way of life which attracted and repelled him.

He confessed that he and John had been worsted at least in words by the blandly self-confident Allison, who was sure of himself, his position, and his world. But Frederick, full of doubts about the North, many of which he admitted, still argued still with himself, if not with Allison, over points he had let the other young man win.

Somehow all their talk revolved around the word "gentleman." Who and what was a gentleman? Where was he to be found? Allison grandly denied the existence of a gentleman in the whole of the northwest free states, particularly in and around Cincinnati. He remembered only a few at Yale, the sons of a small number of commercial or professional men—politely, one supposes, making a generous exception of those present. Fred admitted the ruffianism and want of "high honorable sentiment" among the common farming and laboring people of the North, but pleaded the compensation of the "general elevation of all classes." This failed to impress Allison, and Frederick saw that the young man who called himself a Democrat, and had run on that ticket (and lost to a Whig), was in reality no democrat of any kind. He believed in classes. His gentlemen were few in number; they had no wish for their number to be augmented, but desired only to protect their present interests and to expand the sphere of their command. For the first time—he had not feared it on his first trip—Fred feared slavery's spread, however illogical this spread might be in areas ill-suited agriculturally to the institution. Allison's ideas were grandiose: the Southerners would have California as a slave state; they might move on also into Mexico and Cuba and the Amazon Valley, fit places for slave cultivation of the land. This attractive young man, extreme in his views, gave Olmsted the apprehension of a violent explosion between the two sections. Allison had no idea that anyone in the North would oppose slavery except for material reasons.

Walking the streets of Nashville with Allison, Frederick found it one of the most winning of Southern cities. Stopping at a likely bookstore, looking at the capitol placed on a hill, talking, talking endlessly, his and Allison's dialogue continued. In spite of his singular, and to Frederick almost preposterous, views, Allison remained an attractive human being. Frederick granted to the two Charleses at home, to whom he wrote about this meeting, that these Southern gentlemen probably lived up to their own definition of what a man should be. He groped to express to the friends at home, and to himself, what quality he found lacking in Allison and others like him, and what quality he thought desirable which these fine young aristocrats had not a notion of.

The beautiful manners of the South were a genuine good. But the men who used these manners were also, underneath the clothing of manners, as materialistic in their protection of their interests as the more naked money-grubbers of the North. Frederick expressed dislike for the state of public affairs both North and South:

With such low, material and selfish aims in statesmanship [in the South] and with such a low, prejudiced, partly enslaved and material people [in the North], what does the success of our Democratic Nationality amount to—and what is to become of us. . . . I must be either an Aristocrat or more of a Democrat than I have been—a Socialist Democrat. We need institutions that shall more directly *assist* the poor and degraded to elevate themselves. Our educational principle must be enlarged and made to include more than these miserable common schools. The poor and wicked need more than to be let alone. . . . I do [feel] very much inclined to believe that Government should have in view the encouragement of a democratic condition of society as well as of government—that the two used to go together as they do at the North in much greater degree than at the South or I suppose anywhere else. But I don't think our state of society is sufficiently Democratic at the North or likely to be by mere *laissez allez*. The poor need an education to refinement and taste and the mental and moral capital of gentlemen.

He became more personal and colloquial—writing, as he explained, in the gaming cabin of a steamship with oaths, bets, bad light, and movement of the boat all interfering with thoughts and clear writing: "I can't collect my ideas. But to put some shape to it, Hurrah for Peter Cooper and Hurrah for the Reds." There had come to him, from Charles Brace's Hungarian experience, and from his own experience of poverty in England, Ireland, and Germany, some influx of European democratic and socialist ideas. This was an addition to his native New England faith in a small, self-respecting "democracy." He exclaimed explicitly in the long letter, "I am a Democrat of the European school—of the school of my brave porter of Bingen." This reference Charley Brace no doubt understood, a reference to an encounter with a German workingman which they had shared in the summer of 1850. "And these so-called Democrats [like Allison] are not. They are of another sort, material, temporary, temporizing, conservative. I wish I had Victor Hugo's speech now to read you. The Southern sort are perhaps larger—more generous and braver minds than ours and they act up to their capabilities better, but ours are more expansive and have need to be more humble as being less true to their principles and feelings."

Blind and deaf to the din of gambling, aware only of thoughts becoming luminous in this dark of his mind, Frederick wrote:

The great difference I feel between such fellows as these gentle-manly, well informed, true and brave Southern gentlemen, whom I admire in spite of my Democratic determination, whom I respect in spite of my general loathing of humbugging dignity, the great difference between them and those I like and wish to live among and wish to be is the deficiency in one and the sense in the other of what I must call Religion (the intrinsic religious sense) as a distinct thing from Belief, Obedience, Reverence and Love to Personal Deity. The quality which God must have himself. They do not seem to have a fundamental sense of right . . . I have something which distinguishes me from them whether the above explains it or not. So have you, so has Field, Elliott, all our earnest fellows.

His exhortation—to himself and to his friends—was to a general line of behavior. His life itself would bear him out, proving that this hastily written, crudely expressed letter did indeed come from the deepest recesses of his feeling. He concluded:

Well the moral of this damnedly drawn out letter is I believe—Go ahead with the Children's Aid and get up parks, gardens, music, dancing schools, reunions which will be so attractive as to force into contact the good and bad, the gentlemanly and the rowdy. And the State ought to assist these sort of things *as* it does Schools and Agricultural Societies—on the same plan, with the same precaution that the State of N. Y. now does . . . I *don't* believe that the friction compensates for the increased power of the machinery.

He had not yet built one park, nor know that he was going to. He did advocate one specific thing he thought he and his friends might do when he came back—found a magazine:

And we ought to have that Commentator as an organ of a higher democracy and a higher religion than the popular. And it ought to be great—sure of success. Well founded. Bound to succeed by its merit, by its talent. A cross between the Westminster Review and the Tribune is my idea. Weekly I think to give it variety and scope enough for this great country and this cussedly little people. Keep it before you.

Having thought out his position and gotten through the agony of it, Fred was all the more ready to enjoy the journey west from the Red River headwaters into the new land of Texas. As it turned out, this trip was to be pleasanter than his first one. Slavery itself was a muted aspect of things here, and he had the good company of his brother John. Many of the sights seen going west were not particularly Southern, but were evidences of what all Americans North and South endured to move west. Olmsted responded eagerly both to the open country and the crowded city. He felt a need for both. Perhaps this was a general human need, and a man was not made to rusticate altogether, or to be citified altogether. How bring together these values which he felt spontaneously in his body and in his mind? He could not know that this kind of thoughtful consideration, timed to the deliberate slow jog of a horse making a long journey, was a preparation for a future life work.

The Texas journey had the feel of a happy journey even at the beginning. Learning to make camp, learning to cook over a campfire, accepting mule nature and horse nature and fitting themselves to the animal speed of these creatures who soon became friends, Fred and John entered a time of almost unclouded happiness. The effects of slavery could be observed in the spectacle of a thinly clad girl sitting by the roadside in a downpour of sleet. Poverty could not be missed, as in the cabin where John the doctor fussed over a neglected, bronchial child playing on a bare floor. Happiness had tuned the minds of the travelers to a keenness they had rarely felt before so that they missed very little.

One of the most impressive sights was the scattered, impeded progress of an emigrant train bound for Texas.[15] Frederick had the sense that he was seeing something historic. The road was not a road but "only a way where people had passed along before." Through the piney woods, through groves of oaks and cottonwoods, through the openings where there was usually some kind of shanty, straggled these heavily burdened groups. "Inexorable destiny it seems that drags or drives on, always Westward, these toil-worn people," Olmsted wrote.

There were many difficulties with teams, with broken wheels or traces or shafts of wagons. There were stops for meals, backtracking for stragglers. Fred on Nack had many opportunities for talk as he rode alongside the caravan. This was a spectacle which he overtook with much respectful and compassionate observation. Before he saw them, he heard the cries with which these farmers urged on their cattle. "Then the stragglers appear, lean dogs or fainting negroes, ragged and spiritless. An old granny, hauling on, by the hand, a weak boy—too old to ride and too young to keep up. An old man, heavily loaded, with a rifle. Then the white covers of the wagons, jerking up and down as they mount over a root or plunge into a rut." Leaving behind these slowest ones, he passed next those more able to keep going, "active and cheery prime negroes, not yet exhausted, with a joke and a suggestion about tobacco." Next those who have to ride: "black pickaninnies, staring, in a confused heap, out at the back of the wagon, more and more of their eyes to be made out among the table legs and bedding as you get near: behind them, further in, the old people and young mothers, whose turn it is to ride." Then the head of the procession: "the white mother and babies, and the tall, frequently ill-humored master, on horseback, or walking with his gun, urging up the black driver and his oxen." Last of all, the scout at the head of the procession, "a brother, or an intelligent slave, with the best gun, on the look-out for a deer or a turkey." The way was so hard that the atmosphere was one of dogged hope and of weariness. The women in particular, he noted, often walking to relieve the team, were "haggard, mud be-draggled, forlorn and disconsolate, yet hopeful and careful." The negroes were "mud-incrusted, wrapped in old blankets or gunny-bags, suffering from cold." He saw them "plod on, aimless, hopeless, thoughtless, more indifferent than the oxen to all about them." There was not much "Oh, Susannah" in the winter caravans going to Texas.

A man joined him on the road and asked where he was from, where he was going, where he got his horse, how much he paid for it, what kind of a "piece" (gun) his was, and did he drink anything, and would he drink now? Another traveler told him the settlements existed only to "fleece" the emigrants. Olmsted observed: "Every shanty sells spirits and takes in travelers. Every plantation has its sign, offering provender for sale, generally curiously worded or spelled, as 'Corn Heare.' "

Beyond this mean and difficult area, the land stretched out. Camping could be enjoyed. The brothers played at being frontiersmen. Each evening they found corn at a farmhouse. They unsaddled and unloaded. Fanny, who might stray, was tethered, but the other animals were left free. The mule, his pack off, promptly turned over on his back with feet sticking upward in a comical fashion of almost human relief. A tree was found (at least before they got beyond all trees) for the "back-rope" of the tent; they cut a pole for the other end. They gathered fuel, lit a fire, set water to heating. Such became the unthinking, comfortable routine of Texas travel.

One day all at once they were in the real West. Fording a creek, climbing to the top of a steep hill, making their way through the still continuing trees, they "came out and suddenly, as if a curtain had risen, upon a broad prairie, reaching, in swells like the ocean after a great storm, to the horizon before us.... Horses and gray and red cattle dotted the waving brown surface, and in one of these bays, to our right, were six deer unconcernedly browsing."[16] The way forward through this new land was a continual adventuring—on a small and unalarming scale. They shot game. They combatted a grass fire. They fell in with Mexicans and Indians and Texas Rangers. They savored the Mexican flavor of Austin, San Antonio, Castroville, and New Braunfels. They enjoyed the lonely beauty of the Guadalupe country and half wished they might stay.

Castroville and New Braunfels were German towns. These settlements of the emigrants from repression in central Europe interested the Olmsteds. The animus of who was slave and who was free crept into the interest; by 1854 one could not keep it out. The German settlements were "free"; they kept no slaves, and they lay athwart the advance of the Southerners who did keep slaves. The Germans proved that free settlers could farm the wilds of Texas successfully. They had come poor (although with resources of education and political liberalism) and with ingenuity, intelligence, and industry, despite some disasters due to inexperience, had planted farms, communities, and towns.

The two ingenuous and enthusiastic Olmsted brothers were treated as honored guests of the community of Germans living close-knit in the vast spaces of the new state. While balked of their plans for further western travel when Indian dangers stopped them, they were content for some weeks to explore the German world in Texas. They stopped at a German boarding-house in San Antonio and there were advised to call upon the editor of the *San Antonio Zeitung*, Mr. Adolf Douai. An intense, dedicated, somewhat humorless man, he was yet full of kindness. His influence caused the other Germans to be hospitable to Frederick and John. Douai was their guide for a short journey from San Antonio into the wilder country to the north. Lonely, newly built farmhouses dotted the valleys and limestone hills. When the travelers sought shelter in one such homestead, they found the cooking done outdoors, but "the walls of the two rooms had been made tight with clay, the doors were furnished with latches."[17] Frederick commented on the significance of these homely facts, "No man who has traveled much on the frontier will look upon these indications as trivial." Food was served on china, the tablecloth was clean, and there were engravings on the walls. "Honest labor," he remarked, had done all this.

Following this experience of hospitality, they crossed over a ridge and looked down upon the valley of the Guadalupe. Frederick savored the beauties of this landscape, "a wide and magnificent view of misty hills and wooded streams." Stopped from traveling by a norther, they stayed the night with the largest proprietor of the valley and met all his neighbors, who entertained the young men, starved for such activity, with talk and music and even waltzing. "I have never before so highly appreciated the value of a well-educated mind, as in observing how they were lifted above the mere accident of life," Olmsted wrote afterwards.

It was no wonder that Frederick, seeing virgin soil to be farmed, and John, hoping for health in this clean new land, were elated with the notion that they might pull up their roots at home and strike new ones here. John wrote to Mary asking her what she thought of the idea.[18]

While waiting for her answer, they made a trip down to the border of Mexico. They had as guide a former Texas Ranger, the frontiersman John Woodland. The country through which they were to travel was not quite safe, and they learned to practice certain precautions of watchfulness and preparedness which added a zest to the trip. Woodland taught them how to skewer rabbits on sticks of green mesquite and cook them to a delicious crispness over a small, hot campfire. He told them tales of the Texas Rangers and Indians. It was April and the sun each day warmed the soil until whole expanses of the prairie were in bloom. And the cardinals sang all about them.

A slight taste of danger was a seasoning that spiced the experience. One day they were joined by a band of dirty, sullen Indians who arrogantly asked them for their guns. They kept a tight hold on their weapons. They were prudent but bold in their talk with these wanderers—a creeping of the skin on the back of the neck warning them that these men might be dangerous. The hunch was right. The Indians were a party which, a few days after parting from John Woodland and John and Frederick Olmsted, attacked several isolated ranch houses and killed a number of settlers.

Traveling on in spring weather, the little party of three, cautious of other travelers, crossed over the Rio Grande. In Mexico, Frederick and John tasted a foreign life and puzzled over both oppressed Mexicans and freed Negroes. There was some attractiveness in the backwardness of the country, as strange to the mind as tortillas to the tongue; but Frederick liked tortillas better than cornpone. Officers of the United States Army in a lonely post on the river invited the three Americans to dinner. They discovered the strange ceremoniousness and courteousness of these gentlemen stationed far from eastern luxuries. In the afternoon of another day they swam in the border river.

Wherever they went in John Woodland's company, he told them stories. One, appropriate to the scene, was of a Yankee deserter in Mexico who posed as a doctor in the foreign country to which he had fled. "But Jim," Woodland asked him, "what do you do in real serious cases, now—childbed, for instance?" "Oh, I pile in the calomel, and let 'em slide."[19] Such an anecdote scandalized and amused John, the medically educated, if nonpracticing, physician. He in particular was attracted to the seemingly lazy and sensuous beauties of Mexican girls and this more southerly life. He was from time to time to think of fleeing south to Latin countries when his health bothered him.

Without any trouble, they returned to San Antonio, and having heard from Connecticut that it was not to be thought of that Mary and little Charles should be uprooted and moved to Texas, the brothers started eastward on the first stage of their journey home. This was April 24. The weather was good and they found it possible to travel without a tent. "Having divested ourselves of our pack and of all useless weight, we were prepared for more rapid travel, carrying each a single blanket, to preserve the delightful nocturnal freedom of the prairie. We had learned, like all who make the experience, to love the sweet breath of night and the company of the stars."[20] They determined to go on as directly to New Orleans as possible. This meant a route along the coastal plains of Texas and the waterlogged lowlands of Louisiana. They found their pathways—seldom roads—clogged with water. They had some desperate struggles to save mule and horses when they tried to thread their way through sunken logs and hidden tree trunks in swampy ground. John fell ill again in the heat and almost swayed off his horse in a faint. He got wet repeatedly in the struggle the two solitary men had through ill-marked swampy roads. Still, bravely, when he worked later as Fred's editor, assembling his brother's notes and filling in gaps with his own writing, he recommended such a trip for anyone suffering from the early, nondangerous states of phthisis.

The brothers could not convince anyone who lived in this isolated, scantily populated territory that they were traveling to see the country. This would have been regarded as so clearly frivolous or insane an explanation that they soon gave it up. They simply accepted whatever designation was given them —cattle-buyers, beef-speculators, at best. It would have surprised no one at the farmhouses they came across if they had turned out to be even more dubious characters. The people were hospitable enough, but the travelers suffered from the abject poverty of intellect in that countryside: "Hardly once did we see a newspaper or a book, other than an almanac or a franked patent-office report."[21]

They stopped along the way at a stock farm and saw a cattle drive, and were interested in the work of the men handling the animals. These were prototype cowboys, the type not having completely evolved as yet. At this house, whiskey was always present on the sideboard. Even the young boys of the family partook. At another house whiskey and milk were the only beverages on the breakfast table.

At Beaumont they exchanged Mr. Brown, Fanny, and Nack for other mounts. Judy stayed with them. They had outfitted the dog's sore and ulcerated feet with moccasins, and the wounds earned in following faithfully along beside them were cured. She was now fit and frisky.

Manners changed when they crossed from Texas into Louisiana: "The gruff Texas bidding, 'Sit up, stranger, take some fry!' became a matter of

recollection, of which 'Monsieur, la soupe est servie,' was the smooth sub-
stitute."[22] The Creoles were mostly poor, but polite, and the food was better.
They were served one evening, "venison, in ragout, with a sauce that savored
of the south of France; there was a side-dish of hominy, a jug of sweet milk,
and wheat-bread in a loaf—the first since Houston." Fred and John both had
touchy stomachs. The lighter, more palatable food was most welcome, and the
softness of the manners was pleasing to them. Yet there were queernesses
here too, tasting of the frontier. They were "several times, in this neighborhood, shown to a bed standing next to that occupied by the host and his
wife, sometimes with the screen of a shawl, sometimes without." This
ranked, in their fastidious Hartford minds, with a Texan lapse in domestic
amenity; one fair-sized landholder, owning a number of slaves, and some
fine furniture within doors, directed them for bathroom to the great windy
spaces outdoors, where the privy was any convenient bush behind the house.

The brothers reached at last a tributary of the Mississippi above New
Orleans and subsided contentedly into the comfort of the riverboat *Alice W.
Glaize,* which carried them through alligator-infested bayous to the larger
river. Here they parted. John stayed on board to continue to New Orleans,
to take ship there for New York. Fred, his saddlebags over his arm, disem-
barked to take up horseback travel once more with only Judy for companion.
He was going to ride across the "back country" of the South to Richmond.

CHAPTER X

The Back Country

The whole South is maintained in a frontier condition by the system which is apologized for on the ground that it favors good breeding.

—F. L. O., *Journey in the Back Country*[1]

JOHN OLMSTED reached Southside by June 9 or 10, 1854. Restored to his wife and child and the old farmhouse he had grown to love, he took over the supervision of the farm. He found himself critical of the state of the place. While Fred traveled about criticizing Southern farming, his own farm deteriorated. The pear trees needed pruning and there were suckers growing from the base of every trunk. Fred's brother rather grimly promised himself to try to remedy the disrepair.

In a lighthearted mood, at least in bodily good spirits, the errant farmer set off on a long and roundabout way home from the Mississippi river landing where he had parted from his brother. He would spend the rest of the summer journeying by horseback across the northern part of Mississippi, the little round hills and mountains of northern Alabama, the mountains of north Georgia, east Tennessee, and western North Carolina, the remote valleys of southwestern Virginia, and on to Richmond. After revisiting that city, he would take an easier route home to New York by sea. It was to be a deliberate, wandering pace, in which he was restored to concentration on things Southern, finding some very bad things and some very good ones. He was undistracted by the charming raillery of his younger brother, who had made the Texas journey more of a lark than a serious exploration. Being solitary, he had nothing to draw him away from conclusions which brought him to a darkening view of the South as a society organized upon a certain pattern. He asked himself hard questions and found answers not at all in accord with the hopeful mood in which he had first set out on his Southern journeys.

Astride a good new horse—Belshazzar, Fred named him—and with Judy loping alongside in her dog-moccasins, he made his way across a varied country. He passed first over land divided into giant and efficiently run plantations, each under an overseer or manager reporting to a sometimes remote master, who might or might not live on the land his slaves worked; then as he made his way into the hills, he found the land worked in smaller and poorer divisions of acreage, with fewer slaves, and, at last, in the mountains, with none at all. Traveling slowly, he exposed himself again to the anecdotal, tale-telling nature of the inhabitants, white and black. He talked with almost everyone he met along the way. Humorously, he was to describe how people of different kinds asked him for his dog. "Gentlemen inquire respectfully; 'Would not you like to give away that dog, sir?' Negroes: 'Don't you want to gib me dat dog, sir?' Growing boys: 'Please, sir, gim me that dog, sir?' and children, black and white, demand it peremptorily, 'Gim me dat dog.'"[2] Judy was a splendid success. Belshazzar performed well and faithfully during the long rides. However, the traveler, brooding as he rode, found much to distract him from the physical joys of the journey. Even Judy's popularity with some of her would-be purchasers was suspect. Perhaps they wanted her for a "nigger dog." There were such dogs: especially trained, strong, and intelligent hunting animals used exclusively to hunt down runaways and allowed, if the occasion warranted, to "tear" the fugitive.

It was the dark side of slavery that made his emotions raw. He found he could not control his feelings in every encounter. The mind could not organize handily the emotion he felt one day in seeing a Negro girl punished in an open field.[3] Fred had liked the manager of this plantation, who had courteously offered to ride out with him and show him the workings of this large and complicated estate. The man was sensitive to nature, talked well, and was a generous, open guide. But "The gang of toiling negroes to him, however, was as essential an element of the poetry of nature as flocks of peaceful sheep and herds of lowing kine." When it came to punishing a slave who had not behaved well, he acted in a strictly impersonal way to keep the plantation in good order from an economic point of view. Olmsted had set himself to see the South from the viewpoint of economy, assessing praise and blame as the men of the South violated good common sense in this regard. But here was something else, and his feelings shook him.

About noon, after a long instructive ride with the manager, the two men chanced upon a girl of about eighteen hiding in a ditch, hoping not to be observed. She had disappeared from her cabin that morning, the manager told Olmsted, had not appeared for work, and had till this hour remained hidden. There was, from the manager's sensible point of view, nothing to do but to punish her to preserve discipline. He did this job in an impersonal manner. He told the girl to get on her knees. She did so. "He got off his horse, and holding him with his left hand, struck her thirty or forty blows across the shoulders with his tough, flexible 'raw-hide' whip. They were well laid on, as a boatswain would thrash a skulking sailor, or as some people flog a baulking horse, but with no appearance of angry excitement." The girl repeated an evasive story. It was unsatisfactory to the punisher. It was marvelous to the unwilling onlooker how obedient she was to his orders, and clear at last how helpless was a person, not being treated as a person, in such a situation, apparently not particularly unusual.

" 'You have not got enough yet,' said he, 'pull up your clothes—lie down.' The girl without any hesitation, without a word or look of remonstrance or entreaty, drew closely all her garments under her shoulders, and lay down on the ground with her face toward the overseer, who continued to flog her with the rawhide, across her naked loins and thighs, with as much strength as before. She shrunk, groveled, cried: 'Oh, God, master, do stop!—oh God, master!' "

Knowing there was nothing to be done, Frederick looked on and burned with an agony of sympathetic shame and terror. A "young gentleman of fifteen" came up on the scene and was held up for a moment. He showed only impatience and boredom. What seemed at this moment insane to Frederick were the attitudes of these two persons: "I glanced at the perfectly passionless but rather grim business-like face of the overseer, and again at the young gentleman, who had turned away; if not indifferent he had evidently not the faintest sympathy with my emotion. Only my horse chafed with excitement. The screaming yells and the whip strokes had ceased when I reached the top of the bank. Choking, sobbing, spasmodic groans only were heard. I rode on to where the road coming diagonally up the ravine ran out upon the cotton-field. My young companion met me there, and immediately afterward the overseer. He laughed as he joined us, and said, 'She meant to cheat me out of a day's work.' "

Olmsted was to write three books, and then compress the three into one, largely made up of cool observation and rational analysis, but this scene of his own terror, when emotion flared out to overwhelm thought, was to be the climax of the three books' tale of his progress through his Southern experience. He carefully preserved the scene and placed it to make the proper climax in his final one-volume version of the travels. He made it clear, although he wrote no other passage of as searing a quality, that a naked and honest emotion took precedence over reason, for in this emotion he had found what was intolerable in slavery. That one human being had unlimited and uncontrollable power over another human being counted for more than all the economic reasons he was to amass.

Another event of this trip when emotion drenched thought was an evening's moment of perception on the bluff above the old town of Natchez. It was a scene of great natural beauty, yet neglected by the town authorities. It was sunset and he caught his breath as he looked out westward. He had the place to himself, and he lay right down on the ground for some moments of intense feeling. The scene entered into him—the river, the forests stretching away seemingly without end. He was content to let the unforced loveliness of wild nature play upon him with all its elements. The mind needed such scenes and it needed to respond with a certain quality of giving itself. Because in his writing about it, he so stressed this experience, he seemed to place here for his own edification a crisis of knowledge. It was as if in memory, he was to find that at this particular time and in this particular place, he came fully to the realization of how much a man owed it to himself simply to look and to feel. But then a local Natchez hog came rooting about the area, disturbing his contemplation, and Frederick's busy mind began rooting about among the reasons and causes of things. He could not see why the human and civil arrangements could not be such as to reinforce nature, to intensify the average man's natural aptitudes for appreciation, to lead him on by unobtrusive design to share with more sensitive men all the beauty spread before his usually unseeing eyes.

And he did not see why, in a town of the age, wealth, and pride of Natchez, the human civilities, in particular the public civilities, should not match the natural view. They did not do so: "I could find no reading-room; no recent newspapers except *The Natchez Free Trader,* which has nothing but cotton and river news, and steamboat puffs; no magazines but aged Harpers; and no recent publications of any sort are for sale or to be seen at the booksellers; so, after supper, I went to the cliff again, and most exquisite and solemn was the scene: the young moon shining through rents in the clouds, the great gleaming crescent of water below, the dim, ungapped horizon—the earth sensibly a mere swinging globe."[4]

Where were there in this town provisions for a public magnificence, as contrasted to a private one? Perhaps he did Natchez an injustice. He did not stay long enough to test what it might have yielded to a persistent wooer; there were to be many who would praise the unique civilization of this strange, isolated, and ingrown city on the great river. Olmsted in his critical mood groped toward what he thought would be a good life: a beautiful setting in which nature, improved by design, provided a scene for man's outdoor activities both esthetic and recreational; indoors, civic arrangements which gave men scope for reading, talking, meeting, all the civilizing activities, in addition to those exercised in making a living. Not only here were these elements lacking. In all of America, beyond limited areas, all was frontier of a kind, an unfettered grubbing for individual gain, a tossing aside or an ignorance of civilities.

In spite of his thoughts turning dark, Olmsted's senses were as lively and unrepentant as ever, responding to people and their talk, discovering the pathos, color, and humor in every casual encounter. A companion of the road told him about camp meetings, "I used to go first for fun, and oh! Lord haint I had some fun at camp meetings?"[5] The same man recommended the food at a stopping place ahead, describing it as, "good honest fried bacon, and hot Christian corn-bread—nothing like it to fill a man up and make him feel righteous. . . . It's lucky you'll have something better to travel on tonight than them French friterized Dutch flabbergasted hell-fixins."[6] Olmsted persisted in disliking corn bread.

One evening while it was still light he sat on a fence rail with a small farmer, noticed the fruit trees planted among the stumps of a half cleared-out field, and got down to examine the way they had been set out. Scratching with his pocket knife around the base of a small tree to find its roots, he told the man, "You've planted these too deep, if they're all like this. You should have the ground dished about it or it won't grow."[7] He found he got on well with the smaller farmers, could talk to them easily, and often elicited thoughts and feelings about slavery which it was supposed to be hard for an outsider to hear. He seemed hardly an outsider any more. He had traveled Southern roads for so many months that he knew what to expect and how to talk. He was regarded, in his worn travel clothes, as perhaps an agent for an ore company (in northern Alabama), or perhaps a Texan, buying cattle; his rig seemed western. The small farmers of the hill country who treated him in a friendly fashion seemed to him to have more dignity and bearing than their counterparts "at the North" but with less knowledge of the world and less interest in any world outside their own valleys and ridges. They had less comfort on their farms than small farmers in the Connecticut Valley or on Staten Island, New York, but they did not seem to care about little contrivances to make life easy. They had plenty of time to talk, and individuality flowered. Frederick regarded with scandalized delight this total reversal of the values he had been brought up to admire. He enjoyed the talk and reported it in faithful detail. He deplored the squalor and got very tired of dirt and discomfort. He was cranky about eating; Southern food failed to please him and he longed for smooth, bland New England puddings. He viewed without enthusiasm delicacies which were added to the eternal bacon, corn bread, and coffee. He thought hot biscuits heavy and unhealthy when dripping with buttter.

As for the land itself, he found that the hot and humid lowlands around the tributaries of the Mississippi palled, however odoriferous and beautiful the large perfect cups of magnolia blossoms. He was glad at last to reach the "softly rounded hills"[8] of the area of the Tombigbee River in Alabama. He endured many odd and even funny discomforts, but on the whole, he liked both the country and the people better here where they were poorer and "freer." Interestingly enough, he did not find, nor did he describe, what came to be caricatured as the "hillbilly." It was a kind of life which did not exist at the time he traveled, or did not present itself to him in the light it did to later travelers. He was predisposed in favor of people who did not own slaves and did not want to. And he liked their independence and self-possession. Here, in the hills and mountains, it was not unusual for men to express to him the desire to go west to get away from slavery, or to say frankly that they thought slavery bad. However, none saw any solution in freeing the slaves. They feared freed slaves. In all of the South, even here, slavery had become—it seemed to him—a gigantic and miasmic evil. It was like the weather, it had to be endured and could not be cured, or so these people thought.

He rode eastward by easy stages across hidden "coves" and mountains shaping themselves larger and larger across his path. As the air thinned and cooled, he was happier. This was indeed for him the best of the South. He later wrote, "The generally open-hearted, frank, and kindly character of the people, the always agreeable scenery, usually picturesque, and in some parts grandly beautiful, and the salubrious atmosphere, cool at night, and though very hot, rarely at all enervating at mid-day, made this part of my journey extraordinarily pleasant."[9] Food was plentiful and of the right kind for his horse and dog; Belshazzar and Judy seemed to enjoy the travel as much as he did. He stopped to rest on Sundays, always finding people to talk to, and on weekdays traveled twenty-five miles or more with ease. This part of the South had its own traditions and manners. It was little known to outsiders, either of the North or the South. He enjoyed anxious and considerate hospitality and laughed only to himself when urged to partake of molasses in the plural: take "them molasses."[10] He passed through the town of Murphy in North Carolina and heading toward Waynesville and Asheville, turned aside to climb Balsam Mountain. Here, shaggy firs and dark spruces covered the ground between impenetrable thickets of rhododendron. The climb was difficult, through lowering clouds in which he lost the trail, out at last into openings where he had glimpses of sky and distances. He came out of thick growth into a "bald" when the mists tore aside. He found himself far from slavery, far even from his daily self. Even the stumbling descent, in which he lost his way and tore his feet against roots and rocks, was an adventure. Of Asheville, which he saw on July 11, he was to write, "This is a beautiful place among the hills ... with a number of pretty country-seats about it."[11] He could not imagine that forty years later he would have important work to do in these hills, landscaping the setting for a "country-seat" such as no one in these parts, nor many people elsewhere, had ever seen.

After the rusticity of the "back country" Olmsted came blinking back into civilization in the comparative sophistication of the city of Richmond. He stayed to see things he had missed before, and taking the good Belshazzar and the faithful Judy with him, boarded a ship bound for New York and home.[12]

CHAPTER XI

Yeoman: The Southern Writings

W HEN FREDERICK OLMSTED came home from his second long journey
to the South at the end of the summer of 1854, he brought back
with him emotional luggage as well as handwritten notes and an abundance
of impressions. The experience weighed upon him until he was able to
unburden himself in words. These words took the form of three series of
newspaper articles, published in 1853, 1854, and 1857, three travel books,
published in 1856, 1857, and 1860, and a final condensed volume delivered
to the publisher in 1861 and brought out in both London and New York
that year. During this time he lived through engrossing personal experiences
not much related to his writings. His brother John Hull Olmsted died. He
assumed some of the responsibility for the care of John's widow and children.
He completed a career as the editor of *Putnam's Magazine* and was a co-
owner of the publishing firm of Dix, Edwards and Company, withdrawing
from that firm when it went bankrupt. He began his work on Central Park
and left the park to enlist in war service as secretary general of the newly
organized United States Sanitary Commission. Before following the progress
of his life through these years, it might help one understand the kind of
person Olmsted became by pausing over his Southern writings.

If he had done nothing of note after the 1850s, if there had been no parks,
if he had declined into worthy obscurity, Olmsted would still have a secure
place in American memory. He would be Olmsted of *The Cotton Kingdom*,
the man who traveled through the South before the Civil War and preserved
in words a description of the region, made a judgment, and shaped description and judgment into a loose form. But Olmsted, the writer about the

South, went on to become Olmsted, the designer of parks. The earlier career, after the heat of the war years cooled, was dimmed. When Olmsted was remembered, it was as if later generations recalled two different men. The traveler was the lesser known. These pages are an attempt to make the point that it was the Southern experience that was the hinge between the Olmsted of the earlier, tentative years and the Olmsted of the later years of public accomplishment. In the Southern writings one may see elements of rational judgment and of artistic sensibility which he used in a larger way in his career as a landscape architect and urban planner.

In growing up, Fred Law had not quite fit in with his family or his school fellows. Yet he had drawn nourishment from the wisdom of New England and the Olmsted family. It was a matter of course that he should dislike slavery and the Southern supremacy in the United States Senate, but he did so with the disdainful superiority of the gentlemanly Whig rather than the fire of the Abolitionist. So he went South with the feeling that he could manage the experience. He did not expect the challenge that it was to be to him. He found that he had not only to examine this strange, almost alien, life just next door in America, but that he had to reexamine his own beliefs. It was to be Olmsted's struggle with values in the South which furnished much of his emotional motive power for years to come. His work in landscape design was to be the result not only of opportunity offered to native talent, but the result of a readjustment of his own powers and ideas. The South enabled him to make this adjustment.

When Olmsted's first newspaper piece appeared on February 16, 1853 (he had been traveling since December 11), the paper's editor, Henry J. Raymond, introduced the new correspondent on the editorial page as follows: "We commence on our second page this morning, the publication of a series of Letters from the Southern States, which we commend to public attention. They are written by an intelligent gentleman, of decided ability, large experience, practical habits of action and of speculation, known already to the world by his published works, who visits the South for the express purpose of exploring its character and condition for the instruction of the readers of the *Daily Times*."

The article appeared in a prominent place at the top of page two and occupied the first two columns and a bit more of that page. It was headlined:

THE SOUTH

LETTERS ON THE PRODUCTION, INDUSTRY, AND

RESOURCES OF THE SLAVE STATES

NUMBER ONE

SPECIAL CORRESPONDENCE OF THE NEW YORK DAILY TIMES

The article was signed "Yeoman." The author presented himself here and in the following letters as a small Yankee farmer traveling without fanfare through the South and attempting to find out what the large and small farmers of that region were doing in the management of their land.

Yeoman pledged himself to examine the "wealth and intelligence" of the parts of the South he would pass through and "the elements of happiness possessed by the inhabitants"—thus harking back to the inspiration of the "pursuit of happiness" theme of the Declaration of Independence. Unconsciously, he showed inheritance from the puritan ethic of New England as well as to the later "happiness" principle. And he said: "No man can write of the South and put Slavery entirely in the back-ground. I wish to see for myself, and shall endeavor to report with candor and fidelity, to you, the ordinary condition of the laborers of the South, with respect to material comfort and moral and intellectual happiness. I am disposed to treat the subject with kindness, frankness and candor, and I trust in so doing I may be able to encourage the conviction that it is only in the justice, good sense, and Christian sentiment of the people of the South, that the evils of Slavery will find their end."

Olmsted began his travels on December 11, 1852, and was traveling in the time of the sensation caused by Harriet Beecher Stowe's book. *Uncle Tom's Cabin* had appeared serially from June, 1851, to April, 1852, been published as a book in 1852, and been sold in plain covers to gentlemen boarding a river steamer in New Orleans, as Olmsted had reported.

There had been other discursive and incidental treatments of the South in polite letters (as well as the shrill pamphlets of the committed anti-slavery people), but none had had the impact of Stowe's novel. Olmsted had probably read these earlier writings, as he was to read Mrs. Stowe's novel. In 1838 Harriet Martineau's *Retrospect of Western Travel* exemplified the scornful English traveler's barely contained patronage of the American scene. In contrast to the awkward, gauche Yankee, she preferred the "ease and frank courtesy of the gentry of the South"[1] as she met them in Washington, D.C. Even their touch of arrogance did not displease her. It was in part to prove to himself that the North was not inferior to the South that Olmsted traveled. He was the pugnacious, not-to-be-put-down "Yeoman," seeing what he could see of these great folks who had dominated the nation, and not a bit afraid of asserting the small *d* democratic notions of his own Connecticut Valley.

Another English traveler, Charles Lyell, in 1845 in *A Second Visit to the United States of America,* had had a surprisingly sanguine view of the South. He found society in Richmond "refined," although it was true that they had not in Richmond "that activity of the mind and feeling for literature and science which strikes one in the best circles in New England." But he had liked the company he kept. And he had not alarmed himself about the situation of the blacks: "The negroes here have certainly not the manners of an oppressed race."[2]

Writers from whom Olmsted would have been more likely to take a lead were Bryant and Dickens. The visit to Hartford which Dickens included in his *American Notes,* published in 1850, was the very occasion when Frederick's father had hosted a dinner for the writer. On this same journey, Dickens had found the South run-down and desolate and had attributed the poverty of the land to the influence of the use of slaves as labor upon the land. On the railroad journey from Fredericksburg to Richmond, Dickens observed that the Southern land looked poorly and he supposed that slave labor succeeded "in forcing crops, without strengthening the land."[3] But this was only the chance observation of a bright young man busy glancing from one object to another.

William Cullen Bryant collected his *Letters of a Traveller* in 1850, the year Olmsted walked through a part of England. Bryant had visited the South in 1843 and had reacted with a subdued criticism: "It was impossible to mistake the region in which we were. Broad inclosures were around us, with signs of extensive and superficial cultivation, large dwellings were seen at a distance from each other, and each with its group of smaller buildings, looking as solitary and chilly as French chateaus; and, now and then, we saw a gang of negroes at work in the fields, though oftener we passed miles without the sight of a living creature." In South Carolina he had "enjoyed the hospitality of the planters—very agreeable and intelligent men; been out and in a racoon hunt; been present at a corn-shucking; listened to negro ballads, negro jokes, and the banjo." And he found: "The blacks of this region are a cheerful, careless, dirty race, not hard worked, and in many respects indulgently treated. It is, of course, the desire of the master that his slaves shall be laborious; on the other hand it is the determination of the slave to lead as easy a life as he can. The master has power of punishment on his side; the slave, on his, has invincible inclination, and a thousand expedients learned by long practice. The result is a compromise in which each party yields something, and a good-natured though imperfect and slovenly obedience on one side, is purchased by good treatment on the other."[4]

Olmsted hoped to be broader and deeper in his description of the South than his predecessors. But he determined also to travel in innocence. He had not been there before. He would see what he could see, and report honestly. He had learned much about England from trudging its roads and talking to passersby. He thought he could learn in a similar way about this alien section of his own country. Taste, touch, smell, sight, and sound toned all his impressions. He had essentially an artist's temperament although he was able, by an effort, to abstract ideas from observations. He was somewhat distrustful of his gift and supplemented his personal impressions with facts and attitudes culled from newspapers in all the towns and counties he visited. He accumulated materials, also, from gentlemen who kept books and magazines in their houses. In a city such as Richmond or New Orleans, he consulted bookstores and libraries. Before he returned from his Texas journey, he commissioned certain statistical studies to be made by impecunious newspaper men.

But what he accumulated in memory from direct sensory apprehension of scenes was to matter the most in the long run. This varied. It might be simple, straightforward observation of appearances:

The planter's house is usually a plain two story, clap-boarded building, fifty feet long, and twenty wide, divided in its length by a hall, against each outside door of which is a broad porch. It is commonly shaded by a few old white-oak trees, left from the original forest growth. Scattering about it, without much order, are from two to a dozen log-cabins for the negroes.[5]

Or, he recorded talk: a slave speaks to him—"I was a kine of *pet* boy, you see, Mr. Yeomans. I allers wait on my masser myself till my little brudder got big enough."[6]

Trusting his observations and reactions, Olmsted gained confidence in himself and in these newspaper accounts written in head-splitting circumstances —in the poor light and cold drafts of log cabin inns, in overheated and smoky steamboat saloons, in noisy and dirty trains, in stops alongside the road where he rested his horse—he ventured to write his individual, untutored conclusions. The freshness of both observations and conclusions give the accounts the vivid quality which has made them valuable in helping later historians or common readers to recreate from them what it was like in 1852 or 1853 to journey into the South almost as into a foreign country, where one could, luckily and after a fashion, speak the language of the natives.

The first expedition lasted from December, 1852, to April, 1853, the second from November, 1853, to August, 1854. The newspaper articles were written in three series, two for the *Daily-Times,* signed "Yeoman," and the third, unsigned, for the New York *Herald.* There were forty-eight letters in the first series (Schlesinger counted fifty). They appeared with irregular frequency from February 16, 1853, to February 13, 1854, thus covering a year of prominent display. Only his family and friends knew that Yeoman was Fred Olmsted, but as Yeoman he attracted a wide audience both North and South. There were thirteen numbered letters and one unnumbered one in the second series for the *Daily-Times,* between March 6, 1854, and June 7, 1854. The third and last series, not signed "Yeoman," appeared in nine letters in the *Herald* between June 3 and August 10, 1857. This last series, entitled "The Southerners at Home, from the Journal of a Northern Traveler on Horseback," were not as attractively presented nor as prominently displayed as the earlier ones in the *Daily-Times.*

Before the letters finished appearing, Olmsted began writing the three books which he elaborated from his newspaper accounts. *A Journey through the Seaboard Slave States* was published by Dix and Edwards in January, 1856. It covered the itinerary of Olmsted's first journey, from Washington to New Orleans and a little beyond. The book contained the essence of his experience of the South, the painful initiation he had into the realities of slavery, the wrestlings he undertook in learning how complex and interrelated all the parts of life were in this difficult and interesting South. It contained also his fascination with the wealth of life here as it displayed itself before one traveler's rapt eyes.

A Journey through Texas was published by Dix, Edwards and Company (the slight change in the publisher's name reflecting Olmsted's part ownership in the firm). *Texas* showed Olmsted intrigued by the life of the German settlers in western Texas, the democratic and hardy breed who farmed without slaves. The book showed also his delight in the openness and beauty of the region. Except for his interest in the "free soil" movement, this book was lighter in tone than the first book had been or the third book would be. It was an adventure, a holiday. Its genial tone came in part from John Hull Olmsted's part in assembling and editing his brother's notes. Fred let John make what he would of this volume.

A Journey through the Back Country was published by Mason Brothers (Dix, Edwards and Company had failed) in 1860. It covered Olmsted's solitary return, after he parted with his brother, the long horseback ride from the banks of the Mississippi to the James. He came by way of the plantation country of Louisiana through the hills and mountains of the highlands of the South. He saw a striking contrast between the large slave-worked sugar plantations of the deep South and the small tillage of the independent and non-slave-owning farmers of the mountain region. Here at last he met yeoman farmers in the South. In *The Back Country* were agonizing pages of his final facing up to what slavery meant and, on the other hand, the happy release he felt in getting away from slavery in the mountains.

The three travel books contained, besides descriptive chapters, sections of Southern history and of Olmsted's analysis of Southern conditions. As the years passed, his tone darkened. He persisted in offering a gradualist solution to slavery, but his hope diminished. He began by finding war unthinkable. He ended by finding it imminently possible.

The Cotton Kingdom, a condensation of the three travel books, was published in 1861, first in London by Sampson Low and then in New York by Mason Brothers. In putting it together, Olmsted had the good help of a handy journalist of Southern origins but antislavery views, Daniel R. Goodloe, who in 1846 had written an "Inquiry Into the Causes Which Have Retarded an Accumulation of Wealth and Increase of Population in the Southern States." *The Cotton Kingdom* lacked some of the discursive charm of the earlier books, but it presented the sweep of Olmsted's experience from first to last. Olmsted rearranged a few episodes in order to place them in the center of the narration for dramatic effect (the whipping of the slave girl and his meditation upon the bluff at Natchez).

As compared with the three travel books, there was a sharpening of the antislavery tone and more argument in *The Cotton Kingdom*. It was marked by the urgency of the time in which it appeared, the first year of actual warfare. It was published in the new form because it was considered helpful to the free cause. It has endured because of the historical honesty and accuracy of its observations and conclusions. Since the war prevented the working out of Olmsted's gradual kind of emancipation, the urgency of his argument has evaporated; the observations are now more interesting than his conclusions.

There was always an essential unevenness in the reports from the South, the hitching together of two kinds of writing, but the whole remains interesting, one part for its timelessness, the other for its timeliness to the years in which it was written, the disturbed decade of the 1850s. The perspective of one hundred twenty years underlines the validity of Olmsted's portrayal of the relationship of the two races in their harnessing together in the South.

In the first place, then, Olmsted wrote a sensible book in a time of hysteria. The public, and especially those who prided themselves on forming opinion, both North and South, had become irremediably partial during the generation from 1830 to 1850. It was not as if Olmsted was ignorant of the hot abolitionist temper. Charles Brace had brought both Theodore Parker and William Lloyd Garrison to talk to him at Southside. And although Olmsted detested slavery in the abstract, and particularly the spread of slavery westward, he was inclined to speak for a moderate solution short of any kind of violence. When he began to travel in the South, he let the Southerners speak for themselves. He put the reader on the road and allowed him to overhear conversations and be present at all sorts of encounters.

During a visit to a plantation near Richmond early in his first journey, Olmsted reported, a landowner had spoken to him about the frustrations he suffered in his dealings with his servants. The man had wished that the northern philanthropists would devise a method "to relieve us of it"—i.e., the burden of the care of slaves. The rueful slave owner stated an axiom that bolstered Southern self-esteem: "I am satisfied, too, that our slaves *in Virginia* are in a happier condition than most of the poor laborers of the North, certainly than those of England, or almost any other Christian country. I am not sure that free labor would not be more profitable; the slaves are wasteful, careless, and in various ways subject me to provoking losses." And of these bound servants, the man said to Olmsted: "Oh, they are interesting creatures, Sir, and, with all their faults, have many beautiful traits. I can't help being attached to them, and I am sure they love us."[7] Olmsted quoted another Virginia landowner, who employed free labor by choice, as saying that Jefferson had been right, that slavery had a more evil effect on the white race than on the black. The man said that he knew of cases of cruelty toward slaves but that he thought the case against the South in *Uncle Tom's Cabin* was exaggerated.[8] Yeoman himself went closest toward sympathy with this enlightened Southern view in his *Daily-Times* letter of April 8, 1853, when he wrote for the readers in New York City:

I must declare that the Virginia slave is more happy, more comfortable, in some sense more free; and in better and more manly relations with his masters, than the Irish peasant or the English agricultural worker is to the "higher classes" of those countries. . . . Slavery will not die until the world has humbled itself to learn a lesson from it. Oh, God! who are we that condemn our brother? No slave ever killed its own offspring in cool calculation of saving money by it, as do English free women. No slave is forced to eat of corruption, as are Irish tenants. No slave freezes to death for want of habitation and fuel, as have men in Boston. No slave reels off into the abyss of God, from want of work that shall bring it food, as do men and women in New York. Remember that, Mrs. Stowe. Remember that, indignant sympathizers.

Oh, Christian capitalists, free traders in labor, there is somewhat to be built up, as well as somewhat to be abolished before we repose in the millenium.[9]

This passage did not appear in the later book versions. As Olmsted traveled, he became more absorbed in the Southern system and concentrated his strictures upon the South without very many more references to the ills of the North. So, from seeming to lean over backward to present the South favorably, he came to seem—to Southerners—unfair to the South. He had, at the outset, warned that the reader would be traveling with a "growler," but he added, "But growling is sometimes a duty."[10]

That he wrote a vivid as well as relatively fair book was due to his practicing what he preached to his sister Bertha when she went abroad for the first time, and to Charles Brace when he traveled on into eastern Europe— that one should put oneself in the way of incidents and let things happen to one, rather than carefully engineer and routinize one's journey. It was to be out of the accidents and incidents of his Southern travels that his best and most vivid pages would come. Like John Keats's contenting himself to take part in the movements of a sparrow pecking the gravel, Olmsted could during periods of self-abandonment be happy in taking in the spectacle that life offered to him. This was the opposite of clenching the will to prove a theory or make a point. Olmsted the artist, rather than Olmsted the doer, let the accidents of travel happen to him.

It is these accidents of travel which fill the most brilliant pages of the writings about the South.

He had picked up Joseph (a Negro) from the road in his chaise between Portsmouth and Deep River and held a conversation with him about runaway slaves. There were deep woods near them, a place where runaways could hide for months or years. Joseph said that "it was easy for the drivers to tell a fugitive from a regularly employed slave in the swamps."

"How do they know them?"

"Oh, dey looks *strange*."

"How do you mean?"

"*Skeared* like, you know, sir, and kind o' strange, cause dey hasn't much to eat, and ain't decent (not decently clothed) like we is."[11]

Olmsted observed a poor white family on a train in South Carolina. The man questioned him about New York, thinking it might be somewhere in

New Orleans, and, about to debark, he cordially invited the traveler from New York to visit him on his farm.

The moment the train began to check its speed, before stopping at the place at which he was to leave, he said to his daughter, "Come, gal! quick now; gather up yer young ones!" And stepped out, pulling her after him, on to the platform. As they walked off, I noticed that he strode ahead, like an Indian or a gipsy-man, and she carried in her arms two of the children and a bundle, while the third child held to her skirts.[12]

On board a steamer going upriver from New Orleans a Red River man talked to him about his slaves left idle at home while he traveled:

"I've got twenty on 'em to home, and thar they ar! and thar they ar! and thar ain't a dam soul of a white fellow within four mile on 'em."
"They are picking cotton, I suppose?"
"No, I got through pickin' fore I left."
"What work have they to do, then, now?"
"I set 'em to clairin', but they ain't doin' a dam thing—not a dam thing, they ain't; that's wat they are doin', that is—not a dam thing."[13]

He met an ill-educated German, who began each conversation with the words: "Oh, Christ! gents."[14]

Much of this life seemed in motion. He found he must show the South not as a static frieze, but as a moving procession of people, still searching westward for better lands and opportunities. Owners, slaves, rich men and poor, white and black, moved along the roads, on Georgia's coast, in the Carolina piney woods, on Louisiana swamp roads, and onto the swelling grasslands of Texas where the future also seemed to open out. Yeoman watched the whole human scene. He described with equal vigor three levels of Southern society: aristocrats in a comfortable and well-ordered plantation, crackers in the vital, coarse life manifested in a country church service, and the slaves typified for him (crucially as it turned out) in the runaway girl who hid out from her day's labor and was whipped for it.

The episode had stayed in his mind, and, with an esthetic intuition, he had made the scene the climax of his reporting. However, the years which followed, the bitter decade leading up to the Civil War, made the passions of both North and South sharper. That Olmsted at least unconsciously heightened the color of the scene in his final book account of the episode is shown by a sentence which he included in the despatch to the New York *Daily-Times* but which he omitted from his later book versions: "I must say, however, the girl did not seem to suffer the intense pain that I should have supposed she would."[15] But the whip had touched his imagination, and he would not be the same again.

In addition to presenting pictures, Olmsted felt obliged to make quiet judgments. This he did through a gathering of statistics, a summarizing of Southern history, and conclusions based upon personal observation. The substance of Olmsted's critique is easily stated: slavery is wrong because it makes the wrong use of land and the wrong use of man, and it causes the South to be backward economically and culturally. This basically straightforward and simple view was buttressed for Olmsted by all the impressions and all the smaller judgments he had made in two long and difficult journeys. It was to be variously accepted and rejected in his own time and later. It has, however, continued to have a substantive weight.

Olmsted had a view of man which was consistent with his past. From family and region he inherited an ethic which held that man was a responsible, self-directing being, and that anything which prevented man from being so was wrong. He included the black man under the rubric *man* and so contradicted the habit, North and South, of not taking seriously the proposition that a Negro was as full a person as a white man was. (He had been three-fifths of a man in the United States Constitution.) This starting position was distinctive and original in Olmsted for his time. The impulse to exclude freedmen from the functions of a citizen was already well established and generally approved in the North at this time. This repressive attitude was to have its ugly climax when Negroes were the scapegoats of street riots in 1863 in New York and even Negro orphans were killed and their asylum burned.

A series of quotations from Olmsted's first book of Southern travel shows how one basic idea flowered into many branching ideas, all interrelated. He began as a traveling farmer, who was immediately struck by the improper use of the land. In Virginia, he saw the dramatic degradation of land used for tobacco.

No governmental interference was ever allowed to prevent the planters from defrauding their posterity of the natural wealth of the land. They were, therefore, able to live sumptuously, but ever discontentedly, as spendthrifts do, and always staggering with debt, though spending, with all their might, their capital stock, their land's fertility.

As their exhausted fields failed to meet the prodigal drafts of their luxury, they only made further clearings in the forest, and "threw out," to use their own phrase, so much of the land as they had ruined.[16]

Olmsted did not give enough credit to a native Virginia effort to improve the land with fertilizer—Edmund Ruffin's creditable and to an extent effective advocacy of the use of marl. And he did not link the careless use of land in the South to the careless American use of land everywhere that the frontier advanced in haste. Shocking to him was a farmer's remark that, "if he was well-paid for it, he did not know why he should not wear out his land."[17] It seemed to him that the use of slave labor accelerated this wearing out of the land. On the field labor of slaves, he wrote:

Could the hope of reward for faithfulness be added to the fear of punishment for negligence, and some encouragement be offered to the laborer, to apply his mind to a more distant and elevated result than release from his day's toil—as, it seems to me, there easily might be—it would, inevitably, have not only an improving effect upon his character, but would make way for a vastly more economical application of his labor.

In other words, if a slave were a man, with the hope of a man, he would not work as a slave—that is, under duress, and with only the care and interest that was exacted by the threat of force if not force itself. For, said Olmsted:

Take men of any original character of mind, and use them as mere animal machines, to be operated only by the motive-power of fear; provide for the necessities of their animal life in such a way that the cravings of their body shall afford no stimulus to contrivance, labor, and providence; work them mechanically, under a task-master, so that they shall have no occasion to use discretion, except to avoid the imposition of additional labor, or other punishment; deny them, as much as possible, the means of enlarged information, and high mental culture —and what can be expected of them, but continually increasing stupidity, indolence, wastefulness, and treachery?

Put the best race of men under heaven into a land where all industry is obliged to bear the weight of such a system, and inevitably their ingenuity, enterprise, and skill will be paralyzed, the land will be impoverished, its resources of wealth will remain undeveloped, or will be wasted; and only by the favor of some extraordinary advantage can it compare, in prosperity, with countries adjoining, in which a more simple, natural, and healthy system of labor prevails.[18]

He admitted that a temporary and apparent advantage belonged to the slave states through "certain circumstances of topography, climate, and soil, that give them almost a monopoly of supplying to the world the most important article of its commerce."[19] And he never denied that certain planters for a certain length of time were monstrously prosperous; but their engrossment of the income from the labor of slaves and the wearing out of land was, in his view, shortsighted and would be short-lived. His was a conserving, fostering, and creative view of man and land, in essence, a reverential view.

Much that he found slack in the South he traced back to slavery. No man took pride in work; this was menial. He told a story which exhibited the difficulty of getting handicraft work done. He wished to have an umbrella repaired. He took it to a workman who said it would have to be left and that it would take at least one half hour to fix. Olmsted said that he wished to wait, and that all that was required was a rivet to be tightened. A brief dialogue ensued:

"I shall have to take it all to pieces, and it will take me all of half an hour."
"I don't think you need to take it to pieces."
"Yes, I shall—there's no other way to do it."
"Then, as I can't well wait so long, I will not trouble you with it;" and I went into the hotel, and with the fire-poker did the job myself, in less than a minute, as well as he could have done it in a week, and went on my way, saving half an hour and quarter of a dollar, like a "Yankee."

Virginians laugh at us for such things.[20]

In his impatience to get things done Olmsted could not tolerate the lacka-daisical attention to detail, the lack of energy in doing chores, and the want of finish in workmanship. He was surrounded by sloppiness and indifference to things that would have been handled punctiliously in Connecticut. And yet, he was to enjoy the attention, relish, and care which Southerners lavished upon sides of existence scanted in the North. These were the leisurely arts of living. This was a lively and attentive people where matters of human interest were concerned. It seemed, simply, that human energies had been turned in different directions in the South. He did not admire all the things the white landowners did, and yet he had a sneaking admiration for the lordly freedom and generosity of manner possible to a man so free in himself, so used to command, and so negligent of detail. There was a dearth of formal intellectual exercise, or so it seemed to him—few books, magazines, or news-papers, no public forums of discussion—but, nevertheless, "The social inter-course of the wealthy people of the South is certainly more agreeable, ra-tional, and to be respected, than that of the nearest corresponding class at the North." This Olmsted wrote in his letter of January 12, 1854, for the *Daily-Times*. In the same letter he paid a tribute: "But to the Southern gen-tlemen, . . . as I have often met him, I wish to pay great respect. The honest and unstudied dignity of his character, the generosity and the real nobleness of habitual impulses, and the well-bred, manly courtesy which distinguish him in all the relations and occupations of life, equally in his business, in his family, and in general society, are sadly rare at the North—much more rare at the North than the South. I acknowledge it freely but with deep regret and melancholy."[21]

Having paid his tribute, he wrestled with the problem of how to transfer these qualities of the individual gentleman to a larger group of people in a society not subsistent on slavery. However much he liked the best specimens of this society, they gained their sustenance, as he thought, from living on slavery. And he did not believe in the happiness of the slaves. "The precari-ousness of the much-vaunted happiness of the slaves can need but one further reflection to be appreciated. No white man can be condemned [in a court of law] for any cruelty or neglect, no matter how fiendish, on slave testimony. The rice-plantations [this was written in South Carolina] are in a region very sparsely occupied by whites: the plantations are nearly all very large —often miles across: many a one of them occupying the whole of an island —and rarely is there more than one white man upon a plantation at a time, during the summer. Upon this one man each slave is dependent, even for the necessities of life."[22]

Into this analysis of a highly wrought and interconnected social order, Olmsted with patient and deadly persistence introduced the idea that the labor system as it existed should be done away with and a free labor system substituted. He did not advocate instant abolishment of slavery, but a gradual emancipation. He was confident that the Negroes, whom he thought brutalized progressively by slavery, would grow toward the condition and character of free men if allowed to do so.

Negroes given even the semblance of freedom as the swamp Negroes were in North Carolina came to seem like free men. These black laborers were hired out by their employers to work for other men. During the rainy period of the year they were free to find work for themselves and to keep their wages.

The slave lumberman then lives measurably as a free man; hunts, fishes, eats, drinks, smokes and sleeps, plays and works, each when and as much as he pleases. It is only required of him that he shall have made, after half a year has passed, such a quantity of shingles as shall be worth to his master so much money as is paid to his owner for his services, and shall refund the value of the clothing and provisions he has required.[23]

If these were good men, they might be hired and rehired and spend most of their lives at this work. "The negroes working in the swamp were more sprightly and straight-forward in their manner and conversation than any field-hand plantation-negroes that I saw at the South; two or three of their employers with whom I conversed spoke well of them, as compared with other slaves, and made no complaints of 'rascality' or laziness."[24] He learned of one industrious worker who had bought his freedom although at an exorbitant price, who wished to learn to read and write, and who shipped to Liberia.

Olmsted's "plan" perhaps grew out of such living examples. He was to elaborate his curative ideas in the last of the three books, *Back Country,* but he suggested the essence of them in the first, *Seaboard Slave States.* And his ideas remained curative rather than radically revolutionary. As much as he desired the freedom of the slave, he did not wish the utter destruction of the owner. He did not wish to bring about the freeing of the blacks in a way to tear apart the society of the whites. He clung to the hope that persuasion or reason might cause the southern whites to bring about a change that, in his view, would make their way of life not only morally better but more profitable in the most mundane way. He thought that freed slaves, who had learned to care for themselves, would work more carefully and at more of a profit for wages than under a "driver."

He argued as follows:

The ascertained practicability of thus dealing with slaves [he had visited a plantation where slaves were allowed to sell produce and to keep the money] together with the obvious advantages of the method of working them by tasks, which I have described [rather than in gangs doing the same work by the hour], seem to me to indicate that it is not so impracticable as is generally supposed, if only it was desired by those having the power, to rapidly extinguish Slavery, and while doing so, to educate the negro for taking care of himself, in freedom. Let, for instance, any slave be provided with all things he will demand, as far as practicable, and charge him for them at certain prices—honest, market prices for his necessities, higher prices for harmless luxuries, and excessive, but not absolutely prohibitory, prices for everything likely to do him harm. Credit him, at a fixed price, for every day's work he does, and for all above a certain easily accomplished task in a day, at an increased price, so that his reward will be in an increasing ratio to his perseverance.[25]

There was to be punishment meted for laziness. The family, which he thought had been partially destroyed by slavery, was to be fostered.

When he desires to marry, and can persuade any woman to marry him, let the two be dealt with as in partnership. . . . When any man has a balance to his credit equal to his value as a slave, let that constitute him a free man. It will be optional with him and his employer, whether he shall continue longer in the relation of servant.[26]

Olmsted's plan was based in part on the emancipation process in Cuba where, as he explained, "Every slave has the privilege of emancipating himself, by paying a price which does not depend upon the selfish exactions of the masters, but it is either a fixed price, or else is fixed, in each case, by disinterested appraisers."

Abstract justice, as in the abolitionists' pamphlets, called for immediate freedom and no payment to the owners. Olmsted was pragmatic, concerned with the actual situation, the practical freeing of the slaves, the practical working of the land, the practical substitution of one system of labor for another without destroying the white owners, and, in addition, a method of educating the slaves. Psychological analysis of his motives would uncover deep-lying assumptions in the planner, one of these being that Olmsted did not here hesitate in his mind to play God. (He never did.) That Olmsted was paternalistic and dictatorial in his methods is obvious enough; he was also patient, practical, and had a grasp of the situation as it existed. He said also in utter conviction, "I do not think, after all I have heard to favor it, that there is any reason to consider the negro, naturally and essentially, the moral inferior of the white."[27] He would have had argument on this point in the North as well as in the South.

Although Olmsted's judgments on slavery make the framework of his Southern writings, they are not the residual part that remains today. The war took care of his plan, smashing all its sweet reasonableness to pieces and leaving the whole South, both that of the whites and the blacks, in ruin, out of which it took many generations for both parts, first one and then the other, to begin to find a creative way of life. But Yeoman's world of the 1850s lives. This is because he was a wayward artist content to be more than a fact-collector and fact-arranger. He was able in one part of himself to put off argument and let play upon his senses the whole richness of Southern life. And rather than force everything that was Southern into a logical whole, Olmsted was satisfied to show that spectacle in passages which alternated description with analysis. Therefore, the final chronicle, whether in three volumes or in the one abridged volume, was to be a structure slightly crooked and askew, but true to both sides of his nature. He felt some guilt about devoting too much space to his untutored, unarranged reactions, but this artless kind of art, this laying of himself open to life, was the best of what he brought back. The whole, unwashed South, gross and awkward and rich in its humanity, revealed itself.

A case might be made for awarding Olmsted an honorably high place among the writers of American frontier humor. It would be a niche somewhere between Augustus Baldwin Longstreet's *Georgia Scenes* (1835) and Samuel Clemens's *Life on the Mississippi* (1883). Longstreet's "scenes," written before slavery became an issue, had been milder and lower pitched than Olmsted's. Twain's river life would be more highly wrought and more consciously humorous. All three were true to the life of the region. Olmsted's humor inhered in the characters as they displayed themselves; yet there would be a kinship to the later, more rambunctious treatment of Twain. Clemens was to make a masterpiece of the conversation between the Duke and the Dauphin on the raft arguing as to the foolishness of anybody's talking French. Olmsted's treatment of the man on the train who thought that New York was somewhere in New Orleans had come out of the same background.

Olmsted has been compared to Arthur Young, who wrote his *Travels in France during the Years 1787, 1788 & 1789* (published in 1792). There is a considerable similarity in the circumstances and the treatment of material. Young wrote about a society in the last stages of its overripe development, beginning to break up. Olmsted saw the South in its final decade before the Civil War. Young was an agricultural expert; Olmsted was one also in an intelligent, amateur fashion. Young alternated between personal narrative and analysis of the social and economic conditions of each section of France he traveled through. Olmsted handled his material by a simliar alternation. However, to grant Olmsted his due, his firsthand sections are more colloquial and colorful; he disappeared into his material more easily than the eighteenth century writer did.

It would not be fanciful to say that Olmsted's own earliest traveling experience, his voyage to China, was inspired by reading Richard Henry Dana's *Two Years Before the Mast,* and that his writing of the English book *Walks and Talks of an American Farmer in England,* as well as the series of Southern books, owed much to the way Dana told plainly his adventures and misadventures and described the people he met on his voyage. There was a similar enjoyment of the travel for its own sake, and a relish of human curiosities met.

Olmsted went further in his delight in beauty. Amid the straightforward descriptions of the wealth and poverty of the South, the fine plantations interspersed with gullied fields, the richness of farms contrasting with the staleness of towns, he could not forebear a reaction to beauty. In spite of its faults, the region attracted him powerfully in its individuality and richness and sensual attractiveness. His articles and books on the South were more than studies of farming conditions and labor management. They were descriptive rhapsodies, character studies in which Frederick Law Olmsted lost himself in the language, manners, and attitudes of these people. He celebrated life as well as analyzed it.

Olmsted's original puritan inheritance had been mollified by the flowering of feeling of nineteenth century New England, the culture of Emerson, Thoreau, the elder Holmes, and Lowell. It had been enlightened by German and English romanticism through words and visual stimulations. He embraced the good of man as well as the good of God. The individual qualities of Southerners impressed him, therefore. He wrote about the generic Southerner: "He enjoys life in itself. He is content with being. Here is the grand distinction between him and the Northerner; for the Northerner enjoys progress in itself. He finds his happiness in doing. Rest, in itself, is irksome and offensive to him, and however graceful and beatific that rest may be, he values it only with reference to the power of future progress it will bring him. Heaven itself will be dull and stupid to him, if there is no work to be done in it—nothing to struggle for—if he reaches perfection at a jump, and has no chance to make an improvement."[28]

It was as if Fred Olmsted were describing himself in his at once curiously divided and at last united nature: the dreaming side, appreciative of sensuous impressions, the part of him that had been happy to sit under a tree in his youth and look at the line of the horizon, the inner nature which had never known quite what to do with itself in the busy world of his contemporaries; and on the other hand, the pushing, energetic, doing organism, devising and making things. The career in land design which was to come to him almost by accident was to be a logical outgrowth of the timely jointure of the two vital sides of his nature. His Southern travels helped him complete that joining together.

As he looked outward from the citadel of his being, he applied to society the same insights which had come to seem true to him about individuals. A society of men needed opposite kinds of qualities to flourish and to be fruitful in high, creative ways as well as energetic, ambitious, and righteous ways. It is not too farfetched to say that the lopsided South taught him that Northern society was lopsided too. He wrote in the *Seaboard Slave States*: "Our civilization is one-sided, irregular, and awkward. We must grow accustomed to exhaust our judgment and self-control less in matters of pure business, and apply it more to religion and politics and the good government of our individual bodies and minds, with their various appetites, impulses, functions, and longings."[29]

Out of his earnest attempt to understand the true qualities, so often opposite, of Northern and Southern man, he arrived at an idea of a better man, a small democrat exercising the humane preferences of an aristocrat. It was an impossible and impracticable ideal, but one toward which in some manner he directed all the work he was to do in the remainder of his life.

One can summarize briefly the manner in which Olmsted's contemporaries received his writings. Initial praise contained the taint of a very partial emotion. War passion already gripped Northern and Southern reviewers. Each one wanted his side to be right; for the North, Olmsted made it easier to believe that one was right.

The North American Review noticed each of the three volumes handsomely. *A Journey Through the Seaboard Slave States* was "of permanent interest" the reviewer of July, 1856, stated, and "To all those persons, therefore, who look upon the Slavery question as a problem, requiring a practical solution, this book comes in as a stepping-stone, which will lift that discussion to a range decidedly higher than it has ever held before." In April, 1857, the *North American Review*'s treatment of *A Journey through Texas* stated, "We believe that the wide circulation of these volumes of the 'American Farmer' will do more to enlighten public opinion and to hasten emancipation than any passionate speeches or any works of fiction, however exciting and pathetic." The same journal's review of *A Journey through the Back Country* mentioned the book's "kind, conciliatory tone," but it was October, 1860, and late for conciliation.

The Atlantic Monthly, which had not reviewed Olmsted's earlier volumes, made up for this hiatus by a long and thoughtful review of the *Back Country,* in November, 1860. "Mr. Olmsted is no ordinary traveler," the writer of the review begins. "He leaves home to instruct himself through his own eyes and ears concerning matters of general interest about which no trustworthy information was to be found in books.... Self possessed and wary, almost provokingly unsympathetic in his report of what he saw, pronouncing no judgments on isolated facts, and drawing no undue inferences from them, he has now generalized his results in a most interesting and valuable book." Such were typical Northern reviews. From the South after a short period of favorable attention to the New York *Daily-Times* articles, after which disapproval set in, there was abuse. Southern bookstores returned the books when they found out what they contained, an objective picture of the South coupled with a plan for freeing the slaves. He troubled Southern defenders long after the war. They held onto an inherited resentment of what they conceived as a slur upon the section's honor.

Olmsted's career as a writer was soon over. It was true that Mason Brothers resissued the *Seaboard Slave States* in 1859, 1861, and 1863. The same firm reissued *A Journey through Texas* in 1859 and 1860, and there were German issues of that book in Leipzig in 1857, 1865, and 1874. *A Journey in the Back Country* was reprinted in both New York and London in 1861 and 1863. Other reprintings of these three volumes and of *The Cotton Kingdom* would not be made until the 1950s, 1960s, and 1970s. Even while Olmsted finished assembling the materials for these volumes of Southern travel, he was beginning to veer away from writing to land design. Gradually, with some stumblings, he became altogether absorbed in the various work of landscape architecture. Except for the fact that his plans and reports for parks, school grounds, estate designs, and so forth read well and carried always the implication of large cultural aims, it might have escaped notice that the author of these professional papers had once been considered a promising writer. Olmsted no longer greatly cared. He found writing more and more of a chore as he grew older, and yet continued to write voluminously in the interests of his ideas of design and also in his own private letters.

As the years went on through the decades after the Civil War, when his fame as landscape architect eclipsed his small renown as a writer, Olmsted only occasionally made the acquaintance of someone who had read and savored those old books One of these was Thomas H. Clark, secretary to the governor of the State of Alabama, with whom Olmsted enjoyed a lively exchange of correspondence about the state of the South in the late 1880s. Clark kept the letters and published parts of them in 1904 in *The South Atlantic Quarterly.*

His doing so was a part of the small flurry which occurred in 1904, the year after Olmsted died (1903) when there was a slight revival of interest in his Southern writings. There was a new edition in this year of *A Journey through the Seaboard Slave States,* the first since 1863.

Walter L. Fleming reviewed this new edition in *The Dial,* October 1, 1904, commenting, "Frederick Law Olmsted was a thorough-going abolition-ist of the more sensible type.... In his eagerness to denounce slavery, he reaches the incredible." Fleming, a stiff Southerner of the old school even in 1904, was particularly offended that Olmsted did not find Southern land-owners as hospitable as they were reputed to be. "Olmsted came South with the idea that the Southern people generally were accustomed to forcing hospitality upon the passing stranger of whatever degree, and he was greatly surprised to find that he had to pay his way just as in other sections of the country."

The 1904 edition of *Seaboard Slave States* occasioned a short and slight revival of interest in Olmsted, the Southern traveler. He had died only the year before; there had been obituaries published in a number of newspapers in 1903. An anonymous writer in the *Forum* stated that a rereading of the *Seaboard Slave States* proved the author "a thoroughly just man, a true demo-crat, in the best sense of that ambiguous word, a genuine American." A *Nation* review called Olmsted's book in its original publication a "weapon in the great struggle between two civilizations."

But then Olmsted's writer's reputation died out again. It was only in the 1930s and in the 1940s that serious consideration—first by political scientist Broadus Mitchell—was given to his descriptions of the Southern society in the 1850s. (Critics of his landscape work and his planning for cities and wild parks spoke up one by one, beginning with Lewis Mumford, at about the same time, but that is another story.)

Perhaps Frank L. Owsley's hostile criticism of Olmsted in his *Plain Folk of the Old South* was the signal that Yeoman was to be reckoned with once more. Owsley thought Olmsted to be his principal opponent in his attempt to rehabilitate the place of a sturdy middle class in the Old South. In a way, he wrote his book, *Plain Folk,* against Olmsted.

Most travelers and critics who wrote about the South during the late antebellum period were of the opinion that the white inhabitants of the South generally fell into two categories, namely, the slaveholders and the "poor whites." . . .

Frederick Law Olmsted, perhaps contributed more than any other writer to the version of Southern society sketched above; for he was possessed of unusual skill in the art of reporting detail by subjective comments and generalizations. . . . Indeed, the degradation of free labor by slavery was Olmsted's major premise from which all conclusions flowed regardless of the factual observations that he conscientiously incorporated in his books.[30]

Fabian Linden, in a *Journal of Negro History* article that had repercussions, attempted to demolish Owsley's early proclamation of his thesis by demonstrating that this defender of the Southern independent farmer had used statistics in a shallow fashion. He defended Olmsted. True, Olmsted had demonstrated the existence of a large middle class. But Olmsted, not Owsley, was correct in his theorizing. The yeoman farmer of the old South, who had few slaves or none, did not set the policy of the South. This was a class that willingly, even eagerly, aped the doctrines of the large landowners, if it did not take on the manners of that small but influential group.[31] This was a movement back toward Olmsted's interpretation of the South of the 1850s.

By the 1960s, Olmsted's accuracy of vision at least was accepted. His analysis received support from an angle not to be expected. Eugene Genovese, with his Marxian schooling, followed Olmsted's views in approving Linden's study cited above which to him seemed to have demolished Owsley. "While slavery existed," wrote Genovese, "the South had to be bound to a plantation system and an agricultural economy based on a few crops. As a result the South depended on Northern facilities, with inevitably mounting middlemen's charges. Less obvious was the capital drain occasioned by the importation of industrial goods." And he said, "The fact of slave ownership is central to our problem. . . . The essential features of Southern particularity, as well as of Southern backwardness, can be traced to the relationship of master to slave." As Olmsted had done, Genovese admits a troubling esteem for Southern aristocrats, "The slaveholders' pride, sense of honor, and commitment to their way of life made a final struggle so probable that we may safely call it inevitable." So Olmsted was enrolled on the side of those who were trying to turn back the effort of the "revisionists" to put the blame for the Civil War on something besides slavery.[32]

In any case, historians of the middle span of the twentieth century became accustomed to making use of Olmsted to provide evidence or corroboration. In his study of the South, *Civil War and Reconstruction* (1937), J. G. Randall said mildly of Olmsted, "In contrast to the romance and aristocratic brilliance of the Old South any realistic study would necessarily reveal less happy aspects. Frederick Law Olmsted, though finding much to praise in Southern character, was on the whole critical of Southern conditions."[33] In 1961 Clement Eaton quoted Olmsted as a matter of course as a witness to the dearth of general culture in that place and time: "From the banks of the Mississippi to the banks of the James, I did not (that I remember) see, except perhaps in one or two towns, a thermometer, nor a book of Shakespeare, nor a pianoforte or sheet of music; nor the light of a carcel or other good centre-table or reading lamp, nor an engraving or copy of any kind, or a work of art of the slightest merit."[34] Eaton, himself a Southerner, acquiesced in the new Southern desire for truth to the conditions of the old South. In other words, in the thirty years between the 1930s and the 1960s, Olmsted was appropriated as a source by reputable Southern historians.

An example of the careful scholarship of the twentieth century bearing witness to the truthfulness of Olmsted's sharp and casual observations is in D. Clayton James's study, *Antebellum Natchez* (1968). "Olmsted's observations in 1854," says James, "regarding the aristocratic domination of the agricultural area around Natchez were correct. The number of large farms in Adams County increased steadily from 1820 to 1860."[35]

A place for Olmsted in American letters (whether considered as literature or history) has never been located. His books have been praised as "travel books" with the sense that this kind of writing is somehow outside the pale of serious consideration. Edmund Wilson in *Patriotic Gore* (1962) came closest to serious study of Olmsted as a writer although only briefly. He found Olmsted's syntax awkward and thought that he recorded Southern talk without exercising the art of selection. But Wilson believed that Olmsted had a "knack" and a vivid ear for "the accent and language of the people." And Wilson said justly, "He tenaciously and patiently and lucidly made his way through the whole South, undiscouraged by churlish natives, almost impassable roads or the cold inns and uncomfortable cabins in which he spent most of his nights. He talked to everybody and he sized up everything, and he wrote it all down."[36]

CHAPTER XII

Editor and Publisher

The best writers seem already to have acquired confidence that we can be depended upon.
—F. L. O., to his father, May 28, 1855[1]

FREDERICK OLMSTED, the recent traveler in the South, and long settled farmer on the south shore of Staten Island, became an editor and publisher in Manhattan. Acting upon a notion which seemed sudden to his friends, but not unexpected in Fred Olmsted, he was to move from the Island to the city, occupy a daily desk at *Putnam's Magazine*, and invest a part of his—or his father's—fortune in Dix and Edwards, the firm which published the magazine.

The transformation should not have astonished those who knew him. Frederick had turned from one thing to another several times already and had been equally intense in his energy in mastering a new set of habits. The position at Dix and Edwards was entered into with the enthusiasm of one who envisioned it as a settling of himself for life. That was an outcome perhaps wished for by his father and such friends as Charley Brace, who often wondered what was to become of the brilliant, restless young man.

The interests Frederick brought back with him from the South in the late summer of 1854 made the bridge to the new life. The small number of preconceptions he had carried on his journeys had enlarged into some firmly held ideas. He had quantities of notes which he wished to shape into more permanent form. During the fall and winter, while making repairs upon the farm, he thought out the main sections of the book to be called *A Journey through the Seaboard Slave States*. When he retreated indoors from bad weather, he began in earnest to write this volume.

Besides the outpouring of words, the journey moved him to acts. He and his brother John, who had preceded him home, felt some responsibility for the group of German settlers in Texas who had been kind to them on their travels and who had captured their interest. Frederick spoke for them to his friends in the East and wrote a brochure in an attempt to raise money to keep the German newspaper in San Antonio going.

Adolf Douai, the editor of the San Antonio *Zeitung*, for his part, had no intention of letting the Olmsteds forget him. He had quickly replied when, in Chattanooga on the way home, Frederick wrote to him to ask him for statistics about slave ownership in Texas. Douai, as the voice of a few thousand free settlers across the path of an ever-moving emigration of slave-owning native Southerners, needed help. The Olmsted brothers seemed to promise help or to know where to find it back home in their own New England and New York. Douai was shrewd and persistent as well as high-minded. He called on Frederick and John Hull Olmsted for aid. Even before Frederick reached home, Douai wrote letters inquiring after the health of Dr. John and asking about the success of Frederick's long journey home. He continued this correspondence with one long letter after another making plain to John and Frederick the need in his part of Texas for more "free" settlers, for money, supplies, and public advocacy.

Frederick circulated among his friends and acquaintances a statement which announced, "A Few Dollars Wanted to Help the Cause of Future Freedom in Texas,"[2] and said in part, "A year ago a free German paper was firmly established... It has gradually got to be considered so dangerous by slaveowners that an effort has been made to buy out and silence the paper." The sum of three hundred fifty dollars was needed, he announced. With this help, the editor would be able to "purchase the paper of its proprietors (stockholders) and to secure himself an entirely free position." He would then continue to advocate freedom from slavery for the western part of Texas. The specific means he put forward was the establishment of one or two separate free states to be carved out of west Texas. This was, whether possible or not, legal.

Frederick and his brother collected two hundred thirty dollars for Adolf Douai and on September 15 learned that the money had staved off the silencing of the *Zeitung*, at least for a time. The brothers also helped in the cause of "free" emigration to Texas. Frederick was in addition an occasional worker for the New England Emigrant Aid Society, which helped pay the cost of moving "Free Soil" laborers and their families westward (mostly to Kansas). When Kansas flamed into fighting, Frederick singlehandedly paid for, and had sent to settlers in that state, a brass howitzer and ammunition.

Frederick was restless after he came home from his travels. He was more interested in the world outside Southside than he had been before. He went up to New York and collected from editor Henry Raymond the money the *Daily-Times* owed him for his newspaper articles.[3] By June, 1854, Raymond had run two series of *Yeoman* letters, first a long series running for a full year and covering the "seaboard slave states" and then a short series covering the Texas journey. After Olmsted returned in the late summer of 1854, Raymond seemed not inclined to use any more material from him. The "back country" articles, ten in number, were to appear later in the New York *Daily Herald* in 1857 (June 3 to August 24).

His association with journalists and writers at this time stimulated his ambition to continue writing. He spent less time personally overseeing farm work (allowing John to continue some of the supervisory activity of the farm) and spent more time shaping his notes and new research into pages of the book which was to cover his first journey. He also needed access to other men's books, to contemporary magazines, and to government statistics. He invited his father to accompany him to Washington to look up material, but the two did not accomplish this trip.

Thus Fred had only half a mind on the farm. Yet expeditiously he was able to direct the needed efforts to smarten the appearance of Southside. He found that a landscape firmly outlined in trees and roadways and shapes of fields and ponds was an enduring thing and needed only superficial repair after a period of neglect. The form was there underneath. However, almost cold-bloodedly, Fred Olmsted prepared Tosomock for a possible sale. He was determined to change his life. In February, 1855, Fred proudly wrote to his father of his improvements, "The establishment advances in rank from a farm house to a villa and the whole land surrounding is glorified."[4] And John Hull, who had suffered another hemorrhage, stated to the same correspondent (on February 7), "We have now a first class country seat for sale. Price $30,000 and no less. $230 per acre."[5] But having no expectation of another job or place, he also commented, wistfully, "I should be very sorry to sell the house and pears.... In fact except the fever and ague I can't think of any place I should like nearly as well."[6] By a swift turnabout of Fred's kind of luck, John Hull became owner of the farm, and Fred had his chance to be a man of letters in Manhattan.

It came about because there was an ambitious young clerk in the Putnam publishing house named Joshua A. Dix who decided that he wanted to go into business for himself.[7] He was a friend of Fred Olmsted's and Charles Brace's, and told them the progress of his strivings. He bought into a company that had failed but salvaged from it one asset, a magazine called *Household Words*. At this time his former employer, George Palmer Putnam (a kinsman, incidentally, of Frederick Olmsted), being embarrassed with debts, offered Dix the firm's magazine, *Putnam's Monthly*, which had been in existence since January, 1853, and had an excellent reputation. Dix located another up-and-coming young man who wanted to go into business on his own. This was Arthur T. Edwards, a dry goods clerk who knew bookkeeping and might be expected to handle the financial side of the prospective new publishing house. Frederick Olmsted, hearing of these young men and their venture, being also a friend of one of them (Dix), saw an opportunity for himself as a third partner in what, without his help, might be a shaky affair. The idea of going into the publishing business awakened his keen interest. He was at this moment very much concerned with words and the making of words into books. His own writing about the South had made him aware of the power that published words might have. The firm could publish the book he was writing; and he, as an official of the company, would be in the position to publish other books in which he might interest himself.

How to get out of his farming responsibilities? Tosomock Farm, Southside, however beautiful it was had not been profitable. Times for farmers were getting harder. It was unreasonable to expect the farm to make money for two masters. John and his family needed to live off the farm. Perhaps John could do better if Fred were no longer there taking his share also. Rather than sell Southside to a stranger, why not give it over to John who, with less overhead and less hankering for wandering, might make it pay? It would at least give him a place to live and an occupation.

Fred plunged quickly into a whirlwind of arranging. He transferred his mortgage to John. John was to be nominal owner, assuming a debt of $25,000—"$20,000 a book debt to you—$5,000 a note,"[8] as he detailed it to his father. It was all decided and acted upon too quickly for John's equilibrium or cheerful acceptance. "I regret to be left in the lurch but I suppose things will go on as they did in his absence last summer.... Remember that the place is for sale—that Fred with much more knowledge than I had not made it pay and that I do not undertake to."[9] So John wrote to his father while acquiescing in the new arrangement. He conceded that "some such connection" as the one Fred proposed with *Putnam's* and Dix and Edwards would be "a very pleasant permanent and satisfactory position" for his brother. John doubted that Fred was "capable of editing or of writing much for such a magazine but with good business partners is just the man to publish it and have its general overseeing. And once in that position he will be earning a regular income which is now not only small but precarious. I am not sure he could stand city life—but would like him to try—it *might* be much better for him."[10]

John felt physically wretched himself and was filled with the momentary anxiety of the expected birth of his and Mary's second child. The baby was born on the afternoon of March 15, 1855, while Fred was away. Aunty, who was expected, did not arrive on time. A "black girl in the neighborhood" was called in to help. But "all is right"[11] John wrote his father. The second child was a girl, to be called Charlotte. "Tot," as they called the little boy, was at this time two and a half years old. Whatever anxieties and troubles were to visit John as he began to try to be a farmer, the old Dutch house was to be a lively place, with children crying and laughing in and out of doors. And John, with worry always in the back of his mind, reconciled himself to staying on in the place he loved.

Frederick Olmsted signed an agreement with Joshua A. Dix and Arthur T.

Edwards on April 2, 1855. Several weeks earlier he had taken Dix to see his father in Hartford, and John Olmsted backed Fred once more. He furnished the money to bind the agreement: $500 to come into the new firm on May 1, 1855, and $5,000 the following March 1.[12] On April 1, John Hull, Fred's brother on the farm, wrote to Mary's grandmother, "My dear Mrs. Perkins. . . . Fred moves tomorrow to the city—a partner in the firm of Dix and Edwards 10 Park Place—and the farm is left to Mary and me."[13]

Frederick entered as wholeheartedly into living in New York as he had done at Sachem's Head or Southside, giving all his energy and enthusiasm to mastering a new world, the intense, small world of book and magazine publishing, of newspapermen and magazine writers, of essayists and story writers and poets, of public figures who condescended to write their views when editors asked for them. The publishing house had its office first on Park Place, as John Hull had told Mrs. Perkins, then at 321 Broadway, in the center of the lively life of commercial New York. It was a contracted indoor life for Fred, used to sky and sea and land. But it was a life of new excitements and a city way of living to be got used to.

His flat (as he called it, English style) was a modest place at 89 Moffatt Street—the corner of Moffatt and Broadway. He had always a peculiar sense of *place;* in this case, his rooms looking out on a hospital enclosure, green at least in spring, when he first tried what might be seen from his windows. To his father he wrote, "I have hardly yet got settled, though I slept, very uncomfortably last night, in my room. I am quite confounded at the expense of furnishing a house at all nicely and have been attending auctions and searching pawnbrokers shops since you were here trying to find things to suit me at moderate prices."[14] He got Aunt Maria to come up to help him with the furnishings. Some red-striped toweling reminded him, as he had wished it to, of the farmhouse, and he intended to fill in the emptiness of the rooms with "good strong furniture that will be suitable to use a year or two hence."[15] To stave off loneliness, he had a dog companion. "I have Gip to play with..." (Was Judy on the farm? Had she died? Was this her pup, or a new dog picked up, heedlessly and impulsively, as Fred did?) "and I make my breakfast very easily now and nicely.... Tea and toast for breakfast, crackers commonly and sometimes soup at the Astor House for lunch, and dinner sometimes at a restaurant and sometimes at a French ordinary in Barclay Street—at 50 cts. at 6 o'clock."[16]

Fred delighted in the creative confusion of a beginning, and becoming an officer of Dix and Edwards was a new start for him. He might have been content, if he had had another nature, to invest his money (his father's) and remain a silent partner. He had indeed plenty of work to do to complete his Southern volumes and to get them ready for the publication assured now by the firm of which he was part owner. But Frederick could not take part in any venture without being a principal part of it. So his entry into the publishing world was a strenuous one. Joshua Dix was to see to the selling of the books and the circulation of the magazines published by the firm; Arthur Edwards was to be the money-man, keeping up with income and outgo; Frederick Olmsted was, to begin with, to assist in the editing of the firm's principal magazine, *Putnam's Monthly*. In March, 1855, even before the papers of partnership were signed, he went traveling for the firm, and so was away from the island when John and Mary's second child, Charlotte, was born. He called on people in New York and then set off on a tour of the authors of New England. In Boston he tried to see Lowell but missed him; he went to Cambridge to meet Longfellow, to Concord for Emerson, to Andover to call on Mrs. Stowe. In Providence, he was to collect a manuscript from George Curtis, who had been quietly associated with *Putnam's* since its inception. Frederick believed always in a certain amount of uprooting and disarrangement in order to bring about a new order in which he had a hand. He urged on the two other young men—Dix enthusiastic, Edwards probably, if in character, holding back—to authorize a general refurbishing of the offices: a painting, papering, and refurnishing session. John Hull, down on Staten Island, to whom Frederick made enthusiastic reports when he came to visit, was somewhat disapproving. He thought that Frederick was incautious for the future, and that he and his partners were, at this uncertain initiation of a new business, spending far too much money.

But Frederick was sanguine for the future, his own, and the firm's. For *Putnam's*, he had good reason. It was at this time a magazine of excellent reputation if of short history. Thackeray, who was to write for them and visit their offices when he was in the country, said it was better than *Blackwoods*, that it was indeed the best magazine in the world. It was a feather in the cap of any young man beginning in the publishing world to have something not unimportant to do with the management of *Putnam's*. It was understood, of course, that young Olmsted was inexperienced, but he might try his hand at the everyday business of editorial correspondence, meet authors when they came into the office, and call on others elsewhere. He would be the representative of *Putnam's* to these people and would manage the office, besides. People sensed that Olmsted could be a formidable manager and that when he took things in hand they were likely to go in an exemplary fashion. Olmsted had some confidence in his ability to judge writing.

He was content to have second place in the matter of editorial decision.[17] George William Curtis had been offered the chief editorship of the magazine but had declined to accept the position, at least publicly. He was willing, however, to continue to spend a number of regular hours advising *Putnam's*. (He had in fact done almost as much earlier when George Palmer Putnam was publisher and Charles F. Briggs was the editor.) He would now, behind a closed door and with no public acknowledgement of the fact, read and solicit manuscripts and help guide the general policy of the magazine. He was relieved of many of the onerous daily duties of an editor; these Olmsted was willing to undertake. The firm made rather a game of the secret editor-ship of the magazine. Curtis occupied an office behind Frederick's, the door between them closed, while Frederick dealt with callers; or, as the two men became friends, Curtis often settled down with his papers in Frederick's rooms in Moffatt Street and there did his reading and writing for the maga-zine. In addition to Curtis, Charles Dana gave a hand to the magazine from time to time.

Curtis was already at this time associated with the Harper's firm. He had begun to edit "The Easy Chair" in 1854. He had books of his own to write. He had influence, popularity, and a winning way. For Olmsted, he was an enlarging friend from this time on. They were almost the same age, Curtis only thirty-one in 1855 when Frederick Olmsted was thirty-three. Curtis had come out of a New England background which allowed a quick understand-ing between them—most basic things unspoken, and his politics were of the kind Olmsted was moving toward. As young boys, George Curtis and his brother Burrill had been pupils in the school run by the Brook Farm com-munity. At another period, boarding with a farmer in Concord, the two Curtis boys knew Henry Thoreau and actually helped him build his cabin at Walden. George Curtis had traveled abroad a little earlier than Olmsted and returned from Egypt, Syria, and Palestine with materials for two books, *Nile Notes of a Howadji* (1851) and *The Howadji in Syria* (1852). Curtis was linked at this time, at least superficially and in early reputation, with Herman Melville, who had written "travel books" too. Curtis liked and ad-mired Melville and brought him to *Putnam's* where much of his short fiction was published.

Curtis was to become an admirer of Olmsted's Southern books, and was to consolidate their friendship by becoming a neighbor on Staten Island. After his marriage to Anna Shaw on Thanksgiving Day, 1856, he took up housekeeping on the north shore. He and Olmsted took the ferry together to go home. Curtis's father-in-law Francis G. Shaw was a man of means who helped Curtis several times in much the way Olmsted's father aided him. His brother-in-law Robert Gould Shaw was to become a hero in the Civil War and to march into infinity on Boston Common on St. Gaudens's relief.

Curtis's influence on *Putnam's* was beneficial. At this time the somewhat older *Harper's*, the only rival *Putnam's* had as a magazine of quality, pub-lished principally English writings, which its editors could use without paying a copyright fee. *Putnam's* course was bolder, in opening its pages to native expression, whether in the latest poem of Longfellow or Lowell, a new story by Poe or Hawthorne, a scientific article by Agassiz, a chapter of history from Parkman, or Curtis's own light satire of society, *The Potiphar Papers*. The short career of the magazine was part of a remarkable decade in American publishing. This was a fruition of thought and feeling which had a continuity with the past but also a new confidence and power. The violence and change of the Civil War would interrupt writing and thought, and what was to come after would have to begin again on new emotional bases. *Moby Dick* was published in 1851, *Uncle Tom's Cabin* in 1852, *Walden* in 1854, *Leaves of Grass* in 1855. And belonging to the time in tone and quality, Olmsted's *A Journey in the Seaboard Slave States* was published in 1856.

The lasting distinction of *Putnam's,* and its part in the publishing merit of the decade, was the appearance of Melville's short fiction in the magazine. Before Olmsted came upon the scene, *Putnam's* published in 1853 a critique of Melville, and a portion of *Mardi* and *Bartleby the Scrivener.* In 1854 the magazine published *The Encantadas, Israel Potter,* and *The Lightning-Rod Man.* After Olmsted became an editor, Putnam's published *Benito Cereno* in three installments and *I and My Chimney.*

In the year 1855, when Olmsted's enthusiasm and activity for the magazine were most constant, there appeared in *Putnam's* such things as an article on the new and astonishing "Song of Hiawatha" and also Longfellow's lyric, "My Lost Youth." Politics induced Olmsted and Curtis to accept an article for October on "The Kansas Question."

The magazine was to be generous in its attention to Frederick Law Olmsted too, noticing his books as they came out, reprinting whole sections of them, reviewing them copiously; this was George Curtis's courtesy, for by this time Olmsted himself had either gone abroad for the firm (1856) or had relinquished an active part in the business, while Curtis hung on to an increasingly desperate venture.

In its later months the magazine developed a column called "The World of New York" and in the last half of 1856 ran short pieces on "The National Academy of Design," "History of the Opera in New York," and "Our New York Theatre."

In working together for *Putnam's* Frederick Olmsted and George William Curtis cemented a friendship which outlasted the vicissitudes of the publishing firm. A significant link from the beginning was a mutual regard for the memory of Andrew Jackson Downing. Downing was already a hero to Olmsted. He found that Curtis revered his memory also. His new colleague had edited Downing's *Rural Essays,* which Putnam had published, in 1853. The preface to this volume contained Curtis's biographical and critical notes on the man.

By the end of May, 1855, when he had been working with the magazine for two months, Frederick Olmsted was full of confidence in the future of *Putnam's* and of himself as a member of the firm of Dix and Edwards. *Putnam's* first editor (before the era of Dix and Edwards), Charles Briggs, told him that the June number was the best yet. "There is no doubt," Fred went on in a letter to his father, "that there will be a great improvement in the quality of the Magazine, which can not fail, I hope, to improve its circulation, sufficiently to return our capital. The best writers seem already to have acquired confidence that we can be depended upon to do our duty strongly and boldly and that the magazine is . . . more than ever the leading magazine and the best outlet of thought in the country. If we can get the writers, there is little fear but that we shall get the readers."[18] If they only had a little more capital, they would publish books extensively. Eight books, he proudly told his patient correspondent, had already been offered to them.

In weekend respites from the publishing business, Frederick found he did not have to give up seeing crops grow at Southside, nor visits with John and Mary and the babies. He carried his editing work with him down to the farm for quiet hours away from Broadway. Inexorably, though, with his change of base, he was becoming a city man. And he enjoyed the sensations which accompanied this change in status.

The crowded life of Broadway, Moffatt Street, the Astor House, Delmonico's, *Putnam's*, the New York *Daily-Times*, the *Evening Post*, the press club dinners to which he was now invited, filled his hours with a liveliness to which he responded. In the midst of organizing his rooms, his office, and his responsibilities, he wrote to his father on April 13, "I have been twice to the opera with free tickets and enjoyed it much. The first night of William Tell was really magnificent."[19] He met unusual types. "I had just now a call from a queer fellow whose poetry had been rejected and who wanted to know why, and who struck his heart fearfully and assured me there must be some mistake for he knew that there was no better poetry." At the modest "French ordinary" where he dined for fifty cents, the company was varied and not like the Perkinses and Olmsteds of Staten Island. "The company consists of a dozen Frenchmen, two French women, Mr. Dana of the Tribune and one or two irregulars." It was a world in which, if one did not see Poe, one heard good stories about him. George Palmer Putnam told an anecdote about Poe and the early *Putnam's*.[20]

Poe, somewhat intoxicated, came to the office, demanded pen, paper, and a place to write, and stayed, oblivious of the office force, writing and writing. He outstayed first Mr. Putnam, then the bookkeeper, and at last the janitor, apparently writing on through the night. He came again the next day and went through the same performance, and again a third day. At the end he left the story "Eureka" behind.

Frederick grew acclimated to this literary world to the extent that he could be bored by Washington Irving one night as he sat across from the old gentleman at a press club dinner. Altogether he found himself expanding in this varied, close-knit, shoulder-rubbing world of the city. Hitherto he had been an amateur appreciator of meadows, rivers, and mountains. Now he learned to savor (as he had done first tentatively in Liverpool and London) the landscape of cities: broad or narrow streets, low or tall buildings, vistas, closed-off views, squares, corners, cornices, chance bits of greenery, and the inhabitants who used this territory of buildings.

He lived in a rapidly growing and changing city. Between 1845 and 1860, New York increased in population from 371,000 to 813,000. Emigrants from Ireland and Germany poured in. Poor people, as Charley Brace had taught him to see them, formed a large part of the population and personality of the city. He contemplated them with puzzlement and interest as he had looked steadily at the ill fed but different poor of the South. How could they live? How should they live? Yet for a hopeful young man, the growing city had splendor and daring. Even its avenues aspired northward at a visible and reckless rate. Institutions accompanied the brave squalor northward. Columbia College, in the midst of uncertainty about its future, moved northward to Forty-ninth Street. St. Luke's Hospital uprooted itself to "the desert places"[21] of Fifty-fourth Street west of Fifth Avenue. Beyond this outpost area was a squatter's territory, an ugly, dubious, bony land, with no natural forest, but only a poor brushy growth, where the city fathers had designated that one day there would be a public park.

Frederick had the best of two worlds. He was even happy about the farm. John carried on his brother's plans and seemed to be doing a good job of it, as well as maintaining his family there in a state near content. "I was at the Island Thursday," Fred wrote his father. "The doctor seems to me to be getting on well, directing more efficiently than I did and managing judiciously. The place will be vastly improved by his contemplated completions. Mary was better than I have seen her for a long time."[22] John, however, was not without sarcasm about how well things had worked out for Fred, who had an important position in New York and had succeeded in slipping out from under the burden of the farm. He wrote to sister Bertha on May 6 about Fred's "capital position" and his and Mary's situation. "Mary and I were here on the spot. I must live somewhere so— though I am no farmer and would much prefer to do literary or medical work rather than agricultural or real estate-istical, especially when it requires us to live in the fever and ague and keep 10 servants instead of one, etc., etc., it seemed to fall to me to undertake it."[23] John explained to Bertha the money arrangements made with his father, his being now the one in debt to him. About Fred, he went on: "Of course he has all his own way in such things and I am to endeavor to get along! Seven years ago Fred undertook to do the same thing and has been obliged to call on Father for $1100 a year to keep the farm, himself, and Auntie going. Now I am to undertake the same thing, with Mary's income instead of drafts on Father, $700 instead of $1100, wife, nurse, and two babies instead of Aunty, so here we are receiving visits from Fred instead of Fred's receiving visits from us." The sarcasm existed in brotherly intimacy with the closest dependence on Fred for company, conversation, moral support, and guidance in farming practices. When the office needed Frederick less, and his book needed him more, John and Mary could not but be glad of his coming down to Southside to share the place with them.

Frederick's writing of the book about the South had suffered during the excitement of his becoming an editor. Now that his life had been reorganized, he devoted more time to retracing in words his "journey in the seaboard slave states." He concentrated his efforts to the point that, on November 8, 1855, he could write to his father, "I *am* overworked certainly very much but I am not unusually unwell. I am afraid I cannot come to Hartford until my book is in type, which I hope will be before Thanksgiving.... I begin to print with some fifty pages at the end unfinished—calculating to write them up while the bulk of it was being set. But I have not yet had time to write a page of it."[24] In adding history and argument to the daily experiences of the journey, he had caused his book to lengthen monstrously, or so he thought. The experienced bookman Dix told him that his *Journey* would necessarily run to two volumes, and that the firm would have to charge two dollars and fifty cents a copy for it. This seemed too much to Fred, who was afraid his book would be priced beyond the reach of the many readers he desired. "This ponderosity becomes a goblin of botheration to me." Yet he had faith in the book. "Reputation or notoriety it cannot fail to give me—not perhaps friendship but respect I think for while I strike right and left and strike hard I do so respectfully and with the grace of sincerity." He went on explaining himself to himself, "I have said some unpleasant things from a sense of duty. I thought they ought to be said and nobody else appeared to be ready to say them. If they are true they will now make their way—if not it will be discovered." He had thrown his whole being into the making of the book, and in addition a considerable bit of his father's money. John Olmsted backed his son in paying the extra expenses which Dix and Edwards said were necessary to complete the printing of the book.

Frederick Olmsted's final assembling of the volume took place in a time of intense and growing excitement over North-South differences, much more so than when he traveled southward. There would, therefore, always be a sort of contradiction in the pages of the book, but a contradiction of dialogue, which added a dynamic of the changing time to the volume. Olmsted's preface to the book entitled *A Journey in the Seaboard Slave States with Remarks on Their Economy* was dated January 9, 1856. The book appeared in New York under the imprint of Dix and Edwards and in London under that of Sampson Low and Co., a firm with which the American company had established close relations.

His book published, Olmsted had a sense of relief. He had shed his weighty personal responsibility—to get said what he had to say about the South—and was buoyantly ready for a change. Someone in the firm suggested that he go abroad on a publishing trip, seeking outlets for the books of the firm and writers who might agree to be published in the United States by Dix and Edwards. Olmsted had by no means satisfied his taste for travel abroad by the walking tour of 1850. He was delighted to go and to be agent for his own company. Dix, in friendly trust, wished him to go; Edwards, in some irritation at Olmsted's superabundant energies, was not sorry to see him gone from the New York office. The two young men, Edwards and Olmsted, had already discovered that they got on each other's nerves.

At Southside, Fred left his notes for a second volume, the story of the Texas journey, to be edited by John Hull. John seemed to be in good spirits and in better health than he had been for some time and able to manage both the farm and his editorial job. It helped the younger brother's pride to be given the writing assignment, and he took it seriously. He thought he might add something of his own to the volume; he had shared in the experience; Fred gave him freedom to shape it as he wished.

Therefore, Frederick could leave New York with a good conscience. His decision to go was sudden. Just as impulsive was his resolve to use the trip to introduce his sister Mary to foreign travel. He could be her escort abroad, get her settled with Bertha, who was already over there, and enjoy her company during at least part of his traveling. Mary came innocently to Staten Island from Hartford to pay a visit and was swept into her brother's plans. Infected by Fred's enthusiasm, and sharing some of his impulsiveness, she turned about, went home to Hartford immediately to get ready for the trip. Then she came back to the farm to go with Frederick.

John Hull related the family story to Bertha, whom the brother and sister would soon be joining in Europe. "Father came down yesterday to see to the pecuniarities. He has his usual pleasant excitement at the sudden bustle, of sending off two more children to Europe and rejoices over having kept the secret of his intentions from Mary and everybody down to the last moment when he exploded with eclat while he put on an innocent look as if a February trip to Rome were as ordinary a thing as a summer day's ride to East Windsor. But nobody's hurt and everybody's glad."[25]

Father John and Mary Ann added to the general festive atmosphere by announcing their own intent of going abroad for a grand tour of Europe the following summer. They should all meet over there. Only John Hull and Mary, left behind, experienced (at least John did) some slight pang. His father had said in passing, only half serious, would he not come along too and help with the travel arrangements for his father and mother. But John refused, saying to himself, a little stiffly, that he could not go unless his father offered to pay for Mary and the children.

In London Frederick was full of hope for the prospects of the firm although he found the going slow. He was well received personally, and he was persistent. He felt that after some weeks he was beginning to establish a solid base for foreign operations. He engaged a shipping agent. He made a contract with a literary agent. Filling his days with meeting writers and publishers, he postponed any decision about an early return. He had also to show Mary about London and to see again the parks there, which continued to fascinate him. This of course had nothing to do with Dix and Edwards's business, but he pleased himself in spending time in London's green spaces. It would be this personal side of his second European stay which would remain with him and be a living part of his future existence.

At home things seemed at first to go well. When he left, the company had sold only eleven copies of his book, and those in Hartford, but shortly he had the good news that 2,000 had been sold and 5,000 were expected to move before he came home. The firm expressed confidence in him and urged him to stay abroad some time. During his absence, George William Curtis had joined the company as a partner. He had paid $10,000 for the privilege and promised all his future production of books to Dix and Edwards. From Staten Island as from Manhattan the news was bright and cheerful. John had been making regular visits to Dix and Edwards in the city, and reported the activities there to his brother. He and Mary had been going occasionally to the city for a concert and felt their lives, bound so strictly by the sea, the fields, and the noise of little children, was opening up. "Just now we are rather spreeing," John wrote to Fred, "that is we have got a new piano, a great step in country comfort, and we are painting and papering....26 He had sold a lot from their land to Charles Brace and the money had helped their situation. Calvert Vaux, whom Fred had met at Downing's in Newburgh, had moved to Staten Island also, and was an addition to the friends there.

In London, Fred made friends with young Sampson Low, the son of the publisher who had brought out his book in England. Low agreed to be literary agent for Dix and Edwards abroad and would be paid a salary on a rising scale for two years. Then he might be offered a partnership, another young man to share the hoped-for profits of Dix and Edwards. Frederick found in a family friend, Henry Stevens, with whom he and sister Mary stayed some time, their business and shipping agent. To him, Dix and Edwards would pay a set percentage of all their books sold in England.

Needing to stay in London until he got these affairs settled, Frederick was firm with his sister. She could see Kew Gardens or Hampton Court while he met people. There was no need to rush off to Rome for Easter Week. Seeing London would do her more good, he pronounced, than "an hour of the illumination of St. Peter's or the elevation of the Host."27 However, when the two of them began to travel, he made amusement out of mishaps. After crossing France, bound out from Marseilles, a storm blew their ship into the harbor of Toulon. He described his fellow passengers to his partners in a letter which betrayed only lightheartedness, "We have a bishop and a lady superior and a squad of nuns aboard besides a Virginia parson. It is evident the gale is on their account, and we are conspiring to make the latter marry the two former and then keel-haul him and so have done with it."28 The saltiness of the former sailor came jauntily to the surface when he got on board a ship.

The trip went well. Fred and Mary met Bertha in Rome where she had been staying under the protection—as the phrase of the time had it—of an older American married woman, Sophie Hitchcock, whose brother Henry

Stevens had been helpful in London. Bertha, who had already lived a year in a Paris pension, made a happy third member of their traveling party when they set out on a carriage trip beyond Rome, first to Naples, "then to Amalfi and Pompeii, then to Florence, Venice, across to Trieste, then to Vienna, Prague, and to Leipzig, where we staid several days." So Bertha wrote, explaining the stopover at Leipzig "on account of Fred's business with the Tauchnitz publishers.... Then to Dresden where Fred left us."[29] The brother deposited the two sisters in a boarding school in that city, where they stayed put only until their parents arrived to pick them up and carry them off for more touring.

The family touring group was not to be exhausted. Father Olmsted tended to the monetary details of travel in his own large, comfortable hired carriage, and became the most inveterate viewer of sights of them all—the all being himself, his wife Mary Ann, the child Allie (Albert), and the young ladies, Mary and Bertha. He wrote enthusiastically and in detail of what he was experiencing to Frederick, soon returned to London, to John Hull and Mary in Staten Island, and to his brother Owen in Hartford. He was so wrapped up in this family adventure that he seemed at first not to be aware of difficulties accumulating for both Frederick and John Hull; but then the two sons, delicately considerate of their father who was enjoying himself in a joyful and childlike way, refrained from calling his attention to their troubles.

John Hull had been well enough at first. He had come to like the farm supervision and was reasonably competent in it with the help of a good foreman. He and Mary and the two children, Charles and Charlotte, had a pleasant place to live in. He had a new occupation also, the revising of his brother's cramped notes of the Texas journey. John infused something of his own personality and his own views into the manuscript. He called on Fred toward the end of July to contribute a preface and a final chapter. Fred declared himself happy with what John had done. He used John's preface. The book was to be published by Dix and Edwards in January, 1857, a year after the appearance of the *Seaboard Slave States,* and was to have an excellent reception, the second book's way smoothed and anticipated by the first.

The book, with the long title, *A Journey through Texas, or, A Saddle-trip on the Southwestern Frontier—with a Statistical Appendix,* met some rejections in the South. A book dealer in Mobile, Alabama, returned the seven copies he had ordered with a note to Dix and Edwards: "There is considerable objection made here, as to the sentiments advanced in 'Olmstead's Texas Journey.' We are obliged to be very cautious with regard to selling any book at all impregnated with abolition principle."[30] But the reviews in the North were good and widespread. John had contributed his time and effort freely to Frederick's book and only lightly teased him about the profits to be made. If it should sell a million, would Fred give him two thirds of the profit, or if it did not sell, pay him a salary for having done it?[31] John's horizon seemed brighter at this time, but his health faltered again.

His lungs had seemed well during warm weather, but in the fall, with the chill winds blowing off the Atlantic onto their land exposed to all the blows, he felt ill again and determined to go, at least for the winter, to some warmer climate. This would be a considerable expedition and a considerable expense, for he should want to take Mary and the children with him. His father, on whom he might readily have called for help, was still abroad, so that he was forced to ask Uncle Owen in Hartford for the money needed to buy passage to Cuba. Uncle Owen was kind and generous, and in January, 1856, John Hull Olmsted and his family set out on the beginning of a long, difficult, and disturbed journey of several stops, none of which benefited him.

In Cuba John settled first in the country near Havana, but the warm climate did him no good, and he was incurably bored. Even though it was now winter, and an Atlantic crossing in winter was a fearful matter for a sick man, John Hull and Mary resolved to go on. They crossed to Southampton. Whether they saw Frederick in England there is no record, but they joined the other members of the family in Italy and were able to be with them for some time. Then they settled in Switzerland, near Geneva, for another reprieve. John enjoyed the cool bright morning air, took walks, and awaited with some slight if forced confidence the birth of their third child.

Fred's troubles had begun in the summer of 1856 when he was only beginning to make his way abroad as a publisher's agent. John was still at home and in the habit of dropping in at the office of Dix and Edwards to talk with one or another of the two partners. Then he relayed to Fred news of the firm. All seemed to be prosperous and cheerful at first. George Curtis had put money in. The company planned an edition of Melville and perhaps one of Dickens. But a word of encouragement passed along to Fred abroad was not entirely pleasing to him. John told him that Dix "preferred you should stay abroad partly because you were in a good way and had proceeded in impossibilities, where he or Edwards would have done nothing, partly because there was really nothing for you to do here."[32] Then from John, without warning, and from Joshua Dix in simultaneous confirmation, came the thunderbolt, news that Arthur Edwards was mismanaging things financially. Frederick hardly knew who to be angrier at, Edwards, who at best had behaved carelessly, or Dix, who did not have the courage to face up to Edwards, but now begged Frederick to come home and straighten things out, perhaps buy out Edwards.

This tale of trouble back home came to Olmsted just as things began to go well in his European career, when he felt that he was succeeding in his new position. It was like a crack opening in the path of his stride forward into the future. This, then, was going to fail too. This was not going to be what he would be doing for years, nor would he become fat and comfortable and even rich doing it. His books were receiving praise at this time, even abroad. Writing to his "Dear Sisters," Fred told them that the [Liverpool] *Daily News* had had two columns devoted to the *Slave States* and promised more. "I suppose it is written by Miss Martineau. It is in the highest degree complimentary, ranking the book with those of Bryant, Taylor & Stephens in its attractiveness and attaching still higher value to it for its information, in which it is said to be richer than any previous work on this subject."[33]

John Hull, at home, before he took Mary abroad, had written to his father (about Fred's coming home), "He appears I am glad to see to hesitate a little." But he added, showing his own needs, "I really don't see how we can live entirely alone here."

But Frederick's satisfaction was spoiled. The full story of the firm's troubles seemed spread out before him when he opened a packet of letters, one from John containing another from Dix.

John had written at this time: "Dix wants you to come home in August: and as you and he constitute an active majority of the firm, you will come without regard to 'orders' from D. E. & Co. He don't like to say as much himself but he wishes me to say so. He is not altogether pleased with the way matters are going on here and wants your countenance and help for a general overhauling and reconstruction of mutual duties and confidence, before further progress is made in extending the business. Edwards he finds too much disposed to take matters into his own exclusive management and not sufficiently open in financial affairs. . . . Since Edwards' absence some little things have come to Dix's knowledge which worry him. Edwards had been secretive and had rashly lent firm money to his brother."[34]

Enclosed in John's letter, as in an intrigue, was Joshua Dix's letter. Dix wrote, "I am sick, tired & worn out. . . . I hope you will return in August, even if you have to go back in a short time after. *Come over* let us talk and begin anew. . . . Don't be frightened at what I have said about money matters, for I believe we are all right, but I think an investigation is necessary and some changes should be made *now,* and I don't want to say or do anything till you return."[35]

Despite a soothing letter from Edwards on August 8, Frederick was unhappy and disappointed at the turn of events in the young business in which he had sunk so much of his own money (his father's), and in which, even more recently, George William Curtis had placed his own and his father-in-law's money. He was embarrassed, mortified, and angry. As much upset with Dix as with Edwards, for the former's timidity, he actively disliked Edwards. Earlier, Arthur Edwards had written him in an upbraiding and scolding style about some woodcuts Olmsted had purchased in England. Edwards's reproach had had the tone of a schoolmaster berating a naughty child. Frederick never forgave him. Now, it looked as if Edwards, heedlessly and in stiff-necked pride, had endangered the future of the firm. It was not a good time for a firm to fail. Business in general was in sharp decline. Frederick refused epistolary comfort from Dix, who seemed superficially cheered up after his first gloomy letters. He tried to give Olmsted the impression that some rearrangements he had made were working out: "Edwards, so far, attends to his matters and doubtless will not interfere with me. Curtis gives one or two hours a day about the same as when you were here. Dana also the same."[36]

Frederick precipitately lost all confidence in the ability of either Dix or Edwards to run the business. He sat down and wrote a long letter expressing the intricacies as well as the heights and depths of his feelings, and probably did not send it. The draft exists, with many crossings-out and changes. He threatened to withdraw from the firm but did not do so immediately. He expressed resentment not only of Dix's lack of acumen but of his puerility—asking him to read and destroy letters as if in a melodrama. Dix seemed afraid of the shadow of Edwards, who, however, seemed doubly thick-skinned, lacking Joshua Dix's extreme sensitiveness.

The draft of the letter kept but not sent reveals more of Frederick Olmsted than of Dix and Edwards.[37] One can learn only obliquely the details and drift of the difficulties in which the members of the publishing house found themselves, but one can discern the temper and the tone of Frederick Olmsted when angry. In extreme situations such as this one he was not the flexible, level-headed man he thought himself, and whom he presented himself as being in his travel books, but rather, he resembled much more closely the high tempered and easily outraged character, almost stereotype, of the high-bred Southerner, such a man as he often deplored in his "journeys." Something intemperate in these people and easily let loose had fascinated him in the South, for there was that in himself, which resembled these qualities, which broke things or ruined things. Olmsted, all his life, would have to fight to be what he wanted to be, a reasonable, sensible man. Inside, struggling to get out, was a raging ego. Only occasionally, he expressed that other self, usually suppressing the outward signs as in this letter not sent.

But he wrote such letters, more than once. His friendship, he wrote in this letter-draft of September 4, 1856, was not "impaired," but, "I can't tell how ashamed I am of being involved in such a mess as you describe." About Edwards: "With half the obligations upon me that he has, if he made such a mistake as you describe him to have made, I would not sleep till I had resigned my office and relieved myself of obligations for which I was incompetent." He would, he said, have had a guardian appointed for himself, if he could have done no better. He turned also on Dix, the mild and inoffensive Dix. "That you have known of such a state of things and have still allowed Edwards to manage our money affairs is—I must say more than extraordinary—incredible." Dix must have been "hoodwinked and led in a maze." He himself will certainly come home. He thinks Dix "cowardly" to tell him such things in confidence and not do his duty there at home.

"Have I not reason to be frightened? I would rather be shot dead tonight than fail to meet the obligations I have undertaken on our mutual account here in England." Fearing that their investment was already lost, he demanded a full accounting for both Curtis and himself through a lawyer.

Among the papers preserved is a draft of a document dated October 28, 1856, in which Frederick Olmsted proposed to withdraw from the firm of Dix and Edwards.[38] But he did not withdraw at this time, and he did not go home at once as he had threatened. He wrote and sent to Dix a letter reproving him, but not breaking with him. Cannily, an Olmsted businessman again, he waited and allowed his *Journey through Texas* to be published in January, 1857, before he wound up his affairs with the company.

Olmsted's anger was verified by reason. Edwards had indeed seriously mishandled finances, his own and his partners'. Frederick was effectually finished with the firm in his own mind, but regained his composure, a calm in the midst of a great disappointment. He wrote his father from New York (John Olmsted was still abroad) on February 7, 1857: "The miserable nemesis of haphazard business comes daily nearer and at length begins to be recognized by other eyes than mine. I have been striving ever since I came home to get myself out of the ship. Now I think it is too late and I abide my fate with such composure as I can. I busy myself in my book. Write every night till four o'clock and get on grandly."[39]

This was his third book of Southern travels, the one he was to call *Journey in the Back Country*, which, not unremarkably, Dix and Edwards would not publish, as they would not be in existence to publish. The firm (Dix, Edwards, and Curtis) struggled to continue. It dropped the name Dix and Edwards and with another member became Miller and Company. Meantime, Olmsted got out, with the promise of the payment of interest on his investment for a number of years, and the return of the sum later. Olmsted thought it was foolish of Curtis to stay in, but that was what Curtis did, and put in more money from his father-in-law.

Frederick was relieved to be out, even if he had lost a good deal of money and might lose more, for he did not believe very strongly in the promise to pay in the future. He soothed his father and his brother, who were both still in Europe, by speaking easily of his own future. He told them that, whenever he wished, he could get a position with Henry Raymond on the *Daily-Times*. Perhaps he deceived himself. The job did not work out. Bad times grew worse. Frederick, having finished writing his third book about the South, began seriously to worry about his own working future. He leased the farm on Staten Island for John and Mary, but his renter was in financial straits and fell down on the payments.

Meanwhile in Europe his brother John felt the pinch of something more dire than poverty; it was the breath of death coming toward him. He had managed a precarious hold on his health into the summer of 1857, living with Mary and the two children, Charles and Charlotte, in a village near

Geneva, awaiting the birth of a third child. He was able on July 6 to write to Frederick that they were pretty well. He congratulated his brother on his exit from the publishing business. "You are quit and remarkably well quit of D & E and M & Co. They must have been very glad to get rid of you to offer such terms—a few weeks before you were ready to go with only your shirt—now 10 prct. on 5000 for 5 years and then the 5000. Very well.... Good that you can write for Times easily. If so, nothing better to do. You believe in yourself, go on and convert the public. Make use of Dana to get heard."[40]

John managed a wry kind of happiness when the baby was born. He announced the event in the postscript to a letter to his father, a letter which apparently he was in the act of writing when interrupted for the event. (John delivered the baby himself.) "P.S.   Hallo, here's a baby—Suddenly on the 10th inst. at ¼ to 5 P.M. Mr. Owen Frederick Olmsted having apparently no silver spoon in his mouth and no visible means of support. He was immediately seized and placed in a tub, against his loud remonstrances and afterwards dressed up in petticoats and exposed to the gaze of all the old women of the house. He looks like his father, but especially like his mother and grandpa, and his Uncle Owen and Frederick for which reasons he has received their united names. His own Father was his deliverer and his own mother on the whole had rather an easy time."[41] He wrote with a happy irreverence of the same event to Fred the next day, "Hallo—here's a go—I'm wanted to hold a *baby!* He's just slid into the world without apparent means of support, shouting like a well to do Irishman at a fair.... So goes the world—one every two minutes they say. But what are we going to do with this one? The Lord only knows. However never mind—break a bottle to Owen Frederick and may he drive all the nigger owners out of Texas." And "Communicate this affliction to our relatives, the Perkins family, and believe me,   Yours."[42]

John could for a moment feel bravely gay with a new child in his arms, but he was not well. His cough persisted, his weight was down, he was unable to walk any distance. He decided he must go somewhere farther south for the winter. The children could be left with a nurse under the care of his sister Mary in Lucerne. His wife Mary would stay behind only till Owen was weaned and then join him in Nice.

John, very shakily, accomplished the first stage of his journey, to Paris, by himself. Away from family and friends, faced altogether and only with himself now, he achieved a bleak kind of courage. In Paris he wrote to his father that of course he wanted to go home, but if he did so he would only want to start off again: "I should be getting Fred to go to Havana with me." He saw that he must step off his merry-go-round, a prematurely wise young man with a touch of humor at his own expense: "If a man bumps me on the shoulder on the sidewalk I am ready to tumble into a shop and lie on the floor till I get over it."[43]

This younger brother, who was Frederick Olmsted's closest and most intimate friend until this time, went now straight toward his end. Mary met him at Lyon and with difficulty managed to get him, weak and almost helpless, to Nice. There a doctor, hastily procured, was kind but unable to help him. John saw himself and his situation without pity and with a kind of icy clarity: a leg paralyzed, appetite gone, a ravenous weakness debilitating him. He glanced toward Fred, of whom he heard that he had a new kind of opportunity—the superintending of a park: "I am glad Fred is settled for a while in something and hope it will require duties that he will enjoy —not bookkeeping and paying. $1500 is not enough for all Fred's time and he'll be turned out next election. Does he say what he will have to do?"[44] This to the father, from whom he had heard the news of a by now shadowy, distant older brother out of sight and out of reach.

On November 10, Mary telegraphed John's father to come to Nice, and then wrote him telling him when he came not to be shocked. John told Mary to write to Fred and tell him the details of his illness. This she did, describing to Fred without exaggeration the progressive downward movement of John's ebbing vitality. She apologized for not having written to him while he was still in Europe. She had penned such a letter but destroyed it. The failure of John's last strength had come more quickly than she had expected. The doctor now warned her that an attack of diarrhea or a hemorrhage "would bring on the end at once." And, "I'll write you soon again."[45] In her letters Mary was composed and firm. There was no hysteria, and she did not dodge facing her husband's situation and her own.

John looked, when he could, at the winter sea and the mountains scalloping the northern sky, still touched by a beautiful sight. He was full of self-awareness, particularly of all that he was saying goodbye to. He knew that he would never laugh again with Fred, never argue with him either. On November 13, with a shaky hand, he wrote Fred a letter, knowing perfectly well that it was the last one he would write to him:

Dear dear Fred

It appears we are not to see one another any more—I have not many days, the Dr. says. Well so be it since God wills it so. I never have known a better friendship than ours has been and there can't be a greater happiness than to think of that. How dear we have been and how long we have held out such tenderness.

I am kept wild with opium and am so weak that I suffer from too many little things. I cannot comprehend this suddenness—but I see it. I can barely be got out of bed and have no breath. Give my love to the boys. I want you to have something mine—my watch or cane or something and give something to C. and [illegible] of same sort.

Don't let Mary suffer while you are alive.

God bless you.

John H. O.[46]

When John's father arrived in Nice, he saw at once what he had not realized before, that John was dying. He made himself a bulwark to the young wife, soon to be a widow. On Tuesday, November 24, the father wrote in the firm, lucid Olmsted style of John's death to his daughter Mary in Lucerne: "He took Mary's hand and then mine as if he was conscious of his approaching end.... For the last 15 minutes he breathed very gently and died without a struggle.... [Of Mary:] She was born up most bravely."[47] Local law required that the burial of a person who died on Tuesday be on Thursday. John Hull Olmsted was buried in the Protestant Burial Cemetery on Castle Hill in Nice.

Frederick in New York absorbed in silence the knowledge that the most intimate friendship he had had so far in life was ended. He was now alone in a way he had not been before. Who could he talk to? Even who could he be angry with? The rivalry, love, mutual help, and fertile brotherly jealousy were over. No love could ever again be to him what John Hull had been—brother, friend, almost son, to whom he could say anything. The two of them invading Texas would ride on in his mind forever.

As his father completed his duties in Nice, he found time to write to Frederick both the feelings he had in contemplating this wreck of a young life and the complications the death had left behind in the lives of others. "In his death I have lost not only a son but a very dear friend. You, almost your only friend."[48] John Olmsted, Senior's wife Mary Ann and his daughter Bertha, with young Albert, had already sailed for home before John Hull's death. Mary, John Hull's widow, resolved to spend the rest of the winter in Lucerne with her sister-in-law Mary rather than face a winter passage home across the Atlantic. Cold, nausea, and bad food were real evils of such a voyage. Father Olmsted had no relish for such a winter journey either. He decided to stay in Lucerne near the two Marys and the children.

Frederick in New York, as John sickened and died in Nice, had moved into a new situation. On August 6, 1857, George William Curtis had written to him, "We failed today!"[49] Frederick could not be surprised. He had expected the failure of the company, but he was sorry to see Curtis saddled with liabilities not only for himself but for his partners. Curtis was to spend many years, cheerfully and valiantly, paying back his father-in-law Francis Shaw for this unfortunate venture. He seemed only glad that Frederick Olmsted was safely out of the affair. On August 18, he wrote to him: "My dear copartner in the general book publishing business, I hope you are less and less bothered about it—that you keep comfortably, and hear the sea under your windows, Yours affectionately."[50] Frederick seems to have moved down to the farm again.

As a writer, Frederick was not quit of the publishing business. During the summer, from June 3 to August 24, 1857, ten pieces, his third series of newspaper letters from the South, the ones from his "back country" travel, appeared not in the New York *Daily-Times*, where the others had been published, but in the New York *Daily Herald*. They were entitled "The Southerners at Home," and were signed "From the Journal of a Northern Traveler on Horseback." The fact that the *Daily-Times* did not publish these letters denotes at least a lessening of his access to that newspaper and its editor, Henry J. Raymond. The job with the *Times* did not open up, or Frederick for some reason did not try to gain it. In any case, during the months when he might have been looking for a position, he worked on his third book. He woke up to a worsened condition in the city and the country and to the fact that he was without a job. He had gone beyond the notion of returning to farming. Perhaps he had come to think that he could no longer call on his father for the money needed. Even his father confessed himself somewhat straitened and anxious in this money crisis of 1857. Frederick had written to his father something vague about going west to try his fortunes, but he did not do so.

Finishing up his manuscript in an empty echoing barn of a resort hotel, he dined one night next to an acquaintance who happened to mention the fact to him of the superintendency of the new Central Park being open. He turned his mind toward this opportunity, assented within himself, and characteristically acted with speed and decision. He wrote the following letter:

The President of the Commissioners of the Central Park

Sir,

I beg leave to recommend myself for the Office of *Superintendent* of the Central Park.

For the past sixteen years my chief interest and occupation has been with those subjects familiarity with which is most needed in this office. Economy in the application of agricultural labor has especially engaged my attention, and my observations on this subject have been extensively published and discussed in this country and reprinted in Europe. For ten years I have been practically engaged in the direction and superintendence of agricultural laborers and gardeners in the vicinity of New York.

I have visited and examined as a student most of the large parks of Europe, British, French, Italian and German, and while thus engaged have given special attention to police details and the employment of labor in them. Evidence of this is afforded by my published works, to which I have the honor to add the accompanying testimony.

Respectfully,
Your obedient servant,
Fred. Law Olmsted[51]

New York, August 12, 1857

CHAPTER XIII
Greensward

Our gardens, if nothing else, declare, we begin to feel that mathe-
matical ideas are not the true measures of beauty. . . . It is rather
the soft green of the soul on which we rest our eyes.
—Edmund Burke, *A Philosophical Enquiry into the Origin of Our
Ideas of the Sublime and Beautiful*[1]

I T WAS A DAY IN THE FALL of 1857. In the waste center of Manhattan,
in an area which the city had reached only stragglingly, a sardonic
guide showed the man who was to be the superintendent of works the rough
land which the city had designated for the as yet unformed "central park."
It was a project long hoped for, objected to, dreamed of, derided, wrangled
over, through a succession of years. It did not exist yet except as a legal
entity of which the bare outlines had been determined, its full extent not
settled. The new boss was dressed in city clothes and looked like a gentleman. His guide was roughly dressed and paid only in promises so far. Chief
Engineer Egbert Viele, who had not welcomed a new assistant with enthusiasm, had picked Hawkin as guide out of a crowd of idle, lounging
laborers. The workman, tutored by Viele's unfriendly attitude to the new
superintendent, and himself underemployed and purposeless, had a touch
of envy for this seemingly soft young man who had fallen into an easy,
undemanding job.

Not much work of any importance was being done, only the lining up
of a boundary wall with stones cleaned from the pocky, brushy land which
had deteriorated from farming into an area used by squatters for huts that
could not be called houses, or by followers of occupations best practiced
outside the bounds of the better parts of the city, tanners, slaughterers, and so
forth. The city had acquired the land after an intricate political struggle
involving not only its own government but that of the state, and of rivalries
between parties and men. Poets and visionaries had called for a park; now

the city fathers had the land but did not know how to command a design. The hundreds of men hired for the job often did no work. Employment was so scarce in the city in this year of business panic that men fought for a chance to get on the force. When the new superintendent met the engineer of the works, he found that individual besieged by demoralized, desperate men asking for work.

Fred Olmsted, for it was he of course who was the superintendent, understood the situation at once and endured the hazing which Viele had caused him to be subjected to. Unfortunately, he looked that day the smooth young city man he was not, one who had had no dealings with sick farm animals, the planting of trees, the spreading of manure, the digging of ditches, or living outdoors in rough and primitive conditions for days at a time. Hawkin led the new boss not only through the worst ground possible but encouraged the disrespect of the men they met along the way. These workmen had been hired not for their skills but for their votes at the next election.

Olmsted recalled an exchange that went like this:

"Smith, this is Mr. Olmsted, your new Superintendent; you'll take orders from him after this."

All the men within hearing dropped their tools and looked at me. Smith said, "Oh, that's the man is it? Expect we shall be pushed up, now." He laughed, and the men grinned.

Hawkin led the way onward through "a number of vile sloughs," passing from one loitering group of men to another. Olmsted kept his counsel, remarking quietly that he had not known that the park was "such a very nasty place." That day, when he saw what was to become Central Park, "the low grounds were steeped in the overflow and mush of pig-sties, slaughterhouses, and bone-boiling works, and the stench was sickening." For several days, even when he was more suitably dressed for exploring the ground, the new boss was treated jocularly, as if they were all engaged in some elaborate practical joke. He wrote later, "The most striking illustration occurred, I think, on the third day, when a foreman who was reading a newspaper as I came suddenly upon him, exclaimed, 'Hello, Fred; get round pretty often, don't you.' "[2]

But an elation seized him in spite of the unprepossessing circumstances of the introduction he was enduring. He had gone into the job knowing that the politics of the city were unsavory, that the times were discouraging, that he would be poorly paid, and that no one believed in him. He believed in himself and an instinct told him that here somehow was his chance to turn a private pastime, the enjoyment and care of land, into a way of making a living.

The commissioners of Central Park had been looking for a superintendent of the works. Frederick Law Olmsted, who had tried being clerk, tried being sailor, failed at farming, and had not quite made a success of editing and publishing, determined upon a dogged campaign to get the job. He found out the names of prominent citizens who might influence the commissioners to accept him in the position. The long yellowed and tattered sheets exist: petitions for Mr. Olmsted to be given the job of superintendent of "the central park."[3] George H. Putnam, Henry Holt, Whitelaw Reid, Horace Greeley, Peter Cooper, Clarence King, William Cullen Bryant, Bayard Taylor, and Henry Havemeyer signed. Parke Godwin, Bryant's son-in-law and associate on the *Evening Post,* wrote: "My old and intimate friend, Fred Olmstead [misspelled] is an applicant for the place of Superintendent of the Central Park. Let me assure you that I know no man in the country better qualified than he for such a place. He is a practical farmer —a man of exquisite taste—most diligent habits, and decided character."[4] The Harvard botany professor Asa Gray (who was a kinsman of Olmsted's close friend Charles Loring Brace) wrote: "I do not know another person so well fitted, both on practical and general scientific grounds."[5] Fred's solicitation of the letter had not been falsely modest: "You know that I have had a good deal of experience in working land and in management of New York laborers, that I have planted several thousand trees (and I have been particularly successful with them), also that I have long had a great interest in public parks and have observed them closely (not as a botanist or gardener, but as landscapes and pictures in their popular educative character). I suppose that I am much more trustworthy for the duties, which include police regulations, but are independent of the landscape gardener, engineer, etc., than anyone who is likely to apply or be considered."[6]

At this time Olmsted thought that he would not have any part in the designing of the park. He would watch this activity and carry out the directions of someone else who would have this grand affair in hand, and he would watch with interest, keeping his original ideas to himself. But he believed that he would be given a free hand in the running of the park, the management of it for the people who would use it. Thus he came to park work from the side which had to do with public use. What was paramount in August, 1857, was that he would be working at making a park, however subordinate a part he might play. The emotions he had felt in Birkenhead Park in England, where on his youthful walking tour in 1850 he first saw a large landscape laid out for the enjoyment of the public, would at last have some use in his life. He had ambition and push. He coolly foresaw that he might have difficulties with Chief Engineer Viele, who had not wanted anyone in particular in this job and especially did not want a "literary" man. Olmsted was aware however that he would not have had a chance at the job on the basis of the intensely practical life he had led on the farm down on Staten Island where he had raised grain and vegetables and pear trees. Only his "literary" connections, the endorsements of the men mentioned above, and particularly the signature of old Washington Irving, had secured him the job.

It was a close thing in the commissioners' meeting when his fate was decided. Other candidates included a house-builder, a former city surveyor, a professor, and a man who was the son of the painter-naturalist John James Audubon. Olmsted's strongest advocate on the board was Andrew Haswell Green, the most self-willed and influential member. Green was a man long experienced in the various rungs of city government, a man of stiff integrity, iron purpose, and devotion to the city. He was only two years older than Olmsted (who was thirty-five in 1857) and who had before him a long career in the government of the city. Olmsted endured a long wait in a friend's office over Broadway, a few doors from the commissioners' meeting; the news that he had been elected by a vote of eight to one was brought to him straight out of the meeting.

In spite of foreseen difficulties, and the fact that the salary had been cut recently from $3,000 to $1,500, Olmsted was delighted. He expressed his gladness to his brother in Europe who, unknown to Fred, was now dying of tuberculosis. To John Hull Olmsted, he wrote, "I am elected. . . . On the whole, as the times are, I shall think myself fortunate if I can earn $1500. The times are worse and worse. . . . It seems to be expected that Vielle [Olmsted's spelling] will be jealous of me, and that there will be all sorts of intrigues. I shall try the frank, conscientious and industrious plan, and if it fails, I shall have learned something more and be no worse off."[7]

For some time, Olmsted probably slept at night at the farm and traveled the long way up and over the rural heights of Staten Island, then by boat across the bay, and at last by horse car uptown to the area marked off technically as a park. Later he moved nearer to his work.

The farm continued to be a responsibility. Fred had taken charge of it in John Hull's absence. He had leased it to a farmer who turned out to be a poor manager and who did not even always pay his quarterly rent. After John's death, he felt more than ever conscience-bound to the place, for it belonged to Mary now, or rather was held in trust for her children.

But Fred dropped behind him piece after piece of his old life as he moved into a new one. He did not do so without pain. It was only late in John's illness that he had realized his brother's hopeless condition. His father, whom he habitually consulted whenever he made a change of direction, was unreachable at this time, in Europe where he had taken his family on a pleasure trip, remaining there to watch John die and then to care for Mary and her children after John was buried in the Protestant cemetery in Nice.

Another leftover piece of his old life was the last volume of his Southern travels. He was completing *Journey in the Back Country* at the time he began his work on Central Park. He had waited several years to put this portion of his Southern impressions in book form. It weighed upon him to finish the job.

But whatever else he did, his thoughts were filled with the park. He spent all his daylight hours learning his new trade. Geared to a high pitch of interest, living intensely in his new concerns, he hardly noticed the minor ailments which accompanied the screwing up of his nerves to achieve-ment—toothache, stomach pains, sleeplessness, and rheumatism. But he grew brown and lean and ultimately fit, his outdoor life tuning him to an exceeding fineness and sharpness.

He spent much time with the new friend he had found again in New York. This was Calvert Vaux, the young architect to whom he had been introduced at Andrew Jackson Downing's house at Newburgh. Olmsted enjoyed a good arguer and Calvert Vaux was a lively talker with notions of his own, of the way bright, educable, democratic man in America could be led into an appreciation of beautiful places and beautiful things. The native-born Englishman, married now to an American wife, Mary McEntee of Newburgh, and practicing in the most American of cities, was a fiercer Amer-ican even than Olmsted.

The park on which Fred Olmsted was at work, preparing the ground for the shaping hand of an unknown designer, caught the imagination of the two friends. The daily work of superintending the seven hundred men hired to build a wall and clear brush and fill in swamps did not blind Olmsted to larger views. To Professor Asa Gray at Harvard he wrote on October 8, 1857, "The site is rugged, in parts excessively so, and there is scarcely an acre of level, or slope unbroken by ledges. With a barely tolerable design, tolerably executed, the park will have a picturesque character entirely its own, and New Englandish in its association much more than reflective of any European park. There is no wood but saplings on the ground." In addition to seeing in his mind's eye what might be done, he allowed free play to his private criticism of the Central Park commissioners. "The Board consisting of eleven New York lawyers and merchants, is, of course, most unmanageable, unqualified, and liable to permit any absurdity. Still, I believe it will be a fine thing and I like my place in it much."[8]

He was cheerfully in debt as he began drawing his small park salary. On the very day he received his first check, $80, he wrote to his father of his straits. He had bought a horse to ride over the ground, $200; he had boarded the horse, $20; he had paid $75 for lodging for three months; he had bor-rowed $60 from friends Elliott and Godkin (the English journalist). He needed "hat, shoes, coal, etc." He told his father that in his need, he had also turned to Uncle Owen Olmsted. But now, with his father once more reachable by letter, he asked him, since he was in England, to secure him two coats, one for himself, one for his chief Viele. And he also needed badly "an English hunting saddle." For he had found that the saddle he had brought back from his travels would not do here. "I ride my Texas saddle now, but it is a dangerous thing in slippery fast riding. I came down a while ago, going over my horse's head in the most approved fox-hunting style and not hurt a bit." He needed also spurs and "four of the nice flannel shirts that English gentlemen wear in travelling. They are fine, check patterns, warm colors. Here they ask $5 apiece for them."[9]

While his father doubted the proper dignity of the job, Frederick Olmsted entered into a new and better period in his life. The dream material of his youth wove itself into a way of making a living. It was a wonderful conjunction for him, that his old wandering habit of looking at scenery should now become a career. Even temporary setbacks did not bother him seriously.

The commissioners had ordered him to discharge all the men for lack of funds. But he understood that this was temporary. It was expected that soon there would be one thousand at work again. In his very nature to do so, he began encroaching on Viele's authority. After his study of drainage in England and his practical experience of draining farmland down on Staten Island, Olmsted felt qualified to give advice on the subject. He promptly wrote a paper on drainage for the park and turned it in to the commission. At least some of these merchants and lawyers had been impressed and had wished to print his report. But Olmsted's interest in drainage poached upon Engineer Viele's special area of knowledge; he too had done a study of the problem of draining the malodorous ground which was fed by underground streams, some of them carrying the wastes of hog-slaughtering.

His father and brother at a distance continued to have doubts about the worthiness of Fred's occupation and about his ability to handle money. Some of his friends wondered if this were not another Fred-project which might start bravely and founder. But Olmsted did not doubt himself or his work in the brave beginning period of his new life. He did not know, however, how crucial a testing ground the "central park" of New York would be both of himself and of the city.

Ideas aside—and he was soon picking flaws in Engineer Viele's design, which no one, not even the businessmen on the board of commissioners, seemed to think much of—the physical fact of being where he was was enough at first. He put a firm hand on the direction of the work, and the slouchy, demoralized men responded at once. He aroused their interest in their work. It suddenly made sense to them. No more, after the first days, did any of the workmen try Mr. Olmsted with impudence or an elaborate exhibition of laziness. They were soon vying with each other to do well and to please the new boss. He made working on "the central park" exciting and important and amusing although he had initial problems in the hiring of men made desperate by being long out of work. Many of them were ill qualified. There were, in these early days, even near-riots with men carrying

"Blood and Bread" banners demanding work. The park became a safety valve for the city; many men could be employed in work that demanded brawn rather than skill, and the men could be good tools for the boss's careful and skillful direction. Mr. Olmsted was strict, and his expectation of good performance soon percolated through the ranks. He organized the men into groups and subgroups, gave small responsibilities to foremen and subforemen and held them strictly to accountability. There was as yet not much highly skilled work called for, but Olmsted had a gift for matching men to jobs and even in this early period of supervision he began to exercise this ability. Olmsted's readiness was the result of the meandering progress of his life up to this point, which had led him precisely here. But he could never have foretold the circumstance; there were no great public parks in the United States during his growing up. The public ones he saw in England, France, Germany, and Belgium in 1850 were new things and looked at somewhat askance, a bastard development from the old aristocratic "parks" surrounding gentlemen's country houses. The talents Olmsted began to exercise in this new American situation were a curious mixture, those of a sensuous, dreaming artist, and those of an imperious manager. Perhaps no other career on which he could have embarked would use so well both sides of his character.

Can the direction be traced through the zigzags of the early life? When he was a child, he had been tenderly encouraged to look at raw scenery and to find pictures in it. Being a somewhat lonely child, he had read a great deal and chanced upon old English writers on the picturesque in landscape. In his first youthful walking tour of England, he had browsed intellectually and emotionally in the countryside, following pathways and roadways on foot for the closest possible contact with loam and clay, grasses, brush, trees, and people—not all idyllically happy, as he had noted. In Connecticut and New York, trying to make a living as a farmer, he had handled soils, seeds, plants, plows, cultivators, drains, fences with as scientific a skill as he could. And that wayward impulse that he had toward beauty caused him to arrange these elements so that the result was a pattern. But repetition and drudgery bored him. In his years with *Putnam's Magazine* he had lived a city life and in the city he had become familiar with the need for a central park. He became interested in the campaign led by Bryant and Downing to secure such a park. Yet he was still a bystander to that effort. It was only the collapse of the publishing firm in which he had invested, a chance word about a position being open, his determination to get the job, which had led to his being in Central Park with a sense of his life opening up in a way that was good for him.

Frederick Olmsted was ready for his career; but if there had not been readiness in the city, he would not have had his life in landscape design. The area that was to be the park was a wasteland with the old Boston Post Road running north through its rocky, hilly spaces. The well-to-do people of the city thought they did not need a park. They went to the Adirondacks or to Newport to get away from the summer heat. The poor people of the crowded lower regions of the city did not know that they needed a park. Yet it was the thought of these deprived people, particularly of the children of the poor, which stimulated at least a part of the impetus to secure a park for the city.

In the same years, the early 1850s, when Olmsted traveled south to learn about the life of the ordinary people of the South, his close friend Charles Loring Brace concerned himself with the life of the poor in New York City. Out of the South, where Fred Olmsted was discovering truths about himself as well as about the white and black folks of that unknown region from Virginia to Texas, he sent his "Yeoman" pieces to the New York *Daily-Times*. Out of as unknown a territory, out of the streets of New York City, Brace drew the experience and wrote the story of the poor—often for the same issues of the paper in which his friend's pieces appeared.

A *Daily-Times* editorial on April 26, 1853, when the city government was moving toward authorizing the purchase of land for a central park for all its citizens, exhorted, "Let us act not only for the present, but for the future. The cleanliness and health of the City is a matter of first necessity. Let us lay, or rather remove the dust, that great bane of New York. Let us have a Park that shall correspond with her present growth and prospects, and be a joy to the coming millions which are to dwell upon our island."

The editorial in the *Times* celebrated the winning of the long battle fought by two persistent gentlemen. In 1845 Bryant had praised the English parks for the breathing space they provided. "These parks have been called the lungs of London."[10] He foresaw that New York would need its lungs too. Downing was even more visionary than Bryant. In 1848 he wrote of the means by which a society attained a larger and more fraternal spirit. How was this to be done? "Mainly by establishing refined public places of resort, parks and gardens, galleries, libraries, museums, etc. By these means, you would soften and humanize the rude, educate and enlighten the ignorant, and give continual enjoyment to the educated."[11]

It was an accident of economics that the area to be known as the "central park" was chosen. Earlier, Bryant in the 1840s found a desirable park space in "Jones's Wood," an area bound by Sixty-eighth Street and Seventy-seventh Street and bordering the East River, and other acres adjoining. In some sense, buried under those blocks today are the birds and trees, the clean air and water that was once there, what Bryant described, "A tract of beautiful woodland, comprising sixty or seventy acres, thickly covered with old trees, intermingled with a variety of shrubs. The surface is varied in a very striking and picturesque manner, with craggy eminences and hollows, and a little stream runs through the midst. The swift tides of the East River sweep its rocky shores."[12] Jones's Wood might have been the New York park, matched, as Olmsted later fancied, by a companion park on the Hudson, with a tree-lined avenue connecting the two. Frederick Law Olmsted, Jr., wrote later that the lost chance haunted his father, and that, in some moods, the maker of Central Park believed that Jones's Wood might have been a better park. But then the mighty effort stimulated by the challenge of the waste center of the island might never have been expended.

The rectangle which the city at last purchased, after years of maneuvering and litigation, was, as Olmsted had said, "squalid." Another describer (H. W. S. Cleveland, who, like many of Olmsted's associates, became a distinguished landscape architect in his own right) wrote of it: "The land it occupies was a series of barren ledges, of such forbidding aspect that no one was tempted to incur the expense of improving even so small a portion as was required for a suburban residence, and its only inhabitants were the hordes of squatters, whose shanties, clustering under the shelter of the rocks, served only to heighten the dreary aspect of the place."[13]

The dreariness of the scene which presented itself to public view emphasizes the quality of vision and imagination which the two young men possessed who were to design a park to fill these spaces. Vaux, who was to be Olmsted's partner in the design, who was, in fact, to be the instigator of the design, moved to the city in 1857 from Newburgh, where he had remained a few years after his friend and patron Downing died. The first year in New York was good for Vaux. He designed a bank and the Jefferson Market Court House. He published his book, *Villas and Cottages,* carrying on Downing's tradition of showing houses properly designed to fit into the landscape. He wrote provocatively, knowing that he had the answer, "Some will say America is a dollar-loving country, without taste for the arts; others, that expense is the obstacle, and that the republican simplicity of America cannot afford the luxury of good architecture. The latter of these solutions is clearly incorrect, for it is knowledge, and not money, that is the chief source of every pleasurable emotion that may be caused by a building."[14] He believed that the untutored and widespread love of "nature" in Americans was sufficient cause for hope that the more sophisticated love for art would grow out of this good and healthy ground.

Vaux imagined a land of mechanics and workers, no man ashamed of his labor, but working to produce beautiful objects: "It is worth remembering, too, that no occupation need be undignified, no labor graceless. Adam worked as a gardener, Franklin as a printer, Paul as a rope-maker, Aesop as a slave of all work, and Jesus Christ . . . as a carpenter."[15] In Vaux's mind, the artist was primarily a worker, and the worker, therefore, should be an artist. He would wish all citizens to be workers in this sense. Such was his overweening ambition for the ordinary man in America. A park might help make him such a man. Such an illustration of Vaux's writing allows an imagining of his talk with Olmsted.

The ideas that Vaux expressed were congruent with Olmsted's. They both revered the teachings of Downing. Vaux had loved him as a friend. Both young men, through Downing, through personal experiences, and through books, inherited some ideas from the romantic park-makers of England. Vaux had an originality of his own in his aspiration for the common man of America. Art was to help that man become uncommon. His notions fell in with some things that Fred Olmsted had learned in his travels in the South. There he discovered that the virtuous North was not in all ways superior to the unvirtuous South. What he found out, against all the prepossessions of his upbringing, was that the undemocratic, slave-owning, white Southerner had personal qualities—however expensively attained, at the cost of a whole society out of gear—which his yeomanlike, independent, small democrat in the Connecticut Valley often lacked. Universal education, a careful, economic way of doing things, a respect for the rational, and a prevailing sympathy for doing good had not made Northern man a graceful creature, as the best Southerner often was, reprobated as he must be in his actions and beliefs. What was needed was the development of the esthetic instinct somehow left out of the commendable education of the common man of the North. Olmsted struggled with this contradiction.

The South that produced such exceptional individuals must be done away with (perhaps by these same Southerners in a long, slow change—Olmsted was willing for the change to be slow). But precious qualities which might perish in this eradication must be taught to grow elsewhere, implanted in the free, independent, common man wherever he grew. And Vaux wrote enthusiastically about what might be done with the improvement in the quality of public structures, some of which hardly existed as yet, "public baths, gymnasiums, theatres, music-halls, libraries, lecture-rooms, parks, gardens, picture-galleries, museums, schools, and everything that is needed for the liberal education of an intelligent freeman's children." What was to come about then, effortlessly, enjoyably, would be "a refinement in popular education that will urge the unspoiled, pliable young minds of the rising generation to the study of the beautiful as well as to the acquirement of reading, writing, and arithmetic. The leading principles of good taste should go hand in hand with the multiplication table."[16]

It is no wonder that, having such congenial ideas, the two men should become friends. They found each other's company intoxicating and stimulating; the chance acquaintance they had had several years before when they met in Downing's house became, in New York City in 1857, a comradeship.

On October 30, 1857, the commissioners of Central Park advertised in the New York papers a contest for a design for the park:

PLANS FOR THE CENTRAL PARK

The Board of Commissioners of the Central Park offer the following premiums for the four designs for laying out the Park, which may be selected:—

For the first	$2,000
For the second	1,000
For the third	750
For the fourth	500

The plans to become the property of the Board. . . .

All designs must be presented to the Board by the first day of March, 1858.

Jno. A. C. Gray

Charles W. Elliott

Andrew H. Green

Committee[17]

It was Calvert Vaux who had the idea first to enter the contest. Vaux had to persuade Olmsted, who knew that his superior, Chief Engineer Viele, considered that his own preliminary plan was good enough for the continuing park. The fact that Olmsted thought little of Viele's plan, and the fact that the commissioners by their act of dismissing it showed that they thought little of it, made him rather delicate about offending the man with whom he did not in any case get along very well. But Vaux's enthusiasm warmed him, and Olmsted did not long hang back.

Viele showed contempt and indifference when Olmsted broached the idea to him that he, Mr. Viele's assistant, might be engaged in trying to make a design for the park. That contempt was the stimulus needed to pitch Fred Law Olmsted whole-souled into the project. Thoughts and ideas swarmed. Later Olmsted and Vaux did not sort out, they even purposely agreed never to sort out, whose was this idea, whose was that, in the making of the park. Of their most brilliant idea, the transverse roads, they were to say that they did not know which one thought of the device first, but that it was literally a joint notion. Olmsted was to have everything to do with making the park a place in which people might enjoy themselves, playing, exercising, loafing, looking at green things growing. Vaux was to care little for the daily life of the park after it was once designed; Olmsted was to care as much for the life of the park as for the designing of it, so that in later years he was necessarily more closely associated with it than Vaux. And in this and in all their many years of joint work, Olmsted was to have the more public personality, to be more aggressive, to enjoy the battle with public officials for attaining his own way, to push and push for what he wanted, and to write and to talk about open spaces. So it was going to be inevitable that the more retiring Vaux would become the shadowy figure in the work he and Olmsted had done together and fade out of the public mind when they had separated and worked apart from each other. But all this was in an unimagined future. For everything was fresh and delightful to the two men in the beginnings of their career.

In 1857, it was all a joyous rivalry and harmony of thought. One supplemented the other. Vaux was more highly trained, and his friend deferred to that technical training; but Olmsted had his useful, rough-and-ready surveyor's skills and was daily on the ground, ranging the park's gaunt, scurvy surfaces, imprinting on his mind every hollow in the rocks, every broad space, every ledge. In his imagination he superimposed upon this skeleton of rock the clothing of grass and trees, scooped out lakes, ponds, meres, and directed the flow and fall of streams. All this, of course, in minutes and hours beyond the time of daily conscientious labor for the park, work for which he was paid. He and Vaux spent Sundays or evenings riding or walking the park area together, looking and measuring, dividing areas into meadow and forest, catching ideas to be translated at Vaux's house on Eighteenth Street onto the long plan stretching across the length of an improvised table in the parlor. Some of the best hours the two men had in the park as the fall crisped into early winter were on the moonlit nights when they were the only two human beings upon the scene, continuing their creative and constant revision, making the park in their minds.

They came to respect the raw land underneath the scruff of human debris. And working together, they came to respect each other and to have an almost familial closeness one with the other. Probably at times Olmsted stayed overnight with the Vauxes. Olmsted's sister Bertha, when she visited Fred in New York, stayed with Mary and Calvert Vaux. Bertha, a venturesome Olmsted in her own right, went out with her brother and her brother's friend almost daily during her visit to see what was making these two young men so happy and excited.

Their cooperation was wholehearted and a delight to both of them, but it was not placid. The pattern of Fred Olmsted's most fruitful friendships was never in this style. He had worn out Charley Brace many times with eager argument on the beach at Southside. Now in this new friendship with Vaux, it was again a matter of reaching agreement through an enjoyable kind of arguing. Olmsted's son, Frederick, Jr., later wrote, "They doubtless then entered upon the first of those long, searching, exhaustive and exhausting arguments that were characteristic of their collaboration for years. Both were argumentative, very much in earnest and interminably persistent until fully convinced."[18]

Much of their thought was an American crystallization of a great tradition. Vaux wrote (in his *Villas and Cottages*) as if it were the most normal thing in the world to think in this manner, and not the result of a revolution in sensibility that had taken one hundred fifty years to accomplish: "The great charm in the forms of natural landscape lies in its well-balanced irregularity. ...Human nature, when allowed a free, healthy scope, loves heartily this well-balanced irregularity, and longs for it in life, in character, and in almost everything."[19]

What Burke and Pope and Addison had written, and for Olmsted in particular, what more obscure men had written, Uvedale Price and William

Gilpin; what Le Notre, Kent, and Capability Brown had practiced; what the Reptons, father and son, had done; the strong reinforcement of the example of Downing, a conscious follower of those English exemplars—all these influences played upon the two young men separately and jointly. Yet they were their own men, having thoroughly absorbed these older notions of earlier designers of gardens and parks. They were not burdened by the past, merely helped by it, and determined in their own time and place to make a mark upon the land.

They set about their plan. The size and shape of the area was determined already, and it was not without an initial difficulty and queerness. The park had to be created in a long rectangle stretching from Fifty-ninth Street to 106th Street from south to north and from Fifth Avenue on the east to Eighth Avenue on the west. The east-west dimensions held, but by April, 1859, the park commissioners and the designers persuaded the state legislature to authorize the extension of the boundaries of the park northward as far as 110th Street. This added sixty-five more acres to the original. The total area was to be eight hundred forty-three acres, a parallelogram drawn between streets in a state of sketchy but numbered existence.

Olmsted was to write later, "I reserve the word park for places with breadth and space enough, and with all other needed qualities to justify the application to what you find in them of the word scenery, or of the word landscape in its older and more radical sense, which is much the same as that of scenery."[20] Not the word garden, he emphasized. What he and Vaux were to set out to do here was not what their predecessor Downing modestly called "landscape-gardening" but "scenery-making." Showing his ambition in its dimensions of largeness and lordliness, Olmsted also wrote, "And, by the way again, did not Milton use the word architecture for the working out of the divine design for the heavens? Architecture is not rightly to be limited to works of buildings."[21]

The ragged barrenness of the actual place began to transform itself in their minds into a design of coherence, elegance, and beauty. Friends were invited in to look over the design and were pressed to stipple in grass. There was much careless gaiety surrounding the project. The fondness with which Olmsted and Vaux already regarded the park is seen in the fact that they gave a name to their plan, not just a number. (It was to be the last entered— No. 33, submitted on April 1, 1858, after an extension of the contest.) They called their design "Greenward." And the plan, with the casually stippled-in grass, exists today on exhibit in the assembly room of the old Arsenal. The durability of the design, which has survived changes and additions with its outlines unimpaired, derived from the respect the two designers had for the land itself. They were going to transform that land, but not deform or demolish it.

Two immovable fixtures sat squarely in the middle of the area: the tall brick Arsenal, bare and glaring in its nakedness in 1858, and the old reservoirs, square receiving pools for water for the city from the Catskills. Later a "new reservoir" was to be built, and the old ones were to become a lawn. Curving drives were to carry carriage, horse, and pedestrian traffic around these obstacles in a north and south circular flow, drives to be masked by trees, existing as yet in Olmsted and Vaux's minds only. North of the reservoir area, the land was high, rolling, with long views possible. This land was to be left as wild as possible. The area south of the reservoir was complicated by long, rocky ridges running north and south, and by a variety of depressions and elevations which, by the aid of the designers' art, would come to seem more natural than ever in being transformed into shady glens and grassy open vistas. It would be the naturalness that would impress future generations, fooling them into thinking that the designers had been lucky in finding a beautiful landscape and preserving it. A long broad and regularly tree-lined parade (the "mall") was to add the piquancy of a formal element to the naturalness of the park scene. It was to have a fountain at its head, and the rocky hill above was to be adorned with a tower. Men had designed manor houses and castles in earlier generations with the formal elements near to the house, the wilder elements of scenery increasing in the distance from the garden and the park. The "central park" of the people of New York was to incorporate for the democracy of the city some of the same elements; it was to have its tamer, domestic areas, and always in sight, its reminder of, and imitation of, the gentler elements of the natural.

The inventiveness of the four transverse roads was twofold. These sunken roads were useful; they carried traffic across the long park at a rapid rate and prevented the park from interfering with city traffic. The roads thus also hid the city's busyness and hectic pace; the park pathways and roadways were carried modestly and unobtrusively over the transverse roads. The vistas, whether open to the sun or shady with trees, were therefore uninterrupted for the longest possible stretches. Curves and sinuous lines increased the sense of spaciousness of the area also; this was to be particularly true in future year when trees and shrubs cut off the cruel, open, and ugly view across the dusty hilltops visible to the planners in 1858.

Olmsted and Vaux had in mind not only the land, but the men who dealt in city land. They stated their plan plainly in words to be understood by the business and professional men who would judge the contest.[22] They presented a narrative, a statement of cost, and a folder of sketches. The illustrations showed before and after scenes in the park in the manner of such an earlier designer as Capability Brown. They presented themselves to the commissioners also as practical men in speaking of gravel to be brought cheaply by sloop from the upper Hudson, trees of any size to be allowed to remain, rock for roadbed to be derived from the excavations in the park itself. The thin soil of the northern part was to be enriched by the organically rich soil of the lower part previously occupied by "market-gardeners and dealers in offal." Thus the overflow from the slaughterhouses through which Olmsted had slogged his way on his first day of inspection would contribute to the beauty of grass and trees. They estimated the cost to the city of $1,500,000, a great sum. It came in their day to $16,000,000.

Money aside, the idealism of a people's park showed in their argument: "Townpeople appear to find, in broad spaces of greensward, over which they are allowed unrestricted movement, the most exhilarating contrast to the walled-in floors or pavements to which they are ordinarily confined by their business." Olmsted remembered perhaps the restrictions penning him in when at twenty he was a dry goods clerk on lower Broadway and how he sought the roof of his boardinghouse from which to fly his pigeons. He and his partner pushed the main point, that the park was to be scenery, even if it was also a place of recreation, exercise, and socializing. "Buildings are scarcely a necessary part of the park; neither are flower-gardens, architectural terraces or fountains. They should, therefore, be constructed after dry walks and drives, greensward and shade." The park was not simply for now but for the future: "Twenty years hence the town will have enclosed the Central Park. Let us consider, therefore, what will at that time be satisfactory, for it is then that the design will be really judged. No longer an open suburb, our ground will have around it a continuous high wall of brick, stone, and marble. The adjoining shores will be lined with commercial docks and warehouses; steamboat and ferry landings, railroad stations, hotels, theatres, factories, will be on all sides of it and above it; all which our park must be made to fit."

On April 28, 1858, the Central Park commissioners announced that Plan No. 33, "Greensward," had won the grand prize for the design of the great new park for the people of New York City. The plans were published, the public entered into the discussion through the lively reports in the press, the commissioners directed a committee of their own to sit down with the designers and suggest some changes in the plan. Olmsted and Vaux entered at this point into their combative but adaptable career at treating with city officials. They exercised persuasion and were left to make only certain minor revisions. They had in mind already many small changes which they themselves had thought of, for the park was a living thing. The board passed a resolution that the superintendent (Olmsted) "be required to proceed forthwith to form working plans for the construction of the Park."[23] On May 17, the commissioners passed an amendment to the bylaws to change Mr. Olmsted's status. This was to provide that instead of a superintendent there should be "a Chief executive officer who shall be styled the Architect in Chief of the Central Park."[24]

Olmsted acknowledged the appointment handsomely and with the high spirits of anticipation and courage:

> Gentlemen: I wish to acknowledge the honor I have received in your appointment to the office [of] Architect-in-Chief. You will allow me to assure you with what personal feeling and purposes it is accepted. On the first occasion in my life in which I ventured to address the public [in *Walks and*

Talks of An American Farmer in England, in 1852], I used the words, "What artist so noble as he who, with far reaching conception of beauty and designing power, sketches the outlines, arranges the colors, and directs the shadows of a picture upon which nature shall be employed for generations before the work he has prepared for her hand shall realize his intentions."

. . .

In the first and highest responsibility of the office, I shall steadfastly regard the distant future, when alone it can be fully seen how far I am worthy of it.[25]

So began a great career.

CHAPTER XIV

The Boss of Central Park

I shall venture to assume to myself the title of artist.
—F. L. O., draft, to the Central Park commissioners[1]

LUSHED WITH HERO WORSHIP, a gardener in the Central Park in the early stages of its being dug, blasted, and shaped wrote a piece of doggerel verse to his superintendent, the driving Mr. Olmsted, who had caught the fancy and loyalty of his thousands of workers. Hugh O'Reilly delivered to Mr. Olmsted the following effusion "Composed and Sung by the Bearer."

A NEW SONG ON THE NEW RESERVOIR

In scriptures I hear of great Solomon's works
Of building the Temple so high
But he ne'er could compare to that great architect
I mean Olmstead who does the world defy
That he may gain honour wherever he goes
And all his whole family likewise
For erecting such ornaments in the Central Park
And making the New Reservoir . . .
etc., etc.[2]

So effectually had Olmsted warmed the warmable Celtic temper of his workers. "Hibernians," George Templeton Strong called them, as he surveyed, from the heights of impregnable respectability, the work of these diggers and delvers in the rough ground of the island. Strong was a capable lawyer who loved his native city and was a connoisseur of new urban sensations. He was keenly interested in the park and included descriptions of it in the secret diary he kept. On June 11, 1859, he walked over the ground with his little boy Johnny and his friend George Anthon. "Improved the day by leaving Wall Street early...to explore the Central Park, which will be a feature of the city within five years and a lovely place in A.D. 1900, when its trees will have acquired dignity and appreciable diameters. Perhaps the city itself will perish before then, by growing too big to live under faulty institutions corruptly administered."[3]

The building of the park had become a spectacle. Strong's little party arrived just in time that day for the excitement of the blasting: "Reached the park a little before four, just as the red flag was hoisted—the signal for the blasts of the day. They were all around us for some twenty minutes, now booming far off to the north, now quite near, now distant again, like a desultory 'affair' between advanced posts of two great armies." Strong went into the park at Seventy-first Street on the east side and crossed to what was already called the Ramble.

Its footpaths and plantations are finished, more or less, and it is the first section of the ground that has been polished off and made presentable. It promises well. So does all the lower park, though now in most ragged condition: long lines of incomplete macadamization, "lakes" without water, mounds of compost, piles of blasted stone, acres of what may be greensward hereafter but is now mere brown earth; groves of slender young transplanted maples and locusts, undecided between life and death, with here and there an abori-cultural experiment that has failed utterly and is a mere broomstick with ramifications. Celts, caravans of dirt carts, derricks, steam engines, are the elements out of which our future Pleasaunce is rapidly developing. The work seems pushed with vigor and system, and as far as it has gone, looks thorough and substantial.[4]

Strong was an interested observer of the civic world in which Frederick Olmsted balanced his work between generous and careless corruption and stingy parsimony. Of Mayor Fernando Wood, under whom the park first gained a chance to exist, Strong wrote, "a man of great energy, ambition, and perseverance, and most prolific in resource—pity's he's a scoundrel."[5] He noted the traits—good but inept—of Mayor Daniel F. Tiemann, who overcame Wood and succeeded him for a short term. Olmsted had to do his work inside the circle of politicians, or at least on the periphery of their circle. The board of commissioners of the park protected him and his work to an extent. The zealous guardian angel of that group was its treasurer, Andrew Haswell Green, who became almost as much of a stumbling block to Olmsted as the politicians.

But this much said, and difficulties to be traced out, it should also be said that Olmsted was probably never happier and never more himself. He planned, supervised, bossed, cajoled, and prevailed upon men to do with this piece of ground what he wanted done. If any place on earth supports the impatient, energetic and visionary ghost of the man, this place does. And in this early period of the park, he maintained the most intimate relationship he was ever to have with a piece of ground. For in this case he was not only a vital partner in the plan; he bodily supervised every foot of the transformation of raw ground into finished park.

Strong was to have a part in Olmsted's future in the war years soon to come. At this time the two men did not yet know each other. Any other existence but his present one in the park would have been hard for the fiercely concentrating Olmsted to imagine at this time. As he had been so entirely a farmer and a traveler, so now he was Olmsted of Central Park. He was to plan many other parks, estates, campuses, villages, towns, parkways, a world's fair, and to lay out railway stations, the grounds of asylums, and the design of beaches; he was to be consulted by men of every degree of importance; he was to be listened to with attention in many connections. But assuredly, he never had more joy than in the planning, planting, and peopling of one parallelogram of land. For the perspective it gives on that long and busy future, his intense career in Central Park can serve as a sample of his consistent method of doing things.

He surveyed and learned by heart every foot of the actual unkempt land, every dip and hill and granite ledge, and had in mind images of the future appearances of every vista, both in the horizontal sweep of long lines, in the depth of the shade of grown trees as well as the openness of grassed meadows. In 1858 and 1859 he found that smaller trees were more likely to live and grow than larger ones, so the scale of the future had to be imagined. He kept the work going at a steady pace. According to the fortunes of city finances, he had hundreds and sometimes thousands of men working busily in subdivided gangs on various tasks. There were two thousand men at work in August, 1858; twenty-six hundred in November 1858; and three thousand the following June.[6] On October 17, 1858, the first tree was planted. After this, the planting never let up. Nursery areas, to grow trees within the park, were set aside. Some trees were imported from outside the park, and some from outside the country. Olmsted hungered for fine specimen trees to stand alone in the full freedom of their individuality as well as for groups of trees to give effects of mass and edge. The trees had had to wait until the skeleton and frame of the park could be set: the roadbeds, laid down sturdily, more firmly than any roads designed in this region. The roads were wonders to the town and offered seductive surfaces to the owners of fine carriages. When it was discovered by the amateur owners of trotting horses that the Central Park roads were so fine, these men began to clamor to the park commissioners that some straight roads should be laid out for their benefit. Olmsted resisted this notion with all his might. This was only one encroachment that was urged against his plan. The very fact of the park coming into successful existence made it alluring to people for reasons which had nothing to do with the creators' intentions.

He wrote later,

A purpose more clearly apart from, and inconsistent with, the original comprehensive purpose of the park could hardly be devised than this of a Speeding

Track. . . . No one would have thought of it if it had not been for the chance of stealing the necessary land out of the park and so saving the expense of buying a suitable site for it. . . . If you yield to the demand for a Speeding Track, you yield the principle, adherence to which has thus far alone prevented the complete ruin of the park for its established purpose. It may be asked: would not provision within the city for athletic recreations be more valuation than provision for a sauntering place for the enjoyment of rurality of scenery?

And he answered his own question:

I think not; but what if they would? Would any man in his senses have chosen the site of Central Park for them? A site in which there was not an acre of flat ground, or of ground not broken by outcrops of rock? All these sports require places of flat surface and of even a somewhat elastic surface. . . . A Speeding Track a mile and a half long (from 71st St. to 101st St.) on the west side of the park, . . . would not only require the destruction of valuable existing natural scenery and the blasting out of an immense quantity of ledge rock, but also either the closing of eight of the present entrances to the Park, or a great amount of ugly tunnel and bridge building.[7]

Olmsted intended to provide winding roads and pathways for citizens to ride or saunter along gently at a civilized pace. Speed and competition for place would destroy what he was attempting to create, a gentle, natural-seeming though artfully created area of woods and meadows. But the natural scene was to be a place for people. There were to be shelters, arbors, benches, a ladies' pavilion, and pleasant, rustic rest houses in four locations for mothers with young children. He designed these shelters not for the well-to-do in their own carriages, but for mothers who brought their children on the Third Avenue horsecars. Here fresh milk was sold at five cents a cup and "bowls of bread and milk" at ten cents, and well-designed rest rooms were provided. He and Vaux saw to it that, on a sunken road out of sight and behind the shelter, milk wagons and trash wagons could come and go without disturbing the scene of mothers and children resting in the shelter or on the grass adjoining. There were to be sheep and lambs pastured nearby for the amusement of the children. A handbill was to be circulated to let people know of these advantages.

Young children, when confined in the city during the summer, generally suffer in health, and are specially liable to fall into dangerous disorders of the bowels. When it is impracticable to make a visit of some length to the country with them, great advantage will be gained by spending the greater part of the day occasionally in the open air, and under conditions otherwise favorable to health. Arrangements have been made by which this can be done easily and cheaply by great numbers on the Central Park.[8]

In shelters for children, in easy walks, in ponds for children's boats, in a lake for ice-skating, Olmsted designed amenities which were graceful and fitting; these appurtenances of the seemingly natural landscape were to make that arena easier to enjoy.

Ice-skating in the park became a popular sport very early. Water was let into the lake for the first time in December, 1858, and if one could not be a skater, one could watch skaters. From the signal tower a banner was flown to announce that the ice was thick enough for skating. Olmsted saw to it that a drab and inconspicuous banner was replaced by a large and bright one. He took care of the bodily comfort of the skaters but did not let dealers in food take over the area without restrictions. He persuaded the commissioners to limit the food concessionaires to three—those who had managed their stalls most economically and decorously the first skating season. From the earliest snow seasons in the park, artists painted the scene. In 1860 Winslow Homer showed the gay, self-absorbed skaters in their bulky clothes exercising their skills with comic solemnity, showing also beyond the rim of the lake workmen carrying their hods uphill over a landscape decorated with skimpy, winter-suffering trees and the skeleton frame of some kind of derrick. A Currier and Ives lithograph of 1862 showed snowy hills and a few more trees, a finished building with flags flying from the roof staffs, and a stylish crowd of men, women, children, a dog barking, the waltzing movement indicating a lyrical enjoyment. Homer painted the scene again in 1868, depicting a small group of girls and women skating as if it were serious business, their robust movement denoting physical effort and exertion. The natural scene— white ice against a background of wintry tree trunks—was intensely pictorial. Taking part in the life of the park, seeing it pictured by artists, the people of New York found Central Park becoming an integral part of their city and of their lives. It became a point of reference to them, from the superintendent through all the ranks of those who worked in the park, to the lawyer who strolled there occasionally and made critical notes of the progress of work, and to all those who walked or skated or boated on outings. The park became a center, almost a core of meaning for the city.

It had the most meaning and the most promise for its designer and builder, Frederick Olmsted, for he held in his mind what the park was to be in ten, fifty, or a hundred years. Meantime, he battled with the commissioners for more money, he instructed the public in the proper use of their park, and he taught his workmen and his park police how they should function. He picked good foremen and he subdivided the work to make it intelligible to those who performed the duties and to accelerate the progress of the large and complicated work. In his report to the commissioners in 1858, very early in the park's life, he informed these gentlemen that he had between four and five hundred men doing excavation work for the entrance drive and promenade (mall), four hundred engaged in draining swampy ground and in pond excavation, while seventy were working in the nursery area in "grubbing and tillage."

Very early, he found first-rate men to boss the work directly under him, and he subdivided the work and held these supervisors strictly responsible: "The work is organized in divisions; Mr. Fielder, with two general foremen, directing the first; and Mr. Waring, also with two general foremen, the draining and pond excavation; Mr. Pilat, general foreman, has charge of the grubbing and nurserywork; Mr. Grant, is employed as my principal assistant over all."[9] W. H. Grant was Olmsted's expert on road design. George S. Waring, Jr., knew as much as anyone in the country about sanitary engineering. He devised the miles of drainage pipe underlying the new topsoil clothing rock and boggy swamp. Olmsted's previous study of farm drainage was put to use here.

Ignaz Pilat was perhaps the most interesting of Olmsted's park colleagues. His mark upon the park survives. A man only two years younger than Olmsted, an Austrian who had studied in the Imperial Botanical Gardens in Vienna, he was to remain with Central Park the rest of his life, devoted to the place. Olmsted had a rough and ready knowledge of plants and trees, and an artist's taste in grouping them and placing them in relation to the land, but Pilat was his expert on these matters. Pilat knew things that Olmsted did not know, and Olmsted could use such men. With these men, Pilat and the others, Olmsted was a figure to inspire trust, reverence, and a fierce kind of loyalty.

Olmsted concerned himself with everything that was going on and yet developed responsibility in those serving under him. His care for detail can be illustrated by some of the communications passed back and forth between these busy builders of the city's pleasure ground.

Memo from Grant to Olmsted, June 29, 1860:

Mr. Olmsted will please examine staking of Bridle road West of Brook and S. of Bogardus' Pass.
It is staked at 12 ft. Should it not be 15 to 18 at this point?
I think it desirable to have a look at outline of Lower Pond before the work goes much farther . . .
Please look at filling and shaping W. of Reservoir.

Olmsted to A. H. Green, December 14, 1860:

The ball will be hoisted tomorrow. I have been carefully over the ground, and what is essential, is tolerably complete . . .
More than 2000 came to the pond with skates yesterday.[10]

Olmsted set an order and a style for the "Park Keepers" after he had won the right to have his own force and to banish ordinary city police from the park. These men were to perform the duties of policemen but were to be much more. They were to be protectors of the green growth of the park and instructors to the public. Olmsted wrote a sheet of instructions for the "Keepers," dated March 12, 1859. Each one of them, he said, was to "preserve a quiet, reserved and vigilant manner," and was to salute and return salutes.

In such cares, Olmsted devoted himself almost domestically to the park. His colleagues and workmen developed a loyalty for him tinged with awe, and were also occasionally bruised in their self-esteem by his not coming closer in friendship to them. Olmsted gave himself completely to his work, but found it difficult, except with a few, to be intimate. There was a reserve in him, perhaps engendered by the years when he had received no special esteem from others, when even his family privately considered him a kind of interesting failure. In any case, after John Hull died, after Charley Brace drifted away into his own absorbing concerns, and aside from Calvert Vaux, with whom he quarreled and agreed in quick intimacy, he was unable to give himself in easy friendship. His wife was soon to fill up all this space of need for comradeship as well as love. For he married early in his Central Park career.

Could it have surprised anyone that, in the end, Frederick and Mary, John's widow, married? The outcome seems something that came along at a pace of its own to a conclusion that must have seemed to the two most concerned quite inevitable. All the pieces are not movable and fittable to the hands of biographers. Olmsted in his private life was secret, and in his deepest feelings most reserved.

Returning from spending the winter in Switzerland after her husband died, Mary Olmsted was a good deal with the senior Olmsteds in Hartford. She also visited relatives in the Boston area. She had the aura of being orphaned at this time, orphaned and stranded, with three small children to care for, and if not penniless, at least with not much in the way of income. Yet on October 15, 1858, Mary leased a house of her own on Seventy-ninth Street in New York City between Third and Fourth avenues. This showed some small competence of her own. It also showed independence. She did not stay in the shadow of her father-in-law in Hartford; she did not return permanently to Boston where her Perkins kin lived. She settled near her brother-in-law and almost in sight of his work. Frederick was a witness for her when she signed the document renting the house. The sturdy self-sufficiency of the woman shows. This was a time when it was required of a woman of good family to be almost entirely dependent upon a man, whether her father, her husband, or her brother. Being attached to and interested in a brother-in-law was somewhat eccentric and special. Women of Mary's upbringing rarely even worked for a living. And she had three children, John Charles, Charlotte, and Owen, to care for.

There are no letters between Frederick and Mary surviving from this period. There was no need for letters. They were close to each other. The letters they wrote after their marriage attest to the friendship as well as the love they had for each other. Their relationship was an old and steady one. John Hull's death only changed their perspective upon each other. In the years when the three of them—Fred, John, and Mary—had shared the farmhouse there had been an affectionate and close love among them. Now the brotherly and sisterly relationship changed. John dead, Mary had need of Fred. Frederick had always needed Mary, or someone like her. He had one time got himself engaged and been thrown over. Rebuffed and hurt in his pride, he had apparently contented himself with being a third member of John and Mary's domestic circle. He hungered for a happy domesticity. He had romanticized this condition and been supported in his dreams by Zimmerman's *On Solitude,* which is in part a rhapsody in praise of home virtues. Zimmerman had sung the joys of an enclosed, intimate family circle as the best center for all the doings of a thinking and feeling man. Fred was good with children and fond of his nephews and niece. If more than mutual trust and liking were needed, Fred and Mary were united in an orphaned closeness. They both had lost much in losing John. And perhaps for a long life together, Fred's wiry penchant for doing was more compatible to Mary's own strong character than the charming and gallant way John Hull had had of failing. In Fred's mind, there sounded also the haunting words of John's bequeathing Mary to him: "Don't let Mary suffer while you are alive."[11]

On June 13, 1859, Mary and Frederick Olmsted were married in the Bogardus House in Central Park by the Mayor of the City, Daniel F. Tiemann. It was a quiet affair, but a fitting one for the architect-in-chief of the park, who was finding that all of the important events of his life seemed to be taking place within the boundaries of the park. Mary and Fred planned to move into a house in the park as soon as arrangements could be completed. There was a group of buildings—cloisters, offices, cells, stables, and other outbuildings—that had been a convent, Mount St. Vincent, on the Boston Post Road, which ran straight up through what was now the park. The road was soon to be closed, but the Olmsteds were to give their address at first as on the Boston Post Road. Their new home, which they visited often before they moved in, was on the top of a moundlike hill and had sweeping views, windswept perhaps, but sunstroked also, and its location would give the superintendent of the park a northern vantage point to view the works which were moving rapidly in that direction. Mount St. Vincent was located on the east side of the park between 102nd and 106th Streets.

Meantime the Olmsteds lived in the rented house on Seventy-ninth Street. The children were a rare handful, Charles, seven, Charlotte, four, and Owen two. Frederick legally adopted Mary's children. He was father now, as well as stepfather and uncle to them. Mary began to move flowering plants from one yard to another. The new place looked more promising with every visit. There was a great glass gallery where the children could play in the light but be protected from winter rains and wind. Mr. Green of the commissioners authorized the city to pay for repairing and repainting the buildings. Mary began to plan the colors of the rooms, the kinds of wallpaper to be used and the paint to make halls and living areas lighter and more cheerful. Frederick liked the site of the house very much, but as he was going to do all the rest of his life he left to Mary the practical side of setting up housekeeping. Mary was clever at this kind of work but she was not contained in her housekeeping. She spoke her mind freely and with tough honesty about the larger aspects of Fred's work and in particular about his somewhat difficult relations with the park commissioners. There was always give and take in her relationship to Frederick. She respected her own ideas as well as his, and he listened to her. From the time of their marriage, their letters to each other, when they were absent for any length of time one from the other, reveal happiness, a steady kind of romance united with an everyday kind of friendship.

Frederick continued to drive himself through the hot summer of 1859 and to push the work of the park with extreme energy. He and Vaux not only planned the newly authorized extension of the park from 106th Street to 110th Street but revised their original plan almost as soon as "Greensward" was accepted. A report that the two men made to the commissioners "As to Proposed Modifications"[12] shows the flexibility with which they worked and also the stubbornness with which they stuck to what they thought essentially important. They insisted on keeping the sunken transverse roads which were initially expensive and unnecessary in the view of some of the commissioners. They struck out, probably gladly, "the flower garden" and "the music hall, arcade and casino." They pointed out that the length of the promenade was determined by fitting it to the natural scenery. If it were made longer, it would no doubt be impressive but it would "destroy scenery," that is, God-given scenery. Olmsted and Vaux did not propose to do that, but to use what was there, and with modesty, enhance it: "A simple and unartificial treatment with variety and some degree of intimacy, seems to be preferable . . . to straight lines of trees or stately architecture. These belong not to parks for people, but to palatial gardens."

Part of the job that Olmsted and Vaux had to perform was teaching the commissioners. They told these gentlemen,

> The time will come when New York will be built up, when all the grading and filling will be done, and when the picturesquely-varied, rocky formations of the Island will have been converted into foundations for rows of monotonous straight streets, and piles of erect, angular buildings. There will be no suggestion left of its present varied surface, with the single exception of the few acres contained in the Park. Then the priceless value of the present picturesque outlines of the ground will be more distinctly perceived, and its adaptability for its purpose more fully recognized. It therefore seems desirable to interfere with its easy undulating outlines, and picturesque, rocky scenery as little as possible, and, on the other hand, to endeavor rapidly, and by every legitimate means, to increase and judiciously develope these particular individual and characteristic sources of landscape effects.[13]

Not waiting for the park to be finished, the public found the new walks and proceeded to use the park as it was being shaped into being. This had the approbation and encouragement of the park-makers.

However, there was a stiff opposition to the whole idea of the park from those who feared "the democracy." An editorial in the *Herald* viewed Central Park and its possible crowds with alarm.

It is all folly to expect in this country to have parks like those in old aristocratic countries. When we open a public park Sam will air himself in it. He will take his friends whether from Church street, or elsewhere. He will knock down any better dressed man who remonstrates with him. He will talk and sing, and fill his share of the bench, and flirt with the nursery-maids in his own coarse way. Now we ask what chance have William B. Astor and Edward Everett against this fellow-citizen of theirs. Can they and he enjoy the same place? Is it not obvious that he will turn them out, and that the great Central Park will be nothing but a bear-garden for the lowest denizens of the city, of which we shall yet pray litanies to be delivered![14]

That this was wide of the mark in 1859 and 1860 and that some of the prediction came true one hundred years later, only through the mismanagement and undermanagement of the park, is an irony of the history of the park.

In 1859 the people came and behaved well and enjoyed what was there for them in the midst of the work being done. It was a remarkable year. The rate of employment increased, the largest number put to work at one time, 3,666, occurring in that year. Ten viaduct arches were constructed, and seven miles of walk, ten miles of drainage pipe, while over 17,000 trees and shrubs were planted, and the plan for the extension to 110th Street prepared. In June the Ramble was opened. In July the first concert was performed, with Olmsted moving about from place to place during the program to determine whether the placing of the band was correct. In August the Vista Rock tunnel was cut. Olmsted was the motor that ran the progress of the whole. He was everywhere seeing to everything. By September he was sick in bed.

In September, 1859, he wrote his father that since he and Mary had come back from Saratoga, where apparently they had had a trip together away from the children, they had all been ill, one by one. Charley's eyes were bad, Charlotte was covered with sores, and Mary was "half distracted." "However, we have a good deal of happiness between ... that's a fact." Lying in bed with a fever that rose and fell and that may have been typhoid, coddled by Mary who waited on him and read to him, he laid out the present position of himself and his dependents to his father.

He was sobered at finding himself with a family and not quite sure that his salary was going to cover all the expenses that it seemed necessary to incur. "Our supplies are frightfully expensive and difficult to get. We have to live well—on good food and drink—for there is not one of us in moderate health and never less than three that need careful nursing and bolstering." They looked forward, however, to their house in the park: "We are going, you know, to move into the Convent—taking some low and rather dark but warm rooms, rather conveniently connected. The great comfort is that there is a great extent of glass galleries or piazzas, where the children can be in fresh air without wind or rain. I hope too it will be a little more convenient of access—for grocers, etc." Warming to his efforts to make a new life, Fred confessed the great fact to his father: "I have fixed what I most cared for in the park beyond reconsideration and shall not be so zealous probably in the future."

The continuation of his letter to his father was to be dramatic, for as he wrote it, he said, "Here came in three of the commissioners to inform me that a meeting had been had today and that they had resolved to give me six weeks leave of absence, with a request that I would employ the time in examining European parks, advancing $300 for the expenses. I expect to sail by the 'Persia' next Wednesday."[15] Frederick was to have difficulties in the future with the commissioners but at this juncture they valued him and wished him to recover his health as well as to study what he had convinced them was important, the design of parks for great cities. The commissioners, in particular Green, the curmudgeon of the money box, seem to have been brought conspiratorially by Fred's father and wife into a scheme to send him abroad. Mary was faced with handling alone the move into Mount St. Vincent but was glad to have Fred go abroad for a restful change. Even this early in his career Olmsted gave signs that this was the way he would always work—bouts of fearful energy alternating with exhaustion. This early separation of Frederick and Mary Olmsted is an advantage to the history of their relationship. They began at this point to write letters to each other, and the letters have survived, painting their simple, fond, and straightforward relationship.

They had been married only three months. After going down to the dock and setting off on his voyage considerably enlivened and refreshed, Fred left behind Mary, his father, and his friend Vaux standing together, a support for one another in his absence. Mary sat down and wrote to him almost immediately knowing that he would have to wait for his ship to reach England to receive her communication. She told her husband, in a letter written for his amusement as well as comfort, how the three of them, after saying good-bye, boarded the Staten Island ferryboat, persuaded the captain to pursue the *Persia* down the harbor, and found themselves going under the stern of his slowly moving ship. They enjoyed the pursuit hugely, the young wife, Fred's partner, and the older Mr. Olmsted, always childlike in his enjoyment of excursions. "Our Staten Island boat was delayed by barges which prevented our getting very near," Mary wrote. She did not know if he saw them frantically waving, but Mary thought she saw Fred at the rail of the larger ship.

Mary made up her letter of the small events of her life, how she dined "in the glass place off the kitchen for economy and convenience," how she had gone back to the old house to gather late flowers, how Mr. Vaux had told her of a place on Broadway to purchase wallpaper and that she had picked "a buff oak leaf for the dining room." She would be content if he would get one dress for her in Paris, and new gloves for her and for him too. And to reassure him about herself she wrote, "I have carefully refrained from working too hard—and have been so conscientiously cheerful that I hardly know myself." She ended: "I have no need to say how entirely I wish your well being. Regards to the people I know. Mary your wife."[16]

His letter, crossing hers, began, "Dear little woman at home." He told her how he passed the time on ship board. Card-playing with dry goods men on the ship was not very interesting. He spent some time working on the index to his *Texas* book. He described sea sights for Charles: "Tell Charly I saw five whales, altogether, snorting and turning somersets (so it looked) in the water. Lots of birds, floating and flying, and once, a little sparrow, several hundred miles from land, too tired to move more, dropped on deck and allowed itself to be caught. It is alive—the sailors keeping it."

He wrote his wife that he was "concerned" about her and "a little ashamed of leaving the farm matter in the way it stood." The renters were not satisfactory. Mary had inherited the place from John, and Fred was trying, after a fashion, to manage it. The letter ended as the voyage ended: "The officers to examine luggage interrupt me."[17]

Once in England, Frederick was swept up in new interests and refreshed by the change. He was very well received by public officials and park designers. Several friends, including his partner Calvert Vaux, had written letters of introduction for him. They smoothed his way. Vaux's letter is especially interesting, for it shows clearly his generous spirit and how he credited Olmsted with the entire execution of the plan. Vaux had written to George Goodwin, editor of *The Builder*: "Mr. Olmsted for the last year and a half has been occupied exclusively with the execution of a design we made together for the Central Park, New York—a public work, with which you will heartily sympathise if I judge your antecedents rightly."[18] Letters like this one from Vaux and from the commissioners helped, but Olmsted's reputation had preceded him. When he arrived, he was already a celebrity among designers. This was a pleasant thing for the misprized superintendent of two years before, and not unexhilarating for the man who had had a number of failures or at least failed efforts in his past.

During his visit he did everything he wished to do and saw everyone he set out to see. He was waylaid by new pleasures too. He began collecting books relating directly and indirectly to landscape design, intending to set up a library of such materials somewhere in the offices of the park. From one London bookseller a bill survives for Sowerby's *Farms and Farm Allies, Forest Planter, Parks of London,* and Ruskin's *Two Paths*.[19]

A letter from Olmsted to Thomas Lloyd, Esquire, Mayor of Birmingham, on November 28, 1859, illustrates his direct way of approaching people: "Will you do me the favor, Sir, to state, what effect, if any, the park has been observed [that is, the park in Birmingham] to have upon the habits of those resorting to it."[20] This curiosity about the social effect of parks persisted.

He visited the Birmingham Sewerage and Filtering Works and found their engineering "ingenious and effective." In London, Sir Richard Mayne, commissioner of the metropolitan police, opened up his whole operation to the American visitor, who reported to his own commissioners later that this gentleman gave him "the opportunity of studying the whole management of that admirable body," and that Sir Richard passed him along "to the Superintendent of the division patrolling the West-end parks, and the instructor of recruits, for very detailed information, which I trust will be of value on the Central Park." Olmsted already had his own ideas of how to manage the safety of a park and at the same time protect its qualities. He now quickly made himself an expert on the ways these matters were handled in European cities. He was indefatigable and unstoppable in his curiosity about everything he saw. He crowded in a great number of parks and people in the strenuous schedule he commenced upon setting foot in England. In a half dozen pages he reported to the commissioners of Central Park the most important things he had learned. This was a report dated December 28, after his return.[21]

Every park which could be seen, he saw, and every estate, every plantation of trees. He was in and around Birmingham and Liverpool. He saw Chatsworth, the Derby Arboretum, the Forest of Windsor, and, again and again, the West End parks of London. Introducing himself to the office of the Works of Her Majesty's Palaces and Parks, "I was received with the most frank and generous kindness, and the same day orders were given to the Superintendents of all the public parks in the vicinity of London, respectively, to hold themselves at my disposal whenever I should visit their grounds, and to give me information on every point, without any reserve. I was also offered the use of documents and plans at the office."

He went to Paris and met M. Alphand, "head of the government departments of Roads and Bridges, under which the suburban improvements of Paris are carried on, who kindly supplied me with such information as I required, and directed an engineer to attend me in my visit to the Bois de Boulogne." He spent two weeks in and around Paris, seeing all "its pleasure-grounds and promenades, also visiting the parks of Versailles, of St. Cloud, and the wood of Vincennes." He went eight times to the Bois de Boulogne.

Then he proceeded to Brussels where Dr. Linden, the director of the horticultural department of the Horticultural and Zoological Garden, and Dr. Funck, director of the zoological department and chief editor of the *Horticultural Journal* of Belgium, both greatly interested in New York's Central Park, gave him aid and information. He went to Lille where he visited "gardens, parade-ground, and promenade." Then he returned to London, visited Kew, "the superintendent of which, Sir William Hooker, I found extremely interested in the Central Park." Then Sir Joseph Paxton showed him the Crystal Palace grounds at Sydenham (which he had visited before when he was a traveling editor for Dix, Edwards and Company). He took in the Royal Botanic Garden and the Garden of the Zoological Society in Regent's Park. He accompanied Samuel Parsons to purchase trees and shrubs to be sent back to Central Park the following spring. Parsons was to become a valued member of the New York park staff and eventually, following Olmsted's and Vaux's terms, its superintendent. "The following week, I visited the park at Elvaston Castle, which has the finest plantations of Evergreens in Europe; Trentham, the seat of the Duke of Sutherland, which I believe to be the best private garden in England; Biddulph Grange...Stoneleigh Abbey...Peel Park, and the Botanic Garden at Manchester." Then he went to Ireland and visited Phoenix Park and the Zoological Garden in Dublin. Thence to Cork and so home. He had spent all the money given to him for the trip and no wonder, and suggested also that the commissioners expend one hundred dollars to mount park plans and documents and to exhibit all these materials and a collection of books, photographs, and documents in a special place. He began pushing the commissioners toward making the park an educative as well as recreative place.

In his whirlwind travels he had broadened and professionalized his own knowledge. He was a quick study and never forgot what he once learned. He was, when he returned, simply the only American expert of the first class on parks, with a store of comparative information on hand and a critical judgment honed by experience. He knew also that his own and Vaux's accomplishments rivaled, if they did not surpass, what was being done abroad. (The best effort of English park-making had, by this time, waned, and the best work for the next fifty years was to be done in America.) Olmsted was aware that he was founding an American profession. He returned home with confidence in what he was doing and new ideas of what might be attempted. It was going to be less endurable for him that the commissioners of Central Park still treated him—as he thought—as an amenable underling. He was to forewarn them in a supplement to his report that he desired changes in his duties. He wished the daily hiring of people, the hearing of complaints, the paying of employees, to be delegated to an official directly responsible to him and also the appointment of other supervising officials under him to take care of a subdivision of duties. He was pointedly jealous of his sole authority for decision and suspicious that the commissioners, especially Mr. Green, might wish to share that authority with him. He claimed the professional right to devote himself to "a calm exercise of the imagination, and a just consideration of beauty and a large economy."[22]

With Frederick Olmsted away, Mr. Green, as Fred's wife told him in letters, did indeed enlarge his care for the park. Mr. Green loved Central Park too, and wished to be responsible for it and known to be so. Here was a difficulty for the future. However, all this did not come on immediately. Fred came back not only to a sense of his own powers, but also to confidence in Calvert Vaux's abilities and friendship. Their relationship is shown in the endearing intimacy with which Vaux scolded Olmsted as he went away: "I consider that the only thing to be really regretted in our last two years operations is the absence of jollity. Because you see there are so many aspects of comicality in the whole affair. 'An you love me Hal' get flesh on your bones and forget that you ever had a puritanical marrow."[23] In his partner's absence, Vaux looked after their joint interests. He had met with Stranahan, the influential Brooklyn businessman, and had been out to Brooklyn to look at sites. This seemed to foreshadow a park for that area.

Mary, at home, had been a rock to which to anchor himself. She never failed to let Fred have the benefit of her own ideas. Her letters to him abroad kept him posted on the vagaries and virtues of Mr. Green, the most active of the commissioners and the keeper of the park purse. Mary wrote to her husband almost in the manner of a colleague, above and beyond her care for him as a wife. "Mr. Green was here," she wrote on October 10, 1859. "He talked Park nearly all the time. . . . He likes your taste in planting and wants you to help lay out his place at Worcester. . . . If you feel that you can trust Mr. Green's generosity, stay until you feel quite well—and do not work yourself up in the absurd manner to which you are given. I must confess he frets me with his manner of thinking himself so much more efficient than you or anybody else." And about the Park she said, "Mr. Grant, in reply to my query as to what he might wish to say to you—says—'The work is going on very well with the force allowed us.'" Mary knew how he cared for the welfare of the people in the park. About them, she wrote: "They are all they say shaking in their shoes, as they have been ever since you went away. They come to me and complain in the most naive manner as though it were a compliment to you. I hope I am not indiscreet."[24]

Mr. Andrew Haswell Green wrote kindly to Fred: "I hope you are attending to your health as well as to business. Are you? Let health and repose *be the first thing.* I look for you about the middle of December. [He wrote on October 21, 1859.] Would be glad you were here today in my own account, but want you to recruit."[25] A sidelight upon the formidable Mr. Green came to Fred from one of his superintending foremen, A. I. Dallas, on October 25: "Mr. Green has concluded apparently much to my satisfaction to keep me upon the work. His bark appears to be worse than his bite. Mrs. Olmsted says he is fond of disconcerting people! I am sure he did, me."[26]

On October 24, telling Fred—"My dear old man"—that she was somewhat reluctantly going away for a visit to Hartford from the house she had got in order in the Park, Mary wrote again of Green. "Green here, disappointed in his position. [There had been a reorganization of the commissioners by the politicians in Albany.] He growled a great deal."[27]

Mary supplied the portions of wit, fondness, and a certain sharpness that suited Fred in a wife. Vaux was both soothing and salty in his friendship and in their working relationship. They could say what they pleased to each other and not give a hang about the niceties. So, when Fred Olmsted came back in December, 1859, he returned to a life which, although compounded of struggle and some private tragedy, was to suit him.

A letter of February 6, 1860, to his father tells the story of Fred's contentment: "We are getting on very well. Mary has a bad cold but slides along pretty well. [She was five months pregnant.] The children have bad colds, but recover rapidly. We have had our little porcelain stove put together and up in the parlor and it is pretty and works well. Have had lots of papering, painting, and . . . cleaning [done] and begin to see some prospect of an end in some places for the present. I am fairly well and working more steadily than usual and with less wear . . . Altogether as happy, all of us, as you can imagine possible. . . . What they do at Albany I don't know, but have not much fear—and at all events, they can't destroy the present, which is ours."[28]

His third book about the South, *A Journey through the Back Country,* was being published this year. He was happy in his work in the park— ridiculously so, Vaux told him. His partner could never understand the way Olmsted bound himself to the carrying out of the plan they had made on paper. He himself was interested in a number of other things, and although he had an official position with the park subordinate to Olmsted, he continued to do architectural work on his own. Olmsted, on the other hand, let himself be concerned with every detail of the park and felt an intense joy in its coming into being.

Frederick's reference to Albany was to the threat of an investigation of the park by the legislature. "Somebody's spending a good deal of money in embarrasing [this is Olmsted's spelling] us."[29] Yet meanwhile, whatever the politicians might do to their park, Fred continued to be wrapped up in it. And there was a promise of more city work for the two young men who had planned the Central Park. In April, 1860, they were appointed "Landscape Architects and designers to the Commissioners north of 155th Street." They would henceforth slip into the role of planners for the city beyond the strict limits of park designers. In the next decades they would plan many parks for the city and be concerned with the approaches, the surroundings, and the connections of parks. It became a broad matter of neighborhoods, streets, and the design of the whole city.

And outside Central Park it was not only Mr. Green who desired their private services. He asked them to come up to Worcester and look over the private grounds of the old house he loved and help him lay out trees and lawn in a more fitting way. Very soon in their Central Park career, other private individuals and institutions began to call upon the young men who had made the "Greensward" plan to ask them to make plans for different kinds of projects or simply to give advice. George S. Schuyler, a member of the old family intermarried with the Hamilton family, asked Fred Olmsted for advice about a reservoir for his estate up the river. The Hartford Retreat for the Insane asked Olmsted and Vaux to design the grounds of the institution. Together now, using Vaux's office on Broadway, they surrendered to the lure of doing a small amount of private work in landscape design. Yet if rude circumstances had not shaken Frederick Olmsted loose from his close superintendence of the park, he might, as he thought later, have been happy to stay for decades in that small circle of duties bounded by Fifty-ninth Street and 110th Street. He might never have broken out into the full practice of the profession which was to take him north to Montreal, west to San Francisco, and south to Atlanta.

His only other absorption was in his family, and his family was a part of his park life. He and Mary and the children lived in the park. His own first son was born on June 14, 1860, in the house at Mount St. Vincent. He described the event reverently. In a letter to his father, he wrote, "Just in the earliest flush of dawn—the birds all singing—the boy came, with a great cry—strong and big—a good nine-pounder (P.S. 10½ pounds official. You see I am modest, but the doctor says it is extraordinarily large for so small a woman) with a three cornered nose and other 'Olmsted' marks, which Mary sees better than I do. His name is John Theodore. . . . It was the largest child Mary has borne and she had had her hardest labor, but she seems now remarkably comfortable and is very happy. . . . The children are all delighted, except Charlotte, who would rather God had made a sister."[30]

There was a fullness to life at Mount St. Vincent. The new child seemed to thrive. "He behaves like a young pugilist,"[31] Mary wrote to her father-in-law. Frederick was simply strengthened by the burden of another mouth to feed. It was as if Mount St. Vincent were his stronghold and the park his kingdom when he went out to a summons such as that of his assistant Mr. Grant who asked him on June 29 to inspect the outlines of the Lower Pond before work went any further. Olmsted also spent considerable time beyond the bounds of the park in work for the city, exploring the "very rugged and beautiful ground"[32] of upper Manhattan. It was almost as it had been before it was passed over by Dutch, English, and Yankee invaders of the island. Scattered farms, estates, a few roads, but the high, rocky, and broken terrain was much as the Indians had known it. Olmsted and Vaux concluded that this part of the island was ill adapted to the gridiron pattern of cross streets and north and south avenues which prevailed in the lower part of Manhattan. They intended to say so in their "preliminary plan." Meanwhile it was a joy to take possession in their imaginations of this virgin part of the island.

On August 6, 1860, Olmsted had a carriage accident.[33] Driving in or near the park, he lost his grip on the reins and the horse went out of control. He was thrown violently out of the carriage. Apparently, but this is not clear, Mary and the baby were in the carriage, and were carried along till the horse stopped. Olmsted had to be picked up off the ground, and carried first to a nearby house which strangely turned out to be that of his old friend Charles Trask. His knee was shattered. He was in such bad condition that the leg could not at first be set. When it was set, it did not heal easily. Doctors even debated taking the leg off, but feared that the act would kill him, for he was weak still from a fever.

Even while the doctors debated the proper treatment for his shattered knee, Frederick had men in from the park only two days after the accident and directed them to spread maps and charts on the floor of the bedroom, so that he could carry on his work.

Eight days after the accident, the child John Theodore died. Whether the child died naturally from the kind of weakness and sickness that affected so many newborn children of the time, or whether the carriage accident had something to do with it, is not clear. Olmsted always at least associated the two events in his mind, as one may see in a later letter he wrote to Mary when he was away in war service. That the matter was not clear, at least at first, to his friends is borne out by a letter which Fred Kingsbury in Waterbury, Connecticut, wrote on August 17 to his old schoolmate:

> My dear Fred,
> The papers said that Mary and the baby were unhurt when the horse ran, but the baby's death so soon afterward has led me to fear that they might have both been more injured than was supposed at the time. I shall be very glad to learn that my fears are groundless so far as Mary is concerned.[34]

Outpourings of sympathy and offers of help came from friends.[35] Richard Grant White of the *World* wrote; "I have no brother. Treat me as if I had one and you were he." The engineer Asboth, with whom Frederick had been surveying upper Manhattan, wrote Mary in flowery sincerity, "Whilst expressing my deep regret for the Calamity which has again befallen you, I beg leave to request that you will allow me the privilege of joining Mr. Olmsted's friends in watching at his bedside and will please to indicate what nights my services would be acceptable." Charles Dana, who had been Olmsted's friend since the days of *Putnam's*, sent a gift of wine on August 20. George Curtis, with a similar thought of comfort, wrote that he would come September 2 and "bring that famous bottle of old Madeira." In the meantime, he sent books.

Fred was physically hurt, but he escaped serious emotional hurt, unlike Mary, who was struck double blows, in Fred's injury and in the baby's death. Two months after the accident she was suffering sharp headaches, and Fred came to the conclusion that she would get better rest by going away from Mount St. Vincent. She was sent away to visit relatives. Fred's healing continued slowly and his knee continued to be stiff. After two months, Fred wrote his father that he was only learning to seat and unseat himself. With crutches by the bed, in an emergency, he could dress himself. But he had to wear a splint, and he was bandaged at night "from toe to hip." For help in learning to use the leg, a man was hired to live in. This helper also gave gymnastic lessons to the children, who had remained, it seems, at Mount St. Vincent. The children also had a new governess who gave them school lessons at home. With Fred's strong approval, she introduced regularity and discipline into learning, with short periods of sitting still and intervals of vigorous runs up and down the glass gallery. Up until this time, one has the impression that the children had learned their lessons in a rather hit-or-miss fashion and had moved about and missed school altogether for long periods. The children thrived on this new regularity, and, as Fred drily put it, "I think Charley may be expected to learn to read, after all." Charley was almost eight years old at this time.

Fred had not let himself be absorbed completely in his misfortunes. He had taken a sharp interest in the education of the children. He had insisted that Mary go away to her relatives in Boston when she showed the need for rest and change. He had not for a moment lost his grip on the operations of the park. He had a grim satisfaction in having beaten the doctors' odds. One practitioner had said in the desperate early hours of his injury that his chances were "not one in a hundred." He learned to use the crutches. He would soon be on canes. He prided himself on his agility although he swung himself along with a decided dip. If he could not get out on rough ground in the ordinary way, he would have the men "tote" him.[36]

In November he had an exhilarating day making "a long reconnaissance" at Fort Washington. Two men from the park carried him on a litter. Asboth, the city engineer, accompanied him. When the party came to a tricky fence, Olmsted crawled or rolled through a gap. He had a "fine time," he said. Another day, while Mary was away, he had the carriage hitched up—not stopped by the memory of the accident—and drove Charley and Charlotty, as he called the little girl, on a fine evening all the way to the scene of the surveying on the promontory at Fort Washington, "glorious day and the views finer as the leaves leave openings."[37] One can imagine him looking down on an unspoiled Hudson River where no bridge crossed, knowing what ought to be done in this upper region of Manhattan and what ought not to be done. (His advice would not, in the end, be followed.)

People petted him. The actress Charlotte Cushman and her friend Miss Stebbins came to call and stayed to lunch. Miss Cushman promised him a box at her theater whenever he wished to go. "Wife being away I fall among Bohemians,"[38] he wrote his father. He viewed himself with irony but enjoyed the attention.

War looked possible. Olmsted's park-keepers drilled with muskets in the park. On October 24, "Captain J. T. Walker" of the Keepers invited their boss Mr. Olmsted to a "target excursion and dinner." Mr. Olmsted declined, and Captain Walker was hurt, thinking that the superintendent's declining the invitation was due to Olmsted's consciousness of a difference of "stations" between them. This came back to the superintendent. Fred sat down and wrote a long letter to Walker disclaiming with horror his care about "stations." He tried to explain to Walker how he had himself worked for low pay and educated himself. His explanation is curious, as if he were writing a letter to himself.

Your modest reminder therefore that I should have excused your difference of opinion with me, on account of the difference of our "stations in life," and the lack of advantages on your part are uncalled for. I feel no fixed difference to exist in our stations in life. [And] The best of my travelling has been done on foot at a cost of 70 cts. a day, or working my passage as a common seaman. My practical horticultural education, I mean that not gained by reading, was in part acquired while engaged as a laborer, looking to working men as my masters and teachers. It is then impossible for me to have any hearty or habitual respect for the superiority of one man over another, in stations in life except as superiority of station means higher responsibility and larger duty. . . . I am happy to believe that of the present force no man would remain a month after he felt the duty required of him to be unreasonable or degrading in the slightest degree of his true manhood.[39]

He was not quite candid even with himself here. He had not gone to China as "a common seaman." Although mistreated, he had gone as an apprentice officer. He had been one of the family rather than "laborer" at Fairmount. His background in family and education had, despite his belief in the equality of men through effort, always made a difference.

He held to a complicated and prideful sense of democracy, but he was, in practice, an autocratic and masterful man. He saw to it that workmen with his help set up a sick fund. Yet he fired summarily those who struck in sympathy with a force working outside the park. Even at the beginning of work in the park, when he was hounded by thousands of unemployed carrying "Bread and Blood" banners he had imposed order and discipline by the sheer force of his will: "I had almost no assistance but within a week I had a thousand men economically employed and rigidly discharged any man who failed to work industriously and to behave in a quiet soldierly manner."[40]

The overseers had pride in working under Olmsted. Men who left his employ spoke always later with high regard for the fact that they had worked for Mr. Olmsted in Central Park. Many of his subsupervisors and engineers distinguished themselves elsewhere, carrying not only Olmsted's ideas with them, but his methods of work also.

However much he gratified himself in his work, he lacked a balance wheel, Mary's presence in the house. "Your absence is more and more felt, but the household gets on better than it might.   Affection!"[41] So he ended a letter to her on November 15. Finding he could do without her no more, he gathered himself and the children together and collected Mary in Boston for a Thanksgiving visit to his father's house in Hartford. It was a troublesome, difficult trip. His wounded, balky leg impeded him. But the Olmsteds were reunited and had the satisfaction after visiting Fred's family of stopping in Waterbury to see Fred Kingsbury.

In August, 1860, the same month in which the carriage accident took place and the child John Theodore died, Frederick Olmsted's third book of southern travels, *The Back Country,* was published. The book added to the reputation of the man who was now principally known as the creator of New York's great park. "Thank you heartily for your book," wrote Henry

Bellows to him on November 3. The Reverend Henry W. Bellows, the pastor of the Church of All Souls (Unitarian) on Fourth Avenue, and a battler with the pen in the abolitionist cause, wrote, "It cannot but have a marked influence on public opinion; and to contribute anything to the settlement of this vexatious national question ought to satisfy the moral ambition of the best man."

Bellows had begun his letter by stating his fixed purpose to come up by horseback to visit Olmsted. He had been impeded by a balky horse. "I mean, however, the first fine day next week to start by 10 o'clock and get up to your castle."[42] He had caught the idea, like others, that Central Park was Olmsted's barony.

Olmsted was soon to be tempted by a duty which would take him away from the park. He wrote to Charles L. Brace at about this time something of what the park had meant to him. "It is not yet time to fully estimate the merit of the park as a work of art. There were great difficulties both essential and political (or social). The former consisted in the heterogeneous, barren and imobile [F. L. O.'s spelling] qualities of the ground to be dealt with. I believe that they have been overcome very successfully and that the park will not only be more convenient for exercise than any existing metropolitan pleasure-ground, its details more studied, more varied and substantial in character, but that there will be greater unity of composition, details being subordinate to general effects, than in any other. In anything you say [Brace was preparing to write an article about the park] remember that Vaux is to be associated." However, as to the management of the park, he was clear. "As to the organization and management of the work, I think it more creditable to me than anything I have done publicly. It was within a fortnight of a most exciting election (when Wood was defeated) and during the prevalence of bread-riots, a larger number of men being out of employment than at any previous period of the city's history, that the Common Council voted money to go on with the work and I was unexpectedly ordered to organize a large force for the purpose." As if still thinking that his part might not be recognized, Olmsted told again to his friend the tale of the early days of the park, the desperate men wanting work, the orderly way that tasks and authorities were organized, and how he was praised by a Swiss engineer hired to investigate the workings of the park by the state senate. This inspector carried out his task faithfully without consulting Olmsted and "reported the other day that [in] organization and superintendence it was most excellent and much better than in any other public work in the United States." And in this letter to an intimate, speaking almost as to himself, Olmsted still not quite sure that he was appreciated said, "I think it important to me that the public should know this and that I should have the credit of it. I am anxious to remain Superintendent of the park, that is."[43]

Several complicated emotions unfold themselves here. Olmsted still could not believe in other people's faith in him. He craved admiration which he was, in fact, receiving in abundance. For New York had become enamoured of the park. This green space, this "greensward," was being claimed as a piece of personal property by every citizen of the city who casually or habitually used it. Yet the park-maker still resisted believing in what he had done. The Fred Olmsted who had dreamed away years still lived within the energetic fibers of the doer of public deeds. He was yet to reconcile completely the two sides of his nature and to know within himself both the dreamer and the doer.

The inner struggle to be himself was exacerbated by a struggle he was having with the commissioners. As the most active and forceful of the commissioners, Andrew Haswell Green concentrated upon himself Frederick Olmsted's ire. The man was honest and respectable, but he wished to impose his ideas and his strict control upon the park. There could not be two rulers of this little kingdom. Green's care was real, but it was the money man's care. Green, in an era of careless and corrupt spenders, perhaps all the more so for a general acceptance of loose public morality, wished every cent spent on the Central Park to be accounted for to him. He held a tight rein on Olmsted, and Olmsted could not bear it. He was like a restive horse rubbed raw by bit and bridle. If he was to be given a job to do, let him be treated like a gentleman. He would do the work; he would be responsible both monetarily and artistically; the managers must just leave him alone. And, besides, they must furnish him the wherewithal, not asking questions, for him to do what he told them plainly must be done.

Mary, with the tender license of a wife, had told Fred not to work himself up in that "ridiculous way"[44] he had. It is evident that during the late months of 1860 and the early months of 1861 he did just that. Mr. Olmsted's public dignity rested upon a seething mass of volcanic feeling usually hidden from view. Only chance glimpses, as in occasional letters or notes in his private papers, reveal this truth about the man. Early in January, 1861, he decided suddenly to resign his job. He wrote a dignified letter informing the commissioners of his decision.

Gentlemen:

I cannot without sacrifice of self respect any longer allow myself to be held responsible for the duties implied by the designation, Architect-in-Chief and Superintendent of the Central Park. . . .

If I could be charged with any specific duties of design or of superintendence, or of both, being responsible directly to you and having sole control, the necessary means for a true and honorable performance of those duties, I could nowhere in the world put to better use such talent as I possess or live with more satisfaction to my tastes and inclinations than on the Central Park.[45]

He resigned as of the date of the next meeting of the commissioners, January 22, and proposed to appear before them then and explain his action.

(His swift anger had been caused, apparently, by a somewhat petty restriction put by Mr. Green upon the amount of money Mr. Olmsted could handle without detailed accounting beforehand.)

Having written his formal resignation and sent it off, boiling with emotion, disturbing himself and his household, he sat down to compose on paper what he would say when he came to his meeting with the commissioners. The scribbled pages remain. One doubts that he used much of it in his meeting. But he preserved this heap of paper, forty-one pages of an outpouring of himself.[46]

I did not lack confidence in myself. I knew and felt that the varied experience of my life had given me an eclectic power in which I had great confidence. And I knew that I could trust to that quality of my nature which from earliest childhood had given me a *delight and satisfaction* in landscape beauty, in picturesque beauty, which other children, other men rarely had in the degree in which I was endowed with it. . . . At the bottom of the most important function of my office, Mr. President, there must be something which you can not buy in any market, of good quality, merely for money. It is a natural, spontaneous, individual action of imagination—of *creative fancy.*

And more, in this conversation with his innermost self:

There are circumstances favorable to the action of this good instinct, and there are circumstances under which no amount of good intention and hard labor will produce good design. . . . The work of design necessarily supposes a gallery of mental pictures, and in all parts of the park I constantly have before me, more or less distinctly, more or less vaguely, a picture, which as Suptd. I am constantly laboring to realize. . . . I shall venture to assume to myself the title of artist and to add that no sculptor, painter or architect can have anything like the difficulty in sketching and conveying a knowledge of his design to those who employ him which must attend upon an artist employed for such a kind of designing as is required of me. The design must be almost exclusively in my imagination. No one but myself can feel, and without feeling no one can understand *at the present time* the true value or purport of much that is done in the park, much that needs to be done. . . . Does the work which has thus far been done accomplish my design? No more than stretching the canvas and chalking a few outlines, realizes the painter's. Why, the work has been thus far wholly and entirely with dead, inert materials, my picture is all alive—its very essence is life, human and vegetable.

He digressed to his past. He remembered being the French importer's clerk, entrusted with the petty cash including supper money for the other employees and "never after questioned of his handling of it." His indignation boiled over again. Here were these commissioners putting a pettier kind of accountability on him.

It was a different thing, Sir, when we commenced. [He still speaks as to the President of the Board of Commissioners.] I had no professional reputation, no professional standing, except what you had given—or rather given me the means of gaining myself. . . . And now, I say, after three years trial of me, I feel that if you are, now, unwilling to trust my judgment—to trust confidently and implicitly to my judgment—in such matters as I have referred to, that it is time you were rid of me altogether. I feel this sir, I feel it, and have felt it and spite of my sincere respect for you, spite of my real love for the park, and in spite of my personal habit of discipline and loyalty, which is a very strong and inherent element of my character.

and so on and so on.

Olmsted no doubt spoke with more control at the meeting. The commissioners, seeing and feeling his anger, backed down enough to make him more comfortable. He was "induced,"[47] as he said, to withdraw his resignation. He went on with his work in the park.

But during this year the outside world more and more invaded that place which had been like a kingdom to him. For one thing, Olmsted and his partner Vaux were asked to do more private work. On March 9, Dr. Brown of the Bloomingdale Asylum north of the city thanked them for advice and a diagram, as he called it, a plan for the grounds of the hospital. In May, Hugh Allan, a gentleman of Montreal, wrote them thanks for advice concerning disposition of his ten acres of ground. The other overwhelming outside incursion into their seclusion in the park was the war.

As early as December, 1860, before there was a shooting war, Frederick wrote to Charley Brace: "We intend to have two republics, peacably if we can. Fighting, if we must, don't we? But my mind is made up for a fight. The sooner we get used to the idea, the better, I think."[48] The new year of 1861 found him deeply involved in the thought of a coming struggle. He was conscious that he knew more about the South than most men in the North. As early as January, 1861, his English publisher Sampson Low suggested that he condense his three volumes of travel into one volume, which should be well received at this point. His publisher foresaw that the book would sell well. Olmsted agreed and was not squeamish in getting another man's help in making a condensation.

In February he wrote to Daniel R. Goodloe, a publicist for the abolitionist cause, asking him if he would undertake the job. He himself planned to offer a minor amount of advice and guidance. He did more than he had planned, but he also gave Goodloe some latitude. The editor's hand was on the whole skillful. He made some word changes, which somewhat generalized the vividness of Olmsted's original observations, but his editing of Olmsted's text was mostly a matter of cutting. The overall job was a good one. *The Cotton Kingdom* has a dramatic structure. Its narrative starts with the invasion of a strange territory by a guileless, naive, willing-to-learn traveler, continues with his involvement, and ends with his hard-earned conclusions, sympathetic to the South in intent but condemning all the institutions clustered around and made necessary or possible by the economic system of farming prevailing in the region.

On June 11, 1861, Olmsted shipped off the last of the manuscript to

London. First, an English edition and then an American edition were to come out. It was hoped that there would be a simultaneous powerful effect on the reading publics of both continents. Olmsted received a first copy of the book from his English publisher on October 25. The American edition was out on November 7.

By this time war had invaded the peaceable green and granite kingdom of the park. In April, after Fort Sumter, volunteers of the hastily raised regiments of the city drilled in the park and were quartered in the Arsenal. Writing to his father, Frederick stated on April 17: "We are full of fight. I am organizing a home-guard in the park and shall [have] above a hundred enrolled and under drill this afternoon.... My resignation and all that is before a Committee this week. If they throw me off, I shall volunteer for the navy and you must take care of my wife and children—unless you go too." This letter shows Olmsted entertaining two complicated trains of thought at once—about the park and the war. He continued, "I have told my men that I consider it a religious duty to strengthen the government by any means in my power, therefore they will be required to muster and drill every Sunday."[49] (Many New Yorkers were by no means this zealous. There was much excitement and haste in volunteering, but there was also a hanging back at this time by the merchant class. They had done most of their trading with the South.)

The commissioners refused to accept his resignation—again, as they had half a year earlier. But one day when he was away from Mount St. Vincent, Mr. Henry Bellows, the minister of social causes and advocacies, came to call. He told Mary that he and his friends intended to persuade Mr. Olmsted to accept the directorship of a new organization, a collection of loosely organized groups of volunteers all wishing to do work for the Northern troops. A formal letter concerning the subject came from Bellows in June: "I want to see you in regard to the *Resident Secretaryship* of our Sanitary Committee. I dare say you may think it very bold that we have entertained such *high* notions as taking you bodily from your important duties at the Park, and transferring you to Washington. But I trust I can present the matter in a form in which it will not be, or look, presumptuous. At any rate come see me if possible tomorrow as early as 10 o'clock. I want to see you if possible before the meeting of our Board at 11 A.M. tomorrow."[50]

It was inevitable that Frederick Olmsted would accept. This was his war duty presented to him in an acceptable form. The minutes of the meeting of the Sanitary Commission (as the new organization termed itself) recorded on June 20, 1861, the fact that Frederick Law Olmsted was elected "Resident Secretary of this body in Washington." Olmsted obtained a leave of absence from Central Park at a reduced salary. Mary and the children were to remain at least temporarily at Mount St. Vincent. Frederick Olmsted prepared to go to Washington to see about organizing a relief force for the "sick and wounded of the Army."

CHAPTER XV

Secretary of the Sanitary Commission

It is a good big work I have in hand.
—F. L. O., to his sister Bertha, January 28, 1862[1]

I N HIS FIRST DAYS in wartime Washington Olmsted seemed as if swimming through a motion of men and materials where nothing was orderly or controlled. Not only he, but everyone camped in the hot and humid capital this summer seemed to have lost his bearings. The army seemed a joke, ill provided for, its soldiers often without uniforms, its officers as ignorant as the men they were supposed to command. The volunteers who had joined in this effort were scornful of their lieutenants and often refused to salute generals whom they met in the streets. Each disorderly unit belonged more to its home district or state than to any national army. Its camps were scattered in disarray about the city on unhealthy ground, or ground soon made so by unsanitary practices. Dysentery, typhoid fever, and malaria began to be reported. Beyond the horizon in Virginia there was the rumor of an enemy, troops said to be out there, threatening the capital, but derided rather than feared, for it was all going to be over soon. Then hooray for home. (But Olmsted was soon to see the Confederates' flag from the top of a house in Washington.[2] He knew, beyond rumor, that they were there.)

The work he had in hand involved him in relations with individuals all of whom had strong ideas of their own. The men who organized the United States Sanitary Commission were a masterful and idiosyncratic group— among them a doctor, a lawyer, a preacher, a scientist, and military officers. The three military men appointed to the commission were nominal members; it was the civilians who remained active. Olmsted was to have the closest relations with these men for the next two years and was to be their principal agent. In the weeks of getting started in his work, it is probable that he cast a measuring eye upon them. He was to insist on being an equal among equals, wrestling with the Commissioners as with top-hatted and frock-coated angels or demons. These men were a distinguished group: President Henry W. Bellows, a reform-minded and popular preacher in New York City; Vice President Alexander Dallas Bache, head of the Coast Survey; Corresponding Secretary Elisha Harris, Doctor of Medicine; Treasurer George Templeton Strong, attorney at law and connoisseur of music and New York fires, also a conscientious vestryman of Trinity Church and a trustee of struggling little Columbia College; Dr. Wolcott Gibbs, professor of chemistry at City College; Philadelphia lawyer Charles Janeway Stille; Cornelius Rea Agnew, youthful-looking surgeon general of New York, soon to be in charge of the State Hospital for Veterans; Dr. William H. Van Buren, professor of surgery of Bellevue Hospital; Samuel G. Howe; J. S. Newberry; and others. They conceived their task as a preventive and support-ive one—to make the army of the republic as healthy before battle as pos-sible, as curative of wounds and illnesses during campaigns as might be, and as humane a body as an army could be. Bellows was to say that he poured ten years of his life into the four years of the war. They all worked at this pitch, but none, perhaps, at the wrought up level of their secretary-general. His was the only full-time position among them. He was included in their policy meetings but had also the daily direction of the work of the commis-sion.

Henry Bellows, the minister of the Church of All Souls (Unitarian) on Fourth Avenue, New York City, was an imposing personage, a man only eight years older than Frederick Olmsted himself, but seeming, with his bald dome and sparse hair, straight-gazing eyes, and firm mouth, much older. He usually wore dark ministerial suits with much expanse of white shirtfront. He was straight in figure and commanding in bearing. Persuasive, charming, somewhat overbearing, capable of expressions of religion and patriotism which were overrich in sentiment, he was a man who loved his own power of command and delighted in being important. He was also intelligent, persistent, and devoted to good causes. He disarmed his friends by freely admitting his faults. He was to write Olmsted one day, "You must allow me to prance around now and then on my official horse and wink at folly without publicly laughing." Olmsted understood and respected Bellows, al-though he occasionally made fun of him. There was to be a warm and frank friendship between them which only intense strain threatened. Like Olm-sted, Bellows had had experience of the South before the war. He had preached first in Mobile and before that tutored in a wealthy Louisiana fam-ily. He had gained firsthand knowledge of habits and attitudes very different from those of Walpole, New Hampshire, where he was born, and Northamp-ton, Massachusetts, where he had gone to school.

By the end of July, 1861, the city, the president, the army, the Sanitary Commission and its secretary, were faced with the lowest possible tilt of their fortune. The overconfident army, pursued by congressmen on a picnic, marched out to meet the Southern troops outside the city, were more or less routed, and returned, some without their guns or any other supplies, their wounded abandoned or thirsting and starving. Olmsted, an onlooker in the sweltering streets, saw the shameful condition of the Union Army as it poured pell-mell back into Washington from Bull Run. He suffered in the sight and sat down to write his impressions of the cause of the demoralization of certain of the troops (not all, he was careful to discriminate). His pointed analysis seemed too sharp for immediate publication, but it had circulation among the members of the commission. Treasurer George T. Strong wrote on September 16 in his diary of a commission meeting: "There was much discussion about a queer, clever report by Olmsted as to causes of the volunteer demoralization that culminated in the race to Washington after Bull Run. An able paper, certainly, but its publication would have done mischief—would have retarded recruiting."[3] Some of this paper was published, however, as Appendix IV to the year-end report of the commission and entitled "Some Notes of An Inspection of A Part of the Forces Engaged in the Battle of Bull Run."

Frederick wrote to his wife out of the hot dismay of the moment on July 29: "Many regiments are but a mob, they are part of a disintegrated herd of sick monomaniacs. They start and turn pale at the breaking of a stick or the crack of a percussion cap. At the same time they are brutal savages.... But they are fast recovering." And he said also, "Our commission can do something and I from my position in it can do something to set public opinion in the right direction and overcome in some details the prevailing inefficiency and misery. You would not have me do less than I can."[4] Olmsted was being drawn by his imagination into the war, and he had less and less time for his family and Central Park. Yet he still yearned toward that fast-receding time when his life centered around Mount St. Vincent.

To him, his wife wrote on August 4,

My darling Fred,

I don't know that I have anything much to say to you except that I love you dearly and want to see more of you and wish that this undesired war were over and the times were prosperous again. When are you coming back again? Say when. I see by the paper that your session is over and that Congress adjourned this week so why don't you come?

I think your aids will be able to work splendidly when you have once started them. . . . This time when you come come to stay a fortnight at least if you love me.

Why don't you write. I don't call that rhodomontade you sent me a letter to a wife tho' I dare say that you there in the focus of the trouble are more affected than me who takes a more extended and distant view.

I wanted you to go because I thought you would be happier there, than here with me, on the Park, and if you do not exert yourself to be happy you see I am swindled, besides being as it appears, impoverished.

Mary told him in this letter that she had had word from Mr. Green that he was going to issue his salary check "for only two weeks unless you came back and asked for more. Do so I beg of you. I think they hardly need cut you off this month as you had two weeks leave and it has always been assumed that you have a right to a little holiday." She went on:

> Don't consider that I mean to reproach you dear, only you are, I am afraid, so much given over to the contemplation of the enemy that you will forget all about the temporal wants of your wife and babies—if not constantly reminded, and yet you always seem to feel as tho' I doubted your kind intentions whenever I break out about our not being as successful and rich as I would like. But you must know that I love and respect you so you must let me jog your memory of filthy lucre very often if only for my own gratification. But pray do make lots of money so that we may be freer from anxiety on the children's account than we are now. You cant think how I miss you dear. There is nobody but you who is my husband in spite of all the worry I am in about you. Who do you find pleasant and satisfactory to meet with there! You are cruel not to tell me more of your doing and surrounding. I am so much interested and have so little outside of myself that is entertaining—now that you are away. I see a good deal of the Vaux', but they are neither of them very well or cheerful just now. . . .
>
> Yours lovingly[5]

Olmsted worried about affairs in the Park and at Mount St. Vincent. He returned to New York City from time to time; at the end of the year he noted that he had spent six weeks' time there. Yet it was undeniable that what Mary discerned was true, that he belonged, at this time, less and less to New York, and more and more to Washington.

Affairs in the capital city had a kind of fascination, flattering to those looking on. Like others in the city, Olmsted was interested in the character of the president. Like many others at the beginning of the administration, Olmsted jumped hastily to conclusions about Lincoln, thinking that he was lacking in firmness, would probably be dependent upon others for direction, and was common in his manners. He had seen Lincoln in the street and had not been impressed: "Looked as if he would be an applicant for a Broadway squad policemanship, but a little too smart and careless. Turned and laughed familiarly at a joke upon himself which he overheard from my companion *en passant.*" As for Mr. Lincoln's city in midsummer, it was cursed with flies, "far worse than Staten Is'd in fish time."[6] He found himself in a capital city in wartime in which many of the elements seemed as tentative as his own organization. This was the kind of situation into which Olmsted enjoyed plunging and straightening things out.

The nearest thing which needed order was the Sanitary Commission itself. (He would later try his hand at the more outlying parts of the government which directly affected the commission's operation.) He understood very well what the task of the commission was. The public, in the warmest, most impulsive way, wished to give tangible goods to the men in the army—clothes, food, bandages, nursing help. Professional medical men and officials of charitable organizations saw things more complexly. They wished to avoid the catastrophic mistakes made by other nations in recent wars, such as the Crimean conflict, in which more men died of disease and neglect and lack of knowledge than of wounds. The large task was to bring science to the service of a large body of men involved in the operations of war waged across half the width of a continent.

Henry Bellows had brought into being the United States Sanitary Commission as a pooling of the interests of several organizations. He persuaded the Women's Central Association of Relief for the Sick and Wounded of the Army, the Advisory Committee of the Boards of Physicians and Surgeons of the Hospitals of New York, and the New York Medical Association for Furnishing Hospital Supplies in Aid of the Army to sink their separate identities in one agency to be called the United States Sanitary Commission. On May 18, 1861, the members of the proposed organization petitioned the Secretary of War to allow them to operate under a charter from the government, their stated purpose being to "contribute towards the comfort and security of our troops, by methodizing the spontaneous benevolence of the city and State of New York."[7] They asked only office space and stationery from the government, no funds. And almost immediately their intended and understood scope expanded to take in all "spontaneous" contributions from whatever part of the country for the benefit of federal troops wherever they should operate.

They had to argue persuasively. The war was going to be short, nearly everyone thought. There would not be great numbers of wounded men to care for. Why should professional men in the military require civilian help? But Bellows and the other gentlemen of the commission insisted and would not be put off. It was in this period that Lincoln had doubts of the enterprise and thought that this civilian commission might be the awkward "fifth wheel" to the military undertaking. By good luck, Acting Surgeon General R. C. Wood approved the project. Next Secretary of War Simon Cameron was brought to concurrence. Lincoln, after some demurral and a last minute lobbying appeal from Bellows, agreed at last to the chartering of the organization. On June 13, 1861, Lincoln added to the paper which the Secretary of War had signed ordering the charter of the United States Sanitary Commission: "I approve the above. A. Lincoln."[8]

When Frederick Olmsted was elected secretary-general in a meeting on June 20, 1861, the organization was a legal entity, but not much else. A draft of powers specified that the commission's concern was to be with the health of the volunteers, with diet, clothing, tents, grounds, transport, depots, camp police, military hospitals, women as nurses, hospital supplies, ambulances, field service, the care of the sick and wounded. But the draft also stated that the commission was to exist "for purposes only of inquiry and advice." Under these terms, Olmsted principally, but backed by his executive committee, carved out the shape and forceful edge of the organization. Neither he nor the officers of the commission intended to rest upon the vague and limiting powers defined in their charter. They intended to do more, and soon did.

Olmsted wasted no time. On July 9, 1861, he made his first report on the conditions of installations around the city of Washington:[9] "Your Resident Secretary has inspected twenty of the volunteer camps during the last ten days." Olmsted and a medical member of the commission, Dr. Elisha Harris, traveled together and noted such items as poor drainage in the tents, allowing two inches of water to stand during heavy rains, and the universally bad management of latrines. "In most cases the only sink is merely a straight trench, some thirty feet long, unprovided with a pole or rail; the edges are filthy, and the stench exceedingly offensive; the easy expedient of daily turning fresh earth into the ditch being often neglected. In one case men with diarrhoea complained that they had been made sick to vomiting by the incomplete arrangement and filthy condition of the sink. Often the sink is too near the camp. In many regiments, the discipline is so lax that the men avoid the use of the sinks, and the whole neighborhood is rendered filthy and pestilential."

While Olmsted personally examined hospitals and camps near Washington, other members of the board looked at conditions in the captured coastal areas and the western commands. Reports began coming into the headquarters, which was one room in the Treasury Department. But this space was soon inadequate. The government was going to have to furnish more than one baize-covered table and one row of chairs in a spare room to these energetic gentlemen. After Bull Run, needs were felt and it had to be acknowledged that the commission might help. Under Olmsted's relentless leadership, the organization expanded. The transformation worked itself out rapidly and may be framed by quotations from two of Olmsted's letters to his wife. On July 29, after Bull Run, he wrote, "We are in frightful condition here."[10] On September 18, he wrote, "I have completed a large organization."[11] So speedily did he work and make others work that in two months he had systematized, prescribed, and deputized the operation. He set up routines but made allowances also for emergencies. In one major department of the commission's functions he centralized the soliciting and storing of gifts, which were placed in convenient warehouses. Under the control of his men, these goods could be removed and transported quickly to points near battles and, when called for, to the actual battlefields. In another area of service, he expanded the work of medical inspectors, sending them to every division and, in time, to every regiment, armed with a carefully laid-out course of questions to be answered. He took pride in the office of "actuary" (statistician) which he instituted. His office soon began compiling a formidable set of facts about the conditions of the unprecedentedly large number of men under arms in the service of the nation. The commission was also the publisher on a large scale of simple, practical bulletins of information and instruction for the use of medical men in the army, facts about diseases, wounds, treatments, medicines, sanitation, diet, and other subjects. Olmsted also instituted a different kind of publication, that of scientific monographs by medical men, studies of wounds and diseases in war. In the secretary's mind, the commission was an agency which would not only succor the sick and wounded but would study all the disabilities of a great army in a scientific framework. These records would serve the community after the present convulsion had ended. This was a late fruit of Olmsted's early youthful scientific bent, shown years before in his boyhood following of "experiments" at Yale. It was his ambition to add to human knowledge through the researches of the medical men attached to the commission.

In mid-October the United States Sanitary Commission in Washington moved into its own building, lent by the government, a residence at 244 F Street, known as the Adams House. Frederick Olmsted took possession of this headquarters with pride. He wrote to his wife about this "fine old house occupied once by Madison, John Q. Adams, etc." The commission, he said, "had a room freshly papered ... and bedded, ready for me, opening into a fine board room, which when the Board [was] not in session will be my private office or parlor."[12] Like other older houses in the city, it fronted the street directly, with only a stoop separating its entryway from the passersby. Number 244 was to be a busy doorway on F Street throughout the war, with horses and carriages hitched in front, wagons stopping, civilian and military visitors coming and going. It was to be the center of all the activities of the commission although, later, an office on Broadway in New York City would become important as the principal meeting place of the executive committee; and many depots, warehouses, and subsidiary offices were to be established throughout the North and the West. Here, at least in busy times, Olmsted lived as well as worked. His nominal places of residence had been first Willard's Hotel, then the Paris Hotel, owned by a freedman and frequented by congressmen, and then, as his father noted in his diary, "Fredk's Washington address, 185 South B St., corner of W. 9th, back of Smithsonian."[13] A draft of the powers intended for the commission had stated, "The Secretary should be a gentleman of special competency, charged with the chief executive duties of the Commission, in constant correspondence with its President; be resident at Washington; and admitted to confidential intimacy with the Medical Bureau and the War Department. Under him such agents as could safely be trusted with the duties of inspection and advice in camps, hospitals, fortresses, etc., should work, receiving instructions from, and reporting to, him."[14] From 244 F Street Olmsted filled out this sketch in a robust fashion and never hesitated in the interests of the commission to take the largest interpretation of his duties.

While Frederick dug himself into the work in Washington, Mary yearned toward him, never really agreeing with his proscription of her presence in Washington. She kept up tart good spirits, and was frank in criticism. She was expecting a child again. "Keep a good heart and order me home by telegraph when necessary," wrote her husband to her on September 28, 1861.

In the same letter in which he told Mary to "keep a good heart," Frederick began to show the strain of the perpetual battle he was waging for the commission. After the exhilaration of the initial accomplishment of organization, he realized the difficulties the North faced in the war: "I am disheartened. I can see nothing but humiliation and the destruction of any patriotic hope and pride before us, except a miraculous man such as does not show his head in the least soon appears." He had recently stood upon the White House grounds during a concert. Mrs. Lincoln, whom he did not like, appeared upon the portico accompanied by a known political huckster—"That insufferable beast Wycoff.... We have no greatness; no heroism; no art. Dear me! I am ashamed of myself for talking to you so, but I am sick of it."[15]

But Frederick Olmsted the father took time to write amusing letters to his oldest son John Charles (John Hull's son). To this lively, curious boy, who was nine years old on September 14, he wrote on October 17, 1861, a letter which he printed with painful care. (Ordinarily Fred Olmsted drove his pen across paper with the speed of thought and took no pains to make his penmanship easy to read.

Dear Charley,
    There was a man who had been on picket duty and got nervous and tired. And when he got through, and got some coffee he laid down in his tent with his gun by his side, and his feet out the door of the tent, and he went to sleep and had a dream. He dreamed that Beauregard was comeing. And he woke up, and when he opened his eyes he saw his toes against the sky out of the door, and he thought his toes were Beauregard and a squad of men comeing over the hill; so he pointed his gun, which was already pointed that way, toward them, and pulled the trigger, and shot four of his toes right off. And then I think he woke quite up. And Bishop Clark saw him in the hospital today, and he only had one toe and that was what he said. And the doctor said he thought it was so.
    I went to the White House to-day and· saw the President. He is a very tall man. He is not a handsome man. He is not graceful. But he is good. He speaks frankly and truly and straight out just what he is thinking. Commonly he is very sober but sometimes he laughs. And when he laughs he laughs very much and opens his mouth very deep. He said he was glad to see me and shook hands with me. It seemed as if he was. He did not look proud nor cross but a good sort of fellow.
    Give my love to Mother and Charlotte and let me know if anything goes wrong.

                                                      Your affectionate father[16]

The tenderness and care and good humor of this letter to the small boy were characteristic; as much so were the bad grammar ("laid") and the misspelling ("comeing") of the clever man, who never learned correctness in his vivid writing.

To Mary, Frederick wrote two days later (October 19), "My Dearest Love, I hope this silvery weather is with you and is brightening you." He confirmed to his wife his more favorable impression of the president, "He was very awkward and ill at ease in attitude, but spoke readily, with a good vocabulary, and with directness and point. Not eloquently. 'I heard of that,' he said, but it did not seem very wrong from him, and his frankness and courageous directness overcame all critical disposition." He told her of enjoying the new house of the commission: "I am only ashamed to be enjoying it away from or without you—but let it not be without you. God strengthen and cheer you, darling.   Fred."[17]

On October 25, he received from England the first copies of *The Cotton Kingdom* to be printed and sold for two dollars in New York, and perhaps to be a help to the North in the struggle. "*It is selling well* in advance of publication. They think two editions will be called for."[18]

On October 28, Frederick's first own child to live, a girl to be named Marion, was born, and this child of a creator of the park was born in Central Park at Mount St. Vincent. Frederick was there, at least shortly afterwards. His first letter telling of the event, dated November 6, is to his sister Mary: "We want to call her Content, but Vaux makes such a fuss about it, that it's like to be Contention unless you can settle it. He says we ought to have some regard for her opinion. *Do* folks whose name is Content don't like it? Ask father." He thought the baby "a regular Tom gal, she pouts and makes faces at me, horrid, every time I go near her. Mrs. Lucas says it's only wind, but it's what they used to call spunk when I did it."[19] He told his sister that he should have to go to Philadelphia the next day (November 7) for a commission conference. By mid-November he was back in Washington. The cold weather coming on filled him with anxiety for wounded troops freezing on battlefields, mostly imaginary so far.

Yet in New York, he had seen people strolling the paths and carriages rolling on the roadways he had made, as if the war could not be conceived. Coming back to Mount St. Vincent reawakened Olmsted's bitterness toward the park commissioners, especially Andrew Green. He had not resolved his situation here. On November 12, he wrote and preserved the draft of a letter—probably not sent in the form in which first written—to C. H. Russell, one of the park commissioners to whom on a recent occasion he had incautiously expressed some of his anger.

My conviction is—and it certainly has been acquired with reluctance and deliberation enough—that the limits within which it might have been possible for me to effectually serve the Central Park Commission, have been gradually, skilfully, carefully and circumspectly curtailed. From the day when Mr. Green received the first installment of a salary larger than that of the architect-in-Chief and Superintendent, there has been a constant effort not only to assume more important responsibilities and more valuable duties, but to include all other duties and responsibilities within his own, and to make those of the inferior office not only completely and servilely subordinate but to make them appear of a temporary value only and unimportant even temporarily.

And he went on hotly, "For the means of performing what duties were then yet nominally allowed me I was made so absolutely and to the last detail dependent on Mr. Green's pleasure—not possessing the smallest right by which I could employ my judgment otherwise than in subjection to his." And so on and so on. He admitted handsomely, "Mr. Green's services as a politician have been perhaps essential to the Commission," but "he has continued to pursue a course toward me, of which no honest man could know himself subject without occasionally giving more or less articulate vent to feelings such as I was so unfortunate as to betray to you."[20]

Leaving his affairs in New York unresolved, he returned to uncertainty in Washington, D.C. Yet, for the sake of the Sanitary Commission, he was stiffened by a desire to win through to a time when the public should catch up with a true knowledge of things. For the North, this was a time of sagging away from the high spirits aroused by the drumbeats of the previous spring when the firing on Fort Sumter had awakened a quick and easy patriotism. General McClellan continued to prepare for war, but he did not fight, at least he mounted no major campaign in the East. He organized and drilled into good shape the army which had shown disarray at Bull Run, but at each apparent opportunity for action he found that his army was not ready. A sporadic action like Ball's Bluff was like a warning; Union troops, surprised and unready, were massacred; and for Olmsted, there was an alarming lesson of an ambulance corps untrained and hesitant—men shot by officers to force them into rescuing the wounded.

The delayer McClellan was, however, a protector to the Sanitary Commission. As he made ready his great army for a move southward, he gave every opportunity to Olmsted and his inspectors to carry on their work in all the camps and forts east and west. Olmsted visited McClellan frequently and assessed him shrewdly, coming out on the side of admiration. He found him "a very fine animal. . . . To us his attitude and in effect his words were, 'We are working for the same ends. I have entire confidence in you: you know more of medical and sanitary matters than I do. Tell me what ought to be done and it shall be done. I do not care who is in my way nor what."[21] Olmsted's loyal liking for McClellan lasted through the campaign they were to share and in which the general lost the president's support. Olmsted would never forget that it was this general who gave his commission its chance.

At this time of low national morale, the commission deliberately pushed its influence into matters beyond its prescribed sphere. In doing so, it endangered its future, but its leaders thought the effort was worth it. Strong wrote with his characteristic private vigor in his diary of a recent meeting, "The business before us was to kick out the Surgeon-General; to get our hospital plans approved and the work of erecting them begun."[22] The hospital plans were for "pavilion" hospitals, new buildings to be erected especially to care for the war's wounded, buildings in a new style, with plenty of circulation of air, and ease of movement all on a ground level for doctors and nurses; structures with plumbing facilities especially designed for a new kind of care. The army's sick and wounded had been nursed in old government buildings, often with poor air and light, inconvenient and dirty. What the commission asked for was revolutionary, and it was one of the principal ideas of William Alexander Hammond, the young assistant surgeon who was the commission's choice for surgeon general.

In order to see Dr. Hammond installed in the position of surgeon general, they had to see to it that the incumbent in the position, Dr. Clement A. Finley, was removed. Dr. Finley, who had been in the service since 1818, was, in their blunt terms, unfit for the complicated and strenuous efforts just ahead. When Congress asked him to say what he needed for his Medical Bureau, he made such modest and—in the mind of Olmsted and Bellows and their fellow commissioners—such inadequate requests, that he proved the point of his unfitness for the job. Finley, a fiercely upright elderly man, with a strong sense of the importance of his past service and present authority, resented the commission bitterly; he considered it an upstart civilian and amateur intrusion into the proper business which he had spent a lifetime mastering.

William Alexander Hammond, an assistant surgeon in the medical bureau of the army, had attracted the attention of the Sanitary Commission men by writing unsparing and incisive reports of the bad condition of army hospitals at Grafton, Virginia, and Cumberland, Maryland. The Commission circulated these hospital reports among their own documents. Hammond was thirty-three in 1861, a neurologist with a bent toward scientific research, a talent which he had exercised even in the dusty outposts of duty to which a decade's service in the Indian campaigns had assigned him. In 1857 he had published a study, "Experimental Researches Relative to the Nutritive Value and Physiological Effects of Albumen, Starch, and Gum," which had won a prize from the American Medical Association. In 1859 after ten years in frontier army posts in New Mexico, Kansas, and Florida, and a tour of duty at the United States Military Academy at West Point, he resigned to become professor of anatomy and physiology at the University of Maryland. When the war broke out, he volunteered for the army medical service once more. He reentered at the foot of the list of army surgeons, having lost his seniority by the break in his service. The commission attempted to influence Secretary of War Cameron and President Lincoln in favor of Hammond. These efforts seemed at first to come to little but to earn the commission the reputation for meddling in affairs which did not concern it.

A sharp campaign against the United States Sanitary Commission began in November, 1861, in the New York *Daily-Times*. Strong wrote privately, "The old Surgeon General has been making war on us through the *Times*. Raymond is his personal friend."[23] Olmsted's former employer, Henry J. Raymond, editor of the *Times*, published alternately a series of anonymous letters and editorials, the one abusing, the other solemnly lecturing the commission on its supposed shortcomings. The editorial on November 25 alleged that "the gentlemen who have the direction of its affairs, are in some danger of greatly impairing if not wrecking its [the commission's] usefulness by neglecting their proper sphere of duty and meddling mischievously with matters which are already in competent and experienced hands. We hear serious complaints that the Commission has become less attentive and efficient in what was, at the outset, regarded as its special field of effort,— attention to the sanitary conditions of the soldiers in camps, and is bitten by the ambition of superseding, or at least remodeling, the established Medical Bureau of the regular army."

The anonymous correspondent signed himself or herself "Truth." The writer was reputed to be a Miss Powell, a friend of Raymond's. The article on December 4 was sharp. "Truth" applauded the recent editorial in the paper for "suggesting to the Sanitary Commission that they turn their attention to the sick soldiers in the camps, before assuming to teach an experienced medical officer his duty . . . and has led to the hope that the Commission may yet do some little good, to make up for the vast amount of trouble they have incurred, and the large sums of money,—taken principally from the pockets of New Yorkers—which is necessary to defray their monthly expenses here." (The dateline for "Truth" was Washington, D.C.)

Another editorial on December 7 pursued the subject: "The contributors to its funds are looking with interest for reports of the practical results of its labors in camp inspection and in relieving the wants of our suffering soldiers. A communication from Mr. Olmstead [sic] its Secretary, will be found in another column." The secretary-general wasted no time on reprisals but wrote crisply, "If your correspondent 'Truth' . . . will do me the favor to call at this office, it will give me pleasure to exhibit to him vouchers, signed by officers of Govt., for more than twenty thousand articles furnished to Govt. hospitals during the month of November. Yours respectfully, Fred Law Olmsted."

Another anonymous letter, signed "Miles," appeared on December 16, and additional unfriendly editorials on December 17 and 18.

The members of the commission pursued their precarious course, but warned of danger by persistent criticism, they determined to publish a year-end report in December, 1861, which would convince the public as well as the government that the organization was doing a job worthy of its contributors and its "ambitious" officers. George Templeton Strong and Frederick Olmsted sat down on opposite sides of a table loaded with reports from inspectors and statistics from the "actuary" to block out the paper. Olmsted, who worked almost normally with a furious and sustained economy of energy, somewhat daunted the treasurer, who was an able man but believed in a certain amount of moderation in any effort.

The relationship between these two men during Olmsted's tenure with the Sanitary Commission was to be not intimate but nevertheless close. Strong was to contemplate Olmsted curiously and report on him from time to time in his diary. Strong had steel within him which contradicted his habitual appearance of gentlemanly foppishness. He was a keen observer and spared no man's foibles, not even his own. His observations of Olmsted offer an antidote to the uncritically fond recollections of Olmsted's closer friends. Strong was of Olmsted's own generation, only two years senior, a man reared in a gentle and well-to-do family in New York City, spared the rigors of the Hartford habit of self-examination. He was essentially a more self-indulgent kind of being than Frederick Olmsted, and tended toward a kind of lazy introspection; yet the war, for a time, effectually aroused him from this trait. In December, 1861, the two men worked hard together drinking strong coffee and sleeping little as they blocked out the report that Olmsted filled in and finished after Strong had gone home to New York. Strong noted of this episode in his diary: "Worked harder than I've done for years, writing steadily from Sunday afternoon till Thursday night every day till midnight, Wednesday evening alone excepted. I traced out most of the ground and left a great pile of crude MS matter for Olmsted to polish into shape and comeliness. It will be an interesting and valuable paper, I think."[24] Strong gave himself too much credit, perhaps. Olmsted by this time had all the affairs of the commission in his hands.

In any case, the report made a strong impression. Dated December, 1861, it was delivered formally to the secretary of war, but it was also printed by the firm of McGill & Witherow in the city of Washington and delivered to an audience outside the government. It was entitled descriptively, "A Report to the Secretary of War of the Operations of the Sanitary Commission and Upon the Sanitary Conditions of the Volunteer Army, Its Medical Staff, Hospitals, and Hospital Supplies."[25] (The New York *Daily-Times* devoted almost a full page to reprinting a condensed version of the report on January 20, 1862. This, in effect, was an apology. Raymond behaved as if he admitted that he had been wrong. The *Times* from this date ceased its campaign against the commission.)

The commission's report made no effort to argue with recent criticism. Its authors contented themselves with being thorough, comprehensive, and factual in describing the organization and the work of the past six months. The report related the way the commission took immediate hold of the task in June, 1861, when the officers of the organization went out into the army camps to see firsthand the conditions in which the men lived. The report stated clearly the commission's financial position, which was entirely private and voluntary. At the time the report was written funds had fallen off. In its charter the commission's purpose had been laid out as "inquiry and advice." The report told how this was put into practice: "For this purpose the Commission proceeded, as speedily as possible, to secure the services of a body of physicians specially fitted for the required duty, and to send them into the field at various points from Fortress Monroe to St. Louis." The writers described the free pamphlets distributed to army doctors, as well as the inspectors' questionnaires which enforced "written answers in the most exact and concise form to a series of printed questions." They mentioned with pride their collection of statistics: "The Commission is not without hope, if it should be enabled to continue its operations, eventually to lay before the country a body of military medical statistics more complete, searching, and trustworthy than any now in existence."

The report attacked boldly and straightforwardly the charge that it had overstepped the bounds set for it:

The Commission did not, at first, contemplate furnishing hospital and other supplies to the army on any large scale. . . . It could not refrain, however, without doing violence to the human sympathies of its members, from supplying some few of the more pressing wants which they saw existing in the military hospitals of Washington and elsewhere . . .

The Commission thus found itself in a manner obliged to overstep its strict duty, and was induced to employ a number of experienced young men as hospital dressers; to provide for the washing of the clothing of patients and of the hospital bedding, bandages, and towels; to purchase waterbeds for patients who had undergone amputation, and whose surgeons certified that they could not recover without them; to provide nurses possessed of skill for the handling of badly-fractured limbs; to engage the services of barbers to be constantly employed in the hospitals; to supply from time to time, some small amount of stimulants, and medicines, and surgical appliances to surgeons who were unable to obtain them from the Medical Bureau, either from their own excusable ignorance of official forms, or because the stock at the disposal of the Bureau was exhausted; to provide some means of recreation for men with tedious wounds, and convalescents; to furnish letter paper, envelopes, pens, ink, and postage stamps, or obtain franks, for those wishing to communicate with their friends.

Olmsted detailed a convincing mixture of humble and grand aids that the United States Sanitary Commission did not scorn to perform. Writing the final version of the report, Olmsted became both doer and teller of these deeds, for by this time the commission had become his, as Central Park had been his. At least it was so in his imagination. His claim for the commission was one in which his personal honor was involved: "The Commission has, therefore, for some months past held itself ready to receive and to distribute where most required, among the soldiers of every portion of the army, all supplies, especially of hospital stores, which might be forwarded to its depots by the humane and charitable societies that are working for the northern army in every northern city, town, and village."

The report ended with a protest and a warning: first, a grim notice: "The Commission feels that the duty assigned it by the War Department requires it to protest, as it has already protested, against the grossly inadequate provision for the contingency of a general action." And the warning: that battles would occur soon which would involve hundreds of thousands of men, with wounded "from twenty to thirty thousand men crying to us for relief from agony." The public, and perhaps many of the men of the government, did not believe this extreme claim, but in any case they applauded the report signed:

By order of the Commission

Fred. Law Olmsted,

General Secretary.

Just as, with a favorable reaction to the year-end report, it seemed that the commission might be more generally accepted, a most dangerous enemy entered upon the scene. This was the new secretary of war, Edwin M. Stanton. He came into office in January, 1862, after Lincoln sent the former secretary Simon Cameron to Russia as diplomatic representative of the United States. In Stanton, the president appointed a man of formidable abilities and faults. From the initial viewpoint of the commission, something of friendship was to be expected. Stanton was close to McClellan; McClellan had been a patron of the commission. And Stanton came to visit the headquarters on F Street only three days after he assumed office. But the cautious expectation of good relations with this new man in the War Department was soon dissipated. It was upon the question of the surgeon general that any possible friendship foundered. Stanton did not wish Hammond to be surgeon general for the simple reason that Hammond was not his choice. That Hammond was the commission's choice, and that Lincoln at last appointed Hammond made Stanton the implacable enemy of the commission. While the appointment hung in the balance from January until April, Stanton became a sort of ogre to the Commission. "Thick-set and of medium height; a strong heavy neck supported a massive head thatched with long black, curling hair. His nose and eyes were large, his mouth was wide and stern. A luxuriant crop of coarse black whiskers concealed his jaws and chin."[26] So ran a later description of the man who was a frank and forceful enemy of the United States Sanitary Commission. The only means of preventing Stanton from revoking the charter of the commission was for the organization to become so valuable in the eyes of the public and in the eyes of the president that it developed a kind of immunity from its own superior officer, the secretary of war. And this eventually happened. But as spring came on in Washington, with its redbuds and dogwoods and rumors of actions beyond the Potomac, the situation seemed terribly uncertain. Even so, Olmsted and his peers took on another risk. They determined to work through the Congress and get the Medical Bureau reformed by means of legislation.

Olmsted himself drafted a bill, and persuaded Senator Henry Wilson of Massachusetts to introduce it in the Senate on December 10, 1861. He lobbied for the bill among congressmen. He enlisted his father in Connecticut to help speak up for the passage of the bill.

The commissioners could go home from their commission work each night. George T. Strong continued to concern himself with Columbia College and Trinity Church in New York City and attended concerts with his pretty wife Ellen. Bellows continued his pastoral work with superabundant energy. Olmsted, however, in his usual fashion, let the job become an obsession. He slept often at the office of the commission at 244 F Street, dined on inedible or insubstantial food, drank many cups of coffee and tea, and worked through nights as well as days.[27]

In the intervals during this bleak winter when he lifted his eyes from his work, Frederick Olmsted was lonely. He wrote to Mary of incidental enjoyments he had, one an evening of drinking and talking with several good fellows, mostly newspaper correspondents, William Howard Russell of London among them. (Russell was to publish *My Diary North and South* in 1863. For his wartime travels, he used Olmsted's earlier travel books as a guide.) Olmsted felt easy with journalists. He knew their kind of talk. His days at *Putnam's* had given him a kinship to them. It also gave him an ability to tell them the story of the United States Sanitary Commission in a way that they could understand and in terms that they could report to their readers. But this good fellowship was marginal. Separated from his family, he was essentially lonely. Fred ended one letter to Mary (late summer, 1861): "Do you think often of this day, year ago? That morning when for a moment my heart was broken and yet I felt more the next moment for you than of myself. We must always be far more to each other for that."[28] He was recalling the child who had died, writing to her before the birth of the child who was to live.

It was not easy for Mary even in the most material ways. On January 6, 1862, when Olmsted had been away for half a year, the commissioners of Central Park cut his salary in half. The loss of money was a sore point for Frederick and Mary Olmsted. Mary entered into her husband's perplexities in a frank way, not sparing him her emotions. For weeks and months, they allowed the child Owen (five years old in August, 1862) to stay with his grandparents in Hartford. It was a protection for him, for New York was malarial in summertime; but Mary missed the little boy and was concerned that the arrangement might be an imposition on the senior Olmsteds. Mary was acutely aware of the money they owed Owen's grandfather. She handled the small payments to John Olmsted and was embarrassed at the slowness of the removal of this debt. After the first of the year a new difficulty for the family in the park arose: "They are going to rent this building for a tavern so I shall have to move out shortly,"²⁹ she wrote her father-in-law on February 10.

With these personal complications in the background of his life, Olmsted was also doubtful of the future of the Sanitary Commission. He and his colleagues had angered Stanton, and the secretary of war was not a man in the habit of withholding revenge for what he conceived to be a wrong done to him. If they should succeed in getting passed their bill for the reform of the Medical Bureau and the man appointed who was their choice for surgeon general, they might very well lose in winning. It is not surprising that in this insecure time Frederick Olmsted considered several alternate jobs. That one so blatantly busy should be casting his mind in other directions was simply an evidence of excess energy. The two people to whom he wrote of these opportunities were his wife and his father.

In March and April, he wrote his tolerant father of two possibilities. One was the job of street commissioner of New York, a position offered to him by the mayor. He seemed ready to take, almost to have taken, this job: "I have accepted it on condition that I am not to be trammelled in appointments or keep any practical bargains." But he let go this possibility. Another passing notion was to try for the job of head of the new Bureau of Agriculture. "If the Bill passes constituting a Bureau of Agriculture and Statistics, would you advise me to get the appointment of Commissioner, if I can? . . . It would be respectable, comparatively quiet, and might be exceedingly useful leading all the industry of the country and even greatly aiding banking and finance."

Then he stated the most farfetched alternative of all: "The alternative is going in and trying to build up a landscape gardening business—an alternative that even at forty, I am not likely to follow very steadily, I fear. 'Whenever you see a head, hit it,' is my style of work, and I have not yet sold [sowed] my wild oats altogether."³⁰

Early and late, from at least February, 1862, to April, 1862, he worried the problem of the freed Negroes of the South, and saw a job in it for himself. Those who had come within the federal lines on the sea islands when the plantation owners fled were not technically emancipated, but they were not slaves either. Lincoln was not yet ready to issue the order for the freeing of the slaves, and these "contrabands" as they were called, as if they were bales of cotton or cords of wood, had no real status and were a practical as well as moral problem for the North. Here were thousands of blacks left rudderless on Hilton Head and the neighboring islands; others were slipping through the lines and swelling their numbers. What to do with these charges? They were of some use to the federal army and were promptly pressed into menial jobs when needed. But the larger questions remained: how feed them, how provide work for them, how pay them, how educate them?

"He is trying to do something about the contrabands,"[31] Mary wrote about Fred to John Olmsted on February 16, explaining why her husband could not get home. With his quickness and inventiveness, Frederick Olmsted drew up a bill "for the management of the Port Royal contrabands"[32] and tried, as he had with the Medical Bureau reform bill, to find a senator to sponsor it. "I shall go to Port Royal, if I can," Frederick wrote to his father on February 24, "and work out practically my solution of the slavery question."[33] One can imagine Fred Law, doing Sanitary Commission work in conscientious detail and then sitting up half the night to write letters about the problem of the freedmen to influential men, one of whom was Charles Eliot Norton in Cambridge. His most considered effort was a letter to President Lincoln on March 8, 1862.

> Dear Sir:
>   At the request of several gentlemen—I mention Dr. Howe, Prof. Bache, Dr. Bellows and G. W. Curtis—I shall offer you my thoughts about the management of the negroes at Port Royal. That I can suppose it worthy of a moment of your time is to be accounted for simply by the fact that it chances to be more mature than most men's thoughts on this subject can be, the occasion which has arisen having been practically anticipated by me several years ago.
>   Aside from military considerations, the duty and function of government with regard to the negroes is included in and limited by these two propositions:
>   1. To save the lives of the negroes, except possibly as death may be a natural punishment of neglect of duty.
>   2. To *train* or *educate* them in a few simple, essential and fundamental social duties of free men in civilized life; as, first, to obtain each for himself the necessities of life, independently of charity; second, to regard family obligations; third, to substitute for subordination to the will of their former owners, submission to Laws or rules of social comity . . .[34]

Olmsted outlined some simple rules for preventing the Negroes' being objects of charity. His hard-nosed prescription was inspired by respect. He had no sentimental regard for these people, but a rational desire to make them citizens —a desire not very common even among the warmer-hearted advocates of abolition. He ended, "It would be better for the state, and more merciful to the negroes to guillotine them at once, than to educate them by any means in beggary, distrust of themselves and cowardly hatred of the first duties of freedom."[35] But then Olmsted had always a high view of what a citizen should be. He did not patronize the "contrabands," but he expected, after remedying their present generally helpless condition, to present them with the choices and duties of free men.

It might have made some difference to post-Civil War history if Frederick Olmsted had been charged with the duty of helping to accomplish the transition between slavery and freedom for the black people of the South. He knew in April, 1862, that if he had exerted himself he might have had the job. He said as much to his father: "I suppose that if I was determined to have it, and could neglect other matters to devote myself to it, I could get myself appointed Brigadier General, and assigned to duty as Military Governor of the islands, and then have absolute dictatorial control of it."

But Olmsted was on the brink of a deeper involvement in the work of the Sanitary Commission. On April 19, in the same letter in which he had outlined, almost feverishly, possibilities for himself in other fields, he wrote, "Our success is suddenly wonderfully complete."[36] The bill reforming the Medical Bureau and the appointment of Hammond as surgeon general had come to pass at last, so unbelievably according to their wishes, that he could not quite believe the truth and so continued to look about for other occupations.

In February the president had issued a general order calling for a forward movement by all the federal troops. The call was designed to stir into motion General McClellan, the great preparer. While that result took several months to be accomplished, in April McClellan was ready at last to carry out the attack he proposed. This was to be an attempt, with a great army convoyed by sea, to take Richmond from the Atlantic, from what was thought to be the city's vulnerable side, the "Peninsula," the land between the York and the James rivers. This was an alternative to what had been expected, a straightforward land drive inland from Washington to Richmond down the valleys between the mountain ranges, or more directly across the coastal rivers between the two cities. Reportedly, the president did not entirely approve McClellan's plan but allowed it go forward, giving his commander the opportunity to carry out his strategy.

Lincoln had steered the North out of the doldrums. The attainment of the two long-held aims of the commission seemed consonant with the new atmosphere in the capital. A diary entry of Strong's on April 19 tells of the surprising turn events had taken:

The Commission seems to have achieved at last the work it has been prosecuting for at least seven weary months of hope deferred, of official promises sliding away under its feet like the slopes of a steep sandhill of repulses, snubbings, and misrepresentation, and of late (in my own case, at least) of disgust and despair: the work of reforming the Medical Department of the army; a bill to increase the efficiency of that rheumatic, lethargic, paralytic, ossified, old institution passed a few days ago under the pressure brought to bear on the Congress by the United States Sanitary Commission and by the public opinion we have been educating. . . . It is our bill, except . . . in a few minor particulars.

As for the appointment of Hammond, it had taken place almost simultaneously (the bill on April 18, the appointment on April 25, 1862). Strong wrote familiarly of how the news came to the commission.

Bellows tackled Lincoln while he was being shaven . . . and seems to have talked to him most energetically and successfully. He was with the President again last night and was informed that Hammond was appointed. "Shouldn't wonder if he was Surgeon-General already," said the President, and they shook hands upon it.

Irresistibly, Lincoln supplied Dr. Bellows on this occasion with another saying, to be made into an anecdote to retell: "Dr. Bellows, apropos of something he said, advised him to take his meals at regular hours. His health was so important to the country. Abe Lincoln *loquitur,* 'Well, I cannot take my vittles regular. I kind o' just browze round.' "[37] Strong, along with the other gentlemen of the commission, could not help seeing the president as more countrified and quaint than they were; and none of them found it out of character for their own masterful Dr. Bellows to hesitate not one minute before lecturing the President of the United States about his eating habits.

Even before the success of their long lobbying effort was assured for the commission, the members found the torpid atmosphere of the city cleared by other events. In March the Confederate troops which had been camped within sight of the capital faded away into the Virginia hinterland. Olmsted and several others of the Commission made up an expedition to ride out into this newly opened territory. McClellan's men had marched out smartly to occupy the abandoned ground only to find that seemingly strong fortifications maintained in the face of the city were partly bluff, wooden cannons painted to look like metal, and the whole area lightly held for all the months that this army had seemed to threaten the capital.

The secretary observed these facts with some inward wonder and even a sense of humiliation, yet being in the open—even in the raw and biting air of March—was tonic to Frederick Olmsted after close confinement to his desk. The debris of war scattered about on the ground made all this landscape seem strange and interesting to the little group of civilized gentlemen on a busman's holiday.

Strong, an indefatigable note-taker, described in his diary those who made up the party and the small adventure they had.[38] "Our party was Bellows, Van Buren, Olmsted, Rogers (of Boston, a wealthy stolid citizen who has left his home and taken up his abode in Washington to work for the Commission without pay), Dr. Chamberlain (one of our inspectors) and myself." The group set out with a carriage and a splendid driver, "Uncle Ned," three horses, "forage for man and beast, blankets, buffalo robes, and one revolver." They alternated riding in the carriage or on the saddle horses. They set out in sunny weather and dined outdoors on what was left of the grounds of the Fairfax Court House. When they went on beyond this point, Olmsted, Rogers, and Chamberlain on horseback took the turn to Manassas and got separated from the others following in the carriage, who found themselves in a kind of desolated, deserted land between the armies, possibly dangerous. They turned back to Centreville where they slept on the floor of a vacant house. Strong listened to the others snore: "Van Buren [a distinguished New York City surgeon and professor, a member of the Executive Committee] snored in a steady, severe, classical style; Bellows in a vehement, spasmodic, *sturm und drang* Byronic way."

In the morning Bellows and the carriage party set out again into an area dotted with dead horses. There was a mass of abandoned matériel scattered about. They picked things up at random including numbers of papers, among which were personal letters of the Southern troops. They read them shamelessly and curiously, finding some of them shockingly illiterate, profane, and also comic, and touching. Strong particularly enjoyed this rummaging about in the human detritus left behind by the Confederates. They went on slowly through the rubble, meeting "contrabands" only, each of whom had a pitiful small pack of goods on his back, going on his unknown way, seeking freedom. Looming through the morning fog suddenly appeared their secretary-general. "Olmsted met us, bristling with bowie knives and shooting irons picked up on the ground, and looking like Robinson Crusoe." He and his two fellows had spent the night snugly in a rebel hut. Characteristically, Olmsted was in the best of spirits.

There is a photograph of Frederick Law Olmsted as he must have looked this day: an erect slight figure with lean cheekbones, a straight, light-eyed glance that seemed to assess and to possess whatever it took in. It was a youngish face yet, although its owner deplored being almost forty. The newer wartime fashion of growing whiskers he had not yet honored except in the possession of a drooping moustache. He had plentiful brown hair curling over a coat collar. The billed cap, having a military air, was well pulled down, with a defiant cock over the forehead and the slightly balding dome of the head. The ribbed heavy stuff of the coat looked, like the hat, slightly military, but was worn over a conservative dark suit and waistcoat and white shirt.

Poised at this precarious time in a satisfying balance of desires and ambitions, Olmsted traveled forward in the next months on the currents of the war, into an active part in McClellan's ambitious campaign against Richmond. He let himself go into the heart of action and passion and danger, using his active brain to harness some part of these forces.

CHAPTER XVI

The Chief of
the Hospital Ships

It is no common nation's task that we have undertaken.
—F. L. O., Introduction, *Hospital Transports*[1]

OLMSTED HAD MADE an organization. In April, 1862, he had a chance to prove what it could do. On the nineteenth of the month, while discussing alternatives to his present position as secretary-general of the Sanitary Commission, Olmsted mentioned in an aside to his father in a letter, "As you will see by the papers, I am getting up floating hospitals. I shall probably take command of the fleet in person."[2]

When McClellan made his long delayed move against Richmond in a sea expedition south to the "peninsula" of Virginia, Frederick Olmsted threw aside his alternatives and plunged himself and the commission into the new effort. He gave up the desk work in Washington which had consumed his time for almost a year and left the national guidance of the organization to subordinates in the capital, to agents stationed elsewhere, and to the executive committee in New York City. Under Olmsted's direct command, the Sanitary Commission played a central part in this campaign in succoring the sick and wounded of the federal forces—and sometimes of the Confederates captured. While individual members of the Army Medical Bureau in the field were often brave, industrious, and inventive, the entire official effort was inadequate. On the Peninsula, the Sanitary Commission, a private, voluntary organization, supplemented, and in some circumstances, took the entire place of the Army Medical Bureau. In this effort the commission, therefore, fulfilled its conceived function; it gave aid where aid was needed, and it indicated to the Medical Bureau what its proper function should be.

Much can be learned about the expedition from *Hospital Transports,* a book published in 1863 to help raise money for the commission. The book excerpted the letters of various members of the commission who served in the campaign. Olmsted's along with the others were printed anonymously but can be identified by a key. This source and others, principally Olmsted's letters preserved separately, allow a reconstruction of the history of his part in the episode.

Heading an advance working party, Frederick Olmsted boarded the *Daniel Webster* at the port of Alexandria on a Friday late in April. The ship needed a tug to get over shoals past the city of Washington and none was at hand. The secretary-general went ashore, commandeered a tug, and soon had the *Webster* moving. In this company were "six medical students, twenty men nurses (volunteers all), four surgeons, four ladies, a dozen contrabands (field hands), three carpenters, and half a dozen miscellaneous passengers. There were, besides, five of us members of the Sanitary Commission and of the central staff [Olmsted is writing], and one of the Philadelphia associates, eight military officers, ninety soldiers (convalescents, returning to their regiments), some quartermaster's mechanics, and a short ship's crew and officers."

Olmsted did not allow the officers of the commission, the ladies, the contrabands, the carpenters to enjoy for long the excitement of setting off to war. "I organized all our Commission people on Sunday, in two watches, sea-fashion [his almost forgotten sea experience came back to him]; appointed watch-officers, and have worked since, night and day, refitting the ship. We broke up all the transport arrangements,—they were in filthy condition,— thoroughly scraped, washed, and scrubbed the whole ship from stem to stern, inside and out; whitewashed the steerage; knocked away the bulkheads of the wings of the engine-room section, so as to get a thorough draft from stem to stern; then set to fitting and furnishing new bunks; started a new house on deck, forward; made and fitted an apothecary's shop and when we arrived at Cheeseman's Creek were ready for patients."[3]

Somewhat apart from the activity, admiring it sufficiently, but with a space in his mind to note peripheral happenings, the commission's treasurer George Templeton Strong commented in his diary: "One of the officers, a chaplain from western New York, Cleveland by name, gave us a 'service' Sunday night by invitation, the like of which I do not care to hear again."[4]

When the *Daniel Webster* sailed southward carrying its load of personalities toward the scene of war, the city they were leaving had become more sober than it had been. News had come from the west of the battle of Shiloh fought early in April. It looked as if this war was not going to be an operation of dash and speed but of slow and ponderous movements to gain ground or capture troops. McClellan had made careful preparations for his advance on the Confederate capital. If care could effect a change in the fortunes of the North, this army steaming south would make the difference. This was generously allowed even by the president who doubted the wisdom of the place McClellan had chosen for his attack.

First landing for the commission ship was Cheeseman's Creek, an estuary of the York River. As the *Daniel Webster* made its way through many ships, the passengers saw shores dark with men. White tents were visible through the woods. As night came on they saw fires made from great piles of brushwood. They heard singing from many of the ships they passed. There were "bugle calls and drumbeats"[5] to be heard, George Strong noted, as well as the sound of a heavy gun not too far away.

In the daylight Olmsted, Strong, and several others secured horses to ride overland to the headquarters of the army. Making their way through a disturbed landscape, they found out the kind of place this was in which soldiers were attempting to live and move. As Olmsted wrote, "The original country roads had all been used up; it was difficult even to ford across them, when we had occasion to do so, on horseback. The army wagons, each drawn by six mules, and with very light loads, were jerked about frightfully. We passed many wrecks, and some horses which had sunk and been smothered." The woods opening out, they found cavalry exercising, then more woods, a rise, and "suddenly a grand view of the valley of York River." Moving out of the tangle of honeysuckle and briar it was exhilarating to see on a flat slope "a camp of some twenty to forty thousand men."

The following exchange occurred when they talked to a doctor of the Medical Bureau headquarters: "That isn't the enemy?" "Yes." "Is he so near?" "O yes! we are quite within range here."[6]

They found at the outset that the "medical arrangements seem to be deplorably insufficient. The Commission [some part of it already established onshore] is at this time actually distributing daily of hospital supplies much more than the government." Strong noted in his diary that they found men "lying on bare hospital floors and perishing of typhoid who could be saved if they had a blanket or a bed, or appropriate food and sufficient stimulants and proper hospital clothing instead of their mud-encrusted uniforms."[7]

The small party of commission men rode back to the river landing through sunburning heat, but by late afternoon they passed through a chilling mist rising from the ground. Strong wrote that he saw typhoid patients being carried without protection through this mist turned into rain. He and the others realized early that the land and the weather would be enemies.

Fighting on a large scale had not begun. McClellan had stopped to besiege Yorktown. Strong climbed a tree by way of a dangerous ladder to have a view of the shells coming at them from that place. He was told tales about rebel sharpshooters—"The best rebel sharp-shooters are niggers. One of them seems to bear a charmed life and has been very successful. He is known as the 'irrepressible nigger.' "[8]

Olmsted secured the right for his men to go anywhere into and through the lines. One after another transport was added to his command until he had between one-half dozen and ten. He and his people saw that each one was made clean, equipped with proper bunks and stores of food. This was accomplished by any method possible, including the shooting of a wandering rebel cow when a ship was in desperate need of meat. Reinforcements joined them: dressers, doctors, women aides—among them George Strong's wife Ellie. These "ladies," as the men called them and as they quaintly called themselves, bathed the patients, fed them, clothed them in clean plain gowns after cutting them out of dirty and bloody garments, cooked the food and distributed it to dozens, then hundreds, and finally thousands who poured in upon them from the dark land stretching from their river landings. Ships of Olmsted's command anchored in relay along the river and stream tributaries of the York, or steamed north to discharge sick and wounded in Washington, Philadelphia, and New York. They were loaded in these cities and turned around to return with new supplies, new volunteers, new orders. The names of some of these battered transports were: *Daniel Webster, Ocean Queen, Wilson Small, Knickerbocker, Elm City, Spaulding, Elizabeth, Alida, State of Maine, Kennebec.* The *Wissahickon,* Wicked Chicken," was the tugboat which they used to scour shallow waters for wounded men deposited on the banks, and sometimes for fugitive moments of pleasure running up flowery stretches of undisturbed water with tree and sky reflections, as far away from the war as a bend in the river.

The Union Army from time to time seized one of their ships, often when they had recently made it ready for use. Or the army begged the commission people to come aboard one of the unprepared regular army ships and give aid to poor broken men brought there without any preparation having been made to receive them; the "ladies" and the student dressers and perhaps one doctor would take on with a shrug the extra, midnight-to-dawn job of looking after a full shipload of gasping, suffering men where there was little medicine, no food ready, and no order. This they had to bring with them. It was a life of improvisation, of order commanded to appear and somehow made to appear out of chaos. All activity circled around Mr. Olmsted, the pivot of energy and order. He never seemed rushed, nor upset and angry, never gave way. He preserved his equanimity and caused a quantity of calm to spread around him. The medical officers, the volunteer aides, male and female, the agents dispatched to crucial points at a distance, all conceived a kind of hero worship for him. His co-workers found they could depend upon his reliability, ingenuity, and courage. He was their buffer against the incalculable decisions of higher ups. He had come to them as an unknown quantity, in appearance a thin, partially crippled man, swinging up the gangplank at Alexandria on crutches; but his authority, immediately extended over their lives, was something that they could rest in. Of course it cost him greatly; the calm he displayed hid all kinds of spontaneous dreads, fears, hopes, and angers. But he did in the main thrive in this work. He enjoyed being under the blazing sky or in the misty rain. He was bemused by work and had a sort of joy in struggling to impose his will on stubborn generals, crafty politicians, and all those who believed in doing things the way they had always been done.

"I have no idea what we are to do, and ask no questions. Mr. Olmsted is the law-giver; he knows the facts of my existence, and will use me when he wants me,"[9] wrote one of the women volunteer aides, Katherine Wormeley. Curious was the enlargement these ladies felt in dirty and difficult service. Reared in gentle and protected surroundings, they shed more than the hoops in their skirts in order to do their work better on board the ships. Here unpleasant duties were exacted of them at any hour of the day or night. They bloomed in the dirty, bloody, crowded, hectic atmosphere. George Strong was astonished at his wife, Ellie. Gently bred, petted by him in a hothouse atmosphere in New York City, she showed firmness and administrative ability in her work with the hospital ships, displaying qualities of leadership and decision which would never have been demanded of her in normal, upper class life.

This throwing together of men and women in congenial, hectic work fostered an emotional atmosphere not foreseen. Katherine Wormeley, who was one of the medical aides during the campaign, revealed the complications of her feelings, at least by indirection, in her letters and in her published account of her war experiences. Some of her letters to Frederick Olmsted were preserved by him; some of her letters were excerpted in *Hospital Transports;* her postwar account of the campaign was contained in *The Other Side of the War.* Katherine Wormeley went on to hospital administration during the remainder of the war and she had a career later in writing, in particular, the translation of French novels into English. Her wartime letters are useful in giving one the everyday, working side of commission life aboard the hospital ships as well as the strangled personal emotion the writer had for Mr. Olmsted. Her letters reek of the feeling, somewhat beyond devotion, that she felt, but the admission perhaps not even made to herself was never put in words. During the war, when they had gone to other duties, he back to the direction of the commission in Washington and New York, she to a hospital in Rhode Island, Katherine Wormeley despairingly sent to him letter after letter (which he kept), trying to work up some kind of joint duty again for them. This never came about. Frederick Olmsted must have been aware of the emotion in her letters, but he was blandly and outwardly impervious to it while at the same time gratified by it. Katherine Wormeley was never a threat to the relationship he had with his wife. However much circumstances—children, house, the keeping up of her husband's ties with the Central Park commissioners—kept Mary at home, Frederick's wife was not the model "lady" of her time; she was frank, straightforward, giving as good as she got in conversation, thinking her own thoughts, sharing ideas with her husband. This tied him to her, while Katherine Wormeley's attitude of self-abasement, in the style of the times, did not stimulate him. He praised her as devoted, even to Mary, but it was a patronizing praise. He never patronized Mary.

The work they had come to do in Virginia occurred in spasmodic intervals of wild day and night activity, separated by quiet pools of time. During one of these workless intervals Mr. Olmsted rowed two of the women along the winding curves of the Pamunkey to enjoy the scenery. The headquarters of the commission was an anchorage just short of a broken railroad bridge, beyond which the larger ships could not venture. "Mr. Olmsted rowed us close in shore, where the knotted roots of the outermost trees made a network, or paling, behind which dropped or glowed in their spring beauty the lovely trees of this region, among them the magnolia, the flowering catalpa, and the beautiful white fringe-tree. . . . Mrs. Griffin looked today so like a mediaeval Madonna, with her heavenly complexion, her golden hair, and the extremely angular appearance which we persist in keeping up without our hoops, that I was forced to suggest the idea to Mr. Olmsted, who entered thoroughly into it."[10] The writer was Katherine Wormeley.

The headquarters to which they returned from tree-viewing on the river was known to them as White House, from a small abandoned plantation house with a view downriver. (It had been George Washington's earliest residence after his marriage.) It was to this point that the wounded were brought by rail and by wagon through the forest. There were not many calm days here. A typical sequence of events was retold in *Hospital Transports*. Late one day Olmsted received a message to pick up one hundred sick men at Bigelow's Landing where an ambulance-train had left them "on the ground in the rain, without attendance or food, to die."[11] This place was "up a narrow shoal, crooked creek," and would endanger any vessel sent up to it. However, he determined to move his small fleet (not as many ships as he would have later) to the mouth of the creek and take the one with the shallowest draft up the creek to get the men. This was "at sunset, stormy and cold." Attempting to move his ships, Olmsted was intercepted by a request from a military surgeon that they immediately take off his regular army ship one hundred fifty sick men who had been picked up from the West Point Landing and had had no nourishment that day. Olmsted hesitated but complied, and looking into the crammed cabin found sick men sitting on the floor without space to lie down, one man dying—dead the next time he looked in. At midnight, nevertheless, Olmsted sent Mr. Knapp and Dr. Ware, three dressers, and two of the women aides to find the men at Bigelow's Landing. They found them, brought them back, washed and fed them and put them to bed in the straw-filled bunks of the hospital transport. In this involvement with raw life, Olmsted's leadership provided meaning. His prevention of slackness and his joining them all together in a companionship of effort allowed for a kind of happiness to exist in the middle of much ugliness and suffering. "We all know in our hearts that it is thorough enjoyment to be here," wrote Katherine Wormeley with more effusiveness than Mr. Olmsted would have used, but her words were only the exaggeration of a shared mood: "*It is life,* in short; and we wouldn't be anywhere else for anything in the world." The women aides, doing more than they had bargained for, moved through scenes of pain with a quickly learned stoicism. They covered their ears when the bandages of the wounded men were changed each day; they improvised food from what they had, one day only ten pounds of Indian meal for one hundred sick men.

The three principals of the organization—Olmsted, Knapp, and Ware—moved through the small, tightly organized world as mentors and exemplars. Mr. Knapp was the dependable workhorse, the administrator of everyday affairs, Olmsted's second in command. Dr. Ware was the chief surgeon of the expedition, clever with his hands, charming in his manners and in his person. Olmsted was slightly aloof in his masterful management of all the affairs of the commission, from commanding the fleet to conferring with generals. A picture of that time shows him the only clean-shaven one of the three, with a slender, almost gaunt face, with light eyes under straight dark brows, a high forehead from which his dark hair was brushed back to curl just below the ears. He had high cheekbones, a slightly crooked, prominent eagle nose (the "Olmsted nose," which looked as if it might have been broken), a drooping black moustache, a full mouth, a neat chin. It was a high-strung, sensitive face, hiding turmoil within. The strain of living at the high pitch which had been his consistent rate for many years had creased his forehead. He looked at this time still youthful and had not as yet passed into the appearance of middle age. The war would push him in that direction.

Here, in a letter of the time, is Katherine Wormeley's description of Olmsted. She remarked to her correspondent at home, away from the war, that Mr. Olmsted had given them a routine of work to follow upon the arrival of every batch of wounded. "You may be sure that it is carried out, with Mr. Olmsted at the head of affairs: his are no paper orders." She went on: "I think I have not yet described our 'Chief' to you. He is small, and lame (for the time being only) from a terrible accident which happened to him a few months ago; but though the lameness is decided it is scarcely observable, for he gives you a sense that he triumphs over it by doing as if it did not exist. His face is generally very placid, with all the expressive delicacy of a woman's, and would be beautiful were it not for an expression which I cannot fathom,—something which is, perhaps, a little too severe about it. . . . I think he is a man of the most resolute self-will,—generally a very wise will, I should think; born an autocrat, however, and, as such, very satisfactory to be under. His reticence is one of his strong points: he directs everything in the fewest possible words; there is a deep, calm thoughtfulness about him which is always attractive and sometimes—provoking. . . . He is a great administrator, because he comprehends details, but trusts his subordinates: if they are good, he relies on them; if they are weak, there's an end of them."[12]

Olmsted used willing subordinates angelically and mercilessly. He played his role of leadership on the peninsula with perfect proportion and sincerity. He paid a cost later in damage to his health and nerves, but the result showed only after the effort had been expended. As the tempo of the battles on the peninsula increased into June and July, the chief of the hospital ships and his teams cared for the broken men brought to them with a superhuman energy and competence.

Olmsted's people knew little about the course of McClellan's campaign. They knew that the federal troops moved—whether forward or backward— by the quantity of wounded men brought down to the river to them. There were many wounded after Williamsburg (May 5), after Fair Oaks (May 31), after Gaines Mill and the other protracted engagements of the end of June and the beginning of July.

A typically bad time for them, when they fulfilled the part they had come to play, was in the days after Fair Oaks (when McClellan advanced to within five miles of Richmond and then turned back). William Quentin Maxwell, the historian of the commission, wrote of this time: "The evacuation of over three thousand wounded began on the night of June 1 and was completed on June 7. Surgeons packed living and dead like freight into boxcars with nothing to ease the jolting and bumping; but this was only the beginning of the inferno. When the sufferers reached White House the stench of rotting flesh was rising on the summer air. All Sanitary transports, except the *Spaulding*, were on hand. The *Commodore, Whilden,* and *Vanderbilt* took the worst cases. . . . Olmsted pitched a hospital tent on the riverbank by the railroad track."[13]

From Olmsted's letters and those of Knapp and Wormeley and others preserved in *Hospital Transports,* one can reconstruct the torch-lighted scene at the river's edge, in which the tormented men, some dying, were brought to the tent where the men and women of the commission sorted out this human wreckage, gave them their first food and drink and drugs and emergency surgery since they had fallen in the battles forty miles north near Richmond. The doctors and the dressers (male medical students serving as nurses) and aides worked day and night with little stop. United in a harmony given them by Olmsted's kind and despotic leadership, they organized some sort of order in all this confusion of suffering.

The wounded arrived unattended; no medical officers of the army accompanied them. Their first help at the end of their train ride came from this civilian and amateur organization which had been derided for its impracticality and for its arrogance in previously stating the insufficiencies of the Army Medical Bureau. Olmsted wrote:

The trains with wounded and sick arrive at all hours of the night; the last one before daylight, generally getting in between twelve and one. As soon as the whistle is heard, Dr. Ware is on hand (he has all the hard work of this kind to do,) and the ladies are ready in their tent; blazing trench-fires, and kettles all of a row, bright lights and savory supplies, piles of fresh bread and pots of coffee, —the tent door opened wide,—the road leading to it from the cars dotted all along the side with little fires or lighted candles. Then, the first procession of slightly wounded, who stop at the tent-door on their way to the boat, and get cups of coffee with as much milk (condensed) as they want, followed by the slow-moving line of bearers and stretchers, halted by our Zouaves, while the poor fellows on them have brandy, or wine, or iced lemonade given them. It makes but a minute's delay to pour something down their throats, and put oranges in their hands, and saves them from exhaustion and thirst before, in the confusion which reigns on most of the crowded government transports food can be served them. Meantime Dr. Ware and his dressers work with the men left temporarily with them—sometimes for three days at a time—before they are carried onto waiting ships.[14]

Occasional respites were long remembered. "Our evenings are the pleasantest hours of the day," wrote Katherine Wormeley, of the times between the recurrent racking crises. "The Chief and Mr. Knapp and the staff collect on a broken chair, a bed-sack, and sundry carpet-bags, and have their modicum of fun and quinine. The person who possesses a dainty—chocolate or gingerbread, for instance—is the hero for the time being."[15]

While the people who worked with the "Chief" found him a support for their own infirm thoughts; within, Frederick Olmsted was not so steady as he seemed. His letters to his wife and to Charles Loring Brace gave away his private dreads. On June 11, he wrote to Mary, "We have got through with a terrible week's work." Knapp was coming home for a few days exhausted. He would be able to look up Mary and bring back to her husband news of her and the children. Olmsted had written to his wife six or eight times and he had not had any letters from her. She was to move out of the park and he wondered about her circumstances. He wanted her to know what his had been. "Let Knapp tell you what it has been. It is worth while to have seen such awful suffering to have also the recollection of such relief and such gratitude. If we had not been just where we were, I cannot tell you what a horrible disgrace there would have been done here to our country." He had seen a crowd of those looking for their kin among the dead and wounded. "Thank God this comes not to us. Pray God it comes not again in our time or with our children. The horror of war can never be known but on the field. It is beyond, far beyond all imagination." He begged Mary to send him word of herself with Knapp. "It will go far to break me down, if I cannot at least be sure of hearing of you often hereafter. Your husband."[16]

With the best will, Charles Brace had written his old friend Fred Olmsted asking if he might come as a volunteer medical aide. Frederick answered him, with some sharpness, that he needed no such volunteers (although he wished he would come as a chaplain—most of them were so mediocre). The best practical nurses, he found, were other soldiers. "Consequently, in the way of business, I don't want you;—for any man without a clearly defined function about the army is a horrid nuisance and is treated as such unless he comes with a peremptory edict from the Secy of War.... I have seen enough of it and it's not an entertainment to which I would invite a friend."

He had had up to forty-five visitors recently, including assorted congress-men. They generally got enough in one day and night and were glad to leave "sour and seedy." And he went on with feeling: "There is just one thing which a man can usefully bring to the army of the Potomac, reinforce-ments of sturdy musket bearers. There is but one other service to which a true patriot and christian could as well devote his energies—the guillotine-ing of the aforesaid Secretary of War." And he went on to "My dear Charley," that while General McClellan made mistakes and was not worthy of the hero worship he received, "but as between him and his enemies, I am a McClellan man to the backbone."[17] Olmsted was immersed in this small corner of the war. He was partial and passionate.

McClellan disappointed his most ardent supporters. Failing to take Rich-mond, he ordered a general retreat, but not to the York and the Pamunkey. His troops were to pick up their supplies and move across the peninsula to the James River, cleared now for the entry of Northern ships. White House was to be abandoned. The commission was to load what it could on its ships and move down the York and around the peninsula to Harrison's Landing. The members of this volunteer force saw from the decks of their own ships the grand spectacle of the destruction by the federal army of all the supplies it could not take to the other side of the peninsula: "All the material that could not be put on board the transports were burned; the engines and cars, some of the latter loaded with supplies, were put under a full head of steam and were run into the river."[18]

Before he left White House, Olmsted saw one of the spontaneous and touching events of the retreat, the pouring forth to them of the slaves, "flocking from all the country nearby, bringing their little movables, frying-pans and old hats and bundles, to the river-side. . . . Fortunately there was plenty of deck-room for them on the forage boats, one of which, as we passed it, seemed filled with women only, in their gayest dresses and brightest turbans, like a whole load of tulips for a horticultural show." Smoke went up from the ruin on shore, but these women, as Olmsted noted, quietly nursed their babies and sang hymns and were convinced that "the day of their deliverance had come.

"All night we sat on the deck of the *Small,* slowly moving away, watching the constantly increasing cloud, and the fire-flashes over the trees toward White House; watching the fading out of what had been to us, through these strange weeks, a sort of home where we had all worked together and been happy."[19]

CHAPTER XVII

The End of Olmsted's War

As the clergymen say when a rich parish bids for them against a poorer; I think the call to California is a *clear* one, if not as loud as that to battle here.

—F. L. O., to his wife, August 12, 1863[1]

O N THE EVENING of July 3, 1862, Frederick Olmsted began a letter to his wife describing the scene spread out before him as he sat on the deck of the hospital ship *Wilson Small*. This was his headquarters ship, which had moved with the Union Army from its base at White House on the Pamunkey River to its new base on the other side of the Virginia peninsula at Harrison's Landing on the James River. He had a grand view here of a large human action, and he relished the drama of it as if he were only a spectator.

"The beach, below the broken bank is filled with soldiers, some bathing, some washing clothes, many reading newspapers which have just arrived from New York." At the pier, wounded men were being led down to the hospital ships lined up to receive them. Wagons pulled loads up the slope from the water. Lifting his eyes upward, he saw artillery pieces being maneuvered along a hill crest. In another direction a body of cavalry moved out of sight over the hill. Through trees he saw "a city of tents." Transport ships anchored nearby. Farther out in the wide river were the gunboats. They began firing as he wrote. These guns were the protection of the army which had retreated from Richmond down the peninsula to this landing.

The letter continues, "Our grand army is very nearly destroyed. I wonder whether they will let you know it.... The majority of our men have lost tents, knapsack and blanket, have saved only musket and cartridge box. Many in the line of battle are bareheaded and barefooted. Think what their condition will be in this shadeless plain when the July sun comes out tomorrow. I am going to get if possible, first tents, or something that will cast a shade for the wounded."

Olmsted completed the first pages of his letter as the ship pulled away from shore and made its way downriver through a maze of transports and gun boats. As night came on, the *Small* moved without lights and without a pilot carefully and precariously down the James and at dawn out into Chesapeake Bay. He explained his mission to Mary, "Letterman, the new Medical Director, has been on board and I am to go with the *Small* as quickly as possible to Washington to tell the Surgeon-General more fully than he can write what the condition of the medical needs of the Army are, and to bring back direct what it most urgently wants."[2]

Olmsted had not yet had time to look back at the campaign and see what they had all done, he and his people of the United States Sanitary Commission. But shortly it would be clear that, while the military campaign had failed, the Sanitary Commission had accomplished a great deal. Dr. Charles Stille, one of the medical men of the commission, who composed the official history of the organization very soon after the war (1866), wrote of this first great test that the commission had "succeeded in transporting from the Peninsula in a comparatively comfortable condition, more than eight thousand sick and wounded men."[3] They had tended the wounds and illnesses, and fed and clothed these men when there was no one else to do it. The chief of the hospital ships had not only set the example of order in the midst of which compassion could exercise itself, he had cleared a way for himself and other agents of the commission later to find scope for their talents and services. Olmsted had in a manner invented the hospital ships; Elisha Harris, a medical man of inventive talent, shortly designed and made practical hospital trains. Olmsted, upon returning to his Washington office, worked with the surgeon general in plans for a field ambulance service, for pavilion hospitals, and for other improvements. The Sanitary Commission had demonstrated what it could do. It was a respected, expanding service for the remainder of the war.

On July 25, 1862, the members of his expedition saw their chief leave Harrison's Landing, this time not for a hurried visit to Washington to expedite supplies, but for the last time. Katherine Wormeley wrote, "The last I saw of Mr. Olmsted, he was disappearing down the side of the 'Webster,' clad in the garb of a fashionable gentleman. I rubbed my eyes, and felt then that it was indeed *all over*."[4] The secretary-general's normal wear in the war area had been a vaguely military and rakish jacket and a cap cocked over one eye.

Dr. Bellows had had reports from the commission's doctors that Olmsted was not well. The president of the commission was told by one of them, as he said, "that Mr. Olmsted does not and will not live as he ought to, and that he thinks him liable to break down. I have written him again and again to *return;* but he is *fanatical* about his duty."[5] But when Frederick did in fact leave the peninsula, which had been the scene of so much of his concentrated effort, he did not at once reform his ways. He received good advice from the commission's Dr. Agnew to go to Saratoga and rest; instead he attended commission meetings in New York City, visited the park he had missed intensely, and returned to work in the headquarters in Washington.

Meanwhile, he worried about his family. It seemed likely that he should settle them again at the farm on Staten Island. But then he would have to devote time and thought to crops and marketing and would need to borrow at least four thousand dollars to put the place in order, and, since his brother had left the farm in trust to his children—Charles, Charlotte, and Owen— Frederick was in something of a quandary. He wrote frankly to his father, "I should have accumulated nothing else probably and my own children—in distinction from John's would have but a back-door title to any part of this."[6]

Frederick did not get better during the month of August as he continued to work in the Washington office. By the twenty-third, he wrote Mary, "am deeply yellow and otherwise liverworn."[7] And he emphasized the unpleasant details of his ailment, "I am weak, yellow, itchy and have not been out for several days." Fred was at last glad to agree to Dr. Agnew's suggestion of a rest cure in Saratoga. By this time he needed someone to go with him. Dr. Agnew agreed to accompany him on the train. Mary was to stay in Litchfield until, as he said, "I am bleached again." And "Love to Charley, Charlotte, Owen, and Marion." A queer kind of spartan resolution to endure pain in private caused him to resolve to be alone while getting well. This—in addition to the practical problem of Mary's having all the children to care for. He did not, however, spare his wife the horrid details of his discomfort. "I grow daily more yellow," he wrote her from Union Hall at Saratoga, "until I could have passed for a rather dark mulatto; the whites of my eyes gave place to a queer glistening saffron colored substance, and my skin became flabby leather, dry and dead. I itched furiously and where I plowed the surface with my fingers' ends, it presently became purple.... I hope to hear daily from you." He became also more lame in his illness, finding it difficult to get about even on crutches. He slept poorly. There had been excess in his devotion; there was extremity in the way he paid in the flesh and spirit. While it had been indeed a time for heroes (as Olmsted said), the hero faced the continuance of life. A minor theme running through all his letters at this time was how to make a living for his family. He had not been making one during this time, but constantly falling behind.

His difficulties were rubbed in on his return from Saratoga through New York. Here he found a depressing circumstance, the failure of the Mason Brothers publishing house, which had brought out his *Back Country* and *Cotton Kingdom.* "Their stock and plates are to be sold, perforce, at auction, and they do not hope to get more than 20 prct. of their late estimated value. They say they hope to pay me in full—about $100 due. They have managed

FREDERICK LAW OLMSTED
American Landscape Architect ∞ 1822–1903

Frederick Law Olmsted during the Civil War; etching by
Jacques Hnizdovsky. (*Courtesy, Jacques Hnizdovsky*)

Anchor off "Hong Kong", September 5th 1843.

Dear Parents,

We arrived at this port day before yesterday one hundred and thirty two days from New York.

I wrote you at "Anjier" on the 9th of August - which place we left on the following evening, having procured a supply of Yams, sweet potatoes, Plaintains, bananas, cocoa nuts - Tamarinds, Fowls, Ducks, & Paddy (rice in the "hull") to feed them on, pumpkins, and fresh water. Of these the yams & water alone were intended for the benefit or use of the "people". To be sure we would occasionally get a plantain or banana smuggled out of the main top by a boy setting to'galn't stud'n sails in the night, and we were welcome to the cocoa nuts shells, rings, I should say, after the Capt's had drank their contents - East Indians never think of eating them except with a spoon when in a pulpy state, as it were. We bought "amongst us" two large Green turtle - but when the first was killed, the best part of it was taken for the Captain's table, & supplied for some days, while we had but one meal - The other was launched overboard, they called it sick, but the way it struck out for Cochin China was a caution to doctors.

We had a most remarkable passage through the "Straits". We had anticipated a very hard & dangerous time. There is a beautiful clipper built Eng: vessel now lying by us which was over three weeks getting through; anchoring every night - I think we were but three days, and did not anchor once - The 2nd night we were becalmed and all hands kept up some time expecting to anchor; the magazine was opened, guns loaded with grape, &c. for you know this sea (Java Sea) is infested with Malay pirates, who very often attack vessels;) but just as we were about to drop the kedge, a light breeze sprung up. It soon became strong & so favorable that we could lay our course - Sunday (12th I think) P.M. Land was made right ahead, and at dark we were almost enclos'd by it - Before midnight we pass'd Gaspar Island at the head of the "Gaspar" or "Caspar" Straits, & were in the China Sea. The next morning I made three sail from the royal mast head; before night we were near enough to see that they were "Malay Proas", Our course was altered a little & next morning they were out of sight. We were now standing before the regular "Monsoon" which gave us plenty of work. - Thus at day light we are right before it, carrying lower, topmast, tog'll, & royal studn sails on both sides - The wind shifts a little over our starb'd quarter, "Brace the yards!" "Let go to star'bd", "Man the lee braces fore brace! - Hold on to star'bd! "Haul'em taut" "Well!" "make fast - top'sail brace - well!" Tog'lt brace well! royal brace a small pull - belay! "Haul tuts to stab'd! - - - So! all well

Page from a letter of Frederick Law Olmsted to his parents, from the *Ronaldson*, off Hong Kong, September 5, 1843. (*Courtesy of the Library of Congress, the Collections of the Manuscript Division, Frederick Law Olmsted Papers*)

The five friends in New Haven days *(from left to right)*, Charles Trask, Charles Loring Brace, Frederick J. Kingsbury, Frederick Law Olmsted, John Hull Olmsted. *(Reproduction courtesy of the New York Public Library)*

Portrait of George Geddes, painted in 1836 by Charles Loring Elliott. *(Courtesy of the Onandaga Historical Association, Syracuse, N.Y.)*

Yale College in 1845. (*Engraving in* Yale Life and Men, *by Timothy Dwight,* 1903)

The Farmhouse at Southside, Staten Island, a sketch probably by Olmsted, about 1849. (*Courtesy of the Library of Congress, the Collections of the Manuscript Division, Frederick Law Olmsted Papers*)

Olmsted in 1850 (from Fred-
erick Law Olmsted, Landscape
Architect, 1822–1903).
(Courtesy of the New York
Public Library)

Temporary Station,
U.S. Sanitary Commission
(from *Photographic History
of the Civil War*, 1911)

Central Park, the Lower
Lake, 1865, Skating Scene;
oil painting by J. M. Culverhouse. (*Courtesy of the
J. Clarence Davies Collection, Museum of the City
of New York*)

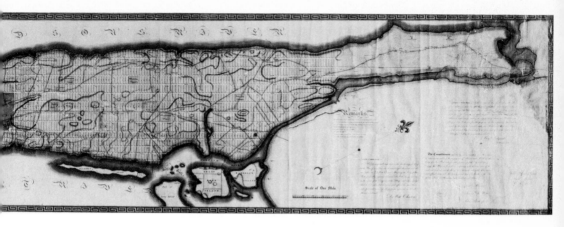

How Manhattan might have grown without a
Central Park; New York's First City Plan, 1811;
the Bridges Map, or Randel Survey. (*Courtesy
of the J. Clarence Davies Collection, Museum
of the City of New York*)

Central Office of the U.S. Sanitary Commission,
244 F Street, Washington, D.C.
(from *Photographic History of the Civil War, 1911*).

Harrison's Landing, Berkeley Plantation, Virginia, spring 1862. (*Courtesy of the Berkeley Plantation, Charles City, Virginia*)

Calvert Vaux. (*Courtesy of the Calvert Vaux Papers, Manuscripts and Archives Division, The New York Public Library, Astor, Lenox & Tilden Foundations*)

Near Bear Valley, Mariposa County, California.

OSO House, Bear Valley, California, in the
1860s. (*Courtesy of the Bancroft Library, University of California, Berkeley*)

John Charles Olmsted. (*Courtesy of Olmsted Associates, Inc.*)

Olmsted house and office at Brookline, Massachusetts, 1894. (*Courtesy of Olmsted Associates, Inc.*)

Prospect Park centennial plaque with heads of
Olmsted and Vaux; Neil Estern, sculptor.
(*Courtesy of the City of New York Department
of Parks*)

Frederick Law Olmsted in the late 1880s (from
*Frederick Law Olmsted, Landscape Architect,
1822–1903*). (*Courtesy of the New York Public
Library*)

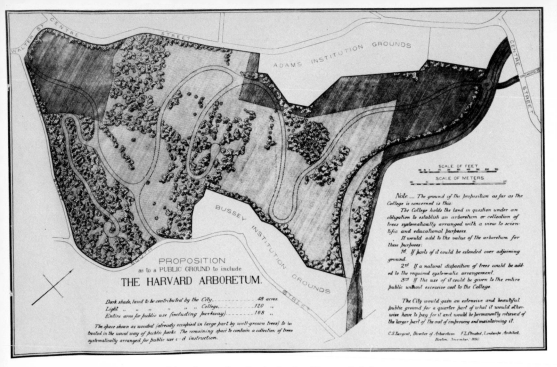

Proposition As to a Public Ground to Include the Harvard Arboretum,
November 1880; and Preliminary Plan of Jamaica Park, 1892 (Boston).
(*Courtesy of the Collection of Regional History and University Archives,
Cornell University*)

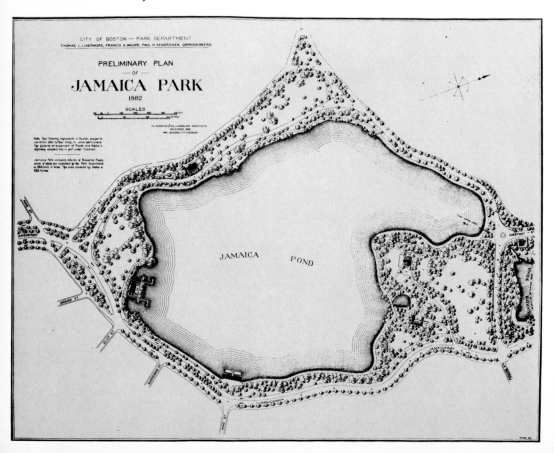

Henry Sargent Codman. (*Courtesy of Olmsted Associates, Inc.*)

Portion of a letter dated 21 December 1887 from Frederick Law Olmsted to the architectural critic Mariana G. Van Renssalaer. (Olmsted here pays tribute to Calvert Vaux.) (*Courtesy of the Library of Congress, Collections of the Manuscript Division, Frederick Law Olmsted Papers*)

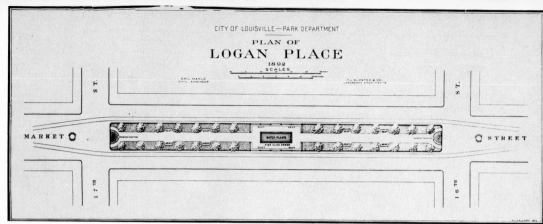

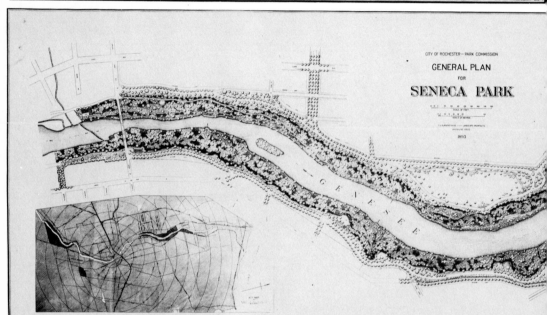

Plan of Logan Place, 1892 (Louisville, Ky.); and General Plan for Seneca Park, 1893 (Rochester, N.Y.). (*Courtesy of the Collection of Regional History and University Archives, Cornell University*)

Charles Eliot. (*Courtesy of Olmsted Associates, Inc.*)

Olmsted in his later years; engraving by T. Johnson from a photograph by James Notman (originally published in the *Century Magazine*). (*Courtesy of the Yale University Library, Stokes Autograph Collection*)

Frederick Law Olmsted, Jr. (*Courtesy of Olmsted Associates, Inc.*)

John Singer Sargent por-
trait of Frederick Law
Olmsted on the grounds of
the Biltmore estate. (*Courtesy of Biltmore House and
Gardens*)

Mary Perkins Olmsted in
1895. (*Courtesy of Olm-
sted Associates, Inc., and
Dr. Stephen P. Gill*)

Mrs. Frederic Law Olmsted 1895
[... in Biltmore 4 Wochen ...]

to keep my plates and copy right out of the sale on the ground that as they had no contract with me they were my property."[8] Olmsted wrote this letter on Central Park stationery, showing that he had been in the office of the park commissioners and in the park.

He felt a genuine division in himself. Here was his place, this park, green and growing, toward which he felt a more than proprietary affection— a real passion of concern. His friend Calvert Vaux was not well. More than ever the park needed him. On the other hand, there was the war stretching out toward an unknown future, and he had enlisted. To Mary, Frederick wrote: "I am greatly perplexed and perhaps not in a position or state of mind to consider healthily and with confidence what I ought to do. I wish you would advise. I don't mean to tax your energies but give me your impressions from your superficial general view. The park and Vaux's interests pull me toward New York. I am intensely held here. It don't seem as if I could do justice to both. Which shall be paramount? Self interest says the park I think. Benevolence, duty, and gratitude say Sanitary Commission. The Sanitary Commissioners are gentlemen, liberal, generous, magnanimous." He even looked with a real eye of appraisal at some houses on Seventy-eighth Street where, he said, "the situation is as nearly right for me as possible."[9]

This was the puzzlement of his mood after staying in Saratoga during the end of August and the beginning of September—where, in a kind of void, he not only began to recover his health but began to look about at the real world in a way he could not during the days on the peninsula. He was busy soon enough with the Sanitary Commission work. During his absence, on August 29 and 30, the second battle of Manassas had been fought with many casualties. Bellows encouraged Olmsted by telling him how well his agents had behaved during this period. Olmsted determined to go back to his duties in Washington as soon as he could, but he was held for a number of days in New York by Calvert Vaux's shocking illness.

His friend suffered from an unspecified kind of fever and was out of his head in a delirium. Olmsted found the Vaux household in confusion. He persuaded Mrs. Vaux to let him call in some of her friends to help her. He thought of calling on Mary but refrained from doing so for fear of damaging her health. A number of his references to her and her health at this time seem to mean that his wife was not, at least at this time, able to stand any kind of strain. He himself attended methodically to Vaux's affairs, presumably those connected with Central Park and those deriving from his private architectural business. His friend's illness was such that the doctor warned Olmsted not to come near the sick man. To Mary, Fred wrote on September 15, "Dr. Brown advised that I should not be at the house, lest Vaux should somehow hear me, or hear of me—he is very acute—and insist on having me to argue with and talk business. He is incessantly philosophizing about glass and colors and drapery and insists on a floating capacity—tries to repose on air, etc." Olmsted admired the quality of his friend's mind even in delirium: "He has said, of course some very clever and sensible things."[10] Among others, he had said to keep Green out. Olmsted feared that this mental difficulty might last, but he had to go on to Washington, leaving Vaux in a precarious state of health.

Vaux, when well, had already let his partner know that he himself desired to resign from the park. He had found himself even less able than Olmsted to work with the tightfisted Mr. Green. Olmsted at this time felt that Vaux was wrong. The importance of the park struck Olmsted forcibly. Great battles determining his future and the future of his fellow citizens were being fought, but people strolled without a seeming care in the pleasure ground that he and Vaux had made out of a desolate wasteland.

What the intelligent stroller might see was noted down by George Templeton Strong in his diary on August 31: "We went after dinner to the upper end of Central Park and walked down. Great progress made since my last visit. The long lines of carriages and the crowds of gents and giggling girls suggested peace and prosperity. There was nothing from which one could have guessed that we are in a most critical period of a great Civil war, in the very focus and vortex of a momentous crisis and in imminent peril of grave national disaster."[11]

Olmsted returned to his work in Washington. But having tasted action on the Pamunkey and the James, he could not stay long in his chair in the house on F Street. He could not forswear going out into the field during the large battles which came this year and the next. He coordinated and checked the work of his agents near the fighting.

At the news of the battle of Antietam in Maryland (fought September 17), Olmsted sent supplies forward. He loaded some on rail cars, "but fearing the trains would choke the road, bought, hired, and borrowed waggons and horses and sent them through by turnpike ('National Road'). The Rail Road did get choked, and all the government medical stores as well as ours were held back some where in twenty miles of cars, behind ammunition and subsistence, so that our waggon train passed them and were twenty-four hours ahead of anything else on the battlefields.... [to his wife] Of course I have been working my brain like fury and my blood boils."[12] This was written September 21.

Olmsted was in Frederick City the day of the entry of the federal troops and saw a girl throw her arms around McClellan's horse. He wrote Mary, "I find the hospitals here in admirable condition, under the circumstances, and [our] agent a splendid fellow."[13] On the twenty-ninth, he wrote again to Mary of having visited hospitals set up in farmhouses and churches in the Maryland battlefields and he said that he was "affected by the great heaps of suffering and death. I saw evidence of the great value of our work."[14]

He could not get away to see his family very often although he worried about them and their situation and about that of his friend Vaux, who was reported still to be ill. "I hear favorable accounts of Vaux.... [but] Brown thought for a time he was going to be deranged badly—and yet holds it a danger." Mary sent him some pictures of herself. "The full length is the most agreeable one I have seen of you.... I don't much like the cold surroundings ...you should be in the garden." He ended this letter (September 29) emotionally: "Kiss all the young ones. I thought of them when I saw hundreds of men dying for them."[15]

Mary was less and less satisfied with their long separation. She protested Frederick's excessive devotion to labor. He found himself glad to have the case argued with him: "You say you did not know that you had reproached me. You hadn't, I was reproaching myself and arguing the case with you. Thank you for encouraging me. That I suppose is what I need."[16] He outlined to her in his fluent way two alternatives: 1) he could come to New York and work in the park regularly, saving several afternoons a week and his evenings for the Sanitary Commission, or 2) he could have her come to live in Washington where he could continue to concentrate his time on the Sanitary Commission. The latter was the more probable alternative and it won. He planned through the fall of 1862 to move his family to Washington. He could endure it no longer alone.

The times he was able to see his wife were often haphazard and had the quality of romance, as if he were not forty and she thirty-two with four children. "If you should be in town on Sunday, leave a note for me with the toll man at the ferry house," he wrote on October 27, 1862, expecting a chance to come up and find her either down on the island or in the city; "I shall come if I can with any conscience. Yours affectly."[17]

He found a house to rent in Washington and described its dimensions and location to Mary in detail and set about preparing for her arrival. While seeing to the cleaning and refurbishing of the house, he entertained a friend, having a kind of picnic with him in the half empty house. The friend was the English newspaperman, Edwin Lawrence Godkin, whom he had come to like and to trust earlier in New York. Godkin, after arriving a complete stranger in New York, intensely curious about all American things, made friends quickly with Fred Olmsted of *Putnam's* and was soon accustomed to visiting the Olmsted farm down on Staten Island. When Godkin came to Washington in late 1862 he looked up Olmsted again.

The two men in recent encounters had found much to talk of together and their friendship was strengthened. Olmsted had written to Charley Brace a little more than a month before this Washington meeting, "Give my dearest love to Godkin. I would limp ten miles to talk an hour with him."[18] Here in the house which Olmsted filled in his imagination already with the noise of his children, the two friends had a narrow escape. When he wrote to his wife about the incident, Frederick spoke of it with comical emphasis as if to take the sting out of the real danger there had been: "Godkin and I came as near heaven [as possible] today because a green servant made a fire of charcoal in the furnace stove down stairs, turned on the damper into the chimney and turned off that into the parlor. We managed to get to the window and open it in time, but have both been in a queer way ever since. Getting all right."[19]

Mary, later in the winter, having settled in Washington, wrote to her "Dear Grandmama" with a sense of satisfaction at leading a normal family existence. "We have recovered from our colds and are flourishing accordingly. Marion is the brightest of little tots. She can get down stairs now quite fast.... You can't think how comical she looks going backward and dropping so fast down from one step to another. Charley and Charlotte are well and are progressing *slowly* in their reading and so on. I have found no school so continue to teach them myself."[20] Owen, not mentioned here, was often with his Olmsted grandparents in Hartford.

Although his family was with him, Frederick had little time at home. He was busy in the grim winter of 1862–63 devising ways of serving the federal troops in the battles which interrupted routine behind-the-lines existence. In Virginia, Fredericksburg was fought on December 13; in Tennessee, Stone's River, December 30 and 31.

As confident as he was in the enlarged role of the commission and his own direction of this function, Olmsted became aware of a certain discomfort in his position, something he had not had to face in the first year in Washington or on the Virginia peninsula. During the time he was loading hospital ships with wounded, the executive committee, which was a close-knit little group in New York City, felt compelled to take into their own hands the daily direction of affairs which Olmsted temporarily abandoned during McClellan's spring campaign against Richmond. They met conveniently during this period every day, and afterwards continued to do so. When the secretary-general returned to Washington after recuperating from his bout with malaria, the executive committee in New York continued to meet frequently and regularly. Its members had caught the habit of command. They wished to keep their hand upon the control of all the activities of the organization. Olmsted was not willing to accede to this fact; he had had it all his own way in the preparatory first year, and he was accustomed to running the commission. The commissioners, when they came up against Olmsted's will, were not quite ready to enforce their authority over his. They valued Olmsted and did not wish to quarrel with him. The ambiguous feelings which these able men, used to controlling large affairs in their own and other men's lives, had toward the masterful man whom they had made their deputy shows in the mixture of opinions George Templeton Strong recorded about Olmsted in the privacy of his diary.

Strong was aware of the energy with which Olmsted had run the hospital ships and noted the terrible results in Olmsted's ill health. When he showed up at the executive offices on sick leave, Olmsted, in Strong's words, was "jaundiced—yellow as butter; the poison of the Pamunkey and the James River malaria is in his very bones."[21] This was on August 29. Almost a month later, after Olmsted had gone back to work, Strong wrote admiringly of the man, naming him in conjunction with the one other competent leader he knew (the quartermaster of the Union Army): "Probably Meigs is the strongest man in the service. Would that he or F. L. Olmsted were Secretary of War! I believe that Olmsted's sense, energy, and organizing faculty, earnestness, and honesty would give new life to the Administration were he in it."[22] But on December 17, Strong wrote after an executive committee meeting at No. 823 Broadway, "We had much debate...about the relative authority of the Commission (or Executive Commission when the Commission is not sitting) and our executive officer, F. L. Olmsted, to wit. Were he not among the truest, purest, and best of men, we should be in irreconcilable conflict. His convictions as to the power an executive officer ought to wield and his faculty of logical demonstration that the commission ought to confide everything to its general secretary on general principles, would make a crushing rupture inevitable, were we not all working in a common cause and without personal considerations."[23]

At stake at this particular meeting was the degree of autonomy the western branches of the commission should have. The commissioners were willing to tolerate a certain amount of independence in the western units if they pledged allegiance in a general sort of way to the United States Sanitary Commission. Olmsted wanted a centralized authority.

In addition to this difference of opinion about policy, the commissioners viewed with some alarm Olmsted's intemperate working habits. They distrusted his power to hold out. Strong's diary notation of January 3, 1863, reported at second hand the observations of another member of the commission, Cornelius Rea Agnew: "Olmsted is in an unhappy, sick, sore mental state. Perhaps his most insanitary habits of life make him morally morbid. He works like a dog all day and sits up nearly all night, doesn't go home to his family (now established in Washington) for five days and nights altogether, works with steady, feverish intensity till four in the morning, sleeps on a sofa in his clothes, and breakfasts on strong coffee and pickles ! ! !"[24]

Probably an exaggerated report, but the intensity of effort of which Olmsted was capable frightened more moderate people. And supporting evidence of the critique was to come later from other firsthand observers. Olmsted was, in fact, immoderate when highly wrought up by emotion or effort, and harmful to himself in the excitement of work. This had been true before, and was to be true again later in life. The Civil War experience, in which every occasion was a crisis of national life, emphasized this trait in the man.

Strong went beyond observation to private conclusion in the January 3 entry: "It will be a terrible blow to the Commission if we have to throw Olmsted over. We could hardly replace him." He, Bellows, Agnew, and Wolcott Gibbs met for supper to talk about this delicate problem. "We agree fully as to the necessity of a radical change in the relations of the Washington office to the Commission and the Executive Committee. Olmsted is unconsciously working to make himself the Commission without advice or assistance. If so, I for one am inclined to withdraw and let him have the credit for doing it."[25]

However, Olmsted and the commissioners got through the winter without an overt break. But it was a situation to make Strong note grimly on March 11: "I fear Olmsted is mismanaging our Sanitary Commission affairs." He went on to analyze Olmsted in a kind of exasperated fascination. "He is an extraordinary fellow, decidedly the most remarkable specimen of human nature with whom I have ever been brought into close relations. Talent and energy most rare; absolute purity and disinterestedness. Prominent defects, a monomania for system and organization on paper (elaborate, laboriously thought out, and generally impracticable), and appetite for power.... I think without horror of the possibility of our being obliged to appoint somebody else General Secretary."[26] Strong was intelligent and sharp. He was also something of a dilettante, never having given himself away to anything completely except perhaps to his love for music and his private vice of enjoying conflagrations.

On his side, Olmsted felt the same dissatisfaction with the executive committee of the Sanitary Commission as he had felt with Haswell Green and the commissioners of Central Park. He had an intense and essentially esthetic point of view toward any task he undertook; it had to be his; it had to be as perfect as he could make it. The explosion point earlier in Central Park had come over the accounting of money. The same kind of irritation arose when the executive committee of the Sanitary Commission attempted to limit the amount of money the secretary-general could spend in an emergency without a specific accounting. Olmsted won this particular battle for the time being.

He growled and grumbled at the commissioners through the winter. The commissioners wisely sent him west on an inspection trip in the spring of 1863. This journey postponed the mutual difficulties of the commissioners and their secretary-general until later in 1863. Olmsted was refreshed in his body and in his mind by new scenes. He recovered his zest always by traveling.

The first segment of his travel was in February to Pittsburgh, Cincinnati, and St. Louis. Cities began to fascinate him. "Pittsburg is a most wonderful reproduction of Birmingham. All the colors and smells and grease. Great steep cliffs opposite, up which I clomb, cinders, coalmines . . . a very grand, mysterious, obscure, gloomy sentiment in the view over the town."[27] This was a different kind of human settlement from those he had known in the villages of Connecticut, the county seats of the South, the less inhabited boroughs of New York.

At the beginning of March, Olmsted visited the Army of the Cumberland headquartered at Murfreesboro, Tennessee. This was the army that had fought the fearful, draining battle of Stone's River the previous December.

He rode out on patrol, saw an unoccupied plantation, sat by a campfire during a thunderstorm with the officers of the unit, shared camp food with these men—"fried ham and coffee. . . . After three hours yarning, went back to the house where we—the general and staff—slept on the floor and on feather-beds."

Next day he and Knapp, the good Mr. Knapp of the Pamunkey, found themselves suddenly representing to these "western" soldiers the whole of the East in their own persons. Brought on horseback before assembled troops they were grandly introduced by the general: "Men! We have some friends here from the East. From the Army of the Potomac, Mr. Olmsted and Mr. Knapp. They will be glad to give you a few words of greeting." They said sixteen words, wrote Fred back to Mary, and were cheered. He found the easy good will of these seasoned men heartening. "All well," he wrote, "but I can hardly walk from the bed to the table, my leg so stiff. . . . A nice bit of amateur campaigning, eh? No letter yet from Charley. No letter from Charlotte. Dada."[28]

On a long tedious train ride across the Illinois prairie, Olmsted amused himself by writing his impression of the people he saw in houses along the tracks, glimpses caught and conclusions made in haste. He thought of writing a book of impressions. (He thought of himself as a writer yet and had had encouragements recently to write. George Curtis had offered to open the doors for him at the Harper's publishing concern. The editor of the London *Spectator* had written asking him to write whatever he wished about "the political and social aspects of your great struggle."[29] Charles Eliot Norton, who admired Olmsted's books about the South, asked him to join him editing or writing notes for the publications of the "Loyal League," an organization that sent material to abolitionist newspapers.

He saw a poor family in a log cabin and wondered about them. They were surely poor Southerners who had moved here and were already finding their neighborhood too crowded. Of the head of the family, he speculated, "I could swear that he has never written a letter in his life; that he takes no newspaper, that he thinks the Vice President is a mulatto, that the President is a despot, that he means to resist the execution of the Conscription Act and to refuse to pay any more taxes; that he thinks Northern and Southern Illinois ought to be two states, and that he hates a Yankee 'worse than a nigger'; . . . He helped drive the Indians away from here, as well as the panthers and the wolves. . . . He has not the smallest particle of servility; I should not be surprised if he were a member of some church and meant to do God's will, according to his light; and on the whole, I must say that I think that the average English agricultural laborer leads a[n] even less enviable life than this poor man on the prairies. He never had any fear that he could not get food for his children or that . . ."[30] The sketch trailed off unfinished.

Diary entries such as this remained intact for his own amusement, or his family's. The war and later activities prevented his making up another book of impressions.

At the end of March he reached the Mississippi. He saw that the commission's delivery of fresh vegetables—"230 barrels of potatoes and onions" —had fended off the scurvy for Admiral Porter's river fleet.[31] He secured General Grant's support for commission activities in this area. Spring coming on warmed Olmsted into an enjoyment of the natural scene, the characters of privates and generals, and his own reactions. He tended to business, but he also took in life through his pores.

Of Grant, he wrote that "no general [was] more beloved or belovable, by his men." And he said, judging his abilities, "As a general his quality is dependent on the quick and sure, snap judgments of commonsense and simple unselfish humble purpose." He found that "Sherman commands a worshipful sentiment from those familiar with him which leads me to suspect that he was more *genius* than any other of our generals."[32]

On a more companionable level, Olmsted made friends with one of Sherman's staff officers, an engineer, Captain Jenney, "with whom I rode a couple of hours in the afternoon" after dining outdoors in a plantation yard surrounded by willow oaks and Pride of China trees. "He has had a half artist education in Paris and was warm on parks, pictures, architects, engineers and artists."[33] Olmsted expanded in gratitude in the chance delight of such talk. War had starved him of what had become essential to his existence.

The inspection trip was good for him as a person. However, the slipshod management of the commission's affairs in this part of the world disgusted him. In the midst of his rhapsody about spring air along the Mississippi, he wrote gruffly to Bellows, "I should herewith send you my resignation. I think, however, that my skirts are clean."[34] But this was *pro forma* only. He came back from this experience in high gear, full of what he knew and impatient of restrictions put upon his right way of doing things. It was inevitable that the following summer, even in the midst of great battles, he should engage in a running struggle with the commissioners. Olmsted had seen new worlds, opportunities for the commission to do a greater work in the war, and incalculable opportunities for himself, in the land stretching north of the Ohio and out to and beyond the Mississippi. Full of his own power and vision, he was affronted to discover that the commissioners were determined to keep direction of affairs in their own hands. He was not one tamely to submit. He fought with vigor.

There was embarrassment among the commissioners, who resisted somewhat dumbly the persuasive Mr. Olmsted, but were also obstinate. It seemed to Olmsted and to the others occasionally during 1863 that there must be a break, but for month after month, there was no final one. The executive committee continued to meet and to direct policy while Olmsted objected. Olmsted won on small points, but he continued to lose on the larger ones.

Olmsted's reactions, Strong's sidelong glances at their difficulties, and Bellows's fatherly worries were all written down in the form of letters and diary entries which give the flavor of the time. All this time the war went on, and these individuals performed creditably and industriously in trying to save their country.

While carrying on his duties, for the Sanitary Commission and to an extent for Central Park, Olmsted continued to think about his personal affairs. Discontent with the policy of both sets of commissioners allowed him the luxury of complaining privately. He received a letter from John Olmsted in April in which the father by the evidence of the son's reply made some kind of proposal to Frederick that they go into business together, or that the son undertake some kind of business. Frederick outlined his financial situation, which, for a large family, was meager: "While I am in the service of the Sanitary Commission, I can lay up no money. I take for services $2500....I still get $100 a month from the park (out of which Weidenmann has been paid) though I expect any day to hear that this is stopped." (Jacob Weidenmann became distinguished later in his own right. Apparently at this time he substituted for both Olmsted and Vaux in the management of the park.) Olmsted went on in this letter to his ever patient father. "With the general rise in prices, I find myself constantly dropping a little behindhand....I never find myself quite square up. So that if I leave the Commission Sanitary [*sic*] as I am liable to do at any moment, I should be obliged to call on you to tide me over to the next berth."

If the executive committee was not happy with their secretary-general, he in his turn was critical of them: "The Commissioners blunder so in their business, whenever I am away." This was written in the letter quoted above to his father. And he went on, "The Commissioners must either submit to a system and discipline in their own transactions—or I must be relieved of responsibility." What scorched his mind was that he was "practically relieved of all general responsibility at this moment"; and he would "refuse to resume it except upon better conditions of personal security than before."[35]

The step down did not in fact take place. In actuality, he continued to direct the day-to-day operations of the organization, to lay out plans for the future, and to keep a tight rein on all its operations wherever he could control them. He found in late spring that he worked more effectively in New York, where he met personally with the executive committee. He effected a gradual transfer of his operations to that city.

But as late as May 22 he wrote to his father from Washington, where, as he said, "It is very hot and noisome here but we are all pretty well. Charly learning to fiddle, Owen to climb over the house, and Marion to say 'dada.' She is uncommonly backward and only half pint pot size, but lively and clever enough."[36]

It was in this season also (in May, 1863) that he and Vaux resigned with finality, as they thought, from their Central Park connection. Frederick to

John Olmsted: "Vaux has been finally badgered off the park and my relations with it are finally closed. He couldn't bear it even as *consulting* architect. They wound it up with a very innocent complimentary resolution."[37] He and Vaux were united in this backing out of the relationship they had entered so youthfully and triumphantly six years before. But the park was there, growing with every season. People enjoyed it and made it a part of their lives. Olmsted had lived in it and with it, and could not rid himself of an affectionate interest and proprietary concern for it. On August 2, after having followed great armies through unimaginable battles, he was to write to his father in a quiet moment: "I am going out this evening to see the park, which I have not before this summer."[38]

The thunderhead clouds of summer piled over New York, and heat filled its streets. Frederick was staying alone in the city while his wife and children remained in Hartford with the older Olmsteds. As he directed supplies from southerly depots to points ahead of Lee's advance into Pennsylvania, he watched the developing campaign with grim absorption. On June 23, he wrote to Mary: "Chief thinks Hooker will attack.... The Pennsylvania defence is a horrid, tragic comedy.... I think we shall see what Lee is after, in another day at the furthest." He said also, "I cannot come to Hartford this week.... It is very lonely here, now.... If I can possibly manage it, I shall get to Hartford next week." To Mary he ended with a combination of affection and nonsense, "Take the air, hang care, eat clams, laugh and grow—into your place.   Affectionate husband."[39]

On June 26, he wrote that he must remain in New York. The Westerners were threatening to resign from the commission if he put through his reforms, i.e., made them dependent for orders on him; and "I can manage the Executive Committee while here, very well but they would put the fat in the fire as soon as I left them."[40] This was egotism, but his strong will was almost a naked force in him which he was helpless to resist. Purpose had gathered in him since his days of solitude and quiet contemplation when the qualities that were in him strengthened to a powerful equilibrium which allowed him now to be his own man whether winningly or not so winningly.

He continued in this letter to his wife to express the keen emotion he felt during this national emergency, the Lee invasion, while people strolled carelessly in his park: "I never felt so near taking a musket myself."[41] He advised Mary to go on to Litchfield, and he would come there as soon as he could. And he envisioned all of them, himself, Mary, and the children, settled here in this city, where he felt at home.

During these tense days he stayed at the Brevoort Hotel. He dined evenings often with Godkin. (Already he and Godkin were planning a splendid weekly newspaper or magazine which they would edit together.)

Alone, he sometimes walked out at dusk to catch his breath. "It is like going to the mountains to go to Murray Hill. I have walked out there merely to enjoy fresh air."[42]

He sent his wife a picture of himself on July 2, looking, as he said, like Ben Butler, "the beast of New Orleans." "Please write me more about the children. I have not anything to tell you about myself. You ought to write four times as much as I do—letting alone that you are a woman and don't shirk details."

He bullied Mary and teased her and in the next breath asked her advice: "Help me to a name for the project [the publication he and Godkin were planning]—Comment, Examiner, Reviser, Inspector, Tide, Key, Scrutiny, National, Faggot, Yeoman."[43]

It was at this time also, in the midst of all his duties, that Olmsted assisted several friends in the organization of a club. He was asked advice by Wolcott Gibbs and George Templeton Strong in their desire to institute a strong organ for conserving into the future the kind of public effort and good will temporarily embodied in the Sanitary Commission. Olmsted fluently supplied rules, admissions procedures, guidelines for the kinds of men to be admitted, and significantly stressed the need to search out persons of talent and promise in the arts as well as of good family and money. The club became a fact, the Union League Club. Inevitably in later years it became, par excellence, a haven for heavy men of affairs and money, hardly what Olmsted had suggested, but then he was elsewhere. He was never a member himself; he seemed not to have wished to have any regular part in it after having lightheartedly helped to found it.

The battle of Gettysburg concentrated the secretary's attention. Olmsted was a general to his forces during this time and after surely as Meade was on the field. The battle was fought July 1 through 3. Olmsted forwarded supplies to the scene of actual fighting. From July 2, a short note survives from one of his agents. Writing on that day in the middle of it, J. H. Douglas wrote to F. L. Olmsted: "Two wagons are now at the front with the 11 and 12 Corps. Shall get forward supplies to them as soon as I am able."[44]

Olmsted supervised the strategy of getting supplies ahead of the movement of troops. On July 7 he wrote to his wife from Baltimore,

I left New York Saturday night, spent Sunday in Philadelphia, where I got the first conclusive account of the victory of Mead [Olmsted's spelling]. . . . While in Philadelphia we bought several tons of fresh eggs, butter, mutton, chickens, fruit, milk, etc. which were delivered Monday morning to a refrigerating car (with a ton of ice), which we chartered for the purpose. Coming here ahead of it, we bought a lot of larger camp-meeting tents, and a larger lot of miscellaneous furniture, loading another car, last night got our ice-car over to the Northern Central Road, and both cars attached to the first train through to Gettysburg after the battle. . . . Our regular waggon force was on the ground during the battle, and the waggons visited all the field-hospitals as fast as they were established and hours before they received supplies from other quarters. We have to-day purchased four pairs of horses and four sutlers' waggons, which will start tomorrow for Frederick. I shall also go tomorrow to Frederick, and there load the waggons and send them scouring all the country where we had been skirmishing. I have arranged to receive and take care of about forty tons of supplies a day, for the present, if the people supply them, as I think they will.

I am pretty well tired with day and night work, but not ill.[45]

On July 15 Olmsted wrote to his wife from Frederick, Maryland; his organization had been feeding one thousand men daily since the battle and "doing a great deal for stragglers and broken down men along the roads." As usual, he was cheerful after effort:

I had two good days of campaigning, camping three nights, and enjoyed it. I went through our line of battle and crawled up among the trees and rocks to our most advanced skirmishers in the midst of the Indian fighting, our men advancing from tree to tree and driving the rebel skirmishers back from tree to tree. There was a good deal of sharp shooting but the chances of a hit on either side was very small. Finally we advanced so far there through the trees we could see the rebels throwing dirt on their earthworks.[46]

By wagon and horseback, the secretary-general inspected Sanitary Commission "stations" and then finished with his tour of duty, in the middle of an afternoon boarded a train carrying wounded. They reached a junction point and he had to detrain. "Here I was very sick, got a vile bed at a nasty tavern and nearly fainted asleep. Woke up a couple of hours [later] and waited on the track till 11 o'cl. P.M. Then got upon a chance train out of place with wounded rebs and from there to 3 A.M. was lying on the floor of a car which yesterday carried hogs and had not been cleaned, and was now occupied with wounded rebels and a dead Pennsylvanian the whole producing the most shocking stench I ever endured. Came to Baltimore station at daybreak and thence walked into the Eutaw House, toting my luggage on my shoulder." The badness was not all bad; he saw himself getting through it with a kind of bravado. He did not dislike his desperate expeditions.

As if he remembered something the other side of the big battle, he wrote, "I don't hear anything more of the paper. I am afraid the war has knocked it out of their heads."

He was heading toward Washington and then back to New York, and ended his letter, "With love to Charly and Charlotte and Owen and Birdy I am all love to you. Fred."[47]

In this disorganized summer, Mary visited his and her relatives and friends. She was in Hartford in late July. Frederick at this time asked about his father, seeming to have some worry about him. He asked her if she might meet him in Litchfield, for he was going there to visit Fred Kingsbury on one of his journeys, writing, "Cd. you meet then?"[48]

The battle of Gettysburg had spared Frederick the firsthand sight of the burning, murdering draft riots in New York City which began July 13, when men were drafted for the first time. Resenting the purchasable exemptions of the rich, the draftable poor attacked every object of their fears and prejudices. The recent immigrants and the native poor whites particularly resented the free blacks who had been coming into the city. The blacks were the greatest sufferers in this lawlessness—even black orphans being attacked and a black orphanage burned.

After he came to a stop from his exertions in the field, Olmsted was peculiarly prey again to discontent. On July 29, he wrote to Mary: "I don't feel as if I could stand the Sanitary Commission any longer."[49] Yet only six months before (on January 31) Olmsted had written passionately to one of the members of the executive committee, Wolcott Gibbs, "It looks to me as if the question of popular doggedness of purpose in the war was soon to be determined, and might be turned by a hair. It is only necessary that a certain number of men should commit themselves to go through with it whatever comes, and whoever drops out; to give no hearing to any suggestion of quitting, come what will, to make final success sure."[50] Yet after the mental and physical exhaustion of the summer battles, Olmsted himself felt that he might quit. He and Edwin L. Godkin had struck fire off each other both personally and professionally. Olmsted spent weeks of feverish activity promoting a publication that he and the congenial new friend might edit together as if this were the alternative to which he were going to turn full-time when he left the commission. (That he believed that he could not go back to the work he loved in the park was tragic to him but he put that behind him, as he thought.)

It is not clear which man had the idea, but a May 9 letter of Godkin's gives evidence that they had written and talked of it previously. On this date he wrote Olmsted, "I have been thinking and talking a great deal about a first class weekly paper ever since I saw you, and am thinking and talking of it still." He asked Olmsted if he were "in earnest" to go into such a scheme: "I should be very glad to make some such arrangement."[51] On June 25, Olmsted brought the scheme to a Union League Club meeting and shared it with his friends. Strong noted the episode in his diary, that Olmsted presented the "project of a weekly paper, independent of mere party politics, and upholding sound principles of loyalty and nationality. What vast good such a paper might do." Next day Olmsted visited Strong with a more practical proposition. Strong and three others were to be trustees of "a fund to be raised by subscription."[52] Olmsted described to his wife his efforts among "gentlemen" and "capitalists" getting money for his project. Apparently he and Godkin prepared a sample issue, or possibly an advertising brochure. "The paper I had prepared by Godkin and myself was much liked and is printing. I can only say that so far, the enterprise is initiated as I could wish, in all respects. We meet . . . on Tuesday night and shall then go ahead for subscription . . . I shall go into it strong, meaning to succeed. Your affectionate man."[53]

This was no flighty plan. The weekly became the *Nation*, which Edwin L. Godkin was to edit for many decades, making it an influence and a power.

Almost forgotten for the part he had in its beginning, Frederick Law Olmsted was to be gone from the scene by the end of the summer. (Some of the quality of the partnership of the summer of 1863 can be sensed in the tribute which an editor of the *Nation* paid forty years later when Olmsted died: "Would that the hand which clasped his in the small beginnings of this enterprise, could now portray that modest and lovable character, warm-hearted and yet sane, well-balanced, equable, gentle as a woman or as those growing things which he wrought into lines and tracts of beauty for the personal adornment of his native land.")[54]

The magazine was only one of several alternatives considered at this time.[55] He had also considered management of the freedmen, as a letter to his father had shown. But Olmsted was restless with ideas beyond these. When he had traveled west recently he had seen possibilities for wealth in Chicago: "I couldn't help speculating for [about?] accumulation at Chicago. There is such an obvious want of a pleasure-ground there, I think that by a small admission-fee, a handsome interest on a large expenditure of capital could be got." Even Olmsted felt momentarily the fever of speculation blowing across the North during wartime. He seemed to be thinking of running a park for profit. This, however, he was never to do. The idea brushed him, but never took hold, and when later he discovered that there was permanency in the profession of landscape architect, he never needed to.

But his situation of near bankruptcy had come home to him. He knew that men regarded him as competent, "a man of unusual capacity and good judgment in certain respects, and there are some matters which it is getting to be thought I can handle better than anybody else in the country." Yet he was not able to support his family without occasionally turning to his father. The farm, which belonged to his wife and was held in trust for her children by her first marriage, was now merely a bother: "The farm is going to the dogs and no help for it that I can see. Its value for sale would be very small now—which shows what speculators think of it. It is a great drag on my comfort. An elephant to carry about."

Yet at this season he felt well again and ambitious—"I am much better for my western scrabble, weigh more than I have in fifteen years." The subsequent displacements of sleep and rest during the summer battles were temporary and stimulating rather than debilitating. Olmsted alarmed people by his irregular habits, yet when the lightning bolt of a new chance came to him in August, 1863, he was poised ready to take advantage of it.

A letter marked "Private" came to him at the end of the first week in August. He opened it to find it from his friend Charles Dana, a newspaperman whom he had known since his days at *Putnam's*. Dana had been recently with Grant at his headquarters as a special commissioner of the War Department; he and Olmsted may have seen each other on the Mississippi and renewed the acquaintance that had begun in New York restaurants frequented by journalists. (Dana was to be assistant secretary of war.) The letter, which was to change Olmsted's life, read:

My dear Olmsted,

I came from Washington four days since on the summons of the new proprietors of the Mariposa estate. They have offered me the Superintendency of that vast establishment. I have refused it, and have recommended you. The salary offered me is ten thousand a year, including a furnished house to live in . . .

You are less rooted than I am. . . . It seems to me a chance you may like to accept.

I communicate with you at the request of Mr. Opdyke, who may also write to you himself. Whether he does or not, please write to him on the subject, or what will be better come to New York and see him at once. They are in some haste.[56]

From references in letters near to this time, it seems likely that Frederick had gone visiting to Hartford where his father was, to Litchfield where Mary was staying, and to Walpole, New Hampshire, where his sister Bertha and her husband and baby were living. He came back immediately to New York to try to make up his mind whether to go after the job.

Olmsted went through much outward debate about this change, but inwardly he was strongly pulled toward it. The argument that he had made against quitters in the war effort must have told against him in his inner dialogue, but a trait of his character operated here with a force he could not resist. When Olmsted had done his utmost, when he had given a certain satisfactory shape to an effort, he was done with it and ready to move on to another project. He was deeply and essentially the artist rather than, as he seemed, the man of affairs. In arguing his case, Olmsted wrote voluminously to his wife, his father, and Dr. Bellows of the Sanitary Commission, who was both shocked and relieved at Olmsted's imminent leavetaking. Frederick conscientiously lined up reasons for and against going, but in this specious exercise of rationality there shines through the emotional attraction of Mariposa. Frederick was dazzled by a new prospect for the exercise of his talents.

Out West, in an unknown territory, was a whole estate of land and people which he was called upon to organize and make flourish. General Fremont had failed to make Mariposa prosper, but vast mining holdings were waiting there for proper development as well as unknown resources of grazing land and timber. The present owners were a group of Eastern investors. Of them Olmsted had some suspicions but could find nothing particular to justify his feelings. He believed that if they were honest, and if he was left alone to manage this large affair, then Mariposa might bloom. And he would incidentally be freed from the embarrassing financial worries in which he found himself year after year. The war would go on without him. The

United States Sanitary Commission was well organized and well established. He had done his part here.

The largeness of the challenge snared his imagination. To his father he wrote on August 10: "It is a whole county 5 × 40 miles, with a tenant population of 7000." But, "It is 200 miles from the coast and dreary, I have no doubt." Arguing against himself, testing himself to see how he felt, he went on, "I am rather disposed to decline it chiefly, or partly, because I think it might be too much for me. I should have complete, entire... management. There are seven mines opened besides a large amount of Chinese placer mining, a railroad and more to be laid out, and a great commercial business established."[57] One day later, on August 11, he wrote his wife, "I incline to think this afternoon that I can hardly afford to decline the offer they are prepared to make." The tone in which he went on might well have told Mary what his decision would be. "It is in the mountains—with the best air in the world, and grand scenery. [But] I don't see anything else attractive except the money-making."[58] The attraction of an unknown land to be shaped, and the infernal temptation of money-making, worked together on him. He was caught up in a current of desire which was not without murkiness, but which he enjoyed as it pulled him along.

He knew that this move would involve a great change in all their lives. To Mary he wrote, "I think, therefor, you had better be considering what you want me to do for you—where and how you will live, etc."[59]

Still arguing against himself, he wrote to Mary, "Don't think I fail to see the immense labor, anxieties, and heroisms, which acceptance will impose upon me. I hate the wilderness and wild, tempestuous, gambling men, such as I shall have to master, and shrink from undertaking to encounter [?] them, as few men would."[60] (The ideas here deserve to be sorted out. He did not hate the wilderness of nature, but the wilderness of man. He savored the attitude of the civilized man looking at the wild, not of the wild man matching himself against raw nature. The piquancy was in the contrast.)

At the very time he slipped nearer to acceptance, he continued to have suspicions about the management of the company with which he might be going to associate himself. "As I am now forty-two years old," he wrote John Olmsted, "I cant afford to go on board a rotten ship."[61]

When Henry Bellows, the president of the Sanitary Commission, learned of Olmsted's possible resignation from their organization, he wrote on August 13 rather harshly to his colleague, "I think the faith of many, already pinned unconsciously to you, would fail and grow cold, if you should quit the field under what would seem to be a pecuniary temptation."[62] These words hurt, for it was indeed in part the devilish attraction of money and ease that constituted a great deal of the pull of the offer.

Olmsted's reply, probably explosive and indignant, went to Bellows between August 13 and 17. Bellows replied with some asperity of his own, allowing to show some of the doubts that he and his fellow officers had felt about Olmsted's management of the Sanitary Commission. "With the feelings you have about the Commission, and your confessed loss of interest in it—if they are your habitual feelings—I do not see that you can hesitate to leave it for the excellent and inviting opening in California. I was not fully aware of how deep and fixed your dissatisfaction was. Not being able to understand clearly *what* you have aimed to make the Commission or what its ideal in your own mind is—of course I can have little sympathy with your declarations about its failure. It has failed to realize *your* ideal for it. It has not failed to realize that of the Board, or that of the Nation, or that of its contributors. It has affected ten times over all I ever had in view in starting it."[63]

He asked Olmsted, if he decided to go, to keep their differences about the commission private. This Olmsted did, and it was allowed to be thought, and has been repeated since, that Olmsted left the United States Sanitary Commission to go to California principally for reasons of health.

Having disposed of their joint business and called it quits, the honest and formidable Bellows, a man Olmsted admired even when making a little fun of his solemnity, gave it to his correspondent straight about his assets and defects:

I have long felt that your constitutional qualities, both bodily, mental and moral, made you a difficult subordinate. You ought not to work under any body. I think you the most singular compound of the practical philosopher and the impracticable man-of-business I have ever encountered. I don't believe any Body of Directors could get along two years with you. And this—because your own notions are so dominant and imperative, and prevent [?] conscience, heart, will and body and soul in a way to make concessions to ordinary judgements—which are none the less valuable for being instinctive and the result of contact with average people—utterly impossible. When was there a Board of more liberal and enlightened views, more considerate, flexible, patient, and respectful than ours? You complain that you have not been able to win it over to your views. Might they not complain with more reason that they have never succeeded in making any impression upon you? . . .

My ambition for you has been to see you in some independent function, the Head of a Bureau, a Department, the Editor of a great newspaper. . . . With *subordinates,* you have, and would have, no difficulties. It is only with *peers* or *superiors* (official) that you cannot serve. I still think the country will lose a power it can very ill afford to overlook or dispense with, when you retire from public affairs into Mariposa! Yet, it is very likely that your imperfect health, your irritable nerves and your fastidious character—your ever teeming and brooding brains—give to practical men, a certain doubt of your qualifications for affairs. It must be this which has kept you in Washington two years without being seized upon by the sagacity of the Government for some high position. . . .

In regard to the pecuniary question. I did not know your embarrassments, nor your necessities. I think they alter the case considerably. I shall not think it strange if you yield to the argument of bread and butter.

Bellows ended this letter with an expression of friendship as characteristic as his expression of opinion.

My dear Olmsted, I write you with the plainness you have always practiced with me. I can't say a thousandth part all I think and feel, but what I do say I mean. I am inexpressibly grieved at the thought of parting with you; grieved at your disappointment with our common work. . . . But I shall always rejoice to have known so intimately and worked so long with, a man—of such peculiar genius, such extraordinary disinterestedness, such tender affections, and such deep and unalloyed patriotism.   Ever yours truly and affectionately.[64]

The exchange did not irremediably crack their friendship.

Whatever he felt about leaving the Sanitary Commission, Olmsted went straight ahead. He wrote to his father on August 20 the terms of his acceptance: $10,000 salary; a bonus of stock, $50,000, of which he was to forfeit $40,000 if he left at the end of one year, $30,000 if he left at the end of the second year, etc.[65] He was going hastily to Washington, to Walpole, New Hampshire (where Bellows was), and to Hartford to make final arrangements for resigning from the United States Sanitary Commission and going to work in the position of superintendent of the Mariposa Company. "Shall take Mary and all, if found practicable"[66]; otherwise, he would have to go and go soon alone, and send for them later after he had found a place for them to live in what he knew would be primitive surroundings in the wilds of California.

This was found to be the course he would have to pursue, a solitary voyage to his new world at the end of the continent. The New York *Daily-Times* on September 14, 1863, carried the following item: "Mr. Frederick L. Olmsted sails today for California."[67] In the way that was characteristic of him—always resilient and hopeful in beginnings—Olmsted faced the unknown future with remarkable cheerfulness and expectation, able to leave behind the cares which had worn him out, and his own part in the large accomplishment of the United States Sanitary Commission.

In the lives of a number of people, he left a rather large void. Godkin, with whom Olmsted had been planning a joint project until a few days only before he changed his direction, wrote musingly to Charles Eliot Norton (with whom Olmsted had made him acquainted) about the dreary prospect that "such an excellent fellow, so clean a brain, should be buried in Bear Valley. . . . He was so much to me that perhaps I exaggerate his importance to the public, but I feel satisfied we shall all feel his loss sorely when the work of reorganizing the South comes to be done."[68] G. T. Strong, who had criticized Olmsted and been irritated by him, wrote in his diary, "Olmsted has completed his arrangement with the Mariposa people and is to bury himself for five years in a mountain gorge in California. We can ill spare him."[69] Dr. Walter R. Steiner, one of the medical men of the Sanitary Commission, wrote, "It seems as though the light of the Commission was being lost."[70]

CHAPTER XVIII

Mariposa

The white peaked Sierras were very beautiful. They are to be
remembered.

—F. L. O., to his wife, January 8, 1865[1]

"I DON'T KNOW when I have had such a day of delight,"[2] Frederick Olmsted wrote to his wife Mary about his crossing of the Isthmus of Panama
in September, 1863. He was leaving the war behind, going west to California
to try his fortune in gold mining. He was joining the westward movement of
his countrymen which went on irresistibly even though a civil war was being
fought in the East.

Olmsted sailed from New York City to the Atlantic side of the Isthmus,
then crossed the narrow neck of Panama by way of the first American transcontinental railway, which had been in operation for eight years. Olmsted,
forgetting the war, found the novelty of tropical scenery a joy. Forests
fantastically draped with vines passed his moving train window. A deep
river, the Chagres, flowed past. At dusk, giant bats laced the quickly darkening sky. Olmsted responded sensitively, as if sloughing off all the busyness
of the past two years. "Simply in vegetation it is superb and glorious and
makes all our model scenery—so far as it depends on beauty of foliage—
very tame and quakerish. You will see it and I will not go into particulars.
[He was writing to Mary, who was to follow at some future time.] I think
it produces a very strong moral impression through an enlarged sense of
the bounteousness of nature."[3]

He thought how such an effect of profusion in foliage might be used
in Central Park: "I could not help asking whether the idea I had of producing some such effect about the island in the park was preposterous with our
Northern trees and shrubs and vines."[4] As if he were yet working for the
Park, Olmsted wrote to chief gardener Pilat the same day he wrote to Mary

suggesting that he try such an effect. Pilat was to reply to Olmsted in California that, if the commissioners allowed it, he would make the attempt.

Continuing his journey on the ship *Constitution* northward toward California from the Pacific side of the Isthmus, he saw mud villages of Indians backed by bare hills. Beyond was a high range "which is grave and makes grand cloud effects."⁵ He was repelled by the first sight of land near San Francisco, "dreary in its aspect, dry, brown, smooth hills."⁶ (It was not only the dry time of year, but California was enduring one of its worst droughts in years.) As his ship passed into the bay, he had nothing with which to compare the scene but what he remembered of other places. "The Golden Gate is a narrows about as wide as New York's, with mountainous hills on each side and low cliffs at the edge. The hills are quite like the English downs—perfectly bare of trees or shrubs—and most awfully bleak." The port itself struck him as "the noblest possible." On the other hand, San Francisco did not seem anything remarkable. "The town is what you would expect, a multiplication of Stapleton, Staten Island (Brooklyn, Jersey City, etc.—along the river) and so far as I have seen in the interior, much like any western town."

Getting through the crowd on the wharf, he was kicked on his bad leg by a dray horse. "It has made me quite lame."⁷ He spent one day in his hotel room but then went out to meet the agents of the Mariposa Company to plan his first journey to the mines. He found himself enjoying the mellow, windy air, the sea-washed colors of the buildings, and the lively movement of this new people.

His mood in coming west had been one of self-congratulation. He had had his wits about him, he thought, in accepting this job. He had not followed the easiest way; he had taken advantage of a great chance. He had had some subdued doubts about the company and its claims, but his discreet enquiries in New York had uncovered nothing tangibly wrong with the operation. He believed substantially in the weight of the charge made to him by the officers of the company in naming him superintendent:

> Your offices will be peculiarly directed to the development of the mineral resources of the estate and the use of the means necessary to that end. . . .
> Your authority, in the premises, is full and unlimited. . . .
> Our banker, Messrs. Donohue Ralston & Co. of San Francisco, will give you all necessary financial aid, in honoring checks drawn by you as Manager, for all purposes of your Trust.⁸

He had been led to believe that the estate, which had gone bankrupt under the inept management of General Fremont, was still possessed of resources which could be made to pay. His hope was that he and his family would share in this prosperity. First, he believed that he would be able to save money, at least eight thousand dollars a year. To accomplish this goal, he would put behind him all foolish, unattainable, well-loved ambitions and concentrate instead on getting money in his purse. He had had years of semidependency upon his father. Now, with his own immediate family enlarged, he expected to achieve at least monetary independence, if it meant coming to the end of the continent away from all green vegetation.

His father, still devoted, watched his son disappear into the distance. And he had a prospect of the whole family, Mary and the children, disappearing soon also. He asked that Owen be left behind to comfort him. "Old age has few pleasures. A child in the family is a great joy,"[9] John Olmsted wrote to his son. This wish was not fulfilled. When Mary followed Frederick, she brought all the children with her.

The Olmsteds of Hartford, and the friends whom Frederick left behind, ranged themselves in circles near or far in his imagination. There were his father and stepmother, the one modestly doing his private good deeds but saying little, the other enlisted in public good works, particularly for the Sanitary Commission, carrying on efforts in which Frederick had started her. In Maine lived sister Bertha and her husband Mr. Niles, as she spoke of him, a young minister. In Hartford, with the senior Olmsteds, was Frederick's closest sister, Mary. In Hartford, also, was brother Albert, who had served for a time in the army, but who was now out and at loose ends. He was to write Frederick in California about a choice of a career. Should it be engineering, law, or what? Others of the numerous family—uncles, aunts, cousins—took on shadowy outlines; they were farther away from Frederick's active consciousness. But there was one persistent and familiar ghost who continued to haunt both Frederick and Mary. The figure of the dead John Hull stood over them, or at least was beside them, all their lives. And he lived on in the active and engaging traits of his children, John Charles, Charlotte, and Owen, whom Frederick now fathered.

Frederick had to shake off past ties, past concerns, upon taking up a new life in California. He had not come here, as he thought, to look at scenery. He intended to be practical and businesslike. He had undertaken the conquest of Mariposa in as determined a fashion as he had, six years before, stormed the bastions of Central Park. But when he began discussing financial arrangements with the banking agent of the company, he found that the grand affairs he was to manage seemed sadly diminished by a close look.

Frederick told the tale of his initial disappointment to Mary in a letter written on October 12. Instead of the mines' producing the $100,000 a month that he had been led to expect, they were producing only $25,000, and that sum was expected to fall lower. The Mariposa Company's account with the bank was at the moment overdrawn. He tried to reason out the situation, which seemed due to "bad management": "It will increase my cares and, if I can be equal to the demand, the importance of my services. It damages the value of the stock and reduces my compensation for the present, but it will the better prepare the company for radical changes and for giving me free swing in establishing a policy."[10]

The beginning was bad, but Olmsted plucked up his heart in action. He walked about looking at the city, and he began to meet interesting people. One of them was the transplanted New England Unitarian pastor, the Reverend Thomas Starr King. He had come west only three years before and had written articles about California for the Boston *Transcript*. Olmsted knew him to be a mainstay of the United States Sanitary Commission; through him a good deal of money had come east to the commission from this region.

But his beginning to acclimate himself in San Francisco was cut short by his first journey into the interior. Martin, his personal servant, who had come out with him, set out on the regular conveyance for Bear Valley, but Olmsted, as the new manager, and a Mr. Billings, acting for the bank, went in considerable style, by "a special service, with relays, so as to get through in thirty-six hours." (Olmsted had hired an accountant and an engineer in the East. Presumably they came on to Bear Valley also, by a different conveyance.)

The trip began with a ferry ride across the bay. It was the end of a long, dry summer and fall. Olmsted was impressed first by the dust. The great domed swellings of the coastal ranges through which they passed were a pale dun brown in the glare of light descending from a wide sky. Beyond the swellings of these giant hills was a flat, bare plain, the inland valley of California, stretching monotonously before the traveler. Stockton was a stopping place upon the way, and Olmsted looked eagerly beyond to the ramparts of the Sierra. To attain those blue distant mountains there were many weary miles to go across the valley, then upward through tilting foothills. The stage climbed at last precariously around and across great bare mountains, alongside almost dry riverbeds. Trees appeared, not in masses as at home, but singly, dotting the swelling hills. Over a pass, down through thicker woods, upward again and then braking to assist the horses, the coach swayed downhill into a high open space, more a crossing or a plateau than a valley, the town of twelve hundred souls called Bear Valley, plain and ugly, a mining town scattered about helter-skelter in shacks and tents. But there was a pure sky overhead, and the outcroppings upon the mountainsides glittered in the sunlight.

Frederick tried to describe the place to Mary.[11] A great shouldering mountain reared up, Mount Bullion, "so different from our mountains that I can't readily describe it." The human scene was as foreign as the raw hills. There were shanties where the Chinese laborers lived. The company store was clean and neat, but, after all, only a store. As for Bear Valley, the village, to which he proposed to bring his family, "It is just a miner's village—no women and everything as it must be where men don't live but merely camp."

He settled in temporary quarters, apparently at first in the OSO Hotel and later in the top floor of the company's store. He looked about trying to get beyond reports, rumors, and tales, to see Mariposa for himself. He found the human encrustment on the brown and dusty valley floor small and small-minded. He had never before been concerned with a mining venture, and he found the tearing up of the ground disturbing. "I rather think that if I had known what the place was I should not have asked you to come here. You must be prepared for a very hard life; I can hardly face it yet and see what you are going to do. But it is too late to retreat; so the sooner we trim sail to the wind the better. You will have to live in the mountains—a region possessing less of fertility—less of living nature you scarce ever saw. The style is Cyclopian, but the vegetation Liliputian. The population—roving adventurers, Chinamen and diggers—...the dust is everywhere."[12]

So his first thoughts had been for his family. He plucked up hope, however. He told Mary that they should build a "chalet" on a "rocky spur of the mountain"[13] and have water forced up by pump. Incorrigibly, he had an eye for sites and views. In spite of the drought, the air was exhilarating and seemed to be restoring his health. Three days after his first view, having traveled to the borders of his estate, forty miles from end to end, he found rewards in the undergrowth, the trees, the light upon the mountains, and the views of the Sierra. Eleven miles southward from Bear Valley was the settlement of Mariposa, with a narrow main street grooved between opposing mountains, a newspaper office, a primitive hotel, and a courthouse which looked like a transplanted New England church. He began to see the humorous picturesqueness of the human scene. He drew for Mary a sketch of a Chinese miner perched like a bird upon the rickety framework of a treadmill working a waterwheel. He wondered about and began to pity the Digger Indians. He noted down sayings and stories out of the lives of the careless, drifting miners.

Even before he investigated the mines proper, he began thinking of what he could do to restore the damages caused by them. It was as if he could not help looking at land as proper for growing things rather than as a place for ripping, blasting, and desolating. "The Mariposa river the most important stream running through the estate, is, at the least, six inches deep and ten feet wide: the diggings on it are enormous, and, in the landscape, horrible." His imagination carried him forward: "What the estate wants and must have if a million or two dollars would get it—is water. I am germinating great plans of washing all the gold out of the surface of the valley and then, making a garden of the debris. I think it is possible. The hills below here will make the finest sheep range imaginable—say 20,000 acres, and I have a plan budding for that." He never succeeded in persuading the New York City corporation to finance the digging of a canal to divert river waters into the estate.

Then there were the "mines proper" which he mentioned almost as an afterthought in this letter. He began systematically examining them. He had soon seen twenty veins. He went to the bottom of the first one, knocked out quartz, and, by the light of a candle, saw particles of gold. He believed there was much in them, but "for all that, it will be an enormous work to 'realize' upon it." And, meanwhile, he was lonely—"I have not heard a word from any of you since I left New York."

But the close of the letter shows Olmsted beginning to enjoy himself. (And he really meant to stay. He sketched a house and asked Mary to secure professional advice from Vaux. "It should have deep piazzas or galleries with low shades. It should have a bold rough-hewn character in outline as well as detail.") "The natural death of the country is cold lead in the brain. There are no churches in Bear valley but we had a horse race in the main street, at which a great deal of money changed hands, at noon today." It was Sunday. He remarked ironically, "Evn'g services consist of a dogfight—a deep interest is felt by the whole population."

But he had already discovered a Sunday evening walk which he enjoyed. He climbed a knoll which resembled "a sugar loaf" in shape. "The view down the valley, with a perfect Indian summer haze, with the heathery hill of Mt. Ophir closing up the vista, birds singing softly, in minor key, with a very rich deep color (violet grey, Martin says) which (so far) always follows sunset here for a few minutes—all made up a most soothing Sunday evening."[14]

As Olmsted, with ruthless clarity and unremitting attention, familiarized himself with every part of the operation, he found that he filled a real vacancy. There had been no real manager on the scene for some time. The interim superintendent had been "a mere bookkeeper"[15] and nobody knew or cared much about the estate. Olmsted's emotions, as he faced the task, had three pushes from his will. He felt the simple interest of unfettered curiosity. He wanted to see what made up the human and natural scene of Mariposa, so far from the cool meadows of the Connecticut River Valley or the shore of Staten Island. In addition, Olmsted wished to master the operation. Appointing foremen, dividing and subdividing work, getting intimate with everything that could or could not be done, he very quickly felt that he was accomplishing just that. He wrote to Mary, "I have got pretty good command of the machinery and shall soon knock something out of it or burst the boilers."[16] His third feeling, tinged with bitterness, was the sense that he must overcome the fact that he had been in part deceived. He stated this new understanding plainly in a letter to his father on October 30: "The estate is in very bad condition, and is paying so poorly,—yielding so little gold—that the suspicion could not be avoided that deception had been practiced upon the company purchasing it."[17]

He knew that he was going to have to perform a salvage operation which might or might not be successful, but he intended to use the men and materials at hand to work what was left of the gold. By the following summer, in 1864, he would have achieved a short-term prosperity for the Mariposa

Company. He introduced more efficient devices in the processes, and he got more gold out of the ground and to the market. He worked old veins and retrieved ore which had been missed by careless methods. For a short time Mariposa looked good. He was later to confess, however, that he knew that this was only an appearance of prosperity.

In organizing and inspiriting what had been a slack, demoralized, almost moribund community, he journeyed back and forth on the dusty and difficult road to San Francisco to meet with bankers and others with whom he had to deal in operating the mines and in transporting the metal out of the back country. He wrote peremptory letters or sent telegrams to New York for authority, instructions, and information, but he was often ahead of a decision in the East. Occasionally telegraphic communications were cut off by Indians on the plains. For the most part, he acted on his own understanding of needs. The owners had left Mariposa to him. The men of the mines found that they had a superintendent who was interested in everything, missed nothing, and by a deft suggestion or order, put into their hands tools and supplies. He built new roads to the ore. He reopened certain mines and closed others. He thought about developing other resources, a copper mine, sheepherding, agriculture. He restocked the company store, ordering initially twenty-five thousand dollars' worth of goods from the city. He decided upon a second store at the reliable Princeton mine at Bullion.

He took less in funds, personally, from the mines than he had expected to do and he stopped a strike with some harshness, both efforts justified to himself as helping to save the estate. But he was prudent with what he did take in salary. He converted this into gold bars and shipped the weighty produce back east to his father.

On his first Thanksgiving Day in the West he invited his superintendents and their wives, the few women who were in the valley, to dinner in his own improvised quarters. He longed for talk to go with the meal, but he found that no one wished to talk of anything but what made them all feverish with desire, gold. However, Olmsted wrote home with some complacency about his civilized meal, about which he had taken some care. It was an attempt to make an occasion, a human occasion, of an hour of leisure.

He longed for the advent of his family. Looking at the land with eyes now accustomed to the place, he tried to see what Mary would see when she came. "All the tolerable, big trees have been wasted—and still are being wasted, though I am checking it. The trees don't look nearly as badly to me, as they did at first. I don't know why, but I see considerable beauty in them, and in the shrubs especially, great promise for the spring. Indeed, the spring must be glorious here—spring and early summer. I want to know more about the plants, and hope you may bring some information, for I can't find any one here, who knows one from another. You will find an ample field in which to exercise your mineral-mania—if it lasts. My table is loaded with quartz."

And, direct in his appeal, as if saying, come, come!—"Come well prepared to ride in the dust and among the briars. Beyond them, it is fine. The moonlit mountains are superb, and there is no malaria."[18]

Olmsted suffered from being surrounded by people none of whom belonged to or loved the land. "This sojourning habit of the people who are here is shown in their want of interest in the fixed qualities of the place. Nobody knows what the trees and plants are. They are all like ourselves—strangers."[19]

In a similar vein he wrote to his colleagues at the Sanitary Commission headquarters in Washington, to Knapp, Jenkins, and Bloor: "There is very little civilization here now, but a very queer mixture of camp, squatter and town life, leaving out the better part of all, a good deal. Nobody feels fixed or settled. Men walk about with their effects tied up in a blanket, ready to take a house, shantee, tent, or tree as it may happen when night comes. Of course they don't build houses of worship nor 'call' ministers. The towns are wooden camps. I have it in mind to form a different kind of town and shall begin next summer if the company will let me."[20]

The tasks of building pastures on top of washed-out land and of creating a livable town where there was only a collection of shanties for wanderers was to be too much for him in the two years he was to remain in California. But the impulse to think in this direction could not be resisted. He engaged in this kind of mental play even while he and the others were engaged in the ripping and destroying which was to make the place pay them handsomely.

As the fine fall prolonged itself, Olmsted discovered that the landscape of this high country was a place with which he was at last on terms. First of all, the air was healthful and exhilarating, and he worked well outdoors whether walking or riding. He lost his tiredness from the months of war. Through the clear air he traced the patterning of a large, extended land which lay open to the uninterrupted light. The burned gold of the dry grass on the giant hills was like a lion's hide. The sky above was a fierce blue. The final turning of the key of his entry into this land was his experience of the big tree grove forty miles to the south and east and higher in the Sierras. Olmsted went on an exploratory trip in November, partly in the interest of the hoped-for canal. He and his small party went in by pack train; there were no roads. Beyond trails they struck off through wilderness. After encountering the first snow of the season, Olmsted came out tired but calmed by the experience.

He wrote to his wife on November 20:

I had a highly interesting journey in the mountains—exploring the South Fork. We passed through the Big Tree Grove. The big trees are in a dense forest of other trees a few standing free. They don't strike you as monsters at all but simply as the grandest tall trees you ever saw although among others as tall or nearly so. You recognize them as soon as your eye falls on them, far away, not merely from the unusual size of the trunk but its remarkable color—a cinnamon color, very elegant. You feel that they are distinguished strangers [who] have come down to us from another world,—but the whole forest is wonderful. I never saw and I don't think you ever did any trees to compare with the pines, cedars (arbor vitae) and firs—generally 200 to 250 feet high and as thrifty and dense and bright in foliage as saplings. Trunks of 4 feet are ordinary; of 6 feet not uncommon. The scenery otherwise is fine and at some points grand—terrible. One or two annual trips into it are the highest gratifications peculiar to the country that you have to look forward to.

In this manner, speaking of the delights that were to come, he reached out to his wife so far from him. He had at last heard from her in a letter written in Litchfield and was sorry to find her upset at planning her journey: "It grieves me that you are so flurried and bewildered." He said simply, "I long for the children and you here."[21] All during the time of waiting, words in letters from the East had entangled him in emotions of that other world.

The men of 244 F Street in Washington, D.C. had written, and he had answered with quick if passing feeling, "I got your letter, damn your eyes; it made me snuffle. Tell me all about what you are doing—and the fellows. I am homesick for 244."[22]

George Curtis wrote, trying to interest Olmsted in concerns of the moment, halfway glad that his friend was somewhat disappointed in California, hoping that he might be persuaded to come home to head the Freedmen's Bureau. "My dear boy, the wind blows drearily, and it rains heavily. Why can't you come in at the library door, and sit quietly by my fire?"[23]

Edwin L. Godkin advised him of the progress he was making in initiating the publication of the new magazine. Charles Eliot Norton invited Olmsted to write for the *North American Review*.

Katherine Wormeley continued to write Olmsted from time to time, recalling their war days, trying to piece out that experience into a longer existence.

Charles Brace wrote Olmsted about the death of Louisa Schuyler's mother. Louisa had been a stalwart worker for the Sanitary Commission. Frederick wrote to Charles to convey his "dearest love and condolence to Louisa."[24]

His father wrote him about a fire at the farm at Southside. Frederick's collection of books and papers, including his manuscripts and notes of the Southern journeys, had all been burned. Frederick replied with more equanimity than might have been expected. But the event recalled what the farm meant to him. He resisted his father's advice to sell the place. He doubted that he could get more than fifteen thousand dollars and "It is home to me —and I confess that I am sadly homesick. It is hard to make up my mind to adopt this as my home or to begin life over again in making friends here. I don't see how I can hope to make Mary contented to live here—or to endure it. It is dreadfully rough, and I even when on horseback, can't help turning many a long, lingering look back upon civilization and homes. I detest this intermediate state between bivouacking and home living. [But] Individually, I am comfortable enough. I have made my office comfortable; I have comfortable meals, I have a loveable horse and I enjoy the air and the landscape."[25]

What Olmsted was most homesick for was perhaps his park work. Every exchange of letters with Calvert Vaux touched him deeply. It was at this time that his relations with his partner entered into a curious and difficult time. Olmsted heard from Vaux frequently, but misunderstandings occurred and were hard to cure across the wide space which the letters had to travel. Vaux's attitude toward Olmsted moved through a succession of moods— anger, hurt pride, affection, jealousy, and admiration. Not many of Olmsted's letters to Vaux of this time have survived, but Vaux's are extant. Olmsted saved them.

On October 19 Calvert wrote that he was sorry he had missed seeing Fred off. He had been ill and had reached the Brevoort only in time to shake hands with the elder Mr. Olmsted and to see him start back from New York City to Hartford. After some trivial matter, Vaux launched into a long passage intimating that a matter concerned him which he thought his friend should agree to rectify, namely, the proper distribution between them of credit for Central Park. "The public has been led to believe from the commence- ment of the Central Park work to the present time that you are pre-eminently the author of the executed design, and such we all know is the general im- pression throughout the country today." And: "Now, however, that our con- nection with the park has ceased for the time being, we may as well ex- change views on this point." Calvert Vaux, naturally retiring and shy in public relationships, credited Olmsted's superior title in the partnership, and his having been "Architect-in-Chief" of the park as having been the cause of people's not understanding that their design had been a "simple partner- ship." He did not dispute Olmsted's greater part in the management of the park after the design was completed. He was stiffly and pridefully unhappy with Olmsted for not having rectified a false impression. He signed this letter, not affectionately as usual, but "Yours faithfully."[26]

Olmsted had never consciously claimed more part in the design than was due him. Yet he had always made himself known. It was almost inevitable that, given the character of the two men—the one withdrawn and private, the other aggressive and able to make a point in public—Olmsted should be the better known. One cannot capture a particular moment when Olmsted ever knowingly tried to make more of himself than of Calvert Vaux in the origin of Central Park. There were to be many occasions when he pointedly gave credit to his partner, but the inevitable result to the great public was of graciousness and generosity on Frederick Olmsted's part. Vaux was correct; he was never to get proper credit for his share of the design of Central Park, nor of his part in later works they did together. The fault lay more in himself and his own nature than in Olmsted; but he could not help, as he grew older and to an extent bitter and morbid, but blame his old friend.

The difficulty between the friends in 1863 and 1864, when they were separated by a great distance, was to be passing and mixed with other emotions. When Vaux wrote again on December 1 to Olmsted, he relayed agreeable details of his daily and professional life, the kind of life Olmsted was homesick for. He had been to New Haven to consult with some "gentlemen" who proposed to "agitate" for a park.[27] He was pressing his claim for back salary on Central Park. He was told by one of the commissioners that he might be asked to come back to work for the park. Vaux, however, did not think, he told Olmsted, that he would do so "on any terms." Vaux was delicately fastidious. "The park connection was too devoid of any agreeable impression to be either healthy or practicable for so long a time without demoralization in some form; my business is in good shape and I have formed a partnership wth Mr. Withers."[28] (This was Frederick C. Withers, another architect.)

A letter written on January 18, 1864, found Vaux saying, "I have received your letter it makes me sick and sad but I know that I have but one feeling towards you which is and always has been sweet and pure. My error seems to have arisen thus. When we went into the competition I knew you were superintendent, but did not attach the meaning to the word that you did." And: "To me it seemed that I brought as much as you to the park. . . . I became convinced that our estimates of each other's value differed." He ended very stiffly "Yours very truly."[29]

However, twelve days later (January 30), Vaux wrote in friendly fashion about the "Marion House" he was working on, apparently a design for a house which Olmsted might build for his family in Bear Valley.[30] He also informed Olmsted that the two of them were involved in a legal difficulty. Viele, the former engineer of the park, was suing the Central Park Commissioners, claiming that his plan had been stolen by Olmsted and Vaux. Vaux attended court and heard judgment; Viele was initially awarded eight thousand dollars. Developments in the case were to be reported later to the interested friend in California. Vaux visited the park too. He reported that he had been ice-skating there. But being there and not of it "seemed strange and hateful." He reported matter-of-factly that he had heard some people "using foul language" and he threatened them with the police. And, yearningly to this friend to whom he had said harsh things, he said, "My own impression is that you will not stay there forever." They could discuss their differences in the years ahead and, "I have only to hope that you will understand me, on the whole rightly. I remain, my dear Olmsted, yours assuredly."[31]

By February 5, 1864, the quick-tempered, mercurial, warm-hearted Vaux had shifted in the wind of his emotions. He suggested that Frederick write a piece about Central Park and their part in it, a sort of history for the public—in the face of the unfair and dishonest claims Viele had been making. While still holding out rationally for his proper share of the credit, he apologized for the hard, unfeeling way he had written. "In my first letter it...was not possible to get at the facts without leaving out all the love all the heart all the life for the time being, it would have been much better to have left the whole thing for time to settle." He thought he had written in a "plain business way...but I see that it could not fail to be read by you, as you read it—and thus at one blow, the whole delicate structure of an affectionate personal relation, invaluable to me, was, I am afraid, destroyed, but I cannot, I will not believe that this is really so, I feel that I have well deserved your affection and that I have returned it with earnestness. My letter was ill conceived, over-done and ungentle." He hoped to see Mrs. Olmsted before she left and sympathized with her in her "long tedious journey." He looked forward to a reunion one day with his friend. Meanwhile, his own wife expected daily "to be confined." He ended "I look forward to our meeting again here at no very remote period. I used to tell you that you would be wanted for the public service even in the old romantic days, but you would not listen. Perhaps you will not now but I think you will allow me to be always, Yr. affectionate friend, Calvert Vaux."[32]

The connection could not be broken on either side. Olmsted's life, seemingly a series of disjointed jumps from one intense experience to another, was yet linked by emotion into one channel of experience. Vaux was one tie to all that he had been before he left the East, and Vaux was a part of what he would return to.

The manager of Mariposa needed very much to have his family come out to California. He had quickened the pace of work. He had reduced wages and his own income and he had quelled a strike. And he had spent a good bit of time early in 1864 in writing a report to the absentee owners spelling out to them the straitened circumstances of the mines. The exercise of energy and will told upon him. He had written Mary as early as December 6, 1863, "Since I left New York the trouble I used to have in my head has been frequently recurrent so as to be a serious check upon my writing."[33] Just before the arrival of his family, for whom he had waited months, he became convinced that he had a serious heart condition. To his father on March 11, 1864, he wrote, "I have been under examination by Dr. Ayres, who finds my heart is enlarged. The disease is incurable but not necessarily fatal. . . . It will oblige me however to live very quietly and carefully. . . . By great care and avoiding fatigue, especially through writing and brain-work, I can avoid any distress, such as I have sometimes had lately."[34]

Frederick's old friends, doctors in the service of the Sanitary Commission, disagreed decidedly at a distance and informed Olmsted that the doctor in California must be mistaken. In any case, Olmsted did not for very long behave as if he thought he had a serious heart condition. But in the meantime he obtained full value from his discouragement. "If the mines fail—rather if my experimentations don't succeed in the latter part of the summer—I may be glad to find some employment involving less responsibility and anxiety. I have had my full share of bustling life and shall be better content to live quietly for the rest or to die where I am, than most men are. I only want to see the children provided for and I am for the present making money pretty fast for such a vagabond as I am."[35] That he was working against the grain of his nature, his next words show: "I am enjoying this visit to San Francisco, meeting many pleasant people and a strong contrast to Bear Valley."[36]

At this time, when he seemed so full of foreboding, Olmsted was about to enter the happiest period of his life. He would find congenial work in the West and would return to the East to take up a long, energetic, and rigorous career requiring the utmost mental and physical effort. But he was to have recurrent moods of acute self-depreciation. He ended this letter to his father in a curious, not quite sane way, striking out his signature, and saying to his father that he hated the autograph "enterprise," and demanded of him who was the least likely person ever to trade upon his son's signature, "You will never give my autograph to anybody. Take them back if you can."[37]

It was probably at this time that he began to meet men in San Francisco to whom he could talk about a public reservation for the Big Trees of Mariposa and the Valley of the Yosemite. There were men in the professions, in business, and in the state legislature with the same idea. Olmsted, by reason of his being located in Mariposa right up against the territory in question, was a valuable man to include in their counsels and one who entered into these discussions as a leader. He had had some experience in the Sanitary Commission lobbying for pet projects. He, probably among others, saw that a federal bill in the United States Congress would be the best method of preserving these areas.

This was a kind of concern which he considered proper to civilized men. What he had said in an aside to his father in the letter of March 11 was deeply significant of his character: "I hate barbarism and like civilization in all its forms."[38] The very name Mariposa had had a flowerlike appeal when he started west. But what he had found in this isolated mountain upland was raw mining and raw life, men not settled in any kind of community, stripping minerals from the land, fighting, killing, sporting, lusting, not interacting in any of the gentler rituals of life. Much of this life was colorful, and he had a keen eye for noting its humors. Yet he was tired of such reactions in himself. He had had his fill of backwoods crudity in the South in the 1850s. It might seem to those not following his train of thought that his love of the uncultivated woods and mountains looming just beyond Bear Valley was a contradiction to his love of civilization. He did not see it so. For him, the love of the nonhuman land was something that could be most relished by one steeped in "civilization." Cultivated man looking at wild nature made a delightful equation. Olmsted had said earlier that he hated the "wilderness,"[39] but it was the wilderness of man that he hated, not the wilderness of nature.

Lobbying efforts by Olmsted and his friends achieved their purpose. On March 28, 1864, Senator John Conness of California introduced a bill to set aside the Big Tree Grove and the Yosemite Valley on the condition that the area "shall be held for public use, resort, and recreation for all time." The bill passed the Senate in May, the House on June 29. On June 30, 1864, Lincoln —in the middle of the war, performing an act not much noticed at the time— signed the bill. This was the genesis of all future national parks although at this time Yosemite was not national, but state-owned; the land having been taken out of the public domain of the federal government and given into the keeping of the State of California. It was not to revert to the federal government for some years and after much controversy and misuse. But the beginnings of the whole national park movement were here brought to birth in the middle of the Civil War at the far end of the continent by a small group of men of whom one was Frederick Olmsted.

This kind of interest was to be as typical of the rest of Olmsted's stay in California as his mining activity. Apparently it was the coming of his family which made a difference in his life. Olmsted had missed "civilization" when he first came into Bear Valley on the fast stage from San Francisco. Almost half a year later Mary and the children brought to him a private kind of "civilization" which could sustain him. It was a whole tribe which arrived in March, 1864, on a ship from Panama. There were his wife, the four children, the children's governess, Miss Harriet Errington, who had been a friend of Mary's in Staten Island and her former teacher, and Henry Perkins, Mary's cousin, who was to be Frederick's confidential secretary in the world of Mariposa, which the superintendent saw more and more as a kingdom deserted by its owners and beset by dangers.

A sign that he was not merely and only the superintendent of Mariposa was a letter he received from J. H. Brayton who, with some other gentlemen in Oakland, was preparing to lay out a new cemetery and who called upon the designer of Central Park for advice. Olmsted agreed to make a plan. On March 23, 1864, Brayton informed Olmsted that he was laying the plan before his cemetery board and asked matter-of-factly, "What are your own charges?"[40] The exchange signifies that, by this time, Olmsted, without nailing up a shingle, was practicing landscape architecture in California.

The ground of the cemetery lay behind the town. Here was first a level floor and then a tilted arena cupped by great brown hills and looking down beyond the houses to the bay. Within this natural amphitheatre the first purpose, Olmsted believed, was to honor the dead with dignity and beauty. But at the same time he thought one must create a setting compatible with the naturally dry climate and the vegetation adapted to this western air. Here, for the first time, Olmsted worked beyond the limits of the English or New England style which he and Vaux had used to clothe or set off the rocky ledges of Manhattan. His Oakland design was somewhat severe, a straight-edged area enclosed from robust Pacific winds by hedges and walls. (The cemetery, which has continued to grow and to be used, has been enlarged in conscious or unconscious imitation of Olmsted's original eastern park style.)

When Olmsted was not in San Francisco, he was often in the wild country above and beyond Mariposa. He established his family in some style in Bear Valley and also exercised for them the privilege of leaving comfort behind and going for weeks at a time to live in the country of big trees and granite domes. As he had explored the land beyond Bear Valley, he had been converted into a lover of that region. He wished to make Mary and the children lovers of it too. By mid-July he instigated an extended family expedition into the wilderness.

In spite having been a city-bred woman, Mary came to delight in riding and camping. The children, with the adaptability of little animals, thrived in walking, exploring, collecting. Even Miss Errington, terrified at first by the steep and narrow canyon trails which duty compelled her to traverse with the children, began to enjoy the experience. She sketched in watercolors some of the scenes which being a member of the Olmsted family caused her to visit.

The midsummer expedition moved on the backs of horses and donkeys. Pack animals carried supplies. A camp cook traveled with them. The party advanced by easy stages along the South Fork of the Merced and set up camp near the Mariposa Big Tree Grove. This area had been first visited by white men not more than fifteen years before, and it was unchanged from its thousands of years of growth when Frederick and Mary and the children set up temporary housekeeping here. The air was dry, clear, and bracing—cold at night. The smell of the woods was aromatic, and among the varied greens, other colors were bright, reds in the manzanita stalks and in the large trunks of the incense cedars, plated brown and rust scales on the trunks of the Ponderosa pines, and iron gray in the bark of the sugar pines. Unmistakable in size and cinnamon color, as Fred had written Mary, were the occasional "big trees." The area in which the redwoods grew was rough and hilly. Camp was set up on a level space among some firs.

From beside the trout stream which made a pleasant noise near the tents (in a letter partially preserved, to an unknown correspondent), Frederick wrote on July 20, "We have trout, venison, grizzly bear and Indians in plenty and are within a day's ride of the estate to which I shall return next week for a short visit. After that we expect to go to Yosemite. The women have tents, the boys and I sleep out. Fine air and scenery. Mr. and Mrs. Ashburner are with us. [Ashburner was a member of the state geological survey, an enthusiast for Yosemite.] ... It is warm, but not excessively so at noon and cold enough at night to make us who sleep out careful about our fire and blankets, but we don't suffer. The woods are on fire all around us and the atmosphere hazy with smoke." And he spared a word for the war: "We are in great anxiety about the army and disgusted beyond endurance with the confidence and boasting and bragging of the Eastern papers."[41] (In that other world, Grant was pushing his army through the morass of Virginia's swamps, and Sherman's forces had put Kennesaw behind him and was on the way to besieging Atlanta.)

While so far from the scene of war that he could think of it only as something in another world, Olmsted began to believe that his colleagues of the Sanitary Commission were right and that he did not have an alarming heart condition. He was better, and Mary and the children thrived. To his father, Frederick had written earlier from Bear Valley, "Mary has gained quite markedly in courage and patience and Charlotte is growing to be a nice young woman, simple, straight-forward and self-possessed. She is John's master in everything, and makes nothing of mounting an unbroken donkey, taking Owen on behind and cantering off . . . for miles. Mary who turned ill and threatened to faint the first time she followed me over a mountain trail, now gallops over the worst places faster than I want to go, and dashes up the steepest declivities, where I a little prefer not to follow. She generally over-does it, and is half crazy with nervousness for a while afterwards, but these turns are getting less frequent and less protracted and severe. Owen is a perfect cub—the climate seems only to make him more clumsy, imperturbable, ravenous and prone to fall anywhere but on his feet than ever. Marion has improved as much as any of them and, talking German, French, Spanish and English all together, talks very much. We have been exceedingly favored in the season."[42]

Frederick and Mary spent more time together this year in California than they had done in several years of war separation. Frederick initiated his wife early into a mineral-gathering expedition into difficult high country near Bear Valley. "It was very rough riding and the weather filthy warm, but we both enjoyed it." He taught her to recognize gold-bearing quartz, and when he rode out with the children he taught them to recognize plants and trees as he had learned them. "If California does nothing else for them it will educate them to be clever observers in geology and botany."[43]

In August the general family expedition which had stopped first at the Big Trees moved over a height of land and then down a steep trail to enter the Yosemite Valley proper from the south, coming to rest in a meadow beside the Merced with the great white granite cliffs standing up steeply north, south, and east. The children hunted rocks and flowers. Mary enjoyed horse-back rides. Harriet Errington sketched in her leisure after finishing morning classes with the children. Frederick wandered up and down the long narrow valley, learning its heights and depths by heart.

Into the Olmsted camp one day in mid-August walked Clarence King, a young geologist who had come into Bear Valley the winter before and been pressed into service assaying the Mariposa ores. This twenty-two-year-old had crossed the continent in 1863 with almost as cool a nerve as one might have in going from Hartford to New Haven (and he came from these places, too, having attended grammar school in one and the Scientific School at Yale in the other). King may have reminded Olmsted of himself at a similar age when he sailed away to China. King had found a job on the state geological survey and become a part of the team which was working under Josiah Whitney. His companion in the field was usually William H. Brewer, another graduate of the Yale Scientific School. As Frederick wrote his father on the seventeenth of the month: "We have also had Clarence King.... We hope to be joined here by Prof. Brewer."[44] King, Brewer, and Whitney all became friends of Olmsted. Olmsted found them congenial and their intellectual interests stimulating. They savored the country as well as measured it. The three men named many of the mountains and ranges of the area.

It was easy to believe in brilliant futures for these men, especially for the least known of them, Clarence King. He was ambitious in his profession and seemed to be learning quickly everything to be known in his field. He was also a good storyteller, full of tales of Sierra mountaineers, goldminers, and Indians, and he told tales of incredible mountain climbs with a gentle easy self-assurance tempered by a disarming humor. "King has been heroic in his explorations,"[45] Frederick wrote his father. King apparently walked up and down mountains as easily as other men tramped fields. He had climbed the highest mountain in the California ranges and named it after his chief. Sitting before the campfire, with the big and little Olmsteds gathered about and raptly listening, the young man told his respectful listeners some of the stories he was to publish shortly in *Mountaineering in the Sierra Nevada*.

In his sojourn in the wilderness Olmsted now had the kind of talk he had been craving. Later in the season, Dr. Brewer guided Frederick and John Charles higher into the mountains. This experience gained Olmsted a closer knowledge of the fierce, stark territory he was trying to save.

In the fall, Governor F. L. Low of California named Olmsted as a member of the first board of commissioners to have authority over Yosemite. Olmsted was willing to accept, if, indeed, he had not engineered his place on the board. The Governor wrote Olmsted on September 29, 1864: "By today's mail I send you the Yosemite Commission."[46]

There were nine members of the board, including the governor, Olmsted, J. D. Whitney, head of the Geological Survey, and William Ashburner, with whom Olmsted had become acquainted in San Francisco and with whom he had shared a family expedition to Yosemite. This was a group willing to work and to work quickly. By agreement among themselves, Olmsted became president of the commissioners. With his quick grasp of what was important and his gift for doing things swiftly, Olmsted hired Clarence King, who was on the scene and obviously the best man to do the job, to survey the boundaries of the new park. In a letter on October 14, 1864, the geologist reported to Olmsted the progress of his work.[47] Olmsted paid for the survey out of his own pocket since the commissioners had no money. There was only a possibility that he would be repaid by the state legislature "two years hence."[48] Olmsted's ambition was for a new kind of park, a "wild park" for the people of the future.

While his belief in Yosemite was strong, his faith in Mariposa failed. He became convinced that the managers of the company were not going to support him. He informed his father that he had instructed the owners to sell his Mariposa stock and convert what they had promised to pay him in that article into cash. He had some doubt that they would do so. Meanwhile he continued to convert his monthly salary into gold and ship gold bars back East to his father. This substance out of California's ground was going to help him reestablish himself in the East. He now knew that he would return to the East. But carrying on his present responsibilities in the failing kingdom of Mariposa brought on a return of the illness he thought he had shaken. "Old symptoms returning as soon as I came back to the desk,"[49] he wrote to his father after returning from an invigorating journey to San Francisco.

He had hardened in his attitude toward Mariposa, but he continued in his work as superintendent. The job made possible the easing of the burden of his indebtedness to his father. By late November of the year 1864 Olmsted had taken out of his salary sufficient funds to repay John Olmsted for the long years of support given him. This much at least Frederick Olmsted was to owe to the mines.

When Henry Bellows came to California for a six months' visit, the East did not seem so far away. The energetic minister had learned of the Reverend Starr King's death and traveled west to fill the dead man's pulpit and to take his place as a fund-raiser for the Sanitary Commission. That Olmsted could show Bellows a substantial personal establishment in Bear Valley was a satisfaction.

Bellows's world, the world back home, did not give up Olmsted. John Olmsted wrote to his son, "Cambridge has made you Master of Arts. Good enough for them. Yale ought to have done it before."[50] It helped Frederick's sense of himself to have this tangible award from the academic world of which he had inhabited only the fringes many years ago. Other ties with the East remained strong. In the campaign of 1864, Olmsted in California helped a little in the electioneering for President Lincoln. Edwin Godkin kept in touch with Olmsted, giving him news of the struggling young magazine, a project Olmsted had once shared with this friend. Godkin wrote to him, "Your quitting the East was ... a great blow to me ... I looked forward to your settling down somewhere within my reach, so that we could grow old and grumble over the ways of the world together."[51] Olmsted, cogitating a possible future for himself in California should he not go back East, asked Godkin to come out to him. They might found a paper together in this new state. Godkin, with justification, hesitated. He saw that Olmsted himself did not make his fortune as handsomely as he had thought he might in California. And in his familiar way, he questioned Olmsted's manner of living, foreseeing a difficult road ahead for them in partnership, particularly in the trying career of the daily newspaperman:

I am a good deal troubled about your health. I have felt satisfied for years that you would at last suffer from your insane way of living. I have always wondered how a man of your intelligence could go on acting on that theory of yours about night work.

Olmsted had apparently described his symptoms to Godkin (the letter does not survive). Godkin wrote,

I have had every symptom you describe, with palpitation so violent as to keep me awake at night. I have been *six* times examined for disease of the heart, and once blistered for inflammation of the pericardium. There never was anything the matter with my heart except functional derangement caused by the state of my nerves .... Doctors are constantly mistaken on this point. ... I would have wagered 100 to 1 any time these four years that your mode of life would end in laying you up with your present ailments. I offer the same odds that two years hence, if you avoid fatigue,—especially mental,—do no work in the afternoon, go to bed at 10 P.M., and totally abandon tea and coffee, you will be as well as ever.[52]

The length of the quotation is justified by the insight it gives, indirectly, into what Olmsted may have told him about his symptoms. In any case, Godkin was not going to come west, for he wrote Olmsted shortly that his weekly would soon be appearing, and with "ample capital."[53] Olmsted continued as superintendent of Mariposa for another year.

That he could do design work in California was a boon. The Oakland Cemetery was only the first landscape task which he was asked to undertake. He was able to agree to other jobs in the Bay area because, beginning in January, 1865, he spent long weeks in the city awaiting instructions by wire from the company's directors in New York.

This winter journey from Mariposa to San Francisco gave him one of the clearest views he had yet had of the mountains he might at any time now be leaving. To Mary from Stockton he wrote, "The white peaked Sierras were very beautiful. They are to be remembered."[54] He prepared himself and Mary for the failure of Mariposa by writing his thoughts to her in the lonely hotel room where he had established himself. "I shall be quite content either to leave or remain in Bear Valley. The enterprise is a failure and it will be a relief to drop it. On the other hand if we should be required to stay, I really think we never lived as comfortably and happily anywhere else, and I don't believe the children could be situated better than they are."[55]

At a distance, he teased Mary and domineered over her: "I have an increased and increasing positive respect for you as well as decreased disrespect for your occasional perversities."[56] In February, he asked Mary to come down to the city to go with him to Santa Cruz to look at some oil properties. It seemed that oil might become a more and more lucrative resource, and Olmsted was interested. She was unable to come at the time, although she did get away from the children and the household in April. Mary, for the most part left alone at Mariposa in this early part of 1865, feared for their future and expressed some of her forebodings to Frederick in letters. He reproved her for doing so: "What do you mean by saying 'We should arrive in New York certainly destitute?' We have over $6000 in gold now." He reassured her but went on: "I don't think I can stand the pressure much longer unless you encourage me."[57] Two days later Frederick sent Mary a present. "The pineapple is my valentine to you and your friends."[58]

Olmsted did not wish to save the company. He thought it not worth saving. But he had qualms about what Mariposa's failure was doing to the miners. "I don't want to turn my hand to save the Company from failure if it ought to fail. I think the men have all been very lenient and forbearing to me and we should feel grateful and generous. . . . I feel their interests and mine are identical, not rival. . . . I am sorry for them and want them to know it, but whether they believe it or not I am sorry and would befriend them if I could even if they believed me to be their enemy, as it is natural they should do."[59] Still Olmsted was not quite candid with himself. He had saved considerable money from the wreck of Mariposa; the men were in no position to do this. Olmsted was able later to get a certain amount of mining work going again to enable the men to pay off their debts.

Olmsted had worries, but he had paid off his own debts, and after receiving one thousand dollars for the Oakland Cemetery job, a portion of his fee, he had hope of making a secondary income from his design work. As it turned out, the payment for the cemetery design was the largest amount he was to receive from this kind of work in California. Both from his inner desire to do this kind of work and from a hope of monetary reward, Olmsted took on additional landscape tasks even while remaining superintendent of the slowly dying Mariposa.

Across the bay from San Francisco, north of Oakland, the coastal range rose up in large shouldering hills bare of vegetation, imposing but not seductive to the eye. Against this overhang, the promoters of the newly organized College of California intended to place their institution. The trustees, having heard of Olmsted's reputation, requested his advice about the placement of the buildings of the college. As a cold spring advanced with fog, rain, and the blooming of the plains flowers, Olmsted began crossing over regularly by ferry to the site of the proposed school.

He walked over the ground or hired a horse. He slept out at least once on the ground and looked down at dawn to the bay and the narrows of the "golden gate." He became convinced that the hither side of the bay, the mainland side, was a milder, more beneficent climate than San Francisco's, and that here were softer winds, milder days and nights, and that a gentle society of learners and learned could live together sweetly upon this ground. He tried to overcome his repugnance at the lack of greenery and imagined strategic tree plantings. He saw with a practiced eye what fine views there would be from streets curved lassolike along the side of the ridge. He sited the bay from various heights and locations, imagining houses built, and pleasant resting places carved out at turns in the roads. A whole settlement grew up in his mind where he stood, the only human being upon the scene. Down toward the water, there were a few blocks and streets laid out and some houses built, but here upward toward the hills, there were only two farmhouses. The rest was emptiness with the wind blowing through the spaces in which he took his stand.

After he laid out in his mind the location and number and siting of a number of simple, convenient school properties, he spent his thought upon what was to him the key to the founding of a successful educational institution, and his own contribution to the scheme, the planning of an accompanying residential area. Here the professors and their families would live, near to the school, near to the city across the bay, but not too near. This congenial nucleus would attract other residents, who would not be excluded, so that the village would make an attractive setting for the school. There would be households living in domestic content, and yet with an intellectual liveliness acquired from the manner of occupation of most of the homeowners. The students would have the benefit of the nearby community and would not live as boarders nor in dormitories set up barracks style, but, according to Olmsted's prescription, in "buildings erected by the College...having the general appearance of large domestic houses, containing a respectably furnished drawing-room and dining-room for the common use of the students, together with a sufficient number of private rooms to accommodate from twenty to forty lodgers."[60] Or so went Olmsted's dream of an ideal school, as he put the dream in words in his prospectus.

In addition to ruminating over the landscape of Berkeley, as the new community was to be called, Olmsted pondered the development of San Francisco proper. It was inevitable that he should see a better future for this raw western town in the creation of a park. And it was almost inevitable that the influential citizens of San Francisco should call upon the creator of New York's Central Park to make suggestions for a park. He said, as Mariposa failed, that he stayed on "If by staying I could drive the San Franciscans into undertaking a park."[61] A park would signify the coming of age of the place where he had found work and friends. "A liberally devised public pleasure ground with its accessories, would be the most effective entering wedge that can possibly be conceived of by which to open the way to a better state of things [to overcome] the dead weight of indifference to all municipal improvements, which is characteristic of the transient speculative class. When the better element asserts itself in a positive way, then the real life of the city of San Francisco will begin. Worthy to be, and destined to be one of the largest, if not the largest city in the world, it must at some time escape from the influences that happen to be associated with the discovery of gold in California."[62]

His plan, to be finished after he left the city, and to be published both in San Francisco and New York City, was solicitous of the geographic and human climate of the city.

"In any pleasure ground for San Francisco the ornamental parts should be compact; should be guarded from the direct action of the north-west wind, should be conveniently entered, should be rich in detail, close to the eye, and should be fitted to an extensive system of walks, rides, drives and resting places.... At the same time it should have such a form that when the city shall be much enlarged it may so divide it that, without subjecting the trees and shrubs it contains to destruction during great conflagrations, it shall be a barrier of protection to large districts, which would otherwise be imperilled."[63] (When the great earthquake occurred, the park served just this function.) Olmsted did not, after all, design Golden Gate Park. It had to wait for a better time and another designer. However, as will be seen, his ideas were solicited and in part followed.

There were indeed attractions in San Francisco. Olmsted might have stayed, but one importunate Easterner, Calvert Vaux, bombarded him with reasons for his return to New York. Olmsted told his partner at first that he was simply too busy. This was difficult for the New Yorker to understand after he had learned that the mining business was failing. "I'm bound to go through with the college," wrote Olmsted, and "I should like too to be free to do more gratuitous work for the Yo Semite, than I shall be likely to if I cut away in September."[64]

Vaux wrote to Olmsted that there was a good chance that they might be able to work together on a new large city park, this one in Brooklyn. Vaux had already been engaged to give advice to the promoters. For the veteran creators of Central Park, it was stirring to think of working on a new large design. It seemed to open up to them again the opportunities of their younger ardent days. Olmsted knew that his chances of laying out the San Francisco park were not good. More urgent than George Curtis's telling him to come home and do his duty by the freedmen, more interesting than Godkin's desire for him to help with the *Nation*, were these words of Calvert Vaux asking him to come home to his true profession. Only for a time Olmsted resisted the suggestion, arguing that the Brooklyn park would not pay him enough to support his family properly. But the idea beguiled him, and Vaux's friendliness, after their recent quarrel, warmed him too.

His friend wrote, almost in self-abasement, about their past work, "If you had been disheartened there very likely might have been no park to chatter about today, for I alone was wholly incompetent to take it up." Vaux felt, he said, the need (of Olmsted's partnering) "very little less;—now, and enter on Brooklyn alone with hesitation and distrust, not on the roads and walks or even planting which Pilat would have to attend to, but in regard to the main point,—the translation of the republican art idea in its highest form into the acres we want to control."[65]

Olmsted felt a rising excitement at the prospect of going home to New York and working on another park there. A few words excerpted from a letter written on March 12, 1865, show his mood. "My heart really bounds (if you don't mind poetry) to your suggestions that we might work together about it [the Brooklyn park]. . . ." He offered objections for reasons of health and money, but went on, "I can't tell you—I say again how attractive to me the essential business we had together is; nor how I abhor the squabbles with the Commission and politicians. Both are very deep with me—I feel them deeper every year. It was a passion thwarted. . . . I have a perfect craving for the park, sometimes." (He meant Central Park, this time.) He told Vaux that he thought his preliminary plan for the new park in Brooklyn looked excellent and that he hoped that "the Commissioners are wise enough to comprehend it."[66]

The exchange with Vaux rekindled his thinking about the art. He wrote fluently to his friend about the particular virtues each one of them possessed, and about the profession they had tried to found. He deferred, he said, always to his friend's professional skills, but had faith in his own judgments. "If I don't wholly adopt or agree with all you say, at least I respect it very thoroughly. . . . I do not wholly sympathize with your views of the guild of art. I think you are a little idolatrous and in danger of losing sight of the end in devotion to the means but I am *inclined* to go with you,—at least, after you." And what should one call their occupation? "I am all the time bothered with the miserable nomenclature of L.A. *Landscape* is not a good word, *Architecture* is not; the combination is not. *Gardening* is worse. . . . The art is not gardening nor is it architecture. What I am doing here in Cala especially, is neither. It is the sylvan art; *fine art* in distinction from Horticulture—Agriculture—or Sylvan *useful* art."

Trying to make clear at least to himself what he was, Olmsted went on,

I am sorry to say that I do not feel myself capable of being a landscape gardener —properly speaking—but I have a better and more cultivated taste in that department of art than any other, very much, having none in any other—and if I had the necessary quality of memory, or if my memory had been educated in botany and gardening when I was young, I might have been. But I can do anything with proper assistants, or money enough—anything that any man can do. I can combine means to ends better than most, and I love beautiful landscapes and rural recreations and people in rural recreations—better than anybody else I know. But I dont feel strong on the art side. I dont feel myself an artist, I feel rather as if it were sacriligious in me to post myself in the portals of art. Yes, I know you are indignant and vexed with me, but I speak one truth, and it has got to be reconciled with all the rest—like Dr. Bellows's sermons.

I have none of your feeling of nauseousness about the park. There is no other place in the world that is as much home to me. I love it all through and all the more for the trials it has cost me.

Olmsted descended abruptly from this high level of esthetic discourse to his everyday life at the end of the long letter to Vaux. He told his friend that he had sent another report to the directors of the Mariposa Company. He hoped that they would publish it, for it "exposes the main facts of the swindle." Whether he meant a swindle which had victimized the present company for which he worked, or which had been continued and perhaps enlarged by those same people, is not quite clear. Olmsted seemed to think that a sign would be given him by the company's publishing, or refusing to publish, his report:

There was not one of the deposits which gave the Estate its repuation which had not been completely worked out and exhausted before I took charge of it. I have tested them at a cheap rate, have reduced the current rates of expense in my department and have proved the Estate to be nearly worthless under present circumstances, so no more swindling can well be done with it. If the report is not published by the Trustees, I think it most likely, I shall be relieved, and then I will publish it myself—if that seems proper—the substance of it, I will, anyhow.

He told Vaux that he expected to go on another trip into the Yosemite. Meanwhile, he sketched a picture of domestic content. He and Mary rode each day to the height of the great rounded dome of a foothill near their house. There they gardened, "doing some child's play gardening work,"[67] and had tea together, where at five thousand feet they had a view of the peaks toward Yosemite. It was an escape from the summer heat of the valley; it was a retreat from care; it was comradeship.

That there was some fieriness in their relationship is shown by Frederick's half admiring, half amused, testimony to a feat of horsemanship which Mary accomplished.[68] Some time after his return to Bear Valley from his long stay in San Francisco, Olmsted rode up into the Yosemite accompanying a Miss Whitney, showing her the sights and acting as her guide. Mary was held back from going on this particular expedition by a transitory illness that had afflicted the children's governess, Miss Errington. She felt honor bound to stay behind and nurse her friend. However, as soon as her patient showed signs of recovering, Mary set out on a mighty ride which was to become a legend in the family. She was an accomplished horsewoman and used to rough going, and she did not fear the California weather or solitudes. Following Frederick and Miss Whitney, she accomplished a forty-mile ride in one day. And she caught up with her husband who had ridden on, showing off the Big Trees and the entrance into Yosemite to an interesting young lady seeing all this for the first time.

In addition to having a last family camp in the Yosemite, Olmsted was determined also to do some long-lasting business for the park. He invited the other commissioners to come into the Yosemite for a meeting in order to plan a strategy of management for the future. Olmsted intended to make an oral report to his colleagues gathered around a campfire. Later he would write a more polished version of this report and send it to the California legislature. He hoped to make a guide for the future for this kind of wild park which had never existed before. It was a kind of park he had never imagined until he came west.

But his ideas had broadened. In addition to created parks, in which man as maker not only imitated but improved on nature—in adapting land to man's recreational and contemplative use, there was justification, as here, for larger natural parks. The point to be made was that man had no need, or right, to touch these wild areas or to change them; in fact, the less man did to shape them the better. He might make them accessible, that was to be all. Olmsted was aware, before many other people were, that these mountains and forests, which during millions of years of growth had taken shape without man's intervention, were now of first importance to man—if he could be brought to appreciate the wild.

Olmsted groped his way toward a philosophy of preservation and, thinking aloud, tried out his ideas first on the men chosen to sit with him on this first board of commissioners of the first public or national wild park. Olmsted never attempted anything halfway. He saw what had to be done here. He had written to his father on July 5, "I am preparing a scheme of management for the Yosemite, which is far the noblest public park, or pleasure-ground, in the world. I expect to have a meeting of the Commission there early in August."[69]

The report to the legislature which resulted from this meeting contained words that would echo across a century of preservation of the wild: "The first point to be kept in mind . . . is the preservation and maintenance as exactly as possible of the natural scenery: the restriction, that is to say, within the narrowest limits consistent with the necessary accommodation of visitors, of all artificial constructions markedly inharmonious with the scenery or which would unnecessarily obscure, distort or detract from the dignity of the scenery."[70] Other persons, principally John Muir, helped in later decades to rescue Yosemite from the abuse that, in spite of these brave words, came. Yet it was Olmsted who honorably instigated the movement of preservation to be followed, abandoned, and then re-adopted here and elsewhere in the national park system and later in the wilderness system.

In 1864 and 1865, the solitude of a single family in the great wilderness meant as much to Frederick Olmsted as his exertions for the public use of the park. He and his family were happy in the Yosemite, but with a poignant kind of joy. They knew that this might be their last experience of the free, generous, and open life they had been leading. They were certainly going to return to the East soon. They had no way of knowing how long it would be before they saw again the great cinnamon-trunked trees, the splintered granite walls, the great domes towering over their campground, and the flower-bordered river winding through gentle, natural meadows.

In 1890, twenty-five years later, Olmsted wrote for publication a few pages about Yosemite, at a time when the area was suffering from several kinds of abuses—lumbering, grazing, and general neglect. He recalled, in a way that allows one to imagine his going off from the others, that last time in 1865, to wander and to look. "The distinctive charm of the scenery of the Yosemite does not depend, as it is a vulgar blunder to suppose, on the greatness of its walls and the length of its little early summer cascades; the height of certain of its trees, the reflections in its pools, and such other matters as can be entered in statistical tables, pointed out by guides and represented within picture frames. So far, perhaps, as it can be told in a few words, it lies in the rare association with the grandeur of its rocky elements, of brooks flowing quietly through the ferny and bosky glades of very beautifully disposed great bodies, groups, and clusters of trees. . . . I felt the charm of the Yosemite much more at the end of a week than at the end of a day, much more after six weeks when the cascades were nearly dry, than after one week, and when, after having been in it, off and on, several months, I was going out, I said, 'I have not yet half taken it in.' "[71]

This savorer of scenery could not stay to enjoy Yosemite in unalloyed content. Frederick could not remain with the others in the delightful solitude of the park. He had to return to the practical affairs of Mariposa and left Mary and the children for some time in the wilderness. He went down hurriedly, spending a night on the way in a haystack because he could not travel on, having fallen ill. In San Francisco, he found that he had been formally offered the directorship of the new Freedmen's Bureau at a salary of seven thousand dollars a year.[72] He declined the job by telegram without much of a qualm. He hoped, by this time, to return to park work when he returned to the East.

Meanwhile, Calvert Vaux did what he said he would not do and concluded negotiations with the Commissioners of Central Park, who had been after him and presumably his former partner to return to professional positions under their jurisdiction. A formal letter, dated July 26, 1865, from the Central Park commissioners was addressed to Olmsted and Vaux and resolved "that Messrs Olmsted & Vaux be . . . appointed Landscape Architects to the Board."[73] Thus, for all that they had said about not renewing this bond, the old relationship was renewed. Frederick wrote to his father about this new appointment to Central Park: "I propose to accept it, but cannot until I am finally relieved of Mariposa."[74] He told his father that he planned also to help Godkin edit *The Nation.*

He wrote to Vaux on September 19 that he anticipated momentarily his legal release from Mariposa, and "We are now packing for the voyage." He signed himself to his former and future partner, with whom he had had some stormy passages, "Very Affectly."[75]

Much had been happening in the East to which Olmsted proposed to return. The shock of Lincoln's assassination had been felt shudderingly by Frederick Olmsted in California. It had taken him almost from April until October to recover in his emotions both from the news of the end of the war and of Lincoln's death. After Lincoln's death, being away from Bear Valley, he wrote to Mary and instructed her to drape their house in black. He fell into a dark mood. While listening to the bells tolling in San Francisco churches, he wrote, "All I ask of fortune is to be saved from growing weak and incapable before my time. My brain and nerves tire so easily and I am so incapable without excitement and excitement is so destructive to me."[76]

But following this black and lonely spring, Olmsted recovered his nerve. He had taken his family up into the Sierras again. He had completed his college and village plan. He had proposed a park for the reluctant San Franciscans. The Oakland Cemetery was virtually laid out. And Mariposa had succumbed to its ruin. When bankruptcy became a fact, Olmsted disposed of the failing affairs of the company in a civilized manner, staying on good terms with the foreclosers, officers of a bank in San Francisco. Olmsted lost nothing of local community respect as he presided over these last rites of Mariposa. He was considered only the upright and honest agent of a firm mismanaged by the owners. The slow death of Mariposa had told on Olmsted, but he was able to dissociate himself in his own mind from the company's failure, and he had comforted himself with other activities.

On September 28, he wrote John Olmsted that he had asked Howard Potter, the New York attorney who had helped him and Godkin finance *The Nation,* to notify the Mariposa Company officially that he was leaving the estate and leaving California. On the same date, he asked Calvert Vaux to begin looking for a house for him and Mary and the children.

On October 23, off Guatemala, on the steamer *Moses Taylor,* Olmsted continued to work on the San Francisco park design. Mariposa was already far behind, shuffled off his conscience with an equanimity which, once he had made up his mind, Olmsted practiced all his life about past endeavors. What was important now to a continuity and a sense of purpose was his park work, what he would do in the future linked to what he had done in California and, before that, what he had done in New York.

He was back in New York City at least by November 22, 1865. On the twenty-fifth, he sent his official quittance letter to the Mariposa Company and repeated the gesture on the thirtieth, finding it difficult to get an answer out of the officers of the luckless company. In December a new firm announced itself in New York City. Letters were being written under the letterhead:

Olmsted, Vaux & Co.

Landscape Architects

No. 110 Broadway[77]

CHAPTER XIX

Between Two Worlds

A condition is necessary . . . the unbending of the faculties which
have been tasked . . . a diversion of the imagination.
—F. L. O., *Preliminary Report . . . For Laying Out a*
Park in Brooklyn, 1866[1]

T HE YEAR 1866 was to be the hinge on which Frederick Olmsted
turned, a time when he determined finally upon the career which
he had tentatively begun before the Sanitary Commission and Mariposa interrupted and diverted him. He was ready to enlarge his scope. He returned to a
New York City bigger and busier than he had remembered it to be, a place of
dangers as well as opportunities. He was conscious of the difficulties first and
conserved himself against failure by taking on an extra job, that of serving
as a kind of unofficial associate editor on the staff of Godkin's magazine *The
Nation*. Olmsted relieved Godkin of some of his duties. He renewed acquaintanceship with writers and public figures and assisted in persuading a number
of them to make the *Nation* a place in which to express their views.

More quickly than if he had been solely occupied with park work, he
became knowledgeable about the New York world which had grown in his
absence. His old friends George William Curtis and Charles Dana were
powerful men in this world. Through these and other friends, and through
the magazine connection, Olmsted widened his circle of acquaintances
beyond the inevitable architects, horticulturists, enlightened or unenlightened
commissioners, politicians, and well-endowed owners of private land with
whom his work in land design inevitably led him.

Perhaps the most important new friendship which this life gained him
was with Charles Eliot Norton of Cambridge, Massachusetts. He had known
Norton slightly before he left the Sanitary Commission. Now he sought out
Norton again as a *Nation* contributor. Olmsted asked Norton to write something about education and then, in his own irrepressible fashion, proceeded to

tell Norton what he himself thought on the subject. Schools should not establish class distinctions. All students should start together, be friends together, go as far as each one could, and only then drop out at the appropriate year. He wished an emphatic "Yes" as answer to several questions: "Can we associate a superior education for men who will be engaged in pursuits other than 'professional' or scholarly with an university?" "Can the university be democratized? To draw such a line between an education of head-workers and hand-workers ... will go far to establish in the minds of each class a very undemocratic habit."[2] He groped toward a kind of education for the whole man, an education of the senses and perceptions and physical skills as well as of the mental aptitudes and strengths. Olmsted soon found that the scholar of Shady Hill did not share all his admiration for an education that democratized, that, in fact, Norton had already given up on democracy. But Olmsted was able all his life to be tolerant of differences between himself and his friends if, as in this case, he could like the man himself. And, as he came to know better the retiring, fastidious, aristocratic Norton, he became fond of him.

Norton and his wife urged the Olmsteds to come visit them in Cambridge or at Ashfield, later in the summer. While delaying the visit, the Olmsteds linked themselves to the Nortons by an exchange of letters. In January, Mrs. Olmsted thought the children too ill disciplined yet to come. "My children after so long a run at grass are very likely to kick in the traces and to require a strong hand for a while with the bridle we won't mention the whip."[3] (She was speaking, of course, in metaphor.) In February, the children had the measles. In June, Frederick had to spend "a day or two" in bed, so they could not come then. And the family was inconveniently separated. "Mrs. Olmsted still remains in the remote parts of Staten Island—she might almost as well be in New Jersey or Bermuda. But I hope for a visit from her tomorrow, and even that next week I may have my whole family about me in my own boarding house."[4] (Frederick was living temporarily in Brooklyn, near the new park.) He continued this written conversation with the Nortons in July: "As my wife said 'Oh! I would like of all things to go to Ashfield' but I can't think of it for the present." And he went on to explain his own circumstances:

The Brooklyn Park has been put for the present wholly into our hands and the Commission having but one meeting after our appointment when they passed an appropriation bill upon my estimate, put everything into our hands and then dispersed for the summer. The various engineers and other assistants whom we selected were all employed elsewhere and could not be at once relieved. We have had to get underway therefore with a very imperfect organization. Hence, as I have taken the duty of superintendence of the work I am held more closely to it than I expect to be when it is fully underway. We have put four hundred men at work and are getting on very nicely. I did not much like the ground at first, but it grows upon me and my enthusiasm and liking for the work is increasing to an inconvenient degree, so that it elbows all other interests out of my mind.[5]

Olmsted also discussed public political affairs with Norton. He was not pleased with the way things were going. "Mr. Johnson as a representative of the better sort of poor men of the South, has by showing his own essential barbarism of character, confirmed and established the apprehension that it would not be just, merciful, prudent or economical to hastily adopt Mr. Johnson's policy. We can not safely hand over the negroes nor can we risk the national welfare by giving the degree of responsibility to the whole body of whites of the South which Mr. Johnson proposes to do." Yet he did not like Andrew Johnson's enemies either: "I wish that a strong subdivision of the republican party could in some way make itself known, feared and respected, as being strongly distinct from that which accepts Stevens and Greely [Olmsted's spelling] as its leaders and authorized attorneys."[6] The world of Andrew Johnson and Thaddeus Stevens was not the world he had wished for when he did his part in the war. He feared that in the ugly and confused dispute about what to do about the South, he and those others who had endured and suffered in the mud on the peninsula (and elsewhere) were going to lose whatever it was for which they had suffered.

Olmsted at this time rather stiffened in his politics. He was far beyond the humble, piquant, objective view he had had—at least in his early journeying —of the people of the South. He made small allowance now for those who, as he conceived, had willfully precipitated the country into the war. He came finally to agree, in simply suspension of qualifying thought, with the radical wing of the Republican Party, although he did not like its leaders.

He found himself willing to expatiate on other general topics, and he found that other people were listening to him and were deferential to his views. His having been chief of the Mariposa estate, a vague, grand situation in the Eastern mind, gave him additional prestige. And his reputation as a designer of great unprecedented public parks was growing. He and Vaux were in the public eye in a way that they had not been when they designed Central Park. They had become something in the way of heroes to the knowledgeable public. They could no longer work secretly, silently, and privately as they had done in planning the first park.

Yet the enjoyment Olmsted himself experienced in the work was almost unsharable. As he negotiated the rough ground of the new Brooklyn park with his lame gait and energetically pushed stick, propelling himself from one end to another of the considerable expanse of land, he saw this raw territory taking shape in his mind's eye. Where at present were pyramided heaps of topsoil or gouged-out dry lake beds, he saw a great meadow, a winding lake, a place for concerts, a skating house, trees, grass, and shady and sunny places. Prospects brightened, and it seemed fitting that the park should be named Prospect.

During the first months after returning from Mariposa, the Olmsted family lived haphazardly in one place or another. At last, in the spring of 1866, they settled in a house on Amos Street at Clifton, Staten Island, across the Narrows from Brooklyn. From Vanderbilt's Landing, Frederick Olmsted took a daily ferry ride across the neck of the harbor and a short ride or walk to the ground of the new Brooklyn park. For certain periods he stayed in Brooklyn, away from Mary and the children. The growing family absorbed almost all his interest away from his work. He took the boys, John Charles and Owen, rowing in the harbor after he came home at night.[7] Or he and Mary, on holidays, drove John Charles, Charlotte, Owen, and Marion into the countryside for a picnic at the local beer works. John Charles was fourteen, Charlotte, eleven, Owen, nine, and Marion, five. The family group was close-knit, lively, and argumentative.

In Manhattan, Olmsted and Vaux had been restored to their authority over both design and superintendence of Central Park, a parallelogram which had already become an institution in the city growing steadily northward toward this open space, but not yet entirely surrounding it. The Central Park commissioners promised also to use the talents of these two men in the new wards which were to be added to the city in the northern area of Manhattan beyond the park. In the meantime, the park across the river in Brooklyn was Olmsted's major interest.

The enjoyment that Olmsted had in the new park was proprietary. He had added his part to the design which Vaux had originated, and he knew, from the moment ground was broken, that his part would be larger than Vaux's in bringing the plan into physical shape. He considered no design set as long as work was being done. Later in his career he would learn to delegate work, but in its early stages, Prospect was shaped under his personal direction, much as Central Park had been. He (and Vaux) had some authority even outside the boundaries of the park, and here, for the first time, they were able to relate a large park to the total life of a city. Since the park was, first of all, a refuge from ordinary, everyday life, they made it private from the nearby streets. The design remolded the very ground of the park's borders. They raised up artificial hills enclosing the park in a world of its own. In their design, Olmsted and Vaux also insisted that public buildings planned for the future (unlike the art museum and the natural history museum in Manhattan) should not take up park land but should be given separate territory outside the park proper. As he had told Vaux, thinking always of the proper end of their means, Olmsted intended the park to be a place into which Brooklyn citizens might walk for easy refreshment, but he did not propose for this generous space to exist in meaningless isolation. He planned "parkways"—an early use of the word, perhaps an initiation of the word—to connect the park with the south Brooklyn shore and, as he hoped, by way of a bridge with his New York park. These generosities of his imagination did not come into full being. Some of the streets leading away from Prospect Park were to be wider than normal city streets and to be tree-shadowed, but his great connected park system linking the two cities never became a reality.

The complications of municipal politics were to intrude upon the joys of park-making, but the partners, at least early in the history of this second park, had substantial support for their aims. James Samuel Stranahan had been president of the Brooklyn park board since 1860 and was to continue in the position until 1882. A man of influence and weight, he became an important personage in Olmsted's career, giving stability to the Brooklyn work. Stranahan had been a merchant, an investor in ferries, and a Whig congressman. He was distinguished by his imaginative insight into the public good. He worked many years, as his counterpart Andrew Green in Manhattan did, for the welding of all the communities of New York into one city. He was to be for Olmsted and Vaux a powerful supporter of the Brooklyn park, one who protected the integrity of the designers' aims. And the partners had other business which built their confidence. They had some freedom to practice their art privately. Their personal professional work increased in 1866.

Olmsted during this time gradually weaned himself from westward yearnings. He sued the Mariposa Company for the costs of having to give up his position before his contract expired. He turned in a finished report for a public pleasure ground in the city of San Francisco and in June received five hundred dollars for his plan. But the project stalled. On May 9, 1866, J. W. Coon of San Francisco wrote to Olmsted:

> By the steamer which arrived two weeks ago, I received your Manuscript Report—and the tin box containing the Coast Survey map, with delineations of the contemplated pleasure grounds and sundry documents. By the last steamer I received your printed Report—and also by Express a package containing a dozen or more of the printed copies of your Report. I submitted the whole matter to the Board of Supervisors at their meeting night before last and it was referred to an appropriate committee. . . .
>
> We did not procure the necessary legislation for carrying your Report into practical operation and I do not think the Supervisors will see the way clear to go on with the work for the present, but the subject will be kept before the people and thus I think their minds will be prepared for action when the necessary legislation has been procured.[8]

Olmsted had already turned in a plan for the college of California and a village to be called Berkeley. A university and a city were to grow later on the space Olmsted had surveyed, but his plan was lost and his report was to be used only in an advisory way.

Olmsted received letters from time to time about Yosemite from those who had been his colleagues on the first governing board of commissioners, of which he had been president. But the "wild" park was to fall away from the high aims he had had for it, and it was to be a long intermediate generation before, with the help of other men, Yosemite began to be preserved in the way Olmsted had prescribed.

In 1866 he allowed active concern for the college, the city park, and the wild park in California to fade away. He plunged in a fashion typical of his nature into the activities of the present moment in the thickly populated, complicated life of the East. Here money, much of it new and raw, did great and terrible things, but at least a certain amount of it spilled over into his projects for green spaces for the cities. Abetted by Vaux, Olmsted found an intoxication in getting involved in one thing after another, finding that he could very well indeed handle each one successively. After many preparations and failures, Olmsted had discovered within himself a steadying balance-wheel for this kind of activity. It might have seemed rather late for him. He was forty-four in the spring of 1866. But the way he took on new jobs at this time was youthful.

In the curious life Olmsted had led among various kinds of men and in a wide range of circumstances—farming on the poor soil of Connecticut's Sachem Head and the sandy loam of New York's Staten Island, editing *Putnam's Magazine* in Manhattan, walking English footpaths, riding horse-back and rocking in crude stagecoaches through the pine forests of the South, designing and supervising the first large city park in America, managing a volunteer war service, supervising gold mines in California—he had had a wide experience. And he had ideas in plenty for new opportunities as they presented themselves.

In 1866 he began to be called on to design schools or the setting of schools in the East. The first of these was a school for the deaf. In March, 1866, E. M. Gallaudet wrote three letters (March 10, 19, and 27),[9] asking the Olmsted and Vaux firm, but Mr. Olmsted in particular, to advise him on the improvement of the grounds of the school for the deaf he was establishing in the open countryside on the northeast side of the national capital. Olmsted returned to the familiar Washington scene to meet the strong-minded Mr. Gallaudet, who greeted him at the train station and conducted him over the grounds of his new school. Olmsted was intensely interested in helping to provide a humane and beautiful setting for the education of these children whom Gallaudet proposed to board and to teach. Vaux was to be brought into the project to design several of the buildings of the school.

Olmsted's San Francisco park plan was read in Chicago by William T. Brass, a businessman, who inquired of Olmsted on April 28, 1866, if the designer did not think that something might be done in the way of a park for Chicago.[10] Much was to result in the next few decades from this innocent query.

On May 12 and 22, Henry F. French, president of the Massachusetts Agricultural College at Amherst, wrote to Olmsted arranging for him to visit and "to advise about our college grounds."[11] This visit resulted in an interesting report, but, in the end, the firm did not do the design. Olmsted drew upon this experience to write a pamphlet, "A Few Things To Be Thought of Before Proceeding to Plan Buildings for the National Agricultural Colleges (1866)." The publication attracted inquiries to the firm from Maine and Minnesota, as well as other states which had boards planning schools under the new Morrill Act. Olmsted visited Orono, Maine, but failed to get a job.

General Montgomery Meigs, who had been quartermaster general of the Union Army, now busying himself with many federal constructions and installations, wrote to Olmsted, whom he had known in the Sanitary Commission days, telling him, "I shall be glad to see you if you come and to talk with you on a subject which I have much at heart just now, a public park [for] this City of Washington."[12] Out of this vague proposition would come much varied work, including supervision of the grounds of national arsenals and cemeteries and in time the redesign of the grounds of the United States Capitol.

On July 23, William Dorsheimer, an influential attorney in Buffalo, New York, wrote to Olmsted and Vaux and inquired about the possibilities of a Buffalo park. "Many of the . . . citizens of Buffalo are talking about establishing a park here, and I desire to obtain from you such information as you may be able to give about the subject."[13] Much grew out of this connection, first a park system and hospital grounds for this western New York city, and later, other works in the state of New York, and a long enduring friendship with Dorsheimer.

On August 2, Olmsted's friend Howard Potter called upon him to go down with him to Long Branch, New Jersey, where he owned some land, in order to advise him on the proper use of the area.[14] Thus Olmsted moved into the design of residential and resort areas, a natural outgrowth of the tentative ideas he had had for a village such as Berkeley.

A considerable portion of Olmsted's and Vaux's joint work, and later Olmsted's alone, was henceforth to be for private individuals. An example of the way such jobs came to the partners in 1866 was a letter from G. M. Atwater of Springfield, Massachusetts. He wrote on October 2, "I may decide to develop the wooded land and meadow about my residence—and be glad to receive your advice and visit here. What are your terms."[15]

On September 14, Olmsted was asked to serve as a juror for the Paris Exposition to be held the following year.[16] On October 18, he was notified that he had been elected a director of the American Social Science Association.[17]

So 1866 brought him offers of various kinds of jobs quite accurately forecasting many ways in which he would exercise himself in the next three decades: in municipal parks, in campus design, in real estate development, in work for individuals. And also there came to him honors and summonses to serve publicly in various positions.

The press of work seemed to leave little time even for friendship. In

August Fred Kingsbury wrote Fred Olmsted how he had come down to the city one day in spring on purpose to see him, found him gone from the office, waited about, got impatient, and left. "Have you gone to work *malice prepense* to kill yourself with labor? Is your life insured? If not you ought to have thought of that before you worked yourself into a condition where no company could take a risk on you."[18] Kingsbury learned later that this was a day when the Olmsteds had moved. He was sorry, he said, to see his friend so seldom. The two Freds had always enjoyed crossing the swords of their wit one against the other.

In all this work Olmsted was finding the postwar world one of many opportunities. Nearly all the chances were tied to interesting temptations. But Olmsted was not attracted to corruption, and he never had any desire to gouge. He was straightforward about the rates he charged, which were handsome but not exorbitant and tempered to the client's pocketbook. He furnished each client a rate sheet: $100–$200 for a preliminary survey plus traveling expenses, $2,000–$5,000 for a large design.[19] Olmsted insisted on a gentlemanly relation in his professional dealings. A landscape architect was, like a lawyer, called on for his superior knowledge, and he treated clients as equals. If, after a preliminary look at what the client wished done, he found that with good conscience he could not do the work, then he withdrew. Olmsted and Vaux accepted a lot or two each as a portion of pay for work they would do shortly at Riverside, Illinois, in addition to the fee promised, but they did not ever go in for land speculation. Olmsted had invested in Godkin's magazine, which was, after all, his brainchild too. He put some modest funds in Dana's newspaper, and he invested, more for the sake of friendship than for business reasons, in another friend's cranberry bogs. He held his California investments for a number of years. But he was not interested in stock speculation. Land design was too large a passion to allow room in his imagination for what in others was a devouring interest. And before long, landscape architecture paid, as he thought, rather well.

What enabled Olmsted to work his own purposes through the tangle of other men's motives which surrounded his profession was the fact that he had a steadfast aim. He knew what he wanted and he had persistence. Opportunities were large enough for a confident man to achieve a great deal of what he wanted to do for a public or a private purpose by slipping through and around the many rapt and selfish aims of other men. There was room in this careless time for the odd, the eccentric, even the creative, to find waste places for growth, just as Olmsted's parks were usually laid out on abused or neglected ground.

Walt Whitman, in the years after the war, wrote in his *Democratic Vistas,* his excoriation of the bad and his hope for the good in this time. Olmsted and Vaux's great city parks were included in his poem in prose: "The tumultuous streets, Broadway, the heavy, low, musical roar, hardly ever intermitted, even at night; the jobbers' houses, the rich shops, the wharves, the great Central Park, and the Brooklyn Park of hills (as I wander among them this beautiful fall weather, musing, watching, absorbing...these I say, and the like of these, completely satisfy my senses of power, fullness, motion, etc....)"[20]

Olmsted tried to state what his intent was in this postwar world in the occasional reports, plans, and prospectuses he wrote for boards of commissioners. In spite of his partner's fear that Fred was casting pearls before swine, he persisted. Vaux's opinion of Olmsted's lengthy work upon a report on the Brooklyn park had contained these very words. In the engineer's office of the Brooklyn park, Vaux sat down one day in August to write to the absent Olmsted, who had gone on vacation, apparently carrying the unfinished report with him. He asked his partner not to be so long. "I note what you say about report,—something compact an you love me.... Attempts to convince by elaborate deductions of first principles will fall rather flat on our Brooklyn clients. However, I will think it over as you request." And his concluding words show the good terms of their present partnership: "Have a good time and rest assured that I will take the earliest opportunity to communicate anything that is disagreeable."[21]

Despite the disproportion of "first principles" to dull ears, the report was to be one of Olmsted's basic statements:

The great advantage which a town finds in a park, lies in the addition to the health, strength and morality which comes from it to its people.... The reason is obvious: all wealth is the result of labor, and every man's individual wealth is, on the whole, increased by labor of every other in the community.... but as there cannot be the slightest use of will, ... nor the slightest exercise of skill of any kind, without the expenditure of force, it follows that, without recuperation and recreation of force, the power of each individual to labor wisely and honestly is soon lost....

But to this process of recuperation a condition is necessary, known since the days of Aesop, as the unbending of the faculties which have been tasked, and this *unbending* of the faculties we find is impossible, except by the occupation of the imagination with objects and reflections of a quite different character from those which are associated with their bent condition. To secure such a diversion of the imagination the best possible stimulus is found to be the presentation of a class of objects to the perceptive organs, which shall be as agreeable as possible to the taste, and at the same time entirely different from the objects connected with those occupations by which the faculties have been tasked. And this is what is found by townspeople in a park.

And so, while specifying all the means by which his park should be psychologically useful to the citizens of the city, Olmsted could not help going on beyond usefulness. His park should be also "rural, natural, tranquilizing and poetic" in character. It should "produce a general suggestion of sympathy with human gaiety and playfulness."[22]

Thinking over his report, perhaps carrying a draft with him, Frederick went with Mary and the children to pay a long delayed visit to the Charles Eliot Nortons, conveniently on the way to the White Mountains. The Nortons were at their rural summer home in Ashfield in the northern part of Massachusetts where little brooks ran clear and the air was fresh all summer long. The two families found an easy agreement, and Frederick confirmed a friendship. Norton was thirty-nine, a handsome man with sharply chiseled features. His wife was younger and companionable to Mary. Through Norton, Olmsted renewed himself in a New England atmosphere. Later, coming to visit him at Cambridge, he began to meet a circle of thoughtful people in that community.

Norton had already traveled in Europe to see paintings and famous men. His views were fastidious and refined although his great career as a teacher was still ahead of him. He had written about Dante and about travel in Italy. The calm with which Norton surveyed the world was unlike Olmsted's own attitude. The two men had a friend in common in George William Curtis, who was more active and more radical in his political and personal sympathies than his pose of *dolce far niente*. Norton was helping James Russell Lowell edit and reinvigorate, as they hoped, the old *North American Review*. Lowell had reviewed Olmsted's Southern travels and was still, to Olmsted, the hero of his youth, as the author of *Biglow Papers*. So Norton put him in touch with a world he admired. If he did not always agree with Norton, that fact did not at all spoil their warm friendship.

Norton wrote fondly to Olmsted after the latter had set off with his family from Ashfield northward into the White Mountains and on to Quebec: "I wish you could come here again this autumn for a longer and quieter visit to us. I wish we did not live so far apart."[23] To Norton Olmsted wrote about getting back into the New England mountains, so different from the chasms and cliffs of Yosemite: "We felt a little cheated of our enjoyment of the mountains by the crowd of infidels—philistines—which occupied them. We enjoyed, very much indeed a few hours we spent in a ramble up one of the neglected mountain streams, such a stream as you may perhaps have within a mile of your house. The peculiar charm of the White Hill scenery I find in the underwood, mass and water, not in that which is grandest."[24] Savoring a difference was important.

Variety in scenery was to be desired. In the great wild parks (such as Yosemite), human creatures were to be inconspicuous, quiet, watchful, listening rather than acting. Man in city landscapes, such as he and Vaux had made, was to be a more animated figure, engaged in movement, sometimes noisy and demonstrative, with balloons flying overhead and even fireworks exploding, an active figure, hitting baseballs, flying across ice on shining skates, also strolling slowly, or moving rapidly seated at ease in a carriage. No landscape, however, was thought of as an empty picture. Man had to be there as a reference point (even if men were there in too great a number, as in the late summer in the White Mountains).

In his work and in his recreation, Olmsted had shaped a way of life by the year 1866. He had placed in one perspective his professional public work and his private and personal thought. He was ready to go on with a long life of park-making.

CHAPTER XX
A Wider Work

You are a magician.
— Miss McCagg of Chicago to F. L. O., April 12, 1871[1]

IN THE FALL OF 1871, one of those poking about in the ruins of the Chicago fire was Frederick Olmsted. He had occasional business in this western city and, finding himself there shortly after the disaster, could not resist reverting to being a reporter and writing an account of the situation for the *Nation*.

The desolation was amazing. An area half as large as Manhattan, four miles long and one mile wide, was completely gone, except for the straight streets which Olmsted traversed in an omnibus which was operating in the midst of nothingness. The very stones and bricks of substantial buildings had disintegrated, and the level mud flat was newly raw. Across this open space, one could see a man standing upright three miles away. The shadow of this citizen, or any Chicago inhabitant, needed to be very long, if he were to rebuild what had been destroyed.

Olmsted was delighted by the way these self-reliant Westerners were already digging and hammering and putting things together. "The City is again supplied with water, most of it with gas; it is as well sewered and paved as before. Omnibuses and streetcars are running on all the old lines; newspapers are published, schools are open and full...a new public-library is started in the basement of a Baptist meeting-house.... Chicago, in short is under jury-masts, and yet carries her ensign union down, but she answers the helm, lays her course, is making fair headway."[2] Olmsted, full of feeling, used sailor's lingo. He subscribed one hundred dollars to Chicago relief.

The fire interrupted the landscape work Olmsted and Vaux were doing in Chicago. But Olmsted found an interest, nonetheless, in redoubled activity after the disaster. He was hopeful for the kind of human life he found here. Chicagoans, doing what needed to be done, seemed a fulfillment of what he had hoped the late war had redeemed, a proud and independent citizenry working hard for the general welfare.

The way Olmsted reacted to the great fire was an instance of his curiosity and concern for the world he had left when he went out to California and which, when he returned, he saw with new eyes. He thought, or hoped, that he had helped create this new world by his part in the war. He wished to share in a new kind of postwar society. He believed, at least for a time, that the new time was to be a wider kind of democracy. He had a basic sympathy for the lives of the people who made up the nation. But there was in him also an artist-critic who could not long be borne forward on a surge of mindless energy; the critic in him desired to curb or shape the life of this people, to give it flavor and direction where it had none.

One of the symbols of the new city of Chicago was a friend, Ezra Mc-Cagg, a wealthy and enterprising lawyer and businessman. He had met McCagg in the war years in the Sanitary Commission work. McCagg was the son of a New York farmer who had graduated from a small college, worked for the Ogdens in lumber and railroads, and become rich. He was interested in an art museum for the city and had a valuable private collection of books. McCagg lived in a fine house, but he and his family were basically simple folk, much like the Silas Laphams. Olmsted fell ill at his hotel during one visit to Chicago, and the McCaggs moved him to their house and took care of him. Thereafter, whenever he came to the city, he was an intimate who charmed the younger members of the family, and he counted on McCagg to support his and Vaux's various projects for the good of the community.

Olmsted described the family to Alfred Field, a friend in England, as rich folks who invited drifters to meals and aided such men in finding jobs. They lived in a house full of flowers and music and wanted Chicago to become as wealthy in the arts as in flour, lumber, and rails. "In short while they seem to be very simple, almost frivolous and playful in their habits of mind they must have a serious instinct, strong humane sympathy and very clear common sense, and I really feel as if they were about as good a production of our western civilization and Christianity as I ever hope to see.... In one word, I love them very much and could write a great deal more."[3] Olmsted, in his new happiness in the practice of the art he loved, became himself more lovable, more open to new friendships, flexible in a way that increased with age rather than decreased.

On their side, the McCaggs young and old recognized in this visitor from New York a remarkable man who did not hesitate for a moment to take on himself the task of transforming their city in some important respects. "Puss," the clever daughter, wrote once to Olmsted when he had gone home to New York, "Our gift was superfluous, you need no charm but the one you carry in your own person, for you are a magician yourself, at least I believe so, or how else could you have known that I had been wishing for a note of yours. . . . The evening you left, I lamented so piteously, as I rose from the table, my loss in having no one to push back my chair, as you had done, that Bob [her brother] was moved to compassion, and has taken that charity upon himself ever since."[4]

An intimacy such as he had with the McCaggs probably taught Olmsted in a quiet way that he was an important man. His easy camaraderie with the McCaggs of the world also told him how far he had come in his profession since he was an underpaid superintendent of workmen in Central Park. The letter from Miss McCagg, marking the stage of his friendship with this Chicago family, was dated April 12, 1871. Olmsted looked forward, seldom back. But in this sixth year of work since his return from California, he might have seen in his happy situation in Chicago, and in other cities outside of New York, that he—he and Vaux, still working together—had traveled far in the profession which they had named and almost invented. Their work in landscape architecture, and similar work of a few other men, had become national in scope. Olmsted had traveled much and become a familiar figure to municipal commissioners and private investors.

New circumstances had called for novel solutions. Each opportunity—a sandy beach south of Chicago to be made into a park, a scrubby and undistinguished neighborhood of Buffalo to have parks and parkways laid down upon it, a site in Massachusetts to have a hospital for the mentally ill given a proper setting—called for ingenious ways of thinking. Olmsted, who often did the original surveys and usually wrote plans and reports for the firm, caused city fathers and business leaders to feel an alliance between their ambitions and the solutions proposed by Olmsted and Vaux.

But even in the successes of his new career in design, he had not fully recovered from the emotions which the war had churned up. He felt pity for the condition of the postwar South even if he had no sympathy with what he conceived to be the politics of the leaders of the South. He took on the job of being recording secretary of a new organization, the Southern Famine Relief Commission. He enlisted his own stepmother as a volunteer, among others, to assist in raising funds and supplies. Mary Ann Olmsted wrote with some dismay to Fred, "I think I must have been unfortunate in my selection [i.e., of the local Hartford ladies she had tried to interest in the cause], for I found them *very* bitter toward the South, and entirely opposed to doing anything for the sufferers—thought the very best thing that could be done was to 'let them starve.' "[5] She went, however, to the editor of the Hartford *Press* and persuaded him to publish some circulars her stepson had sent her. She and the editor both thought Fred should "come and talk with the ladies, in the parlors of one of our churches." (This was in February, 1867.)

Whether Frederick went at his stepmother's behest to talk to a gathering of women in Hartford, one does not know, but he did other things, under the pressure of personal news out of the South. He received a dignified but plaintive letter from one William M. Browne of Athens, Georgia, who recalled to Olmsted their acquaintanceship during the travels of "Yeoman" and described to him the hunger and raggedness of a countryside that had been rich in crops when his Northern friend had seen it little more than a decade before.[6] Olmsted, who was the principal mover and agent of the organization, saw to it that Southern Famine Relief shipped corn and other food to North Carolina, South Carolina, Georgia, and Alabama. Knowing that the federal government could do more than any small, private agency, Olmsted went to the quartermaster general and inquired sharply (in October, 1867) how much relief his office had given the South since the war.[7] He received a not very satisfactory answer on the twenty-sixth of the month.

Olmsted also attended a number of meetings of the United States Sanitary Commission after the war during the time the executive committee was winding up the affairs of what had been the most successful relief organization.

He continued to receive word from California of his activities there. Governor F. F. Low officially acknowledged his resignation from the Yosemite Commission on January 18, 1867.[8] Private correspondence from California informed him that his careful report on the preservation of Yosemite had been held back. Alex Deering of Mariposa related a story of intrigue, of a kind to disgust Olmsted, that his friends Ashburner and Whitney of the Geological Survey had had something to do with suppressing his report.[9] They were, according to Deering, jealous for the use of state funds and wished their work to receive moneys which might otherwise go to the new state park. Olmsted was a proud man with quixotic views about friendship. Rather than involve Whitney and Ashburner in a public quarrel, he let an injustice pass and paid no public attention to it. He worked later, behind the scenes, to get signatures from influential friends for a petition to Congress on behalf of the sanctity of the Yosemite. He secured, among others at Yale University, the signature of J. D. Whitney, who had returned to his professorial career. Whether Deering's allegations (and Galen Clarke's, too) against William Ashburner and Josiah Whitney were true or not, Olmsted did not let either of these men know that he had heard them. Ashburner and his wife were his and Mary's friends and continued to correspond with the Olmsteds. William Ashburner continued also to act as Olmsted's financial agent in California, attempting to collect architectural fees long owed by the University (once College) of California and by the Oakland, California, Mountain View Cemetery. Henry Perkins, Mary's cousin, had remained in California and worked for Ashburner for a period. Perkins married in California and succeeded Ashburner as Olmsted's agent managing Olmsted's modest investment in western stocks and land properties. But the report on Yosemite sent to the Governor for transmission to the California State Legislature was lost, and its message lost too, until found, reconstructed, and published by Laura Wood Roper in 1952.[10]

Another friend appeared out of the West from time to time, Clarence King, the geologist whom Olmsted had employed to assay the ores of Mariposa and to survey the boundaries of Yosemite. King was ambitious to organize a national survey of the western territories. Olmsted was one of his friends to whom King announced that he had gained his object. King wrote Olmsted on March 7, 1867, "After a very hard battle my bill came safely through, and yesterday afternoon, I received, verbally, from the Secretary of War, my appointment as chief of the new Survey [the 40th Parallel Survey]. I hope to cut the Gordian knot of red tape which surrounds me here within the week and get away from this suffocating atmosphere of circumlocution. I shall be in New York, certainly, within ten days and will call on you. Perhaps after I am a little more organized you will give us a brief notice in 'The Nation.' "[11]

Olmsted's friends assumed that he had influence at the *Nation* and this was true. He continued to contribute a certain amount of editorial attention, and some financial support, to the magazine for a number of years. He and Edwin L. Godkin were in close touch, often writing letters to each other from one part of New York to another, meeting occasionally to discuss magazine policy as well as for the sake of their easy friendship. This friendship was not to preclude Olmsted's arguing with Godkin about politics in the next decade. He remained obstinately "stalwart" while Godkin flirted with dissent from Republican regularity although he came round in the end. But Olmsted's active interest in the *Nation* diminished as he had less and less time for it.

But various kinds of jobs in land design engrossed him. Friendship caused Charles Eliot Norton to call upon Olmsted to take on the task of making a design for some land he owned which he planned rather timorously to open in part to the public. "There is a risk of its being misused by the low population of the neighborhood and of Boston."[12] But Olmsted went ahead quietly with the plan in spite of Norton's fears and carried the owner along with him. Charles Norton's was only the first claim Boston made on him.

In January, 1870, James Haughton of Boston attempted to interest Olmsted in a future for parks for that city, and was half frightened off by Olmsted's immediate, specific ideas. "I had not the slightest idea that you would be the advocate of any particular scheme or project."[13] However, Haughton accustomed himself to Olmsted's importunate definiteness and was carried along by him to an unBostonian enthusiasm. Olmsted visited Boston at Haughton's invitation, looked about, and made more suggestions. On October 15, 1870, Haughton wrote a letter to the firm: "Our park bill passed by the Legislature of the Commonwealth last winter, will come up for acceptance at the general election in November. It requires a two thirds vote, to be accepted by the city.... I wish to place in the hands of Gov. Claflin your last report."[14] So that, although the movement for a refurbished and extended park system for Boston progressed slowly, it was at least started. Much of Olmsted's future was set toward Boston.

In the meantime, his life seemed settled in New York where he and Vaux had a renewed care for the Manhattan parks as well as the big Brooklyn project in hand. If Olmsted traveled to other cities or towns or campus sites, it seemed pleasant to return home to Clifton, Staten Island.

Olmsted continued to superintend the work on the new Prospect Park. He was out in a bad snowstorm in December, 1867. But the experience rather exhilarated him: "I was out all day in the park, getting things in winter rig, and unable to get home at night, but though much knocked about suffered no serious harm. Some of our engineers were badly frost bitten. I have never experienced a more blinding and bewildering storm."[15]

Staying close to this large project, Olmsted mentally stepped back and gained perspective on the kind of work he was doing. His personal taste grew, during these years, for an unobtrusive simplicity in fitting means to ends. And he was developing, through practice, an ability to employ with ease the diverse abilities of many men and the qualities of trees and plants as well as stone and masonry to make a design that answered a craving in his own being. There was a slight but significant and growing difference between him and Vaux. It was the difference between the school-bred professional and the self-educated maker (artist, though he would not at times claim it). Olmsted was concerned equally with the initial design, which came to him through an attentive contemplation of the ground itself, and the social usefulness of the plan. He possessed to a remarkable degree the often mutually exclusive qualities necessary for a landscape architect: the ability to find within himself ideas and intuitions, and the ability to translate those self-pleasing notions into projects for which one group of men were willing to pay and which other men would want to walk into and enjoy.

Olmsted disliked, as Vaux did, the ugliness and grossness of many of the politicians with whom they had to deal. Central Park had been at least partially protected in the earliest years by its commission form of government under the authority of the state and not of the city. Most of the first set of commissioners had been relatively free from corrupt pressures except those of providing jobs. The most energetic of these men, Andrew H. Green, was icily correct and clean. It was only with the creeping power of the ring of politicians headed by William Marcy Tweed, from 1869 on, and the eventual seizure of the parks by that group, that Olmsted and Vaux found themselves watching helplessly as their aims in park-making were flouted and their positions became subject to the whim of the bosses.

While Olmsted flinched at the quality of these men rising into power, he had a wider tolerance—as long as his health held out—of difficult working conditions than Vaux did. Eager to attain his ends, he was a whirlwind of energy and will, magnetic and winning to a variety of men. He attracted even men of the buccaneer class and got along with some of these men as long as they would accept his terms.

It was pleasanter to find men with large ideas and strong wills who shared his general kind of morality, that one's aims must fit in with some kind of improvement of the future. Andrew D. White, the first president of the new Cornell University at Ithaca, New York, was one of these forceful and idealistic men with whom Olmsted got along well. As early as May, 1867, White was bombarding Olmsted with messages, trying to arrange an early visit of the New York land designer to the site of the new school. "Mr. Cornell absent and cannot meet us next week."[16] Old Ezra Cornell, who had given a great sum for the new school, let Andrew White take the lead in planning the institution but kept a keen old eye on details. Olmsted paid a preliminary visit. White wrote Olmsted subsequently, "Even more glad was I that you like our surroundings at Ithaca.... I have long wished to meet Mr. Norton of whom you speak and hope to do so this summer.... Don't I beg of you lose faith or hope on account of this doubt regarding our buildings. You must take an interest in us."[17] Some bricks and mortar were already committed, buildings which Olmsted seemed to think would not be appropriate.

Not one to hang back, Olmsted gave White the benefit of his advice. He passed on to White also the names of several of his friends as possible professors in the new institution: Charles Eliot Norton, Clarence King, and Edwin L. Godkin. King, while awaiting consummation of his survey plans, carefully considered becoming a professor of geology at the new school, but declined when the federal government authorized his great western work. The other two responded cautiously while testing their alternate opportunities for the future. Godkin's magazine survived another crisis, so he turned down the chance to teach political science, and Norton, declining Cornell, eventually became famous as a fine arts professor at Harvard. A few years later, White persuaded Olmsted to serve as a trustee of Cornell, a connection which kept him available for advice on landscaping. George Geddes, who had taught young Fred Olmsted scientific farming at Fairmount, near Syracuse, was also brought into the circle of advisers to President White of Cornell. Geddes counseled White on the practical matter of the repair and maintenance of the school's water reservoir. The connection brought him and Olmsted into contact again.

In his service to Cornell, Olmsted gave himself to a free play of emotion and exertion. Despite his crippled leg, of which he made as little complaint as possible, he rambled energetically over the hilly grounds. He visited the school in September, 1867, while President White was absent, and wrote to him, "We have done little else than tumble up the streams and over the hills. I have blocked out a tolerably complete plan for the general subdivisions and formed a theory of the probable progress of closer settlement on the hill outside of the necessary university grounds. I think I can accommodate most of Mr. Cornell's wishes more satisfactorily to myself than I had supposed I could when I was here before ... We [Mary was with him] are going on to visit some relations of Mrs. Olmsted at Genesea and shall probably reach home about Wednesday of next week when I hope we may see you."[18]

Calvert Vaux sketched the original design for President White's house although he did not complete it. The advice which Olmsted gave on the original plan for Cornell was not to show later in any traceable detail, but his informal influence was to have considerable lasting effect. The historian of the campus, Kermit Carlyle Parsons, wrote in 1968:

The formative ideas for Cornell's early architecture and campus development were determined by its Founder Ezra Cornell, and its first President, Andrew Dickson White. But Frederick Law Olmsted, the University's first landscape advisor, prophesied the final outcome. . . .

In 1867 he told them they should seek variety within unity in the arrangement of the campus. . . .

He thought the new land-grant colleges and American communities would assume almost identical forms in which growth and change would require flexible, extendible plans. He also predicted a movement in American society from what he termed a Puritan reaction to 'merrie England' toward a new freedom where many men would participate in community affairs, enjoy full family lives, carry on intellectual pursuits, and still have time to make their daily bread.[19]

The advice Olmsted gave at Cornell signified to himself his continuing effort to further an enlarging, inclusive kind of education. The new school at Ithaca seemed a hopeful institution where new kinds of learning might thrive. Here generations of farmers were to be educated to be open-minded, liberal men; here, also, within a cautious interval of time, women would be educated to take their place in a humane society.

One should note that at this same time Olmsted's friend Charles Brace was establishing schools for boys and girls rescued from the New York streets. No doubt the two friends had a fellow-feeling about their diverse educational projects. Brace wrote about his industrial schools, "These schools are not, first of all eleemosynary; their principal purpose is not to give alms to the poor, but to prevent the poor from needing alms." And, in tune with Olmsted's ideas, he wrote, "A child's mind grasps knowledge most of all through its senses and its imagination. A good teacher should keep these continually in play."[20]

In the specific situation at Cornell, with its loose and flexible arrangement of buildings, its spaces and directions for growth, Olmsted happily endorsed a break with the mentality which had built schools like barracks in a rigidly aligned order. For young people—in fact, all men and women in whom native sensitivity had not been deadened—learned through their senses and their imagination. This was the educational premise of his parks.

As his children grew up, Olmsted spent personal attention upon their education, perhaps too much for their comfort. From the time he married (and even before that time, through reading Zimmerman, he had conceived a romantic idea of family life), he was devotedly a father. With Mary, he shared his thoughts as well as feelings in an imperious, demanding way, and yet often left her physically alone to deal with household problems. That his wife had her share of slight depressions, irritations, and nervousness at thus being left out of the active life he led was normal to her generation of carefully reared women and yet unconsciously hard to bear. If she could have shared his war experience, as Ellie Strong had shared that of her husband, George Templeton Strong, she might have had fewer ailments. (Mrs. Strong served as a capable administrator on the hospital ships.)

As for the children, subject to the devouring interest of an ever solicitous father, it was sometimes to be difficult for them to be the object of such concentrated attention. This was to be particularly true for the oldest, John Charles. John, as he had quietly determined to call himself in a first gesture of youthful independence, became early a kind of loving problem for his father. The father was conscious that this bright boy's schooling had been erratic. The years in California had given John advantages not to be measured, but had hardly prepared him for a scientific education. Olmsted decided to send John to his friend Frederick Knapp's small school at Sutton, Massachusetts, to prepare to enter the Yale Scientific School. Good-natured little Owen was already there and happy. From this time on, vacations for the Olmsteds became often a matter of boarding with or near the Knapps, first at Sutton and then at Plymouth, where Knapp moved the school. Frederick, taking longer and longer trips away from the New York area in the summers, had the satisfaction of knowing that Mary and the children were with congenial friends where the children could have plenty of outdoor exercise.

Knapp, who was of course the good right hand of Olmsted's war service, gives the impression in his letters of being a guileless man, incapable of taking advantage of anyone, and perhaps not sharp at managing his affairs. He had formed a small company and invested in cranberry bogs. Olmsted, out of friendship, put money in Knapp's cranberries. Their colleague of the war days, George Strong, wrote sarcastically in his diary on November 12, 1867: "Poor Knapp! He has given up philanthropy and is speculating in cranberries. He has got up a great cranberry company in New Jersey, and the more feeble-minded of his friends are taking stock therein."[21]

Olmsted regarded Knapp's simplicities with tolerance. He thought these qualities were virtues when used to educate young boys. He also offered a great amount of advice to Knapp about what to teach the pupils, for in time, he came to think of this boys' school as in a manner his school. The pupils lived together as in a family, playing, studying, mingling sports and chores with mental exercises. Knapp idolized Olmsted and endured his interest with a good grace. He invited his former chief to talk to the boys. Knapp wrote to Olmsted from Plymouth on February 7, 1870:

Our course of 'talks' on familiar and practical subjects has commenced. The boys take hold of the idea. . . . If you come on, this spring, you will I trust give them a talk on perception and culture of the beautiful. . . . John is doing well decidedly. . . . Owen is doing well also but of course his short legs don't carry him as fast as John goes. We are much attached to both.

Whenever, Mr. Olmsted, a thought occurs to you that would be valuable to me let me have it.[22]

With some interruptions, the two Olmsted boys were to stay with Knapp until they were ready for college. While the boys were with Knapp, Charlotte attended school, at least for a time, in Boston. To Frederick's attentive mind, she seemed sometimes a worry too, a sensitive, nervous, but bright and conscientious young girl, growing up thin and apparently without resistance to moods. Olmsted wrote to friend Knapp about Charlotte, fifteen at the time, on July 11, 1870: "We find her decidedly improved by the Boston experience —more so than we had expected. She is a very nice girl, now, as far as I can see. But she is very slight and on the least provocation turns down [?] almost to the bottom, pale, thin, blue and hysterical."[23]

Being able to talk to Knapp about intimate family matters, as he seldom did to others, was a resource. In his turn, Knapp leaned upon his now famous friend. He worried himself about the momentous matter of the move from Sutton to Plymouth until he prevailed upon Olmsted to go to Plymouth with him to look over the ground. This Olmsted did and Knapp wrote to him gratefully for "helping me to *steady* myself."[24] Olmsted considered at one time (December, 1867) getting out a book of social statistics in collaboration with Knapp, perhaps mainly to help Knapp, but the project died.

Young John Olmsted, happy enough at Knapp's school, was developing as a person. He picked up outdoor enthusiasms and skills easily. He built a sailboat at Plymouth and sailed it himself, with the other schoolboys. He was the leader in making an ice-skating rink at the school, and in other ways took a natural kind of lead among his fellows. As he grew up, he found friends among the children of his father's friends; among them were Downing and Bowyer Vaux and Loring Brace.

The vulgar life of the new rich proliferating in New York City made John's father uneasy, but sometimes, as in one particular case, a boy like John might be dazzled and excited by an opportunity which the father scorned. John was invited to a showy, expensive party for boys of his young and privileged circle at the fashionable St. James Hotel. The partygoers were to dress up like men, and the affair was styled in a manner which the father found objectionable and unsuitable for unformed boys (his son was some months short of being eighteen). "This to my mind," he wrote to Frederick Knapp, on June 20, 1870, "is quite on a par with the little children's parties we heard of in the shoddy part of Fifth Avenue last winter in which the girls wore chignon and diamonds and were served with champaign, etc.... It is akin to the worst form of public demoralization—that which now as in old Rome indicates a rottenness in the foundations of society—and it is the merest snobbish aping of a sort of life which if not wholly bad is anything but worthy of being followed senselessly....I wish he [John] could be made to feel this."[25]

Not only was this new low manner, as he thought, threatening to invade his private life, it was walking into and trampling upon the verities of his professional life. Until 1870, the commissioners of Central Park, appointed at state level and ruled by the inflexibly honest Andrew Green, had preserved a minimum of decent support for Olmsted's and Vaux's work in the parks. Now with the rise to power of the Tweed Ring, this protected circle was threatened. While honest citizens like Vaux and Olmsted watched, the clever rascals gained control of both the state and city governments. In November, 1868, they had secured the governor's job (Hoffman), the mayor's (Oakey Hall), and the comptroller's (Connolly). Two years later, at the behest of this ring, which used the average citizen's decent pride in his city's having self-government, the passage of a new city charter was manipulated through the state legislature. All the old commissions, of which the Central Park commission was one, were revoked, and the parks became a city department under the control of the men who were milking money out of every transaction of the city administration.

Vaux wrote to Olmsted, who was out of town, on April 6, 1870: "The Charter is passed without protecting the Central Park Commission. I saw Mr. Green this morning on his return to town. The vote was taken last night. He says that 20 days is all the legal life the commission has....I do not have any clue to the extent of the change contemplated, but will write you further in a day or two."[26]

Vaux wrote again to a still absent Olmsted, whom he was finding in less of a fighting mood than usual: "I hold that we are the final guardians of this interest as long as we live and as you have always argued that the commission element must from the nature of the case be a transitory one. I wish you felt as disposed for active hostilities as I do but you don't and I am not going to be caught again on the war path alone so shall follow your lead and resign peacefully if such a course seems called for....A law has been introduced making it illegal for any Commissioner to accept a salary. Of course aimed at A. H. G."[27]

Perhaps because he saw the hopelessness of fighting this gang of accomplished thieves, Olmsted was strangely quiescent. Or perhaps it was because he was ill in Chicago. To his partner, immobolized in Ezra McCagg's house, Vaux wrote on April 18, "Dear Olmsted,...Am sorry you feel so blue but consider it to be attributed to your being out of health with diarrhoea. I hope Mr. McCagg's hospitality may bring you round again. I do not see the force of your feverish anxiety for my immediately leaving New York. The

Riverside matter will keep another week.... I hope you can get the Parkway matter in shape to be yielding cash in hand before we leave Chicago.... Keep your spirits up, nothing is so demoralizing to me as muddle."[28]

So while they were having difficulties in bringing to a conclusion certain business in Chicago, their New York business seemed threatened with a stoppage. Olmsted and Vaux knew that while Tweed and his henchmen were in control of the city government the professional and esthetic ideas they held would receive no consideration, or very likely even ridicule. Their appointments were likely to be terminated.

It turned out the way they feared. In April, 1870, the Tweed Ring took over the Central Park area, metamorphosed by the new charter into the New York City Parks Department, and one of the inner Ring, Peter B. Sweeny, was handed the ripe plum of the department. He was named president of the Board of Public Parks. Olmsted and Vaux were reappointed at the beginning of the new regime, but were disregarded. The two men made a test of their position by writing letters to Sweeny recommending certain things to be done in the parks. They were not answered. On November 12, 1870, Frederick Olmsted, for Olmsted and Vaux, wrote a bland-sounding letter to the Honorable Peter B. Sweeny, asking permission to go ahead with certain plantings intended for some time.[29] It was gall to Olmsted to have to ask this ignorant, bloated member of the Ring anything about the park. He was not answered. Within two weeks (November 25), the official landscape architects of the New York parks found that the bosses were instituting plans without consulting them. On November 30, 1870, Olmsted and Vaux resigned from their city positions with the public parks; this happened only one day ahead of their being dismissed. On December 1, 1870, the Board of Public Parks passed a resolution terminating the city's arrangement with Frederick Law Olmsted and Calvert Vaux.[30] There was a vague suggestion of possible new arrangements, but it was lip service only.

Shut out of New York's parks by the Ring, Olmsted and Vaux were free of the onerous and beloved duties which had held them so long. They should, perhaps, have rejoiced in being at large and able freely to engage in their private activities, but the break hurt more than a little. (This gap in their relationship with the city was to stretch no further than one year, but they did not know it.) Olmsted felt anger, disillusionment, and a sort of ache at seeing slip out of his hands the care of the land on which he had lavished the closest if intermittent attention since 1857.

Yet setting aside the New York parks (Manhattan only at this time), Olmsted had reasons for hope and a justifiable ambition in his professional life at this time. Brooklyn was another city, and the work in Brooklyn continued uninterrupted. Street development contiguous to Prospect Park, as well as other small city parks, were placed under the Olmsted and Vaux firm. Requests from communities elsewhere had been coming in steadily to Olmsted and Vaux asking them to do municipal work. From the office at

110 Broadway, which had been and still was Calvert Vaux's architectural office, Olmsted or Vaux or Fred Withers—who doubled as a member of both firms—had been going out regularly to do landscape work away from the New York area. In 1867 citizens of New Britain, Connecticut, and Newark, New Jersey, requested designs for parks. There was also a call for a ground plan for the state school at Orono, Maine. In 1868 the firm considered work at Vassar College and in Albany, New York. In 1869 Montgomery Meigs called again on the firm and asked Olmsted to advise him on the proper drainage of the grounds of the national cemetery at Vicksburg. In the same year, with a kind of boyish enthusiasm, Olmsted, finding himself at Cataract House, looking at the beautiful energy of Niagara Falls, became a part of a spontaneous and happy gathering of gentlemen who found themselves together in the hotel. They determined to start a movement to preserve the area of the falls from an already visible encroachment of commercialization.

In 1870 Olmsted's city of Hartford requested a plan, Amherst College wanted advice, Fall River desired an improvement scheme, and a new area of residences at Tarrytown gave Olmsted the opportunity to travel up and down the Hudson, a trip he always enjoyed.

In March, 1870, Frederick Olmsted, Henry Hobson Richardson, and Dr. Elisha Harris were named members of a group of experts who were brought together to make an overall plan for an entire community: Staten Island. The island was as yet sparsely settled; it was much loved by residents like Olmsted, Richardson, and George William Curtis, who liked its quality of being country near the city. But they also believed that Staten Island could attract many more residents for the enjoyment of an uncrowded and companionable kind of life. There was one drawback; the island had a reputation for bad health conditions. Malaria hovered over the easygoing island settlements. The cause of the disease was not yet understood, but some of the conditions which decreased the prevalence of the disease were. The Staten Island plan devoted much sensible attention to the sanitation of all the neighborhoods which were to be bound into one comprehensive community. Upon this foundation of health, the members of this study commission built a plan. Water supply, sewage disposal, convenient roadways, a restriction of undesirable developments, attractive siting of residences, the segregation of areas of natural beauty, the protection of the waterfront: all these matters were touched on in a comprehensive plan in a thoroughgoing treatment.

It was Olmsted speaking in the words of the study: "It may seem hardly necessary to say that views of woods which will soon be felled, streams which will be turned into sewers, meadows that will be built on, landscapes that may be shut off, are of no permanent value in a home, but it is certain that they are accepted as such in thousands of cases, and that they enter largely into the fictitious valuation of real estate."[31] So the signers argued mildly for planning, a kind of growth which would be going against the grain of normal practice.

Unfortunately, the plan remained merely a plan. It was not followed. Staten Island grew haphazardly, protected to a certain extent by its remoteness, but the beautiful fitness of parts adapted to the needs of a community was not to be.

The Social Science Association asked Olmsted to deliver an address to a meeting to be held at the Lowell Institute on February 25, 1870. Olmsted took pains with the talk, using the occasion to say much that was on his mind. He gave the talk the title "Public Parks and the Enlargement of Towns," and had the satisfaction of seeing it printed and distributed by the association. He was able to respond to unsolicited requests for copies from architects, municipal officials, and private citizens. In this talk, reprinted as a pamphlet, his influence spread in many directions, both to the geographical regions of the nation and to various levels of society.[32]

Olmsted said goodbye here to the old America he had known in his innocent and neglected childhood in rural and small-town Connecticut. The small agricultural centers were decaying, he stated, "the meeting house closed, the church dilapidated; the famous old taverns, stores, shops, mills, and offices dropping to pieces and vacant." Cities would be the centers of the future. This was where we would all live. And it was not at all a bad change: "I will refer but briefly to the intimate connection which is evident between the growth of towns and the dying out of slavery and feudal customs, of priestcraft and government by divine right, the multiplication of books, newspapers, schools, and other means of popular education, and the adoption of improved methods of communication, transportation, and of various labor-saving inventions." He was hopeful for the future of cities. For here, did not even the poor have advantages? "Compare advantages in respect simply to schools, libraries, music, and the fine arts. People of the greatest wealth can hardly command as much of these in the country as the poorest work-girl is offered here in Boston at the mere cost of a walk for a short distance over a good, firm, clean pathway, lighted at night and made interesting to her by shop fronts and the variety of people passing." If she seldom took advantage of her opportunities, at least being in the city put her in the way of education.

Olmsted's statement of the virtues of city life was almost romantic. He was, of course, aware of the kind of monstrous wrongs his friend Charles Brace had encountered in the city. Yet he remained convinced that the hopeful and aspiring American democrat might live well in cities. He had earlier, in his young years, chosen rural life, the farmer's life, as the proper one for a civilized man with a scientific bent. This had been his idea of himself at Southside. But life there had proved impracticable. So he had moved to the city. And he proposed, in his profession, to make city life more civil, more healthful, more beautiful, more amenable to a good life for its inhabitants. Cities need not be ugly, dirty, densely crowded. The green of the country might with propriety invade the city. "It must be remembered, also, that man's enjoyment of rural beauty has clearly increased rather than diminished with his advance in civilization."

The problem of men living closely pent together in cities was the major problem of the future. He put it stoutly: "[There will] soon be larger towns than any the world has yet known, and...the further progress of civilization is to depend mainly upon the influences by which men's minds and characters will be affected while living in large towns." He identified the distinctive character of town life as "the devouring eagerness and intellectual strife of town life." But city man, who lived so intensely, had a need to intersperse intervals and spaces of peace between his bouts of activities. Therefore, a great city park should have "the beauty of fields, the meadow, the prairie, of the green pastures, and the still waters. What we want to gain is tranquillity and rest to the mind." Parks were to civilize, but by an appeal below the level of the rational. "A great object of all that is done in a park, of all the art of a park, is to influence the mind of men through their imagination."

Although he was interested in certain reforms in his private life, Olmsted did not in his profession specifically plan an amelioration of the living conditions of the poor except through their access to his open spaces. His less compacted residential sections benefited only those who could afford the move out to them. The poor, in his hope, would eventually be those who moved out, but then they would no longer be the poor. For city life would sharpen their wits; city life would educate them, and they would eventually climb out of their limiting conditions.

The particular psychical benefit of parks (so he continued his argument in the talk to the earnest social scientists) was twofold: the *gregarious* and the *neighborly*. He was conscious, in defining the virtue of gregariousness, of reacting against his own background of puritanism. "Purely gregarious recreation seems to be generally looked upon in New England society as childish and savage, because, I suppose, there is so little of what we call intellectual gratification in it. We are inclined to engage in it indirectly, furtively, and with complication." But he justified this quality as answering emotional needs starved not only by the old straitened Puritan tradition but by the harsh crowding energies of the new cities:

Consider that the New York Park and the Brooklyn Park are the only places in those associated cities where, in this eighteen hundred and seventieth year after Christ, you will find a body of Christians coming together, and with an evident glee in the prospect of coming together, all classes largely represented, with a common purpose, not at all intellectual, competitive with none, disposing to jealousy and spiritual or intellectual pride to none, each individual adding by his mere presence to the pleasure of all others, all helping to the greater happiness of each. You may thus often see vast numbers of persons brought closely together, poor and rich, young and old, Jew and Gentile. I have seen a hundred thousand thus congregated, and I assure you that though there have been not a few that seemed a little dazed, as if they did not quite understand it, and were, perhaps, a little ashamed of it, I have looked studiously but vainly among them for a single face completely unsympathetic with the prevailing expression of good nature and lightheartedness.

He justified the opposite quality of neighborliness with equal warmth. He praised "what I have termed *neighborly* receptive recreations, under conditions which shall be highly counteractive to the prevailing bias to degeneration and demoralization in large towns.... [i.e.] the close relation of family life, the association of children, of mothers, of lovers, or those who may be lovers.... There will be room enough in the Brooklyn Park, when it is finished, for several thousand little family and neighborly parties to bivouac at frequent intervals through the summer."

The confidence that Olmsted showed in this talk in 1870 came from several years of good work. He was a weightier man from having gone west. The initiation of two large works in Chicago and two large works in Buffalo were accomplishments which had given him a strength he might not have had if he had remained peacefully and undisturbedly in charge of Central Park, although this was, as he once wrote, a life he would have enjoyed without the rewards of higher ambition. Or thus he said, pretending that his own character would not have driven him on.

A natural kind of division of labor began to develop in the firm in these years. Olmsted more often than Vaux went away from New York City to find new landscape business, although Vaux shared in the designs resulting from the jobs found. Vaux did architectural work of his own in addition to his landscape work with Olmsted. He was architect for Frederic Church's "Olana," the painter's castle on the Hudson. Vaux designed the original Metropolitan Museum and, across the park, the Museum of National History.

Church came into the circle of friends which the two partners had among the artists of the time. For his part, Olmsted's ability to find new kinds of jobs brought him a friend and collaborator in the architect Henry Hobson Richardson, who was attaining his solidity of reputation in the 1870s. It was probably some time in 1869 that they first met, and found that they had Staten Island in common. They took on together the task of making a plan for the island which was home to them both. And a joint task in Buffalo was soon commissioned of them. The generous and open-hearted Richardson brought Olmsted also into the circle of his friends Augustus Saint-Gaudens, John La Farge, and Henry Adams and his brother Charles Francis. It was an enrichment of Olmsted's life that he had in knowing the strenuous, difficult, and delightful Richardson.

The architect was sixteen years younger than Olmsted. He had had already the beginning of some modest success in his career after years of deprivation and apprenticeship in Paris, where he had remained when the Civil War cut off his home in Louisiana. This grandson of Joseph Priestley had made a place for himself after the war in New York and in 1867 married Julia Hayden of Boston, whom he had met when he was a classmate of Henry Adams at Harvard. Conscious of his powers, of a robust, handsome, stout appearance, with auburn hair and beard and brown eyes, a man with frank keen manners and a contagious hearty humor, Richardson carried himself with an air. A great talker, with a slight stammer, he radiated charm and conviction. Having made a beginning of a reputation with the design of the Church of the Unity in Springfield, Massachusetts, and the Grace Episcopal Church in West Medford, he was asked by the prominent Buffalo politican William Dorsheimer in October, 1868, to build a new house for him.

There was a connection between Olmsted and Dorsheimer as well as between Richardson and Dorsheimer. Dorsheimer had been a leader during the war days in the voluntary work in Buffalo for the United States Sanitary Commission. Olmsted had also already unfolded ambitious plans for parks for Buffalo businessmen among whom Dorsheimer was prominent. He had laid before them not only the idea of two large parks and a number of smaller squares, but of parkways, streets to be lined with trees for pleasant walks and drives, giving access to these open areas of turf and shade to all the people of the city.

William Dorsheimer was also at this time the moving spirit in the planning of a state hospital for the insane. Richardson was to design the building. It was natural at this time, when Olmsted impressed the planners of the park, to ask him to design the grounds of the hospital and to confer with the architect about the proper siting of the structure. Richardson designed an original and useful scheme of ground-level pavilions receding to left and right of a central administration building. In their joint work in Buffalo, Olmsted and Richardson made firm their friendship. Dorsheimer made it his custom to invite them together to stay at his house in Buffalo.

Through this influential lawyer, the two men gained a friend destined to be more and more active in New York state politics. Dorsheimer was to be the political right arm of the three-man commission (Richardson, Olmsted, and Leopold Eidlitz) charged with the completion of the New York State Capitol in Albany. By this time, Dorsheimer would be lieutenant governor of New York.

Dorsheimer was a broadening experience for Olmsted. Here was a man who maintained a high integrity even while moving from party to party. He joined the original Republican Party before the war, but took part in the 1870s in the "liberal" Republican revolt. Dorsheimer then returned to the Democratic Party to which he had once earlier belonged and when Samuel J. Tilden was elected governor, served under him as lieutenant governor. In the 1880s he was to write Grover Cleveland's campaign biography and to feel cheated when, under that national Democratic administration, he did not receive the high office he thought he deserved.

Olmsted eagerly met suggestions from Chicago citizens for two projects, a public park and a new detached residence village. It was he who went west to this new booming town on its inland lake, a place of infinite flatness and sandiness, with only energy to show for the future, and persuaded the town fathers to entrust the jobs to the Olmsted and Vaux firm. Although both designs were slowed first by the great fire and then by the severe depression of the midseventies, work on South Park, as it was called in its early stages, and Riverside, the suburban village, continued with satisfying complexity, at slow or fast speeds for a decade.

Vaux had complained of Olmsted's "first principles" in reports written for those who might not understand such reasoning; but it was for himself, perhaps, that Olmsted wrote out his reasons. He wished to put in words the tale of his wrestling with each particular unlovely piece of ground, for it was usual for town officials to designate wasteland for parks.

The Olmsted and Vaux company's "Report Accompanying Plan for Laying out the South Park" (March, 1871) explained step-by-step the designers' analysis of the problem of transforming a sandy lakefront south of the inhabited city into a green park. The land was poor in trees; the horizon was dully flat; the only enhancement was the bordering beauty of a tideless blue lake of apparently limitless expanse. It was a completely different kind of problem from that of the rocky ledges and scrubby growth in the center of Manhattan that had become "the central park." But Olmsted and Vaux were in the habit of beginning with what was given, of respecting what was on the scene, and going on artfully to underline and make significant that intrinsic quality.

Olmsted's report stated that a flat space was not necessarily bad. Restfulness was the first quality to be desired in a park. The lake alone would supply an element of "grandeur." And: "An irregular border formed by massive bodies of foliage will in a great degree supply the place in landscape of moderate hills and particularly will this be the case if it contains water in some slight depression, so situated as to double these masses." The draining of the shore area to make lagoons would have the effect also of working for the practical good health of the nearby area as a place of residence. Raising up the level of the ground above water level would make trees, shrubs, gardens, and a healthier air possible. This would be serving beauty and social usefulness at the same time. As he looked forward to doing the work, Olmsted wrote here with some pride that, therefore, generations to come would be proud of "their fathers' work upon a sandbar."[33]

The laying out of a complete village of residences outside of but connected with the city of Chicago by rail, and to be linked also, the designers hoped, by a fine tree-lined parkway, was to go a step beyond what Olmsted had planned for the living quarters adjacent to the College of California in Berkeley. Here was ample brushy and woodsy land, with a fine small river, the Des Plaines, running through it for ornament and amusement. And for the time, there seemed to be sufficient support from a corporation of ambitious businessmen.

Riverside was to develop, from the Olmsted and Vaux plan, irregularly and slowly, but was to become and to endure as a modest but substantial and agreeable community with some sense of unity, tied together by shadowing trees and knit in upon itself by curving streets, a place apart but in convenient reach of a great city. Its houses were not to be as far apart as rich men's villas in the country, but were to be in visible communication if not elbowing each other across lawns uniform only in their measurement from curb to house. There were to be play areas scattered through the curving streets, a common, and central buildings such as a railway station, a water tower, a hotel, and shops.

The "Preliminary Report" stated: "The most prominent characteristic of the present period of civilization has been the strong tendency of people to flock together in great towns.... Yet ... there are symptoms of a change; a countertide of migration, especially affecting the more intelligent and fortunate classes." And: "Hence a series of neighborhoods of a peculiar character is already growing up in close relation with all large towns."

The Des Plaines River was to be the scene of innocent fun for his villagers. "It will probably be best to increase the height of the mill-dam so as to enlarge the area of the public water suitable for boating and skating.... A public drive and walk should be carried near the edge of the bank in such a way as to avoid destroying the more valuable trees growing upon it, and there should be pretty boat-landings, terraces, balconies overhanging the water, and pavilions at points desirable for observing regattas, mainly of rustic character."[34]

While working at various plans which took him often away from home, Olmsted wrote frequently to Mary. He told her about his work, sharing triumphs and anxieties and mixing professional matters with the cares and interests of his domestic life, in fact making little difference between them, having strong naive emotions in all directions. His life was all of a piece and not compartmented.

He told Mary in a letter on August 14, 1868, not to worry about John, who had gone west at the invitation of Clarence King to share in the excitements of the 40th Parallel Survey and to learn something about scientific methods. "I have just got yours of the 12th announcing the disastrous retreat of the ... Expedition. I don't think you need to be alarmed about John's castdownedness. He needs a little real roughing and not mere playhouse roughing and he can't have it without its being rough. He cannot learn prudence except by paying for imprudence ... it will do him no harm, I think."[35]

Writing to Mary again during the same prolonged absence, traveling on a train of some outstanding discomforts, he found only three-by-five slips to write on, and pieced out his story on these stray pieces of paper: "The cars all furnished with all sorts of patent contraptions for producing drafts, one diabolical one passing through an ice box. I took a terrible cold which I have not yet worked out of. I was kept all of one day in Chicago with a fire in my room." But he had kept his engagements: "Conferences, debates, single plans, treaties about terms consumed the time till we had to run for the train. To-morrow we make an examination of the Buffalo ground and sketch outlines of a larger scheme."

He was searching for a name for the Des Plaines River village. He told her that the place had been a picnic place and a racetrack and was known as Riverside Farm. "They had proposed calling it Riverside Park but I objected and they told me to suggest a better. This I refer to you.... The river should be the important circumstance.... Please write me a name or some names. All the old English river names are out of my head.... River Groves is the best that has occurred to me but a more bosky word than grove would per-haps be better." (But Riverside it was, at last.) He was returning to New York; Mary was apparently somewhere northward in New England. "Will you come down for a day or two soon if I cant go? Your affectionate hus-band."[36]

Whoever had gone with Frederick Olmsted on this trip, it had not been his partner. Calvert Vaux and his wife had set off on a long anticipated tour of European parks during this season, his first visit back to England and the continent since he had come to America to work with Andrew Jackson Down-ing. Calvert Vaux wrote expansively to Frederick Olmsted of the sights he was re-seeing with new eyes—American eyes, now. Olmsted replied with a long letter on August 29, 1868, mixing personal and professional matters.

Yours of Aug. 18th (Killarney) is received, and is admirable; I hope you will keep it up on that line. But I should have liked one line about your welfare, Mrs. Vaux, the passage, etc....

I returned yesterday from the West. The enteprise there is a big speculation....

I send a newspaper report which gives as good an idea of what I actually did at Buffalo as newspaper reporters' work generally does. I did a good deal of talking privately and publicly, was cross-examined, etc., and got through very well. At least the project was advanced materially, I was told, and they will go to the Legislature in January for a Commission....

Work goes on well at Brooklyn. Entrance Arch complete and people using the road on it. Stranahan just returned from Saratoga. The Rustic Shelter is well advanced, nearly ready for the thachers [Olmsted's spelling]. The dairy cottage walls are half up. Piers of Lull Wood bridge are complete. Miller is still be-hindhand and grumbling and explaining. He can't afford to give an hour to the Flagstaff. Earth work is getting on less rapidly for want of men.

The Chicago operation is to make a suburban village out of the whole cloth on the prairie and connect by a park-way with town....

My wife has been thrown from a wagon and dragged, but escaped, so far as yet appears, without serious injury. Weather sultry. With love to your wife. Affec'tly[37]

There was not only a lively exchange of emotion and opinion between Frederick and Mary Olmsted; Frederick was dependent to an extraordinary degree in his own sense of balance and happiness upon this close relationship.

However far off he flung himself in his travels, he was pulled back toward this family center by a magnetic attraction to Mary. A prolonged absence made him literally ill. The series of journeys he made in the summer of 1868 was prolonged and became wearisome to Frederick. In June the house on Staten Island was closed. Mary went away to Sutton and Litchfield. Frederick had remained at first near work in Brooklyn and Manhattan but then he traveled to his western work. He returned to New York between trips to makeshift boarding places, and did not like the situation. He kept Mary apprised of his small and homely doings. On July 14 he told her about visiting the Godkins and seeing their new baby. He told her about checking the condition at midsummer of Central Park, complained about the midseason heat, and told her he was not sleeping well. Toward the end of the long hot season he grew more and more homesick for her. In New York or Brooklyn he wrote to Mary on September 10, "I am quite unwell but able to be about. Weather sickening, dog days."[38] He was low in his mind when he wrote to her on September 22: "I had a bad attack of wakefulness and the blues last night. I don't see how I can begin to do justice to the work before me and am presently in a shamefully demoralized condition. I think that I have experienced something of the kind before even when I had a home to go to at night but I am none the less homesick.   Yours affectionately."[39] He wrote successively to his wife who remained away on September 24, 25, and 26.

But John came home and that cheered him. "You might as well make it the 3d or 4th or 5th ..."[40]—to Mary. The season wound down. Mary stayed away late into the fall. John went back to Yale. Knapp sent Olmsted a good word about Owen at the school in Sutton. Calvert Vaux wrote entertaining letters from abroad. Frederick handled all the affairs of the firm while his partner was away. Mary and the girls came home when the heat in New York abated, and life settled into a satisfactory routine for Frederick. Vaux returned and spelled his partner in dealing with the firm's business.

The substance of the daily life of the summer and fall of 1868 suggests the tone of Olmsted's life during the postwar years when a wider work meant for him a growing hopefulness and confidence. This, in spite of the ugly difficulties he and Vaux had had with the city government which had led to their removal from their Manhattan parks work. They had a busy and congenial headquarters at No. 110 Broadway. The Brooklyn parks work operated out of another office across the river. In their increasing landscape work, Olmsted and Vaux did not at this time depend very much on helpers in their own office. They performed most of the firm's detailed work, going out to meet clients, drawing up plans, and then hiring other engineering or horticultural firms or individuals to do specific jobs for them on large projects.

Olmsted's long-lasting comradeship with his partner, which had often expressed itself by humorous disagreement and had occasionally sharpened into a crisis, seemed in the late sixties and early seventies to have healed into a firm renewal of friendship. The two men signed their letters to each other "affectionately" and their children grew up playing together. Vaux's architectural work was a handy supplement to their joint landscape design. Calvert Vaux, along with Jacob Wrey Mould, an insouciant, clever young man, continued (after the demise of the Tweed Ring) to design the modest structures of the New York parks. Vaux found patrons for house designs at Riverside. Although both Vaux and Olmsted disapproved of structures within Central Park, when it became clear that both a museum of art and a museum of natural history would be built, Vaux undertook the designs.

Not everyone found Vaux agreeable. A. J. Bloor, who had been a Sanitary Commission staff member under Olmsted in Washington, D.C., appealed to Olmsted for help on February 10, 1867, stating that he came to him because, "Mr. Vaux is too egotistical and irritable to make my talking with him profitable."[41] It is probable that Vaux suffered fools rather poorly. Olmsted, perhaps because of the past Civil War association, endured many somewhat incoherent and confused appeals from Bloor about his various business ventures. With Olmsted and his wife, Vaux could be full of charm. He made an entertaining tale to them of an overnight boat trip to Boston sometime in late 1868. He painted a picture of the disagreeable passengers on board, made a joke of his not being able to find a decent place to lay his head, and told them of enjoying being on deck all night watching "the glimpses of the moon," and ending "Love to your wife who will I hope come back to S. I. [Staten Island]."[42] This during Mary's protracted stay with the Knapps in Sutton, Massachusetts.

Vaux showed understanding of his partner's tendency to push himself too hard. Vaux in Brooklyn, at the headquarters of the park project, wrote to Olmsted in Chicago in June, 1869, when Olmsted was trying to arrive at some kind of orderly agreement with the entrepreneurs planning the Riverside development,

The Riverside matter looks somewhat fluent in the light of your letters but we must hope for the best.

I do not feel disposed to go on without we are indemnified and a clear future made apparent but we can discuss this when you return. . . . Try and secure our money interests. . . . I speak however without information and only touch on this that you may understand that neither Withers or I think you should vex your weary soul to an indefinite extent.[43]

The Olmsted and Vaux firm counted on the sanitary engineer, George E. Waring, for advice and professional work in large drainage problems. Waring had done the drainage system of Central Park and since that time had remained not only in professional association with Olmsted but a firm and admiring friend. He had set up a business of his own at Newport, Rhode Island. Olmsted and his wife visited the Warings in Newport, where Olmsted was also beginning to secure landscape work for the firm.

Waring wrote Olmsted on June 28, 1868, complaining about a review in the *Nation* of a technical book he had written.[44] Olmsted probably passed on the letter or substance of the complaint to Godkin, but by this time he had little to do with running the magazine. That connection had about run out through a slow erosion. However, Olmsted and Godkin remained close friends.

The firm extended its influence through another individual who became a particularly important western follower of Olmsted's and Vaux's leadership in land design. This was H. W. S. Cleveland (Horace Cleveland) for whom, in March and April, 1868, both George Curtis and Charles Norton wrote letters of introduction to the Olmsted and Vaux firm. From his office at *Harper's* where he edited "The Easy Chair," Curtis wrote to Olmsted on March 30, "Mr. Cleveland is a landscape gardener and I have told him that you can advise him better than anybody I know."[45] On April 10, Norton wrote to Olmsted asking him to give Cleveland a job if this were possible: "He is one of the most upright and trustworthy men I know, and possessed of considerable faculty."[46] Cleveland was already set up in business as a landscape architect but was having difficulty finding engagements. He and a partner had submitted a losing design for Central Park when Olmsted and Vaux were the winners, but he had no apparent rancor about this past event. Frederick Olmsted and Horace Cleveland came into correspondence when Curtis and Norton introduced the older man to him. They found each other congenial. On Cleveland's side, it was always a relationship in which he was disciple writing to master—this in spite of the fact that he became, in his own right, one of the outstanding men in landscape work in the Midwest in later years.

Cleveland did not go to work for Olmsted and Vaux at this time but found engagements for himself in Chicago. There he established himself for some years. He remained in touch with Olmsted, telling him from time to time what he was doing. His correspondence was always with Olmsted. In 1873 he was to publish a series of lectures as *Landscape Architecture, As Applied to the Wants of the West.*

Olmsted's family continued to interest and absorb him. Friends multiplied. Therefore, in spite of losing battles with the likes of William Marcy Tweed and Peter B. Sweeny, life had compensations during this period. Olmsted, with allies such as his partner Calvert Vaux, Horace Cleveland, and George Waring, was initiating a revolution in the design of open spaces in large cities, and was even affecting street design and the flow of transportation. Cleveland wrote to Olmsted from Chicago, September 7, 1870, how Westerners, in laying out their new cities, knew only straight lines: "It seems a hopeless task to try to move their rectangular lines." But he was going to try. "Your examples," he wrote, "of the improbability of making radical changes in an old city are very valuable as arguments in favor of doing it right in the first place."[47] It was no small thing to Olmsted that Cleveland was, so frankly and, in his own way, so masterfully, a conscious furtherer of ideas Olmsted had initiated.

In July, 1870, a great event loomed in the lives of Mary and Frederick Olmsted. He wrote to Frederick Knapp on July 11, asking him to arrange for John and Owen to stay two weeks longer than usual at Plymouth. "Mary's confinement is expected last of next week and she could not have the boys coming home for a week or two after.... As to funds, etc. command me."[48] Mary herself at this time was forty years old. She had given birth to John Charles, her first child, in 1852, eighteen years before. Then had come Charlotte in 1855 and Owen in 1857. After Mary and Frederick were married, the intensely domestic Fred had been at first cheated of paternity. The two-month-old child, John Theodore, had died in August, 1860, from what was called infant cholera, in the midst of the family disorder caused by Frederick's serious carriage accident. His little "tom-girl" Marion was born in 1861. A boy child was born in November, 1866, but died within six hours, and Mary was ill for a number of months. At last, fulfilling a great need, a son who was to live and eventually to honor his father's name was born on July 24, 1870.

The infant was regarded with almost religious veneration by the father and was spoken of generically as "Boy" through his first, anxiously observed years. He was supposed to be named Henry, but the name did not stick; and at last the father's fond regard fastened upon the child his own name. So that from this decade of the 1870s on, there was, tugging the hand of an older than usual father, and dogging his footsteps, a little Frederick Law Olmsted. Samuel Bowles, editor of the Springfield, Massachusetts, *Republican*, who had traveled west and met the Olmsteds at Mariposa, and who was by now a privileged friend, wrote to Frederick Olmsted a teasing letter when he heard of the birth of the little boy: "We heard of the new boy over there [that is, in Europe, where he and his wife were vacationing], and celebrated the miraculous gift to your old age with enthusiasm."[49] Frederick Olmsted was forty-eight at the time.

CHAPTER XXI

A Humane Life

Don't forget that I am now fifty years old (all but) and that I am responsible for the nurture of five children, what is more I love them.
—F. L. O., to Fred Kingsbury, April 20, 1871[1]

FREDERICK OLMSTED'S IDEAL LIFE was a humane, calm, free, and steady existence with time apportioned for quiet leisure as well as hard, engrossing work. This was the way he wished to live. By designing decent settings for everyday work and play, he hoped to enable other people to live in this manner. Then a majority of the population might lead sane lives with an allowance for emotion and imagination as well as for rational and normally selfish activity. This was the life he advocated enthusiastically in letters to friends.

And yet to the same friends he often addressed an amount of intemperate feeling. He had been shaken by gusts of emotion all his life. He had enjoyed wild arguments with Charles Brace on the piazza of the stone farmhouse at Southside, Staten Island; he had relished disagreements with Calvert Vaux about artistic ends and means. And as he matured, he did not find life settling into calmer ways. He put all his feeling as well as thinking into his acts, accomplishing much in periods of highly wrought activity, falling back, inevitably, into sloughs of exhaustion. He was able only at times to lead the kind of moderate life he admired.

A letter written to Fred Kingsbury on April 20, 1871, allows glimpses of the good humor he was able to enjoy in the happy role of paterfamilias of a numerous and growing family and the angers to which he occasionally gave himself. The occasion of his twenty-five-page letter was his having received from Kingsbury a communication, rather innocuous in tone, about the Sunday question being debated in New York City at this time. It had been possible only recently for a New York newspaper to bring out a Sunday issue with propriety. This, the New York *Daily-Times* was presently doing. A mutual friend of the two Freds, the conscientious minister Henry Barnes, had written to Kingsbury telling him how he had given up writing for that paper because of this breaking of the Sabbath rest. Kingsbury had mildly acquiesced and sent along Henry Barnes's letter as well as his own.

Olmsted replied with feeling, telling Kingsbury how he had deliberately brought up his children in a complete reaction against the restrictive Puritan Sunday of his own childhood. What he had endured then made him indignant yet; and the possibility that laws might enforce on thousands, even millions, the iron restrictions which he believed destructive of a humane life made him furious. "I realize with some difficulty," he wrote his friend, "that you still remain essentially in a position from which I have drifted so far." And he went on, "I am in the ranks of the 'enemies of the Sabbath' fully and unreservedly."

He displayed to Kingsbury the kind of Sunday he had made his own. He was, he said, subject to much interruption during the week and so had to do a good bit of work on Sundays and so on that day made "no distinction between holy and unholy work—secular and sacred. I recognize nothing of the kind. I undoubtedly greatly overwork myself.... [But] I do try to get a little more rest also on Sundays of a certain kind, but it is mainly anti-Sabatarian rest. I lie longer in bed, I am longer in dressing, I am longer at breakfast.... I read two Sunday newspapers. I smoke after breakfast as I usually do not. Being on the coast and near shipping I reciprocate their courtesy, and pay the day the compliment of hoisting my ensign or seeing that the children do it. I play with the children more. Generally late in the day I go out with some of them—in summer we go rowing—sometimes drive back in the island—go to the Brewery and I treat them to sangaree or a little beer; in winter I have been to the skating ponds with them. My wife generally goes with us. She has often been—at least more than once or twice —to the Brewery. Sometimes we go picnicing either by boat to the Long Island shore or to the high woods by wheels. I wish these excursions were more frequent, but I rarely get through or get too tired to go on further with my work till near sunset, and it is too late for anything but a row. I have taken the boys to a Beer Garden concert. I never took them to a church." He went on to say that in the evening he might read a book such as *Robinson Crusoe* aloud, or play backgammon: "Mary and the other ones play cards. I never had head for cards." He rather quaintly thought of this kind of Sunday as his German or Lutheran Sunday. He had become acquainted with this more human kind of celebration of the Sabbath when he and John Hull Olmsted stayed in the German communities in Texas. He had at once approved this relaxation of the standards on which he had been reared. The idea that someone wished, in any respect, to deprive him of these pleasures kindled him into anger. "I should be very angry with the man or men who prevented me from having my newspapers, my boat, my conveyances, my wine or my cigar...my Robinson Crusoe. If the Times should drop its Sunday edition, I should drop the Times, as I should drop my cook if she dropped my Sunday breakfast."

He was sorry that Fred Kingsbury and Henry Barnes could not agree with him. A fury overcame him, as he wrote faster and faster and in a more and more difficult and crabbed hand. This restricting of Sunday freedom was "what I regard as a persistent, fanatical attempt to fasten upon our religion and social order an emasculated Jewish Sabbath.... [and it was] obstruction to desirable progress."

And a strictly observed Sunday had certainly not given a high tone to the nation. Olmsted pointed out, "It can hardly be that in any heathen country men of wealth, influence and power have been more thoroughly licentious, selfish, conscienceless than those who occupy the most important public stations in this community of New York."

His handwriting became almost illegible as he wrote with an obviously increasing tension of feeling. He stuttered forth phrases: "those most powerful mutual admiration clubs called churches...I believe that men would be better for more real amusement—recreation—and less preaching.... I am in the ranks of the 'enemies of the Sabbath,' fully and unreservedly."[2] Fred Kingsbury must have wondered what he had written to call forth this diatribe.

Months later, in October, Olmsted, feeling more equable, apologized to his friend for writing as he had. Kingsbury had asked to have back the letter which had "stirred up" Olmsted so. Olmsted had lost it meanwhile and said, "It was not your letter that stirred me, but a combination of circumstances, and your letter gave me the opportunity of blowing off. Sorry I wrote feverishly. I don't very often now."[3] The contrasts in mood are typical of the man: a complacent happiness at the kind of good life he had achieved, and a hot anger at all possible obstructions to that good life. The early years of the productive 1870s illustrate not only the achievements possible now to the mature talent, but also the ups and downs of his barometer of happiness.

During most of 1871, Olmsted and Vaux remained outside the management of the New York parks watching the careless and stupid misuse of their creations by the Tweed Ring. That the handiwork of these men suffered less than they themselves believed might be deduced from an objective and spontaneous reaction of a clever observer of city life. George Templeton Strong visited Central Park on a late day in May, 1871, and wrote in his diary, "The Park is lovely and leafy. These things should exert a civilizing and humanizing influence upon 'the masses.'"[4] He went farther afield than usual from his beloved Manhattan in July and visited Prospect Park. He was happy in the experience, recording that Prospect "beats Central Park ten to one in trees."[5]

It was in the sultry midsummer of 1871 that the New York *Daily-Times* began to publish the series of stories that would lead at last to the breaking of the power of the Tweed Ring. The papers had come to the editor through the defection of a supposedly well-controlled and innocuous bookkeeper of the Ring who had felt abused by the leaders of the organization, grew more and more disgruntled, and at last approached the newspaper with proofs of the financial chicanery and profit-making of Tweed and his gang. One can only imagine the satisfaction that Vaux and Olmsted had in the disclosures. Early in September, 1871, Calvert Vaux attended a meeting at which the editor of the *Times* was cheered as a public hero. This was the beginning of the end of the Ring. Vaux saw that he and Olmsted were affected personally and should be ready to act to make the parks more safe for the future. Vaux to Olmsted, September 5: "You should be thinking of some strong man who ought to be in [i.e., in the board of commissioners governing the New York parks] and whose appointment can be urged on public grounds."[6] Eventually Olmsted and Vaux saw to it that the painter Frederic Church received this appointment. Thereafter, he was their ally.

With the fall of the Tweed Ring, the return of the two landscape architects to municipal office was assured, and they were not unwilling to come back into the care of their parks. On November 23, 1871, Olmsted and Vaux were reappointed as landscape architects to the Parks Department, with Olmsted still in the senior position. They found that they had a new kind of restriction under Andrew Green's parsimonious management of funds as comptroller of the city. A hero of the recent unthroning of William Marcy Tweed, Green had more power than anyone in city administration. He had determined not to spend city funds for any purpose which he did not himself approve. He infuriated Olmsted almost as much as the loose-living crooks had done. George Strong, sitting on the sidelines as an amused spectator of the drama of city life, could see no reason for objecting to Green. He wrote in his diary on September 18: "Green has taken possession of the comptroller's office.... The only person I ever heard speak ill of him was F. L. Olmsted, who had relations with him in Central Park Administration, and Olmsted had a rather *mauvaise langue*."[7]

Coming back to Central Park and other New York City parks projects, Olmsted began to clear away the temporary damage effected by the greed, stupidity, or neglect of the Tweed Ring. He felt a great stimulus to clearing his mind also in written directives and reports on many topics of parks management. There was a stream of these papers issued in the midseventies enriching the general outlines of his theory with statements addressed to particular and narrow problems. He continued to be a "park-maker" in the most practical sense. He had a compulsion to fit his design to the lives of the people who walked his pathways and rolled in fine carriages along his drives; he wished also to teach these temporary inhabitants how to behave themselves within his vistas, even how to learn to appreciate them.

In "A Review of Recent Changes..." (1872), Olmsted addressed H. G. Stebbins, president of the department, deploring the "fantastic" proposals that had been made or were presently being made for additions to Central Park: that the park

should be used as a place of burial for the more distinguished dead of the city; that all religious sects should be invited to build places of worship upon it . . . ; that it should be an exhibition and advertisement of the goods for sale in the city; that it should be many other things as diverse in character as the worship of God and of Mammon. . . . A street railway through the midst of the Park has been called for; steamboats, and even a full rigged ship have been proposed to be placed in its waters. New roads have been called for, crossing and practically destroying, for their original purpose, the most important features of the design. . . . The use of various parts of the ground, assumed to be at present unoccupied, has been asked for horse-races, for steeple-chases, for experiments with sundry new machines, for various kinds of advertising, for the sale of various wares, for popular meetings, for itinerant preaching, for distributing controversial tracts.

He was aware that as the city grew, applications for such uses would become more and more "plausible." And he answered, in caps:

THE ONLY SOLID GROUND OF RESISTANCE TO DANGERS OF THIS CLASS WILL BE FOUND TO REST IN THE CONVICTION THAT THE PARK THROUGHOUT IS A SINGLE WORK OF ART, NAMELY, THAT IT SHALL BE FRAMED UPON A SINGLE, NOBLE MOTIVE, TO WHICH THE DESIGN OF ALL ITS PARTS, IN SOME MORE OR LESS SUBTLE WAY, SHALL BE CONFLUENT AND HELPFUL.[8]

Olmsted might not expect Mr. Stebbins, or the other members of the board, to understand fully what he had in mind, but he continued with all his force to try to educate not only the board president, but engineers, park-keepers, gardeners, and the general public. He had handbills printed and had them passed out to everyone who came through any one of the fancifully named gates, the Artizans', the Artists', the Scholars', or the Childrens'.

He opposed gas-lighting of the park at night. Gas illumination, sufficient to make the park safe for promenaders at night, would be harmful to the trees. And the fact was, he said, the park could not be made altogether safe at night. Its "coverts of rock and low foliage"[9] made impossible absolute safety; better to close the park in the late night hours.

Olmsted did not disdain the homeliest considerations in internal management. He considered the proper design of "retiring rooms, respectively for women and for men." These should be "buildings . . . with low roofs . . . so placed that while one could always be reached by a short walk by visitors needing to make use of it, in whatever part of the Park they might be, they would yet be scarcely to be seen by those who had no occasion to look for them. . . . All necessary refreshment rooms, privies and urinals can be arranged so as to be perfectly convenient without being obtrusive or injuring the rural character of the park."[10]

The year 1872 was not only a busy one for Olmsted, but a curious one. He was to be much in the public eye. Henry Stebbins, the president of the Board of Park Commissioners, went abroad at the end of May and did not return until the end of October. Stebbins went through the form of resigning for this period and persuaded Olmsted to allow himself to be appointed a commissioner of the public parks and then to be elected president and treasurer of the board for this interim period. Calvert Vaux stepped up temporarily into Olmsted's job as principal landscape architect to the board. Therefore, Olmsted had added to his normal duties many administrative and financial oversights. And they were of various and ridiculous detail. No one could buy a pencil without his authority. With his penchant for close survey, he found himself overworked.

He had larger worries too which his seat on the board opened to him. This was supposed to be the beginning of a new era of reform after the deposing of Tweed and his henchmen, but he saw little of that quality. He was surrounded by commissioners anxious to give parks department jobs to incompetent friends. He was called a "fool" by "practical" men (words he remembered and used when years later he wrote "The Spoils of the Park"). He was abused in the press, besieged by callous and importunate office seekers even in his own house, and threatened with violence at least once. Olmsted found that to do his own real work, he had to practice it almost secretly as if it had been some kind of vice. He observed that nearly all the other public officers in other departments spent all their office hours filling jobs or fending off those seeking them.

Olmsted was also, as he thought, victimized by an attempt to honor him. He was nominated for vice president of the United States by a splinter group of "liberal" voters unhappy with Grant. Mrs. Olmsted in 1920 recalled the incident, looking back to June, 1872: "In 1872 when the 'Fifth Avenue Convention' nominated Groesbeck of Ohio for President, they nominated Mr. Olmsted for Vice-President. When Mr. Olmsted heard of it, he hid, so that when the reporters came to the 46th St. house, Mr. Olmsted was nowhere to be found. The 'Nation' was much amused at the incident but Mr. Olmsted's friends kept the matter rather quiet because it made him [as he thought] ridiculous."[11] (Mrs. Olmsted's memory was hazy about the house they lived in then; they were to move to Forty-sixth Street later.)

No one was less suited to political life than Frederick Olmsted. He was both too shy of public attention and also too arrogant, in his quiet way. He gloried in his private kingdom, not in a public one. He worked for objects which would live publicly and would be used multitudinously, but he preferred always to be an anonymous observer of that thriving life, perhaps walking about unnoticed in one of his parks, watching a swarming public life taking over the object he had made.

In addition to the city parks in both Manhattan and Brooklyn which required close attention, Olmsted and Vaux, as partners in their own professional business, were asked to lay out a residential community in Tarrytown, New York, to design the grounds of Trinity College in Hartford, Connecticut, and had other civic and private work in Poughkeepsie, New York; Providence, Rhode Island; and in Massachusetts, where Olmsted was asked to help locate the site for the "Retreat for the Insane."

George Radford, a competent engineer in Buffalo, directed the firm's continuing work there. Later Radford was to be replaced by William McMillan, who continued to consult Olmsted and Vaux at every step of the laying out of the rather complete system of parks and roadways which the ambitious city fathers of this lake-port city had authorized. Radford moved to New York and set up his shingle outside No. 110 Broadway and worked either on his own or with the Olmsted and Vaux firm for many years. His children joined the circle of the younger Olmsteds, Vauxes, and Braces.

The South Park work in Chicago slowed, stopped, and resumed, no longer directly under the Olmsted and Vaux firm but, when renewed, under the direction of Horace Cleveland, who kept Olmsted abreast of what the shaky finances of the city allowed to be done and, insofar as he could, followed the original design of Olmsted and Vaux.

An example of Olmsted's influence was the way his name continued to count in California. William Hammond Hall tenaciously sought Olmsted's advice and blessing on the work he was doing in designing the park which Olmsted had urged in San Francisco.[12] Hall asked Olmsted's advice, too, about work to be done at the college, now a university, across the bay. A curious fact about this project was the loss of Olmsted's plat of the ground. Hall related to Olmsted the possible circumstance of the loss: an old gardener entrusted with the responsibility for keeping up the grounds departed and apparently took the plan with him, and so it vanished forever. Olmsted's report survived.

"Your name has been on my lips almost daily for the last three weeks," wrote President Daniel Gilman to Frederick Olmsted in December, 1872, "because I have been trying to find the plot [Gilman's spelling] of the grounds at Berkeley which you made for the College of California but which nobody can or will produce.... I have been greatly instructed by your printed report on the site. You know probably that the University has inherited these grounds from the college—that they have been partially laid out and planted with trees, and that large costly buildings are going up.... I wish every day that you were here that the University might avail itself of your counsels during the development of the estate."[13] He wrote again later in the same month, "The only thing to be done is *to get you here again*. Would you consider the subject next summer?"[14] It must have seemed a temptation, but Olmsted did not go again to California for a number of years and he did not do work again on the grounds at Berkeley. But Gilman kept up with Olmsted and was to employ him when he had himself moved east to found a new university.

Despite professional concerns, Olmsted had energy to spare to pour out his scorn on the nomination of Horace Greeley for president in 1872. This attempt to unseat a bad president aroused only his intolerant wrath. "A thousand years of Grant, say I, before one minute of Greeley,"[15] he wrote to Sam Bowles. Bowles, who disagreed, replied lightly, "Clearly you need the cooling presence of the country. Come out here, and we will figure out Greeley's defeat, and the country's salvation on my back piazza. Very cordially yours."[16] "Here" was Springfield, Massachusetts, where Bowles exercised his sway as editor of the Springfield *Republican,* which had come out for the liberal Republican faction in an attempt to defeat Grant and the greedy crowd of corrupt hangers-on of that unseeing, unknowing great man.

Olmsted was not soothed, and he was not through arguing; he wrote hotly to Bowles on May 13: "I know he is an imposter. You knew he was an imposter before you went to Cincinnati . . . but now you soberly ask me to help him impose on the country. If I do I'm damned. If all the world went for him and I stood all alone it would be the unforgivable sin to my moral nature to have any patience with such an outrage to it. . . . When such a man can have the countenance of such a man as Sam Bowles in asking to be made President of the United States, it is the darkest day I have known. Bull Run was bright to it . . . am I mad, or are you?"[17]

Bowles replied on May 15: "You are certainly laying yourself open to suspicion of having positive views on the subject. I am not so terribly earnest on the other side as to feel inspired to wrestle with you in behalf of brother Greeley. . . . though your wrath is something refreshing to behold in these days of easy compliance and feeble virtue." Bowles insisted mildly that Greeley was yet better than Grant and ended, "What with Greeley's nomination and the killing of so many evergreens this winter we all need to study the higher philosophies."[18]

All Olmsted's friends had to learn to "wrestle" with him, or give him up altogether; his was a warm but wearing comradeship. Occasionally, he alarmed such friends by his vehemence.

It was to the tender and humorous Bowles that Olmsted confided his greatest trouble during these years. On April 26, 1871, Bowles had asked Olmsted to come to Springfield, which he described as a sort of country paradise, to lay out for him and a group of friends a new residential neighborhood for which they had secured a piece of acreage.[19] Bowles's cheerful letter struck a nerve in Olmsted. He was tired, still not recovered from the illness he had recently suffered in Chicago, and was worried about money— the children growing up and needing to be away from home at school. Bowles replied sympathetically. Olmsted answered again, offering a new ill for the view of his friend, an unhappiness in his business partnership with Vaux. This letter of Olmsted's does not survive; it was sufficiently urgent for Bowles to write to him: why not pull out of the firm and go into business alone?

Olmsted's next letter (June 2) said: "You write in view of one horn of my dilemma. I must have more assistance and even if there were no ties of sentiment and obligation I have not courage enough left to dispense with Vaux's cooperation. I feel myself so nearly desperate that I have to school myself against the danger of some mildly foolish undertaking—such as putting all I can together in a farm, cutting the world and devoting myself to asceticism. But against extreme lunacy in this way my wife makes a pretty strong bar. But I say to myself ten times a day that I positively must find some way of living in the country and escaping this drive. I cannot live another year under it."

He allowed a thin ray of humor to shine through this generally gloomy letter when he described to Bowles his recent failure in trying to find an assistant in the landscape work. Without properly interviewing him, he had hired a man who had come to him from England. He found him to be only a "gardener." Olmsted tried him out, not so much in work as in the exercise of his sensibilities, and found him hopeless. He took him up the Hudson on a boat trip and exposed him to the scenery visible in changing patterns in every mile the boat traveled. "I never saw the Highlands under more favorable circumstances. He said 'Yes—very pretty' and turned into the cabin to read the advertising books."[20]

Olmsted did not complain directly of Vaux in these surviving letters, but he gives the impression of a man conscious of suffering a wrong, of not receiving the help he needed in their joint work. Whether Olmsted was fair to Vaux or not, it is impossible to ascertain. He was in a depleted state and subject to mental fatigue due to overwork. It is probable that Vaux devoted a good part of his time to his architectural contracts in which Olmsted had no part. The two men had no full-time capable assistants.

Bowles tried to give advice he thought suitable to his worried friend. He urged Olmsted to settle down in a semirural situation, such as his own Springfield, Massachusetts, and "set yourself up as a consulting landscape architect, to give advice and make general plans for parks and the laying out of grounds, and the location of public buildings; having alliances at all our chief cities, but holding yourself independent of any firm . . . and refusing to go into any detailed work."

He tried to reassure Olmsted about the effect on Vaux of breaking up the partnership. "In the long run, you can do more for Vaux on the new plan than you can by going on as you are. Indeed, you cannot go on as you are. It is killing the goose, instead of preserving her for the continuous golden eggs."[21]

Yet the end of the partnership, when it came, worked itself out with less difficulty than Olmsted had anticipated. If there was any ugliness, both men concealed it from the world, and indeed, their communications with each other have the ease accompanying a sense of relief. The formal sundering of the Olmsted and Vaux partnership came on October 18, 1872. This occurred within the same week when Olmsted thankfully returned the presidency of the parks board to Henry Stebbins. Frederick Law Olmsted and Calvert Vaux agreed to continue their joint work with the New York parks, but to make each one a separate contract with the city. Olmsted returned to his position as landscape architect, Vaux to that of consulting landscape architect; the date of these formalities was November 24, 1872. The letters of the two men to each other bringing these things to a conclusion were perfectly civil and amiable. But civility is different from affection. There were, at this time, no more letters one to the other signed "affectionately." If Olmsted felt relief at the severing of the partnership, it could not have been at having less work to do, for he had immediately more to manage, and that singlehandedly. It seems concludable that personal emotional reasons had as much to do with the break as practical matters of labor division.

There was no ostensible break in personal relations. The young people of the two families remained close, writing letters back and forth, going to parties and on vacation trips together. Olmsted threw business Vaux's way, for from this time on Olmsted seemed to have a weightier influence on those who had land design work to assign. He recommended his former partner to persons inquiring for a competent architect or landscape man.[22] Olmsted and Vaux also occasionally found themselves working together outside New York on certain ventures. Yet something at this time shifted unalterably in their relationship. And there was to be a delayed emotional eruption five years later which seemed a kind of sequel to this apparently civilized separation of their professional interests.

At the time of the breakup, they divided the firm's work in hand between them, Olmsted taking on the superintendence of the larger share of the parks they had designed together (with the exception of the New York parks, in which they continued to share). Vaux, and this was probably in part the reason for the break, had a number of important architectural works in hand, those mentioned earlier—the Hudson River castle of the painter Church, the two museums upon the borders of Central Park—and a new ambitious project, undertaken in 1873, the landscape design for the government buildings in Ottawa, Canada. With Samuel Parsons, who had worked under Olmsted and Vaux for many years, Vaux was also engaged to design what he called in 1873 the East River Park.

The end of the partnership with Vaux could not have been anything but a grave happening in Olmsted's life. Other events at the end of 1872 and the beginning of 1873 gave this time a special emphasis. He and Mary decided in the fall of 1872 to move their residence. They had tried temporary quarters the winter before in Manhattan and had fully realized the inconvenience of Staten Island. They found a house at 209 West Forty-sixth Street. This was to be home and office until 1883, although after 1878, Olmsted's professional work would be for the most part outside of this city in which, for twenty years, with the break of the wartime service and the California experience, he had found a center for his existence.

The memories of Frederick Law Olmsted, Jr., begin to date from this period. He remembered the house on Forty-sixth Street as the earliest scene of childhood memory, recalling in late life a long and narrow "back yard," behind a narrow tall house. The yard was sheltered from its neighbors by walls and contained an irregular narrow ribbon of grass enclosed by flowers and shrubs.[23] From this house the oldest brother John went off to New Haven or came home from there; these were his years at the Sheffield Scientific School. Here the postman delivered letters from Owen, still at the Knapp school. Charlotte was away some of the time in a girls' school in Boston. At home were the two youngest children, Marion, eleven, when they moved into the new house, and Rick himself, a busy two-year-old. The house, for these years, became a satisfactory center for the family although it was not entirely convenient. The father's study was the best room, at the back, overlooking the garden. His work and the family's activities filled the house to the cramming point. Two hundred nine West Forty-sixth Street was a cheerful, happily self-centered place, to which friends came informally and to which Frederick returned gratefully after trips.

It was during these years that John Charles Olmsted, or J. C. Olmsted as he began to sign himself, matured and yet remained in a position of apprenticeship to his father. He had gone west with Clarence King's government survey of the West during the last year he spent at the Knapp school and again in the summer before he entered Yale.

And while Frederick Olmsted almost refused to believe that his eldest son was growing up, he found it as hard to realize that his father was growing old. When the old man died it came suddenly. On January 21, 1873, John Olmsted had an accidental fall near a neighbor's house in Hartford upon ground made icy by winter weather. He was put to bed with a broken hip joint. His brother Albert wrote to Fred that he did not know how serious the accident would be. Fred caught the next train to Hartford. His father was surprised and pleased at Fred's coming. Frederick went home to New York somewhat reassured. In a few days his father grew worse. The old man seemed unable to determine to recover and was suffering from pain and increasing weakness. Albert telegraphed Fred. Fred came home again to find his father sleeping. He sat by to watch. The sick man woke moaning and tossing but when his son spoke to him (as Fred wrote to Fred Kingsbury), "He turned his head quickly toward me and in a pleasant natural voice and with a smile said, 'Why, who's this? Fred? So you've come back!' " The old man weakened steadily and died. Fred and other family members were with him. "He was a very good man," the son wrote his close friend, "and a kinder father never lived. It is strange how much of the world I feel has gone from me with him. The value of any success in the future is gone for me." And he went on, "It is very gratifying to me to find among his papers filed in his private drawer, a number of scraps of newspapers running back 20 years, referring to my books or the parks or other works in which I have been engaged."[24]

There was pain in finding himself so lonely for the man who had been his supporter, helper, and friend, as well as father—and buried deep down, the wondering resentment at the father who had been absent from him when he was a small boy. Olmsted wrote a letter about his father after the funeral to John, who was to pass it on to Owen at the Knapp school, and he asked that Owen show Mr. Knapp the letter too.

The sorrow had seemed matched by a physical disorder, because this was the time he and Mary moved the family into the house on Forty-sixth Street. "We were half moved into our new house, my chief pleasure in which was the hope of making him comfortable in it, when my father died. We return to the disorder of it and go on with our works. Mary is much worn and the children have colds."[25] So he wrote to Frederick Knapp. Ordinary matters such as colds had to be attended to, but the year 1873, beginning with the death of his father who had almost attained the age of eighty-two, and marked by his own personal drama of going into business by himself, seemed significant as a milestone.

His friend Kingsbury answered with consideration and some tenderness, glad to tell Fred Olmsted that he knew that the old man "had taken the greatest possible pleasure in your success and fame. I think it had been the great joy and pride of his old age. And then, beyond all that, I know, what probably few others do, that he had a feeling for you and John as the children of the wife of his youth, which was different and probably a deeper and tenderer feeling from any other."

Kingsbury went on with intimate memories of the senior John Olmsted which might soften the moment for Frederick. "My recollections of him and of the old Ann Street home, of the large loose woolen shoes, in which he used to sit up nights to read; of our crude table discussions on scientific farming, in which he used to take a part, are among the pleasantest memories of my life."[26]

John Olmsted's will named Frederick and Albert as trustees of his estate. Albert Olmsted, by this time an officer in a Hartford bank, necessarily took the larger part in the complex, long-drawn-out business of settling the estate. Mary Ann Olmsted, John's widow, did not take kindly to being placed in a position dependent on her two sons in monetary matters. Her husband wrote the will in such a manner that she did not inherit his estate outright; the estate was put in trust, and his widow, as well as the surviving children, received each a certain portion of income a year. Hers was the largest, approximately $2,500 per year, the others to receive $140 to $250 quarterly, depending upon investments. Her share, Mary Ann thought, was hardly enough, even with her daughter Mary's share added, to keep up the house on Asylum Street where she and Mary lived together, to maintain a carriage, and to make improvements. Mary, from being a bright, unfettered girl of years before, had become, in middle age, a partial invalid and a discontented woman.

Although John Olmsted's interests had been large, the division of his estate did not make for a large income for any of the children. Albert showed himself a steady, careful, and efficient executor and investor of the estate. But he was not tactful. He seemed less able to get along with his own mother than did Frederick, the stepson, who showed compassion for Mary Ann in her periodic tantrums over money matters. There was to be a series of dreary episodes in which the senior Mrs. Olmsted fought against the will, even at one time going to law against her two sons. Frederick was saved a considerable amount of trouble by Albert's cold-blooded skill in money matters. And Frederick came to have a new respect for his younger half brother who, in his earlier days, had seemed irresolute and not good for anything in particular.

Albert Olmsted was a solidly settled family man now with a wife, Lou, and a child, Fritz. A banker in the firm of George P. Bissell and Company, he handled the complicated remnants of his father's investments, sending the quarterly income from the estate to Frederick and the others and explaining the vicissitudes of the rise and fall of this not very large residue of the father's mercantile and real estate holdings. His and Frederick's relation was strengthened although the brothers were not very compatible in temperament or interests. They remained good friends. Albert wrote frequently to Fred. Among other services to his brother, he became his wine merchant, sending him a yearly crop of wine bottled and ready for decanting.

If Frederick Olmsted, at the beginning of the year 1873, had stood still long enough to look back—and he did not—he would have seen an epoch ending. His father dead, and his partnership with Calvert Vaux ended, he at last embarked upon an independent life and career. Like many men, he had attained his full independence only by stages.

CHAPTER XXII

Buffetings and Accomplishments

That is precisely what landscape gardening should do I think,
make improvements by design which nature might by chance.
—F. L. O., to Dr. Henry F. Hill, November 3, 1875[1]

OLMSTED POSSESSED the shy intuitions and judgments that writers and painters entertain in private rooms where such men work with no one to disturb them. But he had to armor his artist's temperament and drag his ideas into the open to find a place in the world of other men's aims and ambitions. The years 1873 to 1876 were filled with buffetings to which his kind of work was naturally subject. They were also years of steady accomplishment. It was remarkable that his work was so continuous; this was a time of severe economic depression for the nation. And it was as if he were beginning again. He had dissolved his partnership with Calvert Vaux and had to find a new way of operating his personal profession. He had also lost the supportive figure of his father, the guardian fosterer of many previous enterprises.

It should be understood that, although his and Vaux's partnership for private work had been dissolved, they continued to work together cooperatively for the New York parks and in some other projects from time to time. Vaux gave up his joint part in the larger works outside New York, those that were already under way; and in these places Olmsted carried on a varying degree of superintendence. It was clear to Olmsted that his new independence required him to think through many aspects of his work and to devise new methods of operation. He took hold effectively at this juncture and enlarged his scope in these years. Satisfaction was just this combination of difficulty joined to achievement.

Olmsted with Vaux's help rather quickly restored Central Park to the purposes for which they had done the design—despite A. H. Green's brake upon expenditures. He distrusted the future of the park, however, and used a free-ranging report to tell the commissioners in the midsummer of 1873 the proper perspective to use toward such a city park. Making a park was not enough; one must keep it. The very idea of such a park was "an experiment, by the results of which the welfare of vast numbers of people in other great cities than New York cannot fail to be affected."

He put his case as strongly as he could: "That it is worth while for civilized communities to use their wealth in this way; that humanity and patriotism and religion require that every community which occupies territory in which it is reasonably certain that a great city is to grow, should, if necessary, at some sacrifice of immediate convenience and comfort and prosperity, begin the formation of a park of this comprehensive and artistically complete character."[2]

He had come to the early conclusion that the policing of these public grounds was a special kind of duty, not to be entrusted to the police force of the city, but to his own especially trained organization of "park keepers." These were men trained by him in devotion to the aims of the park, able to interpret these ideas to the public as well as to enforce the public law within the park borders. It was a crisis for Olmsted when a change in the bylaws of the park board threatened to remove the park police powers from the control of the landscape architect and give it over to the regular city police. Olmsted wrote a passionate defense of his position on July 15, 1873, and threatened to resign.[3] The trouble at this time was patched over, and Olmsted kept precarious control of the internal mangement of park affairs.

His paper "Superintendent of Central Park to Gardeners" illustrates the way he shared his mind with those who worked under him: "The special value of the Central Park to the city of New York will lie, and even now lies, in its comparative largeness. There are certain kinds of beauty possible to be had in it which it is not possible for the city to have anywhere else, because on no other ground of the city is there scope and breadth enough for them." He tried to make his park workers see what he believed special in a large landscape park. It was not flower beds nor single trees; these might be enjoyed on smaller grounds. "The seven hundred acres of the Central Park can be better used. That which is expected to be especially valuable on the Central Park is the beauty of broad landscape scenes and of combinations of trees with trees and with rocks and turf and water." He admonished them: "No man is to use the discretion given him to secure pretty little local effects, at the expense of general effects and especially of broad landscape effects." There were, of course, two kinds of effects to be sought: "Smooth, simple, clean surfaces of turf on which the light falls early and the shadows are broad and trees which have grown freely with plenty of room to stretch out their limbs" were the first. And on the other hand there were to be "trees and bushes and plants which have grown in a somewhat crowded way, bent and mingled together as they generally are where native plants thrive on rough ground."[4]

What Olmsted held onto in Central Park and the other New York parks, this scene of his most intense and intimate work, was the control of two functions, design and superintendence. And in the years to come he was to see a slippage in both these functions. There was not enough money given to the parks to carry out the design properly, and indifference and interference frustrated the proper maintenance of the park after it had been tentatively laid out in accordance with the design. Commissioners, coming and going, sometimes had a rough-and-ready sort of pride in the park, but they rarely allowed this feeling to interfere with patronage in giving out jobs or favoritism in bending to the wishes of important people who wished to use the park in various incongruous ways. Olmsted used up a tremendous store of emotional energy in defending the parks of New York. The result was one of his periodic bouts of exhaustion.

He went on a long vacation trip in the late summer and early fall of 1873, seeing something of Quebec, Newfoundland, and the Gaspé Peninsula. He wrote to friend Knapp from Saratoga, coming home, that the cliffs of the Gaspesian countryside, where the peninsula made a shouldering reach into the Atlantic ocean, was "very fine—much grander than any other coast scenery on the continent so far as I know."[5] But he had not had a trip of unalloyed joy. He had suffered with his eyes. (And Charlotte had not been well—a fact ominous for the future.) When he came home, he had decided to resign from the New York City position. He attempted to do so on September 17 in a paper written to Salem H. Wales, of the parks department.

Mr. Wales refused to accept the resignation. At this point, enough was conceded to hold Olmsted to the position. By November he set off with Charles Dana to look at that gentleman's property at Glen Cove, Long Island. So the crisis had more or less passed.

That he was not entirely well in his nerves shows, however, in a December letter he wrote to Charles Brace about faith. It was compulsively personal. "Did you never hear of a case in which the son of a Christian mother was oppressed with melancholy and reflected on suicide as he began to face his great work in the world? Did you never hear of a Christian woman in whose household there was more of blight than in that of the motherless Mills [John Stuart Mill]?"[6]

In long night sessions of letter-writing, Olmsted could be morbid. Yet he went on with his work in the light of day. He undertook to devise a new method of handling his complicated jobs. Jacob Weidenmann was a landscape man whom Olmsted respected. Olmsted was a man whom Weidenmann almost worshipped. Weidenmann had gained some fame by a book, *Beautifying Country Houses* (1870), but in the financial slump of the seventies he was unable to attract enough business to make a success of an independent firm. Olmsted suggested a method of their working together, which would not destroy the independence of either one, but which would enhance the work and the living of each. Of course, Olmsted had the superior role in the arrangement; Weidenmann did not mind.

Olmsted wrote a set of numbered proposals for the other man to review and to which Olmsted wished him to give his assent, or disagreement. The important points may be summarized as follows:

1. Olmsted was to receive half of the compensation for any plan, the design of which Weidenmann assisted in drawing up; Weidenmann's name was to appear below Olmsted's.

2. Jacob Weidenmann and his staff were to be paid their exact expenses if Weidenmann's firm was deputized to implement a plan which was fully Olmsted's.

3. Jacob Weidenmann was to be Olmsted's "adjutant" in the case of No. 2, and "not associate designer."[7]

Weidenmann was perfectly willing to work in a manner which spelled out ahead of time his subordination to Olmsted. In practice, Olmsted allowed Weidenmann a good deal of freedom on particular projects. On these works, Olmsted held the reins of review. If he did not like any aspect of the work, he required revision. The two men, due to their particular natures, found the contract they had made with each other satisfactory. Olmsted trusted Weidenmann; Weidenmann revered Olmsted. "My object," wrote Olmsted to the other man, "in the proposed arrangement with you being to have the advantage of an office staff always ready without the trouble and expense of maintaining it solely for my private business."[8] In this arrangement, Olmsted could operate out of his house at 209 West Forty-sixth Street and not have his living space cluttered with a staff. Weidenmann maintained his own office and carried on in it his own work and occasional jobs contracted for by Olmsted. As of June 1, 1874, the two men thus formed an amicable, profitable working agreement which at the time each found beneficial.

An illustration of the way the agreement worked may be found in a note Weidenmann wrote to Olmsted on April 20, 1875: "Enclosed please find General Plan for the Saratoga Springs grounds [the grounds of the fashionable hotel with its long veranda for strolling ladies and gentlemen of fashion]. If you approve the design please send it either back to my office or to Mr. C. C. Dawson, 94 Chamber Street. Mr. Dawson wishes to commence drainage."[9]

Olmsted used George Radford in a subordinate position also. In February, 1875, Olmsted sent Radford to Hartford to supervise some aspect of the work he had agreed to do for the grounds of Trinity College.

Another change in the internal workings of Olmsted's office was prefigured when in June, 1875, his eldest son John Charles graduated from the Sheffield Scientific School at Yale and went to work for his father in their home.

It was, however, some little time before the father and son worked out a satisfactory professional relationship. This would come slowly as Frederick relinquished a tight, fatherly control, and as John gained his own sense of responsibility and even freedom in the firm's work.

In addition to his immediate family in New York, Frederick was tied to his dead father's household in Hartford. Pity crept into Fred Law's feeling for the stepmother who had with so good intention harassed his years of growing up with a burden of required piety. In April, 1875, the single sister Mary died. The rebellious and sometimes extravagant stepmother's financial situation became acute. Mary's share no longer cushioned her straitened circumstances. Conferring together, Frederick, Albert, and Bertha gave back their residual share of their late sister Mary's income from the family estate to their mother. Mary Ann Olmsted decided to take in boarders. She ran into Albert's opposition to plans to have the house adapted to this change. She was not entirely practical. He was not patient. Frederick tried ineffectively to mediate between the two, but was bruised in the process. Mary Ann's last days were not happy.

Within his own walls, where children's play was intermixed in a happy disorder with his professional work, Frederick could often be quietly joyful. He watched over the big boys John and Owen, viewed with some fond anxiety the quickly maturing Charlotte, and had pure delight in his little tom-girl Marion, and the baby, who was first "Boy," then little "Henry," growing imperceptibly into "Rick." He could be as young with this child as he had, in truth, remained behind his grown-up mask.

To little "Henry" in Plymouth with Mary in May, 1875, Olmsted, remaining in the city, wrote a fairy-tale passage of his own creation in a letter telling the child about cats in the yard, a superfluity of cats, thousands and thousands.[10] Another time, in a scrawled pack of sheets which must have taken hours to write, the father made up a long, rambling tale for the boy about an Old Colony railway engine called "Old Succotash" who lived in a roundhouse, and his friend, a rat named "Tzaskoe," who lived in the turntable.[11]

Frederick, Senior, remained childlike in many of his traits. He took the most minute and naive delight in telling a tailor how to devise a working suit of clothes for him, so that he should be warm and comfortable and have all his pencils and pads in convenient pockets when he went to Montreal for work in that cold winter climate. He had no regard for fashion. He wanted his own way, and he went straight to it, even in clothes. So he was to have a heavy, loose suit, with all the unusual pockets he might need. One may envision him thus attired the next year, happily climbing up and down the eminence of Mount Royal, determining slants and curves of the road which would allow his imagined park visitor the best views of the roofs of the city below and the great glittering ship-filled river.

Olmsted, as the years went on, made something of a habit of saying he was old, and exaggerating the fact. He felt the strains and aches of endurances and disappointments. Yet in temperament he remained open to the freshest of impressions. He experienced a renewal in his senses each time he came face to face with natural scenes. Also, as he grew older, he became unself-consciously more and more of a teacher. He dispensed advice without taking a high tone.

He continued to tell William Hammond Hall his ideas about San Francisco's park, where Hall remained in charge until 1876, and about the university grounds across the bay. California should develop Californian landscapes. "I think that you know my views in this respect. They are that the principles of English landscape gardening—which in this climate [he meant New York and Brooklyn parks] I am disposed to carry to a greater extreme than they are ever carried in Europe—are out of place in the climate of California. I should seek to cover the ground mainly with anything by which I could secure bodies of color, a simple inoffensive low tone, not unnatural, never suggesting death or constant labor to keep alive....I should then concentrate brightness, cheerfulness and elegance on a few plainly artificial elements—such as terraces, avenues and formal parterres—strictly formal and as unquestionably artificial as a necklace or bracelet. You do less in this way than I should."[12]

Thus, Olmsted, as he grew older in body and nerves, grew freer in his ideas. He might feel constricted in his own person, but not in his ideas which enlarged as the years went on. In the *Nation* on January 22, 1874, in an unsigned article Olmsted reviewed not only his friend Cleveland's book about the landscape needs of the west, but Wilson Flagg's *The Woods and By-ways of New England.* Scornfully, Olmsted excoriated the Flagg book, which uncritically praised nature at the expense of a man-made environment. (It was not that Olmsted had lost his love of the wild. When he and Mary went on vacation the following year with the Richardsons, it was Olmsted who taught the restless architect how to be quiet and sit down in front of nature and wait upon its effects, how, in particular, to see Niagara Falls by approaching it quietly and gradually.) But he saw maundering sentimentality in Flagg's book. He would not praise "country living" without some kind of discrimination. In such scenes: "I have found women living more confined, dull, and dreary lives than in any barbarous country; caring less for simple, natural pleasures than any other women in the world;...it has been in such homes that insanity, consumption, typhoid fever, and diphtheria have found more victims than in those even of the densest and dirtiest of cities."

He went on: "While there are beauties to be found by the side of a cow-path and on the boggy shores of a pond, it is also possible to have them where they can be enjoyed with more convenience, under conditions more favorable to health and more economical of civilized raiment." This kind of enjoyment can be achieved "where many homes are found in a limited neighborhood, as in villages and towns."[13] Olmsted was wrapped up in his work in the new suburbs, such as he was designing at Tarrytown, New York, and the work he was doing guided his words here.

But he had not given up on the great cities. He had seen many changes in Manhattan since that time when he was a very young keeper of the cash in a dry goods firm and amused himself by keeping pigeons on the roof of his boardinghouse. There had been pigs in the streets then to clear the gutters of the garbage carelessly strewn there. The pigs were gone. Even the Tweed Ring, which had infested the city recently, was gone. The only permanence in Manhattan seemed to be the hungry movement toward new living space to the north. He saw beginning to happen what he had long ago predicted as this movement began to surround and pass beyond Central Park.

Olmsted welcomed a chance to express his considered thought about the growth of Manhattan when he was called upon to write a prescription for the settlement of the new wards, the Twenty-third and the Twenty-fourth.[14] "So far as the plan of New York remains to be formed, it would be inexcusable that it should not be the plan of a Metropolis; adapted to serve, and serve well, every legitimate interest of the wide world; not of ordinary commerce only, but of humanity, religion, art, science and scholarship."

The new wards seemed to Olmsted a chance to break away from the monotonous and humanly restricting grid plan which since 1807 had advanced inexorably northward across the varied and interesting ground of Manhattan, reducing that natural landscape as it went to a mean geometry in which houses were squeezed onto narrow lots and all natural contours were lost. That he did not eventually achieve his purpose does not diminish the interest of Olmsted's ideas, nor the pity that they were not heeded. He put the case first for housing for ordinary citizens, a kind of housing which the grid plan made difficult.

Decent, wholesome, tidy dwellings for people who are struggling to maintain an honorable independence are more to be desired in a city than great churches, convents or colleges. They are sadly wanting in New York and why?

His answer was that the grid plan made narrow, poorly ventilated housing necessary, or at least profitable. And the plan prevented a system of alleys behind the houses so that, in consequence, the "dust, ashes, rubbish and garbage" of these houses could not be removed except by the front doors and then were piled up in unsightly and unhealthy heaps in the streets.

The narrowness of these houses, set down meanly side by side, squeezed together for the highest profit from each block, enforced the wrong kind of building.

The practice is one that defies the architect to produce habitable rooms of pleasing or dignified proportions, but this is the least of its evils, for in the middle parts of all these deep, narrow cubes, there must be a large amount of ill-ventilated space, which can only be imperfectly lighted through distant skylights, or by an unwholesome combustion of gas. This space being consequently the least valuable for other purposes, is generally assigned to water-closets, for which the position is in other respects the worst that could be adopted.

He pierced through what had become custom. If one changed the street pattern and the spacing of houses, then all this dreary monotony might be broken up. He thought, also, that this northern reach of the island might be reserved mainly for living space, not for industry or commerce.

Here and there a shop or range of shops will be necessary, but being adapted only for local custom, they are not likely to be lofty or excessively obtrusive. Now and again buildings for other purposes would probably occur; a school with its play grounds, a church set in a proper churchyard; a higher institution of learning with its green quadrangle, academic grove or campus; a public hall, a library or museum; a convent with its courts and gardens; a suburban inn or boarding-house with its terrace, commanding grand prospects over the Hudson.

And he ventured to suggest winding roads built along the natural lines of the precipitous hills of this upper part of Manhattan, with easy grades for carriages and walks, and "fine old trees may be left standing, and, to save them, the wheel-way carried a little to the right or left, or slightly raised or lowered. It may be desirable, simply for convenience sake, to go to the expense of avoiding such conditions, but, as a matter of taste, they are far from blemishes; they add to other charms of picturesqueness, and they are a concession to nature, tending to an effect not of incongruity and incompleteness, but of consistent and happy landscape composition." Thus, good art and good living were to go together.

Olmsted's two interests had come together in his urban work, his *rus-urban* work, as he termed it in this report. He wished to conserve land values and he wished to conserve human values. He desired a city where people might live together on ground which they respected, and where they and their children might derive joy as well as material benefit. City work interested him both emotionally and intellectually, but he did not give up work with small spaces.

He went to Amherst repeatedly, concerning himself with the Amherst College grounds and the grounds of the State Agricultural College, as well as the town common. He took on the design of the private grounds surrounding Frederic Church's "castle" on the Hudson. He was in touch with the commission charged with building a hospital for the mentally ill in Massachusetts; three times he went on site visits with the founders. Yale College called on him for renovation of the college grounds. Would he not, in going to New Haven in the 1870s, have thought back to the shy, unofficial student of the 1840s? Hartford continued to consult him concerning the grounds of the Retreat for the Insane. He went south to Baltimore to advise the president of a new university, Johns Hopkins. This was the same Daniel Gilman who had written him from the developing University of California. These and other projects occupied Olmsted intermittently from 1873 to 1876.

But they filled in only the interstices of his time, for he had also in hand two absorbingly large works, one in Albany, New York, the other, in Washington, D.C.

By the mid-seventies, the construction of the new state capitol in Albany had dragged along until it was an embarrassment to the State of New York. The design by Thomas S. Fuller, in progress since 1867, had not been completed. The legislature set up a New Capitol Commission, of which Lieutenant Governor William Dorsheimer, already the friend and patron of H. H. Richardson and F. L. Olmsted, was chairman. Dorsheimer named as an advisory board to the commission these two men, whose work he knew, and in addition, Leopold Eidlitz, a distinguished New York City architect. The three men had first the task of advising what should be done. When their advice seemed good, they were next charged with the complete authority to oversee the completion of the capitol and its grounds. Olmsted's authority was not limited to grounds; all three were charged with the whole task. Olmsted, Richardson, and Eidlitz regularly reported to each other whatever each one had done; as a board they reported to and were responsible to the commission and to the legislature.

This work threw Olmsted and Richardson more and more into each other's company. When wives and children fled summer heat, they would talk in Olmsted's study and then walk out into the hot streets of Manhattan to dine together. Both men were talkers, Olmsted finding perhaps his match in the gregarious, sociable Richardson. Sometimes this long-lasting conversation became exhausting to Olmsted and he would go home to a sleepless night. The restless Richardson hardly knew how to go home. On the other hand, when the architect, in one of his frequent, debilitating illnesses, took to his bed, he would write Olmsted brief notes, sometimes in the hand of a convenient assistant but always signed in his own characteristic sprawling hand, about things that needed to be done at Albany.

The completing of the building was a long-drawn-out and harassing affair. The politicians complained about the millions spent. They failed to appreciate the luxury of Richardson's taste. He wished even details to be splendid, as when, in the Senate chamber, he designed a great free-standing clock. Rival and possibly envious architects in New York City attacked Richardson's and Eidlitz's decision to change the style of the building from a too finicky Renaissance to a bluffer, stronger Romanesque. Olmsted believed that what was possible to be done had been done decently and even richly by Richardson and Eidlitz, although it was not to be a completely satisfactory building even to the designers. Yet the finished structure was to be a dignified, interesting, and useful building, magnificent in its materials and generous in its spaces. What Olmsted lost in traveling to and from Albany, and in defending the work against criticism (characteristically, it was Olmsted who used words to do this), and in worries about appropriations, he gained in comradeship with these two men.

Through this New York State capitol project, Olmsted became more intimate with a number of architects and artists. He had already a considerable acquaintance with architects through Calvert Vaux. Eidlitz, a man of a pleasant, self-deprecating sense of humor, Olmsted valued. Olmsted had recommended him in February, 1873, to Whitelaw Reid when the newspaper editor required a designer for his house. Olmsted wrote a letter of introduction for Charles McKim when the young architect first traveled abroad. He saw to it that John La Farge, who had asked this favor of him, received a notice in the *Nation* of his exhibit of paintings in Boston.[15] When Augustus Saint-Gaudens was at work in Paris on his Farragut statue for Madison Square, he wrote to Frederick Olmsted asking him just how the statue, when he should bring it back, might be best placed in the square. He sketched various positions and the posture of the statue in his informal letter, and begged Olmsted as a friend to go down to Madison Square, look the place over, and write him his opinion.[16] The fraternity of art was broadened for Olmsted in these years.

Fez Richardson and his wife, Julia Hayden, originally a Bostonian, became intimates of Frederick and Mary Olmsted. Richardson took on young John Charles Olmsted with special kindness and consideration. It is probable that outsiders saw John's abilities more quickly than the boy's mother and father did. When Trinity Church was about to be dedicated, its scaffoldings not yet dismantled, Richardson invited John to come to Boston (where Richardson had moved to be near his large project), to stay with him and his wife, and to receive a special tour of the new church. The architect shared with the young man his own delight in the building. He had poured into it all the gathered force of his career up to this time. He had enlisted La Farge to design the stained glass windows and murals and Saint-Gaudens to assist La Farge, and later to create a Christlike bust of Phillips Brooks, the minister, for an outside site. Henry Adams, at this time teaching at Harvard, and an old friend of Richardson's, watched the progress of Trinity and used the scene in his novel, *Esther*. Olmsted wrote to Norton on December 27, 1876: "I sent my boy on last week to see Richardson's church before the scaffolds were taken down. I want very much to see it myself."[17]

While Olmsted got what satisfaction he could out of the strenuous state project in Albany and other works of himself and his friends he had a livelier interest in another capitol project. In May, 1873, United States Senator Justin Morrill, the author of the Land Grant Bill, wrote a letter to Olmsted's New York parks boss, Commissioner H. G. Stebbins. Morrill feared Frederick Olmsted had not received a note he had written to him, and he asked Stebbins to ask Olmsted to come to Washington. He wanted "to get him to come here and spend a day with me on the Capitol grounds, recently enlarged. We want the highest skill."[18] Olmsted was appointed landscape architect to the United States Capitol early in 1874, the appointment under a salary. He made a preliminary report and, at this early date, proposed the terrace on the west side which was to transform the appearance of the Capitol as viewed from the Mall, giving the building the dignity and strength of a base which the enlarged dome needed.

The work was well under way by the spring of 1874, and Olmsted poured out his interest in the new project to George Waring. Olmsted told his friend that he was starting the work with the east side of the Capitol. Trees would have to be removed and the land regraded for the building to be seen properly. Then the soil, which was very bad, would have to be remade. He asked Waring to advise him by suggesting a drainage expert. (Waring suggested himself.) It was, Olmsted said, "a difficult work in which I am likely for ten years to come to get more kicks than halfpence." But in this deprecation there was also an interest which held him. Difficulties confessed were a smokescreen to hide his sense of joy in the large job. "The matter is one for many reasons of much national importance." But, "I should hardly like the Ways and Means to know that I meant to have $60,000 spent for the improvement of the soil, but I don't see how a tolerable condition can be hoped for at much less cost than that, do you?"[19]

That he would expend himself, his wife and friends might assume. He worked no other way. He took on even powerful senators with some confidence. Senator Don Cameron was one of these, the boss of Pennsylvania, and with a seemingly endless term in Washington, minding railroad interests and other large concerns. A man of urbanity as well as conscious power, he had a fondness for a certain elm tree standing beside the Capitol, which Olmsted said must go. The tree was diseased in any case. It stood in the way of Olmsted's design, and he intended to plant or replace trees as he wished. Olmsted, however, gave careful instructions to J. A. Partridge, engineer of the capitol, about the strategy of removing the elm without offending the senator; he said, in effect, to the engineer, be sure that Senator Cameron understands that we are not against him. This was in a letter of October 18, 1875, in which he also initiated Partridge into the mysteries of a perfect turf: "The rule that the surface for a foot or more should always be flush with the top of the edging and then rise with a *concave* curve. There should nowhere be a convex curve at the outside of a piece of turf." And he mollified criticism with praise: "Except just near the edges where the finish is not fine enough, your lawn making is admirable and I think we shall have charming turf."

He warned Partridge that Senator Morrill was coming to Washington the following week and would, of course, inspect the work so far done. "You must, at whatever cost, have the middle trees removed from the west side, and the ground cleared of rubbish (so that he can enjoy the clear field), before that."[20]

It was not enough to be at work in Albany and Washington; he began to feel the pull of the Boston area as a place to work. One possible new job was the laying out of the new Arboretum.

Charles Sprague Sargent, the strong-minded mover of the plan, wrote to Olmsted to involve him in the Arboretum. Sargent saw with his blunt gaze that his personal idea, the tree garden, might never be planted unless he could somehow tie this Harvard property to city management. "It has occurred to me that an arrangement could be made, by which the ground (130 acres) destined for the Arboretum could be handed over to the City of Boston on the condition that the city should spend a certain sum of money in laying out the grounds and should agree to leave the planting in my hands in order that the scientific objects of the tract could be carried out." The negotiation was, so far, being quietly carried out, not noised abroad, and he needed a plan of the grounds to present to the city authorities. "This plan I want *you* to make as there is no one in whose taste and judgment in such matters I can rely so much. Can you, then, come up at once, and have some preliminary talk on the subject, and look over the ground."[21] Olmsted was to go, probably not knowing that the initial two thousand dollars payment for the preliminary survey had been subscribed to in small amounts by Sargent and his friends, in order to secure these Olmstedian services.[22] President Eliot of Harvard and the Boston city authorities were cool at first to the plan and made no move to pay Olmsted's initial expenses. But the tentative plan was made. The Arboretum, pushed by the stubborn and willful Sargent, was to come into existence at last and to occupy a good deal of the Olmsted firm's time in the next few years.

The other Boston project which exerted a pull upon Olmsted's imagination was the care of the Boston parks. By the mid-seventies the possibility became a probability. Charles H. Dalton, who knew Olmsted already through the design work he had done for the site of the Massachusetts General Hospital, asked Olmsted to come up to Boston in October, 1875, "and devote one day to the trustees" of the hospital, but "also one or even two days to the Park Commissioners' service."[23] Olmsted went willingly. On November 3, Dalton wrote: "The route over which you drove on 26th ulto. is marked in red,"[24] sending him a map or diagram of the proposed parks and parkways to be designed eventually. He informed Olmsted that the boundaries were being run. When this had been done, they should want his advice. He asked him to come again and this time to spend a week. By the spring of 1876 Olmsted had firm ideas about a new park system for the city and on April 8 wrote a prophetic letter about sites on the Charles River, Back Bay, Jamaica Pond, and West Roxbury.

Life was filled with many kinds of things. He was asked about land design by private individuals. He took on those plans, small or large, in which he had a spontaneous interest. In spite of advising artificial elements where he thought appropriate—a mall for promenades in Central Park, terracing for the west front of the United States Capitol, and arcaded roofways for the hot sun of Stanford, California, Olmsted still loved the gentle aspect of uncultivated nature in New England. He enjoyed counseling Dr.

Henry F. Hill of Amherst to take advantage of what was already given in the area where he lived. Landscape design was only a way to do with purpose what God or evolution did in an indeterminate, too time-dragging way. "That is precisely what landscape gardening should do, I think," he wrote his client, "make improvements by design which nature might by chance through the action of earthquakes, storms, frosts, birds and insects." And he told the doctor not to be a purist, not to be dismayed by "exotics." After all, they strayed in natural landscapes. "Does the occurrence of the little red or yellow clover or the buttercups in the pastures of Walpole or the barberry on the hills of Andover distract attention from the loveliness of the Connecticut or the Merrimac vallies?"[25] This passage shows Olmsted still in possession of his childlike relish for natural beauty.

To his sorrow he did not have as much time as he would wish for looking at buttercups in a field. Cares and honors came to him in correspondence during 1875. On March 4 a letter arrived from the editors of *The American Cyclopaedia* telling him that his revision of the article on "Parks" was late.[26] On March 14, he reminded the Central Park gardener, John Fischer, about spring duties: "Fear that you will not have nearly as much thinning out done as is needed before the spring opens. Please call for all the men you can use and take every advantage of the opportunity you can. There are many clusters of evergreens where the trees are destroying one another."[27] April 7 brought a letter from Professor Henry Adams asking him to serve in New York on a committee to honor Carl Schurz at a dinner.[28]

On May 6, General Meigs asked Olmsted to examine the Philadelphia Depot of the Quartermaster's Department, the Schuylkill Arsenal, "with a view to the improvement of its grounds in a tasteful manner but at moderate cost, before the Centennial Exhibition of 1876."[29] On May 18, strain showing, Olmsted wrote out a complaint to H. G. Stebbins about the abuse of the turf in Central Park.

On June 9, his brother Albert wrote him about spruces dying at No. 967 in Hartford: what to do? And Albert continued with another weighty matter in their personal family affairs: their mother was considering a lengthy trip to visit relatives in California; was this advisable?[30]

On July 8 Olmsted wrote a draft for the benefit of the New York Parks Board of a plan to reorganize gardening maintenance for the entire city.[31] In July he also wrote a set of preliminary instructions for the Advisory Board of the State Capitol to guide the careful study of the condition and the future of the unfinished building.[32]

Olmsted's friends noticed that he was overdoing. Frederick Knapp wrote to him in mid-October 1875:

We have enjoyed Mrs. Olmsted's summer here very much indeed; and we feel that it has been of great benefit to Marion and to "Boy."

...I fear Mr. Olmsted that you are working too hard. Don't kill yourself quite yet.[33]

In addition to overwork, Olmsted had a reason for real annoyance. His and Vaux's ancient enemy, Egbert Viele, had written a gratuitous and unsigned letter to the New York *Tribune* again claiming credit for the Central Park design, denying it to Olmsted and Vaux, and saying in part: "That the design on which the Central Park has been formed is a poor copy of one made by a gentleman best known for his modest contributions to Sanitary Science."[34] (Before Olmsted and Vaux composed their winning design, before the design contest was announced by the commissioners, Viele had indeed done a drainage design. Olmsted had subsequently employed Waring to design and oversee the drainage of the park.) George Waring reacted in a letter to Olmsted the very day he saw Viele's communication to the newspaper, saying, "It seems to me that the best thing to do in his case is to leave him alone. His capacity for harm must be very small in the end. And his capacity for annoyance must be just in proportion to the attention we pay him. Of course he will lie about you, and about me, and about the Park."[35]

Waring rallied Olmsted gently in a second letter, as if trying to help his inevitable hurt with a smile: "Thanks for your dateless reply to mine of the 20th. There is one reason why I am sorry that you do not officially reply to Viele's nonsense, that is, that your persistent habit of spelling him Vielli would, I think, be a sweet thorn in his side. Otherwise, I am glad you let him slide. Seriously, I think his false statements about the Central Park are the most impudent and the most ridiculous achievements of his miserable life."

Waring reacted gladly to a suggestion from Olmsted that the drainage system of the park needed overhauling. "If the Department acts on your recommendation I shall be very glad to accept the order to inspect and report upon my old work."[36]

These various communications during 1875 simply illustrate the thicket of concerns in which Olmsted moved, some personal and some professional. A continuing enumeration of his works of this time indicates the variety of them. In 1875 he advised the city of Providence, Rhode Island, on the possibility of a public park. He undertook the revision of the Washington Monument grounds in Baltimore in 1876 and 1877. He prepared a decorative map of the work he had been doing in Buffalo for that city to send to the Centennial Exhibition in Philadelphia. His supervision of Mount Royal Park in Montreal continued.

Nineteen-year-old Owen Olmsted conceived the idea of boarding with a family in the city where his father and his brother John were laying out an ambitious hilltop park. Owen was possessed of a lively and adventurous mind. He thought he would learn French and see something of the world away from his family. The family accepted his idea. Frederick favored strenuous adventures for his young. For some months Owen remained in dismal circumstances with a French-speaking family. Characteristically, Owen made humorous matter out of the drunkenness of the head of the family, his own slowness in learning French, and other physical and circumstantial discomforts in Montreal.

Owen was a slim, good-looking boy, with the pleasantest disposition in the family. He bore a strong resemblance to his long-dead father. Mary and Frederick must have seen the ghost of John Hull Olmsted in the nice set of Owen's head, the clear gaze, and the charming manners of their son. But the boy was not physically strong. It was thought that exercise and a change would be good for him.

Owen was straightforwardly frank to his own father. He told him in a letter on August 22, 1876, that the good bourgeois citizens of Montreal thought that their new mountain park was costing them too much; they blamed the park for a rise in their tax rate. He added, with a family wisdom about crooked politics: "But the Doctor [with whom he boarded] tells me there is a regular Tamany Ring here among the officials and contractors for street improvements which is very likely the reason.... From your affectionate son."[37]

Owen worked on the park job occasionally. The engineer on duty taught him to use a level in the roadwork. "It is very slow work at first," Owen wrote John, and signed his letter in his boyish frank way, "Goodbye from your affectionate brother."[38]

The children came and went at the house on Forty-sixth Street. However scattered in movement, they were dependent one upon the other for emotional support. In May, 1876, the youngest boy's transitory illness made them all feel stricken. But "Boy" recovered and they breathed more freely. In June John studied painting with John La Farge—not earnestly enough, his father thought. Charlotte went visiting the Godkins in Cambridge. When the weather began to thicken in typical New York summer fashion, Mary picked up the younger ones and departed for Plymouth where she had the congenial company of the Knapps. Frederick remained for the most part in the city during the hot weather, going away on trips to various work sites in other cities from time to time.

CHAPTER XXIII

Interlude

I cannot help thinking that your life in New York where the democrats are rampant, odious, and corrupt, darkens your mind.
—Katherine Wormeley, to F. L. O., January 5, 1877[1]

Olmsted was a lonely man in a hot and disorganized city in the summer of 1877. A railroad strike had stopped food and other supplies from coming into New York. There were flare-ups of violence along the railroad lines outside, and threats of destruction flickering elusively nearer. Olmsted had his son John with him in the house emptied of his wife and the younger children, who were away on their usual hot weather vacation; but he and John, at this time, fell easily into conflict and misunderstanding, the kind of differences normal between a son chafing for independence and a father watching that son's development anxiously and too closely.

The older man could not sleep well. He was bedeviled, and had been for over a year, by a disagreement with the commissioners of the New York public parks. He tried to while away night hours by writing fragmentary recollections of his childhood, youth, and of the beginnings of Central Park twenty years before, but he found himself enmeshed in old bitternesses. From his childhood floated back to him the still inexplicable way his father had had of sending a small, shy boy away to country schools where more than once he was as badly treated as any defenseless child in one of Dickens's stories. He remembered the aimless wanderings and wastages of his youth which had yet permitted him to learn to love the lines of nature. He recalled, and choked upon the ugliness of some of the resentments he had encountered when he went to work for Central Park under the jealous Viele.

Frederick tried to write cheerfully on July 24 to Mary at Lake Placid; she had confessed herself bored. He attempted to tell her his exact situation: "The city is essentially under martial law"[2]; but there was no excitement, he assured her. There was no difficulty yet in getting about in the city. For example, John had gone over to Brooklyn that day and walked all over the park. Next day, he let Mary see the rising temperature of the crisis. The price of meats had risen, and "if the embargo is not broken in two days the supply of the city will be exhausted." He broke into fantasy about "basting cats and doves in the yard. When these are exhausted we shall have the rats and spare the canaries to the last." He gave her what other news he had. Nothing from Owen. John was well. Richardson came in to talk every evening, "and we walk to the Fifth Avenue to get the Post news and then to French's."[3] He planned to set out next day, despite the crisis, for a swing around jobs in Baltimore and Washington. Another note told his wife, on July 26, "We are chipper. The strikes will break today, I think. We still hear the drums of the 55th." He meant that he had heard the military tattoo of troops assembled to protect the city from riots. "P.S. Owen has arrived looking well but a little thinner. Has had no adventures."[4]

Although he said "we are chipper," he was to be less and less so that summer and fall, winding down after a long period of living too hard. The downward way had had a shove from the outside the summer before. His salary from the New York City Parks Department was held up by a technicality. In May, 1876, he had accepted a more or less honorary position with the State Survey, without salary. A New York City regulation stated that an officer such as he was of the Parks Board could not hold state position. He envisioned certain members of the Parks Board as seizing gleefully upon this fact and stopping his pay. A letter from his lawyers, the firm of Prichard, Choate and Smith, in July, 1876, implied that it was Olmsted's intransigence that held up a possible compromise. W. M. Prichard had conferred with Andrew H. Green, the city's comptroller, and wrote to Olmsted: "Mr. Jackson said to me 'If Mr. Olmsted will come down himself and see me I think this whole matter can be adjusted.' "[5] The matter remained unresolved into the next year. And by November, 1876, Olmsted's future difficulties were to become less compromisable because Andrew Green had been removed from his position. Once Green was gone, the parks were open to various onslaughts from which that gentleman had protected them.

Olmsted should not have cared so deeply as he did about the New York parks job, but the fact is that he did. He continued his work for the city even while the suit dragged on. Central Park had been the beginning of all his design work, and he had an emotional attachment to the place out of proportion to the time he spent upon it. He wished passionately for his ideas to prevail in New York City.

Olmsted's persistence extended even to ideas he knew to be wrong; this showed in the way he held onto his loyalty to the corrupt national Republican Party. He had been so revolted by the corrupt Democratic regimes closer at hand in New York City that he experienced a visceral reaction against a

Democratic president. His friends, except for Charles Eliot Norton, had deserted the Grand Old Party. After the election of Rutherford Hayes in November, 1876, Olmsted wrote to Norton: "I am very glad that you imagine that I agree with you in politics for since the Nation stampeded I have felt lonely."[6]

Even Katherine Wormeley, keeping in touch, had written critically to her old chief, "I cannot help thinking that your life in New York where the democrats are rampant, odious, and corrupt, darkens your mind, and even narrows it."[7] Olmsted kept his letters from Katherine Wormeley. She continued to ask his advice or his help from time to time in matters of business: an old family portrait to sell or a school to start were excuses to consult Frederick Olmsted and extend a raveling connection. She concerned herself, at a distance, about the health of his body and mind. She owned some property in Washington, D.C., and asked Olmsted's advice about selling lots. He had a competent friend look up her property and informed her of their relatively worthlessness due to their location. He answered her politely, but there was more and more constraint in his replies. She confessed herself surprised that Mrs. Olmsted did not, when she wrote to her, answer her letters. Yet Mrs. Olmsted once invited Miss Wormeley to stay with them; Miss Wormeley declined.

Fred and Mary lived in each other in a settled and yet still mutually fascinated way that no offer of intrusion could disturb. The relationship with his wife was the one constant of Olmsted's personal life. Yet Frederick was thoughtless in his care for her day-to-day satisfactions. He exiled her, for her own good, from him and from the house, during the unhealthy summers. Her letters in the early summer of 1877 show how, with all the willful strength of an acute, lively mind, on vacation, she was bored.

To her eldest son John, with whom she corresponded as if they had been friends rather than mother and son, Mary wrote from Allen's Hotel, North Elba, Lake Placid, on July 2, 1877, requesting first that he send fishing gear for Fred, Jr. And she confessed, "Now the novelty has worn off, I am bored to death. Running after Fred as much as I must tires me. I suppose Lake Placid is the best place for us in the Adirondacks and the young people are very nice."[8] Responding to Frederick's letter about Owen's homecoming, she was anxious: "I am very sorry to hear that Owen has lost flesh. He was about as thin as he could be already. Are you all comfortable? Owing to this Fred care-taking I cannot write letters." She betrayed her impatience at the make-believe of vacationing. "Last evening Mrs. Brace made up a party to Legget's Camp and they built a fire and sang songs and told stories until the morn rose. It was pretty and the young folks enjoyed themselves and I enjoyed seeing them, but I am afraid I am too old for that sort of thing. I kept thinking of the messiness [?—word uncertain] of camp life. Loring [Brace] has taken Charlotte out in the canoe."[9] Mary had not minded camp life when she and Fred went on forty-mile rides in California, but theirs was an equal companionship. Mary suffered from a robust impatience the reason for which she may not have fully understood. Wives of professional men were supposed to be idle except for family responsibilities. But she developed a querulousness, showing from time to time in her letters, a trait not really in keeping with the strength of her character. "I have nobody to stand up for me, and I am afraid that even if you [i.e., John] or Owen came you would go waiting on the girls and abandon Mollie [Marion] and Fred and I. . . . I am so homesick, tell Dad."[10]

Charlotte, an intense and unsettled girl of twenty-two, wrote a letter from the same holiday to her brother John betraying a mixture of admiration and amusement at her independent mother. "Mother didn't like minister who was to conduct services at house, took refuge in Boat House."[11]

Since the strike had confused and paralyzed the city, it seemed a good thing that Olmsted had sent his family away. They stayed away while the threat of violence in New York gradually diminished. Mary was not at home to see how, toward the end of the summer and into the fall, her husband fell into a state of causeless worrying. Their roles were reversed; it was Fred now who longed for Mary to come home; but his wife found occupations at Lake Placid to amuse her and stayed on.

In August Fred wrote to Mary about being ill and in bed for a day, "one of my usual summer attacks opening with a faint, purging and running into headaches and neuralgia with moderate diarhea." He asked her in all naivete —he being the landscape architect—"Should the hollihocks be cut down now that their mission is accomplished for this year?   Affectly, Fred."[12] But Mary was the backyard gardener.

He was lonely for her: "I have become possessed with the impression that you are somewhere near the North Pole."

Being thrown closely together with him, the others away, Olmsted was beginning to see that his eldest son John was moody and perhaps ill. He sent him to a doctor and reported to Mary that he had done so. He thought he might send John on a tour of works in progress, in Washington, Baltimore, Buffalo, Montreal, and Boston. Then happily he recalled his own youthful excitement when he went abroad for the first time. He wrote to ask Mary, "I am strongly tempted to give him a six weeks trip to Europe. . . . What do you think of it?"[13] Not hearing from Mary, he wrote, "You disappoint me by saying nothing about my proposition to John. I have almost made up my mind to it but don't like to speak to him till I hear from you."[14] But having heard, he reported to her, "I counted as much as I could on John's apathetic habit, but after I got your approval of his transatlantic vacation I could not keep down my own excitement in sympathy with him."[15] He told, as if it had been a joke on him, the story of the reversal of roles: the son's calm, the father's excitement. It was settled. The father duly saw the son off to Europe on September 11. He wrote to his wife that day, "I suppose I can live another week without you, but I am somewhat doubtful."

He told her he would come to Albany to meet her on the night boat. And, "I need a Secretary very much and shall put you to work as soon as you come."[16]

When he could not sleep at night he continued to write fragments of memories and paragraphs out of his own doctrine of design[17]: "Our country has entered upon a stage of progress in which its welfare is to depend on the convenience, safety, order and economy of life in its great cities. It cannot prosper independently of them."[18] So far had he come from the boy who had idled his days away upon a hillside looking down at the Connecticut River, all the space of a sparsely populated countryside stretching out from him. He felt as deeply as ever the beauty of a line of trees upon a hill-ridge or the path of a river through a valley bottom, but he had now also an educated concern for people packed close in cities. He had come to relish the quickness and sharpness of people who rubbed in daily life against each other; friction made for flexibility and put an edge on wit. Cities contained the means to make a living and the means to make living a pleasure in the various arts. Therefore, city living should be decent and humane.

This mind, calm and free in its meditations on professional problems, could not, however, sustain with equanimity the particular concussions of bad luck he had suffered in this one particular city for the past year. The action of the Board of Park Commissioners in declaring vacant his office as landscape architect had been rescinded. By that action he had been reinstated in his position. And Judge Spier had ruled in favor of Olmsted in his claim for back pay. But these were technical victories. The unpleasantness between architect and board remained. Some members of the Board of Park Commissioners questioned whether their landscape architect could work part-time, for a salary, for the United States Capitol project and still continue his New York public parks salary. So that with one difficulty ended, another arose. Olmsted, on October 12, 1877, wrote formally to the former president of the Board of Park Commissioners, S. H. Wales, whom he considered his friend, to gain from him a statement that his professional work in Washington for three days a week had been accepted by the board when it was begun and did not indeed interfere with his New York parks position.[19] Olmsted's gaining of the point did not restore good feelings with the commissioners in office.

Frederick was suffering also as a parent in a trouble involving Charlotte. John had been difficult, but Charlotte's case was serious enough to warrant intervention by a friend. Lucia Knapp, the wife of schoolmaster Knapp, wrote a candid letter to her friend, telling him that he was handling one of his children, Charlotte, in the wrong way. The girl was twenty-two in March, 1877, and as yet unsure of herself. She had spent a part of the summer with the Knapps, apparently helping them with the children in the school.

On October 3, Mrs. Knapp wrote to Frederick: "Mr. Knapp was much impressed with the clearness of understanding, and the ability of handling that she brought to the work." She urged Frederick to back his daughter in a new ambition. Charlotte had conceived the idea of organizing and running a kindergarten. Mrs. Knapp went on,

It seems to me a crisis in Charlotte's life and that through the course which shall now be pursued, she may become a happy and useful, or a disappointed and frivolous woman. Charlotte's faults are plainly exhibited to all,—her virtues are carefully hid . . . the most discouraging point in her character so far has been a morbid lack of interest in everything, which almost seemed to amount to heartlessness. Now she has a wholesome interest in one thing, give her a chance to follow it—throw her on her own resources, which are considerable and so give her independence—put her among new people, where she will not be fancying her friends do not appreciate her . . . above all, let her feel that she has that liberty of action which is the right of every sane adult person—and see if she will not succeed. If she fails, at least justice will have been done her. We make a mistake, I am sure, when we try to keep grown up sons and daughters in leading-strings—but it is hard for a girl to strike out without a little encouragement from her home. . .

I have faith in Charlotte,—in her ability and prospects—and if you will only have it too, it will be the greatest blessing to her.[20]

This letter implies much about Mary and Frederick's treatment of their dearly beloved children. John's reactions at this period, when he was twenty-four and still treated as a dependent child by both his father and mother, bears out Lucia Knapp's sharp observations. Yet other elements of the parents' relations to their children should be disentangled to balance a judgment. Owen, in spite of his delicate health, was allowed to go live among strangers in Montreal and to begin, the following year, to make a rough living for himself in the West. John, seemed, at this time, as responsible for his difficulties as his father. And, what is more to the point, Charlotte was to show later that the psychical difficulties she was having at this time were at least partly unalterably interior and deep-seated, probably not altogether related to whether she should teach kindergarten or not. Mrs. Knapp's generous advocacy was, in the end, wasted. Charlotte did not take up an independent career.

The difficult year, with public and private needs claiming attention, wound down. On October 12, Olmsted received thanks from the Hot Springs, Arkansas, installation for his willingness to design the grounds of the watering place. On November 23, Charles Sargent wrote that he had arranged for the two of them to visit Wellesley. If Olmsted had been able to be objective at this time about the ugly maneuvers of the New York parks commissioners, he would have seen that he had many different new kinds of opportunities opening up before him and that he need not care so much about New York. But his perspective was short-range at the time, through his being tired, sleepless, and emotionally shaky. Each particular blow clanged in his mind with an acute penetration.

The city comptroller (no longer Green), without any feeling of colleague-ship or loyalty toward Olmsted, wrote to the parks commissioners on December 12, "The salary of Mr. Frederick Law Olmsted, Landscape Architect [has been withheld for the present], for the reasons that he has been informed. Mr. Olmsted renders little or no service in that capacity; that his duties outside of the City of New York render his absence necessary and frequent, that he had been absent from his duties for twenty-six days during the month of October, and that the parks are in that state of completion that the services of an architect can be dispensed with."[21] (Olmsted's and Vaux's view was that the Parks Department needed a permanent landscape architect in charge.)

When Olmsted was in good trim, he did not hesitate to wage verbal war, but he did not take up the fight this time. He wrote to S. H. Wales, the former president of the board, to try to establish the firm agreement he had made earlier with the department, but he went no further. Olmsted seems then to have given up the kind of aggressive resistance which belonged to his temperament. It was as if the everyday pugnacious Olmsted were no longer there to react in the accustomed way to the blows of life. And evidence negative and positive suggests that he was in some sense ill from the end of 1877 through most of 1878.

His family and friends connived to persuade Olmsted to take a rest in the shape of a trip abroad. John was already in Europe; Frederick would join him there. It was hoped that he would enjoy a rediscovery of parks and gardens and meetings with his peers. The board of commissioners of the New York parks, with a kind of ominous smoothness, granted Mr. Olmsted leave without pay "on account of the state of his health."[22]

As if in a fever of activity to assert the solidity of his position, already toppled, Olmsted continued, up to the moment of leaving, to send professional and official communications to the commissioners. On January 2, 1878, he asserted again his opposition to a "menagerie" in the park. "It is so placed as to be a serious injury to the Central Park."[23] On the same date, he drafted a letter about Manhattan Square and the placing of the new Museum of Natural History.

On January 5, the board abolished the office that Olmsted officially headed, the Bureau of Design and Superintendence. They reappointed Frederick Law Olmsted "Consulting Landscape Architect" to be paid for his services "from time to time, as they are availed of."[24] The job of his chief clerk, H. A. Martin, was also abolished. On January 8, Olmsted was on the way to Europe and apparently from this time protected by his family from most of the repercussions of these events.

Although it is not easy to discern, except by indirection, what happened to Frederick Olmsted when he left New York in January, 1877, it is clear enough what happened to those left behind: Mary was in a state of anxiety; Owen feeling himself grown up assumed a new protective attitude toward the family; and Olmsted's friends, aroused to combat, set about to rectify the dismissal. Howard A. Martin wrote to Olmsted on January 25 that the removal was "in violation of the By-Laws." And he went on, "Godkin and Eidlitz and others are considering now what can be done in the Legislature by way of retribution."[25]

On January 22, a letter of protest had been presented to the commissioners and also appeared in the New York *World*. The letter praised Olmsted "in the main the designer" of both Central and Prospect parks, and stated that New York needed him "for completion of the design." Over such impressive signatures as August Belmont, Henry Havemeyer, Bayard Taylor, A. Bierstadt, Harper & Bros., Roosevelt & Sons, D. Appleton & Co., Henry Holt, Whitelaw Reid, Clarence King, John Jay, and others, the statement represented itself as speaking for many citizens: "It is not unnatural that we, as taxpayers, should ascribe the successful management of the Park for the last twenty years largely to Mr. Olmsted's connection with it. . . . No other enterprise in which the city has engaged and on which the municipal funds have been spent since 1860 has been equally satisfactory."[26]

For Mary Olmsted, there was a distressing complication. She had not only to suffer anxiety for Frederick, and endure her own prideful scorn at the way the commissioners treated her husband, but to have the pain of an old friend joining in an ugly way in the controversy. The generous outpouring of letters in praise of Frederick Olmsted neglected to attribute proper credit to Calvert Vaux in the designing of Central and Prospect parks. The decade had not been very productive of jobs for Vaux. Between 1873 and 1879, he had contributed terraces to the Buffalo Park, but with Olmsted in charge of the superintendence. He had designed independently the government grounds at Ottawa, Canada, as well as an East River Park (with Samuel Parsons) in New York City.[27] He had suffered since the mid-sixties a sense of public opinion's invariably giving more credit to Olmsted than to him. He and Olmsted had had rather tender relations about this matter from time to time, but they had succeeded in getting along. Olmsted had been entirely correct in attributing the proper share of the work to Vaux, but his manner of mixing with men of influence and of being the one to write reports, had put him forward as the dominant figure in the partnership. What finally aroused Vaux's expression of what was usually a painful and hidden emotion was a letter which E. L. Godkin wrote to the New York *Tribune* following Olmsted's departure for Europe in January, 1878. Godkin wished simply to help his friend. He too left out Vaux's part in the New York parks. Vaux, therefore, wrote an intemperate letter to the same newspaper on February 18, 1878:

I have waited a sufficiently long time to allow of Mr. Olmsted's disavowal of the greedy misrepresentations made in his behalf by Mr. E. L. Godkin, in regard to the authorship of the designs of the Central and Brooklyn Parks, of which I am the author in every respect, equally with Mr. Olmsted. . . . I have been throughout [the past 20 years] loyal to Mr. Olmsted under the most trying circumstances. His representative, Mr. E. L. Godkin, who knows all the circumstances of the case, has now the repulsively bad faith to step forward publicly and administer our joint estate: to F. L. Olmsted, everything; to C. Vaux, the cut direct. I call for another administrator.[28]

Apparently Calvert Vaux was unaware that Frederick Olmsted was out of the country. And it is obvious from this letter that Vaux had not been in close touch with the family at this time and was honestly unaware of the illness Olmsted had been suffering. Emotion had darkened his expression of emotion and caused him to think that Olmsted had inspired Godkin's letter.

Godkin, who had not thought one way or another about Vaux, tried to set things right the next day (February 19) in another letter to the *Tribune*. "Allow me to say, in reply to Mr. Vaux's note in your issue of to-day, that my letters relating to Mr. Olmsted's dismissal were written after he had left the country, and that he neither suggested nor inspired them, and is in no way responsible for them. If they have done any injustice to Mr. Vaux, I have no doubt he will correct it whenever he has an opportunity. I believe a friend here has sent him one of them, but his family refrain from troubling him with business matters, as he has gone abroad for his health."[29]

With dignity for one so young, taking his first step into adult life, Owen Olmsted wrote to settle this ugliness for his absent father. Mary Olmsted obviously had a share in composing the letter; it appeared over Owen's name in the *Tribune* on February 20 and said in part:

My father Mr. Frederick Law Olmsted sailed for Europe, as is well known, on the 8th of January, on a three months leave of absence from the Department of Public Parks, with strict orders from his physician to withdraw his mind from all business concerns.

Therefore in view of certain recent communications in the newspapers, I think it my duty to state in his behalf that no one has or can have the smallest authority for claiming for Mr. Olmsted either more or less than an equal share with Mr. Calvert Vaux in the design of the Central and Brooklyn Parks.[30]

Mary Olmsted wrote directly to Calvert Vaux on February 21, explaining Owen's letter to the *Tribune* (which may well have been largely her letter also):

I have done this at the risk of incurring my husband's displeasure for meddling in business affairs, in order to gratify in his old partner what seems to me an injudicious desire for advertisment for there is not the smallest doubt that if you had waited patiently only eight short weeks for my husband's return your interests would have been much better served.

Two gentlemen called on my yesterday to give me intelligence of Viele's operations in support of his pretensions to having himself planned the parks. I trust you will not feel obliged to give him battle until you can have the aid of Mr. Olmsted's sound judgement and practiced pen.

I subscribe myself, though I own you have made it difficult to do so,

Very sincerely your friend,

Mary C. Olmsted.[31]

Calvert Vaux tried to remedy his ill-judged remarks in a note to Mary Olmsted and in a second letter to the editor of the *Tribune* on February 21:

I desire to withdraw the injurious expressions used in my letter with reference to Mr. E. L. Godkin, as I learn that his neglect to give me due credit was entirely unintentional.

Then, in the warmth that was as true to his nature as his hasty anger had been, he wrote his plea for Olmsted's restoration to a position of authority in the parks system.

Mr. Olmsted has for five years occupied a position [Vaux was numbering the years since the most recent renewal of the position] which has secured to the Park that continuity of control which . . . can never be relaxed with safety, and the public interest will for this and a thousand and other reasons be best served by his holding "unhampered," and for as long a period as he can be induced to stay, a controlling position in regard to the development of its manifold possibilities.

He sweated at the "labor" of it at the outset, and only half succeeded. We have worked and played together at the art of it for twenty years, and have only half succeeded. I trust that more than a half success awaits his attempt to develop the poetry of it; to have the right to do this is the romantic dream of a life so fully saturated with the capacity for hard work, that the few steps now intervening between the dream and the reality will be easy enough to take— so let the watchword of the future with all who are interested in the Central Park be "an unhampered position for Mr. Olmsted." Fair play for all concerned, and God's blessing on the work.[32]

Olmsted himself thought that he was done with this rocky piece of ground in which he had invested a good part of himself. His reactions during his months of absence from work were uncharacteristic. The chronology compiled for Frederick, Jr.'s life of his father lists an elaborate and extensive tour which Frederick, Sr., and John Charles presumably followed during the four months, January to April, 1878.[33] The places listed include London, Bruges, The Hague, Amsterdam, Frankfurt, Munich, Venice, Florence, Pisa, Genoa, Milan, Como, Turin, Macon, Dijon. There is no reason to doubt that Olmsted saw these places. He evidently purchased Venetian glass. After his return, almost the only letter in his hand out of this time inquired about the delivery of the glass. But a great silence hovers over the trip. For so active and expressive a man the silence must have been significant. He wrote no letters home to family, to friends, or to business associates. Or they have been destroyed. This was a family which saved every scrap of paper on which any of its members wrote, no matter how trivial. It was a strangely passive Frederick who accompanied John on the trip. One can only picture the older man at this time protected and guided in some manner by the younger man. There is no evidence of pauses for periods of invalidism. However, such gaps in the trip may be at least surmised. Another piece of mute evidence surviving is the collection of letters of introduction which accompanied Olmsted on the journey. They sit quietly in their envelopes, preserved, evidently unused, speaking eloquently of their nondelivery. It is possible that Olmsted, finding himself more famous than he had known, had no need of them, but he was ordinarily punctilious in social courtesies. He would have delivered these introductions in a gentlemanly fashion before asking favors of superintendents of gardens or curators of parks, that is, if he had used them.

After Frederick's return home in late April, 1878, his family stood between him and demands made upon him from the outside. No new business was taken on by the Olmsted firm during 1878; there had not been much new business assumed in 1877. Inquiries from new clients and the keeping of old business going were handled entirely by John. As an instance, on May 11, 1878, John wrote to Eidlitz a long, detailed letter about the installation of electrical lighting in the new capitol at Albany.[34] What is even more significant, John wrote for his father to "Dear Uncle Harry (Albert Harry Olmsted in Hartford), "Father has asked me to write to you for $500. As our cash balance with you, if I am not mistaken, is only $146, and as we shall probably call for more in the course of the summer, I suggest as the best way of meeting the case the sale of one of the $2000 western mortgages."[35] As this letter shows, even personal family matters were being handled by the son.

Albert sent the money and wrote on May 23, not to Fred, but about Fred to John: "Can't Fred come up here so as to be at leisure May 30th, Decoration Day? Lou and I think of picnicing at the Tower and could make room for him in our carriage."[36] It was as if tacitly understood between Albert and John that the father was in the care of the son.

On May 23, George Radford wrote to John rather than to Frederick about business.[37] But on May 27, H. A. Martin wrote to his former superior in the Parks Department: "John informs me that you go to Albany Tuesday night."[38] Olmsted was trying to resume his work. On June 4, however, Albert wrote Fred concerning two gentlemen, Burr and Brown, who wished to see Olmsted: "*If you would,* telegraph to A. E. Burr.... If you don't want to see them, *write me* and I will explain."[39] They were all being careful yet of Frederick and fending off business from him.

During the summer and fall of 1878, Edwin Godkin asked Olmsted to stay at his house in Cambridge. Whatever tentative business Olmsted undertook during this time was in the Boston area. It is probable that he talked with Sargent about the Arboretum and with Godkin about the campaign to save the Niagara Falls setting. On July 1, the Harvard chapter of Phi Beta Kappa made Olmsted an honorary member. There is no evidence that he attended the ceremony.

There are a few penciled drafts of business letters saved which show that by October, 1878, Olmsted began to write to clients; one was a draft of a letter to H. H. Hunnewell (October 11).[40] On October 26 Olmsted addressed to Charles Sargent a sketch of the Arboretum.[41] This project helped pull Olmsted back into activity. Something of his usual firm handling of an obligation to himself shows in a personal letter, the draft of which survives, written to an Italian dealer in Venetian glass, one A. Salviati. On November 4 Olmsted informed him, "I returned yesterday to New York and am glad to say that I have all the articles in perfect order."[42] These were specimens of glasswork which had evidently caught his imagination during that time when John was guiding him about Europe, in one attempt after another, one surmises, to distract his father from his miseries.

In the meantime, the scattered members of the family went about the business of living their own lives, in addition to sharing among themselves concern for the head of the family. Owen, adventurous as ever, had persuaded the family that his good health would be served by his going west, under the sponsorship of Clarence King, to learn cattle ranching. By June he was at a ranch near Cheyenne, Wyoming, waiting for the arrival of King, who was to initiate him into the adventurous business and perhaps assist him in locating a herd. But Owen's ranching career did not go forward as smoothly as he may have hoped in the East. He found it helpful first to apprentice himself as a ranch hand, and it was in this hard-working role that Owen wrote to John from King's Owl Creek Ranch on December 1, asking about his father's business, "Will the Albany Capitol be finished in time and did they put in the electric light as they wanted to?" He prided himself on the way he had fitted into ranch life. He wrote as if he had been a part of this life for a long time: "The last roundup of the season terminated last week so we have now settled down for the winter."[43] He presented a picture of himself to John as relishing the experience of taking his monthly turn at cooking for the bunkhouse mess, of chopping wood for fires on frosty mornings, of getting up early in order to ride out and see a sunrise stretched across the iron-cold plains.

Owen's not always dependable patron, Clarence King, restless as usual, had come back to New York in the fall and found a document which required an immediate answer. He wrote a quick note to Frederick Olmsted after opening his mail: "Coming home last night I found on my table the invitation to Miss Charlotte's marriage which took me all by surprise."[44] Whether the engagement took the family by surprise is not clear. But Miss Olmsted, giving up her plans for a kindergarten, married John Bryant, a Boston physician.

This would be one more tie to the Boston-Cambridge area for Charlotte's father and mother. Here also were stout friends, Edwin Godkin and Charles Sargent. Here was work to occupy Frederick, the Arboretum and the projected Boston parks. After being sunk for some months in a morass of distress and inaction, Olmsted began to see ahead, at last, hope of work, of friendship, of ambition, and of accomplishment—no longer tied to New York.

CHAPTER XXIV

Recovery

You can have no idea what a drug life had been to me for three years or more. I did not appreciate it myself until I began last summer to get better.

—F. L. O., to Charles Brace, March 7, 1882[1]

ON A COLD DAY in January, 1879, Olmsted found himself enjoying his work again, surveying the grounds of the building inside which United States senators resisted appropriating enough money for him to do exactly what he pleased. He wrote to Charles Brace, "My work at Washington being pottering and out of doors though fatiguing agreed with me."[2]

He had assessed his problem with the Capitol building in a fresh and hopeful way. What was lacking was fit ground for the structure to stand on. There were ill-kept grounds on the east front. And viewed from the lower west side, the structure seemed slipping off Capitol Hill. Olmsted saw that the rubbish must be cleared from the east front to make a dignified, leafy, green ground for statesmen and citizens to use as an approach. On the west front, he was determined to do away with the ugly earth mounds piled up across the base. He would create a majestic terrace to shore up the building. The base would then seem properly to bear the weight and authority of the dome.

The carrying out of the idea would take several more years of effort, of pleasing senators, of hiring engineers and horticulturists and guiding them to achieve his plan. Yet the whole idea shone complete in his mind the cold day in January when he renewed acquaintance with the project after a difficult dead interval away from work. This was a beginning again. Before him were to be the most productive years of his life. This was to be true in spite of personal tragedies and continuing difficulties with men not very anxious to give in to his desires. The years from 1879 to 1882 were to be a slow building of a new foundation, a learning of a way to work with less strain. Then year after year into the early 1890s he worked with full imaginative vigor.

But to be true to Olmsted's life, one must to the extent possible find, in his letters and those of friends to him, the tone of that time, the accidents, the sharp pains and griefs, as well as a slow swelling of tranquillity in the midst of a large achievement.

For Olmsted, working was living. He knew no other way to exist than by thinking, feeling, and breathing work day by day; he only fooled himself in believing that he escaped from work in short, half-hearted periods of rest or holiday. He was often abstracted—seeing far off fields and expanses of water and wood, or in his imagination running roads through cities— even while walking absentmindedly from room to room. An affectionate man, Olmsted was happy to have the hum of family life about him. He was customarily courteous to his children and their friends, yet he unconsciously required a great deal of care by the other members of the family for the sake of his peace and comfort. He had a way of talking unaffectedly with little children, but he was less able to converse easily with young people, perhaps shying away from the very kind of pain he had suffered in growing up in his father's house.

He had the most heartfelt need for Mary's support, but he left her alone for long periods of time in which she had to find ways to support her own emotional life. Mary understood very well Frederick's needs and was a sort of arbiter of family behavior to induce the others to help in this task. In the summer of 1879, Mary in Cambridge wrote to John in New York asking tolerance from him: "Take good care of your father and don't contradict him; he is not such a fool as you think him!"[3] With a certain amount of ruthlessness, she put John at the service of Frederick, whom she was devoutly glad to see regaining a normal tempo of self-absorbed activity.

Yet even in the summer of 1879, Olmsted thought of all of his children as largely dependent on him. John, nearing the end of a prolonged adolescence, was twenty-six. Charlotte, married but living nearby, was twenty-four. Owen, in Wyoming, was not yet quite twenty-two. Marion in this midsummer was seventeen. Rick, the youngest, the center of all attention, was to be nine years old on July 24.

Slowly disencumbering himself of a physical and emotional lethargy, Olmsted worked at a number of projects. He joined Richard Morris Hunt in designing the Vanderbilt family mausoleum on a hill at New Dorp, Staten Island, and so renewed an acquaintance with the Vanderbilt family. He continued to visit Cambridge where he and Charles Eliot Norton plotted to save the natural beauty of Niagara Falls. At this time they labored to secure the signature of noted men for a petition which would give public notoriety to this concern. Thomas Carlyle was their proudest coup. Together, Olmsted and Norton sponsored the writing of articles about the attractions of Niagara by a young journalist, J. B. Harrison, who was already something of a protégé of Norton's. Sometimes the two men, or one or another, furnished the funds for the articles or they helped Harrison find a position with a magazine. Olmsted still traveled occasionally to Albany in the long work of completing the state capitol.

He shared with one of the architects of that project yet another work, a large building program for the Ames family of North Easton, Massachusetts. In this town where the original shovel works had initiated the Ames fortune —their shovels being used in California in the gold rush and in digging the pathway for the rails of the first transcontinental railroad—the sons of Oakes Ames were commemorating their father. In good works for their own community they were attempting to wipe out the stigma of the Credit Mobilier Scandal and to make clear a real achievement in helping build the Union Pacific. Oliver Ames, to be lieutenant governor and then governor of Massachusetts, along with other members of the family, enlisted Richardson's and Olmsted's talents to build and site a memorial town hall, a library, and family residences. This work kept Richardson and Olmsted in close touch. Olmsted was, at this time, as imaginatively aware of Richardson's ambitions as of his own.

A few years later, Richardson brought Olmsted into the circle of Henry and Marian Adams in Washington. Richardson had completed a house for Nicholas Longworth Anderson in that city, and Anderson entertained the architect and the architect's friend, Olmsted, one evening in his new house and included the Adamses at dinner. This was on a Thursday evening, November 2, 1882. Marian Adams was impressed with Olmsted and invited him to come to dinner at her table at 1607 H Street the following Sunday night, November 5, along with Olmsted's old and revered friend, Professor Asa Gray.[4] It was probably through seeing what Richardson could do for his friend Nick Anderson that Henry Adams began to think of asking Richardson to build him a house too. It was a small community of taste and learning. Anderson, Adams, and Richardson had all been in the same class at Harvard. Olmsted and Gray came out of the same New England background with friends and associations in common. Gray was related to Charles Loring Brace. Olmsted was already acquainted with Henry Adams's brother Charles Francis. Charles Francis was to bring Richardson and Olmsted together in another joint venture, a design and setting for a new library in Quincy, Massachusetts.

In resuming active professional work in 1879, the most absorbing occupation had become the planning of the enlarged Boston park system. Here Olmsted had what he most loved, scope for a great public project. He loosed his imagination to roam among possibilities. He had his son John write to his former professor, A. E. Verrill, about an idea he had for the proposed Charles River tidal basin. He wished this watery space to add joy to the life of the city by becoming a living museum for certain kinds of wildlife. John questioned the professor about "the feasibility especially of maintaining in it small whales, porpoises, dolphins, narwhals or other cetatious mammals, flying fish, bonito, sturgeon, or other fish that would make some display."[5]

Ideas such as this Olmsted threw off in a healthy superfluity. Playfulness showed in a plan he had for a developer's beach at Rockaway Point, New York. He said that what was needed here was "a general gay, grand, popular holiday effect."[6] There should be "various moveable entertainments" including "a nightly display of colored fires, bombs and rockets ... simple fountains, both wall and jet ... gay awnings ... row-boats more gaily painted and furnished than is usual."[7] Rockaway Beach in his design was not accepted. But Olmsted had regained his imaginative equilibrium.

And he had also the gift necessary and preliminary to the flowering of imaginative decisions. He lost himself within the sensuous outlines of a physical scene, let play upon his senses impressions of color and pattern, and moved among these perceptions like a boat drifting on a stream. Then—and only then—came the sharp decisions necessary to bring feeling into the particular shape of design.

The schedule of travel and work in which he involved himself once more gradually accelerated. He found himself writing more of his own letters rather than leaving them to John. He took on more projects while continuing the larger works in Washington, Albany, and Boston. Thus, during the end of the 1870s and the beginning of the 1880s, Olmsted resumed his commanding position in the profession he had helped devise.

Yet it was also in these years that one anxiety and tragedy after another afflicted his family.

The first anxiety concerned Marion. The Olmsteds' younger daughter was very like one of those American girls about whom Henry James was writing a new kind of novel. Marion was shy but self-possessed, observant, and humorous at nineteen. She had a close relationship with her father which included a familiarity in teasing him. She mothered both her father and Rick. When a chance came to go abroad with her Aunt Bertha and Uncle William Niles, she embraced the idea eagerly.

Uncle William, a prominent clergyman in Litchfield, Connecticut, was not well, and it was thought that a holiday abroad would aid him to recover from a too great emotional and mental excitability, one sign of which was his inability to refrain from talking too much and writing too much. Bertha would be glad to have a young and steady hand and head beside her on this not altogether easy voyage. Marion prepared happily to go, with her family's encouragement, and with a letter of credit arranged by Uncle Albert Olmsted, the banker. Frederick, of course, footed her bills; the Nileses were not well-to-do people. The three travelers undertook the crossing of the Atlantic late in 1880. They sent back reassuring words about a pleasant journey. Long stays abroad were customary when sea travel was an ordeal.

By the spring of 1881, the Connecticut innocents were in Rome. There, in April, 1881, Marion was exposed to what was probably typhoid, the dreaded Rome or Naples fever, depending in which city one contracted the disease. Marion had been in Naples; she went to bed in Rome. She grew dangerously ill there, and the uncle and aunt cabled her parents the exact and frightening bad news. Frederick replied with a steady kind of courage:

"I write you and William and Marion, if the dear girl is living when this comes to you.... We are so sorry for you and afraid that it will be a setback to William.

"The days are very long as we wait from hour to hour for the second message but Mary's courage is rising as it always does in great trials."[8]

A second cable brought the news that Marion's progress was regular and the outlook favorable. Fred wrote again to Bertha: "I had felt before that she was very dear to me but I did not know how much of what of hopefulness in life is left to me depended on her.... Probably Mary feels this more than I do."[9]

William Niles wrote to them that Marion had probably caught the disease in a dirty hotel. He needed more money for doctors and for medicine and special food. Albert Olmsted, with his usual tartness, thought Niles the minister was extravagant even in this dire situation. In midsummer he sent an additional thousand-dollar letter of credit to help the marooned travelers and wrote to Fred: "Of course Marion's illness made extra expense inevitable, but I guess the Bishop, like most other Revs., is careless about money matters and will spend twice as much as he should."[10]

Marion recovered slowly as her uncle and aunt moved her out of fever-ridden towns, first to Florence, later to Vienna, where she went out to dinner for the first time and walked about, then finally to Leamington in England for a rest at the home of Frederick's old friend Alfred Field. Mary and Frederick were at last assured of Marion's recovery by October, 1881. But in the same month they had another anxiety to face.

They had bad news about their son Owen. A telegram came to Olmsted out of the great distances of the Wyoming-Montana border where Owen had set up his own homestead near the Powder River. Owen was gravely, maybe fatally, ill. This was not expected. Although the family was aware that this slight young man, the son who had turned out to be independent and self-reliant to an extravagant degree, was delicate in his health, it was believed that outdoor life in the West would cure him. A note in Frederick Olmsted, Jr.'s, hand, placed a long time after the event among the family papers, states that Owen had gone west with tuberculosis.[11] But, as one will see in an exchange of opinion that Frederick, Sr., had with a competent physician after Owen's death, neither he nor the other members of the family had entirely believed, when Owen went west, that he had a fatal illness, or that what ailed him was tuberculosis. Perhaps they could not bring themselves to believe the fact because John Hull, Owen's father, had died cruelly young of tuberculosis very shortly after Owen was born. It must have seemed too difficult a fact for Mary and Frederick to believe. Frederick was, after the death, to talk of Owen's disease as having been "diabetes," and, of course, it is possible that Owen had this additional trouble also.

Owen resembled his father John Hull in appearance and temperament, and was, with his handsome face and figure, and frank, open temperament, the most immediately lovable of all Frederick's and Mary's children. The trembling anxiety held within the bounds of the family walls can be imagined during the days they awaited news about him.

On October 19, 1881, Olmsted sent Charles Norton his "Mount Royal Report" and added a restrained personal note: "We are again under the tension of a great domestic anxiety. A telegram saying that our boy Owen is 'very low.' He is two days' journey from a telegraph office. We have telegraphed for a doctor to be sent and our John started by train to go to him —will have reached Chicago tomorrow, but without an hour's rest it will take him a week to get to him. We cannot look for another message under ten days."[12] Olmsted also let Calvert Vaux know about Owen's illness and received back an impulsively heartfelt letter from his old colleague: "I was intending to acknowledge your kind note about Downing [Vaux's son] when I received your last card with the grievous news from your boy Owen.... That he may pull through is our sincere trust. He was a brave young fellow and held his own—and other people's, with precocious tenacity. Let us know directly if you receive better news as the suspense will be painful to us as to you."[13] (October 28, 1881). Albert sent an emotional outburst to Fred: "He was always a pet of mine... *And* [if he should die] *will he not the sooner meet his own Dear Father*, whom he never knew, but who undoubtedly has watched over him!"[14] On November 18, Clarence King assured Olmsted that his silence was not "heartlessness." King's mother and brother both had been ill and had required his care. But he would go to Owen if it would do good and he was able to tell Fred and Mary that "the Deadwood physician is a very competent one."[15]

John reached the ranch and found Owen still living and able to know him. The older brother succeeded in getting Owen first to Cheyenne and then on the train heading east. John had brought Owen as far as Albany, New York, when Mary and Fred joined them. Owen was in a coma, beyond knowing his parents, as they leaned over him. Owen, just twenty-four, could not live. After the fact of his death, the father picked up a clean white card and wrote down: "Albany, 21st Nov. 1881. Owen died here tranquilly at noon today. Fred'k Law Olmsted."[16] Owen was buried in Hartford. Albert Olmsted in his tidy way reported to Frederick that the minister had refused any fee and that the funeral expenses came to forty-three dollars and seventy-five cents.[17]

During the week after the funeral, Olmsted wrote a letter to Dr. J. L. Campbell, trying to find a reason for the death of his son. Campbell had apparently reviewed Olmsted's description of the course of the disease. He wrote back, on November 30:

I have read and reread the pathetic story of your son Owen's sickness and death. I thank you for the detailed history.

. . . I greatly admire your expressed thankfulness that he remained at his post with fixed and resolute purpose until the end was near. . . . I am very very sorry you and Mrs. Olmsted were denied the privilege [of Owen's being able to know them] while he was himself but there is much compensation in the fact that John reached him in time to extend a brotherly helping hand in the wearisome journey over the plains.

The final cause of Owen's death (Tuberculosis) is a not infrequent termination of diabetes, and I believe the event was delayed by an enforced outdoors life.

Unless better informed I do not incline to criticize the Cheyenne physician because at that time the tubercular troubles may not have developed.[18]

The parents were somehow able after the bleakness of their sorrow to find a kind of reconciliation to Owen's death, perhaps because his brief life had been so all of a piece and so satisfying in its poise and bravery. Mary wrote to a friend, Ruth Tompkins, on March 17, 1882, about various items of family news, "Charlotte has a second son and is doing well. Marion is pretty well and Rick is *very* well." And preceding these evidences of normal family life, she was able to say about Owen, "He had been very happy in his life out yonder. . . . I am glad to have him away from all the hardships and disappointments of the world however much I miss him."[19] Frederick was to say later that the sorrow of this period had had a kind of calming effect on all of them.

But family tranquillity was shattered again, and by a more difficult kind of sorrow. The trouble this time concerned Charlotte. By the fall of 1883, she was twenty-eight years old, living at Cohasset in a house and grounds on which Richardson and Olmsted had jointly and lovingly worked, married to a young physician, John Bryant, the mother of two little boys in whom Frederick, new to the agreeable experience of being a grandfather, took a great interest. Mary and Fred had had earlier puzzling worries about Charlotte. Before she married, she had seemed an unhappy, intense, sometimes nervous girl, wanting to do something on her own, but never getting to the point of doing it. After she married, went to Europe for her honeymoon, and settled near Boston with her husband and began having babies, the parents expected she would be happier. All the outward appurtenances of a proper, well-ordered, if somewhat conventional life were present. But inwardly, Charlotte could not hold back the emotional disintegration which had threatened her earlier.

Evidence of what had happened survives in a letter written on October 7, 1883, by Calvert Vaux to Frederick Olmsted:

Bowyer [Vaux's son] has had a letter from John about Charlotte's sudden failure in mind, and Mrs. Vaux has just returned from seeing Mrs. Olmsted so we know all that can be known, as yet.

I write to assure you of our sympathy, and scan the probable future in the same questioning spirit that *I* did with my son Downing [when he was ill] . . .

My feeling in regard to Charlotte is that the attack is explicable, in connection with the birth of her third child and that the future depends on appropriate *diagnosis* and treatment. . . . I should naturally expect a total recovery as Charlotte is so happily married, and will lack for nothing that skill and affection can give.

I trust that the diagnosis of the Physicians may be accurate—and that you will be able after a time to send me a more encouraging account than Mrs. Olmsted gives today of the prospect for the future.[20]

Charlotte never returned to herself. She had to be cared for in an asylum for the rest of her life. She died in 1908. Fred and his wife contained their distress within the family circle. Only some time later did Frederick report to Charles Brace, in the intimacy of an old friendship, that there was no improvement in his daughter's condition, but that the children—the three boys—were doing well, under the care of their father and a good and reliable housekeeper.[21]

Under the weight of events like this, Olmsted felt older than his years. And it was true that in this good and steady period of prosperous work he carried about in his person the aggravations of many physical ills and nervous disabilities. But he was more or less able to keep them under control. He overcame short bouts of diarrhea, rheumatism, dizziness, and other ills by stoic pauses at impersonal hotels or rests at home, and then resumed his traveling, inspecting, and instructing with unabated nervous and mental energy.

By the early 1880s, he had regained an emotional equilibrium. What is more, he had attained a kind of control of his temper which he had not possessed in his younger years. His balance now, however fragile, was made up of two complementary impulses holding each other in check: one, a motion of his spirit toward a half humorous self-denigration; the other, an ebullient determination to exercise himself to the utmost in performing even superfluous and exacting deeds simply because an inner need asked this. An example of his better tone is evident in a letter he wrote on June 13, 1880, to Thomas Wisedell, the architect of the United States Capitol, and Olmsted's collaborator in their long-enduring work of rehabilitating the building and its setting. The two men had had differences concerning the work. Olmsted detected resentment in something Wisedell wrote to him. He dissipated his own anger by writing the architect a frank letter:

We are both of us invalids, both suffer from a similar form of nervous ir-ritability, extremely provocative of impatience, and if your malady is the hardest . . . I am much the older man, more hardened in my habits and less tractable.

Therefore as to mere expressions of impatience and petulance we have neither [of] us much to boast of, and between ourselves I dont think we need attempt to cast up accounts. If you do and find a balance against me, it can only be a case for forgiveness. . . . and I ask your forgiveness.²²

The same month (June, 1880), Olmsted brought to conclusion a private project. He schemed a way, with the cooperation of old Sanitary Commission friends, to pay for a trip west for his old friend Frederick Knapp, ill with mysterious pains. The schoolmaster was by no means able to pay for an expensive rest cure. Olmsted made it easy for Knapp to accept the gift. He organized and collected a fund, and, on June 8, 1880, he wrote in a depreca-tory way to Knapp that a half dozen friends wished to make him a present of a journey for the sake of his health. Olmsted hand-lettered a heading for this communication—"U.S. Sanitary Commission Special Relief"—and signed it lightheartedly, as if making small potatoes of this joint effort, by comparing it to the great financial efforts of the day, "For the Syndicate, Fred'k. Law Olmsted, Secretary." In the body of this friendly and un-patronizing offer, as if asking Knapp to do them all a favor by reminding them of their old joint effort, Olmsted wrote, "Let me know your mind and it shall be arranged to suit you and not too much arranged." He knew that Knapp agonized over small things that needed to be done to keep his little school in running order. Olmsted said of this care, "You told me you had nothing to do [before getting away] but a little papering and painting and if necessary I shall come on and boss that so that you can start the day after school breaks up. . . . I don't tell you who we are just yet but I will when I know that it's all right."²³

Knapp agreed to the plan after seeing his doctor, and Olmsted followed his friend's trip to points west with interest and compassion. He could not help telling Knapp just how to manage the trip for the best results, how to rest himself on the sleeper, how to vary his journey with visits to friends along the way, keeping up a steady assurance that all the old Sanitary Commission men had rallied round. On July 17, 1880, he sent an additional amount of money to Knapp, telling the traveler his own personal news of being settled happily in Brookline, Massachusetts, near his Boston work, "very comfortably for the summer, and all send love and good wishes."²⁴

Knapp returned to Plymouth in September, reported that the old ache hung on, but that he had at times been relieved of his pains. He sent back an unused check to his friend Olmsted, in a stiff kind of rectitude, an attitude perfectly congenial and acceptable to that friend.

By early 1882, Olmsted was able to look back upon the past several difficult years with some equanimity. He had struggled through a debilitating illness and several devastating sorrows and rediscovered satisfaction in his work. An article, "The Spoils of the Park,"²⁵ which he wrote toward the end of 1881 and had printed in February, 1882, though flawed by bitterness and obscure in some of its references because he wished not to injure personally some of the public men associated with unworthy acts in the parks of New York City, had helped to clear his mind. It was as if, in writing "The Spoils," he closed out a debt of agony. And it was as if, after this, he could go on beyond all his New York troubles and be a park-maker to the nation. Telling again the story of the kinds of corruptions and irrelevancies of political life which had afflicted the profession of landscape architecture in New York helped him to gain a healthier perspective on his own life.

He wrote to Charles Brace on March 7, 1882, shortly after he had sent copies of the article in printed, pamphlet form to a long list of colleagues and to other public men, that he had been able to perform this difficult act of recollection with some degree of nervous comfort. He had been able to sleep fairly well even during the time he was writing the piece. He took this fact to represent to himself the end of his long period of recovery. He had now moved on to another and perhaps more fruitful period of his life. "The turning point appears to have been our abandonment of New York."[26]

Frederick and Mary had spent increasing periods of time away from New York, first in Cambridge and then in Brookline, and at the time of his writing the article about the parks, were settled in the "Miss Perrin house" in Brookline, leased until May, 1883. The Olmsteds had found a tenant to live in the house on Forty-sixth Street in New York. Frederick and John were kept busy for some time to come renting this house, looking after repairs, and worrying about the condition of the place until they decided they must sell it.

Assessing himself and his situation, Olmsted stated frankly to Brace, "I am still dilapidated—have a great noise in my head and a little exertion sets my heart bouncing but I sleep well and seem to myself to carry on my legs not [a] quarter of the weight I did a year ago. I have done much hard and steady work. The pamphlet of which you speak was mostly written after midnight and did not prevent me from getting regularly five or six hours refreshing sleep. I enjoy this suburban country beyond expression and in fact, the older I grow find my capacity for enjoyment increasing. We have had great trials and agitations in the last year but their result on the whole has been with all tranquillizing. I am to turn sixty with two grandsons."[27]

He told Brace that he could very well have been harsher in his treatment of the municipal officials who had been guilty of mismanagement in park affairs, but his friendship with some of the former commissioners and the present "entente between Vaux, Parsons, Green & Tilden"[28] which seemed about to come into the direction of the parks held him back. Yet the heart of the article, in its vigorous presentation of the kinds of offenses committed against the parks, the city, and himself, was vigorous and sardonic. Among his numbered instances of callous corruption during the year he had served as president of the board, 1872, were several which had a tinge of heavy, sarcastic humor, a mild example being an anecdote about a member of the board of commissioners who "once said in my presence, 'I don't get any salary for being here; it would be a pretty business if I couldn't oblige a friend now and then': this being his reason for urging a most unfit appointment."[29]

Olmsted's article did not make any difference in municipal behavior. His friends in the profession cared and understood, having had similar experiences in other cities. They thanked him in one deeply felt letter after another. Horace Cleveland told him that the pamphlet "stirred my soul to its depths."[30] S. H. Wales, the only former commissioner whom Olmsted named, replied very decently to Olmsted who had sent him the piece.[31] He might very well have been hurt by the writer's implication that he had been at least weak in handling his commissioner's job, but Wales protested only mildly and asked Olmsted to give useful advice for the present and future. Wales told Olmsted that he had sent the "Spoils" to Theodore Roosevelt, the new state legislator who represented the pertinent area of the city. Roosevelt almost immediately (March 19) wrote in his turn to Olmsted, saying that he wanted to help by sponsoring some sort of legislation to stabilize the security of the parks from interference.[32] Apparently nothing effective came to pass, but it illustrates an early yearning on Roosevelt's part to make reforms.

That some better time followed at least temporarily can be surmised from the fact that Olmsted's former partner Calvert Vaux had already accepted a tentative appointment as "Superintending Architect" of the parks. Olmsted did not know this when he began writing the "Spoils." Vaux informed Olmsted in January, 1882, that he was still doubtful of the appointment.[33] When the position was confirmed, Vaux served only until January, 1883; he was forced out of parks management at least for a period when his and Olmsted's old enemy Egbert Viele was named a parks commissioner and became, in fact, president of the board of commissioners. This regime seemed to the two men who had laid out Central Park the very nadir of city parks management. But Vaux was to be in office again, 1888 to 1895, with Samuel Parsons as his assistant. Parsons was to succeed Vaux, and so the original ideas of the designers were never entirely discarded but were to a very large extent guarded and fostered through many years.

CHAPTER XXV
A Liberal Profession

I know that in the minds of a large body of men of influence I
have raised my calling from the rank of a trade, even of a handicraft, to that of a liberal profession—an art, an art of design.
—F. L. O., to Elizabeth B. Whitney, December 16, 1890[1]

O LMSTED DID NOT all at once return to a full vigor of living and working. The pause in his life which began at the end of 1877 was a
grave interruption. But by 1882, a very full year, he was working once more
at the top of his form. He had both regained his insistent energy and discovered within himself a new equilibrium. He worked hard and well in the
following decade. Everything did not go smoothly, but he was enabled to
bear the common troubles of existence, a son's death, a daughter's insanity,
and the stubbornness of other men who could not see things as he did. It is
appropriate to make an emphasis here: Olmsted, in these later years of his
full vigor, was able to organize the outward works flowing from his inward
vision in a better and smoother way than he had before, and he was able to
relish the daily motions of his life.

Fortunately, during some of these years there was a bystander and a partaker in that existence who kept a private diary. This was young Charles
Eliot, who was an apprentice in the Olmsted office from 1883 to 1885. He
was a privileged young man, but one endowed with his family's seriousness
of purpose—his father was President Eliot of Harvard University—and he had
decided that he wished to be a landscape architect because, as his sympathic
but somewhat wondering father said, "No form of ordinary business...had
the least attraction for him."[2] Charles had come to this decision in surroundings of modest luxury, the family's vacation place at Mount Desert Island,
Maine, and with no compulsion but that within himself. He first prepared for
the career by enrolling for some months in the Bussey Institution, the divi-

sion of Harvard devoted to agriculture and horticulture. With the wide world of study or work before him, and no practical barriers except his lack of training, he looked about and chose Frederick Law Olmsted for his mentor. He had friends and relatives who knew Mr. Olmsted. His former teacher, Professor Norton, said a word to Mr. Olmsted. His uncle, Robert S. Peabody, a Boston architect, arranged for the young man to meet Olmsted. The easy way in which Charles Eliot came into an apprenticeship with the most distinguished landscape man of the country might have seemed the result of favoritism. If Eliot had not had talent and ambition, if Olmsted could have tolerated dilettantism, this might have been so. However, Eliot, sure of his purpose, was also naturally gifted, and he applied himself with a graceful if not deadly grim earnestness. He took full advantage of his opportunities. And he recorded almost daily during his time of apprenticeship his impression of Olmsted and his methods.

Eliot was introduced to Olmsted on April 22, 1883. Olmsted judged the young man to be worth teaching and asked him, after this meeting, to come into his firm as an apprentice—Eliot not to be paid a salary yet, but to have the privilege of learning the business and in fact coming into the house for a time, almost, in medieval fashion, as a member of the family. By the twenty-ninth of the month the arrangement had become a fact. Charles Eliot, Sr., looking back at his gifted son's short life, wrote of the beginning of Charles's career: "By the 29th of April Charles was established in Mr. Olmsted's office, and on that day he set out with Mr. Olmsted on a short journey of work-inspection. His courses at the Bussey Institution were thus somewhat abruptly interrupted."[3] Olmsted had, thereafter, for almost two years, in addition to the important help of his son John Charles, who administered the office to a greater and greater extent, the apt aid of a young pupil, who accompanied him on trips, learned quickly from precept and example and from the reading set before him, and was very soon exceptionally ready in drafting, calculating, and preparing "show" sketches for clients. These were the grimy but necessary details of the business. Eliot was also keenly interested in absorbing the first principles of the profession.

John had been Frederick's first apprentice, and was becoming, in these years, a full colleague. The firm became F. L. & J. C. Olmsted in 1884. It was an advantage to father and son in the growing professional work of the firm to have a third member above the clerk status to whom responsibilities could be given.

Eliot was a keen observer as well as a quick study, and wrote laconically in his little black diary what he saw and occasionally what he thought of Olmsted, his ways, his achievements, even his lapses from Eliot's own taste.[4] His first trip with Mr. Olmsted taught him the relentless energy and the all-encompassing attention of his master. As he accompanied Mr. Olmsted from one place to another, he saw the variety and scope of work possible in the profession. He stood by Olmsted's side when the designer advised Oliver Ames on the work being accomplished at the North Easton, Massachusetts, town hall, an enhancement by Olmsted of the naturally rough and rock-ledged pile out of which the new town hall grew. He was introduced to the work and personality of Henry Hobson Richardson, who was erecting the building. Eliot was with Olmsted at Newport where several private estates were being landscaped. At one, he saw Olmsted's passionate argument with the owner, to persuade him to let nature have its way in an unornamented approach to the sea from the house rather than to clutter the view with fussy details. Charles was an interested observer in Olmsted's handling of a "common" ground for all the estate owners at a vacation place, Cushing's Island, in Portland Bay. A beautiful expanse of spruces was dying there, and the diarist recorded Olmsted's solution: "Pine seed should be sown among the dying spruces so as to have a growth to fall back upon when the spruces are removed. Not safe to cut and clear away now for fear of losing the mosses, ferns, etc."[5] And on the art of the possible in landscaping: "Mr. Olmsted chooses, rather than to attempt the impossible, to plant such trees and shrubs as are suited to the given place, in a natural way;—and then to leave it to Nature to work out her own sweet will."[6]

Olmsted involved Charles Eliot intimately in the work on the Arnold Arboretum. The younger man was one of the group including John Olmsted, two Boston city engineers, and the Arboretum's guardian angel, Charles Sprague Sargent, who went together to inspect staked-out drives. Olmsted pointed out to the group that the engineering work, at this early stage, would "need some revision for the sake of saving certain valuable trees."[7] Eliot, with the buoyancy of youth and his own personal sensitivity, reported happily of that day: "Delightful spring weather. Woods full of delicate tints and shades of color—and soft and feathery with young leafage."[8]

Eliot was a tall young man, slender in build and of a delicate digestive apparatus. Mr. Olmsted found him a good companion for walks. Eliot did not easily tire in this kind of exercise. He rode well, and Olmsted may have been pleased by this talent. He himself found it a pleasant luxury to keep a horse again in Brookline where there were semirural spaces to be essayed by a happy rider.

On June 3, Eliot recorded Olmsted's advice to a private client who owned an estate where a considerable aid must be given to nature. This was on the estate of W. C. Cabot in Brookline. The house was already present, set down awkwardly at the bottom of a hill. "Mr. O. [as Eliot invariably designated his mentor] recommends a work of grading of considerable magnitude. The digging of a gentle valley in a line diagonal to the side of the house and leading down the hill a little slantwise: so as to carry the eye away from the swooping hill to the wide view towards Walnut Hill."[9] An even more drastic job of engineering had to be done at a municipally owned pond at

Newport. Easton's Pond was silted up and overgrown with sedge. "Mr. O. has proposed to dredge a winding and irregular water basin and with material thus obtained to raise the level of the remaining area—thus making land and water of a place now neither the one nor the other."[10]

In late June John Olmsted and Charles Eliot went together on a journey for the firm first to New Haven and then to Bridgeport where Mr. Olmsted met them and showed them the land which was to be Beardsley Park, a tract given to the city by a wealthy farmer. Eliot wrote:

> The Park Commissioners expect a general smoothing of everything, a cutting down of the rough sumacs and brambles, a clipped grass surface,—having in mind the almost universal notion of a 'Park'—that of a nicely kept lawn with flower beds, 'carpet gardening,' and trained trees and shrubs.
>
> Mr. Olmsted will oppose all this. The park-land is a fine piece of rural scenery to be religiously preserved as it is in so far as the use and enjoyment of the place by the public will permit—a scene of quiet character, graceful and picturesque in turns, in which only such changes and additions should be permitted as will elicit still further the naturally prevailing character.[11]

Olmsted showed Eliot what he was doing in Washington for the grounds of the Capitol and the Washington Monument, making them accessible and comfortable as well as beautiful. He took Eliot to Detroit where he was engaged in another large municipal project, Belle Isle Park, situated on a low-lying island. In this case, engineering was again of first importance. "Mr. O's scheme involves the building up of roadways by means of the material derived from the canals [canals to cut across the soggy ground of the low island]—this in order to insure the dryness of the driveways even immediately after rain. As things are now in Detroit no one ever thinks of driving into the country or suburbs for pleasure—so dull is the country and so bad the clay roads." Eliot also noted a new method of removing unwanted trees. "Saw dynamite stump-blowing on the island. Very effective process."[12]

On dull days in the office, Eliot read Gilpin's description of English forest scenery, or other books prescribed by Mr. Olmsted. There was soon, early in 1885, to be another bright young apprentice, Harry Codman, Charles Sargent's nephew, joining them in the office, and another, Phil Coolidge, who came in from time to time, to learn by doing some of the work and by precept. This made an association of learners congenial to Olmsted's earnest desire to teach. These alert young men, willing to learn, but also of an eager and independent turn of mind, a trait Olmsted appreciated, soon contributed their own talents and their own ideas to the firm. (Eliot expressed dissatisfaction with Olmsted when the head of the firm did fussy work, in contradiction to his own best ideas, one example being the grounds for the Storrow house in Brookline.[13]) Olmsted approved Eliot's further training in agriculture and horticulture and encouraged him to go back to Harvard briefly for more of this kind of training when he should have finished his apprenticeship.

Eliot's long and searching study of European gardens and parks in 1886 was to be carried out with Olmsted's warm endorsement. The younger man was to write a running report in letters to "Mr. Olmsted," to John, and to Harry Codman.

In trying to reorganize his work, Olmsted had made a beginning of separating execution from design in his working arrangement first with Jacob Weidenmann, who had carried out some of Olmsted's plans with a freedom of effort subject only to an ultimate control by the designer. Olmsted's arrangement with Weidenmann lapsed as John grew to have a larger part in his father's work. Olmsted remained friends with Weidenmann who, on his side, remained a disciple of Olmsted. From time to time, Olmsted threw work Weidenmann's way. And Olmsted for the most part avoided the heartbreaking trap into which he had fallen in both Central and Prospect parks, of trying to supervise every detail of the execution of a plan. After delivering his design, he reserved the right to hire an engineer and a horticulturist who were to execute the work, subject to his supervision and control. These executors of Olmsted's plans remained subject to his artistic direction but were under salary, customarily, to the commission of the park, or to the private patron of the design, rather than on a payroll of the Olmsted firm.

Within his own firm, Frederick shifted a great deal of work onto John who proved, year after year, capable and ingenious. Olmsted was proud of John and thought him more able in certain lines than he himself was. He was never jealous of John's capabilities nor of the other younger members of the firm. He had the kind of large confidence in his own powers which admitted other men's abilities. John, having a gift for organization and administration, more and more, as time passed, shouldered the daily running of the office, freeing his father for the work he loved, the thoughtful peregrination of the ground to be transformed, and the mysterious initiation of the original plan on which they all then lent their talents in the complete and elaborate working out of the conception into plat and finished piece of ground.

Olmsted needed help when he took Eliot into the firm as an apprentice. Steadily the work was growing. On March 15, 1887, looking back at busy years, Olmsted wrote Brace, "We have all the professional work we can well manage to do justice to."[14]

He had always in hand, when he could secure the funds to proceed, the transformation of the Boston parks, a system which was going to encompass a continuous pacing of the city's growth outward by way of green parks and parkways from the heart of the city at the common to the new West Roxbury Park seven miles away. Olmsted was also still the active adviser to the Buffalo and Rochester parks commissions. He had a new city park in hand in Belle Isle Park in Detroit. The United States Capitol and New York State Capitol work went on. Olmsted was the designer of the layout of the new Arboretum south of Boston. He cooperated with Charles Sprague Sargent in actually bringing about what they had earlier schemed, the arrangement by which the city and Harvard were yoked together: the city to own and maintain the area, Harvard, through its agent Sargent, to supervise the plantings.

In addition to large jobs, Olmsted, if he found himself interested, did small ones. He did even quixotic and time-consuming good deeds, such as his small design for the Summit, New Jersey, Ladies Improvement Association for which, in May, 1882, he gravely accepted fifty dollars.

Olmsted came to have the habit, when he was away, of writing personal and business news to John, making of his letter an "almanac" as he called it of his movements so that the office force would be aware of what he was up to. He wrote such a long letter on November 9, 1882, detailing a mixture of personal and professional information all in one rich mixture.[15] He had had what he called "a violent choleriac attack" in Washington but had come on to New York and was better. In the capital city, he had "found the work in a hopeless condition. No one had any thought of finishing it but when I left there was nearly double the force employed and working smoothly." Congress annoyed him, particularly in holding up his appropriations. "They are all so cautious and timid and postponing and improvident and so easily disconcerted." He supposed that he would "Get home Saturday night and prepare the Detroit pamphlet for the printer Sunday." Then he would be off for Providence, Newport, and North Easton. After visits to "the other places"— not naming them—he would see to a "Niagara meeting in New York." Then, "If I can get so much done then by the 18th I can get off for Albany, Buffalo, Niagara and Detroit and from Detroit to Washington before the end of the month." And as an afterthought: "I have been hoping to make both Bridgeport and Providence this trip but it is now too late before Sunday." And his instructions followed for work in the office: "You must do the best you can with the Capitol Ground report and map. It should be ready for me to send on when I get home. There will be no chance for further corrections."

In March, 1883, the Niagara Bill, for which Olmsted and Norton had lobbied for years, passed the New York State Legislature. The bill would mandate the preservation of some of the natural area around the falls and river in cooperation with a similar move by the Canadian government on the other side of the border. Norton generously gave much of the credit to his friend in a letter he wrote on March 15: "You are a standing motive for me for hope in mankind."[16] Olmsted would soon be called upon to make a plan for landscaping the reservation. He engineered the joint participation of Calvert Vaux in this work. They had at an earlier stage done a certain amount of tentative planning for Niagara. Olmsted always insisted that commissions and boards hire him and Vaux together if they had done an initial work on which further elaboration was required. He brought Vaux into later stages of work on Riverside and Morningside parks, green ribbons in New York City which had languished since he and Vaux had made the original plans for these parks.

Another letter from father to son illustrates the continuing relationship of

Frederick and John Charles Olmsted. On February 24, 1884, he wrote from aboard one of the endless trains he used indefatigably from one point to another where he had work progressing. "You must think about going to Detroit. I don't feel quite equal to the duty that may possibly be required there—e.g., discussion of roof-construction of gallery and I think on general principles you should make acquaintance with the place and the people so if I am sick you can go later." And, "Then I think an outing desirable for you especially as you will be overworked as soon as spring comes."[17] Traveling later into that springtime, in May, 1884, he could not forbear to write John in the quick enthusiasm he felt for some wild nature he saw from another train window: "I noticed cattails and bullrushes and calamus and a tall reed and irises growing abundantly on the margins of salt grass and sedge on the Jersey flats." This was a conversational aside in a letter also concerned with the firm's business in guiding the site and layout of a new school, the Law-renceville School. And he reminded his son of their shared responsibilities: "I feel guilty of neglecting Chestnut Hill Station [the station building, the work of Richardson]. Get out there if you can in working hours."[18]

Olmsted defended briskly this son with whom he now shared his professional duties to a client who objected to dealing with J. C. Olmsted, the son, rather than Frederick Law, the father. He wrote to a "Mr. Jesup" on January 31, 1889: "My son has from early childhood been familiar with my works. He has lived with me on some of them. He has systematically taken lessons in our profession upon them. He has traveled thousands of miles with me while I have been inspecting and studying. He has been professionally educated under my directions, has studied abroad under my guidance. He has been at the head of my office ten years, has latterly taken an equal part with me in all my works, public and private. He is in the prime of life—a young middle aged man. More than one of my clients after experience have requested that I would allow him to lead in their affairs, finding him apter than they found me."[19]

Frederick's defense of his son was as passionate as other movements of his mind. He could not help being himself in whatever he did and learned only a little tact very late. Yet he had a manner of conducting himself toward strangers as well as friends which could be winning. He honored other men's motives and feelings until betrayed by them. He dealt with other men as if they might be friends, as they often became friends; if clients did not behave so to him, he had nothing more to do with them. Thus he carried his personal posture into business. And, as for business, he would not behave as he saw other men behave who were still admitted to "good society."

Olmsted had a high pride in the standards he set for landscape architecture. He insisted that it was "a liberal profession," not a craft like gardening, nor a business like building railroads. He put it on a proud level, alongside medicine and the law, and expected men to treat him accordingly. He was profoundly shocked by the attitude of one prosperous English landscape man who paid a call on him and boasted unconcernedly about the smart deals he had made with contractors on jobs. He was also, in general, shocked by the corruption of the shrewd generation of industrialists and speculators who had taken over the national scene since the end of the war. They were often men with whom he had to deal in getting things done; he did not subscribe to their way of living even if, sometimes, he could find himself involved in a personal friendship with one or another of them.

Olmsted's colleague in many of the projects of the 1880s, Henry Hobson Richardson, had preceded Olmsted in moving to Brookline. He had his architectural studio in his own house. There, his young apprentices came and went in rooms cheerful with the noise of children growing up underfoot. Richardson's splendid studies of works in progress and works envisioned adorned the walls. Olmsted, after shaking off his connection with New York and settling in first one house and then another in Brookline, was a neighbor's distance from Richardson. Family friendship and artistic collaboration brought an easy closeness to a relationship which already seemed comfortably old.

Olmsted had at last found a permanent place in Brookline. He had extolled the virtues of the domestic hearth ever since, as an impressionable young man, he had read Zimmerman, but he had moved about from place to place all his grown life. He and Mary had been fond of the Southside location of the Staten Island farmhouse, but it had grown inconvenient. The house at Mount St. Vincent in Central Park had been the best place in the world for a short time. Bear Valley had been an exhilarating camp. The Forty-sixth Street house in Manhattan had been a tolerable base so long as Frederick could endure New York. But the move to the Boston area had not only renewed his working life, it had refreshed his spirit.

After staying with friends in Cambridge, the Olmsteds found their own house on the other side of the Charles, four miles out Beacon Street from the Park Street Station. Brookline was a suburb where Frederick could once more have a horse to ride and places to walk. The Richardsons were in Brookline too, and the Godkins and Nortons were nearby in Cambridge. The Boston parks were handy for daily or weekly visits, and Brookline seemed a secure base from which to set out on longer, more elaborate trips to works in other parts of the country. Frederick and Mary rented first the Perrin house, then the Taylor house. When the lease on the second house could not be renewed, the Olmsteds looked about for a place to purchase, intending to sell the house in Manhattan which they had been leasing, with considerable difficulties about upkeep and repair. Richardson impulsively offered his friends a part of his large plot of land, saying that he would build them a house, even sketching a tentative design on a corner of a letter. But the Olmsteds desired their own private place. They found it in the "Clarksted," an old square house at 99 Warren Street, which had come down in the same family for several generations. The two elderly Misses Clark no longer wished the care of a large house. Olmsted offered to build a cottage for them on the lot and to let them stay out their lives there rent free. He and Mary found it an adventure to buy this dignified old house and to make it over to suit the family and Frederick's professional work.

However, Frederick left the immediate care of the rehabilitation and remodeling to John. He made only a few wistful suggestions for his own comfort. "Since you ask, I should find a dressing closet—or hot water on draught safely at my room a great comfort," he wrote John on July 15, 1883, as he pursued his never-ending travels. And, "It would make the old Clark-sted much more cottagious if the south wing room were octagated. The chimney might be six inches higher than others—suggesting rising ground as seen from the Northeast."[20]

It was an honorable old house, its original construction of the vintage of 1809 or thereabouts, with additions and revisions since that date, located on a green site sloping upward to a hill behind. Warren Street curved downhill northward across the front, the street masked by trees and shrubs. The house was sufficiently old to need work to be done on the brownish, austere, square-fronted, two-storied structure. The front entrance centered upon the east side facing the gate into Warren Street. Two generous windows opened on each side of that front face of the house. The door was sheltered by a modest gable, and the visitor stepped up to the door upon a broad, low stone. But this was only the official face of the house. A visitor might be tempted to follow the green lawn as it lapped irregularly around the left side of the house, as one faced the structure, and find upon this south side a hospitable, outdoor living space where the longer side of the house looked out under bright awnings from windows and a door opening upon this sheltered vista, hidden from alien eyes by a wall of trees. The green lawn continued around the back of the house and ran up against the base of a tree-covered hill, "Green Hill," which blocked the view westward. If the visitor attempted to round the right-hand side of the house, he would find the going difficult. A steeper, rockier slope fell off from this side. A bow window was opened off from the front office room on this side, the north side of the house. And it was on this side that work space was gradually added in the shape of additional rooms. Later, in the time which came after Frederick, Sr.'s active career, another building, of stone, was to be added upon this "work" side. There was space in the back area for stables and other work buildings. Access to the back was by a road lower and hidden from the front. The modest lot was planted and shaped to seem more spacious than it was. And in this establishment, Mary, as she had been elsewhere, was to be the gardener.

With this safe retreat behind his back, Olmsted ventured forth to works springing up in many parts of the country. He was at the height of his powers, known as a master wherever he went, praised by his peers, and, to his own almost childlike surprise, taken into what he thought of as the company of the great men of his time. He was greatly pleased by being invited to join the Saturday Club in Boston which united for dinner at the Parker House once a month. Here were his contemporaries Charles Eliot Norton, Charles W. Eliot, Sr., of Harvard, and Charles Sprague Sargent. But the monthly occasion had a larger meaning for him, the felt presence of those earlier members, some of whom had been heroes of his youth, writers of the New England literary ascendancy who had influenced his turn toward an enthusiastic romanticism: Emerson, Hawthorne, Longfellow, Richard Henry Dana. The living heroes of his young manhood, the elder Holmes, Lowell, and Whittier, were still lingerers from the earlier era. Their presence seemed like a dying echo of a different kind of age in this world in which he and his colleagues in park-making carried on daily business in the world of the new business tycoons. Probably Charles Norton had a good deal to do with Olmsted's being asked to join the old club. To him, Olmsted wrote about the fact on March 11, 1884: "Today I have received official advice of my election to the Saturday Club to which your last note referred, and to which I did not at the time reply because I was not prepared to credit it. It is the highest and most unexpected honor I have ever received and I don't know what to make of it but I am very grateful." He added as if in afterthought, exhibiting again to Norton the breadth of his personal interests: "Could you at all conveniently steal across here sometime this week? Richardson's magazine is finishing and he has several of the most beautiful and interesting architectural drawings (for the Albany Cathedral competition) that I have ever seen. I am almost sure they would delight you."[21]

Olmsted had always wistfully admired *being* as a state and considered it as higher than the state of *doing*, but in his older years he was busier than ever, doing many things in many places, showing a characteristic and determined energy in his dealings with both land and men. If he was not able to subside comfortably into his carpet slippers before his own fireplace for any long period of time, and was often gone from his home place on tours, expeditions, discoveries, mostly outdoors and in all kinds of weather, walking over raw ground in need of transformation, he yet gained in these years a kind of perspective on himself that he had not had earlier.

He recognized that he was less able to manage his relationship with Calvert Vaux, but he still wondered about him and worried about him. He found that he had to be cautious in his dealings with Vaux, for his former partner's business had fallen off and Vaux had grown moody and was inclined to irrational angers. Vaux's latest partner, George Radway, quietly and without telling Vaux, had asked Olmsted to find him work in California since there was little for him to do in conjunction with Vaux.[22] A more difficult situation arose when the commissioners of the New York parks once more approached Olmsted to advise them in the completion of the city parks.

Olmsted stoutly insisted to S. H. Wales (1884) and Henry Beekman (1886) that he would advise the city on Riverside or Morningside parks, or other special jobs, only if Calvert Vaux were included. Vaux had already served for a single year as landscape architect to the New York parks—from November, 1881, to January, 1883. After the park commissioners negotiated with Olmsted in the mid-eighties, the two men were hired to do specified work on Riverside and Morningside parks. Yet, in the midst of correspondence with Olmsted about the New York parks work, Vaux turned difficult and wrote ugly letters to Olmsted. Olmsted wrote back long, unhappy letters in his turn. In the end, Vaux apologized only after Olmsted appealed to him in the name of their old friendship.

The surviving Olmsted side of the correspondence shows an unhappy, tortured relationship tenuously held together.[23]

Olmsted to Vaux (July 5, 1887):

I have yours of the 2nd and 3rd. Both of them strike me strangely as did your previous note. . . .

If you suspect me of trying to get an advantage for myself or for my views at your expense or the expense of your views, tell me so. Of course you don't.

Olmsted to Vaux (July 9):

You write as you might if I had been coming to New York of my own motive with the purpose to obtain some employment of the Park Commissioners and have moved for this purpose in such a manner as to avoid you—at least to take the "lead" out of your hands. . . . I know that you know that there is not the slightest word of truth in it. . . .

Olmsted, in the same letter, went over the sequence of events which had put him and Vaux into this emotional tangle: the commissioners had asked him for his counsel; he had not sought these interviews, and, "The first word I said to them was that you were the proper man for them to consult and that I wished to make no engagements with them." In the midst of writing this letter, he had received another from Vaux, insinuating certain machinations of which Olmsted felt himself innocent. Olmsted, replying, admitted himself to be careless sometimes in what he said, but he grew angry at the imputation of dishonesty put upon him. His feelings heightened as he wrote:

I suppose that there is something lying back of what you say which you expect me to see and I cannot, something "technical." If I were a prisoner before a criminal court and you were the prosecuting attorney I should expect to be hanged by a technical rope. All the same I should know that I really was not guilty. . . . That after all these years we should be no better able to understand one another is one of the strangest of life's experiences. I seem as near to you sometimes as to any old friend—I have not many left. Yet sometimes we have as little insight of each other's meaning and motives as if we were beings of two different planets.

I still hope that what is best on the cards for you and Parsons will come out of all this otherwise wasted time.

But he said firmly that his prime object was not Vaux's and Parson's interest in the matter, but the good of the parks. He added:

I don't want to have to come back to New York but I am not sure that I should not even do that rather than lose all chance of bringing the parks back to the original principles so far as that is possible. To that end, with you or without you, I shall always do what seems to me best. There is nothing else I care so much for.

And for the first time in years Olmsted signed a letter to Vaux "Affectionately yours." This seemed to have touched Calvert Vaux, who replied in a softened manner. Olmsted, in his turn, rejoined humorously and in a self-deprecating way: "I believe you are ahead of me now by six notes, but then you don't write as long ones as I do." (July 13, 1887.)

They came to an agreement. They passed a revised Riverside Plan back and forth in an amicable fashion; they worked later together on Morningside Park—both of these projects temporary, one-time associations with the City of New York. These plans were to be executed not by the Olmsted firm, but by Vaux and Parsons. And it was Vaux who became the permanent consulting landscape architect to the New York parks once more, 1888 to 1895. In private practice, the two men also cooperated again on a revised plan for the public reservation at Niagara Falls.

Olmsted continued to be wary of Vaux's emotional reactions, and was conscious also of how easily his own quick temper might be tripped by this particular association. The two men could not quite let go of each other. Their children remained friends.

While Calvert Vaux's work fell off in the 1880s, not from any lack of a sensitive gift, but probably through difficulties of temperament, Olmsted's work continued to pick up. In his late maturity Olmsted continued to make designs that were more and more his own. He had come to like a certain plainness. He wrote to Vaux in a friendly manner when they were collaborating in September, 1887: "It is obvious that we have been going different ways; you being disposed to a more, I to a less elaborate plan, than that to which we had virtually come last Tuesday. We can't come to a conclusion by which we can both abide without conversation. And as I cannot come to you [he was in bed in Brookline with a temporary disability] you must come to me, for conversation."[24]

He desired each plan to be developed with a sort of simple fitness. And the placing of Grant's tomb in the middle of Riverside Park was not fit. His personal respect for Grant had endured through Grant's presidential misfortunes and mistakes. But Grant's body in his park designed for a people's lighthearted amusement did not please him at all. "It is a very fine site for a public monument. But it will be extremely unfortunate if, on the one hand, the remains of the dead are brought into close association with the gayety of the Promenade at this culminating point."[25]

Aside from the fitness of each plan for its human use, he continued, even deepened, his interest in fit adaptations of the land itself. He was more than ever curious as to what might be done in arid portions of the United States and sent Charles Eliot and Harry Codman, when they traveled abroad, on searches for Italian and Spanish gardens and parks. He was no longer interested only in the green turfs which had made his and Vaux's early parks famous.

And his interest widened in the uses of all kinds of open spaces in cities. This was another theme of his correspondence with his former apprentices when they traveled in Europe: go look at the little parks and squares and circles in these cities; see what they have done. And Codman and Eliot dutifully and with a youthful enthusiasm replied to their teacher what they had found. Olmsted's design for Logan Place in Louisville was one result. Here city congestion enforced a space that was mostly paved and formal, with only a suggestion of greenery where busy people, a short distance from their daily work, might sit, talk, and walk in the midst of urban life without strolling over turf into a rural park.

Yet the rural or rather the landscape park, as he called it, kept its hold upon him, and the culmination of the seven-mile strip of limited kinds of parks, leading Bostonians outward from the center of their city, was for Olmsted the unshaven, mostly unadorned natural-seeming beauties of Franklin Park. It was to seem the happy accident of a blessed countryside into which city people might easily make their way for the sake of contrast to the scenes of their daily struggle to make a living, and also a contrast to the crowded streets and houses where most of them lived.

The old man, already looking older than he was, with gray, ample beard, bald dome, and limping walk, whom Charles Eliot in his two apprentice years beheld out in all weathers energetically changing the scenery of the Boston area, impressed the young man by the boldness of his ideas. It was with an almost Faustian energy—doing rather than being, the mode Olmsted practiced if he did not always admire—that Olmsted directed that land appear where it had not been, that water should run in the opposite direction from the way which it had followed before, that green banks should clothe a stream where ugly bareness had been, and that Boston should have, at his command, seven miles of linked parks and parkways from the common in the heart of the city through all the winding fenways out as far as the new West Roxbury Park (Franklin Park), which imitated a far-off, rural landscape in its climbing up and down hills and through woods. When Charles Eliot came back into the firm as a partner, having had some independent experience, Olmsted welcomed not only the help Eliot gave him in implementing his own ideas, but was glad to incorporate Eliot's own array of ideas, of a broader and wider metropolitan park system.

His father's paraphrase of Charles Eliot's observations of the time of the son's apprenticeship to the Olmsted firm suggests the lively satisfaction that an aspiring imagination could find in the scenes of Frederick Olmsted's activities:

The great dredge was digging into the existing marsh across the channel near the gate-house, and the material there obtained was going to fill the promontory which was to carry Westland Avenue across the reservation. Men and teams were carrying marsh-mud from the vicinity of Westland Avenue and spreading it over the bare gravel slopes near Beacon Street. Teams were carrying marsh-sod for the shores and coves between Boylston and Beacon streets. Trains were bringing gravel for filling, and good soil from the new Sudbury River water-basins of the Boston Water Works; and men with barrows were spreading this loam on the finished slopes north of Boylston Street. Carts were bringing quantities of suitable manure to compost heaps which were being prepared for use when planting should begin in the spring; and plants were arriving and being heeled-in close to Beacon Street, so as to be handy in the spring.[26]

The younger Charles Eliot noted in his diary just what was being done on December 20, 1883:

The Back Bay is approaching obliteration,—it will soon be entirely filled up; —all but the narrow strip which the Park Commission has with difficulty secured and which has come to be called the Back Bay "Park."

This "Park" is in course of construction from Mr. O.'s designs. The work is fundamentally the saving of a little of the original Back Bay, so as to permit the floodwaters of Stony Brook and Muddy River to escape in a natural manner. Wooden conduits (now constructed) will carry the ordinary flow of these streams from the region where formerly they emptied into the Bay, across the filled lands, to their new mouths opening on the Charles River Basin. In time of flood the overtaxed conduits will be relieved of the extra flow by turning the same into the salt creek which makes the principle [sic] feature of Mr. O.'s scheme, and thus the "backing up" of water on the low lands of Roxbury and Brookline will be prevented.[27]

That the large view did not prevent Olmsted's attention to detail may be well seen in the office copy of a severe letter he wrote to the nurseryman entrusted with certain plantings. Olmsted had engaged F. L. Temple to plant native shrubs at the Beacon Street entrance to the Back Bay. In spring, most of the plants had died; those that had survived were of the wrong type. Olmsted outlined firmly to Temple how he had failed in his task. In part, he wrote, "The mere loss of so many plants is the smallest part of the disaster. The whole design is a wreck. Of what remains of your planting that which should be most prominent and characteristic is least so, that which was desired to be an inconspicuous element merging in a mass of certain quality stands out exclusively; that which was to be subordinate, predominates."

He ended sternly: "I don't see how the plantation can be left longer under your management. I don't think you should depend on me to think out your present duty in the premises. It is a question of professional obligation and character."[28] Although Olmsted had learned to delegate some of his landscape supervision to his son John and to the apprentices, he could not give up the primary responsibility to anyone.

Yet, however heavy his overseeing duties became, Olmsted was still capable of an adventure, and of crowing over it. He was in Detroit in late May, 1884. A ferryboat carried him and others on an inspection of the pier work for the Belle Isle park. The party found itself in a boat too heavy and too ill managed by an ignorant pilot to be docked safely. Olmsted remembered his sailor days, took over, made a "lead line of spun yarn and scrap iron"[29] and put the boat about and piloted it safely in to the dock. He was flat on his back and ill subsequently, able to digest nothing, "not even toast and milk,"[30] after an important meeting with the Detroit city fathers, but one can discern the youthful spirit in the old body delighting in the physical dexterity he had exhibited in boat-handling. There was never anything jaded or sophisticated about Olmsted. He never shielded himself from an emotion and was only learning, in old age, to disguise hot feelings. He had the compensations of delicious triumphs as well as the agonies of despair.

There were other occasions in the 1880s when Olmsted devised adventures for himself. Coming back from California in October, 1886, from his first inspection of the land where Leland Stanford wished to establish a university, Olmsted stopped off in Wyoming to inspect personally ranchlands which, after Owen's death, had reverted to him. He had left both Harry Codman, who was now a member of the firm, and Frederick, Jr., in Salt Lake City. Tiring as it was, he made a thorough survey of the conditions of the ranches, assessed the value of the land he owned, and determined the chances of making money from cattle-raising in this remote area. "[It] was a high interest speculation and the luck has not been with us,"[31] he wrote to John at home in Brookline. But he wrote a careful report of his inspection to the manager, putting as hopeful a face upon the facts of ranching in this dry north plains area as possible. "It has been reported that under close feeding the nutritious buffalo and bunch grasses disappear and worthless grasses take their place. I saw no evidence that the Company's ranges had at all deteriorated in this way. The number of antelopes indicated a wild and uncrowded condition."[32] Olmsted had had at least the satisfaction of seeing a new kind of open grassland, and of judging ground, cattle, buildings, men for himself. The notice he took of antelope and bunch grass was in itself a joy.

Olmsted traveled almost constantly and nearly all of this travel was by train. He came to like the experience less and less, slept badly, and hated the rocking motion. Yet upon one occasion at least—almost a half year after his ranchland inspection—he made a long, imperious Union Pacific train obey his command to stop. He behaved here as the master of this transcontinental motion instead of its victim. Passengers upon the long train, traveling through desolate, high country in southern Wyoming, where winds and early snows had blenched the grasses to a dun and flattened appearance, may have been surprised and even angered at finding their splendid monster slowing and coming to a halt in open desert country, with no visible station and no reason given for this stoppage. If any one of them were curious enough to look out the window toward the upslope of the land, he might have seen the figure of a limping but spry gentleman in an unbuttoned coat which was blowing in a cold wind, climbing the rocky ground to a knoll bearing on its top a kind of cairn or monument, so natural in appearance as to be almost a part of the small mountain it crowned.

Olmsted had wished to see the Ames Monument. Richardson had not only designed buildings in North Easton, Massachusetts, for the Ames family, but also this lonely tribute to the construction of the railroad. Olmsted had been to Garfield, near Salt Lake City, at the request of Charles Francis Adams, at this time president of the railroad, to advise in the landscaping of a Union Pacific settlement. Since he had this connection, it was with little difficulty that Olmsted arranged for the train to stop so that he could get out and take a look at the Ames Monument.

The austere memorial to the brothers Oakes and Oliver Ames was regularly exposed to severe weather. Olmsted wished to see if the monument had been damaged. Buffeted by the winds as he made a circuit of the cairn, Olmsted failed to find any change except a weathering which had made the monument only more a part of the bleak country through which the Ames brothers, in both their good and evil roles, had pushed the rails of this first transcontinental railroad. Olmsted found it a fitting tribute and a great achievement of his recently dead friend, Richardson, and of Saint-Gaudens who had designed the bas-relief portraits set into the opposite sides of the cairn. With considerable gusto in the telling, Olmsted recounted to Mariana Van Renssalaer in a letter dated February 6, 1887, his experience of stopping the train and inspecting the monument.[33]

Richardson had died on April 27, 1886. Olmsted had had a last visit with his friend in Washington, D.C.[34] Although on that occasion Richardson was obviously weak and ill, once they began to talk, he regained his usual enthusiasm and discussed with Olmsted all his beautiful unfinished projects, among them two of his greatest, the courthouse in Pittsburgh and the Marshall Field warehouse in Chicago. Shortly after this time, Richardson had come home to Brookline. Olmsted was not to see him again before he died.

Olmsted knew that Richardson's finances had been shaky, in spite of his ease in securing the management of large architectural projects. He and Mary went to Julia Richardson and ascertained the situation in which this good friend found herself. She had a small personal income. The house was to be let to her at a nominal fee by a concerned and friendly landlord. Then Frederick and Charles Sargent talked over what should be done to perpetuate Richardson's reputation in the hurrying, brutal world of which they were all a part. There was a young architectural critic who had already published what Olmsted thought were enlightened criticisms of Richardson and his works. Mariana Griswold Van Renssalaer seemed to Olmsted the person to write a book about Richardson while the mementoes of his career still remained in the heaped-up splendor the architect had affected in furnishing his house. After conferring with Sargent, Olmsted wrote a second letter to her on May 6 (misdating the letter April 6), saying: "Since I wrote you this morning I have been in conversation with Prof. Sargent about Richardson and we agreed that a memorial book, giving some account of him and his works with illustrations should be pursued; that it should be set about at once, before his office is dismantled, his friends dispersed and while memories of him are fresh, and that you would be much the best person to undertake it."[35] The implication of the letter was that he and Sargent would go to New York and find a publisher for her. He wrote Mrs. Van Renssalaer successively several long letters containing his personal memories of Richardson. Mariana Van Renssalaer used much of this material in the book which she very shortly wrote.

Olmsted, whether pursuing his own career or the interest of a friend whether dead or alive, made his way with a spirited determination across the decade of the 1880s. It was not only the age of his parks, but of Clemens's *Life Upon the Mississippi* and James's *The Portrait of a Lady*. It was the time not only of Richardson's buildings but of Thomas Eakins's, James Whistler's, and Mary Cassatt's paintings. The Red Cross, in 1882, founded itself upon the tradition of the United States Sanitary Commission. It was an age of careless and ostentatious wealth and of crimped poverty. Some of that wealth, in cities, and in private hands, made possible Olmsted's work. He hoped that in some intangible way his open spaces in crowded cities would alleviate the life of the poor and make more interesting the life of the rich. He hoped that Boston might become more human by the greenness and apparent naturalness of the connected waterways, little parks, parkways leading from the common to the great rural hilly park, Franklin Park. He continued to develop the Buffalo park system. He took up projects for smaller cities, for schools, private estates. He did exquisite small-scale landscaping for the Boston and Albany railway stations and for libraries in Quincy and Malden, Massachusetts, and Burlington, Vermont. For his home place of Brookline he began a series of municipal improvements. He continued his landscaping care of the McLean Asylum. In Washington, D.C., he began the work of designing the grounds of the National Zoo in Rock Creek Park. He worked in Rochester, Pawtucket, Swampscott, Newport, and for a hotel at Lake Sunapee. In going west again at the call of Leland Stanford, he widened his sphere, opening his eyes to the changes he found in California.

Olmsted, when he thought of himself and of his friends, was amazed at how time had changed the circumstances of existence. He wrote to Charles Brace on November 1, 1884:

> Social changes in our time have been so great that while I feel myself in the full front of the life of today I feel that the life of our early days was almost another life. . . .
>
> You decidedly have had the best and most worthily successful life of all whom I have known. The C. A. [Children's Aid Society] is the most satisfactory of all the benevolent works of our time.
>
> I have done a good deal of good work in my way too but it is constantly and everywhere arrested, wrenched, mangled and misused and it is not easy to get above intense disappointment and mortification.

In the same letter he confessed, "I get very weary of turning so often from one thing to another and of so many long and short expeditions. Perhaps I all the more enjoy my house and place and the bits of quiet work I am able to do in it."[36]

As long as Charley Brace lived, Olmsted wrote to this friend his most intimate and wayward thoughts. On March 15, 1887, he wrote—with more of wishful thinking than of any basis in actuality: "The more important change that age brings to me is a growing disposition to take no thought of tomorrow—none of today; to delay and postpone and be shiftless." The only reason for shiftlessness at the moment of writing the letter was his being laid up in bed with a knee injury sustained in the most damaging of several railroad accidents he had had the bad luck to experience.

The letter reflects the enforced pause. Mary had gone outside in the harsh March weather to see what had happened to her plants. She discovered that some of them were uncovered where the wind had blown the snow away. But Frederick noted, "During the night there was another storm and they were buried again. She does not go out much in winter and is chiefly occupied in novel reading. Marion is visiting in New Brunswick where it is still solid winter. There is no notable change in Charlotte's condition. Her children are coming up very nicely under an excellent governess and housekeeper."

Idleness enforced recollection. "Tap, tap, tap. What a different world it is from those we used to know. I don't give much thought to it but every day it is driven in upon me. I have not forgotten the Sartor Resartus days. I dont concern myself the least bit with speculations. I don't know and I don't care. I am occupied quite enough with 'the duty that lies nearest to you.' The most horrible waste in the world seems to me the waste of mind in what is called Theology and I repent of nothing more thoroughly than my own sin in superstitious maundering. I take pleasure in observing how perfectly healthy our children are in this respect, how completely uninterested they are in all that used to be such a terrifically cruel burden upon me." This to a minister, even if a minister of the streets! Frederick was not perfectly tactful, but he was frank and true, even in the very awkwardnesses of the movement of his mind.

He concluded the letter by being philosophical for both of them. "In the old language I feel that we have been exceedingly blessed. Few men have more of the happy spirit of nunc dimittis. Yours affec'tly."[37]

CHAPTER XXVI

North, South, and West

Good design means an operation of imagination. It is not altogether a process of inductive reasoning. It cannot be done upon the jump. It is a matter of growth; involuntary and unconscious growth. I cannot come to a designing conclusion just when I want to. I must muse upon the conditions to be dealt with, have them upon my mind, and, after a time, I find a conclusion. I do not make it. It has come to be in my mind without my noting it. Of course, if necessary, I can bring myself to a decision quickly, but such a necessity is unfortunate.
—F. L. O., to Dr. Edward M. Moore, January 26, 1889[1]

To CHARLES ELIOT, enjoying his year in Europe, had come a letter from Mr. Olmsted, inviting him to return home early and go with his former employer to California to help pick a site for Leland Stanford's new national university. Eliot was too busy with his own first independent impressions and conclusions to accept. He cabled "Decline" and wrote a friendly negative letter.[2] Olmsted was not surprised and replied amicably on July 20, 1886: "I did not much suppose that you would take a vacation from your European school for a visit to the Pacific.... I don't doubt that you are right." And he told Eliot what he thought was going to be the major problem with the new client: "I find Governor Stanford bent on giving his University New England scenery, New England trees and turf, to be obtained only by lavish use of water. The landscape of the region is said to be fine in its way but nobody thinks of anything in gardening that will not be thoroughly unnatural to it. What can be done I don't know but it will be an interesting subject of study." He kept Eliot advised also about the dangers his United States Capitol landscaping was encountering in the made-up minds of national legislators: "The terrace at Washington is in great peril and I am doing all I can to save it—the danger being that Congress will order the western retaining wall to be pierced with windows. The prime mover in the matters is not a frontiersman but Senator Dawes of Massachusetts."

And as if talking to Eliot across a drafting table, he went on to catalogue his current problems: "Work is still suspended on Franklin Park and on all the Boston parks, the Republicans being afraid to trust the Democratic Commissioners with funds for advancing it. It looks just now as if nothing would be done this year, but I am inclined to think well before election a new light will be seen. They are not good politicians who take the responsibility of keeping laboring men out of employment."

He told Eliot also about a private park for a Dr. Webb on Lake Champlain near Burlington: "I propose a perfectly simple park, or pasture field, a mile long on the lake half a mile deep, the house looking down upon and over it."

He concluded with an expression of the endearing direct feeling which he never tried to disguise: "I enjoy all your letters exceedingly. Pray let us hear as much from you as you can afford."[3] Olmsted had grown fond of Charles Eliot. In his travels abroad, the young man had seemed to enjoy tracing out the course Olmsted had prescribed and had then gone on to open vistas for himself. He had an exquisite kind of courtesy, proper from pupil to teacher. For Mr. Olmsted, he hunted up and found Humphrey Repton's village house and had a photographer take a picture of it. Olmsted had expressed a desire to possess such a photograph.

Showing a hardy adaptability, Olmsted changed his plans and took both Harry Codman, his second youthful apprentice, and his sixteen-year-old son, Frederick, to California. Olmsted saw again the west coast with his eyes as youthfully open to impressions as they had been a little more than twenty years earlier. With lively curiosity, he revisited the scenes of the Mountain View cemetery, the Berkeley school site, and the San Francisco park which he had suggested. Some delicacy of emotion—the fear of finding disappointment in a place of delight—or possibly mere inconvenience and shortness of time—held him back from returning to the Yosemite Valley, although he visited the Mariposa Grove again. He observed the growth of the city of San Francisco, the development of farming in the great valley, and, to his quiet disgust, the rate at which speculative fever had outpaced constructive growth.

On September 23, he wrote to John about a thirty-mile drive to see "the best orchard and vineyard and winter hotel district." He was interested in the forests of yucca in the Mohave Desert, "as large as our larger apple trees," in the barrenness of the land, its luxuriousness when watered, and other natural sights. But he ended with sarcasm: "But the principal occupation of the people is land speculation." And he hinted the derangement of his interior: "I am almost living on grapes."[4]

The principal California object he surveyed was the formidable speculator and railroad builder, former governor and now Senator Leland Stanford. He was a man in whom force was mixed with a certain crudity. Olmsted later showed a delicate and private dislike for the man's ignorance. Olmsted had recommended Augustus Saint-Gaudens as sculptor for a frieze for a memorial arch Stanford wished to erect at the proposed university. Saint-Gaudens was pleased with the opportunity. Olmsted assumed that anyone of Stanford's knowledgeability would have heard of Saint-Gaudens. But a letter from the Senator to the landscape architect casually turned down the suggestion and referred to the name he had heard as "De Gordon." Olmsted related the incident with cool disgust in a letter to Mariana Van Renssalaer.[5] (But St. Gaudens, after all, made the design.)

The coming together of Olmsted and Stanford was eventful. Letters survive between the two showing that they did not always find each other easy.[6] Eventually Olmsted withdrew from the project, but for a number of years, 1886 to 1891, he directed the basic plan of the Leland Stanford University. He traveled several times to California or sent Harry Codman when he could not go. He directed the initial siting and style of the original quadrangles, designed covered walkways for protection against the sun, planned the railroad station and the residence community which became Palo Alto, and directed the engineering of the roads of the university and the proposed town. He never was able to persuade Stanford to try the experiment of planting only those shrubs and trees that belonged in the region. Nor did he win Stanford to a western arboretum. Stanford was closer perhaps to the common sense of the West than Olmsted in this, stating crudely to his landscape architect that he did not want trees all over his hills.

When Olmsted was in California, he sometimes stayed with the Stanfords. One visit coincided with that of the widow of General Grant. She fastened gratefully upon Olmsted when he was able to give her some fresh recollections of the still unknown general gathering his powers, trying new ideas, in his river campaign before the fall of Vicksburg.[7] Olmsted had met Grant briefly during this period in a Sanitary Commission journey of inspection of a time that seemed very long gone in 1887.

From the time of the trip to California to begin work on the Stanford project, Olmsted looked upon Harry Codman as a trusted colleague. After an interval abroad, where he went as Charles Eliot had, to sophisticate his knowledge of gardens, parks, and city squares, Codman was taken into the Olmsted firm as a partner. (Charles Eliot had set up his own landscape design firm in Boston.) Codman became almost another son to the older man, and was on brotherly terms with both John and Frederick, Jr. For a number of years he was to be second only to Frederick Olmsted himself in the sensitivity and originality of his ideas in design. And in his youthful but stockily mature person, he was also a human support to the Olmsted family.

Whether in California, summoned by an imperious private command such as Leland Stanford's, or in Boston or another city at the command of a board of commissioners, Olmsted himself continued to stretch his thought and his imagination. Sometimes he wrote his reports as if to himself rather than to the hard-fisted and hard-headed men who were his official patrons. In his September, 1886, "Notes on the Plan of Franklin Park," he noted dreamily, "The chief end of a large park is an effect on the human organism by an action of what it presents to view, which action, like that of music, is of a kind that goes back of thought, and cannot be fully given the form of words."[8]

The temperament which Olmsted carried into each new project was still, for a man in his late sixties, a comparatively flexible one. Despite protesting that he tired easily and that he liked to go to sleep over his evening paper, he kept on absorbing new impressions and dealing handily with new situations. And in his life away from his work, he began to doubt the efficacy of the political conservatism which, in him, had hardened in his reaction to the bloody efforts of the war. He did not, like his friend Charles Norton, have a general, amorphous fear of "the democracy." For the first time, in 1884, he supported a Democratic Party candidate, Cleveland, over a Republican, Blaine. He became, apparently, mildly, a Mugwump in the Boston arena, when called upon by Charles Francis Adams II to help rally outraged liberal Republican sentiment during this particular election. It was also in the 1880s that his correspondence showed a sympathy for the increasing hard times of workmen in the new kinds of concentrated industry which the postwar years had brought into being.

He had always been a sharp if fair bargainer when he employed labor for his parks. But he carried into these negotiations the assumption (which had seemed true in his youth) that every man owning his own talents and abilities could make a way for himself. He was forced to see, in the decades following the war, that the individual workman did not always find a decent place for himself in American life solely on the basis of his merits. He expressed something of this in a letter he wrote to Norton on March 16, 1886, advice to be passed on to J. B. Harrison, who was going to write a series of newspaper articles on the labor problem. (Norton and Olmsted had secured the assignment for Harrison, who was generally impecunious and desperate for work.)

Olmsted was aware of how difficult it would be for Harrison to be truthful about labor conditions and yet not offend the newspaper and the newspaper's corporate supporters. "It is a very delicate business matter with the *Herald* which must if possible retain the good will of both sides. I believe the employers in the large corporations here, are not in the least disposed to fair discussion. They are generally taking the sea captain's view and regard every grievance and aspiration of the working man as unreasonable and unnatural. The great body of working men are necessarily in a corresponding attitude."[9] In this case the "here" referred to was Lowell, Massachusetts.

Upon another great subject of the day, the woman question, Olmsted failed to be upset. If an occasional woman was found to be doing a man's work, or if he ran across a woman with a good intelligence about public matters, he was not alarmed. His relationship with his own wife had given him this advantage. She had always been interested in what he did, and he did not resent it when she expressed her opinion decidedly. He had used her advice occasionally, as in asking her more than once for names for streets or subdivisions. They had laughed together and grieved together over the vicissitudes of his professional life. She had not been relegated to sharing only family concerns. Olmsted respected her mind and the lively concern she had continued, in maturity, to have for literature and music and even for amateur geologizing. When Frederick, Jr., matriculated at Harvard, the young man was confident that he had no need to take French; his mother could coach him in that language.

Olmsted's letters to Mariana Van Renssalaer show him pleased and stimulated by the admiration tendered him by an attractive, intelligent woman. He also respected her writing and told her so unaffectedly. Because he found communication with her easy, he wrote to her during this period often, not only about building and land design, but about anything and everything. On August 19, 1886, he gave her material for an article describing and criticizing the new state capitol at Albany. He urged her particularly to give Eidlitz as well as Richardson credit for the revised architecture of this difficult building. "I must say that I think no one does justice to Mr. Eidlitz. I wish that you could know him."[10] He told her that Eidlitz and Richardson were two very different men who had worked well together. Richardson had had gusto and originality. Eidlitz had an incisive intelligence which cut through sham. He was remembered as saying: "American architecture is the art of covering one thing with another thing to imitate a third thing which, if genuine, would not be desirable."[11]

Olmsted had written to Mrs. Van Renssalaer about Eidlitz from Brookline, but he carried the letter unfinished to California, and he concluded it with a humorous, personal commentary on his situation there: "Not precisely in the shade of palm trees but at a window looking out on palms and cypresses, laurels and oranges, live oaks and vineyards (muskitoes, dust, smoke, fog and the mercury at 100°)."[12]

Olmsted came to respect another young woman as a professional. He welcomed her without jealousy to the "brotherhood" of landscape architects. This was Elizabeth Bullard of Bridgeport, Connecticut. She had assisted her father in the execution of Olmsted's park work in that city. When her father died, Olmsted recommended that Miss Bullard succeed to the municipal position which her father had held. Surprisingly, the commission acceded, and Miss Bullard became Bridgeport's landscape adviser. Later, Olmsted was to recommend Elizabeth Bullard for a particular design job at the Chicago World's Fair.

As for women's suffrage, he remained complacently unmilitant. Unlike the Reverend Horace Bushnell, the religious mentor of his youth, who had written a pamphlet against votes for women, *Woman Suffrage: The Reform Against Nature*, and unlike his friend George William Curtis, who was publicly for votes for women, Olmsted took no advertised stand. He was undisturbed, or at least indifferent to this issue. Yet individually, he took his women as he found them. Having encountered several formidable ones during the Sanitary Commission days, knowing a number of them then who performed administrative functions with straightforward vigor, he never doubted women's human capabilities. Knowing Mary Olmsted herself, he did not ever express surprise at exceptional women, but rather enjoyed them, respected them, gave them the same kind of courteous advantage as he would a man who might appear in the position of being an expert in a particular field.

The familiarity, easy in its humor and self-deprecation, of his developing relationship with Mrs. Van Renssalaer shows in a letter he wrote to her on February 6, 1887. He had suffered an injury to his already lame leg. He had been in a railroad accident on the CB & Q line.

Thank you very much for writing me. My hurt is trifling, and I keep my bed under the doctor's orders only because I am knocking about and might get really hurt, and also because I want to earn $15 from the Accident Insurance Company.

It had better be a secret between us three that he is too good a fellow to travel for if it should get abroad his occupation would be gone and then an end, for he gets his living by it.[13]

As it turned out, his hurt was not really "trifling," but a cause of considerable pain and increased lameness. But he picked himself up and kept on going, not grimly, but with a kind of stoic joy in moving and doing.

A sign of his trust in Mariana Van Renssalaer was his allowing himself to speak frankly of Calvert Vaux to her. "Vaux and I have some differences but are fairly in accord. In the Niagara report he helped me and I helped him and at some points each of us crowded the other out a little."[14]

Olmsted did not have the time to interest himself vitally in areas out beyond the peripheries of his profession, but that calling stretched in several directions, mixing itself inevitably in politics and economics. With the men of the boards of commissioners who ruled his municipal work, Olmsted maintained a usually polite, if skeptical, relationship. These men were usually powerful economically, but to Olmsted's way of thinking, terribly ignorant of the public good, applying standards to city and town projects which were more appropriately applied to their private businesses, and even there often inappropriate to the good of the community. Yet he saw that, mistaken as they often were, and powerful in thwarting his aims, some of these men were honorable by their own standards. He wished for what did not exist: an overall public guidance for areas of public concern—in his own field, parks, streets, placement of residences, sanitation, recreation, and art. But he did not have a great deal of hope that he would see such a public policy come into being. And he had little time away from his own work to further these ideas. He simply expressed his opinion wistfully in private letters from time to time. (Olmsted's personal career would be fading out in the mid-nineties when at last some of these ideas began to be expressed powerfully in the public arena by such men as Theodore Roosevelt and Gifford Pinchot.)

It was his own art, that of land design, which occupied him during all these years. He believed that he had made landscape architecture a "liberal profession," and he considered himself one of the fraternity of artists, too, of the fellowship of such men as Richardson, Saint-Gaudens, and La Farge.

In his own important work of the past decade, Olmsted had lived and worked in easy companionship with other talented men. His association with architects was fortunate. He had enjoyed being partnered with Henry Hobson Richardson in several major works: the Buffalo mental hospital, the Albany state capitol, railroad stations, the memorial buildings erected by the Ames family. Richardson on his side had thoroughly understood what Olmsted meant by the proper setting for a building. Richardson's death was a blow to a working relationship as well as to friendship. Olmsted, however, continued to explore what could be done by a landscape designer in cooperation with an architect. He had an easy relationship with a number of outstanding architects, by some sort of intuition often recognizing their ability before that quality was generally known. He had encouraged William Le Baron Jenney in Chicago; Jenney designed a house at Riverside. Olmsted had verbal skirmishes with Richard Morris Hunt over the New York State capitol design but got on with him later; the two of them designed the Vanderbilt family mausoleum on Staten Island and shared later a cooperative effort in the George Vanderbilt estate and house in North Carolina. Olmsted had a keen appreciation for the shingle style of Stanford White and pointed out its virtues to Charles Eliot when they had business at Newport. In the next decade he would advise his son Rick to go see Adler and Sullivan's Auditorium in Chicago, and in that city; in the great World's Fair project, he and Codman would become the intimate associates of Burnham and Root.

But one must keep in mind that it was also an overburdened body and a mind stinted of sleep, put through eccentric schedules of travel, which took part in these creative cooperations. He continued to write the reports and plans of the firm although the physical and mental labor of writing became more onerous with the years. He insisted on rewriting, and yet his expression of general ideas was an awkward struggle to express original insights. His earlier writing had been of a distinctly different kind. The best parts of the Southern writings had possessed an almost self-mesmerized quality. He had simply absorbed the human scenery of the South and let the life he had observed flow from his young, untired pen. He had had a gift for the vernacular for conversation, for slang, and he had relished "characters." Even in those earlier writings, the general propositions had made for rather heavy going if worthy reading. This same rotundity of phrasing, so different from the flashing familiarity of his human observations, was characteristic often of his landscape reports. Yet there was much meat in the reports and phrases which achieved a succinct intellectual wit. He wrote about tree-planting in the Mount Royal Report of 1881: "When an artist puts a stick in the ground, and nature in time makes it a tree, art and nature are not to be seen apart in the result."[15] Of cities, in which he proposed to place parks, he spoke with the intimacy of close knowledge: "the devouring eagerness and intellectual strife of town life."[16] Trying to explain the planning and development of parks, he used terminology from painting: "It is a common error to regard a park as something to be produced complete in itself, as a picture to be painted on canvas. It should rather be planned as one to be done in fresco, with constant consideration of exterior objects, some of them quite at a distance and even existing as yet only in the imagination of the painter."[17]

Olmsted wished his ideas to be known. He wrote painfully and constantly himself. In his later years, Mariana Van Renssalaer's articles expressed for him many of his ideas. With Charles Sprague Sargent, he founded a magazine, *Garden and Forest*. Sargent, who was more active than Olmsted in this project, fell ill at about the time the first issue was to come out. Olmsted stepped in and aided the editor, William A. Stiles, in nursing the first number into being, shortly after January, 1888. Thereafter, Stiles, in New York City, acted as a kind of informal friendly spy for Olmsted, letting him know what was happening in the management of the public parks of New York and Brooklyn. Through Stiles, Olmsted's ideas, usually indirectly, found their way into print, in an attractive magazine, too expensively designed for its own survival, and these expressions helped to block or at least mitigate some of the hindrances put upon these public park areas.[18]

Olmsted was happy in returning to New England. Yet his profession caused him to travel farther and farther away from the comforts of 99 Warren Street, Brookline. Not the least interesting of new engagements after 1888 were those that took him south. This was thirty years after his earlier travels in the 1850s, when the same area in very different circumstances had aroused his curiosity, admiration, anger, and despair. His reawakening concern was both historical and personal. In the 1850s and the 1860s Olmsted had been a keen observer and a participant in the North-South struggle. In the 1880s and 1890s he wished to see a hopeful change in the South, a development which would tell him that his earlier involvement had been well justified. He was also incorrigibly interested in what had become of the land and the people of this other part of the United States.

An opportunity to go back to the South and do professional work there came to him from one of the Vanderbilts, a family with whom he had been acquainted on Staten Island. Since the rise of the Vanderbilts to dazzling and blatant power, Olmsted had done work for different members in various places, on Staten Island, at Lenox, at Newport. He had probably met George Vanderbilt while designing the site of the Vanderbilt family mausoleum on Staten Island. And it was this George Vanderbilt, of the fourth generation in succession to the commodore, who called on Olmsted to go down to Asheville, North Carolina, and advise him what to do with an estate he was at this time secretly purchasing, buying up acres upon acres through an agent, so that he might assemble a large aggregation of land without exciting the local sellers.

George Vanderbilt was far enough removed from the creator of the family fortune to be a spender rather than an accumulator, and he was, in addition, something of an introspective dreamer. He had a kind of cloudy ambition to make something distinctive of this new place of his in the southern mountains. And with his inherited share of shrewdness, he called upon the best known landscape designer for help, a man whose reputation he knew already.

When Olmsted came south to see George Vanderbilt's estate, his client was a young man, a bachelor, caring for his mother, for whom in part he proposed this place as a pleasant winter residence. Vanderbilt had been down to Asheville a few times and found the small town an attractive refuge from northern weathers. It was already a resort for well-to-do Northerners, an exotic stock grafted upon a small native mountain community. The land which Vanderbilt began to buy up, at a point four miles south of the town, lay just beyond the French Broad River. His proposed estate stretched over rolling, hilly, wooded land upon a sort of plateau at an altitude of nearly three thousand feet between mountain ranges. To the north, northwest, and northeast the ranges were higher, to the south the mountain country fell off precipitously to the lower foothills. His greatest asset was a long view to the northwest in the direction of the distinctive double peak of Pisgah, the highest elevation in this area of the Blue Ridge which scalloped the horizon. Young Vanderbilt did not play with railroads or steamship lines as the Commodore had, but he had an overweening desire, akin to the chateau-building on Fifth Avenue of other members of his family, to make his place here in the southern wilderness the greatest house and estate of the neighborhood and no fear of making it inappropriate. He had also a land hunger which would keep him buying acres until at last his domain stretched all the way to Mount Pisgah, the exclamation point of the entire region.

Olmsted liked this highland countryside, remembering his pleasure in it when he was a young man traversing it by horseback, but he was not at first impressed by the immediate surroundings of the proposed chateau. Olmsted saw what mankind, hungry for wood in a poor area, had done in destroying the first-growth forest here. It had been a grand and awe-inspiring forest at one time, and there were mountainous areas only a few miles away which were still unruined. But impoverished "poor whites," scratching for a living, had cut down nearly all the trees of any consequence. Vanderbilt had perhaps not even noticed the discrepancy between the coarse new growth on his house site and the nobler original forests higher in the hills. Olmsted candidly pointed out to him the defects and assets of the scene. Both men, in a dry and chilly end of summer, August, 1888, admired the blue line of mountains in the distance. Vanderbilt planned to build himself a hunting lodge among the laurel and rhododendron of the higher elevations.

Vanderbilt had only a vague kind of notion, inspired by his idea of what English country squires did with their land, of making this wild and difficult rank growth roundabout into a park, perhaps with deer grazing, imported deer, probably. Olmsted later reconstructed, for Fred Kingsbury, the conversation he had had with Vanderbilt. According to his recollection, Vanderbilt had said to him about his property:

"Now I have brought you here to examine it and tell me if I have been doing anything very foolish." "What do you imagine you will do with all this land," I asked. "Make a park of it, I suppose." "You bought the place then simply because you thought it had good air and because, from this point, it had a good distant outlook. If that was what you wanted you have made no mistake. There is no question about the air and none about the prospect. But the soil seems to be generally poor. The woods are miserable, all the good trees having again and again been culled out and only runts left. The topography is most unsuitable for anything that can properly be called park scenery. It's no place for a park. You could only get very poor results at great cost in attempting it." "What could be done with it?" "Such land in Europe would be made a forest; partly, if it belonged to a gentleman of large means, as a preserve for game, mainly with a view to crops of timber. That would be a suitable and dignified business for you to engage in; it would, in the long run, be probably a fair investment of capital and it would be of great value to the country to have a thoroughly well organized and systematically conducted attempt in forestry, made on a large scale. My advice would be to make a small park into which to look from your house, make a small pleasure ground and gardens; farm your river bottoms chiefly to keep and fatten live stock with a view to manure; and make the rest a forest, improving the existing woods and planting the old fields." This advice struck him favorably and after thinking it over several months he told me that he was prepared to adopt it. Since then I have [been] giving it practical form and have each division of the scheme in operation.[19] (January, 20, 1891.)

(The forest has become a possession of the people of the United States, the Pisgah National Forest, the first national forest of the United States, its history commemorated in the Museum of the Cradle of American Forestry. The house, sited as Olmsted planned, dominates its acres. The estate is useful to the community in its dairying. The house and estate are perhaps more appropriate in having been transformed into a tourist attraction than they ever were as the residence of a small family.)

In the early 1890s very little of this calm and assured future could be seen by those who visited the dusty, torn-up site. Only Olmsted was able to see what existed at the moment and what might exist there in the future. He foresaw the growth of small straight saplings, young tulip poplars, into a giant double row which would mark the approach to the house. He foresaw a sheltered walk under a trellis protected by an extended wall. He imagined gardens, park, pasture, and forest stretching in succession away toward the mountains.

Biltmore was an absorbing interest to Olmsted for the remainder of his working life. He came again and again to Asheville (Ashville, as he persistently spelled it). He insisted to George Vanderbilt, and to himself, that this rich man's fantastic chateau and generous estate were going to be valuable to the community in which it was situated and an opportunity to him, the designer, whatever the owner thought of Biltmore, as show of wealth or sign of position in society, Olmsted appropriated the place in his imagination for grand experiments in his art.

Having once come south to Asheville, it did not seem difficult, thereafter, to continue coming south, and to extend his field of operations to other southern cities. He found himself making regular swings from Asheville to Montgomery, or Atlanta, and on beyond to Richmond. Sometimes he stopped in Knoxville, or Louisville. These large movements tired but intrigued the man, newly exploring the old land.

In 1889, he visited the former capital of the defeated Confederacy at the request of the governor of the state of Alabama. There was some possibility of refurbishing the grounds of the capitol building. Thomas H. Clark, the governor's secretary, was a knowledgeable man who had read Olmsted's southern writings with little trace of southern prejudice. It is possible that he, who knew the name Olmsted, suggested him as a landscape architect. In any case, it was Clark who opened the correspondence with Olmsted in March and April, 1889. Clark warned Olmsted, even before he came to Montgomery, that the state might not be able to pay for his services. But Olmsted, his curiosity whetted, came on anyway. He was to be in Asheville, in any case, and was to go on to Atlanta, so a detour to Montgomery would not be difficult.

He looked over the grounds, proposed drastic but simple changes in land contours and wall building which he saw as necessary to protect the site. The costs, however, were too severe to be borne at that time by the finances of the state. In addition no competent topographical engineer could be found in the vicinity to do the kind of map-making which Olmsted would require in his absence. Clark had to write to Olmsted, regretfully, that the Governor had decided to make do with local talent for a less extensive job, and that the services of Mr. Olmsted would not be required.

Clark, who had missed seeing Olmsted, wrote to him on July 20, 1889: "I had been anxious to meet you, more particularly because your books on the South made me curious to know something of your opinions on the problems that are before us now, the relics of Slavery."[20] On August 5, Olmsted, eager to express his opinions, replied to Clark. He took a high line about the missed job: "I feel sure that if the property-holders and businessmen of Montgomery know their own interest they would not let funds be lacking for a more substantial improvement than the Governor thinks practical."[21]

He addressed himself to Clark's general question with a readiness that showed how he had continued to think of these matters:

You kindly say you would like to know how I look upon the after troubles of slavery. I will tell you.

It was not reasonably to be expected when the war ended that the great body of intelligent whites of the South should make so great a change in their habits as would be necessary to the placing of the freedmen all at once on a perfect equality with them before the law.

He went on to say that he had, long before the war overwhelmed both North and South, preferred a gradual approach to emancipation.

If I could I would have secured to the freedmen the full rights of intending citizens, yet unnaturalized. I would have placed clearly before them, and at no indefinite or discouraging distance, perfect political equality with white citizens, but this upon conditions making such political equality a privilege to be earned. . . . As far as I could judge, those who differed with me did so, for the most part, because they took a more hopeful view than I did of the condition of the mass of the freedmen.

[But that possibility of gradualism was long past.] I regard it now as one of the fixed conditions of the country, as surely fixed, for all practical purposes, as its geological conditions, that our people of African blood are to stand on the same political footing as citizens of any other blood. . . .

The negroes have been doing a great deal better as freedmen than I had ever imagined it possible that they would. The whites have accepted the situation about as well as it was in human nature that they should.

Olmsted found the measure of prosperity in the South greater than he had expected "in so short a time after so great a catastrophe." He knew that the elections were often not fair to the Negroes. This was not unexpected to one who had traveled in the South before the war, but: "We are only anxious to have the more intelligent people of the South show a disposition and purpose to struggle out of it as fast as possible."[22]

After investing so much passion in the late struggle, Olmsted wished to be hopeful. Perhaps he had more hope than the facts justified. But the decade of the 1880s was, in truth, a more hopeful time in the South than the decades before or after. Earlier, the poverty of all Southerners, white and black, had been too dire and the military occupation too much resented, for any kind of rational adjustment. Afterwards, in the 1890s and 1900s, the Jim Crow laws enforced a stiffening code of public behavior which had been up to this time somewhat fluid.

Olmsted found in both the West and the South a deep satisfaction in linking this late life to his earlier adventures. Going south and seeing what was happening there interested him. Going to California and looking over the changes in that far area of the continent made a kind of closure to his experiences there in the sixties.

He had kept quiet for long years about the bad treatment which Yosemite had received under California state management. But he had watched attentively the growing controversy about how to preserve such a wild national park—national in fact, if not so in law as yet. Journalists such as Richard Watson Gilder and Robert Underwood Johnson wrote frequently on the subject. John Muir, a decade after Olmsted helped to bring the park into being, began his relentless campaign to save Yosemite from logging, grazing, and every other kind of misuse. Olmsted wrote to Gilder: "I have a deep and abiding interest in the subject. I shall be glad if Mr. Johnson's advice to the Yosemite Commissioners through Senator Stanford leads them to consult me." Yet he declined to write an article on the subject requested by Gilder for *The Century*. If he could help without publicity, he would. "I should like to have a talk with Mr. Johnson and with Mr. Muir on the subject. Are either of them likely to come to you at Marion? If so, might he not find it convenient to let me see him in Boston, or to make me a little visit here."²³

However, Olmsted, stung by a false public statement, consented less than a year later to write about Yosemite in a pamphlet to be distributed privately. A copy survives in the Bancroft Library at Berkeley, dated Brookline, Massachusetts, March 8, 1890, and entitled "Governmental Preservation of Natural Scenery." As a writer on the topic, he introduced himself modestly as one who had not been to Yosemite since 1865; but having heard of the damage being done to the park, particularly to the young trees, and having been asked by R. U. Johnson of *The Century* to express himself, he would do so. Olmsted's name had been brought into the controversy in a slighting manner by a public communication from Governor Waterman of California who had spoken disparagingly of the early preservers, presumably naming F. L. Olmsted. He, the governor, was at this time enthusiastic about the possibility of a cable road to ascend the wall of the valley. In this first piece of writing he had done on the subject since 1865, Olmsted reviewed the already almost forgotten origin of the park.

In the year 1864, being then a citizen of California, I had the honor to be made chairman of the first Yosemite Commission, and in that capacity to take possession of the Valley for the State, to organize and direct the survey of it and to be the executive of various measures taken to guard the elements of its scenery from fires, trespassers and abuse. In the performance of these duties, I visited the Valley frequently, established a permanent camp in it and virtually acted as its superintendent. It was then to be reached from the nearest village only by a sixty mile journey in the saddle, and there were many more Indians in it than white men. The office had come to me unexpectedly and in a manner that earned my devotion. So far from a salary coming with it, it was an affair of considerable cost to me, which I have not asked to be reimbursed.

He told of moving away from California, getting the date wrong, as 1867, or being misprinted. "I have not been in the Valley since; but because of some knowledge of this pioneer duty of mine, travelers returning from it have often told me of what they thought missteps in its administration."

He went on to protest vigorously the imminent cutting of the trees in the park. This cutting of young trees would "be equivalent to the destruction, in course of time, of just what the State of California stands voluntarily pledged to 'hold, inalienably, for all time.'" The words were from the federal act ceding the land to California for the purpose of establishing it as a permanent park for the people of the whole nation. Olmsted stated carefully that he did not make a charge against the present commissioners but said in level judgment that these men had "taken a narrow, short-sighted and market-place view of the duty of the State in the premises."

He quoted then the words of his and Vaux's report to those charged with preserving the scenery of the Niagara Falls area, words which would seem appropriate to preservationists of a later time: "Nothing of an artificial character should be allowed a place on the property, no matter how valuable it might be under other circumstances, and no matter at how little cost it may be had, the presence of which can be avoided consistently with the provision of necessary conditions for making the enjoyment of natural scenery available."

In writing these words about Yosemite, or in corresponding with a Southern governor's secretary about postwar conditions, Olmsted knitted his present to his past and, growing older, preserved the wholeness of his life.

CHAPTER XXVII

A Pisgah View

I cannot go out without being delighted.
—F. L. O., to Harry Codman, from Chislehurst,
England, January 30, 1892[1]

IN THIS NEXT TO THE LAST PART of Olmsted's career, the old man, full of works and honors, found it poignantly necessary to come to an agreement with himself. He had reached a time of self-contemplation and of private statements of belief. The force of this need, interrupting him in the midst of deeds, will be shown in a number of letters remarkably autobiographical. It was as if, growing older and frailer, aware of the limits of his strength and efforts, Olmsted was freshly, naively curious about himself and interested in what he had done.

He had an exchange with William James in July, 1891, at a time of enforced rest in bed when he was recovering from an attack of arsenic poisoning which was thought to have been caused by a new "Turkey Red" wallpaper in his wife's bedroom.[2] He and James, it seems, had fallen into conversation upon some joint public or club occasion. James, indefatigable in collecting mental phenomena, had mentioned a case of "open-eyed sleep visions," the words James used in a letter which followed their meeting, a communication inviting Olmsted's experiences.[3] Olmsted responded with an eager interest. He recalled that, on the long voyage to China when he had had scurvy, he had tried to stay awake while on duty on the forecastle in order to prevent himself being washed overboard. He remembered that he had gone to sleep with his eyes open, and not hearing or seeing his captain approach, had invited a reprimand or even a blow. He had had another experience traveling on a train only a year before talking with James when he had dreamed with his eyes open that he had given a conductor his ticket—and found he had not done so in fact. Warming to this confessing of strange experiences, Olmsted went on with a family experience that he and Mary and the others had had in the old Dutch farmhouse at Southside. For entertainment one night, Frederick had made up a story about a ghost, a British soldier-ghost, created to fit the creaky, aging house, a drummer boy locked in the cellar for drunkenness, forgotten there, and left to starve when the British abandoned the place after a short occupation. The young Olmsteds and their lively guests then kept the story going by imagining that they heard him on stormy evenings. They gave themselves a pleasurable shiver and frightened a succession of Irish maids. Then, oddly, as if they had brought a ghost to life, they found the brassplate off the belt of a one-time real British soldier in the old carriage house on the farm.[4] William James sent back a postcard, thanked Olmsted for his highly curious accounts, and added Olmsted's open-eyed visions to his widening collection of curious mental states.[5]

Olmsted was never busier, nor more characteristically involved in the activities of a vulgar growing America. He kept himself so constantly awake in plans, trips, and the writing of reports that his mind quivered from the effort. He was drawn into the earliest planning of the great Chicago fair, the World's Columbian Exposition, as it was so grandly to be named. On August 7, 1890, he wrote to his son Rick about the firm's beginning to take part in the project. "Harry and I are to leave early tomorrow for Chicago on a call from the World's Fair Commission to help them decide about sites."[6] The father wished already to share with the younger son knowledge about projects; in his mind, Frederick, Jr., was already heir apparent to the work he was doing.

"Harry" was Harry S. Codman, who had come back from a period of personal exploration abroad and been taken into the firm, which was now known officially as F. L. Olmsted & Co. John Olmsted and Harry Codman were both partners. Codman was a young man of a winning solidity of appearance, sporting a new moustache. He was one of the family in intimacy. When Olmsted, on his travels in June, 1890, this time at Bar Harbor, Maine, designing vacation landscapes for the Vanderbilts, wrote back to the office, it was to "Dear J. & H."[7] [John and Harry], and he could depart from Brookline in confidence that things would be well handled while he was away. Olmsted could not perform any piece of business without digesting it into his personal life. His home was his office; his office was his home; and each young man passing through a training in the art of landscape architecture under Frederick Olmsted's close tutelage succeeded and became a friend, or failed and disappeared forever.

The Chicago exposition was to give Harry Codman his greatest opportunity to exercise a rapidly maturing ability. He has probably never yet been given the credit his memory deserves. It was a heady experience for the young man to go with Frederick Olmsted to Chicago and to meet on equal terms Daniel Burnham and John Wellborn Root, the architects who were to be the other half of the team designated to make a basic design for the fair. The four men, uniting in the job, exercised diverse and complementary talents in bringing this ambitious western project into being. However, this could happen only after they wrestled the commissioners of the fair into agreeing to a site. Olmsted and Codman let it be known that they would withdraw from the enterprise if the proposed scene did not include a considerable area of lakeshore. Olmsted saw clearly in 1890 what he had known as early as 1869, that Chicago had only one great natural asset, the lake. He thought a north shore area the best choice. When that was vetoed, and he and Codman with Burnham's and Root's help had also overcome inland sites, he was happy to agree to place the exposition on the ground of the undeveloped lakeside park south of the city which he had planned years before. Horace Cleveland, in his administration of the Chicago parks, had been able to refine only Washington Park, the inland part of the old project of South Park. The sandy area alongside the lake was almost as desolate in 1890 as it had been in 1869. Olmsted saw in the exposition a chance to wring from the city fathers of Chicago the promise long ago broken, to convert the area, after the fair should close down, into the park he had planned. This was to become in fact, after his basic design, Jackson Park.

Olmsted believed almost as eagerly as the ordinary civic booster of the city in the future greatness and present vitality of Chicago. He was willing to eliminate other projects of the Olmsted firm in order to throw all the energies they had into the great fair, an enterprise in which a great many interesting talents seemed willing to join together. He wrote to John on October 29 that Chicago was going to take all of Codman's time, half his own, and a quarter of John's for some time.[8] He allowed, or rather encouraged, Rick to come out during his summers and work alongside the others.

But this was to look forward. In the late summer and early fall of 1890, Olmsted found that Dan Burnham was the much-to-be-depended-on battering ram of their joint desires. Complementing Burnham, John Root had the clever, rapid pencil to sketch the heights and shapes of tentative buildings. He seized upon brown paper which was all they had in hand one early day of inspection of the site when the four men walked over the ground together. Under Root's pencil they saw their early, spontaneous ideas taking shape. Olmsted's was the basic plan of land and water shape. Codman's task was to refine and execute Olmsted's first vision. Burnham would implement the whole affair, with a benign but firm authority. Root would stimulate and coordinate work of a handful of other architects.

On August 20, 1890, F. L. Olmsted and Company was retained officially as the consulting landscape architectural firm for the fair. Burnham and Root was in a comparable position as the official firm of architectural consultants. When in Chicago, Olmsted lived usually at a hotel, but sometimes on the grounds of the fair, and took his mess with the workmen. In the city he and Codman shared office space with Burnham and Root in the building the architects had designed, The Rookery. The two firms had stationery printed with a joint letterhead. The architects' finely designed office fireplace was a meeting place on the occasions they could get together for talk, for joyful agreements as well as arguments or discussions of setbacks and other everyday agonies. The four men worked together in an easy, large-minded harmony. No one of them was limited to a particular area of the project. Olmsted might be the molder of the land, but he did not hold back from telling the director of works (Burnham) what he thought about other matters that came to mind. The work was swiftly done in a happy union of opposite personalities. Doubly tragic was the way death was to break up the quartet.

The idea which Olmsted had had more than twenty years before for a park could be used here as the basic design of the fair grounds. Sand would be dredged out of the shallow marshes of this desolate shore to make irregularly shaped lagoons; the land between could be built up to make a solid base for the buildings. Olmsted's particular delight, a part of the fair he considered his own, was to be a "wooded isle," surrounded by shining, peopled busyness, but secluded, unbuilt upon, a place of rest for people tired of the normal bustle of the crowds: nature set over against the creations of man.

The fair complicated itself from month to month and Frederick Olmsted or Harry Codman or John Olmsted in relay came and went during the next three years. Here, a roster of artists—Richard Morris Hunt, Louis Sullivan, Augustus Saint-Gaudens, and others—worked remarkably well together, although later Sullivan was to see more their differences than their harmonies. At least, he saw his personal idiosyncrasy drowned in the likeness of all the others. Root had, at the beginning, as one of the two architectural advisers, envisaged a warmer tone of color in the buildings and perhaps more diversity in styles. If he had lived, the look of the fair would have been different. Only Sullivan's "golden door" through which one entered his Transportation Building answered this original lost idea. Yet the painted white of the buildings, the agreed upon uniformity of their cornice lines, and the harmony of the one approach ("beaux-arts," after Hunt's prescription) had the strength of an easily visible overall style to both the naive and the sophisticated viewer. The effect was transiently beautiful and dazzling, both in the daytime reflections in the waterways created by Olmsted and in the unaccustomed brightness of electrical lighting at night. The coming together of the principal architects, men not randomly selected, but chosen at the beginning under the firm guidance of the two architects and the two landscape architects, had at least the effect of an overall excellence of conception and execution. These were men not all of genius but at least of decided abilities who knew that they had been given an outline and a foundation on which to embroider their temporary elevations.

Aristides Homos in Howells's *Letters of An Altrurian Traveler* found the Chicago Exposition a portent of what American civilization might achieve, if it turned away from selfishness and competition. The author used the fair (and later, Central Park in New York) to make Altrurian points against what he disliked in his contemporary culture.

I first saw the Fair City by night, from one of the electric launches which ply upon the lagoon; and under the dimmed heaven, in the splendor of the hundred moony arc-lamps of the esplanades, and the myriad incandescent bubbles that beaded the white quays, and defined the structural lines of dome and porch and pediment.

Howells's critic from another world reacted, as Olmsted had foreseen a sensitive man might, to the dark element of water just beyond this scene made with human hands: "the lake, whose soft moan came appealingly through the pillared spaces, and added a divine heartache to my ecstasy."[9]

Olmsted kept his head while the fair was going up. He fought for the natural, unobtrusive look he wished his settings to have; hunted for water plants to give his lagoons the appearance of having been there for at least a century; caused the sand-dredging to be adjusted so that it did not destroy plantings; banished from his plan showy, vulgar, cheap displays of even magnificent flowers, preferring a beauty of line. His hardest fought battle was to keep the Wooded Isle free from displays. He was forced to allow the Japanese government exhibit to be placed there; fortunately, the Japanese temperament fell in with his, and these visitors placed an unobtrusive building among Olmsted's green, shadowy spaces. Just before the fair was to be dedicated, Olmsted and his associates feared that they would have failed to complete the plantings in time, but Burnham's heroic push goaded landscape workers as well as architects into doing more than they had thought possible. When a pompous opening ceremony (approximately four hundred years after Columbus's landing) took place, with platform speeches and public salutations, Olmsted stood off upon the ground away from the dais and was an observer rather than a participant. The fair did not open to the public until May 1, 1893, a half year later.

On March 25, 1893, the artists of the exposition held a grand dinner in New York City in Madison Square Garden to honor Daniel Burnham and also to celebrate the completion of their work. It was a civic occasion in the grand style of the decade. At the climax, after dinner, music and a stereoscopic presentation of scenes of the fair took place. Then a giant silver loving cup was presented to Burnham, who had been the merciless pusher and puller of all these united talents. He gracefully acknowledged the tribute and then made in his turn a speech in honor of Frederick Law Olmsted who was not there but on his travels between Atlanta and Washington—as usual, habitually and conveniently absent from a large formal and public occasion.

Burnham said, in part:

Each of you know the name and genius of him who stands first in the heart and confidence of American artists, the creator of your own parks and many other city parks. He it is who has been our best adviser and our common mentor.

In the highest sense he is the planner of the Exposition—Frederick Law Olmsted. No word of his has fallen to the ground among us since he joined us some thirty months ago. An artist, he paints with lakes and wooded slopes; with lawns and banks and forest-covered hills; with mountain-sides and ocean views. He should stand where I do tonight, not for his deeds of later years alone, but for what his brain has wrought and his pen has taught for half a century.[10]

Olmsted had so little vanity (as distinct from pride), there is no record in his letters that he ever reported at length to anyone the gist of this public tribute, nor ever dwelt upon it to friends.

(The story of the fair has been carried here beyond much of the detail of Olmsted's work upon it and concern for it, so that the accomplishment may be seen whole. A return to the circumstances of the months which went into the creation of the fair will not be treated as contradictory to the summary of its completion.)

Olmsted's high and mighty pride in his profession had come to be concentrated in his imagination upon the head of his youngest son, Frederick, Jr. For Olmsted, everything that he accomplished had some sort of private reference to his boy Rick, who was to inherit the legacy which he intended to bequeath to him, an inheritance of work, responsibility, and aspiration. When Rick showed up, a guileless, happy, and unsophisticated freshman at Harvard, the father wrote, behind Rick's back, to Professor Charles Eliot Norton, trying to smooth the path of the new student. "You remember Rick as a child. He tells me that he has official occasion to call on you today, as a Freshman. He is still just a good healthy boy, keeping the boyish condition longer than most, but not puerile." With an attempt at Connecticut restraint, the father characterized the boy "of a slow mind rather than otherwise, he has himself under good discipline, is studious, patient, deferential." But his feelings pushed through this play at being objective: "I like him very much and he is affectionate and confiding to me, more than boys generally are to their fathers, I think."[11] He told Norton, humbly, that he would be grateful for any advice he might give Rick. Norton replied equably two days later that he had met and liked Rick. He turned aside gracefully from Olmsted's almost embarrassing urgency. He had, he said, seen Olmsted's portrait in last week's *Harper's*. "What a good ancient philosopher you look like! But, indeed, what a good old philosopher you are!"[12]

Even before Rick entered Harvard, his father had written to the young man a long letter putting upon him a mission which, perhaps, young Rick did not at this time see with the same importance as his father. The older man admitted that he had himself "been rather grandly successful," but he had only so far kept "the enemy in check." He went on as if, casting his eye back at all the frays and battles in which he had taken part, his life had been a kind of war. He continued with military metaphors. "These young men, John and Harry, Eliot and Coolidge, with Sargent and Stiles and Mrs. Van Renssalaer are the advance of the reinforcements. I want you to be prepared to be a leader of the van."[13] He had named his oldest son, Codman, and the other apprentices in the office, as well as allies like Sargent of the Arboretum, Stiles of *Garden and Forest*, Mariana Van Renssalaer, whose criticism he admired, as if they had all been soldiers in a cause. He had a fierce, un-relenting conception of his work as imperiled by dangers, resisted by huge, implacable forces. In the father's eye, this youngest recruit, for surely he was to be one of them, would go far, perhaps farthest. It was a stiff sort of ambi-tion to thrust upon Rick. Yet the young man let it roll off him. He had the aplomb of youth. He threw himself into the enjoyments of life off Harvard Square as if he did not have on him the heritage of a whole profession. He was conscientious enough in his studies, yet had plenty of time to enjoy foot-ball and patronize his father on that esoteric subject. "Of course," he wrote to "Dear Father," on November 25, 1890, "you have seen accounts of the great Harvard-Yale Foot Ball game in the papers, and it would be no use for me to tell you about the game itself as you could not understand it."[14]

Rick carelessly let his father know that he had studied at night, or been out late, and so lost sleep. Olmsted replied with extreme emphasis.[15] He required that his college son send a weekly memorandum stating what hour he went to bed each night. He had a sudden horror of Rick's behaving as he himself had done all his life, turning night to day, going without sleep to work, finally losing, as he had at last done, the habit of easy sleep altogether. For in these later years, more and more, Olmsted suffered from insomnia.

One can picture Olmsted writing his long letters to friends late at night, after a day of exhausting work or travel. Such a letter he wrote to Charles Loring Brace on January 18, 1890, upon the occasion of receiving Brace's latest book. He thanked his friend and tried to encourage him. Brace had written to Olmsted, apparently, in a tone of some discouragement. Olmsted urged that the two of them might go on producing with "a sufficient chance of our being in working condition ten years longer." He went on about himself. "If I have lost power in some ways I have gained compensatingly in others, and it must be more so with you and your chances of living vigorously and, with your habits, a great deal better than mine. I never had more before me or less inclination to lay off than now, though my arrangements are such that nobody need be dissatisfied if I drop out tomorrow, John and Codman being ready to take up all my work and on an average better qualified for it than I am. My office is much better equipped and has more momentum than ever be-fore."[16]

Olmsted and Brace did not see very much of each other, but Frederick found it easy to reminisce in writing to the grave and important man who had been the Charley of his youth: "Do you remember a night we passed sleeping upon an earthen floor with our feet toward a peat fire with an old woman who gave us a piteous account of her sufferings in the famine? It amused me to find that I was entertaining her landlord in the Earl of Meath."[17] Lord

Meath, visiting the United States, sought Olmsted's acquaintance. He was willing to take lessons from this eminent practitioner of good land preservation. He showed Olmsted pictures of his land. In the contours of the hills in the photographs, Olmsted recognized a place he had been with Charley Brace in their visit to Ireland, a place where the two of them had suffered vicariously in the wants of the Irish peasants. Olmsted, so unknown then, sought out now by the rich, had some private relish at the situation. And he recalled to his friend the intense emotions they had experienced in this youthful expedition.

Charles Brace was to die in the year of this correspondence, putting an end to this kind of exchange. He had gone abroad for his health with his wife, Letitia. Olmsted had been unwilling to think of his friend's illness as fatal. But Brace incontinently died while in Switzerland on August 11, 1890.

To Fred Kingsbury, the only other member of the old circle of friends with whom he had still a relation of intimacy, Fred Olmsted wrote a response to a note he had received about the death. But he wrote only months after the event, on January 20, 1891. "His death was a shock to me (I heard of it while in Carolina) and the shock has been growing greater since."[18] Olmsted had found it easier to write earlier to someone with whom he had not recently been in close touch. Kingsbury had learned from Mrs. Elizabeth B. Whitney that in December Frederick Olmsted had written her a long letter after she wrote him a note asking if it were true that Brace had died. Frederick had filled many sheets of paper with memories of his youth, only some of them concerning Charles Brace, to this woman, little known to him in 1890 but vividly remembered as a youthful mentor. He was somewhat embarrassed for Kingsbury to learn about the letter which had probably caused a great deal of wonder on the part of Mrs. Whitney at receiving it from one from whom she had heard so little over the years. But Charles Brace's death had set Frederick Olmsted wondering. What had Charley done, but also, what had he, Frederick, done. They had started out into adult life eagerly, those long years ago. And Elizabeth Baldwin, as she was then, had been a part of that youthful hopefulness.

The almost unknown older woman to whom he wrote had been then an important person in his life, Miss Elizabeth Baldwin, dazzling to a young man, to whom New Haven society was a new world. She was the daughter of a former governor of Connecticut, who was kind to the little circle of friends from Yale. He who had been simply a hanger-on remembered that she had introduced him to good conversation and good manners, had recommended books for him to read, and had seemed to care who he was or what he might become.

"I am thinking that of all the young men you knew I was the least likely to do what I have and that you cannot know or guess in what way I was led to it." For himself, as much as for his correspondent, Olmsted enumerated his works. "There are, scattered through the country, seventeen large public parks, many more smaller ones, many more public or semi-public works, upon which with sympathetic partners or pupils, I have been engaged. After we have left them they have in the majority of cases been more or less barbarously treated, yet as they stand, with perhaps a single exception, they are a hundred years ahead of any spontaneous public demand, or of the demand of any notable cultivated part of the people. And [yet] they are having an educative effect perfectly manifest to me—a manifestly civilizing effect. I see much indirect and unconscious following of them."

He laid out before her what he thought to be his other accomplishment. "Then I know that I shall have helped to educate in a good American school a capital body of young men for my profession. I know that in the minds of a large body of men of influence I have raised my calling from the rank of a trade, even of a handicraft, to that of a liberal profession—an art, an Art of design."

And for her, but mostly for himself, he turned back to look at his remote past. He puzzled over what he considered his early miseducation when his father had sent him away from home to the "families of country parsons of small poor parishes" where he was "chiefly taught how not to study—how not to think for myself." And "While my mates were fitting for college I was allowed to indulge my strong natural propensity for roaming afield and day-dreaming under a tree." He had then, without a good reason as he recalled, gone to sea. And it was only when he returned from that unfortunate voyage that he came under her civilizing influence.

"[Then] I first met you and you lifted me a good deal out of my constitutional shyness and helped me more than you can think to rouse a sort of scatter-brained pride and [acted] to make me realize that my secluded life, country breeding and mis-education was not such a bar to an 'intellectual life' as I was in the habit of supposing. . . . In some way with which you had to do, I was led up at that time to Emerson, Lowell, and Ruskin, and other real prophets, who have been familiar friends since. (Here they are on my bed-table.)"

He came back to the puzzle of the two halves of his life, "how such a loitering, self-indulgent, dilletante sort of a man as I was when you knew me and for ten years afterwards, could, at middle age, have turned into such a hard-worker and *doer* as I suddenly became and have been ever since?"

There lingered below the assertion of pride in doing the old question: was doing worth the effort he had put into it? It was the same question he had asked himself when in the South he saw accomplished nondoers making themselves happy and attractive. And he stated with simple humility, "I have been selling being for doing."[19]

It was inevitable that he should be puzzled as to how he had settled the war between the two parts of his nature. He thought that he had warped the dreamer away from his dreams in order to work in the world. Yet he might have had some comfort: the dreamer and the doer had worked together to make certain formed spaces open to the sky in which other persons might find freedom to be.

Reverie was for travel time and for sleepless nights. During professional visits to Chicago and Asheville, Olmsted occupied himself with job problems. He enjoyed exercising his faculties on them. Biltmore, which was the southern fixed point of an axis that pulled him southward regularly from Chicago, had become an engrossing endeavor which, through the whim of a millionaire, allowed him scope of space, time, and money with which to play almost at will.

Olmsted had found in Gifford Pinchot the man to place in charge of the forestry enterprise of the estate. The son of well-to-do parents, Pinchot might have engaged in any genteel and easy profession, but he was a young man with a strong sense of mission. Until Olmsted called him to Biltmore he had had no place in which to exercise his calling. He had accomplished his own education in a profession new to America by going abroad to study management of forests in France and Germany. Pinchot had come home from studying such ancient fern-banked forests as Fontainebleau primed with the idea of managing great American forests. Cut-and-slash methods shocked him. He believed that a well-managed forest could yield good timber and yet be an organic, living, and enduring entity. This was a completely novel idea in the American states where trees blocking a passage westward had customarily been expunged. Pinchot badly needed a place to demonstrate his new idea. Olmsted's summons was a godsend to the fervent young man who replied, "I shall be delighted to take advantage of it."[20] He visited Biltmore, and by December 6, 1891, Olmsted had appraised this tall, lean young man of decided opinions and asked him to take the job for at least the time which would be needed to initiate good forest practices.

Pinchot was given a large freedom in which to exercise his competence. Olmsted also, after making do with temporary, local help, appointed an engineer for the works, W. A. Thompson, and a horticulturist, James Gall. These men were to report to Olmsted for instructions, but were to be on Vanderbilt's payroll. This arrangement left the Olmsted firm free of the petty details of paying workmen, once the general design was set. Pinchot in the forestry work, Gall in horticulture, and Thompson in engineering engaged their own helpers. Olmsted, or whoever he sent south, conferred with Pinchot about the forestry work and kept a gentlemanly rein upon Gall's plantings and Thompson's construction work. Frederick or John Olmsted or Harry Codman continued to develop the original plan and laid out continuing lines of development during the succeeding years. Olmsted encouraged Frederick, Jr., to study under the various chiefs at Biltmore. He considered this place a kind of miniature university of all the branches of knowledge useful to a landscape architect. He placed Frederick, Jr., under the tutelage of Dr. Carl A. Schenck when that forester and teacher of foresters succeeded to Gifford Pinchot's place in the Biltmore scheme.

Olmsted had everything to do with the place except the actual design of the French chateau which Mr. Vanderbilt had agreed with Richard Morris Hunt should be set down among the pines, dogwoods, and rhododendrons of the southern mountains. Although the two men had had their public differences in the architectural dispute about the New York State capitol, Olmsted and Hunt worked together amicably, having already cooperated in another Vanderbilt project, the siting and design of the Vanderbilt mausoleum on Staten Island. Hunt apparently did not resent Olmsted's close instructions to him as to the siting of the house, how it should be placed in relation to the points of the compass and in relation to the lay of the land. It was Olmsted who decreed the giant terraces to be added to the house, and the walls protecting the private garden from the northwest winds. The house, eccentric as it was to its place in the world, was to be solidly set in the ground Vanderbilt had chosen, buttressed and landscaped in a large manner to give its small family of occupants the best of the view of Pisgah, the privacy for walks in the shrub garden and the formal garden, seats for resting under a grape arbor, and, as one strolled away from the house, a grand extension of grounds growing from formal to less formal in distance from the house. Here Olmsted had all the private pleasure of using his knowledge of previous country house landscaping—from England and from America—to choose suitable elements for the enhancement of this house of fantasy, and to allow the owner of the house, as he walked or rode away from it, to move all the distance from civility to the wild. Hunt placed a conservatory of noble proportions and warm brick colors at the foot of the descending terraces of formal gardens and located barns for various purposes in the folds of hills.

Pisgah, the name of the mountain peak in the distance, to be seen in all its shades of blue and in various weathers, might have seemed to serve as guardian for the late Olmstedian mood. It was a Pisgah view Frederick Olmsted had attained, not without difficulties and backslidings into anger and exasperation, not without doubts. He developed a particular fondness for Biltmore, as he had had for Central Park at the beginning of his career.

Pinchot remembered Frederick Olmsted in the early days at Biltmore.

He was a quiet-spoken little lame man with a most magnificent head and one of the best minds I have ever had the good luck to encounter. . . . It was Mr. Olmsted who was responsible for the plan to make Biltmore Estate the nest egg for practical Forestry in the United States. . . . Here was my chance. Biltmore could be made to prove what America did not yet understand, that trees could be cut and the forest preserved at one and the same time. I was eager, confident, and happy as a clam at high tide.

But to me, as I set down at the time, what was worth almost more than the opportunity to work was the fact that Mr. Olmsted took my profession seriously, and took with equal seriousness the assumption which he made that I was able to practice it. I have never forgotten what it meant to a youngster just getting started to be treated to some extent as an equal, and I shall always hold myself deep in his debt for what he did for me.[21]

Of the land he surveyed he wrote, "Half of it was woodland. It had been put together from small impoverished farms, the forest on which had been burned, slashed, and overgrazed until it was little more than the shadow of its former self."[22] Olmsted and Pinchot working together with the backing of George Vanderbilt preserved and, in a sense, created not only Biltmore Forest, the land surrounding the house, but Pisgah Forest, the great area of semiwilderness which became the Pisgah National Forest, the first scientifically managed forest, and the first national forest, of the United States.

Pinchot, who was a rich young man himself, but with a puritanical streak, could not altogether approve the French chateau which another rich young man was causing to be built in the southern wilderness. Pinchot's style was rather to organize a Sunday School for the poor children, black and white, of the neighborhood. Frederick Olmsted recommended Rick to take part in this effort.

Olmsted studied his patron and found George Vanderbilt a man with whom he could work: "He is a delicate, refined and bookish man, with considerable humor, but shrewd, sharp, exacting and resolute in matters of business."[23] This he wrote to Fred Kingsbury on January 20, 1891.

Olmsted took, as a matter of course, the necessity of solving such practical problems as a road for wagons to bring in heavy materials, and eventually a railroad branch-line to make delivery easier. These matters were absolute and necessary preliminaries to the delicate problems of the adjustment and transformation of the ground which his imagination loved to play with. He did not give up thinking about Biltmore and teasing his mind with these things when away from there. He wrote to W. A. Thompson, the resident engineer, about the importance of saving native trees and shrubs when a road was put through the forest; rhododendrons, azaleas, and kalmias should be dug up and replanted, not destroyed or replaced by expensive and foreign plants imported from nurseries. And "The felling of Beech, Black Gum, Sweet Gum, Sourwood, Chestnut and Hickory trees of more than sapling size is to be avoided as far as practicable; even (where they are of particular value) by specific curves in the course of the roads."[24] To James Gall, the horticulturist, Olmsted wrote, "Since I left you, I have been meditating more or less every day upon the Ram Branch work, the prospects of which I find exceedingly fascinating." This was to be a wild-seeming creek in the woods away from the formal gardens nearer to the house. Don't clear up natural circumstances, he told Gall. "Rotting roots, sticks and bits of stone should not be moved unless there is a positive reason for a change of surface."[25] He advised Gall on another occasion about making streams artificially introduced imitate nature. "There are several points where small mossy rocks, so laid as to appear ends of the ledges deflecting the stream, are very desirable." And "Where the water falls over a flat-faced dam, looking too much like a piece of masonry, or where such a fall is seen too directly in the face of it, try the effect of blows with a sledge designed to flake off chips. In such places also, place stone just *under water* below the dam where the falling water will strike and rebound from it. This will make foam and sparkle, will confuse the sight and will add to the purling sound."[26]

It was not forest work alone that fascinated Olmsted in this newer South. He had certain city work in hand soon, in Atlanta, where he did the initial planning for what became the residential area of Druid Hills and its connecting parkways, and in Richmond, for what became the suburb to be called Sherwood Park. It was in Atlanta first and in Richmond later that Olmsted found signs of a new kind of commercial and emotional life being born in the very places for whose subjugation he had once most fervently hoped.

Toward the end of October, 1890, coming from being ill at Biltmore, he stopped the first time in Atlanta. He had been summoned by Joel Hurt, an energetic entrepreneur of this new, tentative period of growth in Southern cities such as Atlanta, a place rising from its Civil War ashes with determination and hardly a backward glance. The creator of a new street railway system for the city, Hurt was a small, intense man of many ideas and projects. He wished Olmsted's expert advice in his scheme to transform into a new residential suburb a piece of land his company, the Kirkwood Land Company, had purchased. Beyond the last settled streets in a northeast direction from Five Points, this was a rare and valuable woodland. It was almost raw wilderness when Olmsted saw it first, its great straight pines with copper-plated trunks, spanish oaks with scimitar-shaped leaves, its dogwoods and rhododendron and wild azalea growing along little streams threading miniature valleys between small hills. Olmsted saw here a possibility for a complete design in the tradition he had begun at Riverside. Houses placed on generous lots on winding roads would have the benefit of woodland preserved and enhanced; a system of efficient transportation with a divided roadway—park space between the shaded lanes for carriages and a separated roadway for the electric trolley cars—would connect this living space with commercial space downtown. He was to plan additional spider-arms of parkways, Lakeshore Drive and East Lake Drive, to connect Druid Hills with other residential areas in which Hurt's land company had an interest. The complete plan was never finished; the lake for Lakeshore Drive was never filled in. Only years later, after Olmsted's death, was his original plan implemented by the Olmsted firm; the irregular and winding resident streets, all at right angles to the parkway of Ponce de Leon, were to have names with an Olmstedian flavor: Oakdale, Springdale, Lullwater, and were to preserve into another century the illusion of a rural neighborhood.

However, in October, 1890, nothing was settled. Joel Hurt was out of town; Olmsted saw only the land and its interesting possibilities. Turning away from these untouched woods, he returned to the city to drive down Peachtree Street and to take a sympathetic look at the bustling business center of Atlanta, a place full of naive hope and unsolved problems, thriving in spite of poverty upon all its edges.

It might seem from the way that large and small private jobs multiplied that Olmsted had turned away from public designs. But this was only apparent. The firm continued to oversee the development of the Boston park system; it had under way a large public park development in Rochester, New York, and continued to act as consultant for the older Buffalo, New York, system; Olmsted had also undertaken plans for Lynn, Massachusetts, as well as for Louisville, Kentucky, and Wilmington, Delaware; he would, within a few years, do work for the municipalities of Kansas City, Milwaukee, and St. Louis. He continued to yearn over the fortunes and misfortunes of both the New York and Brooklyn parks and did a few jobs for them on a consultative basis. Olmsted did not feel bound by monetary considerations. If he disapproved of what a private developer wished to do, he withdrew. This happened for a vacation cottage development outside Denver. After both he and Codman visited the site a number of times, he gave it up and let go a considerable fee.

He had more than ever an idiosyncratic and particular view of what large public landscape parks, as he called them, were for. He expressed his anger to architect and critic Henry Van Brunt on the subject of the general bad judgment of city fathers, who believed that park space was vacant space, suitable for dumping any and every municipal project: "for parades, for athletic sports, for fireworks, for museums of art or science, such as botanic gardens." But, he argued, "It [a great city] also needs a large ground scientifically and artistically prepared to provide such a poetic and tranquilizing influence on its people as comes through a pleased contemplation of natural scenery, especially sequestered and limitless natural scenery." "Tranquilizing," as Olmsted spelled it, would have an unfortunate meaning in the future, but the usage of later days was not Olmsted's meaning. He did not desire to quiet the unsatisfied poor by a soporific enjoyment. He, too, Olmsted, needed the requisite tranquillizing effect, and he did not consider himself soothed into a state of unworthy quietude. In his meaning this was a state of mind of the highest quality, not a deadening, but a heightening, of faculties. He paid the "poor" the compliment of believing them capable of the rarest kinds of enjoyment.

In the same letter to Van Brunt he went on extravagantly about the ways his parks had been abused:

Suppose that you had been commissioned to build a really grand opera house; that after the construction work had been nearly completed and your scheme of decoration fully designed, you should be instructed that the building was to be used on Sundays as a Baptist Tabernacle, and that suitable place must be made for a huge organ, a pulpit and a dipping pool. Then at intervals afterwards, you should be advised that it must be so refitted and furnished that parts of it could be used for a court room, a jail, a concert hall, hotel, skating rink, for surgical cliniques, for a circus, dog show, drill room, ball room, railway station and shot tower? . . .

Again, suppose that once in three or four years an ordinary house painter and paper hanger, or even a theatrical scene painter should be called in to revamp and improve your decoration of the auditorium? . . .

But that, more or less, is what is nearly always going on with public parks. Pardon me if I overwhelm you; it is a matter of chronic anger with me. Cordially yours. . . .[27]

On January 1, 1888, Calvert Vaux had been reappointed landscape architect to the New York parks. Vaux wrote the news immediately to Olmsted and sent him a copy of his acceptance. Olmsted had the comfort of believing that the worst depredations against the parks might be held off by his old colleague. He wrote his approval of the appointment to H. R. Towne, one of the commissioners: "The freedom of the Park and the absence of fees and drink money—the denial of advantages to the rich man that the poor man cannot command—is, I remember, a point in which Vaux has a certain chivalric interest. Don't be deceived by what you hear to Vaux's disadvantage. In certain lines—problems of planning for convenience—he is unsurpassed. He is apt to greatly misrepresent his own mind in talking; a nervous defect."[28] This letter is interesting as much in Olmsted's lasting admiration for Vaux's talents as for his trying, behind Vaux's back, to defend the man from the kind of personal antagonisms he seemed now regularly to arouse. Olmsted very likely did not see that he might, fatally, in this way, be introducing to Towne hitherto unknown faults in Vaux's character. Olmsted could no longer work with Vaux, but he believed in his integrity and knew that the New York parks were safe under his care just so long as the commissioners heeded the advice of their consulting landscape man.

Calvert Vaux's former partner continued his energetic schedule of travel to the sites of old and new projects as if he would never run down. But in fact he was prone to occasional illnesses. He had to stop over in hotels and call in strange doctors to patch him up. Then he picked himself up and went on, or he stayed home a few days in the upstairs bedroom at 99 Warren Street, Brookline, and wrote letters to clients, friends, and children.

The father wrote many letters to his youngest son whenever he was separated from him. He was full of advice to Rick: what to read, how to get a good night's sleep, who to meet, not to be too forward. He reproved Rick for staying too long at the Glessners' house in Chicago on one occasion. Rick arrived to pay a visit to his friend, the son of the household, George. George had gone off. Rick, all unselfconscious of himself as a care, stayed on. Mrs. Olmsted heard of it; she and Frederick were embarrassed that their son might have been a nuisance. Yet the fond father was glad that Rick had seen Richardson's fine work in that house.

During the summer of 1891 Olmsted agonized for a few days over the propriety of Rick's being put on the payroll of the firm in the Chicago fair work when the young man went there to spend his vacation helping and learning. It was finally decided that it would be suitable for him to be paid. The father told his son that he would be under strict orders from various engineers and overseers of the work.

The young man was the center of an old man's care for the future. He wished Rick to learn every detail of work the firm did, from engineering to horticulture. Rick was also admonished, somewhat illogically, to take time to dream, to let impressions sink in, to go look at pictures, to read books, to meet people who might be advantageous to him later in his career.

The pressures did not bear down too heavily at this time upon a healthy, high-spirited adolescent who enjoyed his work and play. Rick planned a north country trip late in the summer and eventually Olmsted, Sr., joined Olmsted, Jr., in a journey which combined vacation with work for the firm at Marquette where there was a tentative plan for a park. They went on for lake views of sky and woods from a boat on Lake Superior.

The father parted from the son after this brief expedition into idleness and traveled southward again by way of Evansville to Asheville. He was to meet John Olmsted in Washington. A letter written on September 12 shows the matter-of-fact, brotherly trust he had invested in this oldest son by this time. Olmsted wrote, "Give me a full account of what you have advised, and what you have me do—making me as far as you can master of the situation."[29] This comradely relationship had resolved, at least for the father, the impatience he had felt toward this son in his awkward period of growing up. One is clear that for the father the difficulties had been resolved. About the son, one is not so sure. If he was overworked, if he sacrificed for a time a home of his own, he was also self-controlled, efficient, and altogether indispensable.

John's main duty was to relieve Olmsted, Sr., of the responsibility for managing an office which had grown to have a complex staff and many jobs to organize. John introduced modern methods; as early as June, 1888, letters from the firm were typed instead of being handwritten as they had been for so many years. There were typewriters, as the typists were then called, an increasing number of draftsmen and clerks, and a succession of apprentices passing through. These promising young men were not only taught in an informal way by the older Olmsted, but trained and used by John in the everyday work of the firm.

Harry Codman, once an apprentice learning the trade, was now a partner. The old man cared for him as if he were another son. On September 25, 1891, Olmsted wrote to John from Louisville that he had sent Harry home with a fever: "I wanted to send Rick with him but he would not let me.... I shall be anxious to hear of Harry."[30] Apparently Codman's illness was not prolonged.

By spring of the following year, for the enlarged Olmsted firm and family, it was the health of the head of the firm which worried all of them. Olmsted had been feeling the downward pull of tiredness in his bones. He had had one episode after another of illness. It seemed a good thing in April, 1892, that he should go abroad with two of his apprentices, his son Rick and Harry Codman's younger brother Phil, for a period of recuperation for himself and for the further training of the young men in European landscaping. Olmsted himself set out with an unjaded eagerness. He would visit Henry Perkins and his wife Hannah. Henry, Mary's cousin, who had been his secretary in California, was living at Chislehurst in England. Marion would go along and be free to pursue her own excursions. In addition to helping his young men to see landscape art in England and France, Olmsted wished to renew for himself old impressions and perhaps to learn a new thing or two.

His initial pleasure in the English landscape of soft greens and finished edges was keener even than he had anticipated. These gentle scenes recalled all the joys of his first visit when he had walked pathways and roadways with his brother John Hull and their friend Charley Brace. But this spring the weather was unusually cold and he suffered from fatigue and exposure and on occasion had to stay wrapped up in an inn while the "boys," as he called them, went off to see Stonehenge or Olmsted Hall, of his ancestors. Hoping for better weather and leaving Marion behind in England, Olmsted and young Rick and Phil went earlier to France than they had first planned. Many scenes new to him were keenly interesting to Olmsted, but his intense and youthful eagerness spurred on the little expedition at too fast a pace for his old body to endure with any grace. Intellectually, he did not admire much of the contemporary landscape design he saw in either England or France, but he enjoyed very much the enveloping natural and farming scenery of this northwestern corner of the old continent. Here, generally, nature was softer and kinder than in America, and men had expended more care in preserving an old and beloved land. The gentle airs, especially of England, which had nourished splendid turfs and raised up trees of noble proportions, enchanted him once more.

"I am too old for elation, but instead of regarding the elation of my youth (I was 27 years old) with surprise, I only wonder that it was not greater. As a result of 45 years of special study of landscape, I have a much higher and more intelligent regard for England."[31] Olmsted wrote such confidences back to "Dear Harry" in America, telling him how he admired English neatness and elegance and finish, which seemed natural to all the citizens of the island. He wished that he could impress on Burnham this kind of care for the great fair in Chicago, and passed this duty on to Codman.

In stopping over in Paris, and going out from the city on expeditions, Olmsted found himself disappointed in the remains of La Nôtre's work at Versailles and Chantilly, a "grand design in outlines, not well carried out in foliage results and with considerable dreary vacancy."[32] This to "Dear Harry &

John," who were carrying on the firm's business with pertinacity and style.

Apparently a number of letters of this period between Frederick and Mary were not preserved, for Frederick refers to one from "your mother" to John, a letter which is missing. But one survives which Frederick wrote to Mary from Tours on May 3, 1892, expressing a mood of quiet enjoyment. First of all, he told her, there had been no first of May disorders; all had been peaceful politically. The weather was cold and he was hoarse, "But I am having a great deal of enjoyment, and I hope laying in a good stock of better health. I get tired and leg-weary, but not enough to prevent me from getting rather more sleep on the whole than I get at home, and getting up fully recovered from fatigue. I have a good appetite without much tonic-taking, and diet exactly suits me. Rick and Phil both very well, are indefatigable in taking care of me. We have visited four of the notable chateaux of the Loire, all interesting.... But I think I am more interested on the whole in the peasant life and peasant villages that we pass through.... Your affectionate husband."[33]

He watched the young men with a quiet tolerance. They were eager to do something practical. From his point of view they did not ever stop long enough to let impressions sink in. He wrote to John from Torquay where he and the others had crossed over again to meet Marion and the Perkinses, "I don't think that either Phil or Rick realizes the value which close observation of all sorts of things that may come under observation (but observation [much] of which is not recordable, or even to be given form verbally) may come to have in future practice, in aiding inventive design." It was with almost a wondering happiness that Frederick Olmsted, feeling his age, acknowledged his late good fortune: "I feel as if I were learning a great deal more than I ever did in traveling before.... I am gaining—so it seems to me— amazingly in education. My enjoyment of sylvan beauty, and of picturesque combinations—accidental as well as designed—has never been as great. I hope the young men are gaining in like manner."

He went over the grounds, still preserved, of the recent Paris Exposition, to compare what he found there with what he had been doing in Chicago. "It seemed to me that at the best it [the landscaping] must have been extremely disquieting, gaudy and childish, if not savage and an injury to the Exposition, through its disturbance of dignity, and injury to breadth, unity and composure. I do not mean to suggest any change of our plans or limitations on their development; only I hope that in elaborating them simplicity and reserve will be practiced and petty effects and frippery avoided."

Still looking over his shoulder at the firm's work going on, he remembered the young woman whom he had encouraged in the art: "I hope Miss Bullard of Bridgeport is employed for the roof-garden."

The unattended, unpolished, or inadvertent in landscape beauty was what touched him now: "The two finest things we have seen are the New Forest ...and a little farm with a little park, very wild, in Guernsey." And (all this

to John): "The finest flower effect in all Europe is an old dilapidated hawthorn hedge, and the next a barren hillside of gorse."[34] It was as if in his old
age Olmsted returned to the earliest kind of relationship he had had as a boy
with nature—the reaching out of his imagination to the wild.

In early June, expecting Frederick's imminent return, John Olmsted and
Harry Codman set up meetings with clients for the head of the firm. It was
expected that he would sail home in mid-June. But by that time Olmsted was
too ill to return. He had written with some anxiety to John on May 18 about
the necessity of having to go straight south to Biltmore as soon as he got off
the boat. "I am not sure that I shall be up to the work."[35] And he was not.
On May 25 he had to admit to himself that the trip had not been the cure
he had hoped it would be. At Henry Perkins's house, lying in bed, where
he could look only wistfully at the outdoors through a window, he dictated
to Rick a letter for Harry Codman: "I suppose I must admit that it appears
now that you were right in thinking that I was travelling too fast and doing
too much when in France. At least, with the access of the first period of hot,
moist summer weather here, I am very much pulled down." But, he pleaded
ingenuously, "It was very undesirable that I should be thinking of myself
and my infirmities.... It was best that I should be thinking of the young
men and their education as well as myself.... I can only conclude now that
I am older and more used up than I had supposed." He ended gallantly: "But
I have enjoyed the journey very much and I think if I should live a few years
longer and be able to work, it will prove to have been very profitable."[36]

The question arises, what was wrong with Olmsted? It is true that he had
from time to time colds, a sore throat, neuralgia, vertigo, and other physical
ills. But what he had to face as the basis for most of his troubles was simply
his old tendency to sleeplessness, exaggerated to an alarming degree. Far from
home, under the strain of traveling too far and too fast, his mind received
stimuli and could not rest. His insomnia had become a chronic ill, frightening
Rick, Marion, and Phil.

The young travelers decided to ask the help of Dr. Henry Rayner, whose
American wife the Olmsteds knew, as a person to whom they could entrust
their debilitated father-friend-employer. Dr. Rayner found Olmsted an interesting person as well as a fascinating case. He had sympathy for the disease
of sleeplessness. He assured Olmsted that he had suffered from this ailment
himself and found a cure for it. Rayner took Olmsted as both guest and
patient into his home and devoted himself to trying to cure him, on condition
that Olmsted would give himself into his care and remain in his house until
the doctor said he was ready to go.

Olmsted wrote to those at Brookline in a curious state of mind—admitting
himself to be ill but looking outward beyond the wall of that illness. To
Harry Codman he wrote, "You know that I am practically in prison here. I
am fairly successful in enforcing patience and resignation upon myself, considering what attractive prospects lie just without the walls, but I am still a

reasonable being and do not exclude myself from thinking of the concern which my disappointments must bring to you." He went on to explain his case. "He [Dr. Rayner] regards my present trouble (apparently) but as a variation in form of the troubles which led me to come abroad. He thinks that my course has not been unwise; that it would probably have been best for me to take more rest than nature prompted; that it is a peculiarity of my case that over-exertion does not produce the sensation of fatigue. He fully expects that I shall be set up again."[37]

Olmsted was not literally so much a prisoner as he felt. The doctor or one of the young people took him on daily drives. He became interested in exploring the northward groping tentacles of London (Dr. Rayner's place was in Hampstead), and in trying to understand the new way in which, as he said, "London is colonizing its suburbs."[38] Marion, or Rick and Phil, or, after Phil went home, Rick and George Glessner, who was visiting England also, made these journeys into enjoyable expeditions. Olmsted interested himself and the younger members of the party in photographing samples of architecture and landscape. They soon collected one hundred photographs of gates, entryways, street corners, and vistas of estates where the little group stopped and looked without making themselves known. Olmsted stayed at Dr. Rayner's without going away at night for at least one full month, from mid-June to mid-July, 1892, suffering from intermittent and sometimes frightening insomnia. He had one setback when George Radford called and talked about a recent humiliation Calvert Vaux had suffered from the insolence of certain New York City parks commissioners and of his old friend's general professional and personal decline.

Vaux had not been well, and at a bad moment he had been questioned by some of the commissioners as if to determine, insultingly, whether he were qualified for his position. One of these commissioners had adopted a sneering manner which wounded him deeply. He was asked by this questioner abruptly, and as if it mattered, what was the botanical name for the Rose of Sharon. Vaux could not think of it and was confused and angry in consequence. The occasion was engineered by a faction which wanted to rid the parks of Calvert Vaux because he opposed a raceway for trotting horses in Central Park. W. A. Stiles had earlier told Olmsted something of the same sad history. Since that occasion, he said, Vaux had been wearing himself out in self-justification, "on the verge of insanity."[39] When Radford elaborated on this story to the tired and sick man who had been Vaux's friend and partner, Olmsted wrote to Harry Codman and John Olmsted: "I fell in with his view of Vaux's character and failings at the time, but afterwards felt indignant with myself that I had done so and exceedingly sorry for Vaux and that I could have done and could do nothing for him and his." And the result for him was "It distressed me greatly and I had no sleep of value for the next two nights and days."[40]

By July 17, Olmsted left Dr. Rayner's for an expedition by electric launch along the upper green reaches of the Thames and was pleased with the innocent pleasures he observed in the people in boats and along the shore. He savored the experience acutely after having been so confined. He recommended even more strongly than he had before the practicability of electric-motored boats for the lagoons of the Chicago exposition. And the plants and trees growing along the lush shores of the little English river gave him new ideas for plantings for his American water channels. He had been sleepless before the Thames trip, but slept well along the way. The doctor next gave Olmsted permission to go to the British Museum to look up old books on London's growth. He was making himself a master of "the progress of suburban improvement chiefly; the history of commons, heaths and parks, and of roads and building operations."[41] But he nagged himself about work going on in another city: "I am anxious to hear how you have got on with the Muddy River work—planting and all."[42]

He resolved to look forward to more life and work, not less. He was as full of interest in problems and solutions as he had been when very young. And he seemed to himself, viewing himself critically, to have reached his highest pitch of understanding of his art. At the end of the summer he sailed for home, carrying with him, as if it were a full cup precariously balanced, a delicate equilibrium of physical disability and moral resolution.

It was a rough crossing. All the young people were seasick while Olmsted, triumphantly the old sailor, was not. As if it were the most natural thing in the world, and not a matter to which he was giving much attention, he reported from the dock in New York in a note to his wife that he had been sleepless on shipboard. But he was hopeful that once he reached home, with his customary cup of tea before bedtime, and with a good book in hand to lull him to sleep, he would continue his recovery. Irrepressibly he announced: "I shall be glad, as will Rick, to run over the Central Park while the English parks are fresh in my mind.... All send love & I am, affectionately, Fred."[43]

CHAPTER XXVIII
The End before the End

I can't come to you and often dream of a ride through our old haunts and meeting you and others but have pretty well surrendered to Fate. I must flounder along my way to the end.
—F. L. O., to Fred Kingsbury, September 6, 1893[1]

OLMSTED CAME HOME to a busy time. The pace of work in Chicago was hectic. The fair had to be ready to open by May 1, 1893, and in October, 1892, when Olmsted was once more upon the scene, he saw lumber, dust, and confusion where there should soon be bright buildings, smooth water, and tranquilly strolling spectators. "The whirl of business is tremendous and I hardly catch on yet,"[2] he wrote on October 1 to son John in Brookline. He pretended that he had not been ill and met with the architects, each one planning his own building, as well as with his own gardeners, dredging engineers, draftsmen, and, of course, with Harry Codman, chief of staff for the Olmsted firm in Chicago. While he pushed his workmen hard to complete the exposition plan, he had another end in view, a basic design which would take a permanent lease upon the ground. He would be content when all the buildings of the great fair should crumble, as they were in fact designed to do rather easily after the crowds had gone, for then he would have his park. It was for this end that he laid out the lagoons and the wooded isle. He would then bring to a conclusion the plan he had first conceived for Chicago twenty-three years before.

He trusted Codman to further his plans. He felt the old wanderlust and wished in particular to go south again. He believed that the future of the firm lay in the undeveloped territories of the South and West where new kinds of landscape work might be undertaken. He entrusted himself once more to the cruelties of overnight railroad travel and headed south toward Biltmore. After his absence, he saw Vanderbilt's clearing in the forest with fresh eyes. He savored the natural scene, the clarity of the fall air making the line of mountains a dark blue, and he took heart from the good work being pushed with vigor. Gifford Pinchot had thirty-five men in the forest. George Vanderbilt had indulged his fancy and bought sixteen thousand additional acres to add to the estate and to the Olmsted firm's responsibility. "Things are going ahead here,"[3] he wrote cheerfully to John. Olmsted pursued his rail journey to Atlanta where he found work lagging. From Atlanta he continued to Baltimore and tended to the firm's business there. It seemed as if he could sustain the load he wished to carry.

But the new year brought pain and confusion. On January 13, 1893, Olmsted's friend and partner Harry Codman died unexpectedly after an operation for appendicitis. His was the second death to strike a blow at the Chicago enterprise. Earlier John Wellborn Root, Burnham's partner, had died of the effects of pneumonia on January 15, 1891. With Olmsted away during a large part of 1892, the burdens of the firm's work had fallen heavily on Codman. Now, with Codman dead at twenty-nine and with the date of the fair's opening at hand, Olmsted had not only a grief to bear but a heavy load of work. On January 19, four days after Codman's death, Olmsted wrote to Gifford Pinchot, "You will have heard of our great calamity. As yet, I am as one standing on a wreck and can hardly see when we shall get afloat again."[4] The sailorlike words came naturally to him in moments of crisis.

Yet the tragedy stimulated Olmsted and seemed to give him back the ability to work at top speed and with high energy. He handled first one thing and then another without pause. "I am at Harry's desk with stacks of his papers and memoranda to be examined,"[5] he wrote John on February 4. He had, like a general who had lost his trusted deputy, taken on the field command himself. He decided also that Charles Eliot should be plucked from his quiet private practice in Boston and offered a partnership in the firm. The thing was quickly done, although Eliot hesitated momentarily, valuing his individual freedom but valuing even more a chance to work in the Olmsted firm. The name of the firm was changed on March 1, 1893, to Olmsted, Olmsted and Eliot. "Tell Eliot that I shall expect him *not later* than Thursday next," Frederick wrote to John Olmsted on February 5. John laid out before Charles Eliot in the Warren Street office all the concerns of the business. Chicago was the most urgent concern of the moment: "No end of work to be done here. It is appaling (Olmsted's spelling)."[6]

Eliot went straight out to Chicago and was troubled on arriving to find "Mr. O." as he customarily denoted the head of the firm to be visibly ill after his recent efforts. Planning to go to Milwaukee where new work was being planned, Frederick asked John to send him at once all the names of those concerned with the work in that city: "I don't remember *one*."[7] Eliot may have foreseen future difficulties. He told Olmsted at this point that his own health was poor. Yet he became for a time not only the partner but the traveling companion of an older man who needed a good deal of care in getting about the country on his errands. That Eliot was close to despair over the situation shows in a notation in his private diary (April 3, 1893): "Problem of Mr. O.'s traveling. I strike!"[8] Under duress, from time to time Frederick allowed himself to be persuaded to stay home and rest or go on enforced vacations, but he chafed at these interruptions. Between illnesses, he recovered and performed heroically.

Eliot brought personal qualities to the firm although he was not as various in his accomplishments as Codman had been. His particular contribution was the idea of the public preservation of natural areas out beyond city boundaries as a resource for people living closely bound to such urban areas as Boston. This was a refinement of Olmsted's concept of public preservation as expressed in the mid-sixties in his Yosemite Report. Eliot had already worked in a private organization devoted to such state preserves. The State of Massachusetts had been persuaded by this small but enthusiastic group to set up such reservations as Beaver Brook, Blue Hills, the Middlesex Fells, Revere Beach, and Stony Brook. Eliot brought the care of such areas to the firm. Eliot also wrote fluently and was to publish Olmstedian articles such as one in the *Engineering Magazine* of May, 1895. (The article was to be wrongly attributed to Olmsted who, by this time, was unable to do this kind of work.) In "General Principles in Selecting Public Preservations and Determining Their Boundaries," Eliot wrote about the special difficulties of landscape parks. For this kind of work, "The directors of the work need to be more than ordinary men. Real-estate dealers must necessarily be excluded from the management. Politicians, also, if the work is to run smoothly. The work is not purely executive, like the work of directing sewer-construction or street cleaning.... Its directors must thoroughly apprehend the fact that the beauty of its [the park's] landscape is all that justifies the existence of a large public open space in the midst, or even on the immediate borders of a town."

In 1893 when Eliot joined the firm Olmsted was at the height of his contemporary fame, known to be the creator and leader of his profession, appreciated by his peers, widely praised in magazines and newspapers. Honors poured in upon him. If Olmsted could have died at the end of 1894, it would have been well for him, for his life would have had a kind of rounded artistic symmetry. In addition to the happy completion of the Chicago Exposition grounds, other ancient struggles seemed coming to fruition. Robert Underwood Johnson wrote to Olmsted during 1893 that at last it looked as if Congress were going to repeal the act granting Yosemite to California and would merge the Valley and the Big Trees with a new national park already surrounding this area.[9] On May 31, 1893, President Charles W. Eliot of Harvard wrote to Olmsted that the University wished him to be present at commencement on June 28 to receive the doctor of laws degree. He must be present at Harvard to receive the degree, and the matter must be kept secret.[10]

Olmsted nevertheless told Mariana Van Renssalaer about this honor on June 17, saying, "It seems to [me] the queerest thing. But I am to take it because it gives a standing to my profession which it needs."[11] Then an official communication from New Haven informed him that Yale wished to award him the same degree on the same day. Apparently he did not need to be present to receive Yale's higher degree. His friend Fred Kingsbury wrote to him on July 8: "I doubt if a man ever came to such honor before as to have an L.L.D. from both Yale and Harvard the same day, and I suspect that nobody ever cared so little about it."[12] Still it mattered to Olmsted, and he was pleased.

Olmsted was ill at the end of the summer and spent time at Deer Isle, a place which was already a favorite with Mary and Marion Olmsted, but which he found something of a bore. He wrote to Fred Kingsbury on September 6 how in hot weather his "excessive sleeplessness" had returned. He also poured out to his friend how he cared for and yearned over his children, John, Marion, and Rick. The boys were robust, but Marion was delicate and suffered from "rheumatic trouble and I don't know what. And she is just the nicest girl—little old maid—possible; patient, happy, indefatigable. I shall leave her and my wife tolerably provided for." He informed his friend with pride that Rick would be a senior this year at Harvard. And he went on: "I enjoy my children. They are one of the centers of my life, the other being the improvement of scenery and making the enjoyment of it available. Spite of my infirmities which do drag me cruelly, I am not to be thought of as an unhappy old man."[13]

In an astonishing revival from prostration, Olmsted was active once more in October, inspecting the forest about Biltmore, exulting to John that he had spent "six hours in the saddle."[14] Biltmore absorbed more and more of his attention. He wished here to plant his own arboretum. For once George Vanderbilt's large ideas were outrun by his adviser's. It took a long time and was to be bitter to Olmsted that this particular scheme did not gain assent from the owner of the estate. By fall, 1893, Olmsted had quite unconsciously come to think of Biltmore as his own, and for the remainder of his life it occupied the principal place among all his plans.

While he was overtaxing his strength in the forests of North Carolina, his portrait and Mariana Van Renssalaer's long article about him ornamented the October, 1893, issue of the *Century*. Olmsted had poured out to her without restraint a torrent of autobiographical memories for her use in letters written the previous June 13 and 17. But when he read her article he was embarrassed by whatever was personal and acutely distressed that she had given him sole credit for the transverse roads in Central Park. He knew how easily Calvert Vaux was hurt and that at this time Vaux was especially vulnerable, being badgered by the New York parks commissioners. Readers of the magazine came upon the portrait of Frederick Law Olmsted opposite the first page of the issue. The likeness was a fine piece of work, an engraving by T. Johnson from a photograph by James Notman of Boston, and showed a benign head, with an expression both keen and benevolent. The pale eyes gazed outward into the future or into the heart of a problem from a face three-quarters averted from the viewer. The photographer had caught a moment of grave ease and happiness. The article was appreciative and informative and marked in its way an emphasis in the fame that Olmsted's work had earned him.

Olmsted himself seemed to feel that he had reached some kind of end. He wrote strict admonitions to his "Dear Partners" when he was separated from them, telling them what to stress in the business of the future, saying with a straightforward and commonsense emphasis, "If I should die this winter." For this reason he wished Eliot to study on the ground the work going forward in the Biltmore estate and in the suburban development in Atlanta. He was able, at the moment, without bitterness, to think that he could put the firm into their hands: "Remember, in any broad organizing view of your siuation, you cannot reckon on my help. My health is extremely frail and I may be tipped out any day."[15] This letter was written in October, 1893.

He was less active the remainder of the year and nursed his health during the winter of 1893–94. Yet he was in Atlanta again in March, 1894, impressing the money-raisers and becoming an actor in that city's excitement over its ambitious Cotton States Exposition to be held in an area already known as Piedmont Park. The officers of the project called upon Olmsted as the most distinguished man they knew for the kind of advice they wanted, and the Atlanta *Constitution* made a front page story of his visit. Atlanta, having a second growth after being destroyed in the war, was simply delighted in Olmsted as an important outsider seconding the city's ambitious plans for an exposition, a smaller, Southern version of what Chicago had just accomplished. The fund-raising for the fair had been carried on at fever pitch for many days.

Olmsted thought privately the grounds were too small, but he was diplomatic and praised the project in general terms while refusing to go into details as yet. He had also, from the experience of several years' familiarity with the region, a sense of participating in a rather remarkable revival upon the part of the once defeated city. The newspaper editorial of a few days before his arrival had crowed over the raising of $140,750, rather than the goal of $125,000 from private citizens, $75,000 having already been appropriated by the city government. The newspaper listed daily individual contributions, among them modest sums from the men of the fire department, "even the two colored men."[16] On March 18 the *Constitution* turned Frederick Law Olmsted's visit to the city into a celebration, an enhancement of all that the city had done so far. The event was headlined on the front page of the newspaper:

Mr. Olmstead Talks

He Says The Grounds Can Be Made Very Beautiful

His Visit For Consultation Only

He Does Not Go Into Details—To Send A Written

Statement Of The Opinions He Has Formed

From Observation

And the story contained the following passages:

A very important visit was paid to the exposition grounds yesterday morning. It was one that will doubtless have an influence on the work of the board and especially upon the arrangement of the grounds.

Mr. Frederick Law Olmstead, the famous landscape architect, reached the city at 10 o'clock yesterday morning. . . .

Mr. Olmstead is the most famous man in this country in his profession—probably the most famous in the world.

The paper reported upon Olmsted himself with a gush of enthusiasm, continuing to misspell his name:

Mr. Olmstead is a distinguished looking gentleman, a fluent talker and brilliant conversationalist, and certainly a genius in his profession.[17]

Olmsted wrote to John from the Kimball House: "Thousands are to be used here as millions were at Chicago. They are collecting subscriptions from firemen and policemen and Sunday schools, apparently. But it will be the best of distinctively Southern Expositions and a more national advertisement than Chicago, and will be sure to lead to other things."[18] The city was to have its exposition, but Olmsted was not to be the designer. The board of directors found a less demanding and less expensive landscape man. Yet the park that survived the fair owed something to the Olmsted tradition. It had an irregularly shaped lake, which was later partially drained and turned into a golf course; it had winding roads and tree-bordered meadows. Many years after Olmsted's death, the firm was called in to refurbish the park.

Olmsted's ease of manner in dealing with the people in Atlanta was a brilliant mask made from elements of his character and used mercilessly all his life, but behind this front he was weary, shaken, and near collapse. He had a temporary breakdown later in the summer in St. Paul, Minnesota. Fortunately John was with his father and could put him to bed. But physical debility was not all. It became evident, to himself and to those closest to him, that his failings and falterings were the stumblings of his mind as well. Persuaded to go again to rest at Deer Isle on the Maine coast, the father began writing a series of long, overwrought letters to Rick. These were frantic pleas to the son to excel. He wrote and rewrote these communications, often occupying a whole sleepless night in writing one, then tearing it up, and

beginning again. He felt that he had lost sight of Rick and what he was doing. "Really I depend for my comfort largely upon you and you must manage
to write me so that I shall not feel so."[19] This was on October 23, 1894. Im-
mobilized at Deer Isle into the fall and later at Brookline, and no longer
taking part in any important way in the firm's work going on tirelessly and
competently in the hands of John Olmsted and Charles Eliot, old Frederick
concentrated a fearful and almost unbalanced attention upon his youngest
son, ignoring almost entirely the rest of the family.

Frederick, Jr., was doing a creditable job learning the business at Biltmore,
but he found it hard to endure the burden of excessive attention and excessive love. For a short time the young man considered throwing up his career
in landscape architecture.[20] But Rick learned to understand and to pity. Even
in the midst of peremptory advice, the old man wrote to his son, "I ask myself if I have been getting at all snarled up in regard to Biltmore affairs."[21]

George Vanderbilt invited Mary and Marion with Frederick to stay at
Biltmore. He turned over to them a cottage, River Cliff, fronting the French
Broad. They were there for a month late in 1894 and again in the spring of
1895. Olmsted attempted to take charge, but by this time the partners
simply worked around him and tried not to embarrass him or their client
by unobtrusively ignoring him.

At about this same time, Calvert Vaux was being bullied and disregarded
as architectural and landscape adviser to the New York parks. Olmsted was
aware of the trouble his old partner was in. He wrote to W. A. Stiles of
Garden and Forest on March 10, 1895: "It makes me grind my teeth to see
how Vaux is treated. . . . They have struck down Vaux and are doing their
best to kill him."[22]

(On November 19, 1895, Vaux walked off a foggy pier at Gravesend Bay.
His body was not found for two days. Whether he had fallen in the water
by accident or gone in a suicide, no one was to know. By this time Olmsted
was being shielded by his family from any news too exciting for him to bear.
He did not learn of Vaux's death until much later when illness had removed him even further from any active part in the profession that he and
Vaux together had effectively founded.[23])

In the chilly spring of the Blue Ridge Olmsted was not happy. He wrote
to his "Dear Partners" on March 13, three days after his letter to Stiles, "A
continuous downpour locks me in the house, makes me neuralgic and per-
plexative."[24]

Mary wished to take Frederick home, but they were held up by Vanderbilt
who desired Olmsted to stay a little longer to sit to John Singer Sargent for
his portrait. Vanderbilt had asked Sargent to paint companion portraits of
both his architect Richard Morris Hunt and his landscape designer Frederick
Law Olmsted and consented to have his own likeness done. The small,
enigmatic picture of young Vanderbilt and the larger-than-life portraits of
the two artists were to enliven an upstairs gallery at Biltmore House. Olmsted

was to stay for only a few sittings; his son Rick was to stand in for the figure part. Sargent, seeing beyond present perplexities in the old man, discerned in the old face and figure lineaments of thought and emotion which he caught in his quick way in a brilliant stoppage of life: the old man outdoors among the dogwoods and mountain laurel, striding forward with the careless aid of his stick in the living green, his coat flapping open, his face and figure expressing the perpetual onward hopefulness of his life as he had propelled it on its way.

It was from this spring season at Biltmore, a time which should have been pleasant, that Olmsted wrote a tragic letter. It was as if he were given a moment of self-realization to see that he was failing and to need to confess the fact, for the good of his family, his firm, and his profession, regardless of the consequences to himself. He wrote to his son John on May 10, 1895, that he realized that his memory of recent events was failing, that Rick had saved him from embarrassment in front of George Vanderbilt, and that, "I try to look at the situation from an outside and impersonal point of view and so looking at it I see that I ought no longer to be entrusted to carry on important business for the firm alone."[25] He was of course unable to maintain this highly conscious and heroic note for long. He was even to forget that he was forgetful.

It is clear that his family was aware that Frederick was failing. In a letter of a later date (January 23, 1896), Mary wrote to Rick: "If we had not been in such a state of nervous irritation last spring how lovely the life would have been at Biltmore."[26] But from this time quiet enjoyment vanished. Getting away from Biltmore in May, 1895, became an agony of indecision for Olmsted. He wrote letter after letter and finally a telegram to John betraying uneasiness about traveling alone and making professional stops on the way back to Brookline. He planned to meet John in Washington, but his son realized that his father was not able to fulfill this plan. John at last took charge and wrote to his mother: "He need give himself no further concern about his trip but simply wait for me and I will direct his movements after I join him. It is not worth his while to burden his mind further in the matter—certainly not to write any more long letters about it."[27] From this moment, John Charles Olmsted was the effective head of the firm. Frederick, Jr., was soon put on a salary as a lesser member.

John handled his burden of a tragic and difficult father with unemotional strength or with the confusion of feeling firmly put down. John had something of Frederick's own clarity of vision about what one must do when it was necessary to do it and a strong will to set his hand to the task. In John's youth the father and the son had not been satisfactory to each other. But as the years had brought John to his sensible, capable majority, Frederick had taken pride in the virtues John possessed and he himself lacked. Now, not without rebelliousness, he was necessarily subject to that calm will.

John Olmsted and Charles Eliot, yoked together, sustained the business of the Olmsted firm with vigor, scarcely letting the dropping out of the senior member of the firm affect the works they had in hand. The smooth succession was the happy result of Frederick Olmsted's conscious bestowal of freedom and responsibility on those who had worked with him, but the situation in which it placed the troubled old man could not make him happy.

Within the new partnership of wills there was a faint stirring of resentment upon the part of John Charles reflected in a private letter: that Charles Eliot might with his head start take over the rightful family place in the firm which belonged in the future to Frederick, Jr. It was at least partially for this reason that he pushed Frederick, Jr., at an early age into a fully salaried position in the firm.[28]

John remained cool and firm in his handling of his father; to that perplexed, sleepless, forgetful, and pained old man he wrote on September 2, Frederick being safely out of things at Deer Isle once more:

Your failing memory will in time necessitate some slight readjustment of firm matters but you need not give it further thought for some weeks to come. You have probably forgotten that you agreed last December to a reduction in your share of the firm's earnings. This quite satisfied your partners for this current year. It is all right to leave the initiative in this matter to us. We understand the whole thing and will do what is right. It doesn't help us a bit for you to worry about it.

It would be well for you to review the letters we have written you since you went to Deer Isle each time before you write your daily letter to us. You cannot trust your memory as to what we have written you. It would help us very much if you would constantly bear in mind that your memory for current events is no longer a working basis for your thoughts. Until you do so realize you will give us no end of trouble and worry. I fully sympathize with your condition of mind but until you "give in" about your memory ailment there seems to be nothing I can do to make life easier for you. Affecly . . .[29]

The facts made John cruel to his father. And also a habit of repressing strong feelings impeded him at this time from proffering a tenderness which would not have cured anything but might have helped to smooth rough moments. Frederick, Jr., was naked to emotion and suffered confusion, rebellion, and helpless pity. Marion suffered in body as well as spirit from the assault upon her feelings which the sight of her father's condition was to her. Only Mary remarkably kept her equilibrium in the midst of her own suffering. She held on to an ability to face the truth and also to do all that she could to alleviate the results which this dire objective condition caused for all of them. She continued to try to mitigate the effects of Frederick's illness for him and for all her children. She was fortunate in possessing a strong ego even through all this trouble.

The business had to go on; the lives of the others had to go on. The old man, when he came into the office from the living quarters in the house at Brookline where life and work had always been a mix, had become an embarrassment. A memo of a staff member of the Olmsted firm, J. G. Langton, recalled (in 1921) Olmsted's last day in the office, presumably a day in 1895: "He wrote three separate letters to Vanderbilt each without slightest memory of previous letter. Charles Eliot found this out and wondered if similar things had been getting out before."[30]

From this time Frederick Olmsted became a person to be dealt with and cared for, no longer an independent individual, standing on his own feet, making his own life and affecting others in a complex world of many shapes and colors, some of which he had created out of his own gifts. Frederick was not tranquil in his broken state. And even for strong-willed and clear-thinking Mary, it was too much at times. She took to her bed at Brookline, and Eliot one day noted that they were "both poorly"[31]; John being away, Eliot wrote to his partner to tell him the situation.

In the cracks of vivid consciousness which lighted up his loss of continuity, Frederick lived in the pain of certain obsessive ideas. He wrote to Rick from Deer Isle, completely unaware of the beauty of the Maine coast: "I am lying awake nights in a perplexed state of mind about Biltmore affairs and your professional training, especially in matters of foliage."[32] This was on July 11, 1895. In August he wrote to Rick again: "I am still here because Mother and Marion seem to have arranged that I should be, and I see no sufficient reason for contending with them, but I can't say that I am enjoying myself or that it does not continue to be hugger-mugger. I am thinking of you more than anything else."[33] Frederick showed a touch of his old power in writing to his youngest son about the possibility of designing a "manufacturing village" near Pittsburgh, a job the firm was considering. This was, he said, "the sort of work that I would like best, as being more comprehensive and more fully touching social problems."[34]

The unhappy trio came home to Brookline. The doctors there shook their heads negatively over Frederick, and Mary determined with Marion's help to take her husband to England. Mother and daughter fought for hope. The subject of their care had none: "Here I am at home again, dear Rick, and at present I suppose, waiting further examinations by the doctors, etc., still with the expectation of being taken out to England to die, by Mother and Marion."[35]

So they picked up their lives and went, Rick going along and staying a short time. In England, sometimes in a house as a family, sometimes boarding in a nursing home where Frederick could have separate quarters and a male nurse-guardian, then with Frederick quartered for a time away from his wife and daughter in a doctor's house in the country, they twisted and turned in agony of trying and failing to find a solution. Steadily Frederick grew worse. Mary expressed herself to Frederick, Jr., at home telling him that she wrote "despairing letters" only to the family and letting him know how bad it was for her and Marion. "We positively cannot live in the house with father."[36] Marion, frail and oversensitive, suffered the most from seeing her father unhappy, angry, disconnected from his old self. She was in danger of going under emotionally from the strain, as her mother saw. Mary feared that Marion would go the way Charlotte had. She herself held onto her balance with a tough resiliency. She was quite straightforward about Marion's fragility and her own strength: "She cannot stand the loneliness and the constant distress of seeing your father's condition. I think that I get on better than she does."[37] This to Rick on February 14, 1896. While Frederick boarded with Dr. Potts, Mary saw to it that she and Marion got away in a little escape from the hospital atmosphere in which they had been living and saw people and places. And then she prepared to send her daughter home. Beyond that despatching, she decided on another, that she would take Frederick home since his sojourn in England had done him no good.

But as characteristically, filled with an irresistible vitality for living, she seized upon a little time out of this great misery and went by herself first to Paris, then to Geneva, and on to Nice before turning back to her problem. Near Geneva she looked up the house where she and John Hull had lived and where Owen was born. In Nice she stood in front of John Hull's grave. The lot was neglected. She gave an order for it to be repaired. And her involuntary cry in a letter to John was of one released from torment: "I feel as though [I] had been in heaven."[38] (Mary's energy for life would carry her beyond the troubles of this time. She lived to be a little over 91 years of age, dying on April 23, 1921.)

Mary returned to her care of Frederick and the continuation of a transatlantic discussion with those at home as to what they were to do. John wished her to keep Frederick abroad at least for a time, but she could not face an indefinite prospect. Early in her stay with her characteristic blunt truthfulness she had written to Rick, "I am so homesick at the idea of staying here. I do so dislike the English—and I can't understand the language."[39] After months of attempting an unnatural, transient life, with Frederick cared for first in one way and then another, and no satisfactory result gained, she realized that the experiment was pointless. She got also from Dr. Rayner a grim diagnosis. She wrote to John on April 2 that the doctor had told her that Frederick "has had one or two or more slight hemorrhages on the brain the effects of which are now passing off and that there is every likelihood that he may with care and proper diet live to be a very old man. He advises that we take him back to the states and provide him with what he says he wants—duck raising and that from our description he would think that Deer Isle was a most suitable place. He says that if he gets too restless and will not stay willingly that as a last resort we must take legal measure of restraint. The brain being injured past recovery from 'starvation.' "[40]

The members of the family separated by many miles twisted and turned in the pain of their quandary. Mary returned again and again to the idea of a place at Deer Isle and won John only reluctantly to agreement. She told him that her boys must build her and their father a little house there, that she and one attendant would be sufficient, and that she liked the good people of the island. John replied with some impatience that his father had never cared for Deer Isle, that this beautiful place had never meant to him what it had to her and Marion.[41] At other times Mary wrote to her sons as if she and Frederick would return to live at the Warren Street house, and in that case she advised that Marion and the boys should then set up housekeeping elsewhere and have an office in Boston. John, thinking properly of the business of which he was at this time the virtual head, thought it would be a disadvantage for the firm to leave the place with which it was identified, and expressed further to Marion and Rick that moving to Boston would give Charles Eliot a larger share of the business.[42]

But in the spring, 1896, consideration of possibilities could not be prolonged. On April 10 Mary wrote, "I repeat that Dr. Rayner says that I must prepare for a long future *probably* and the *best we can hope for is imbecility.* As to Marion's living at Deer Isle that is nonsense. She must live with you. As to whether I am to live with father that is to be decided according to the best judgment of the family. Nothing we can devise will, in his present condition, content your father, and Dr. Rayner thinks that we shall have to take legal measures to restrain him."[43] Mary felt that the doctor was washing his hands of a sad case. She waited for her cousin Henry Perkins to return from an absence to advise her and perhaps help her get Frederick home. John in Brookline began planning the little house with a duck pen to be built at Deer Isle. He did not believe that his mother would be able to stand the solitary winters on that rough coast. Frederick, to the extent that he understood the plans, agreed to going to Deer Isle but insisted that he was going to spend the winter at Biltmore, as Mary wrote to Rick, May 29.[44]

(John's worries about the family's hold upon the business were at this time unnecessary. Charles Eliot was to die less than a year later in March, 1897, from a cruel case of meningitis, leaving a young family behind, and the promise of a long and brilliant career cut off. After this time and for many decades the Olmsted firm was to be called Olmsted Brothers, and John Charles and Frederick, Jr., were to expand the professional work and competence which their father had founded in opportunities offered by the enlargement of urban centers and the expansion of natural park areas. John was to marry and set up a long delayed household and was to have a full and honorable career until his death in 1920. Frederick, Jr., was to marry also and fulfill in his turn all the hopes which his father had heaped upon his young head. He was to carry on the work of the firm far into the next century.)

At this point, it was as if Frederick Olmsted sailed off into limbo. The letters carefully collected by his son Frederick, Jr., break off in 1896 and resume fully only to memorialize the father's death in 1903. It was as if a protective hand sponged out the written record of family distress over the prolonged embarrassment of a life outlived. One can only infer the emotion which surrounded the short-lived experiment of staying at Deer Isle. Frederick could not be happy. He was sometimes angry, sometimes even physically difficult.[45] Mary and her children reached a decision in September, 1898, to find a place for Frederick away from the family. Frederick, Jr., was appointed legal guardian to his father. Frederick, Sr., was committed to the McLean Asylum in Waverly, Massachusetts. Here he lived for the next five years, no happier than he had been before but cared for with consideration. The great thrust of will was thwarted and the questioning mind was broken into jags of disconnected thoughts. He died on August 28, 1903.

After the old man's death, Dr. Edward Cowles, the medical superintendent of the McLean hospital, wrote to John Olmsted to thank the family for the gift of Frederick's warm outdoor clothing, relics of the patient left behind to be given by the doctor to one or another of the patients. Dr. Cowles's words about the fur coat, the warm cap, and the gloves call up an image of the old man, confused, afflicted, yet still passionately alive, walking under the trees and upon the turf which he had called into existence by the power of his conceiving mind. One can only ask, did he in fitful moments recall not only the people, but the scenes, of his life: the glacier-streaked ledges of Central Park, the red-barked trees of the great Mariposa Grove, or the soft green of spring at Biltmore?

NOTES

The sources referred to most frequently are keyed to the following abbreviated titles. For complete publication data, see "Selective Bibliography."

BC   *A Journey in the Back Country* by Frederick Law Olmsted.

CAC   *Civilizing American Cities: A Selection of Frederick Law Olmsted's Writings on City Landscapes,* edited by S. B. Sutton.

CED   Charles Eliot Diary.

CK   *The Cotton Kingdom* by Frederick Law Olmsted.

CVP   Calvert Vaux Papers.

FLO–LA   *Frederick Law Olmsted, Landscape Architect, 1822–1903,* edited by Frederick Law Olmsted, Jr. and Theodora Kimball.

FLOP   Frederick Law Olmsted Papers.

HT   *Hospital Transports* by Frederick Law Olmsted and Others.

JNT   "From the Journal of a Northern Traveler on Horseback" by Frederick Law Olmsted.

LIC   *Landscape into Cityscape: Frederick Law Olmsted's Plans for a Greater New York City,* edited by Albert Fein.

SSS   *A Journey in the Seaboard Slave States* by Frederick Law Olmsted.

TEX   *A Journey through Texas* by Frederick Law Olmsted.

WT   *Walks and Talks of an American Farmer in England* by Frederick Law Olmsted.

YEO   "Yeoman Letters" by Frederick Law Olmsted.

I. A BOY IN THE CONNECTICUT WOODS

1. From fragmentary manuscripts written by Olmsted in the late 1870s; published first in FLO–LA, 1:50. Other quoted childhood memories, otherwise unidentified in this chapter, are from the same source, pp. 45–63.
2. From John Olmsted's diary, entries published in FLO–LA, 1, as part of a chronology of Frederick Law Olmsted's life, "Biographical Notes, 1822–1903."
3. Frederick Law Olmsted to Elizabeth Baldwin Whitney, December 16, 1890, FLOP. The letter, without identification of Olmsted's correspondent, appears in partial form in FLO–LA, 1:68–71.
4. Benjamin Silliman, *A Tour of Quebec in the Autumn of 1819,* p. 3.
5. Timothy Dwight, *Things as They Are, or, Notes of a Traveller through Some of the Middle and Northern States,* p. 218.
6. To Elizabeth B. Whitney, December 16, 1890, FLOP. See note 3.

II. IDLER

1. FLOP.
2. John Olmsted's diary, FLO–LA, 1:4.
3. "Autobiographical Passages," FLO–LA, 1:61.
4. To Elizabeth Baldwin Whitney, December 16, 1890, FLOP.
5. "Autobiographical Passages," FLO–LA, 1:61.
6. Mariana G. Van Renssalaer, "Frederick Law Olmsted," *Century Illustrated Monthly,* vol. 46 (Oct. 1893).

7. September 13, 1838, FLOP.
8. September 27, 1838, FLOP.
9. 1840, FLOP.
10. FLOP.
11. July 21, 1840, FLOP.
12. FLOP.
13. Ibid.
14. To Charles Loring Brace, June 22, 1845, FLOP.
15. Described by George Templeton Strong, September 28, 1840, *Diary*, vol. 1, p. 147.
16. Strong, *Diary*, October 1840, 1:150.
17. March 20, 1841, FLOP.
18. *American Notes* (London, 1957), p. 53; orig. ed., 1842.
19. Timothy Dwight, II, *Memories of Yale Life and Men, 1845–1899*, p. 22.
20. To John Hull Olmsted, June 23, 1845, FLOP.
21. Dwight, *Memories of Yale*, pp. 55–56.
22. October 3, 1842, FLOP.
23. December 7, 1842, FLOP.
24. Quotations in this paragraph are all from letter of April 8, 1843, FLOP.

III. SAILOR

1. To John Hull Olmsted, FLOP.
2. FLOP.
3. November 20, 1843, FLOP.
4. "Thanksgiving Day," 1843, FLOP.
5. To family? (address lost), April 24, 1843, FLOP.
6. Ibid., through "One of the pigs. . . ."
7. Description from time before he sailed, Frederick to John Hull Olmsted, April 8, 1843, FLOP.
8. From long letter to family (see note 5), FLOP.
9. To "Dear Parents," September 5, 1843, FLOP.
10. To his father, September 24, 1843, FLOP.
11. September 8, 1843, FLOP.
12. To "Dear Parents," September 5, 1843, FLOP.
13. To "Dear Brother," (John Hull Olmsted), September 8, 1843, FLOP.
14. To "Dear Parents," August 6, 1843, FLOP.
15. FLOP.
16. December 27, 1843, FLOP.
17. To "Dear Parents," November 20, 1843, FLOP.
18. Continuation of letter of September 8, 1843, to "Dear Brother," FLOP.

IV. COMPANY AND SOLITUDE

1. FLOP.
2. *Memories of Yale*, pp. 65–66.
3. Letter to Frederick Kingsbury, 1846, in Emma Brace, ed., *Life of Charles Loring Brace*, p. 27.
4. Ibid., p. 9.
5. Ibid., p. 10 (through "I have to be much more careful . . .").
6. Frederick Law Olmsted's recollection, quoted in FLO–LA, 1:65, footnote.
7. F.L.O. to Fred Kingsbury, September 1, 1845, quoted in FLO–LA, 1:65–66.
8. September 13, 1845, FLOP.

9. FLOP.
10. FLOP.
11. FLOP, and reprinted, FLO–LA, 1:69–70.
12. To his father, FLOP.
13. And other quotes from John G. von Zimmermann, *Solitude.*
14. February 1845, FLOP.
15. This and preceding quotes in this paragraph, June 17, 1845, FLOP.
16. September 13, 1845, FLOP.
17. December 30, 1845, FLOP.
18. All these family letters about faith, April 1846, FLOP.
19. May 27, 1846, FLOP.
20. And the following episode, described to John Hull Olmsted, June 19, 1846, FLOP.
21. FLOP.
22. July 14, 1846, FLOP.
23. July 1, 1846, FLOP.
24. July 23, 1846, FLOP.
25. August 12, 1846, FLOP.
26. July 30, 1846, FLOP.
27. August 12, 1846, FLOP.
28. November 12, 1846, FLOP.
29. December 31, 1846, FLOP.
30. FLOP.

V. SCIENTIFIC FARMER

1. FLOP.
2. FLOP.
3. February 7, 1847, FLOP.
4. To Fred Kingsbury, March 12, 1847, FLOP.
5. Ibid.
6. Ibid., March 27, 1847, FLOP.
7. John Hull Olmsted to Fred Kingsbury, May 1847, FLOP.
8. Fred Kingsbury to John Hull Olmsted, May 8, 1847, FLOP.
9. "Nasty" and "juicy" description to John Hull Olmsted, February 16, 1847, FLOP.
10. February 14, 1847, FLOP.
11. To John Hull Olmsted, February 16, 1847, FLOP.
12. May 23, 1847, FLOP.
13. John Hull Olmsted's views of Fred's farming, June 1847, FLOP.
14. July 26, 1847, FLOP.
15. Charles Brace, on Bushnell's influence on his and others' youthful days, in Theodore T. Munger, *Horace Bushnell: Preacher and Theologian,* pp. 277–78.
16. H. Shelton Smith, ed., *Horace Bushnell,* p. 378.
17. Horace Bushnell, "Christian Nurture," quoted in Munger, op. cit., p. 76.
18. July 26, 1847, FLOP.
19. November 21, 1862, Worthington C. Ford, ed., *A Cycle of Adams Letters,* vol. 1, p. 196.
20. March 22, 1847, FLOP.
21. *First Essays* (1841).
22. September 9, 1847, FLOP.
23. Mrs. Olmsted's description quoted in FLO–LA, 1:78–79.
24. March 24, 1848, FLOP.
25. Charles Brace to Fred Kingsbury, 1848, quoted in Brace, ed., *Life of Charles Loring Brace,* p. 61.

26. March 9, 1848, FLOP.
27. March 16, 1848, FLOP.
28. March 20, 1848, FLOP.
29. To Fred Kingsbury, September 4, 1848, FLOP.
30. These recollections of Mary Perkins Olmsted recorded in 1920, quoted in FLO–LA, 1:79.
31. March 9, 1848, FLOP.
32. September 23, 1847, FLOP.
33. March 25, 1848, FLOP.
34. Brace, ed., *Life of Charles Loring Brace*, p. 57.
35. Ibid., p. 59.
36. Ibid., pp. 61–62.
37. Ibid., pp. 62–63.
38. Ibid., pp. 82–83.
39. Ibid., p. 76.
40. FLOP.
41. September 4, 1848, FLOP.
42. April 2, 1849, FLOP.
43. Fred to John Hull, February 29, 1850, FLOP.
44. John Hull Olmsted to Fred Kingsbury, December 11, 1849, FLOP.
45. January 7, 1849, FLOP.
46. To his father, November 4, 1849, FLOP.
47. FLO–LA, 1:84–85.
48. March 12, 1849, FLOP.
49. Brace, ed., *Life of Charles Loring Brace*, p. 87.
50. March 16, 1850, FLOP.
51. February 29, 1850, FLOP.

VI.   A WALK IN ENGLAND

1. WT, p. 59.
2. Ibid., p. 24.
3. Description of Liverpool docks, WT, p. 29.
4. WT, p. 31.
5. Ibid., p. 49.
6. Park description, WT, pp. 51–52.
7. English countryside, WT, p. 59.
8. At the inn, WT, pp. 68–69.
9. Farmers' methods, WT, pp. 71–72.
10. WT, p. 279.
11. Ibid., p. 82.
12. Ibid., p. 98.
13. Ibid., p. 281.
14. Ibid., pp. 228–29.
15. Ibid., p. 79.
16. Ibid., p. 235.
17. Ibid., p. 37.
18. Ibid., p. 46.
19. Ibid., p. 150.
20. Ibid., p. 241.
21. Ibid., pp. 239–41.
22. In essay, "Heroism," Modern Library ed., p. 256.
23. Reprinted in Bryant, *Letters of a Traveller*, Letter XXI, June 24, 1845, pp. 168–70.

24. Also in *The Horticulturist*.
25. Ibid.
26. Quoted in Brace, ed., *Life of Charles Loring Brace*, p. 110.
27. To John Hull Olmsted, Ibid., p. 112.
28. Ibid., p. 142.
29. Ibid., pp. 146–47.

VII. A VISIT TO NEWBURGH

1. FLOP.
2. May 27, 1851, FLOP.
3. FLOP.
4. September 12, 1851, FLOP.
5. August 11, 1851, FLOP.
6. October 12, 1851, FLOP.
7. December 4, 1851, FLOP.
8. "Memoir," in Andrew Jackson Downing, *Rural Essays*.
9. Ibid.
10. CVP.
11. Reprinted, Downing, *Rural Essays*, p. 139ff.
12. Reprinted, Downing, *Rural Essays*, p. 147.
13. From two accounts, George Templeton Strong, *Diary*, 2:100, and George William
    Curtis, "Memoir," in Downing, *Rural Essays*.

VIII. JOURNEYING SOUTH

1. SSS, preface of 1856 edition, p. ix.
2. Newspaper clipping, FLOP.
3. October 17, 1852, FLOP.
4. February 24, 1852, FLOP.
5. October 17, 1852, FLOP.
6. SSS, p. 4.
7. Ibid., p. 2.
8. Olmsted's recording of his initial impressions in this and the following paragraph
    from SSS, pp. 17–18.
9. This and other Richmond impressions from SSS, pp. 26–31.
10. SSS, p. 44.
11. The several quotations from the adventure of finding Mr. Thomas W.'s place, SSS,
    pp. 62–86.
12. Truman Nelson, ed., *Documents of Upheaval*, p. 55; from Garrison's article of De-
    cember 29, 1832.
13. Quoted descriptions of stagecoach journey in this paragraph and succeeding para-
    graphs, SSS, pp. 319–32.
14. The "good" plantation, SSS, p. 410ff.
15. SSS, p. 414.
16. Ibid., p. 530.
17. Country church service, SSS, p. 455.
18. SSS, p. 160.
19. Ibid., p. 565.
20. Ibid., p. 562.
21. FLOP.
22. SSS, p. 606.

23. The stevedore's song and other quotations from the river journey on the *St. Charles,* SSS, pp. 606–19.
24. SSS, p. 659.

IX. NEW YORK STREETS AND TEXAS TRAILS

1. TEX, p. 2.
2. About Mr. Brown and Nack, TEX, pp. 45–46.
3. TEX, p. 75.
4. About Judy, TEX, p. 93.
5. TEX, p. 75.
6. Description of New York streets and buildings from Bayrd Still, *Mirror for Gotham,* pp. 125–26, 138.
7. G. T. Strong, *Diary,* 2:142.
8. This quotation and those which follow illustrate Brace's writing in pamphlets in support of work among the children of the streets.
9. These quotations concerning the "Newsboys' Lodging-houses" are from Charles Loring Brace, *Sketch of the Formation of the Newsboys' Lodging-house, No. 128 Fulton Street* (1867).
10. Ibid.
11. Preface, Downing, *Rural Essays,* p. xix.
12. F.L.O. reported this conversation to his father, June 16, 1853, FLOP.
13. The material which follows, paraphrased and in quotation marks, about the beginning of this journey is from TEX, pp. 1–5.
14. FLOP. In this long letter, dated December 1, 1853, Olmsted used the experience of meeting and talking with Allison to clarify his own ideas and aims.
15. Paraphrase and direct quotations about emigrant train from TEX, p. 55ff.
16. TEX, p. 98.
17. About the people and land where the Germans had settled, this and successive quotes in TEX, pp. 189–98.
18. March 12, 1854, FLOP.
19. TEX, p. 352.
20. Ibid., p. 356.
21. Ibid., p. 365.
22. Descriptions of Creole manners and habits, TEX, pp. 382–96.

X. THE BACK COUNTRY

1. BC, p. 413.
2. Ibid., p. 214.
3. Episode of Negro girl being punished, BC, pp. 73–85. Some of the darker experiences of his travels, including this episode, were moved, for a redoubling of moral and esthetic effect, from an earlier period. The emotional climax of this book, and later the climax of his condensed, one-volume version of all his southern travels, *The Cotton Kingdom,* was to be this description of the punishment of a female slave.
4. BC, pp. 38–39.
5. Ibid., p. 132.
6. Ibid., p. 135.
7. Ibid., p. 147.
8. Ibid., p. 162.
9. Ibid., p. 232.
10. Ibid.

11. Ibid., p. 251.
12. BC, p. 283: "From Richmond I went with my horse and dog direct to New York by the steamer."

XI. YEOMAN: THE SOUTHERN WRITINGS

1. Vol. 2, (New York, 1838), p. 145.
2. (New York, 1849), p. 224.
3. (London, 1957 ed.), p. 133.
4. (New York, 1850), pp. 71–82.
5. YEO, no. 1, February 16, 1853.
6. YEO, no. 36, September 1, 1853.
7. YEO, no. 2, February 19, 1853.
8. YEO, no. 4, March 4, 1853.
9. YEO, no. 10.
10. SSS, Preface, p. ix, dated January 9, 1856.
11. SSS, p. 161.
12. Ibid., p. 402.
13. Ibid., p. 561.
14. Ibid., p. 643.
15. YEO, no. 44, November 21, 1853.
16. SSS, pp. 240–41.
17. Ibid., p. 90.
18. On field labor, SSS, pp. 478–79.
19. Ibid.
20. SSS, p. 147.
21. YEO, no. 46.
22. SSS, p. 487.
23. SSS, p. 154.
24. Ibid., p. 155.
25. Ibid., pp. 443–44.
26. Ibid., p. 444.
27. Ibid., p. 446.
28. YEO, no. 46, January 12, 1854.
29. SSS, p. 627.
30. (Baton Rouge, Louisiana, 1949), pp. 1–2.
31. "Economic Democracy in the Slave South," vol. 31 (April 1946), p. 164.
32. *The Political Economy of Slavery,* pp. 8–23.
33. P. 25.
34. Cited in an essay, "Growth of Southern Civilization," in Albert D. Kirwan, ed., *The Civilization of the Old South; Writings of Clement Eaton,* p. 131.
35. (Baton Rouge, Louisiana), p. 149.
36. Chapter 6, "Northerners in the South," (New York), p. 221.

XII. EDITOR AND PUBLISHER

1. FLOP.
2. FLOP.
3. $130 at this time; $720 in all. Frederick to his father, on December 31, 1854, FLOP.
4. FLOP.
5. FLOP.
6. December 17, 1854, FLOP.

7. John Hull Olmsted told the story of this new business venture of Fred's to Bertha, in a letter dated May 6, 1855, FLOP.
8. April 8, 1855, FLOP.
9. March 9, 1855, FLOP.
10. About Fred, Ibid.
11. About Charlotte's birth, March 15, 1855, FLOP.
12. Agreement in FLOP.
13. FLOP.
14. April 13, 1855, FLOP.
15. April 1, 1855, FLOP.
16. To his father, April 27, 1855, FLOP.
17. In the 1880s, Olmsted told Sylvester Baxter about the editorial arrangements at Putnam's; Mary P. Olmsted also told the story, FLOP.
18. May 28, 1855, FLOP.
19. This, and succeeding quotes about his daily life, April 13, 1855, FLOP.
20. *A Memoir of George Palmer Putnam*, pp. 234–36.
21. Strong, *Diary*, 2, April 19, 1856.
22. April 27, 1855, FLOP.
23. May 6, 1855, FLOP.
24. This and other remarks about his book from the same letter, FLOP.
25. February 7, 1856, FLOP.
26. April 20, 1856, FLOP.
27. February 1, 1856, FLOP.
28. March 19, 1856, FLOP.
29. Bertha's notes about trip in FLOP.
30. William J. Osborn of Middleton & McMaster, May 6, 1857, FLOP.
31. John Hull to Fred, November 10, 1856, FLOP.
32. July 10, 1856, FLOP.
33. July 19, 1856, FLOP.
34. July 27, 1856, FLOP.
35. Ibid.
36. Date uncertain, letter in FLOP.
37. Draft, whether sent or not, dated September 4, 1856, London, FLOP.
38. FLOP.
39. FLOP.
40. July 6, 1857, FLOP.
41. August 10, 1857, FLOP.
42. August 11, 1857, FLOP.
43. September 25, 1857, FLOP.
44. October 3, 1857, FLOP.
45. November 13, 1857, FLOP.
46. November 13, 1857, FLOP.
47. FLOP.
48. November 28, 1857, FLOP.
49. FLOP.
50. August 18, 1857, FLOP.
51. FLOP.

XIII. GREENSWARD

1. J. T. Boulton, ed., *Philosophical Enquiry*, pp. 100, 111.
2. From F. L. Olmsted, "Passages in the Life of an Unpractical Man," reprinted, LIC, pp. 61–62.

3. FLOP.
4. FLOP.
5. FLOP.
6. FLOP.
7. September 11, 1857, FLOP.
8. FLOP.
9. October 9, 1857, about his needs, FLOP.
10. William Cullen Bryant, originally in *The Evening Post,* reprinted in *Letters of a Traveller,* p. 169.
11. "A Talk about Public Parks and Gardens" in Downing, *Rural Essays,* p. 142. (Originally published in *The Horticulturist,* October 1848).
12. Quoted by Allan Nevins in *The Evening Post* (New York, 1922), p. 193.
13. H. W. S. Cleveland, *Landscape Architecture, as Applied to the Wants of the West,* p. 37.
14. Calvert Vaux, *Villas and Cottages,* pp. 14–15.
15. Ibid., p. 25.
16. Ibid., pp. 36–38.
17. Clipping, New York *Herald,* Friday, October 30, 1857, FLOP.
18. FLO–LA, 2:42–43.
19. Vaux, *Villas and Cottages,* pp. 39–40.
20. From Olmsted and Vaux, *Report to the Commissioners of Prospect Park, 1866,* quoted in FLO–LA, 2:212.
21. Ibid.
22. *Description of a Plan for the Improvement of the Central Park, 1858;* reprinted in, among other places, FLO–LA, 2:214–33. The following quotations are from this preliminary plan before Olmsted and Vaux began their joint design work in the park.
23. FLO–LA, 2:48.
24. FLO–LA, 2:49–50.
25. FLO–LA, 2:50.

XIV. THE BOSS OF CENTRAL PARK

1. Draft of letter to Central Park commissioners, about January 1861, FLOP.
2. Undated, FLOP.
3. Strong, *Diary,* 2:454–55.
4. Ibid.
5. Ibid., p. 350.
6. Figures from FLO–LA, 2:534 (Appendix 1).
7. F.L.O. to Paul Dana, December 22, 1890, quoted in FLO–LA, 2:527–28.
8. Central Park handbill quoted in FLO–LA, 2:417–18.
9. Report quoted, FLO–LA, 2:51.
10. These various park communications in FLOP.
11. FLOP; this letter is quoted in full in Chapter XII.
12. "Designers' Report as to Proposed Modifications in the Plan," dated May 31, 1858; reprinted in FLO–LA, 2:235–39.
13. Ibid., p. 239.
14. Published in the newspaper during 1858.
15. September 23, 1859, FLOP.
16. October 2, 1859, FLOP.
17. October 6, 1859, FLOP.
18. September 29, 1859, FLOP.

19. FLOP.
20. November 28, 1859, FLOP.
21. To the Board of Commissioners of Central Park, December 28, 1859, reprinted in FLO–LA, 2:55–58. (The quotations which follow, describing Olmsted's visits in England, France, Belgium, and Ireland, are taken from this report.)
22. "Selection from Report on European Visit," 1859, in FLO–LA, 2:307.
23. Undated (1859?), FLOP.
24. FLOP.
25. October 21, 1859, FLOP.
26. October 25, 1859, FLOP.
27. FLOP.
28. FLOP.
29. To his father, March 12, 1860, FLOP.
30. June 14, 1860, FLOP.
31. June 29, 1860, FLOP.
32. Description, to his father, July 22, 1860, FLOP.
33. Retrospective full accounts of this accident in Mary's recollections, July 16, 1920, and in Frederick Olmsted's letter to Elizabeth B. Whitney, December 16, 1890; both in FLOP.
34. August 17, 1860, FLOP.
35. All in FLOP.
36. To his father, about his physical progress and about the children's education, October 21, 1860, FLOP.
37. About November expeditions, to Mary, November 15 and 17, 1860, FLOP.
38. November 15, 1860, FLOP.
39. November 1, 1860, FLOP.
40. To Charles L. Brace, December 8, 1860, FLOP.
41. FLOP.
42. FLOP.
43. December 6, 1860, FLOP.
44. October 10, 1859, FLOP.
45. Undated copy, filed with draft of material for meeting of January 22, 1861, FLOP.
46. Draft of material in preparation for meeting with commissioners, January 22, 1861, FLOP.
47. Explanation to his father, March 22, 1861, FLOP.
48. December 8, 1860, FLOP.
49. FLOP.
50. FLOP.

XV. SECRETARY OF THE SANITARY COMMISSION

1. FLOP.
2. F.L.O. described this sight to his son, John Charles, September 11, 1861, FLOP.
3. Strong, *Diary*, 3:180.
4. July 29, 1861, FLOP.
5. August 4, 1861, FLOP.
6. To Mary, July 2, 1861, FLOP.
7. *Documents of the United States Sanitary Commission*, vol. 1, no. 1, p. 1.
8. Ibid.
9. July 9, 1861, no. 17, *Documents of the United States Sanitary Commission*.
10. FLOP.
11. FLOP.

12. October 13, 1861, FLOP.
13. From Chronology, John Olmsted's diary, FLO–LA, 1.
14. In "Plan of Organization," dated June 13, 1861, in *Documents of the United States Sanitary Commission,* no. 3.
15. FLOP.
16. FLOP.
17. FLOP.
18. FLOP.
19. Content was an Olmsted family given name, FLOP.
20. FLOP.
21. To his father, September 12, 1861, FLOP.
22. Strong, *Diary,* 3:186.
23. Ibid., p. 196.
24. Ibid., pp. 195–96.
25. Also printed in *Documents of the United States Sanitary Commission,* no. 40.
26. From article on Stanton in A. Howard Meneely, *Dictionary of American Biography.*
27. Description of Olmsted's working habits by George T. Strong, *Diary* (January 1863), 3:291.
28. August 6 or 8, 1861, FLOP.
29. FLOP.
30. FLOP.
31. FLOP.
32. FLOP.
33. FLOP.
34. Copy, FLOP.
35. Ibid.
36. April 19, 1862, FLOP.
37. Strong, *Diary,* 3:217–18.
38. Episode recounted in Strong, *Diary,* 3:211–13.

XVI. THE CHIEF OF THE HOSPITAL SHIPS

1. HT, introduction. (Boston, 1863).
2. FLOP.
3. The roster and initial activities of the hospital ships, HT, pp. 18–19.
4. Strong, *Diary,* 3:221.
5. Ibid.
6. Overland ride of F.L.O. and others, HT, pp. 21–23.
7. Strong, *Diary,* 3:222.
8. Ibid.
9. Katherine Prescott Wormeley, *The Other Side of the War,* p. 25.
10. Ibid., pp. 70–71.
11. Episode of Bigelow's Landing, HT, pp. 60–61 and Wormeley, *Other Side of the War,* pp. 36–37.
12. Wormeley, *Other Side of the War,* pp. 60–64.
13. William Quentin Maxwell, *Lincoln's Fifth Wheel,* p. 155.
14. Quotation identified by key as Olmsted's, HT, pp. 109–10.
15. Wormeley, *Other Side of the War,* p. 90.
16. June 11, 1862, FLOP.
17. June 28, 1862, FLOP.
18. Alexander S. Webb, *The Peninsula; McClellan's Campaign of 1862,* pp. 136–37. (Orig. ed., 1881.)
19. HT, pp. 135–36.

XVII. THE END OF OLMSTED'S WAR

1. FLOP.
2. FLOP.
3. Charles J. Stille, *History of the United States Sanitary Commission,* pp. 158–59.
4. Wormeley, *Other Side of the War,* p. 206.
5. Letter of Henry W. Bellows, July 12, 1862, FLOP.
6. July 25, 1862, FLOP.
7. Running description of ailments in several letters of August 1862, FLOP.
8. F.L.O.; a memo or letter (correspondent's name missing), dated September 13, 1862, FLOP.
9. To "Dear Wife," from Washington, D.C., September 21, 1862, FLOP.
10. September 15, 1862, FLOP.
11. Strong, *Diary,* 3:251.
12. FLOP.
13. September 26, 1862, FLOP.
14. FLOP.
15. About Vaux, Mary's picture, and "the young ones," September 29, 1862, FLOP.
16. October 11, 1862, FLOP.
17. FLOP.
18. October 4, 1862, FLOP.
19. "To My Dear Wife," "November 13 I believe," FLOP.
20. February 16, 1863, FLOP.
21. Strong, *Diary,* 3:248.
22. Ibid., p. 276.
23. Ibid., p. 280.
24. Ibid., p. 290.
25. Ibid., p. 303.
26. Ibid., p. 304.
27. To Mary, February 28, 1863, FLOP.
28. Description of Murfreesboro visit to Mary, March 8, 1863, FLOP.
29. Edward Dicey to F.L.O., FLOP.
30. Sketch dated March 13, 1863, at Cairo, Illinois, FLOP.
31. To Dr. Henry Bellows, from on board the *Dunleith,* April 1, 1863, FLOP.
32. Ibid.
33. To his father, April 1, 1863, FLOP.
34. April 1, 1863, FLOP.
35. About Central Park and the Sanitary Commission, April 18, 1863, FLOP.
36. FLOP.
37. In May 22, 1863 letter, F.L.O. to his father, FLOP. (Vaux sent in his official letter of resignation on May 12; Olmsted did so, apparently, within days.)
38. August 2, 1863, FLOP.
39. FLOP.
40. To Mary, FLOP.
41. Ibid.
42. June 29, 1863, FLOP.
43. July 2, 1863, FLOP.
44. FLOP.
45. FLOP.
46. FLOP.
47. July 20, 1863, FLOP.
48. July 29, 1863, FLOP.

49. FLOP.
50. To Dr. Wolcott Gibbs, one of the Commissioners of the United States Sanitary Commission, quoted in Henry W. Bellows' *Historical Sketch of the Union League Club of New York,* p. 29.
51. FLOP.
52. Strong, *Diary,* 3:325.
53. June 26, 1863, FLOP.
54. *The Nation* (September 3, 1903), vol. 77, 191.
55. Various schemes and doubts, about the freedmen, Chicago, the farm, his health, and ambitions, to his father, April 18, 1863, FLOP.
56. August 7, 1863, FLOP.
57. FLOP.
58. FLOP.
59. Another letter to Mary, August 12, 1863, FLOP.
60. Ibid.
61. August 13, 1863, FLOP.
62. FLOP.
63. August 18, 1863, FLOP.
64. Ibid.
65. FLOP.
66. Ibid.
67. Clipping, FLOP.
68. Edwin L. Godkin, *Life and Letters,* 2 vols., 1:226.
69. Strong, *Diary,* 3:350.
70. Walter R. Steiner, *A Physician's Experiences in The United States Sanitary Commission* (pamphlet), p. 175.

XVIII. MARIPOSA

1. FLOP.
2. September 25, 1863, FLOP.
3. Ibid.
4. FLOP.
5. October 10, 1863, FLOP.
6. First impressions of San Francisco, October 12, 1863, FLOP.
7. Ibid.
8. September 1, 1863, FLOP.
9. October 4, 1863, FLOP.
10. Undated, but certainly in 1863, FLOP.
11. First impressions of Bear Valley, October 14, 1863, FLOP.
12. October 15, 1863, FLOP.
13. Ibid.
14. About the river, the possible sheep range, the mines, the planned house, death in Bear Valley, and the view on Sunday evening, October 18, 1863, FLOP.
15. October 31, 1863, FLOP.
16. Ibid.
17. October 30, 1863, FLOP.
18. October 31, 1863, FLOP.
19. Ibid.
20. November 21, 1863, FLOP.
21. FLOP.
22. Ibid.
23. March 30, 1864, FLOP.

24. December 21, 1863, FLOP.
25. January 1, 1864, FLOP.
26. FLOP.
27. December 1, 1863, FLOP.
28. Ibid.
29. FLOP.
30. The house, as dreamed of, was apparently not built.
31. FLOP.
32. FLOP.
33. FLOP.
34. FLOP.
35. Ibid.
36. Ibid.
37. FLOP.
38. Ibid.
39. To Mary, from New York City, August 12, 1863.
40. FLOP.
41. July 20, 1864, F.L.O., in a letter partially preserved, correspondent unknown, FLOP.
42. June 25, 1864, FLOP.
43. Mineral-gathering and botanizing, Olmsted to his father, Ibid.
44. August 17, 1864, FLOP.
45. Ibid.
46. FLOP.
47. FLOP.
48. F.L.O. to his father, October 16, 1864, FLOP.
49. September 14, 1864, FLOP.
50. July 24, 1864, FLOP.
51. May 31, 1864, *Life and Letters*, 1:229.
52. Ibid., p. 230.
53. Ibid., p. 235.
54. January 8, 1865, FLOP.
55. January 16, 1865, FLOP.
56. January 18, 1865, FLOP.
57. February 10, 1865, FLOP.
58. February 12, 1865, FLOP.
59. All this discussion of business to Mary, Ibid.
60. Frederick Law Olmsted, *Report upon a Projected Improvement of the Estate of the College of California at Berkeley, near Oakland;* reprinted in CAC, p. 289.
61. F.L.O., August 1, 1865, CVP.
62. Frederick Law Olmsted, *Preliminary Report in Regard to a Plan of Public Pleasure Grounds for the City of San Francisco;* reprinted CAC, p. 115.
63. Ibid., p. 119.
64. August 1, 1865, CVP.
65. Source, Frederick Law Olmsted, Jr. This letter of Calvert Vaux to Frederick Law Olmsted, Sr., quoted in FLO–LA, 2:79.
66. March 12, 1865, CVP.
67. About his art, about Mariposa, and about his and Mary's domestic life, a long letter, August 1, 1865, CVP.
68. Told by F.L.O. in July 5, 1865, letter, FLOP.
69. FLOP.
70. Frederick Law Olmsted, "The Yosemite Valley and the Mariposa Big Trees: A Preliminary Report, 1865" rediscovered and reconstructed by Laura Wood Roper; reprinted, *Landscape Architecture*, 43 (October 1952):22.

71. Frederick Law Olmsted, *Governmental Preservation of Natural Scenery* (pamphlet).
72. F.L.O., letter to Mary, August 23, 1865, FLOP.
73. FLOP.
74. End of August, 1865, FLOP.
75. CVP.
76. April 16, 1865, FLOP.
77. FLOP.

XIX. BETWEEN TWO WORLDS

1. Reprinted, LIC, pp. 100–01.
2. Typed copy, April 26, 1866, FLOP. The original of this and a number of other Olmsted letters to Charles Eliot Norton are held in the Charles Eliot Norton Papers.
3. January 6, 1866, Mary Olmsted to Mrs. Norton, typed copy, FLOP.
4. Olmsted to Norton, typed copy, June 2, 1866, FLOP.
5. July 15, 1866, typed copy, FLOP.
6. September 12, 1866, typed copy, FLOP.
7. Rowing expeditions described by Olmsted to Norton, July 15, 1866, FLOP.
8. FLOP.
9. Letters in FLOP.
10. FLOP.
11. Quote from May 22 letter, FLOP.
12. June 23, 1866, FLOP.
13. FLOP.
14. Letter in FLOP.
15. FLOP.
16. J. C. Derby to Olmsted, Letterhead, U.S. Agency for the Paris Universal Exhibition of 1867.
17. F. B. Sanborn to Olmsted, from Boston.
18. August 24, 1866, FLOP.
19. Sample rate sheets, FLOP.
20. (New York, 1949 ed.), p. 11.
21. FLOP.
22. *Preliminary Report . . . for the Laying Out of a Park in Brooklyn, N. Y.* (1866); reprinted, LIC, pp. 100–04.
23. September 2, 1866, FLOP.
24. Typed copy, September 12, 1866, FLOP.

XX. A WIDER WORK

1. FLOP.
2. "Chicago in Distress," *The Nation*, November 9, 1871.
3. April 11, 1871, FLOP.
4. FLOP.
5. February 26, 1867, FLOP.
6. March 7, 1867, FLOP.
7. FLOP.
8. FLOP.
9. Letters of January 7, 1867 and August 15, 1867, FLOP.
10. In *Landscape Architecture*, October 1952.
11. FLOP.

12. January 17, 1867, FLOP.
13. January 28, 1870, FLOP.
14. FLOP.
15. Typed copy of a letter to Charles Eliot Norton, December 14, 1867, FLOP.
16. May 24 (?), 1867, FLOP.
17. June 22 (?), 1867, FLOP.
18. September 10, 1867, Andrew D. White Papers.
19. Kermit Carlyle Parsons, *The Cornell Campus*, p. 2.
20. Two quotations from Charles Loring Brace, *Address on Industrial Schools Delivered ... November 13, 1868*, pp. 9–13.
21. Strong, *Diary*, 4:166.
22. February 7, 1870, FLOP.
23. FLOP.
24. August 2, 1869, FLOP.
25. FLOP.
26. FLOP.
27. April 16, 1870, FLOP.
28. FLOP.
29. FLOP.
30. FLOP.
31. Frederick Law Olmsted et al., *Report to the Staten Island Improvement Commission of a Preliminary Scheme of Improvements 1871*; reprinted in LIC, pp. 184–85.
32. The several quotations from *Public Parks and the Enlargement of Towns*, as reprinted in CAC, pp. 54–96.
33. Quotations from reprint of "South Park Plan," in CAC, pp. 162–65.
34. Quotations from Olmsted, Vaux & Co., *Preliminary Report upon the Proposed Suburban Village at Riverside, near Chicago*, as reprinted in CAC, pp. 293–94.
35. FLOP.
36. August 23, 1868, FLOP.
37. Typed copy, FLOP.
38. FLOP.
39. FLOP.
40. September 25, 1868, FLOP.
41. FLOP.
42. Undated, except "Fri. morning" [1868], FLOP.
43. June 18, 1869, FLOP.
44. FLOP.
45. FLOP.
46. FLOP.
47. FLOP.
48. July 11, 1870, FLOP.
49. November 25, 1870, FLOP.

XXI. A HUMANE LIFE

1. FLOP.
2. The long letter of April 20, 1871, from which several quotations are taken, FLOP.
3. October 8, 1871, FLOP.
4. Strong, *Diary*, 4:361.
5. Ibid., p. 374.
6. FLOP.
7. Strong, *Diary*, 4:385.

8. In FLO–LA, 2:247–48.
9. July 15, 1872, "Inquiry Regarding Park Lighting," signed by F.L.O. as "President of the Department of Public Parks," a position Olmsted held for part of one year; FLO–LA, 2:417.
10. To S. H. Wales (Parks Commissioner), December 26, 1873, FLO–LA, 2:485.
11. Notation taken down from talk of Mary P. Olmsted, July 16, 1920, concerning events of June 21, 1872, FLOP.
12. Several letters, FLOP.
13. FLOP.
14. December 21, 1872, FLOP.
15. May 7, 1872, FLOP.
16. May 14, 1872, FLOP.
17. FLOP.
18. FLOP.
19. FLOP.
20. FLOP.
21. June 14, 1871, FLOP.
22. And Olmsted lent Vaux money once, July 1874.
23. FLOP.
24. January 28, 1873, FLOP.
25. January 29, 1873, FLOP.
26. January 31, 1873, FLOP.

XXII. BUFFETINGS AND ACCOMPLISHMENTS

1. FLOP.
2. "Instructions to Keepers," 1873; reprinted, FLO–LA, 2:101.
3. Letter to the President of the Board of Commissioners, July 15, 1873; excerpt, FLO–LA, 2:102.
4. Excerpt, reprinted, FLO–LA, 2:357.
5. September 9, 1873, FLOP.
6. December 21, 1873, FLOP.
7. May 19, 1874, FLOP; paraphrased.
8. May 19, 1874, FLOP.
9. FLOP.
10. To "Henry," May 13, 1875, FLOP.
11. October 1, 1876, FLOP.
12. Typed copy, n.d., except 1874, in answer to Hall's letter of March 12, 1874, FLOP.
13. The review was entitled "Country Living," January 22, 1874, p. 64.
14. Quotations which follow are from F. L. Olmsted & J. James Croes, *Preliminary Report of the Landscape Architect and the Civil and Topographical Engineer, upon the Laying Out of the Twenty-third and Twenty-fourth Wards...*; reprinted, LIC, pp. 349–73.
15. La Farge to Olmsted, undated letter, about 1876, FLOP.
16. February 28, 1879, FLOP.
17. Typed copy, December 27, 1876, FLOP.
18. May 10, 1873, FLOP.
19. July 19, 1874, FLOP.
20. Typed copy, FLOP.
21. June 26, 1874, FLOP.
22. S. B. Sutton, *Charles Sprague Sargent and the Arnold Arboretum* (Cambridge, Massachusetts, 1970), pp. 52–53.

23. Typed copy, FLOP.
24. FLOP.
25. November 3, 1875, FLOP.
26. FLOP.
27. FLOP.
28. FLOP.
29. FLOP.
30. FLOP.
31. Olmsted to park commissioners, FLOP.
32. Draft, FLOP.
33. October 17 or 19, 1875, FLOP.
34. Copy, November 20, 1875, FLOP.
35. November 20, 1875, FLOP.
36. November 30, 1875, FLOP.
37. August 22, 1876, FLOP.
38. August 26, 1876, FLOP.

XXIII. INTERLUDE

1. FLOP.
2. To "Dear Mary," July 24 [1877], FLOP.
3. July 25, 1877, FLOP.
4. FLOP.
5. July, 1876, law firm to Olmsted, FLOP.
6. Typed copy, December 27, 1876, FLOP.
7. January 5, 1877, FLOP.
8. FLOP.
9. FLOP.
10. To John, July 2, 1877, FLOP.
11. July 29, 1877, FLOP.
12. August 3, 1877, FLOP.
13. August 10, 1877, FLOP.
14. August 15 (?), 1877, FLOP.
15. Probably misdated August 10; by context should be September 10, 1877, FLOP.
16. FLOP.
17. Probably late 1870s, preserved by F.L.O., Jr.
18. Reprinted as "The Beginning of Central Park: a Fragment of Autobiography (ca. 1877)," in LIC, p. 52.
19. FLOP.
20. October 3, 1877, FLOP.
21. FLO–LA, 2:110.
22. Ibid.
23. FLOP.
24. FLO–LA, 2:110–11.
25. January 25, 1878, FLOP.
26. Reprinted, FLO–LA, 2:112–13.
27. This account of Calvert Vaux's work between 1873 and 1879, from a memo in his own handwriting, CVP.
28. Calvert Vaux's letter, preserved as a newspaper clipping, CVP.
29. Ibid.
30. FLOP and CVP (newspaper clipping).
31. February 21, 1878, FLOP.

32. Newspaper clipping, CVP. And Vaux wrote a polite reply to Mary Olmsted on February 24, signed "Always your friend, C. Vaux," FLOP.
33. FLO–LA, 1:22.
34. FLOP.
35. May 13, 1878, FLOP.
36. May 23, 1878, FLOP.
37. FLOP.
38. FLOP.
39. FLOP.
40. FLOP.
41. FLOP.
42. FLOP.
43. December 1, 1878, FLOP.
44. October 15, 1878, FLOP.

XXIV. RECOVERY

1. FLOP.
2. January 2, 1879, FLOP.
3. July 16, 1879, FLOP.
4. Marian Adams, in her customary letters to her father, noted these occasions; see Marian Adams, *Letters of Mrs. Henry Adams, 1865–1883;* ed. Ward Thoron, pp. 395–96.
5. February 8, 1879, FLOP.
6. From *Report of a Preliminary Survey of Rockaway Point* (1879), reprinted in LIC, p. 313.
7. Ibid., p. 323.
8. Frederick Olmsted to Bertha Olmsted Niles, April 15, 1881, FLOP.
9. April 26, 1881, FLOP.
10. July 29, 1881, FLOP.
11. FLOP.
12. FLOP.
13. FLOP.
14. November 9, 1881, FLOP.
15. FLOP.
16. FLOP.
17. FLOP.
18. FLOP.
19. FLOP.
20. FLOP.
21. FLOP.
22. Pencilled draft of letter, June 13, 1880, FLOP.
23. FLOP.
24. FLOP.
25. Reprinted by Albert Fein in LIC, pp. 391–440.
26. Misdated *1881,* FLOP.
27. Ibid. (March 7, 1882.)
28. Ibid.
29. LIC, p. 405.
30. March 10, 1882, FLOP.
31. FLOP.
32. FLOP.
33. January 9, 1882, FLOP.

XXV.   A LIBERAL PROFESSION

1. FLOP.
2. [Charles W. Eliot, Sr.], *Charles Eliot, Landscape Architect,* p. 32.
3. Ibid., p. 34.
4. Charles Eliot's manuscript diary is held in the Frances Loeb Library, Harvard Graduate School of Design; quotations from this diary are denoted CED.
5. May 6, 1883, CED.
6. Ibid.
7. May 27, 1883, CED.
8. Ibid.
9. CED.
10. June 3, 1883, CED.
11. June 27, 1883, CED.
12. July 8, 1883, CED.
13. September 9, 1883, CED.
14. FLOP.
15. FLOP.
16. FLOP.
17. FLOP.
18. From Detroit, May 24, 1884, FLOP.
19. FLOP.
20. FLOP.
21. FLOP.
22. FLOP.
23. FLOP. Olmsted's letters in this sequence survive because copies were held in Olmsted's files.
24. September 3, 1887, CVP.
25. FLOP.
26. *Charles Eliot, Landscape Architect,* p. 42.
27. CED.
28. March 15, 1886, FLOP.
29. "Decoration Day" 1884, FLOP.
30. Ibid.
31. October 9, 1886, FLOP.
32. October 10, 1886, FLOP.
33. FLOP.
34. Olmsted told Mariana G. Van Renssalaer about this visit in a letter, May 2, 1886, FLOP.
35. FLOP.
36. FLOP.
37. March 15, 1887, FLOP.

XXVI.   NORTH, SOUTH, AND WEST

1. FLOP.
2. June 27, 1886, FLOP.
3. July 20, 1886, FLOP.
4. September 23, 1886, FLOP.
5. June 14, 1888, FLOP.
6. A file of letters between Stanford and Olmsted and their agents is held in the University Archives, Stanford University Libraries, which sheds light on the rela-

tionship of the two men and the part the Olmsted firm had in the early planning of the campus.

7. Mrs. Leland Stanford to Frederick Olmsted, October 30, 1887, FLOP.
8. *Notes on the Plan of Franklin Park;* reprinted CAC, pp. 259–60.
9. FLOP.
10. FLOP.
11. Quoted by Montgomery Schuyler in *Dictionary of American Biography* article on Leopold Eidlitz.
12. Op. cit., August 19, 1886, FLOP.
13. FLOP.
14. May 17, 1887, FLOP.
15. Frederick Law Olmsted, *Mount Royal, Montreal;* reprinted CAC, p. 204.
16. *Public Parks and the Enlargement of Towns* (pamphlet).
17. Ibid.
18. Olmsted contributed a number of short signed articles in the early years of publication (1888, 1889, 1890), but not in the later years. His son, J. C. Olmsted, and Harry Codman, Charles Eliot, and Mariana Van Renssalaer also contributed articles.
19. FLOP.
20. FLOP; also in *South Atlantic Quarterly,* vol. 3 (1904), where Clark reprinted his and Olmsted's correspondence.
21. FLOP.
22. Ibid.
23. July 11, 1889, FLOP.

XXVII. A PISGAH VIEW

1. FLOP.
2. Frederick Olmsted to his son, Frederick, Jr., June 28, 1891, FLOP.
3. Undated, probably June 1891, FLOP.
4. Paraphrased from Olmsted's letter to James, July 8, 1891, FLOP.
5. July 11, 1891, FLOP.
6. FLOP.
7. FLOP.
8. FLOP.
9. "Letters of an Altrurian Traveller," *Cosmopolitan Magazine,* November 1893 to September 1894; also in *The Altrurian Romances;* vol. 20; a Selected Edition of W. D. Howells; introduction and notes, Clara and Rudolf Kirk, pp. 201–202.
10. From a report in the New York *Tribune,* quoted in Thomas S. Hines, *Burnham of Chicago,* p. 114; and Charles Moore, *Daniel H. Burnham;* vol. 1, p. 74.
11. September 24, 1890, FLOP.
12. September 26, 1890, FLOP.
13. September 5, 1890, FLOP.
14. FLOP.
15. Undated, probably about December 1, 1890, FLOP.
16. FLOP.
17. Ibid.
18. FLOP.
19. From "I am thinking. . . ." December 16, 1890, FLOP.
20. November 3, 1891, FLOP.
21. Gifford Pinchot, *Breaking New Ground,* pp. 48–49.
22. Ibid.
23. FLOP.

24. November 11, 1889, FLOP.
25. June 11, 1890, FLOP.
26. March 12, 1891, FLOP.
27. January 22, 1891, FLOP.
28. October 2, 1889, FLOP.
29. September 12, 1891, FLOP.
30. FLOP.
31. April 21, 1892, FLOP.
32. April 29, 1892, FLOP.
33. FLOP.
34. From: "I don't think that either Phil or Rick realizes...," all to John C. Olmsted, May 15, 1892, FLOP.
35. From Southsea, England, FLOP.
36. May 25, 1892, FLOP.
37. June 16, 1892, FLOP.
38. To "Dear Partners," July 1, 1892, FLOP.
39. April 18, 1892, FLOP.
40. In letter quoted earlier, July 1, 1892, FLOP.
41. Ibid.
42. Ibid.
43. Undated except "Noon—1892," FLOP.

XXVIII. THE END BEFORE THE END

1. FLOP.
2. FLOP.
3. November 27, 1892, FLOP.
4. FLOP.
5. FLOP.
6. FLOP.
7. FLOP.
8. CED.
9. Undated, but about 1893.
10. May 31, 1893, FLOP.
11. FLOP.
12. FLOP.
13. September 6, 1893, FLOP.
14. October 27, 1893, FLOP.
15. October 28, 1893, FLOP.
16. Atlanta *Constitution,* March 16, 1894.
17. Ibid., March 18, 1894.
18. March 15, 1894, FLOP.
19. FLOP.
20. Frederick, Sr. to Frederick, Jr. in reference to this crisis, undated, probably 1895, FLOP.
21. December 28, 1894, FLOP.
22. FLOP.
23. Mary Olmsted to Frederick, Jr., February 23, 1896, FLOP.
24. FLOP.
25. FLOP.
26. FLOP.
27. May 24, 1895, FLOP.
28. J. C. Olmsted to Frederick Law Olmsted, Jr., November 6, 1895, FLOP.

29. September 2, 1895, FLOP.
30. Pencilled memo dated January 31, 1921, FLOP.
31. July 26, 1895, FLOP.
32. FLOP.
33. August 13, 1895, FLOP.
34. July 23, 1895, FLOP.
35. October 15, 1895, FLOP.
36. January 18, 1896, FLOP.
37. FLOP.
38. April 10, 1896, FLOP.
39. January 18, 1896, FLOP.
40. April 2, 1896, FLOP.
41. May 8, 1896, FLOP.
42. May 8, 1896, FLOP.
43. To John, April 10, 1896, FLOP.
44. FLOP.
45. The family memory of this time was conveyed by Frederick Law Olmsted, Jr. to Laura Wood Roper. See her *FLO,* pp. 473–74.

SELECTIVE BIBLIOGRAPHY

Manuscript and Other Unpublished Sources

Frederick Law Olmsted Papers, and supplementary Olmsted firm papers, Manuscript Division, Library of Congress, Washington, D.C.

Records, Olmsted Associates, Brookline, Massachusetts.

Frederick Law Olmsted letters and Andrew D. White letters in Andrew D. White Papers, John M. Olin Library, Cornell University, Ithaca, New York.

Olmsted firm plans and drawings, John M. Olin Library, Cornell University, Ithaca, New York.

Frederick Law Olmsted letters, Henry E. Huntington Library, San Marino, California.

Frederick Law Olmsted letters and other letters and materials, Sterling Memorial Library, Yale University, New Haven, Connecticut, in the Samuel Bowles Papers, the Whitney Family Papers, and the Stokes Autograph Collection.

File of letters between Frederick Law Olmsted and Leland Stanford and their agents, Stanford University Archives, Stanford University, Stanford, California.

Topographical maps and plans, F. L. Olmsted & Co., Stanford University Museum, Stanford, California.

Calvert Vaux Papers, Manuscripts and Archives Division, New York Public Library, Astor, Lenox and Tilden Foundations.

Charles Eliot Diary, Frances Loeb Library, Graduate School of Design, Harvard University, Cambridge, Massachusetts.

Picture collection, Bancroft Library, University of California, Berkeley.

Olmsted/Vaux plan for Central Park, Arsenal, Central Park, New York City.

Photographs and paintings, Berkeley Plantation, Charles City, Virginia.

Periodicals

The Atlanta Constitution, March 1894.

Garden and Forest, 1888, 1889, 1890, 1893.

The Nation, 1866; May–June 1872; July–Aug. 1877; Jan. 1878.

New York Times (known early as *New York Daily Times*), Feb. 16, 1853–Feb. 13, 1854; Mar. 6, 1854–June 7, 1854; Nov. 16, 1861–Jan. 20, 1862; Dec. 1871.

New York *Daily Herald,* June 3, 1857–Aug. 10, 1857.

Putnam's Monthly Magazine, Jan. 1853–Sept. 1857.

A Selective Chronology of Books and Articles by Frederick Law Olmsted (and Other Publications Containing Substantial Material by Olmsted), Published During His Life and After

Walks and Talks of an American Farmer in England. New York: G. P. Putnam, 1852.

"Yeoman Letters." *New York Daily Times*, 1st series, Feb. 16, 1853 to Feb. 13, 1854; 2nd series, Mar. 6, 1854 to June 7, 1854.

A Journey in the Seaboard Slave States, with Remarks on Their Economy. New York: Dix, Edwards & Co.; London: Sampson Low, Son & Co., 1856.

Introduction to *The Englishman in Kansas, or, Squatter Life and Border Warfare*, by Thomas H. Gladstone. New York: Miller & Co., late Dix, Edwards & Co., 1857.

"From the Journal of a Northern Traveler on Horseback." New York *Daily Herald*, June 3, 1857 to Aug. 10, 1857.

A Journey Through Texas, or, A Saddle-Trip on the Southwestern Frontier with a Statistical Appendix. New York: Dix, Edwards & Co., 1857.

Description of a Plan for the Improvement of the Central Park, "Greensward," by Frederick Law Olmsted and Calvert Vaux. New York: John F. Trow, Printer, 1858.

Journey in the Back Country. New York: Mason Brothers, 1860.

The Cotton Kingdom, 2 vols. New York: Mason Brothers, 1861; *Journeys and Explorations in the Cotton Kingdom*, 2 vols. London: Sampson Low, Son & Co., 1861.

"Park." *New American Cyclopaedia*, vol. 12 (1861), 768–75.

Report of the Secretary with Regard to the Probable Origin of the Recent Demoralization of the Volunteer Army at Washington. Read before the [United States Sanitary] Commission September 5th. Referred to the Committee of Enquiry and Ordered to Be Printed for Members, September 11, 1861. Washington, D.C.: McGill & Witherow, Printers, 1861.

Hospital Transports, A Memoir of the Embarkation of the Sick and Wounded from the Peninsula of Virginia in the Summer of 1862 [by Frederick Law Olmsted and Others]. Compiled and published at the Request of the Sanitary Commission. Boston: Ticknor & Fields, 1863.

Preface to the Plan, *Organization of Mountain View Cemetery Association.* San Francisco, Calif.: 1865.

A Few Things to Be Thought of Before Proceeding to Plan Buildings for the National Agricultural Colleges. New York: The American News Co., 1866.

Preliminary Report in Regard to a Plan of Public Pleasure Grounds for the City of San Francisco. New York: William C. Bryant Co., 1866.

Preliminary Report upon a Plan for the General Arrangement of the Premises of the Massachusetts Agricultural College, 1866. Printed by order of the Building Committee for the use of the Trustees.

"Report of Olmsted, Vaux & Co.," 110 Broadway, New York, July 14, 1866 (with diagram of grounds). *Reports & Circulars*, Columbia Institute for the Deaf and Dumb, 1857–72, Washington, D.C.: 1873.

Olmsted, Vaux & Co., Landscape Architects, *Report Upon a Projected Improvement of the Estate of the College of California.* San Francisco, Calif.: Towne & Bacon, Printers, 1866; New York: W. C. Bryant & Co., 1866.

Olmsted, Vaux & Co. *Preliminary Report Upon the Proposed Suburban Village at Riverside near Chicago.* New York: Sutton, Browne & Co., 1868.

Preliminary Report Respecting a Public Park in Buffalo. Bound with the By-Laws of the Park Commission. New York: Matthews & Warren, 1869.

Public Parks and the Enlargement of Towns. Read before the American Social Science Association at the Lowell Institute, Boston, Massachusetts, Feb. 25, 1870. Cambridge, Mass.: Printed for the American Social Science Association at the Riverside Press, 1870.

"Chicago in Distress." *Nation,* vol. 13 (Nov. 9, 1871), 302–05.

New York City, Staten Island Improvement Commission, *Report of a Preliminary Scheme of Improvements,* by Frederick Law Olmsted and others, January 12, 1871. New York: J. Sutton & Co., 1871(?).

Review, "Country Living," *Nation,* Jan. 22, 1874.

Report of the Landscape Architect upon the Construction of Riverside Park and Avenue. New York City, Parks Department, Doc. no. 60. New York: 1875.

Preliminary Report of the Landscape Architect and the Civil and Topographical Engineer, upon the Laying Out of the Twenty-third and Twenty-fourth Wards [and] That Part of the Twenty-fourth Ward, Lying West of the Riverdale Road, by Frederick Law Olmsted and J. James R. Croes. New York City, Parks Dept., Doc. no. 72. New York: 1876.

Report of the Civil and Topographical Engineer and the Landscape Architect, Accompanying a Plan for Local Steam Routes in the Twenty-third and Twenty-fourth Wards, March 21, 1877, by J. James R. Croes and Frederick Law Olmsted. New York City, Parks Dept. New York: 1877(?).

A Consideration of the Justifying Value of a Public Park. Boston: Tolman and White, 1881.

Mount Royal, Montreal. New York: G. P. Putnam's Sons, 1881.

"Report of Frederick Law Olmsted, Landscape Architect," in *Annual Report of the Architect of the United States Capitol for the Fiscal Year Ending June 30, 1881,* by Edward Clark. Washington, D.C.: Government Printing Office, 1881.

"A Paper Relating to the Trees, Shrubs, and Plants in the United States Capitol Ground . . . with Some Observations upon the Planting and Care of Trees in the District of Columbia," by Frederick Law Olmsted, L. A., in *Annual Report of the Architect of the United States Capitol for the Fiscal Year Ending June 30, 1882,* by Edward Clark, Architect. Washington, D.C.: Government Printing Office, 1882.

The Spoils of the Park, with a Few Leaves from the Deep-Laden Note-Books of "A Wholly Unpractical Man." Detroit, Mich.: 1882.

"Report Relating to the United States Capitol Grounds by Fred'k. Law Olmsted, Landscape Architect," in *Annual Report of the Architect of the United States Capitol, for the Fiscal Year Ending June 30, 1884,* by Edward Clark. Washington, D.C.: Government Printing Office, 1884.

Report of Frederick Law Olmsted, Esq. to the Park Commissioners of Wilmington, Del. Wilmington, Del.: Ferris Bros., 1884.

Notes on the Plan of Franklin Park and Related Matters. Printed for the City of Boston, Parks Department, 1886.

[Material from Frederick Law Olmsted] in *Report of the Architect of the United States Capitol to the Secretary of the Interior,* 1886. Washington, D.C.: Government Printing Office, 1886.

General Plan for the Improvement of Morningside Park, by Frederick Law Olm-
    sted and Calvert Vaux. New York: Evening Post Job Printing Office, 1887.
General Plan for the Improvement of the Niagara Reservation, by Frederick Law
    Olmsted and Calvert Vaux. New York: M. B. Brown, 1887.
"Plan for a Small Homestead," Garden and Forest, vol. 1 (May 2, 1888).
The Projected Park and Parkways on the South Side of Buffalo: Two Reports by
    the Landscape Architects, 1888. Buffalo, N.Y.: Printed by Order of the
    Buffalo Park Commission, 1888.
"Remarks About a Difficulty Peculiar to the Park Department of City Govern-
    ments," addressed to the New England Club, June 26, 1889. In 14th
    Annual Report, Boston Dept. of Parks. Boston: 1888.
[Excerpts identified as Frederick Law Olmsted's on the Capitol Grounds and Ter-
    races] in Report of the Architect of the United States Capitol to the Secre-
    tary of the Interior, 1888. Washington, D.C.: Government Printing Office,
    1888.
"Report of the Landscape Architects on Provisions for the Playing of Games," by
    F. L. and J. C. Olmsted. In 14th Annual Report of the Park Commis-
    sioners. Boston: Dec. 31, 1888.
"Terrace and Veranda—Back and Front," Garden and Forest, vol. 1 (June 6,
    1888).
Observations on the Treatment of Public Plantations, More Especially Relating
    to the Use of the Axe. Boston: T. R. Marvin & Sons, 1889.
Governmental Preservation of Natural Scenery, Brookline, Massachusetts, March
    8, 1890. In Pamphlets on Yosemite, Bancroft Library, University of Cali-
    fornia, Berkeley.
"Landscape Gardening." Johnson's Encyclopedia, 1890 edition.
The Landscape Architecture of the World's Columbian Exposition. Prepared by
    invitation of the American Institute of Architects, to be read at its annual
    convention, but by its courtesy made a part of the programme of the
    Congress of Architects. n.d. (c. 1893).
"Frederick Law Olmsted on the South, 1889," by Thomas H. Clark. The South
    Atlantic Quarterly, vol. 3 (Jan.–Oct. 1904), 11–15.
"The Beginning of Central Park: A Fragment of Autobiography," Landscape
    Architecture, vol. 2 (July 1912), 149–62.
"The New England Emigrant Aid Company and English Cotton Supply Associa-
    tions: Letters of Frederick Law Olmsted, 1857." American Historical Re-
    view, vol. 23 (Oct. 1917–July 1918), 114–19.
"The Yosemite Valley and the Mariposa Big Trees: A Preliminary Report, 1865."
    Reproduced with a foreword by Laura Wood Roper. Landscape Architec-
    ture, vol. 43 (October 1952).
Landscape into Cityscape, Frederick Law Olmsted's Plans for a Greater New York
    City. With an introductory essay and notes by Albert Fein. Ithaca, N.Y.:
    Cornell University Press, 1967.
Central Park Country: A Tune Within Us. Containing excerpts from the profes-
    sional papers of Frederick Law Olmsted, Sr. Mireille Johnston, text; Nancy
    and Retta Johnston, photographs; introduction by Marianne Moore; fore-
    word by David Brower. San Francisco, Calif.: Sierra Club, 1968.

Olmsted, Frederick Law, Jr., and Kimball, Theodora. *Frederick Law Olmsted, Landscape Architect, 1822–1903.* 2 vols in 1. New York: Benjamin Blom, 1970. (Orig. ed., 1922, 1928.)

Civilizing American Cities: A Selection of Frederick Law Olmsted's Writings on City Landscapes. Edited by S. B. Sutton. Cambridge, Mass.: MIT Press, 1971.

Books and Articles Concerning Frederick Law Olmsted and His Works

Back Bay Boston: The City as a Work of Art, with essays by Lewis Mumford and Walter Muir Whitehill. A publication accompanying an exhibition at the Museum of Fine Arts, Boston, Mass., Nov. 1, 1969–Jan. 11, 1970, under the direction of William Alex. Boston Museum of Fine Arts. Boston: 1969.

Barlow, Elizabeth. *Frederick Law Olmsted's New York.* Illustrative portfolio, William Alex. New York: Praeger Publishers, in association with the Whitney Museum of American Art, 1972.

Barlow, Elizabeth. "The Once and Future Island." *Audubon Magazine,* Mar. 1971.

Bender, Thomas. *Toward an Urban Vision.* Lexington: University of Kentucky Press, 1975. Chapter VII and Epilogue, 159–94.

Billings, Robert W. "City's Forgotten Island." Chicago *Daily News,* July 24, 1972.

"Birthday of New York's Central Park." *Nation,* vol. 177 (Aug. 1, 1953), 83.

Blodgett, Geoffrey. "Frederick Law Olmsted: Landscape Architecture as Conservative Reform." *Journal of American History,* vol. 42, no. 4, (Mar. 1976).

Bullock, Helen Duprey. "The Personal and Professional Papers of Frederick Law Olmsted." *Library of Congress Quarterly Journal,* vol. 6, no. 1 (Nov. 1948), 8–15.

Campioli, Mario E. "The Proposed Extension of the West Central Front of the Capitol." *Records* of the Columbia Historical Society, 1969–70. Washington, D.C.: The Society, 1971.

"Cities and Parks." *Atlantic Monthly,* vol. 7 (Apr. 1861), 416–29.

"A Day in Central Park." Editorial. *New York Times,* Aug. 15, 1860.

Dunham, Austin C. *Reminiscences of Austin C. Dunham.* Privately printed, n.d., in the collection of the Connecticut Historical Society, Hartford.

Fabos, Julius G.; Milde, Gordon T.; and Weinmayr, V. Michael. *Frederick Law Olmsted, Sr., Founder of Landscape Architecture in America.* Amherst: University of Massachusetts Press, 1968.

Fein, Albert. "The American City: the Ideal and the Real," in Henry-Russell Hitchcock et al., *The Rise of an American Architecture.* Published in association with the Metropolitan Museum of Art by Praeger Publishers. New York: 1970, 51–112.

———. *Frederick Law Olmsted and the American Environmental Tradition.* New York: George Braziller, 1972.

———. "Frederick Law Olmsted: Design for the American City." Illustrated lecture at a meeting of The Friends of Central Park, in the Arsenal, Central Park, New York City, Mar. 31, 1969.

Fleming, Walter L. Review of Olmsted's *A Journey in the Seaboard Slave States,* new ed. *The Dial,* vol. 37 (Oct. 1, 1904), 203–05.

Frederick Law Olmsted: A Register of His Papers in the Library of Congress. Library of Congress, Manuscript Division. Washington, D.C.: 1963; revised, 1975–76.

"Frederick Law Olmsted: Portrait." *World's Work,* vol. 6 (Oct. 1903), 3938.

"Frederick Law Olmsted: Portrait by Sargent." *National Geographic Magazine,* vol. 80 (Aug. 1941), 196.

"Frederick Law Olmsted: Sketch." *Nation,* vol. 77 (Sept. 3, 1903), 191.

Frederick Law Olmsted/U.S.A. Brochure and exhibition, National Gallery of Art, Washington, D.C., Oct. 21, 1972–Jan. 7, 1973. William Alex, designer.

Fridlington, Robert. "Two *Nation* Portraits, Frederick Law Olmsted: Launching the *Nation.*" *Nation,* vol. 202 (Jan. 3, 1966), 10–12.

"Green Pastures and Still Waters: Central Park." *Time,* vol. 58 (July 23, 1951), 58–60.

Harrington, Michael J. "Addition to the West Side of the Capitol." *Congressional Record,* Jan. 28, 1970, E415–18.

[Harris, Elisha]. *The United States Sanitary Commission.* Boston: Crosby and Nichols, 1864. Reprinted from *North American Review* (Apr. 1864).

Harvard University Graduate School of Design. "The Achievement of Frederick Law Olmsted." Cambridge, Mass.: 1964. (In the Frances Loeb Library.)

Heidrich, Robert W. "A Village in a Park: Riverside, Illinois." *Historic Preservation,* vol. 25, no. 2 (Apr.–June 1973).

[Hubbard, Theodora Kimball]. "Olmsted, Frederick Law." *Dictionary of American Biography,* 1934 edition.

Huxtable, Ada Louise. "Up in Central Park." *New York Times,* Mar. 19, 1967; reprinted in *Will They Ever Finish Bruckner Boulevard?* New York: Macmillan Publishing Co., 1963–1970.

Johnson, Norman. "The Frederick Law Olmsted Plan for Tacoma." *Pacific Northwest Quarterly,* vol. 66, no. 3 (1976), 97–104.

Johnson, Robert Underwood. "Amateur Management of the Yosemite Scenery." *The Century,* vol. 40 (Sept. 1890), 797–98.

Johnston, Laurie. "Olmsted Will Be Honored Around Country." *New York Times,* Jan. 15, 1972.

Jordy, William H. Review of *F.L.O.* by Laura Wood Roper. *Frederick Law Olmsted's New York* by Elizabeth Barlow, "Frederick Law Olmsted and the Dialectical Landscape," by Robert Smithson in *Artforum,* Feb. 1973; and *Forty Years of Landscape Architecture* by Frederick Law Olmsted, Jr. and Theodora Kimball. *New York Review of Books,* June 13, 1974.

Kalmbacher, George, and Graff, M. M. *Tree Trails in Prospect Park.* New York: Greensward Foundation, Inc., 1968.

"The Legacy of Frederick Law Olmsted: Parks Where the People Are." Brochure with photographs. New England Olmsted Sesquicentennial Committee, Kevin H. White, Chairman; Francis X. Meaney, Director.

Elizabeth Anne Mack Lyon. "Frederick Law Olmsted and Joel Hurt. Planning the Environment in Atlanta, 1892–94." Southeast American Studies Conference, Atlanta, Georgia, Apr. 27–29, 1972.

McLachlan, James. *American Boarding-Schools: A Historical Study.* New York: Charles Scribner's Sons, 1970.

McLaughlin, Charles C. "The Capitol in Peril? The West Front Controversy from Walter to Stewart." Delivered before the Columbia Historical Society on Mar. 18, 1969. *Records* of the Columbia Historical Society, 1969–70. Washington, D.C.: The Society, 1971.

————. "Letters of Frederick Law Olmsted." Report of Committee on Research, Grant No. 411—Johnson Fund (1961). Reprinted from the Year Book of the American Philosophical Society, 1963.

Martin, J. S. "He Paints with Lakes and Wooded Slopes." *American Heritage,* vol. 15, no. 6 (Oct. 1964), 14–19.

Mitchell, Broadus. *Frederick Law Olmsted, a Critic of the Old South.* Baltimore, Md.: Johns Hopkins Press, 1924.

Motion Picture on the Beginnings of American Forestry. National Forest Service Museum, The Cradle of Forestry in the United States, Pisgah National Forest, North Carolina.

Mumford, Lewis. "The Renewal of the Landscape." *The Brown Decades.* New York: Harcourt Brace, 1931.

Nash, Roderick. *Wilderness and the American Mind.* New Haven, Conn.: Yale University Press, 1967.

Neil, J. Meredith. "Olmsted: A Dubious Heritage." *Journal of Popular Culture* (Summer 1974).

Nevins, Allan. "The United States Sanitary Commission and Secretary Stanton." *Proceedings* of the Massachusetts Historical Society, vol. 67 (Oct. 1941–May 1944), 402–19.

Newman, M. W. "A Great Man Named Olmsted, Shaper of Our Parkland," in Supplement of the Chicago *Daily News,* May 27–28, 1972 (*A Tribute to Frederick Law Olmsted: Green Grow the Parks*).

Nolen, John, and Olmsted, Frederick Law, Jr. "Frederick Law Olmsted and His Works: An Appreciation." *House and Garden,* vols. 9–10 (Feb.–July 1906), 76–83, 117–28, 217–22, 3–11.

Parsons, Kermit Carlyle. *The Cornell Campus: A History of Its Planning and Development.* Ithaca, N.Y.: Cornell University Press, 1968.

"The Prescient Planner." *Time,* Dec. 11, 1972.

Ranney, Victoria Post. *Olmsted in Chicago.* Chicago: R. R. Donelley & Sons, 1972.

Reed, Henry Hope, Jr., and Duckworth, Sophia. *Central Park: A History and a Guide.* New York: Clarkson N. Potter, Inc., 1967.

Review of *Hospital Transports. Atlantic Monthly* (unsigned; attributed to George William Curtis by James F. Rhodes), vol. 12 (Sept. 1893), 398–99.

Review of *The Cotton Kingdom. North American Review,* vol. 94 (Jan. 1862), 272.

Review of *Journey in the Back Country. Atlantic Monthly,* vol. 6 (Nov. 1860), 635–37.

Review of *Journey in the Back Country. North American Review,* vol. 91 (Oct. 1860), 571.

Review of *Journey in the Seaboard Slave States.* Reissued in 1904. *Forum,* vol. 36 (Oct. 1904), 246–51.

Review of *Journey in the Seaboard Slave States. North American Review,* vol. 83 (July 1856), 278–79.

Review of *Journey through Texas. North American Review*, vol. 84 (Apr. 1857), 565–66.

Review of *Walks and Talks of an American Farmer in England. Harper's Magazine*, vol. 6 (Dec. 1852).

Roper, Laura Wood. *FLO: A Biography of Frederick Law Olmsted*. Baltimore, Md.: Johns Hopkins Press, 1973.

———. "Frederick Law Olmsted and the Port Royal Experiment," *Journal of Southern History*, vol. 31 (1965), 272f.—84.

———. "Frederick Law Olmsted and the Western Texas Free-Soil Movement." *American Historical Review*, vol. 56 (Oct. 1950), 58–64.

———. "Frederick Law Olmsted in the 'Literary Republic'." *Mississippi Valley Historical Review*, vol. 39, no. 3 (1952–53), 459–82.

Schickel, Richard. "Frederick Law Olmsted, Creator of 'The Central Park'." *New York Times Magazine*, Dec. 31, 1972.

"Serious Accidents on the Road." General City News, *New York Times*, Aug. 8, 1860.

Simutis, Leonard J. "Frederick Law Olmsted's Later Years: Landscape Architecture and the Spirit of Place." University of Minnesota Dissertation, 1971.

"The South Before the War." Review of Olmsted's *Journey in the Seaboard Slave States*, with a biographical sketch by Frederick Law Olmsted, Jr. and an introduction by William P. Trent. *Nation*, vol. 79 (Aug. 4, 1904), 102–03.

Steiner, Lewis H. *A Sketch of the History, Plan of Organization, and Operations of the U.S. Sanitary Commission*. Read before the Maryland Historical Society, Feb. 1, 1866. Philadelphia: James B. Rodgers, Printer, 1866.

Steiner, Walter R. *A Physician's Experiences in the United States Sanitary Commission during the Civil War*. Read before the Charaka Club, Feb. 16, 1938; reprinted from the *Proceedings* of the Charaka Club, vol. 10 (1941).

Stille, Charles J. *History of the United States Sanitary Commission, Being the General Report of Its Work During the War of the Rebellion*. Philadelphia: J. B. Lippincott & Co., 1866.

Tatum, George B. "The Emergence of an American School of Landscape Design." *Historic Preservation*, vol. 25, no. 2 (Apr.–June 1973).

United States Sanitary Commission, *Documents*, vol. 1, nos. 1–60. New York: 1866.

Van Brunt, Henry. *Essays of Henry Van Brunt*, ed., William A. Coles. Cambridge, Mass.: Harvard University Press, 1969.

Van Renssalaer, Mariana G. "Artistic Triumph of the Fair-Builders." *Forum*, vol. 14 (Dec. 1892), 527–40.

———. "At the Fair." *Century*, vol. 46 (ns24) (May 1893), 2–13.

———. "Frederick Law Olmsted." *Century*, vol. 46 (ns24) (Oct. 1893), 860–67.

White, Dana F., ed. *Frederick Law Olmsted: A Southern Exposure*. Papers presented at the Southeast American Studies Conference, Atlanta, Georgia, Apr. 27–29, 1972.

———, and Kramer, Victor A., eds., *Olmsted's South: Old South Critic/New South Planner*. Westport, Conn.: Greenwood Press, 1977.

Wilson, Edmund. "Northerners in the South: Frederick L. Olmsted, John T. Trowbridge," in *Patriotic Gore: Studies in the Literature of the American Civil War*. New York: Oxford University Press, 1962.

Wormeley, Katherine Prescott. *The Other Side of the War*. Boston: Ticknor and Co., 1888.

[Wormeley, Katherine Prescott]. *The United States Sanitary Commission, A Sketch of Its Purposes and Work*. Boston: Little, Brown and Co., 1863.

Yosemite, Saga of a Century, 1864–1964. Oakhurst, Calif.: Sierra Star Press, n.d.

Predecessors and Contemporaries

Adams, Marian. *The Letters of Mrs. Henry Adams, 1865–1883*. Edited by Ward Thoron. Boston: Little, Brown & Co., 1936.

Anderson, Larz. *Letters and Journals of a Diplomat*. Edited by Isabel Anderson. New York: Fleming H. Revell Co., 1940.

Bade, William F. *The Life and Letters of John Muir*, 2 vols. Boston: Houghton Mifflin Co., 1924.

[Bellows, Henry W.]. "Cities and Parks." *Atlantic Monthly*, (April 1861).

Bellows, Henry W. *Historical Sketch of the Union League Club of New York: Its Origin, Organization, and Work, 1863–1879*. New York: Club House, 1879.

———. *Unconditional Loyalty*. New York: Anson D. F. Randolph, 1863.

Bowles, Samuel. *Across the Continent: A Stage Ride Over the Plains, to the Rocky Mountains, the Mormons, and the Pacific States, in the Summer of 1865, with Speaker Colfax*. Springfield, Mass.: Samuel Bowles and Co.; and New York: Hurd and Houghton, 1869.

Brace, Charles Loring. *Address on Industrial Schools Delivered to Teachers of the Schools, November 13, 1868*. New York: Wynkoop and Hallenbeck, 1868.

———. *Country Homes for Dependent Children: A Review of the Placing Out Work of the Children's Aid Society of New York*. New York: The Society, 1898.

———. *The Dangerous Classes of New York, or, Twenty Years Work Among Them*, 3rd ed. New York: Wynkoop and Hallenbeck, 1880.

———. *Short Sermons to Newsboys*. New York: Charles Scribner's Sons, 1866.

———. *Sketch of the Formation of the Newsboys' Lodging-House, No. 128 Fulton Street*. New York: Children's Aid Society, 1867.

Brace, Emma, ed. *Life of Charles Loring Brace, Chiefly Told in His Own Letters*. New York: Charles Scribner's Sons, 1894.

Bryant, William Cullen. *Letters of a Traveller, or, Notes of Things Seen in Europe and America*. New York: George P. Putnam and Co., 1850.

Burke, Edmund. *A Philosophical Enquiry into the Origin of Our Ideas of the Sublime and the Beautiful*. Edited by J. T. Boulton. New York: Columbia University Press, 1958.

Bushnell, Horace. "Christian Nurture," in *Horace Bushnell*. Edited by H. Shelton Smith. New York: Oxford University Press, 1965.

———. *Woman Suffrage: The Reform Against Nature*. New York: Charles Scribner's Sons, 1869.

Cary, Edward. *George William Curtis*. Boston: Houghton Mifflin Co., 1894.

Cecil, William A. V. *Biltmore: the Vision and Reality of George W. Vanderbilt, Richard Morris Hunt, and Frederick Law Olmsted*. Biltmore Estate. Asheville, N.C.: 1972.

Cheney, Mary Bushnell. *Life and Letters of Horace Bushnell*. New York: Harper and Bros., 1880.

Cleveland, H. W. S. *Landscape Architecture, as Applied to the Wants of the West*. Edited by Roy Lubove. Pittsburgh, Pa.: University of Pittsburgh Press, 1965. (Orig. ed., 1873.)

Curtis, George William. *Early Letters of George William Curtis to John S. Dwight: Brook Farm and Concord*. Edited by George Willis Cooke. New York: Harper and Bros., 1898.

——. *The Life, Character and Writings of William Cullen Bryant: A Commemorative Address Delivered Before the New York Historical Society, at the Academy of Music, December 30, 1878*. New York: Charles Scribner's Sons, n.d.

——. *Lotus-Eating: A Summer Book*. New York: Harper and Bros., 1852.

Downing, Andrew Jackson. *The Architecture of Country Houses, Including Designs for Cottages, Farm Houses, and Villas*. New York: D. Appleton and Co., 1850.

——, ed. *Rural Essays*. With a Memoir of the Author, by George William Curtis, and a Letter to His Friends, by Frederika Bremer. New York: George P. Putnam and Co., 1853.

——. *A Treatise on the Theory and Practice of Landscape Gardening, Adapted to North America, with a View to the Improvement of Country Residences*. New York: George P. Putnam and Co., 1853. (Orig. ed., 1849.)

Dwight, Timothy, II. *Memories of Yale Life and Men, 1845–1899*. New York: Dodd, Mead and Co., 1903.

[Dwight, Timothy], *Things as They Are, or, Notes of a Traveller through Some of the Middle and Northern States*. New York: Harper and Bros., 1834.

[Eliot, Charles W., Sr.]. *Charles Eliot, Landscape Architect*. Boston: Houghton Mifflin Co., 1902.

Emerson, Ralph Waldo. *First Essay*. Boston: James Munroe and Co., 1841.

Furneaux, Rupert. "The Man Who Lifted Captain Kidd's Treasure," in *The Great Treasure Hunts*. New York: Taplinger Publishing Co., 1969.

Garrison, William Lloyd. *Documents of Upheaval: Selections from William Lloyd Garrison's The Liberator, 1831–65*. Edited by Truman Nelson. New York: Hill and Wang, 1966.

Gilpin, William. *Observations, Relative Chiefly to Picturesque Beauty, Made in the Year 1776, on Several Parts of Great Britain, Particularly the Highlands of Scotland*, vol. 1, 2nd ed. London: Printed for R. Blamire, 1792.

——. *Picturesque Beauty*, 2nd ed. (Bound with *An Essay on Prints*). London: 1794.

Godkin, Edwin Lawrence. *Reflections and Comments, 1865–95*. New York: Charles Scribner's Sons, 1895.

Green, Samuel Swett. "Andrew Haswell Green—a Sketch of His Ancestry, Life and Work." *Proceedings*, American Antiquarian Soc., vol. 16, n.s. (April 1904).

Head, Franklin Harvey. "Captain Kidd and the Astor Fortune: A Remarkable Lawsuit." Commentary by Frederick Law Olmsted, Jr. *Forum*, vol. 86 (1931), 56–64.

Higginson, Thomas Wentworth. *Army Life in a Black Regiment*. Boston: Fields, Osgood and Co., 1870.

Hines, Thomas S. *Burnham of Chicago, Architect and Planner*. New York: Oxford University Press, 1974.

Hitchcock, Henry-Russell, Jr. *The Architecture of H. H. Richardson and His Times*. New York: Museum of Modern Art, 1936.

Hoffman, Donald. *The Architecture of John Wellborn Root*. Baltimore, Md.: Johns Hopkins University Press, 1973.

Howells, William Dean. *The Altrurian Romances*. Bloomington: Indiana University Press, 1968.

Longstreet, Augustus Baldwin. *Georgia Scenes: Characters, Incidents, etc., in the First Half-Century of the Republic by a Native Georgian*. New York: Harper and Bros., 1897. (Orig. ed., 1835.)

Lyell, Charles. *A Second Visit to the United States of America*. New York: Harper and Bros., 1849. (Orig. ed., 1845.)

McGeary, Martin N. *Gifford Pinchot, Forester–Politician*. Princeton, N.J.: Princeton University Press, 1960.

Marsh, George Perkins. *The Earth as Modified by Human Action*. New York: Scribner, Armstrong & Co., 1877.

Martineau, Harriet. *Retrospect of Western Travel*, 2 vols. London: Saunders and Otley; New York: Harper and Bros., 1838.

Maxwell, William Quentin. *Lincoln's Fifth Wheel: The Political History of the United States Sanitary Commission*. London: Longmans, Green and Co., 1956.

Merriam, George S. *The Life and Times of Samuel Bowles*, 2 vols. New York: Century Co., 1885.

Milne, Gordon. *George William Curtis and the Genteel Tradition*. Bloomington: Indiana University Press, 1956.

Monroe, Harriet. *John Wellborn Root*. Park Forest, Ill.: Prairie School Press, 1966. (Orig. ed., 1896.)

Moore, Charles. *Daniel H. Burnham*, 2 vols. Boston: Houghton Mifflin Co., 1921.

Munger, Theodore T. *Horace Bushnell: Preacher and Theologian*. Boston: Houghton Mifflin Co., 1899.

Nevins, Allan. *Fremont: Pathmaker of the West*. New York: D. Appleton-Century Co., 1939. (1st ed., 1928.)

Norton, Charles Eliot. *Letters of Charles Eliot Norton*. With Biographical Comment by His Daughter, Sara Norton and M. A. De Wolfe Howe. 2 vols. Boston: Houghton Mifflin Co., 1913.

Ogden, Rollo. *Life and Letters of Edwin Lawrence Godkin*, 2 vols. New York: Macmillan Co., 1907.

Pinchot, Gifford. *Breaking New Ground*. New York: Harcourt, Brace and Co., 1947.

———. "Prevention First." *Survey*, vol. 58 (July 1, 1927), 367–69.

Pope, Alexander. "Epistle IV, to Richard Boyle, Earl of Burlington, on the Use of Riches." *Complete Poems*. Boston: Houghton Mifflin Co., 1903, 1931.

———. *The Guardian*, No. 173, September 29, 1713. *Eighteenth Century Prose*. Edited by Louis I. Bredvold et al. New York: Ronald Press, 1932.

[Potter, Howard]. *In Memoriam* [Charles Loring Brace]. New York: Children's Aid Society, November 1890.

Putnam, George Palmer. *A Memoir of George Palmer Putnam,* 2 vols. New York: G. P. Putnam's Sons, 1903.

Putnam, George Haven. *Memories of a Publisher, 1865–1915.* New York: G. P. Putnam's Sons, 1915.

———. *Memories of My Youth, 1844–1865.* New York: G. P. Putnam's Sons, 1914.

Russell, William Howard. *My Diary North and South.* Boston: T. O. and H. P. Burnham, 1863.

Saint-Gaudens, Augustus. *Reminiscences,* 2 vols. Edited by Homer Saint-Gaudens. New York: Century Company, 1913.

Sigle, John David. *Calvert Vaux, an American Architect.* Master's Thesis, University of Virginia, May 8, 1967.

Silliman, Benjamin. *A Tour to Quebec in the Autumn of 1819.* London: Printed for Sir Richard Phillips and Co., 1822.

Smith, H. Shelton, ed. *Horace Bushnell.* New York: Oxford University Press, 1965.

Strong, George Templeton. *The Diary of George Templeton Strong,* 4 vols. Edited by Allan Nevins and Milton Halsey Thomas. New York: Macmillan Co., 1952.

Stroud, Dorothy. *Humphry Repton.* London: Country Life Ltd., 1962.

Sutton, Stephanne Barry. *Charles Sprague Sargent and the Arnold Arboretum.* Cambridge, Mass.: Harvard University Press, 1970.

Tharp, Louise Hall. *Saint-Gaudens and the Gilded Era.* Boston: Little, Brown and Co., 1969.

Thomas, John L. *The Liberator: William Lloyd Garrison.* Boston: Little, Brown and Co., 1963.

Van Rensselaer, Mariana G. *Henry Hobson Richardson and His Works.* New York: Dover Publications, 1969. (Orig. ed., 1888.)

Vaux, Calvert. *Villas and Cottages.* New York: Harper and Bros., Publishers, 1857.

———. *Villas and Cottages.* Review in *North American Review,* vol. 85 (July 1857), 276–77.

Weidenmann, Jacob. *Beautifying Country Homes: A Handbook of Landscape Gardening.* New York: Orange Judd and Co., 1870.

White, Andrew D. *Autobiography,* vol. 1. New York: Century Company, 1905.

———. *The Diaries of Andrew D. White.* Edited by Robert Morris Ogden. Ithaca, N.Y.: Cornell University Library, 1959.

Zimmermann, John G. [Johann Georg von], *Solitude, or, the Pernicious Influence of a Total Seclusion from Society upon the Mind and Heart.* Exeter, England: J. and B. Williams, 1836.

Other Sources

Adams, George Worthington. *Doctors in Blue: The Medical History of the Union Army in the Civil War.* New York: Henry Schuman, 1952.

Addison, Daniel Dulany. "Theodore Parker" and "Horace Bushnell," in *The Clergy in American Life and Letters*. New York: Macmillan Co., 1900, 229–67, 268–303.

Andrews, Kenneth R. *Nook Farm: Mark Twain's Hartford Circle*. Cambridge, Mass.: Harvard University Press, 1950.

Andrews, Wayne. *Architecture, Ambition and Americans*. New York: Harper and Bros., 1947–55.

———. *Architecture in America: A Photographic History from the Colonial Period to the Present*. New York: Atheneum Press, 1960.

———. *Architecture in Chicago and Mid-America*. New York: Atheneum Press, 1968.

———. *The Vanderbilt Legend: The Story of the Vanderbilt Family, 1794–1940*. New York: Harcourt, Brace and Co., 1941.

Boorstin, Daniel J. *The Americans: The National Experience*. New York: Random House, 1965.

Brooks, Van Wyck. *New England: Indian Summer, 1865–1915*. New York: E. P. Dutton and Co., Inc., 1940.

Brown, John. *Slave Life in Georgia*. Edited by F. N. Boney. Savannah, Ga.: Beehive Press, 1972.

Callow, Alexander B., Jr. "The Crusade Against the Tweed Ring," *American Urban History: An Interpretive Reader with Commentaries*. Edited by Alexander B. Callow, Jr. New York: Oxford University Press, 1969.

———. *The Tweed Ring*. New York: Oxford University Press, 1965, 1966.

Chesnut, Mary B. *A Diary from Dixie*. Boston: Houghton Mifflin Co., 1949. (Earlier ed., 1905.)

Craven, Avery O. "Background Forces and the Civil War." *The American Tragedy: The Civil War in Retrospect*. Lectures, Hampden-Sydney College, Hampden-Sydney, Va., 1959.

———. *Civil War in the Making, 1815–60*. Walter Lynwood Fleming Lectures in Southern History, State University of Louisiana, Baton Rouge, 1959.

Creese, Walter L. *The Search for Environment*. New Haven, Conn.: Yale University Press, 1966.

De Bow, J. D. B. *The Industrial Resources etc., of the Southern and Western States*, 3 vols. New Orleans, La.: The Office of *De Bow's Review*, 1852–53.

Dickens, Charles. *American Notes and Pictures from Italy*. London: Oxford University Press, 1957. (*American Notes* first published 1842.)

Donald, David. *Charles Sumner and the Coming of the Civil War*. New York: Alfred A. Knopf Co., 1960.

Douglass, Frederick, *Narrative of the Life of Frederick Douglass, An American Slave, Written by Himself*. Edited by Benjamin Quarles. Cambridge, Mass.: Belknap Press of Harvard University Press, 1960.

Dutton, Ralph. *The English Garden*. New York: Charles Scribner's Sons, 1938.

Eaton, Clement. *The Civilization of the Old South: Writings of Clement Eaton*. Edited by Albert D. Kirwan. Lexington: University of Kentucky Press, 1968.

———. *The Mind of the Old South*. Baton Rouge: Louisiana State University Press, 1964.

Eaton, Leonard K. "The American Suburb: Dream and Nightmare." *Landscape*, vol. 13, no. 2 (Winter 1963–64), 12–16, in Robert G. Putnam et al., *A Geography of Urban Places*. Toronto, Ont.: Methuen, 1970.

———. *Landscape Artist in America: The Life and Work of Jens Jensen*. Chicago: University of Chicago Press, 1964.

Egan, Joseph B., and Desmond, Arthur W., eds. *The Civil War—Its Photographic History: The War in the East*. Compiled from actual photographs taken at the Time of Action by Mathew B. Brady and Others. Wellesley Hills, Mass.: Character Building Publications, 1941.

Fitch, James M. *Architecture and the Esthetics of Plenty*. New York: Columbia University Press, 1961.

Fogel, Robert William, and Engerman, Stanley L. *Time on the Cross: The Economics of American Negro Slavery*. Boston: Little, Brown and Co., 1974.

Ford, Worthington C., ed. A Cycle of Adams Letters, 2 vols. Boston: Houghton Mifflin Co., 1865.

Gay, Mary A. H. *Life in Dixie During the War, 1861–65*. Atlanta, Ga.: Foote and Davies Co., 1894.

Genovese, Eugene D. *The Political Economy of Slavery: Studies in the Economy and Society of the Slave South*. New York: Pantheon Books, 1961–65.

———. *The World the Slaveholders Made*. New York: Pantheon Books, 1969.

Hadley, Arthur T. "Yale," in *Four American Universities*. New York: Harper and Bros., 1895.

Hampton, H. Duane. *How the United States Cavalry Saved Our National Parks*. Bloomington: Indiana University Press, 1971.

Helper, Hinton Rowan. *The Impending Crisis of the South: How to Meet It*. New York: Burdick Brothers, 1857.

Hosken, Fran P. *The Language of Cities*. New York: Macmillan Co., 1968.

Howat, John K. *The Hudson River and Its Painters*. New York: Viking Press, 1972.

Hussey, Christopher. *The Picturesque: Studies in a Point of View*. New York: G. P. Putnam's Sons, 1927.

Huth, Hans, *Nature and the American*. Berkeley and Los Angeles: University of California Press, 1957.

———. *Yosemite: The Story of an Idea*. Reprinted by the Yosemite Natural History Association from the Sierra Club Bulletin, March 1948.

Jackson, John Brinckerhoff. *American Space: The Centennial Years, 1865–1876*. New York: Norton, 1972.

James, D. Clayton. *Antebellum Natchez*. Baton Rouge: Louisiana State University Press, 1968.

Johnson, Philip. "Why We Want Our Cities Ugly." Smithsonian Annual II: *The Fitness of Man's Environment*. Washington, D.C.: Smithsonian Institution, 1968.

Langsam, Miriam Z. *Children West: A History of the Placing-Out System of the New York Children's Aid Society, 1853–1890*. Madison: State Historical Society of Wisconsin, University of Wisconsin, 1964.

Lee, Brother Basil Leo. *Discontent in New York City, 1861–65*. Washington, D.C.: Catholic University of America Press, 1943.

Lewis, Oscar. *The Big Four: The Story of Huntington, Stanford, Hopkins and Crocker, and the Building of the Central Pacific.* New York: Alfred A. Knopf and Co., 1938.

Linden, Fabian. "Economic Democracy in the Slave South, An Appraisal of Some Recent Views." *Journal of Negro History,* vol. 31 (April 1946), 140–89.

Lynes, Russell. *The Art Makers of Nineteenth-Century America.* New York: Atheneum Press, 1970.

McHarg, Ian L. *Design with Nature.* Garden City, N.Y.: The Natural History Press, 1969. Published for The American Museum of Natural History.

McKinney, John C., and Thompson, Edgar T., eds. *The South in Continuity and Change.* Sponsored by the Southern Sociological Society and the Center for Southern Studies, Duke University. Durham, N.C.: Duke University Press, 1965.

McKitrick, Eric L. *Andrew Johnson and Reconstruction.* Chicago: University of Chicago Press, 1960.

Mandelbaum, Seymour J. *Boss Tweed's New York.* New York: John Wiley, 1965.

Marx, Leo. *The Machine in the Garden: Technology and the Pastoral Ideal in America.* New York: Oxford University Press, 1964.

Mitchell, Henry. "Keeping Nature in the City." *The Washington Post,* October 21, 1972.

Morris, Lloyd R. *Incredible New York.* New York: Random House, 1951.

Mumford, Lewis. *The Culture of Cities.* New York: Harcourt, Brace and Co., 1938.

———. *The Myth of the Machine: The Pentagon of Power.* New York: Harcourt, Brace & Co., 1964, 1970.

———. *The Urban Prospect.* New York: Harcourt, Brace and World, 1968.

Mumford, Lewis, ed. *Roots of Contemporary American Architecture.* New York: Grove Press, 1959. (Earlier ed., 1952.)

Mumford, Lewis, and Osborn, Frederic J. *Letters: A Transatlantic Dialogue.* Edited by Michael Hughes. New York: Praeger Publishers, 1972.

Nevins, Allan. *The Emergence of Modern America, 1865–78.* New York: Macmillan Co., 1927.

———. *The Evening Post: A Century of Journalism.* New York: Boni and Liveright, 1922.

Nichols, Roy F. *The Stakes of Power, 1845–1877.* New York: Hill and Wang, 1961.

Novak, Barbara. *American Painting of the Nineteenth Century: Realism, Idealism, and the American Experience.* New York: Praeger Publishers, 1969.

Owsley, Frank Lawrence. *Plain Folk of the Old South.* Baton Rouge: Louisiana State University, 1949.

Peisch, Mark L. *The Chicago School of Architecture: Early Followers of Sullivan and Wright.* London: Phaidon Press, 1964.

Pevsner, Nikolaus. *Sources of Modern Architecture and Design.* London: Thames and Hudson, 1968.

Phillips, Ulrich Bonnell. *The Course of the South to Secession: An Interpretation.* Gloucester, Mass.: Peter Smith, 1958. (Orig. ed., 1939.)

Potter, David M. *The South and the Sectional Conflict.* Baton Rouge: Louisiana State University Press, 1968.

Randall, James G. *The Civil War and Reconstruction*. New York: D. C. Heath, 1937.

Rhodes, James Ford. *History of the United States from the Compromise of 1850 to the Final Restoration of Home Rule at the South in 1877*, vol. 6, 1866–72. New York: Macmillan Co., 1906.

Saarinen, Aline B. *The Proud Possessors: The Lives, Times and Tastes of Some Adventurous American Art Collectors*. New York: Random House, 1958.

Schmitt, Peter J. *Back to Nature: The Arcadian Myth in Urban America*. New York: Oxford University Press, 1969.

Shepard, Paul. *Man in the Landscape*. New York: Alfred A. Knopf, 1967.

Silver, Nathan. *Lost New York*. Boston: Houghton Mifflin Co., 1967.

Simms, Henry H. *A Decade of Sectional Controversy, 1851–61*. Chapel Hill: University of North Carolina Press, 1942.

Smith, Elbert B. *The Death of Slavery: The United States, 1837–65*. Chicago: University of Chicago Press, 1967.

Stampp, Kenneth M. *The Peculiar Institution: Slavery in the Ante-Bellum South*. New York: Random House, 1956.

Still, Bayrd. *Mirror for Gotham: New York as Seen by Contemporaries from Dutch Days to the Present*. New York: New York University Press, 1956.

Sumner, Charles. *Expulsion of the President*. Opinion of Hon. Charles Sumner of Massachusetts, in the Case of the Impeachment of Andrew Johnson, President of the United States. Washington, D.C.: Government Printing Office, 1868.

Sweet, Frederick A. *The Hudson River School and the Early American Landscape Tradition*. Whitney Museum of American Art, New York, Apr. 17 to May 18, 1945. Chicago: Art Institute of Chicago, 1945.

Taylor, William R. *Cavalier and Yankee: The Old South and American National Character*. New York: George Braziller, 1961.

Thayer, Eli. *A History of the Kansas Crusade, Its Friends and Its Foes*. New York: Harper, 1889.

Tunnard, Christopher, and Reed, Henry Hope. *American Skyline*. Boston: Houghton Mifflin Co., 1953, 1955.

Turner, Frederick Jackson. *The United States, 1830–50: The Nation and Its Sections*. New York: Henry Holt and Co., 1935.

Udall, Stewart L. *The Quiet Crisis*. New York: Holt, Rinehart and Winston, 1963.

Webb, Alexander S. *The Peninsula: McClellan's Campaign of 1862*. New York: Charles Scribner's Sons, 1886. (Orig. ed., 1881.)

Whitman, Walt. *Democratic Vistas*. New York: Liberal Arts Press, 1949. (Orig. ed., 1871.)

Williams, T. Harry. *Lincoln and His Generals*. New York: Alfred A. Knopf and Co., 1952.

Williamson, Joel. *After Slavery: The Negro in South Carolina during Reconstruction, 1861–77*. Chapel Hill: University of North Carolina, 1965.

Woodward, C. Vann. *The Burden of Southern History*. Baton Rouge: Louisiana State University Press, 1960.

Reference Works

Dictionary of American Biography, Edited by Allen Johnson and Dumas Malone under the Auspices of the American Council of Learned Societies. With supplements. New York: Charles Scribner's Sons, 1928–1936.

Encyclopedia Americana. New York: Americana Corporation, 1918–75.

Encyclopedia Britannica. Chicago, London, etc.: William Benton, Publisher, 1943–73.

Encyclopedia of American Biography. Edited by John A. Garraty and Jerome L. Sternstein. New York: Harper and Row, 1974.

Index